Use and Abuse of Law in the Athenian Courts

Mnemosyne Supplements

HISTORY AND ARCHAEOLOGY OF CLASSICAL ANTIQUITY

VOLUME 419

The titles published in this series are listed at *brill.com/mns-haca*

Use and Abuse of Law in the Athenian Courts

Edited by

Chris Carey
Ifigeneia Giannadaki
Brenda Griffith-Williams

BRILL

LEIDEN | BOSTON

Cover illustration: Digital image by Chris Carey based on exhibit of voting discs in the Agora Museum, Athens.

Library of Congress Cataloging-in-Publication Data

Names: Carey, Christopher (Classicist), editor. | Giannadaki, Ifigeneia, editor. |
Griffith-Williams, Brenda, editor.
Title: Use and abuse of law in the Athenian courts / Edited by Chris Carey,
Ifigeneia Giannadaki, Brenda Griffith-Williams.
Description: Leiden : Brill, 2018. | Series: Mnemosyne supplements ; 419 | Includes
bibliographical references and index.
Identifiers: LCCN 2018034735 (print) | LCCN 2018035137 (ebook) |
ISBN 9789004377899 (e-book) | ISBN 9789004377875 (hardback : alk. paper)
Subjects: LCSH: Courts–Greece–Athens. | Practice of law (Greek law) | Law, Greek.
| Justice, Administration of (Greek law)
Classification: LCC KL4115.A75 (ebook) | LCC KL4115.A75 U84 2018 (print) |
DDC 340.5/385–dc23
LC record available at https://lccn.loc.gov/2018034735

Typeface for the Latin, Greek, and Cyrillic scripts: "Brill". See and download: brill.com/brill-typeface.

ISSN 2352-8656
ISBN 978-90-04-37787-5 (hardback)
ISBN 978-90-04-37789-9 (e-book)

This book is printed on acid-free paper and produced in a sustainable manner.

Printed by Printforce, the Netherlands

Contents

Abbreviations

Ancient Authors and Works

Aesch. *Eum.*	Aeschylus *Eumenides*
Aischin.	Aischines
Anaximen. *Rh. Al.*	Anaximenes *Rhetorica ad Alexandrum*
Andok.	Andokides
Antiph.	Antiphon
Ar.	Aristophanes
Av.	*Birds*
Nub.	*Clouds*
Plut.	*Plutus*
Vesp.	*Wasps*
Thesm.	*Thesmophoriazousai*
Arist.	Aristotle
Eth. Nic.	*Ethica Nicomachea*
Pol.	*Politics*
Rh.	*Rhetoric*
[*Ath. Pol.*]	*Athenaion Politeia*
Dem.	Demosthenes
Dein.	Deinarchos
Dio Chrys.	Dio Chrysostomos
Dion. Hal. *Is.*	Dionysios of Halicarnassos *De Iseo*
Etym. Mag.	*Etymologicum Magnum*
Harp.	Harpocration
Hes. *Theog.*	Hesiod *Theogony*
Hom. *Il.*	Homer *Iliad*
Hsch.	Hesychius
Hyp.	Hypereides
Athen.	*Against Athenogenes*
Diond.	*Against Diondas*
Eux.	*For Euxenippos*
Lyk.	*For Lykophron*
Phil.	*Against Philippides*
Isa.	Isaios
Isok.	Isokrates
Lex. Rhet. Cant.	*Lexicon Rhetoricum Cantabrigiense*
Lex. Patm.	*Lexicon Patmense*

Lex. Seg.	*Lexicon Seguerianum*
Lykourg.	Lykourgus
Lib. *Hyp*	Libanius *Hypotheses*
Lys.	Lysias
Paus.	Pausanias
Phot.	Photius
Pind.	Pindar
Nem.	*Nemean Odes*
Pyth.	*Pythian Odes*
Pl.	Plato
Ap.	*Apology*
Leg.	*Laws*
Plut.	Plutarch
Mor.	*Moralia*
Sol.	*Solon*
X Orat.	*Vitae decem Oratorum*
Polyb.	Polybius
Theophr.	Theophrastos
Thuc.	Thucydides
Xen. *Hell.*	Xenophon *Hellenica*

Modern Publications

FGrH	F. Jacoby, *Fragmente der griechischen Historiker*
IG	*Inscriptiones Graecae*
LSJ	Liddell, Scott, Jones, *Greek-English Lexcicon*
MPC	Model Penal Code
SEG	*Supplementium Epigraphicum Graecum*
TLG	*Thesaurus Linguae Graecae*

Journal Titles and Encyclopaedias

AJP	*Americal Journal of Philology*
BICS	*Bulletin of the Institute of Classical Studies*
CA	*Classical Antiquity*
C&M	*Classica et Medievalia*
CJ	*Classical Journal*
CP	*Classical Philology*

CQ	*Classical Quarterly*
CR	*Classical Review*
GRBS	*Greek, Roman, and Byzantine Studies*
JHS	*Journal of Hellenic Studies*
PWRE	Pauly/Wissowa *Realencyclopädie*
TAPA	*Transactions of the American Philological Association*
ZPE	*Zeitschrift für Papyrologie und Epigraphik*

General

accus.	accusative
esp.	especially
fr.	fragment
lit.	literally
n.	note
pl.	plural
repr.	reprinted
trans.	translated

Notes on Contributors

Kostas Apostolakis
is Assistant Professor in the Division of Classical Studies of the University of Crete at Rethymnon. He is the author of two books on Lysias and Demosthenes, and of a series of articles on Attic Rhetoric and Comedy. He is currently preparing a Commentary on Timocles, the poet of Middle Comedy.

Ilias Arnaoutoglou
is a graduate of Law Faculty, Aristotelean University of Thessaloniki, PhD (Glasgow) on Ancient History, Assistant Editor in *LGPN* (Oxford) and Director of Research in the Academy of Athens, Research Centre for the History of Greek Law. His interests include the legal history of classical and Hellenistic Athens, and legal institutions of the Greco-Roman Mediterranean and ancient associations.

Mirko Canevaro
is Reader in Greek History at the University of Edinburgh. He has studied in Torino and Durham, and has also held fellowships and visiting positions in Athens, Mannheim and Cagliari. An expert of Greek law and political institutions, he has published most notably *The Documents in the Attic Orators* (OUP 2013), *Demostene, Contro Leptine. Introduzione, traduzione e commento storico* (De Gruyter 2016), and more recently (edited with B. Gray) *The Hellenistic Reception of Classical Athenian Democracy and Political Thought* (OUP 2018) and (edited with A. Erskine, B. Gray and J. Ober) *Ancient Greek History and the Contemporary Social Sciences* (EUP 2018).

Chris Carey
is Emeritus Professor of Greek at UCL. He has published on Greek lyric, epic, drama, politics, oratory and law.

Michael Gagarin
is James R. Dougherty, Jr. Centennial Professor of Classics Emeritus at the University of Texas in Austin. His latest book is *The Laws of Ancient Crete c. 650–400 BCE*, written with Paula Perlman (OUP 2016). He is currently finishing a book on Athenian law.

Ifigeneia Giannadaki
is a Research Associate at University College London. Her publications focus on aspects of Athenian law and oratory. She is currently completing her *Commentary on the Speech of Demosthenes,* Against Androtion (Oxford University Press).

Brenda Griffith-Williams
is an Honorary Research Associate in the Department of Greek and Latin at University College London. She has published *A Commentary on Selected Speeches of Isaios*, and several articles on Athenian law and rhetoric.

Edward M. Harris
is Emeritus Professor of Ancient History at Durham University and Honorary Professorial Fellow at the University of Edinburgh. He is the author of *Democracy and the Rule of Law in Classical Athens* (CUP) and *The Rule of Law in Action in Democratic Athens* (OUP). He has translated Demosthenes 20–22 and Demosthenes 23–26 (Texas) and co-edited *The Law and the Courts in Ancient Greece*, *Law and Drama in Ancient Greece*, and *The Ancient Greek Economy: Markets, Households and City-States* (CUP).

Rosalia Hatzilambrou
is Assistant Professor in the National and Kapodistrian University of Athens. Her research interests lie in the fields of Attic Oratory, Rhetoric, and Greek Papyrology. Her PhD thesis has been published in *The Oxyrhynchus Papyri*. Her book on Isaios' third speech (critical edition, translation, and commentary) is scheduled to be published in 2018.

László Horváth
PhD, associate professor with habilitation of the Greek Department of ELTE Budapest; director of Eötvös József Collegium, the Hungarian partner institution of the École Normale Supérieure; and head of the Byzantium Centre. He earned world-wide acclaim through the critical edition of the text of the Hypereides Palimpsest.

Christos Kremmydas
is a Reader in Greek History at Royal Holloway, University of London. His research focuses on the areas of Greek oratory, rhetoric, law, and historiography. He is currently co-editing two volumes of conference papers and working on a new research project that examines rhetorical strategies of deception in Athenian forensic oratory.

Robin Osborne
is Professor of Ancient History at the University of Cambridge and a Fellow of King's College Cambridge and of the British Academy. His work has ranged widely over Greek social, political and economic history, Greek settlement archaeology, and the history of Greek art. His most recent monograph, *The Transformation of Athens: Painted Pottery and the Creation of Classical Greece* was published by Princeton University Press in 2018.

David D. Phillips
is Professor of History at the University of California, Los Angeles. His recent publications include *The Law of Ancient Athens* (2013) and *Polybius Book 1: A Commentary* (2016).

Lene Rubinstein
is Professor of Ancient History at Royal Holloway, University of London. She is the author of *Adoption in IV Century Athens* (Copenhagen 1993), *Litigation and Cooperation: Supporting Speakers in the Courts of Classical Athens* (Stuttgart 2000), and a range of articles and chapters on Greek legal and social history in the Classical and Hellenistic periods.

Noboru Sato
is an Associate Professor at Kobe University, Japan. He received his PhD at the University of Tokyo. His thesis concerned the discourses on bribery in Democratic Athens. His fields of research are the Athenian socio-political history, law and rhetoric in Democratic Athens, and ancient Greek historiography.

Stephen Todd
is Professor of Ancient History at Manchester. Among his published books are *The Shape of Athenian Law* (OUP 1993) and *A Commentary on Lysias, Speeches 1–11* (OUP 2007). He is currently working on a second volume of the Lysias commentary.

Eleni Volonaki
is Assistant Professor of Ancient Greek Literature in the Department of Philology, University of the Peloponnese. She teaches both undergraduates and postgraduates Attic Oratory, Attic Law, Historiography, Philosophy, and Homer. Her PhD thesis was 'A Commentary on Lysias 13 (*Against Agoratos*) and 30 (*Against Nikomachos*)' (published by Papazisis editions) and she is now working on the publication of a Commentary on [Dem.] 47, *Against Evergos and Mnesiboulos*. She has published articles on Athenian Greek Law, forensic and epideictic oratory and rhetoric, Hellenistic poetry, Epic poetry and social values.

Victoria Wohl
is Professor of Classics at the University of Toronto. She studies the literature and culture of democratic Athens. Her publications include *Love Among the Ruins: The Erotics of Democracy in Classical Athens* (2002), *Law's Cosmos: Juridical Discourse in Athenian Forensic Oratory* (2010), and *Euripides and the Politics of Form* (2015).

Introduction

Chris Carey

Greek law has always been a Cinderella. Roman law has long held a respected place in the study of the history of law. Unsurprisingly, because in a very real sense it is living law. Roman law became the object of serious study after the rediscovery of Justinian's *Digest* in the eleventh century and its influence radiated outward from Italy throughout Europe to become the basis of the European *ius commune*.[1] The fact that most of the legal systems of mainland Europe ultimately derive in structure and principle from Roman *ius civile* gives Roman law a relevance not just to the historian but also to the student preparing to enter the legal profession. It even features in the law schools in common law jurisdictions. Greek law, which for the purposes of this book is Athenian law,[2] in contrast is childless.[3] Unlike democracy (however reinterpreted), moral and political philosophy, mathematics, historiography, epic, lyric and drama, no ancient Greek legal system of any period has made any direct impact on any modern system. Even the modern Greek legal system, despite the use of terminology which harks back to the ancient world, such as *Areios Pagos* for the supreme court, belongs to the continental civil law tradition.[4] So ancient Greek law has never had the salience in the world of scholarship which Roman law continues to enjoy.

Until recently. The study of Athenian law has changed dramatically over the last few decades in terms of scale, centre of gravity and method. Athenian law is now big business, and the interest shows no sign of abating.

1 See among others Schiller 1978: 3–4, Mousourakis 2015: 243–257, Mayall 2015, Du Plessis 2015: 368–374.

2 This is not the place to enter into the debate on the unity of Greek law, which after the magisterial dismissal by Moses Finley has come back into focus in recent years. The debate is ultimately irresolvable and the question is probably misguided in its current formulation. We can see both procedural and substantive convergence between the Greek states which results from a prolonged interaction from the archaic period onward, possibly earlier. And we can see similarities in the formulation of law which Greece and Rome share with many other cultures in and around the Aegean. But we also find divergence in both substance and procedure. And unlike mainland European civil law, the laws of the Greek states had no identical origin in a single authoritative source. We should probably think in terms of family resemblance rather than 'unity' in any literal sense.

3 Todd 1993: 3–4.

4 Lavdas 1997: 50, Perakis 2008: 23–25, Yessiou-Faltsi 2004.

 | DOI:10.1163/9789004377899_002

The first two strands of change noted above can be taken together. The most cursory glance at the *Nomoi* database of publications in Greek law will show that the volume of outputs in this field has increased dramatically in the past three decades.[5] Much of this is due to the spurt of interest in the subject within the Anglophone world. The nineteenth and early twentieth centuries witnessed some ground-breaking work on Athenian law, most of it from scholars working on mainland Europe. One of the great milestones (possibly the single greatest milestone) of research in Athenian law, Lipsius' magisterial revision of Meier-Schömann, *Das attische Recht und Rechtsverfahren*, was published in several fascicles from 1905 to 1915. Over a century after the appearance of the last section this remains an invaluable work, erudite, authoritative and copiously referenced. Its influence is still visible. Scholars working in civil law jurisdictions continued to dominate the field throughout the twentieth century. The major contributors were either Italian (Paoli in the middle of the century) or German (scholars such as Hans Julius Wolff from the 1940s onward and Ruschenbusch from the 1950s). The tradition still persists in the prominence of scholars such as Alberto Maffi and Gerhard Thür, whose book on the *basanos* will not be superseded for many decades to come.[6] The tradition was enriched immeasurably by the entry into the field of Mogens Hansen,[7] whose enormously important work on Athenian democratic institutions included three deceptively slim volumes on key legal processes relating mainly to political offences.[8]

The Anglophone world was far less productive for much of this period. The exceptions were from the USA, principally R.J. Bonner and Gertrude Smith. As well as collaborating with Smith on the two volume *The Administration of Justice from Homer to Aristotle*, Bonner, a trained lawyer, also wrote two more slender volumes, *Lawyers and Litigants in Classical Athens* and *Evidence in Athenian Courts*. The other US name of note is Calhoun, whose *The Athenian Clubs in Politics and Litigation* is interested in part in the courts. But after these contributions the common law world had largely lost interest in the study of Athenian law by the start of the Second World War. This meant that the Anglophone common law tradition had little impact on research into Athenian law. This picture begins to change in the 1960s. The shift begins with MacDowell's book on homicide law, a very slim volume which, despite its brevity—an increas-

5 http://www.sfu.ca/nomoi/.

6 Thür 1977.

7 Though Scandinavian law has affinities with civil law, it is sufficiently distinctive, and sufficiently coherent, to be classed as a distinct family in its own right. See on this Bernitz 2010.

8 Hansen 1974, 1975, 1976; the last was a revised version of his 1973 doctoral thesis.

ingly rare virtue in classical scholarship—remains invaluable;[9] in fact, it is still the standard work on its subject. The end of the decade saw the appearance of Harrison's two deeply learned volumes on Athenian law (though Harrison's work, unlike MacDowell's, remains firmly anchored in the civil law approach to the study of Athenian law).[10] MacDowell followed up his book on homicide with a general book on Athenian law and legal procedure fifteen years later, still the most accessible general introduction to the subject.[11] Three years later Gagarin published his first monograph on Athenian law devoted to homicide,[12] followed at a short interval with a book on the emergence of written law.[13] The spate of important monographs continued in the two decades following, with major works from Todd, Johnstone, Lanni, and collections of themed papers from Harris.[14]

One could continue to multiply citations; the selective list above largely excludes many specialised works dealing with a particular aspect of the system. But the few works cited should suffice to underscore both the rapidity and scale of the recent growth in scholarly interest and the change in the centre of gravity with the increase in scholarship from researchers working within the common law systems. One reason for the surge is probably the growth in interest in oratory as a genre and the increase in the number of modern commentaries available to support the close study of the orators, both of which proceed *pari passu* with the growth in interest in the law and the lawcourts of Athens, naturally enough, since one cannot understand the one without the other. The interest in the orators arises partly from a steadily widening concept of the literary canon and an increased awareness of the value of the orators as a source for social and political history. The increase in the volume of publications has important consequences in itself, since it creates a base for teaching both at undergraduate and at graduate level and consequently a growing cohort of potential researchers with their own questions to ask. The books of MacDowell and Todd are especially important in this respect. Each makes a distinct contribution and they complement each

9 MacDowell 1963.

10 Harrison 1968, 1971. It was the roots in Roman law which (in part) made MacDowell reluctant to complete Harrison's second volume as co-author rather than edit for publication; see Carey 2011: 242.

11 MacDowell 1978.

12 Gagarin 1981.

13 Gagarin 1986.

14 Todd 1993, Johnstone 1999, Lanni 2006, and collections of themed papers from Harris 2006, 2013.

other well. But in the recent past they have in turn been complemented by the sourcebook of David Phillips[15] and a dedicated volume in the *Cambridge Companions* series,[16] soon to be joined in turn by an Oxford handbook edited by Edward Harris and Mirko Canevaro. The other major resource worth signalling in this context is the comprehensive collection of translations of the orators edited by Michael Gagarin and published by the University of Texas Press.

The reason the entry into the market by scholars from the common law systems matters is that these systems share some features with the Athenian system. One is the presence of a judicial panel in some types of cases, where the civil law systems always use a professional judge. Athenian law uses judicial panels on a scale unimaginable within any common law system. But the dynamics of persuasion of a panel give the common law systems a greater affinity with Athenian courts. Another is the adversarial model and with it the limitation on the power of the adjudicator. Unlike the civil law magistrate, who can open up lines of investigation, the jury (Athenian or common law) has to work with the information provided. At the same time, the adversarial system unlike the inquisitorial requires both sides to state their case in competition as the best way of arriving at the truth. Common law remains a world away from ancient Athens. Among the many differences perhaps the most significant are the absence of a central public agency to pursue offences, the role of the litigants as the source of law in the courts, the reliance on continuous speech from the opposing parties as the medium of narrative and proof and the combination in a single group (the dikasts) of the role of judge and jury.[17] But despite the huge gap common law is a couple of paces closer to Athenian experience than civil law. The result is not that an approach from the direction of common law gives the answers; but it does change the perspective and reformulate some of the questions.

The other significant development is the diversification of method. Here the study of ancient Athenian law is simply responding to the broader context of changes in the study of ancient history and history more generally. The move from an inductive approach, which reconstructs from the bottom up by amassing evidence, to one derived from social sciences and based on the test-

15 Phillips 2013.

16 Gagarin and Cohen 2005.

17 For the modern researcher one result of this combination of roles which we would separate is a problem of translation. Some render the Greek word *dikastes* 'judge', others 'juror'. Contributors to this volume are divided. Since neither precisely renders the Greek, we have not sought to impose uniformity.

ing of a hypothetical model is now fully naturalised in the study of ancient history (including ancient law) as in other fields of historical research. It is perhaps most clearly exemplified in the debate about the role of feuding[18] or in Robin Osborne's influential article on the dynamics of the Athenian prosecutorial process,[19] most of all in the pioneering work of Sally Humphreys on the sociology of Athenian law.[20] The other (interconnected) strands which have expanded the ways in which the subject is studied are the impact of legal anthropology and comparative studies. It is now respectable to invoke Inuit nith-songs or the practices of the Tiv in a way that, if not unthinkable, would have raised an eyebrow thirty years ago. The milestone in this respect was the appearance of the *Nomos* collection in the early 1990s.[21] The comparative method is also at the base of the two volumes by Cohen on different aspects on the law.[22] The results of these approaches are often contentious. But again the effect is to expand the perspective of the field and to offer new questions as much as new solutions.

Despite the remarkable growth in interest in ancient Athenian law, open international conferences[23] dedicated to the theme have been relatively few. It was against this background that we organised an international conference on the use and abuse of law in the Athenian courts at UCL in 2013. To cover the whole subject would have been inconceivable, so the idea was to use one large and broadly defined theme as a means to sample the current state of study. It was a deep and narrow drill designed to illuminate current strands of thinking, not a field survey of work in the terrain. The speakers included a number of established scholars who have contributed much to our knowledge of Athenian law over recent decades, together with younger scholars working in the field who represent the future of the discipline. The talks themselves are available on the internet. This volume assembles a selection from the contributions, chosen both for their intrinsic merit and because through convergence or divergence they create a dialogue on the theme of the law in the courts of Athens. The book explicitly does not seek to impose a single coherent perspective on Athenian law but to open space for further ongoing debate. And it does not

18 See in particular Cohen 1995, Harris 2013: 60–98, Alwine 2015.

19 Osborne 1985.

20 See especially Humphreys 1985, 1988.

21 Cartledge, P., Millett, P. and Todd, S.C., eds, 1990.

22 Cohen 1991, 1995.

23 Mention should however be made of the symposia on the subject of Greek law with contributions from invited speakers, initiated by Hans Julius Wolff, published in the ongoing *Symposion* series.

attempt to do the work of a companion, which would require something far more comprehensive. As noted above there are better alternatives available for this purpose.

As will become obvious to the reader, we very rapidly found ourselves moving away from the premise of our title, *Use and Abuse*. The theme suggests that we can locate a firm dividing line within Athenian culture between proper and improper use, map practice from the evidence available and place individual authors and works on one side or the other of that division. It soon became clear that, once one gets beyond the most obvious cases of questionable ethics (such as use of the courts to intimidate, common enough in modern jurisdictions), inappropriate choice of procedure or outright misrepresentation of a law, it is exceedingly difficult within Athenian culture (possibly in most legal cultures) to label a tactic or a strategy as abusive in a meaningful way. We found ourselves with varieties of use, some mischievous, rather than a chiaroscuro of use and abuse. The issue is further obscured by the depth of our ignorance on so many specific aspects of substance and procedure and the limited direct evidence for the content of Athenian laws. Nonetheless we have kept the title, since it is a useful way of bringing into focus attitudes and practices in relation to the law and litigation and mapping the degrees of tolerance within the system and within the culture.

The papers in **Section 1: Conceptualising the System** all address larger structures, practices and processes at work in the Athenian legal system. Michael Gagarin's chapter (Chapter 1: *Abuse Is in the Eye of the Beholder*) tackles head-on the binary opposition in the book's title, arguing that we cannot meaningfully distinguish 'abuse' from 'use' in Athenian forensic oratory, partly because it is difficult to map the boundary between use and abuse, partly because of bias and distortion inherent in the material at our disposal (allegations of abuse come from hostile sources) and the lack of direct access to the laws themselves. In Chapter 2, *The Elasticity of Athenian Law*, Robin Osborne argues that talk of 'stretching the meaning of the law' misunderstands the nature of Athenian law, and that understanding Athenian law demands taking seriously the way in which law was constituted in every Athenian court as much as in the statute book or in the understanding of legal experts. The chapter explores ways in which the framing of law encouraged or restricted its elasticity, and demonstrates how the way in which a case was brought to court allowed prosecutors and defendants to 'try out' arguments and so discover whether or not they were likely to persuade a court. In Chapter 3, *The Athenian View of an Athenian Trial*, Edward Harris takes a diametrically opposite view. He takes issue with theoretical approaches to the dynamics of the system and argues that the Athenian primary sources available to us indicate that contemporaries believed that the dikasts enforced the law as their oath required. Accounts of trials show that the Athenian courts did not take public service or social identity into consideration and did not make *ad hoc* judgments. Unjust verdicts were thought to result from false testimony given by witnesses or from procedural violations. The chapter contains an appendix with references to all trials mentioned in the Attic orators. In Chapter 4, *Bridging the Divide Between Public and Private: dikē exoulēs and Other Hybrids*, Chris Carey argues that the Athenian legal system responds pragmatically to the needs of different situations to create hybrid actions which mix different kinds of procedure. He notes in particular that despite the (undeniable) bifurcation between public and private cases which formed the bedrock, the penological boundaries between public and private were permeable, with consequences both for plaintiff and prosecutor.

Section 2: Procedural Manoeuvres, while still dealing with larger aspects of the system, turns more specifically to the way in which litigants exploit different procedures available within the Athenian courts. In Chapter 5, *Isaios 6: A Case of Procedural Abuse (and Scholarly Misunderstandings)*, Brenda Griffith-Williams examines the possibility of abuse of the *diamartyria*, a procedural device for blocking a legal action. In the fourth century *diamartyria* was largely superseded by the more supple *paragraphē*, and from 380 BC its use is attested only in inheritance cases, where a direct descendant of the deceased could block a claim from a collateral relative by producing a witness to testify that the estate was 'not subject to adjudication'. Most of our evidence for the *diamartyria* comes from speeches by litigants who accuse their opponents of using it to gain an unfair advantage and it is often difficult for us to distinguish between a legitimate grievance and a rhetorical ploy, because we know little about the circumstances in which a *diamartyria* would have been considered acceptable. On the basis of an analysis of Isaios 6 Griffith-Williams concludes that, if the dikasts accepted Isaios' version of the facts, they would probably have agreed that the opponent had abused the *diamartyria*. But the system did not allow them to decide the procedural issue separately; they had to consider the prosecutor's objections to his opponent's choice of procedure alongside the substantive question whether the statement made in the *diamartyria* was true.

Chapter 6, *Anakrisis and the framing of strategies of argumentation in Athenian public trials*, by Christos Kremmydas, turns to the shadowy pre-trial process of *anakrisis*. Modern scholars agree that this stage involved an exchange of questions between the *archōn* and the litigants, a presentation of key pieces of evidence to be used by the opposing parties, and a brief mention of key arguments to be used at the trial itself. In this chapter, Kremmydas focuses on public trials and examines how the *anakrisis* may have helped the opposing parties shape their strategies of legal argumentation for the trial itself. In principle, this pre-trial stage was supposed to operate in the interest of fairness by making evidence available to both parties and shedding light on key legal arguments they were going to employ. But it is argued here that in practice it may have favoured the prosecution. In Chapter 7, *The Postponement of the Trial by Jury in Athens: The Timing of the graphē paranomōn*, László Horváth examines the postponement of jury trials in prosecutions against the proposer of an illegal decree, for which the best known classical example is the suit arising from the crown proposed for Demosthenes by Ktesiphon (Aischin. 3, Dem. 18). Horváth's interpretation of the relevant passages from Hypereides' recently discovered speech *Against Diondas* confirms that Demosthenes' and Aischines' Crown case was not exceptional; in certain circumstances any legal case, even a *graphē paranomōn*, could legitimately be postponed for years after the indictment. On the basis of the 'Diondas phenomenon' he suggests that many indictments did not proceed to trial and might be left to 'fade away', which may explain Aristophon's supposed boast that he had 'been acquitted (*apephygen*) in seventy-five *graphai paranomōn*' (Aischin. 3.194). Delay again forms the theme for Chapter 8, *Use and Abuse of Legal Procedures to Impede the Legal Process*, by Noboru Sato. Sato argues that, for Athenian litigants, the period after filing a case was not just waiting time before trial but an important stage for strategic negotiations based on litigants' individual circumstances. This chapter deals with litigants' use (for reasons good and bad) of the legal procedures available before trial in court, such as *hypōmosia, paragraphē*, and public and private arbitrations to retard the legal process. In some cases, delaying tactics may have helped them to obtain information that enabled them to win in court; but in other, presumably many, cases, the delay gave them opportunities to negotiate with their opponents with a view to out of court settlement. He argues that these developments give us an insight into Athenian attitudes towards disputes and formal legal procedures.

Law is, however, not just a basis for the pursuit of offenders and the resolution of disputes. It is itself both object of dispute and a theme for rhetorical exploitation. **Section 3: The Rhetoric of Law**, turns to the way in which speakers in court argue with, around or about the law. In Chapter 9, *Clauses Out of Context: Partial Citation of Statutes in Attic Forensic Oratory*, Lene Rubinstein discusses the practice of citing parts of statutes, decrees, and oaths in isolation from their original context. Athenian litigants often cited and interpreted individual clauses without calling upon the court attendant to read out the text in full. Modern scholars have debated the extent to which the practice of partial citation may have broadened the scope for interpretation and application of individual statutes, decrees, and oaths beyond what may originally have been envisaged by those who had drafted the texts. Rubinstein's chapter focuses on the evidence for the Athenians' awareness of and reflections on the practice, and on the extent to which they found it problematic (not least when it was resorted to by their opponents). Chapter 10, *Twisting the Laws in Ancient Athens*, by Ilias Arnaoutoglou, turns from citation to interpretation. He begins by considering whether modern concepts of abuse of law and abusive exercise of individual rights may be applied to the idiosyncratic legal framework of classical Athens. For this purpose Arnaoutoglou defines 'use' of law as the invocation of legal provision(s) to circumscribe litigants' actions and construct their arguments, and 'abuse' of law as any treatment of legal rules by a litigant so as to confer an unfair advantage on his case. On this basis he surveys the range of purposes for which laws are cited and the opportunities for distortion which coexisted with more straightforward deployment.

In Chapter 11, *(Re)constructing the Athenian Legal System*, Ifigeneia Giannadaki continues the theme of the space for exploitation created by the role of the litigant as source for the text of the law in court and moves from the deployment of individual statutes to depictions of the system as a whole. Law too has its story, but until recently little attention has been paid to the study of the dynamics of law as a coherent story in the orators and its effectiveness in the absence of a unified law code and jurisprudence as we find it in modern legal systems. Athenian law had no formal legal theory. But speakers in court readily provide us with confident rationalisations of the corpus of law which offer a consistent and coherent dynamic. Though such rationalisations have to possess a degree of plausibility to convince the judges and all come from people well versed in the courts and the laws, they are at base rhetorical constructs just as much as the narrative of the 'facts' of the case. Building on the work of Victoria Wohl (2010) this chapter looks at the various ways in which speakers create larger narratives to offer their audience a jurisprudence favourable to their case.

With the following two chapters we move to test cases of the rhetorical use of law. Chapter 12, *Liturgies and the Rhetoric of Law in Fourth-Century Athens: a Case Study on an antidosis* ([*Dem.*] 42), by Kostas Apostolakis, examines the speech *Against Phainippos* ([Dem.] 42) as an example of the rhetoric of law in disputes concerning the liturgy system and in particular the *antidosis* procedure. The speaker manipulates the law skilfully in a number of ways. He systematically interweaves law and character. In his own discussion of the *antidosis* law itself he implicitly extends its wording. He also exploits legal provisions which seem to be susceptible of partial interpretations and contests his opponent's readings. Chapter 13, *Jurisdiction and Jurisprudence: the Topography of Law in Demosthenes 23 Against Aristokrates*, by Victoria Wohl, examines Demosthenes' speech for the prosecution by *graphē paranomōn*, of Aristokrates, who had proposed a decree granting personal protection to the condottiere Charidemos, the local agent of the Thracian king Kersobleptes. Like most *graphai paranomōn* this speech combines legal arguments and political considerations. The latter are complicated, involving the negotiation of Athens' interests beyond its own borders, and the thorny questions of jurisdiction they raise are not addressed directly. Instead, as Wohl argues, in a tendentious reading of Drakon's homicide laws and (most unusually) a verbal tour of the homicide courts themselves the speech deploys a spatial rhetoric that equates law with legal procedure and localises that procedure within clear spatial limits: a well-defined (*horismenos*) law is one that respects borders (*horoi*). Demosthenes uses the laws not only to demonstrate the illegality of the *paranomon* decree but also to articulate a spatial logic of law that roots justice (*dikē*) in the physical topography of Athens itself. That same logic allows him to represent the Thracian Chersonese as an extension of the *polis*, a monument to Athenian justice not unlike the court buildings (§§ 207–208). The speech thus uses, if not abuses, the law to draw distant politics near and to evade difficult questions of jurisdiction by bringing Thrace within the close physical boundaries of Athenian law.

In the final chapter in this section, Chapter 14, *'Theft' as a Metaphor for the Abuse of Legal Process at Athens*, Stephen Todd looks not at argument but at terminology, specifically the extension of the terminology of theft to denote some form of trickery in legal procedure. There are at least ten such instances in the orators, plus a few others in the rhetorical theorists. Several of these passages allege a literal act of misappropriation, either of documents or else the hiding of a witness or other potential informant. Other examples of the *topos* are more obviously metaphorical, and include allegations of collusive prosecution designed to remove the defendant from the threat of punishment, the deceit of the audience, the use of logical trickery or of an evasive defence. Such language in the orators is normally aimed at the opponent (with one exception) and the aim is routinely to describe the opponent's behaviour as transgressive. Todd suggests that the language of theft has a convenient ambiguity in Greek, because *klopē* is one of a very limited number of offences that can be the subject both of a private *dikē* and of a public *graphē*—or, to put it another way, that can be easily manipulated so as to denote transgression either/both against the opposing litigant and/or against the wider community as represented by the jury. Metaphorical theft in the Athenian orators therefore becomes not so much a victimless but a victim-ambivalent crime. Another significant factor may be the absence of a distinct concept and language of fraud, which facilitates the identification of chicanery as theft.

Our final section, **Section 4: Specific Areas of Law**, turns to the role and practical use of specific areas of legal provision. Chapter 15, *Laws Against Laws: The Athenian Ideology of Legislation*, by Mirko Canevaro, discusses the ideology that underpinned the procedures of legislation (*nomothesia*) in fourth-century Athens. Several modern studies have isolated features of fourth-century discourse that seem to suggest a conservative ideology, which sees the legal system as characterised by absolute fixity and which refuses any change. Canevaro offers a more nuanced discussion. In the first part of the chapter he surveys the 'ideological' concerns which underpin the legal discussions of Dem. 20 and 24 and which construct a narrative of Athenian laws as a stable, clear and consistent whole with a defined *ēthos*. The figure of Solon as the 'original' legislator (*nomothetēs*) makes the Athenian laws into a coherent whole with specific intentions, and his *ēthos* is reproduced by abiding by the correct procedures for legislation. In the second part Canevaro analyses those passages that seem to reject legal change altogether. In the light of the ideology singled out in the previous section, these passages are more easily understood as providing extreme counterpoints to malpractice rather than offering positive examples of law-making to be followed in Athens.

In Chapter 16, *Abuse of the eisangelia in the Latter Half of the Fourth Century BC*, Eleni Volonaki focuses on the use or abuse of the impeachment (*eisangelia*) after the defeat of Athens in the battle at Chaironeia in 338 BC. Volonaki explores the argumentation presented in court between 335 and 325 BC concerning the allegedly common 'abuse' of the procedure. In particular, she examines the defence speeches of Hypereides *For Euxenippos* and *For Lykophron*, as well as Lykourgos' prosecution *Against Leokrates*. Originally intended for use against public figures or for major offences against the security of the state, after the middle of the fourth century BC impeachment is often directed against ordinary Athenian citizens (*idiōtai*) and for less serious offences such as flight from the city of Athens at a time of national alarm, adultery, and bribery for the announcement of an oracular dream. The charges brought after 338 BC apparently stretched the meaning of the words 'against any citizen who tried to overthrow the democracy' to a remarkable degree, a fact that may reflect an anxiety to secure the democracy against tyranny or any form of subversion. Nevertheless, there is reason to believe it was not always easy even for public figures with enormous authority to persuade the majority of the people that the scope of the offences subject to the impeachment law could be extended to cover any kind of misconduct or misbehaviour by a public figure or an ordinary citizen.

In Chapter 17, *Athenian Homicide Law and the Model Penal Code*, David Phillips turns to homicide, an area of law marked by very distinctive features relative to the rest of the corpus. Phillips argues that a more precise and nuanced understanding of Athenian homicide law can be obtained by applying the offence elements (conduct, circumstance, and result) and levels of culpability (purposeful, knowing, reckless, and negligent) found in the Model Penal Code (American Law Institute 1985). Part I adapts these categories to Athenian law and demonstrates their antecedents in Platonic and Aristotelian legal theory. Part II shows that conduct, circumstance, and result are frequently treated as discrete factors, with differing volitional requirements, in Athenian statutes governing homicide; Part III investigates the use, abuse, and critique of the law in Athenian homicide trials (actual and hypothetical) and beyond. Finally, an analysis of the insoluble problems of joint liability posed in Antiphon's *Second* and *Third Tetralogies* reveals that these works inaugurate the formal criticism of Athenian homicide law that culminates with Plato and Aristotle.

Chapter 18, *Abuse of Inheritance Law in Isaios?*, by Rosalia Hatzilambrou turns to inheritance law, a field in which Isaios was especially expert. Isaios has often been accused (by Dionysios of Halikarnassos and especially by Wyse (1904), whose commentary has been profoundly influential) of abusing the law in his speeches, which have consequently been regarded as an unreliable source for Athenian inheritance law. Hatzilambrou examines the laws cited in the corpus of Isaios' works to determine whether he did abuse the law, that is, whether he intentionally used an existing law wrongly; and, if so, to what extent and in what way. Hatzilambrou's close reading and checking of the citations of law in Isaios against the relevant external evidence (citations and invocations of law in other fourth-century oratorical works, the *Athenaion Politeia*, Plutarch, also Menander and Roman comedy) enable her to sketch out Isaios' approach to the use of law in his extant speeches. Her observations lead her to argue that with one probable exception Isaios *did not* abuse the law in his extant speeches: he merely interpreted vague statutes, and his interpretations, as known verdicts reveal, were the expected ones at least as regards his primary audience. He did employ legal arguments *a fortiori* when there was no legal provision relevant to his case, he did stick to the letter of the law when it favoured his argumentation, and he did suppress limitations on the provisions of the statute he was citing, if they were irrelevant to his case, but he did not intentionally misrepresent the substance of a law.

Bibliography

Alwine, A.T. (2015) *Enmity and Feuding in Classical Athens*, Austin.

Bernitz, U. (2010) *What Is Scandinavian Law? Concepts, Characteristics, Future*, Stockholm.

Carey, C. (2011) 'Douglas Maurice MacDowell', in *Proceedings of the British Academy* 2011, 233–248. (Reprinted in Arnaotouglou, I./ Kapparis, K./ Spatharas, D. (eds) (2018) *Studies on Greek law, oratory and comedy*, Douglas M. MacDowell, London and New York, pp. xiii-xxv).

Cartledge, P., Millett, P. and Todd, S.C., eds (1990) *Nomos: Essays in Athenian Law, Politics and Society*, Cambridge.

Cohen, D. (1991) *Law, Sexuality and Society: The Enforcement of Morals in Classical Athens*, Cambridge.

Cohen, D. (1995) *Law, Violence, and Community in Classical Athens*, Cambridge.

Du Plessis, P. (2015) *Borkowski's Textbook on Roman Law*, 5th edn, rev. Paul du Plessis, Oxford.

Gagarin, M. (1981) *Drakon and Early Athenian Homicide Law*, New Haven.

Gagarin, M. (1986) *Early Greek Law*, Berkeley.

Gagarin, M. and Cohen, D., eds (2005) *The Cambridge Companion to Ancient Greek Law*, Cambridge.

Hansen, M.H. (1974) *The Sovereignty of the People's Court in the Fourth Century* BC *and the Public Action Against Unconstitutional Proposals*, Odense.

Hansen, M.H. (1975) *Eisangelia: The Sovereignty of the People's Court in Athens in the Fourth Century* BC *and the Impeachment of Generals and Politicians*. Odense.

Hansen, M.H. (1976) *Apagoge, endeixis and ephegesis Against kakourgoi, atimoi, and pheugontes: A Study in the Athenian Administration of Justice in the Fourth Century* BC, Odense.

Harris, E.M. (2006) *Democracy and the Rule of Law in Classical Athens: Essays on Law, Society, and Politics*, Cambridge.

Harris, E.M. (2013) *The Rule of Law in Action in Democratic Athens*, Oxford.

Harrison, A.R.W. (1968–1971) *The Law of Athens*, 2 vols, Oxford.

Humphreys, S.C. (1985) 'Social Relations on Stage: Witnesses in Classical Athens', *History and Anthropology* 1, 313–369.

Humphreys, S.C. (1988) 'The Discourse of Law in Archaic and Classical Greece', *Law and History Review* 6, 465–493.

Johnstone, S. (1999) *Disputes and Democracy: The Consequences of Litigation in Ancient Athens*, Austin.

Lanni, A. (2006) *Law and Justice in the Courts of Classical Athens*, Cambridge.

Lavdas, K. (1997) *The Europeanization of Greece: Interest Politics and the Crises of Integration*, Basingstoke/London.

MacDowell, D.M. (1963) *Athenian Homicide Law in the Age of the Orators*, Manchester.

MacDowell, D.M. (1978) *The Law in Classical Athens*, London.

Mayall, L. (2015) 'The Legacy of Roman Law', in Johnston, D., ed., *The Cambridge Companion to Roman Law*, Cambridge, 374–396.

Mousourakis, G. (2015) *Roman Law and the Origins of the Civil Law Tradition*, Heidelberg.

Osborne, R. (1985) 'Law in Action in Classical Athens', *JHS* 105, 40–58. (Reprinted in Osborne (2010) 171–204.)

Osborne, R. (2010) *Athens and Athenian Democracy*, Cambridge.

Perakis, E. (2008) 'Contract Law in Greece', in Ansay, T. and Basedow, J., eds (2008) *Structures of civil and procedural law in south eastern European countries*, Berlin, 23–33.

Phillips, D.D. (2013) *The Law of Ancient Athens*, Ann Arbor, Mich.

Schiller, A.A. (1978) *Roman Law: Mechanisms of Development*, The Hague.

Thür, G. (1977) *Beweisführung vor den Schwurgerichtshöfen Athens: die* Proklesis *zur* Basanos, Vienna.

Todd, S.C. (1993) *The Shape of Athenian Law*, Oxford.

Yessiou-Faltsi, P. (2004) 'Civil Procedure in Greece (Nineteenth and Twentieth Centuries)' in van Rhee, C.H., ed. (2004) *The Law's Delay: Essays on Undue Delay in Civil Litigation*, Groningen, 377–391.

PART 1

Conceptualising the System

CHAPTER 1

Abuse Is in the Eye of the Beholder

Michael Gagarin

The title of this volume, *Use and Abuse of Law in the Athenian Courts*, posits an obvious polarity: just as legal systems are used by those who litigate and by others, so surely they can be abused. But is this so obvious? If we press the question, exactly what it means to abuse the law, we find that the answer is elusive. Criteria for identifying abuse are not easy to specify, even for legal systems that are far more authoritarian than the Athenian legal system. In this chapter I will argue that it is in fact impossible to objectively distinguish use from abuse in Athenian law. Rather, to describe any particular use of the law as abuse is merely to state a subjective disapproval of that use; there is no way to support such an opinion with objective criteria. To provide some context for my argument, I begin with a brief consideration of a legal system in which authoritative standards of correctness can more easily be established, and for this purpose I will use the system I know best, U.S. Common Law.

In 1972, in the case of Roe *v.* Wade, the Supreme Court decided that the right to an abortion was guaranteed by the constitution, which contains, according to the Court, an implicit right to privacy. As a result, no state is allowed to enact a complete prohibition of abortion, and anyone who argues in court that the right to an abortion is not guaranteed by the constitution is, as a legal matter, wrong. Thus a lawyer who claims that the constitution allows states to prohibit abortion is simply wrong, and we can say objectively that he is abusing the law. This does not, of course, prevent people from arguing, as many do, that the decision in Roe *v.* Wade was wrong, and a number of observers fear or hope (as the case may be) that the court may one day reverse itself. But as of today, the constitutionality of abortion is a matter of settled law.

Even here, however, one should be careful in speaking of abuse, because someone can legitimately challenge a decision of the Supreme Court as a means of getting the court to change an earlier decision. In 1954, for example, in Brown *v.* Board of Education, lawyers succeeded in persuading the Court to reverse a ruling it made in 1896 that allowed so-called 'separate but equal' schools for different races. In the same way a state today could enact a law making abortion illegal, and then argue in court in defence of this law that there is no constitutional right to an abortion. To those who point out that this argument contradicts a matter of settled law, the state could respond that it is

 | DOI:10.1163/9789004377899_003

seeking ultimately to persuade the Supreme Court to reverse its decision in Roe *v*. Wade, and if lower courts rejected its arguments, as they likely would, the state could appeal to the Supreme Court. In this way, even an argument that clearly contradicts settled law might be defended as a legitimate use of the law. In short, even in the U.S. it is not easy to determine objectively that someone is abusing the law.

How then could someone abuse the law in the Athenian legal system, in which no judge or other official existed who could rule authoritatively on the validity or meaning of that law?[1] The final authority in court was the jury, but even when we know the verdict in an Athenian case, and we rarely do, we cannot know on what grounds the jury reached that verdict. Even if the verdict was unanimous (which must have happened very rarely with juries numbering several hundreds), different jurors would have had different reasons for their vote. If the same verdict was delivered in many similar cases, it is possible that over time the meaning of a law could be authoritatively established, but even then, a litigant could legitimately try to persuade a new jury otherwise, just as one can always try to persuade the Supreme Court to change its mind.

To illustrate the difficulty of identifying abuse in Athenian law, let us consider some specific examples of cases that may be thought to involve abuse. I begin with substantive law.[2] When a litigant wants to make use of a law (or part of a law), he may introduce the text in court as a document, read by the clerk, or he may simply speak about the law, perhaps quoting a few words of it but without presenting the actual text. When a speaker introduces the text of a law and a text is preserved in our manuscripts, only very rarely can we confirm the accuracy of that text. On the other hand, we can have some confidence that litigants generally quoted the texts of statutes correctly because we are told that a law prescribed death as the penalty for anyone who cited a non-existent law (Dem. 26.24).[3] Litigants were required during pre-trial proceedings to submit the texts of the laws that they wanted to introduce at trial,[4] and the opposing litigant would thus have been able to check the quotation and bring suit if the law as quoted did not exist.

1 Modern scholars often cite Aristotle's statements on law as if they were authoritative, but Aristotle is sometimes demonstrably wrong (Carey 1994: 95–106), and in any case he would not be considered an authority in any Athenian court.

2 I will consider the possible abuse of legal procedure below.

3 θάνατον μὲν ὡρικέναι τὴν ζημίαν, ἐάν τις οὐκ ὄντα νόμον παράσχηται.

4 The requirement is reported for cases in which there was an arbitration hearing (*Ath. Pol.* 53.2–3), but likely applied to all other cases as well (Todd 1993: 129).

Litigants regularly made minor changes in wording or cited only part of a law, and these normally went unchallenged; indeed, partial quotation was probably the rule, since many Athenian statutes were rather lengthy and in most cases would contain provisions that were not relevant to the litigant's argument. Thus in [Dem.] 58.14 the speaker asks the clerk explicitly to 'read out this part of the law for me' (καί μοι λέγε τοῦτ' αὐτὸ τοῦ νόμου). In one case, Dem. 43.57, we can compare the introduced text[5] with the original law, which was part of Drakon's law on homicide, preserved in a fifth-century copy.[6] The order of provisions in the law and in the quotation is different and one clause of the law has been omitted in the quotation, but otherwise the quotation is accurate.[7] The speaker in this inheritance case is interested in degrees of family relationship not homicide, and so he also omits many other provisions of the homicide law not relevant to his case. But this amount of modification was evidently accepted.[8] Thus when Demosthenes complains (18.121) that Aischines removed parts of a law he cited, he is only accusing him of doing what many litigants do in quoting laws: they cite that part of a law relevant to their case, and as long as the quotation is accurate, this use of the law is proper. There is also nothing improper if a speaker quotes laws that support his case but says nothing about laws that may not support it, though of course, he may be well advised to deal with a law that poses obvious difficulties for his argument and try to counter its force, as Epikrates does in Hyp. *Athen.* (see below).

---

5 προειπεῖν τῷ κτείναντι ἐν ἀγορᾷ ἐντὸς ἀνεψιότητος καὶ ἀνεψιοῦ, συνδιώκειν δὲ καὶ ἀνεψιοὺς καὶ ἀνεψιῶν παῖδας καὶ γαμβροὺς καὶ πενθεροὺς καὶ φράτερας. αἰδέσασθαι δέ, ἐὰν μὲν πατὴρ ᾖ ἢ ἀδελφὸς ἢ υἱεῖς, ἅπαντας, ἢ τὸν κωλύοντα κρατεῖν. ἐὰν δὲ τούτων μηδεὶς ᾖ, κτείνῃ δὲ ἄκων, γνῶσι δὲ οἱ πεντήκοντα καὶ εἷς, οἱ ἐφέται, ἄκοντα κτεῖναι, ἐσέσθων οἱ φράτερες, ἐὰν ἐθέλωσι, δέκα· τούτους δὲ οἱ πεντήκοντα καὶ εἷς ἀριστίνδην αἱρείσθων. καὶ οἱ πρότερον κτείναντες ἐν τῷδε τῷ θεσμῷ ἐνεχέσθων.

6 *IG* I[3] 104, lines 13–23:

[αἰδέσασθαι δ' ἐὰμ μὲν πατὲ]ρ ἐ̑-
ι ἒ ἀδελφὸ[ς] ἒ *h*υε̂ς, *h*άπαντ[α]ς, ἒ τὸν κ̣ο[λύοντα κρατε̂ν· **ἐὰν δὲ μὲ**] *h*ọῦ-
τοι ὄσι̣, μέχρ' ἀνεφ[σι]ότετος καὶ̣ [ἀνεφσιô, ἐὰν *h*άπαντες αἰδέσ]α̣σ-
θαι ἐθέλοσι, τὸν κο[λύ]οντ̣α [κ]ρα[τε̂ν· ἐὰν δὲ τούτον μεδὲ *h*ε̂ς ἐ̑ι, κτ]έ-
νει δὲ ἄκο[ν], γνõσι δὲ *h*οι̣ [πε]ντ[έκοντα καὶ *h*ε̂ς *h*οι ἐφέται ἄκοντ]α̣
κτε̂ναι, ἐσέσθ[ο]ν δὲ *ḥ*[οι φ]ρ[άτορες ἐὰν ἐθέλοσι δέκα· τούτος δ]ὲ *h*ο̣-
ι πεντέκο[ν]τ[α καὶ] *h*ε̂ς ἀρ[ι]στ̣[ίνδεν *h*αιρέσθον. καὶ *h*οι δὲ πρ]ότε[ρ]-
ον κτέ[ν]α[ντ]ε[ς ἐν] τô[ιδε τôι θεσμôι ἐνεχέσθον. προειπε̂ν δ]ὲ τôι κ-
τέν̣α̣ν̣[τι ἐν ἀ]γορ̣[âι μέχρ' ἀνεφσιότετος καὶ ἀνεφσιô· συνδιόκ]εν
δὲ [κ]ἀνεφσ[ιὸς καὶ ἀνεφσιôν παῖδας καὶ γαμβρὸς καὶ πενθερὸ]ς κ-
αὶ φρ̣[ά]τ[ο]ρ[ας.

The words in bold face are omitted in Dem. 43.57.

7 Stroud 1968: 49.

8 See Bonner 1905: 59, who concludes, 'it was sufficient if the quotation was not materially different from the original law.'

The law prohibiting the citation of non-existent laws would only have applied to texts that were formally introduced in court; it would not have prevented speakers from seriously misrepresenting these laws when they discuss them in their speech. Several examples of such misrepresentation, possibly amounting to abuse, are generally accepted by scholars. First, in Lys. 1.30, Euphiletos has the clerk read a law that a person is not to be convicted of homicide for killing a man found in bed with his wife. The text of this law is preserved in Dem. 23.53; it reads in part: 'If someone kills a person … after finding him on top of his wife or mother or sister or daughter or concubine kept for producing free children, he shall not be exiled as a killer on account of this.'[9] Immediately after introducing the law, Euphiletos tells the jury that the law expressly says that 'a man is not to be convicted of homicide if he captures an adulterer in bed with his wife and exacts this penalty from him.'[10] The paraphrase is accurate until the last clause, which speaks of death as the penalty for adultery, effectively changing a law that allows justified homicide into one that punishes adultery. This is in line with Euphiletos' earlier assertion that Eratosthenes 'met the fate which the laws prescribe for those who behave like that' (1.27, cf. 1.29). Technically, this is a distortion of the law, but because in practice the law can easily be understood as one that declares seduction punishable by death, and because all Euphiletos needs for an acquittal is that the law allows him to kill Eratosthenes, as it clearly does, the distortion has rhetorical effect (supporting Euphiletos' account of events, which sees Eratosthenes as the criminal and Euphiletos himself as the punisher) but is legally insignificant.

Shortly after introducing the law on justified homicide, Euphiletos introduces a law about rape (1.31). The text is not preserved, but he immediately summarises the law: 'you hear, gentlemen, how it provides that if anyone forcibly shames [i.e. rapes] a free man or boy, he is to pay double the damage; if (he forcibly shames) a woman—one of those for whom it is allowed to kill—he shall be liable to the same penalty.'[11] Euphiletos' conclusion is that the legislator prescribed a more severe penalty for seduction, namely death, than the

9 ἐάν τις ἀποκτείνῃ … ἐπὶ δάμαρτι ἢ ἐπὶ μητρὶ ἢ ἐπ' ἀδελφῇ ἢ ἐπὶ θυγατρί, ἢ ἐπὶ παλλακῇ ἣν ἂν ἐπ' ἐλευθέροις παισὶν ἔχῃ, τούτων ἕνεκα μὴ φεύγειν κτείναντα.

10 τούτου μὴ καταγιγνώσκειν φόνον, ὃς ἂν ἐπὶ δάμαρτι τῇ ἑαυτοῦ μοιχὸν λαβὼν ταύτην τὴν τιμωρίαν ποιήσηται. (Lys. 1.30; translations of Lysias are from Todd 2000.) 'Adulterer' is Todd's term, but 'seducer' would be more accurate, as intercourse with a man's sister or daughter is not called 'adultery' in English.

11 ἀκούετε, ὦ ἄνδρες, ὅτι κελεύει, ἐάν τις ἄνθρωπον ἐλεύθερον ἢ παῖδα αἰσχύνῃ βίᾳ, διπλῆν τὴν βλάβην ὀφείλειν· ἐὰν δὲ γυναῖκα, ἐφ' αἷσπερ ἀποκτείνειν ἔξεστιν, ἐν τοῖς αὐτοῖς ἐνέχεσθαι.

double-damage fine for rape. This conclusion is accepted at face value by some scholars, but at the very least it oversimplifies matters.[12] As is also true of other offences, both rape and seduction were subject to several different laws and could be dealt with in different ways. The law just introduced by Euphiletos probably provided for a *dikē biaiōn* (lit. 'suit against the use of force'); but the law on justified homicide which Euphiletos introduced earlier (see above) would have applied to a rapist caught in the act as well. Rape, though perhaps not seduction, could also be prosecuted by the more serious procedure of *graphē hybreōs*, for which the penalty could be death. Thus serious punishments were possible for rape. On the other hand, it may well be true that, as Carey (1995: 407–417) has argued, Euphiletos' position 'is in its broad outlines correct.' The *dikē biaiōn* may not have been the only procedure, but it was probably the most common charge brought in cases of rape. And although the law on justified homicide could technically be used for rape, it appears clearly to be aimed at seducers (as would a similar law of ours allowing someone to kill a man found in bed with his wife). Finally, the *graphē hybreōs* appears to have been more talked about than actually used. Thus although Euphiletos may be distorting the law in a technical sense, he may well be representing legal practice accurately.

Although the prosecution's speech does not survive, they probably disputed Euphiletos' interpretations of these laws as well as his presentation of the facts. Similar disputes over the meaning or application of a law are fairly common in the surviving speeches. In Lys. 10.6–7, for example, Theomnestos is accused of slandering the speaker by claiming that he killed his father. His defence will apparently be that he never used the word 'killer' (*androphonos*), which was explicitly prohibited in the law against slander, and that accusing someone of killing is not the same as saying he is a killer. Against this, the speaker argues that by prohibiting use of the word *androphonos*, the law also intended to prohibit the use of equivalent expressions, such as 'he killed.' Most scholars consider the speaker's interpretation of the law reasonable, but Theomnestos' narrow, letter-of-the-law interpretation can also be defended.[13] Thus both interpretations are plausible, and neither can be said to be abusive.

In Isa. 11, on the estate of Hagnias, the parties dispute the meaning of a word in the law concerning intestate succession, which is introduced by the speaker Theopompos before he begins his speech. The law is not preserved at

12 See Harris 1990.

13 See Todd 2007: 635, who adds, 'there was at Athens no system of case-law or jurisprudence whereby an interpretation could be authoritatively established.'

this point, but is almost certainly the law cited in Dem. 43.51. The relevant part reads 'if there are no [kinsmen] on the father's side [of the deceased] as far as the *anepsiōn paidōn* ('children of cousins'), those on the mother's side are entitled to inherit in the same way.'[14] The dispute concerns *anepsioi*: does this mean children of cousins of the deceased—his first cousins once removed, to use our terminology—or children of cousins of the deceased's father—his second cousins?[15] Only on the second interpretation does Theopompos qualify as a close enough relative to inherit the estate in question, and so naturally he argues for this view. Another claimant evidently argued for the first view. The estate of Hagnias had been in dispute for quite some time, and we know that Theopompos won at least two earlier cases. Thus at least two juries have agreed with his argument for the second interpretation of *anepsioi*. However, their verdicts clearly did not end the dispute, or he would not have to defend this interpretation once more in Isa. 11. We do not know the reasoning behind either of the two previous verdicts, but I suspect this law was truly ambiguous. Interestingly, there is no sign that any legislation was enacted, or even contemplated, that might determine authoritatively the meaning of the word in this context.

A similar ambiguity seems to exist in the laws on adoption. The speaker in Dem. 44 claims that Leochares and his family have contrived a series of posthumous adoptions over three generations; he argues that this is against the law (44.23): 'Well, isn't it contrary to the laws for a man who is himself an adopted son to leave behind adopted sons and return home?'[16] He returns to this point later (44.64), quoting the lawgiver as saying 'a man [clearly referring to an adopted man] is [allowed] to return to his own family upon leaving behind a legitimate son;'[17] he interprets this to mean that the adopted son is not allowed to adopt.[18] The speaker is very likely referring to a Solonian law that is introduced in [Dem.] 46.14: 'Everyone who has not been adopted when Solon entered on his archonship in such a way that he could neither renounce nor claim the inheritance is permitted to dispose of his own property, however he wishes, provided he has no legitimate sons, unless he is mad due to old age',

14 ἐὰν δὲ μὴ ὦσι πρὸς πατρὸς μέχρι ἀνεψιῶν παίδων, τοὺς πρὸς μητρὸς τοῦ ἀνδρὸς κατὰ ταὐτὰ κυρίους εἶναι. Translation of Dem. 43, 44, and [46] are from Scafuro 2011.

15 On the meaning of *anepsioi paidōn* see Thompson 1976: 4–7, Scafuro 2011: 131–132.

16 πῶς γὰρ οὐ παρὰ τοὺς νόμους, ὁπότ᾽ εἰσποιητὸς αὐτὸς ὢν εἰσποιητοὺς υἱοὺς ἐγκαταλείπων ἐπανήει;

17 υἱὸν γνήσιον ἐγκαταλιπόντα ἐπανιέναι.

18 Cf. Isa. 6.44 and 10.11, which may refer to a different law from the one cited at [Dem.] 46.14, or perhaps to a different part of the same law.

etc.[19] Some scholars[20] have agreed with the speaker that an adopted son was not legally allowed to adopt, but others understand the law differently[21] and it appears that two or three successive adoptions had in fact occurred in the family in question. Thus Scafuro is probably correct to conclude that there was no law explicitly prohibiting an adopted son from himself adopting, but rather that this may have been common practice rather than a matter of law.[22] If this is correct, then it appears that, as in Isa. 11, the dispute here concerns a point not explicitly covered by the law; thus reasonable arguments can be made for both the speaker's position and his opponent's. Here too, the Athenians apparently made no effort to clarify this point.

Litigants may also seem to abuse the laws when they cite them as evidence. For example, Aischines begins his speech against Timarchos (1.6–25) with an account of some laws which he says will illustrate proper conduct. He attributes these laws to Drakon and Solon, and says that the legislator enacted them in chronological order—first boys, then young men, and then others, so he will follow the same order in his speech.[23] Whether all these laws really were enacted by Drakon or Solon is unknown, though orators conventionally attribute all laws to Solon, so we can hardly consider this abuse.

Moreover, no one could have known in what order Solon (or someone else) enacted these laws, but because the order of citation has only rhetorical value as evidence for the proper conduct of boys and young men, it does not affect the legal case. Aischines, like many other speakers, also explains the legislator's motives in enacting these laws. Most such explanations were undoubtedly fabricated, but here too, no one could have known the legislator's actual motives. The jury was undoubtedly aware of this, and as long as the assertions are plausible, they probably saw nothing wrong with it. One could also complain that none of the laws Aischines cites in this passage is directly relevant to the legal issues in the case. But it is common in the orators to cite a law in order to illustrate something else, in this case general standards of proper conduct, in comparison with which Timarchos' conduct is clearly deficient. Today we would probably disallow this kind of evidence, but in Athens laws were treated as evidence, and thus the use Aischines makes of them here would have drawn no objection.

---

19 ὅσοι μὴ ἐπεποίηντο, ὥστε μήτε ἀπειπεῖν μήτ' ἐπιδικάσασθαι, ὅτε Σόλων εἰσῄει τὴν ἀρχήν, τὰ ἑαυτοῦ διαθέσθαι εἶναι ὅπως ἂν ἐθέλῃ, ἂν μὴ παῖδες ὦσι γνήσιοι ἄρρενες, ἂν μὴ μανιῶν ἢ γήρως …

20 E.g., Todd 1993: 222.

21 See Harrison 1968: 85–87.

22 Scafuro 2011: 185–190.

23 For Aischines' narrative of the laws in this speech see further Giannadaki in this volume.

My last example of possible substantive abuse on the part of the speaker is from Hypereides' *Against Athenogenes*. As the speaker Epikrates tells it, he had fallen in love with a slave boy and had proposed to their owner, Athenogenes, that he buy the boy's freedom, but Athenogenes, with the help of a woman named Antigona, persuaded him to buy the boy together with his father and brother and the perfume workshop which the slaves managed. In this way, Athenogenes argued, Epikrates would have the boy he loved under his complete control. Athenogenes mentioned that Epikrates would be responsible for the slaves' debts, but assured him (so Epikrates says) that these were much smaller than the assets of the workshop. Epikrates was persuaded; he brought the agreed sale price of forty minas to Athenogenes, who had prepared a written agreement, which he had read to Epikrates. In his eagerness to obtain the object of his desire, however, Epikrates paid little attention to it. He quickly signed and handed over the money. Only later did he discover that their debts amounted to almost five talents, much more than the trivial amount Athenogenes had claimed. Epikrates thus sued Athenogenes, seeking to be relieved of the obligation to pay these debts.

Epikrates faces an immediate and obvious difficulty: as he tells the jury, 'Athenogenes will at once tell you that the law declares that any agreements made by two parties are binding' (*Athen.* 13).[24] Since the agreement specified that Epikrates would assume Midas's debts, this law, if interpreted strictly, would fatally weaken his case. Therefore, Epikrates immediately adds his own qualification: 'Yes, agreements that are just, my good fellow. But for unjust agreements, the law says the direct opposite; they are not binding.'[25] He then says he will make things clearer from the laws themselves and proceeds to mention four other laws: one prohibiting lying in the Agora (14), one requiring that a slave's defects be disclosed before a sale (15), one stating that children are legitimate only if their mother was justly betrothed (16), and one stating that a will is valid unless made under the influence of a woman or some other constraint (17). None of these laws is directly relevant to his case, and it seems very likely that no law existed that explicitly affirmed that agreements had to be just, or else Epikrates would have cited it.

He then adds several other arguments, in particular that, as an experienced businessman, Athenogenes must have known the size of Midas's debts very well, whereas he (Epikrates) could not be expected to know them (19–20). But

24 ἐρεῖ δὲ πρὸς ὑμᾶς αὐτίκα μάλα Ἀθηνογένης, ὡς ὁ νόμος λέγει, ὅσα ἂν ἕτερος ἑτέρῳ ὁμολογήσῃ, κύρια εἶναι. Translations of Hypereides are by Cooper from Worthington, Cooper, and Harris 2001.

25 τά γε δίκαια ὦ βέλτιστε· τὰ δὲ μὴ τοὐναντίον ἀπαγορεύει μὴ κύρια εἶναι.

the heart of his case is that the agreement he signed was unjust, at least with regard to these debts, and thus it is crucial to determine whether the law on agreements required an agreement to be just in order to be binding. In other words, is the addition of 'just' to the meaning of the law valid, or is it an abuse of the meaning of that law?

The law on agreements is often mentioned in the orators and is introduced in court once, though the text is not preserved (Dem. 47.77). Some speakers add the qualification that the agreement had to be just or lawful, or had to be voluntary, or had to be made in the presence of witnesses. Phillips surveys all these mentions and makes a good case that the law as written did not contain any qualification.[26] Assuming he is correct, is Epikrates' addition of 'just' to the text an abuse? Phillips argues that the law could not have intended that only just agreements be binding, because in fact unjust agreements were considered binding in Athens. He cites Dem. 48, where Kallistratos and Olympiodoros agreed to join forces in seeking an inheritance and to divide equally whatever amount either one received; Kallistratos later sued Olympiodoros for his share of the estate, claiming that Olympiodoros had violated their agreement. Thus Phillips argues, Kallistratos is seeking to enforce an illegal and unjust agreement. But was this agreement illegal? Claimants to an Athenian estate engage in all kinds of strategies, many of them quite devious, in order to make their claim succeed over those of other claimants, but nothing suggests that joining forces with another claimant was illegal or immoral.[27] The agreement in Dem. 48 was made in public before reputable, named witnesses, and Kallistratos reports it with no hint of embarrassment or excuse. In fact, he presents the agreement as a positive legal development.[28] Clearly he does not expect the jurors to see anything wrong with the agreement, and Olympiodoros almost certainly did not argue that the agreement should not be enforced because it

26 Phillips 2009: 89–122. Harris 2000: 49 gives no grounds for his statement that 'actually the complete version of the law included the word "willing".'

27 Cf. Isa. 11.20–21, where Theopompos denies that he could have made an agreement to join forces with Stratocles in contesting the estate because their two claims competed with one another; he suggests, however, that two other claimants might have made such an agreement because their claims did not compete directly. There is no hint in his argument that either agreement would have been unjust or unlawful.

28 See MacDowell 2009: 89–90. Carawan 2007b: 77 argues that the fact that the agreement settled a previous dispute between the two men is the reason the agreement was binding. But Kallistratos nowhere attributes any significance to the fact that the agreement was also a settlement. He cites the settlement to reinforce the idea that the two agreed to an equal division of property, but, as he repeatedly emphasises, his case rests on the agreement to divide the estate equally in the future, not the fact that they divided proceeds equally during a settlement of their past differences.

was illegal or unjust. Nothing, therefore, supports the view that an unjust or unlawful agreement was nonetheless binding.

Indeed, it is difficult to conceive of an agreement that was clearly unjust being enforced in court. For example, if X made an agreement with Y that he would pay him money to murder Z, if Y then killed Z but X did not pay, would Y bring suit against him for payment? It seems unlikely, to say the least. Thus I think we need to take seriously Epikrates' claim that only just agreements are binding. This qualification is, as he suggests, implicit in the law itself. Epikrates does not need to interpret the law by analogy or from legislative intent, methods regularly attributed to him by scholars.[29] He is not using either of these methods of interpretation. Instead, he takes for granted, and assumes his audience will also take for granted, that laws must be just, that they do not and cannot condone unjust acts, and therefore that unjust agreements cannot be binding.[30]

This being so, the case turns on whether the agreement was unjust, and all of Epikrates' arguments are directed at this point. The four other laws that he cites are all intended to provide examples of types of behaviour that these laws implicitly identify as unjust—behaviours similar to the alleged behaviour of Athenogenes. Epikrates implies, moreover, that Athenogenes will argue in his defence that the agreement was just, that Epikrates signed it willingly in front of witnesses, and that he, Athenogenes, had no knowledge at the time of the amount of the slave's debts. He certainly does not expect Athenogenes to argue that the law applies to all agreements, even unjust ones, and that therefore the agreement should be enforced even if it is unjust. This would not be a tenable position. We may conclude, then, that Epikrates' understanding of the law on agreements as applying only to just agreements is not an abuse of the law; it is arguably the correct way to understand it.

Thus far I have argued that the uses which speakers make of the laws can always be supported by arguments that cannot be objectively shown to be invalid. Speakers also accuse their opponents of abusing laws. Such accusations are usually impossible to assess, because the opponents' speeches are almost

29 It may be relevant that although the maritime courts required the parties to have a written contract, the courts would not hear a case concerning a contract to ship grain to a port other than Athens, because this was prohibited by law ([Dem.] 50–51; see Dimopoulou 2014: 268–269).

30 E.g. Phillips 2009: 106–117. Harris 2000: 47–54 argues that Epikrates is exploiting the open texture of Athenian law, seeking to find in other statutes an indication of the legislator's intentions that could then be used to interpret the law on agreements. But Epikrates' argument does not depend on legislative intent but on the general principle that all Athenian laws are just.

never preserved. For the trial 'On the Crown', however, both Aischines' prosecution speech and Demosthenes' defence speech on behalf of Ktesiphon survive (Aischin. 3, Dem. 18). The trial stems from a *graphē paranomōn* brought by Aischines against Ktesiphon for proposing a decree that would award a crown to Demosthenes 'because he consistently speaks and acts in the best interests of the *dēmos*' (Aischin. 3.49).[31] Aischines charges that the decree is illegal. As a requirement of this procedure, the accuser must specify a law that the decree allegedly violates; in this case, Aischines specifies two laws. Also, as is common in such cases, the substance of the decree is also alleged to be illegal.

As one might expect, the litigants present very different views of the meaning and application of the two laws Aischines cites. The first prohibits the award of a crown to any official who has not yet passed the required audit (*euthynai*); Aischines argues that Demosthenes had not yet passed his audit as Commissioner for Walls (3.9–31) and thus the decree was illegal. Demosthenes responds that because he was to be crowned for deeds that had nothing to do with this position, the law Aischines cites does not apply to him (18.111–119). Aischines' second law states that crowns are to be awarded in either the Council or the Assembly; he argues that since Ktesiphon's decree proposed awarding the crown to Demosthenes in the theatre, the decree was illegal in this respect as well (3.32–48). He warns the jury that they should not be deceived by a law that Demosthenes will introduce that may appear to allow the award of crowns in the theatre; this law, Aischines argues, only pertains to crowns awarded by other cities, not those awarded by Athens. As Aischines predicts, Demosthenes does introduce another law that, he argues, allows crowns to be awarded in the theatre if the people so vote (18.120–121). He ignores Aischines' argument that this only applies to crowns from other cities, noting that he himself and many others have been crowned in the theatre. He ends his argument with an attack on Aischines' treatment of the laws (18.121): 'are you not ashamed … to rewrite laws or snip off parts of them, even though citizens sworn to render judgment according to the laws should hear them in their entirety?'[32]

Here, each litigant accuses the other of abusing the law. Most scholars have concluded that Aischines has the stronger position on both laws; Harris, how-

31 ὅτι διατελεῖ καὶ λέγων καὶ πράττων τὰ ἄριστα τῷ δήμῳ. Translation of Aischines is from Carey 2000.

32 αἰσχύνει φθόνου δίκην εἰσάγων, οὐκ ἀδικήματος οὐδενός, καὶ νόμους μεταποιῶν, τῶν δ' ἀφαιρῶν μέρη, οὓς ὅλους δίκαιον ἦν ἀναγιγνώσκεσθαι τοῖς γ' ὀμωμοκόσιν κατὰ τοὺς νόμους ψηφιεῖσθαι; Translation of Dem. 18 is from Yunis 2005.

ever, has maintained forcefully that Demosthenes' responses are correct.[33] Can we determine which litigant (or which modern scholar) is correct? We cannot. We may choose to agree with one or the other side of this debate, but there is no way to determine objectively or authoritatively that one or the other is correct. All we can say is that both sides present interpretations of the law that are not unreasonable. We do know that Ktesiphon was acquitted, but from this we cannot conclude anything, not even that a majority of the jury agreed with Demosthenes' interpretation of either law. Some jurors undoubtedly agreed with his view of one or the other law (or both), but some almost certainly agreed with Aischines; and in the Athenian legal system, no authoritative decision could be made on these points. Scholars can only state their preference for the arguments of one side or the other. In short, each side argues reasonably for its position, and neither is abusing the law.

I turn now to the possible abuse of procedural law. I begin with the notorious trial of the generals after Arginousai, which in the view of some Athenians, at least, was *paranomon* ('against the law').[34] It does not appear, however, that any specific statute was violated, and critics at the time were probably using *paranomon* in the sense of contrary to traditional practice rather than contrary to a specific law.[35] For the possible abuse of specific procedural laws, we need to turn to individual prosecutions.[36]

The clearest example comes from Antiph. 5, where the defendant in a murder trial argues that the prosecution should not have used *apagōgē* (summary arrest), a procedure never before used for homicide, but rather a *dikē phonou*, the regular homicide procedure (§§ 8–19). The prosecution apparently defended their use of *apagōgē* (§§ 9–10) on the grounds that this procedure was meant to be used against wrongdoers (*kakourgoi*) and that homicide was surely a great wrong (*kakourgia*), and the official in charge must have seen some merit in this argument, because he allowed the case to proceed. Thus use of *apagōgē* for homicide, though perhaps unprecedented, was only designated as abuse in the rhetoric of the defendant.

Another homicide case prosecuted by means of *apagōgē* was Lys. 13. Here the procedure was probably used because the recent amnesty agreement pro-

33 For the majority view, see Gwatkin 1957; cf. Harris 1994a, 2000. MacDowell 2009 is an attempt at a balanced assessment.

34 The word is used in Pl. *Ap.* 32b and Xen. *Hell.* 1.7.25.

35 Carawan 2007a.

36 I ignore the possibility that someone might use a completely inappropriate procedure, say a homicide procedure for an accusation of theft. If someone attempted this, the official in charge would presumably advise the plaintiff to file a different charge.

hibited the use of *dikē phonou* except for homicides that were committed by the accused's own hand, and Agoratos was only accused of giving information against Dionysodoros, which led to his death at the hands of the Thirty. When the case was first brought to the officials in charge, they refused to accept it, but they advised the prosecution to revise their indictment by adding to it the expression *ep' autophōrō* ('in the act' or 'red-handed').[37] It seems a stretch to characterise Agoratos' alleged crime as *ep' autophōrō*, but after the prosecution added the phrase, arguing that the informant was the direct cause of Dionysodoros' death, the Eleven allowed the case to go to trial. Evidently, they did not feel certain that this was an abuse of the law. Whether any members of the jury thought that it was is unknown.

The expansion of *apagōgē* to include homicide,[38] which these two cases illustrate, also occurred with the procedure of *eisangelia*, or impeachment, as we learn from Hypereides' defence of Euxenippos. Hypereides begins (§§1–3) by complaining about the broad use of *eisangelia*, a procedure originally devised for cases of attempted tyranny. Recently, he notes, *eisangelia* was used to prosecute someone who hired out flute girls for more than the allowable price; in the present case, Euxenippos is accused of misreporting a dream. Hypereides has parts of the law on *eisangelia* read out in court and argues that Euxenippos' actions have nothing to do with tyranny. The prosecution apparently argued that Euxenippos was bribed to mislead the Assembly, and that this was equivalent to tyranny. Here too, then, we must conclude that because all these cases were allowed to proceed, use of this procedure was considered legitimate, at least by the officials in charge.[39] It seems, however, that the expanded use of *eisangelia* may have led to its overuse, for the law was amended sometime in the late fourth century to make the prosecutor who did not receive one-fifth of the votes subject to a fine.[40]

In addition to cases such as these, where various officials allowed certain procedures to be used, there may have been some cases, though probably not many, where a procedure was disallowed. Because these cases were not tried, they have left no trace in our records. It is clear, however, that at least *apagōgē* and *eisangelia*, and perhaps other procedures, were gradually allowed to expand their scope and be used for cases that do not appear to fit the origi-

---

37 The precise meaning of the term does not affect my point, For the meaning see Harris 1994b.

38 For which see Gagarin 1979, Hansen 1981, and Volonaki 2000.

39 The list of offences covered by the law (quoted in sections 7–8) was quite broad and probably left room for a plausible argument that Euxenippos was subject to the law.

40 Harrison 1972: 51 with n. 3.

nal intent of the law.[41] And the repeated use of these procedures for cases that probably did not fall under the original scope of the law would have had the effect of providing de facto authorisation for these new uses. Thus the authorisation to use a particular procedure would not come from the wording of the law but from repeated acceptance by officials. Some such process seems to have been at work with regard to *eisangelia*, where Hypereides' complaint about the broadened use of the procedure can be read as confirmation that these broad uses were now established as legitimate. Repeated acceptance may not have the same degree of authority as a Supreme Court decision, but in Athenian law it was the only way, besides enacting a new statute, to allow procedures to adapt to different circumstances. And if we are willing to allow the authority of repetition with regard to procedures, we may want to consider a similar process of establishing authority in the case of substantive interpretation of laws, though here we would have to rely on repeated jury verdicts rather than decisions of officials.

To conclude, I have argued that because the Athenian legal system did not provide an official means of making an authoritative determination of the meaning of a law, it is impossible to say objectively that any of the arguments we find in the orators concerning the meaning of a law are wrong or constitute an abuse of the law. Speakers are always ready to brand their opponents' use of laws as abuse, but as scholars we must see such charges for what they are: subjective claims of abuse by an interested participant in the proceedings. Thus they have no more authority than any statement anyone might make about Athenian law. To be sure, ordinary language usage put some constraints on the interpretation of laws, and it may have been virtually impossible to challenge repeated acceptances or rejections of certain interpretations. But this would still leave a wide scope for arguments about the meaning of laws that could not be considered abusive.[42]

---

41 Procedural expansion is not uncommon today. In the U.S., the Racketeer Influenced and Corrupt Organizations Act (RICO) of 1970 provides special procedures to make it easier to prosecute the Mafia and other organised crime, but since then it has also been used to prosecute other quite different crimes. For example, RICO cases have been brought against Catholic dioceses for their cover-up of alleged sexual abuse, against pro-life groups who blocked access to abortion clinics, and against Michael Milken for insider trading. Defendants protested that these prosecutions were an abuse of the RICO law, but they were all upheld by higher courts (though the courts have also rejected use of RICO in other cases).

42 I am grateful to the organisers of the conference where an earlier version of this chapter was delivered for the invitation to speak, and to all the participants for their questions and comments in response. I am especially grateful to Chris Carey, Ifigeneia Giannadaki, and Brenda Griffith-Williams for their many comments on my text, virtually all of which have been incorporated into the final version.

Bibliography

Bonner, R.J. (1905) *Evidence in Athenian Courts*, Chicago.

Carawan, E. (2007a) 'The Trial of the Arginousai Generals and the Dawn of Judicial Review', *Dike* 10, 19–56.

Carawan, E. (2007b) 'Oath and contract', in Sommerstein, A.H. and Fletcher, J., eds (2007) Horkos *The Oath in Greek Society*, Exeter, 73–80.

Carey, C. (1994) '"Artless" Proofs in Aristotle and the Orators', *BICS* 39, 95–106.

Carey, C., (2000) *Aeschines*, Austin.

Dimopoulou, A. (2014) ''Άκυρον ἔστω: Legal Invalidity in Greek Inscriptions', in Gagarin, M. and Lanni, A., eds (2014) *Symposion 2013: Vorträge zur griechischen und hellenistischen Rechtsgeschichte* (Cambridge, Ma., 26–29 August 2013), Vienna, 249–275.

Gagarin, M. (1979) 'The Prosecution of Homicide in Athens', *GRBS* 20, 301–323.

Gwatkin, W.E. (1957) 'The Legal Arguments in Aischines' *Against Ctesiphon* and Demosthenes' *On The Crown*', *Hesperia* 26, 129–141.

Hansen, M.H. (1981) 'The Prosecution of Homicide in Athens: A Reply', *GRBS* 22, 11–30.

Harris, E.M. (1990) 'Did the Athenians Regard Seduction as a Worse Crime than Rape?' *CQ* 40, 370–377.

Harris, E.M. (1994a) 'Law and Oratory', in Worthington, I., ed. (1994) *Persuasion: Greek Rhetoric in Action*, London, 130–150.

Harris, E.M. (1994b) '"In the Act" or "Red-Handed"'? *Apagoge* to the Eleven and *furtum manifestum*, in Thür, G., ed., *Symposion 1993: Vorträge zur griechischen und hellenistischen Rechtsgeschichte* (Graz-Andritz, 12–16 September 1993), Cologne, 129–146.

Harris, E.M. (2000) 'Open Texture in Athenian Law', *Dike* 3, 27–79.

Harrison, A.R.W. (1968–1971) *The Law of Athens*, 2 vols, Oxford.

MacDowell, D.M. (2009) *Demosthenes the Orator*, Oxford.

Phillips, D.D. (2009) 'Hypereides 3 and the Athenian Law of Contracts', *TAPA* 139, 89–122.

Scafuro, A.C. (2011) *Demosthenes, speeches 39–49*, Austin.

Stroud, R.S. (1968) *Drakon's Law on Homicide*, Berkeley, Cal.

Thompson, W.E. (1976) *De Hagniae Hereditate: an Athenian inheritance case*, Leiden.

Todd, S.C. (1993) *The Shape of Athenian Law*, Oxford.

Todd, S.C. (2007) *A Commentary on Lysias, Speeches 1–11*, Oxford.

Volonaki, E. (2000) '"Apagoge" in Homicide Cases', *Dike* 3, 147–176.

Worthington, I., Cooper, C.R. and Harris, E.M. (2001) *Dinarchus, Hyperides, and Lycurgus*. Austin.

Yunis, H. (2005) *Demosthenes, Speeches 18 and 19*, Austin.

CHAPTER 2

The Elasticity of Athenian Law

Robin Osborne

It is not uncommon for scholars to talk of 'stretching the law'. When the advertisement for the conference from which this volume derives invited papers on 'stretching the meaning of the law', it glossed this phrase in an immediate parenthesis as ' (manipulation of substantive issues)'. Talk of 'stretching the meaning of the law' requires us to think that laws are relatively inelastic, and that stretching them is somehow improper, an 'abuse' (which is presumably why discussion of 'stretching the law' was thought appropriate for a conference concerned with the use and abuse of law). But was 'stretching the law' abusive in classical Athens?

In any legal system, there is a tension between the need to ensure that laws do indeed constitute general rules that apply in the same way to everyone, and the fact that the very operation of the rule of law demands adapting particular rules to individual circumstances.[1] In a system with legally qualified judges and lay juries, one way of conceiving of the role of each is that juries make judgments about how successfully prosecutors have made the case in question fit the law in question, and that judges keep control of the degree of Procrustean activity by which the prosecution (or defence) have made the law fit the case.[2] But classical Athens did not operate with judges and juries, but just with juries.[3]

The absence of professional judges did not, of course, mean that there was no limit to the elasticity of Athenian law. There are a variety of ways in which laws can be made more or less 'elastic'. Some of these concern how laws are

1 This is a basic concern of jurisprudence and goes back in explicit form as far as Aristotle. See Arist. *Rh.* 1.1 especially 1354b5–8. Cf. Lanni 2006: 175.

2 Cf. Coke's determination that in a common law system the jurors concern themselves only with the facts of the case, the judge only with the law (*ad quaestionem facti non respondent judices, ad quaestionem juris non respondent juratores*); but as many scholars have recognised such a division is not always easy to observe, see the classic discussion of Thayer 1890 and Sunderland 1919–1920: 255. The essence of the issue, though with the law itself taking the place of the judge, is already discussed by Aristotle at the very opening of the *Rh.* 1354a26–34.

3 Todd 1993: 90–91 on the *dikastēs* being the judge of law as well as of fact. Whether one translates *dikastēs* as judge or as juror is itself an issue; our tendency is to think of the popular courts as manned by a jury, but we might be more inclined to think of the homicide courts, manned by ex-magistrates, as courts composed of judges (cf. below n. 28).

 | DOI:10.1163/9789004377899_004

framed, others concern how procedures are operated—where use of professional judges is just one possible relevant aspect of procedure.[4] In this chapter I use the notion of elasticity to think further about how law was used in classical Athens. I will end up putting most emphasis on procedure, but I start by looking at the framing of the laws.

At a very minimum we have to admit that Athenian laws were not consistently framed to be inelastic.[5] We can certainly find laws, such as Solon's on easements, where the elasticity is indeed limited:

> If someone builds a wall beside someone else's land or a bank, it is not to cross the boundary. If it is a wall, it should leave a foot gap, if a building, two feet. If he digs a ditch or a hole, he should leave a gap as big as it is deep. If a well, a fathom. One may plant an olive or fig tree nine feet from someone else's land, and other trees five feet.[6]

Here the issues are limited to whether it is a wall, whether the wall is part of a building, how deep the hole is and whether a hole is a well, and what the species planted is. Potentially one might dispute what constituted building or digging or planting, but it is hard to think that there was much ambiguity in real life about such familiar activities (self-seeding is hardly a problem with olives or figs).

We might compare the notorious Solonian law on heiresses (once more a law about property), which required that the heiress and the man to whom she is married off should eat a quince together in the bridal chamber and have sexual intercourse three times a month.[7] Here again—where we seem to have only Plutarch's paraphrase rather than the words of the law—the stipulation looks pretty inflexible. Both what and how often is clearly stated. Or is it? Whereas in the case of the law on boundaries it is easy to understand the aims of the law, in this case that is less easy. Did it have to be a quince, or would sharing

---

4 This chapter looks again at issues variously examined by Carey 1998, whose interest is in how laws are framed, and Lanni 2006, whose interest is in how laws are operated.

5 Carey 1998 suggests that there was a pattern, and laws framed to be inelastic concerned particular topics, especially property, the family, the constitution, and religion (see Carey 1998: 107). I am more sceptical—the law on slander does not obviously fit into any of these categories, and the laws on such matters as marriage (see Carey 1998: 99), damages and impiety seem not to have attempted to limit elasticity at all.

6 *Digest* 10.1.13 cf. Plut. *Sol.* 23.76; Ruschenbusch 2010: fr. 60a and b, Leão and Rhodes 2015: 103–105.

7 Plut. *Sol.* 20.2–5; Ruschenbusch 2010: fr. 52a (cf. fr. 51a and b), Leão and Rhodes 2015: 88–91 (who make the case for a genuine Solonian core here).

any fruit satisfy the legislator? Did it have to be eaten in private, and how many other people could be present before the occasion ceased to be private? Did the three times a month have to be evenly spread out? Could an heiress's husband be brought to court for having had too much sex? Plutarch already anticipates these difficulties, not only by introducing this as 'strange and laughable' but by supposing in his explanation that it was simply the degree of intimacy that the quince-eating was supposed to engender that was important, not any aphrodisiac qualities. Rather unexpectedly, Plutarch is happy to think that Solon thought sex good in and of itself, rather than for the children it might produce: 'even if no children were to be born, this is still a way of a husband showing a measure of honour and kindness towards a modest wife, doing away with many of the annoyances which develop on any occasion and not allowing them to be torn apart by their differences'.[8]

A nice case of an apparently inelastic law of Solon whose elasticity was tested in the courts in classical times comes from Solon's law on slander. Although this is summarised by Plutarch as simply concerned with 'speaking ill of' (*kakōs legein*), it is clear from Lys. 10 that there were certain particular phrases the use of which was actionable.[9] Since we do not have the words of Solon's law we cannot begin to tell whether it is reasonable to think that Solon was indeed concerned only with these particular terms, or whether the terms the law happened to use have come to be treated as co-extensive with actionable abuse. The speaker in Lys. 10 attempts to restore elasticity to the law by asserting that it would be absurd to condemn only the use of particular words, and not the expression of equivalent sentiments in other words. And he attempts to do so once more by finding ridiculous (cf. *atopos* in 10.12) the thought that a jury might interpret the law more narrowly.[10]

Many laws, notoriously, made no attempt to limit elasticity.[11] Take Solon's law on *stasis*.[12] If that law is at all correctly summarised by the ancient sources, it took essentially the form of 'If at a time of *stasis* a man does not take one side or the other he is to lose his civic rights'. 'Taking part' may have been glossed here as 'adding his arms', as is implied at *Ath. Pol.* 8.5, but that hardly helps, since even without metaphorical uses of the phrase all sorts of actions involving arms might be held to be covered. Equally, it is hard to conceive that 'at a

8 Plut. *Sol.* 20.5; cf. Plut. *Mor.* 769A.

9 Plut. *Sol.* 21.1, Lys. 10.2, 6, 8–9; Ruschenbusch 2010: fr. 32a and fr. 32b, Leão and Rhodes 2015: 49–53. For further discussion, see Todd 2007: 634–635 and see Gagarin in this volume p. 21.

10 See Wohl 2010: 301–309.

11 Cf. Lanni 2006: 67–68.

12 Ruschenbusch 2010: fr. 38 a–g, Leão and Rhodes 2015: 59–66.

time of *stasis*' can have been glossed in any way that helped determine where the boundaries between normal and abnormal political argument fell.[13]

I have dwelt upon laws ascribed to Solon since it is not least among those that we find what look like deliberate attempts to limit elasticity.[14] But very similar observations can be made about laws that we know to have been passed in the fifth and fourth centuries. Take two epigraphic examples, the fifth-century 'Athenian decree enforcing the use of Athenian coins, weights, and measures' (as Meiggs and Lewis entitled it), and the Athenian law on approvers of silver coinage of 375/4.[15]

The law enforcing the use of Athenian coins, weights, and measures prescribes in detail what is to be done and not to be done. In terms of procedure there is no ambiguity or flexibility. But in terms of the offence itself, the definition is minimal—minting silver coinage, not using Athenian coins, weights or measures, using 'foreign' coins, weights or measures. The minimal nature of the definition may derive in part from the fact that we have the clause preserved only as summarised in the addition to the Council oath—but the prohibition on bringing proposals to repeal the law talks only (as restored) of 'using or lending' foreign money which does not suggest significant expansion in the way the core of the law may have been stated. But what did 'using' coins mean? Handing them over in payment, whether to purchase an item or to pay a wage, certainly. But was possession itself a part of use? Might one continue to keep non-Athenian coin for use outside the Athenian empire? Might one still keep one's accounts in local coinage (or Cyzicene staters) even if what one then handed over was Athenian *drachmas*? Similar questions arise for weights and measures. If weighing and measuring in the market place was now in Attic feet and Attic *medimnoi*, was one obliged to assess one's own farm crops in those forms, or might one continue to reckon up what one produced in the local units, converting only at the point of sale? There remains plenty of room for dispute about what constitutes use here; just how intrusive this law was for Athens' allies would depend crucially on how their own magistrates interpreted 'use'.

The fourth-century law on silver coinage is very similar. Here again the procedural elements are specified in great detail (who the 'approver' is to be, where

13 Though Ruschenbusch 2010: 75 wonders whether *stasis* was actually the Solonian term for war with an external enemy. For the phrase θέσθαι τὰ ὅπλα see Rhodes 1981: 157–158.

14 For discussion of the most notorious of all attempts to limit elasticity, the Solonian law on testaments (Ruschenbusch 2010: fr. 49a–d), see Osborne 2010: 177, 280–281. On the question of whether the 'shape' of Athenian laws changed over time, and for powerful arguments that it did not, see Carey 1998: 107–109.

15 Meiggs and Lewis 1969: no. 45 (Osborne and Rhodes 2017, no. 155); Rhodes and Osborne 2003: no. 25.

he is to sit, when he is to be there), but the basic requirement of the law is simply stated: 'if anyone does not accept the silver which the approver approves, he shall be deprived of what he is selling on that day' (lines 16–18, expanded in 30–32 to cover the case where the seller is a slave). Yet, ironically, the very inflexibility of that way of putting it ensures that the law had to be somewhat elastic. What, for instance, about all those things that the *polētai* sell—taxes, leases of mines, and so on? Or what if the sale was of a person's own body in the context of prostitution? Could a person in that case refuse to accept coin that had passed the approver? Or was such a person who refused to accept approved coin to be deprived of all they could earn in a day of prostitution? How would the provision of a half share to 'the man who exposes' (lines 28–29) work in such a case? How could the moments of sexual pleasure be split between the person bringing the prosecution and the state? Or what about banks not accepting that coinage in repayment of some earlier loan? What counted as 'what he is selling on that day' in that case? And in any case where a number of individuals were selling the same goods, how did one decide which of the goods the individual who refused to accept the coin was selling? It is not hard to see that the questions arise here because the law is not in fact primarily concerned to enforce the acceptance of approved coin, it is primarily concerned to set up a mechanism for removing from circulation counterfeit coin or coin that is not otherwise of good silver. It was simply a necessary by-product of the primary aim of the legislation that it also made provision for the coin that was not removed from circulation by the official mechanism set up to be accepted.

What emerges from this discussion is that although ancient theorists sometimes thought laws should be inelastic, an inelastic law becomes a useless law: if Solon's law on abuse was conceived as inelastic, once language use had changed (in part because of the law) what we take to be the purpose of the law could only be served by treating that law elastically.[16] So too it is hard to think that a court would have had trouble extending the principle of the law on approvers of silver coinage to bankers, even though the specific provision of the law could not be applied. Appeals to the legislator's intention, and to analogous laws, were with reason familiar in the Athenian courts.[17]

This observation will surprise no one. It goes closely with Stephen Todd's insistence 25 years ago, and modified only in detail by subsequent work, that there was no technical language of law.[18] Technical language makes sense only

16 For the belief that law is best if it gives no discretion to the jurors, see Arist. *Rh.* 1354a31–34.

17 Johnstone 1999: 29–33; Lanni 2006: 69, 118; see also Giannadaki in this volume pp. 209–212.

18 Todd 1993: 61–62 on absence of statutory interpretation. Note also Gagarin 2008: 207

if there is some hope that a law can be rendered inelastic, that it should refer to acts very precisely. But technical terms can only be kept technical if their use is policed. There can be no technical language to Athenian law because inelasticity could not be policed. In the absence of a judge to impose an interpretation, Athenian law was always a matter of contestation, as in Lys. 10.[19] And in a matter of contestation, inelasticity might win. If not last time, then this time.

But if inelasticity could not be policed, how could elasticity be policed? If the Athenians did not treat verbal abuse as limited to particular terms, what prevented any terms at all being alleged to be abusive? My answer to this is procedural. There were two aspects to this. On the one hand the range of possible descriptions of any action against which a potential litigant wished to prosecute an offence was often matched by a choice of legal procedures.[20] Depending on how he chose to describe the offensive behaviour, a litigant might have a choice between landing a rather soft blow—in as far as the penalty awarded against his opponent would not be enormous if he won—at little risk to himself, or landing a distinctly heavier blow at considerable risk to himself. Although there was no formal use of precedent in Athenian courts, litigants would have been able to judge on the basis of earlier decisions the sorts of behaviours that had been regarded as fitting a particular law, and hence the chances of their making the particular form of offensive behaviour that they objected to one a court would recognise as appropriately prosecuted by a particular procedure.[21] Faced with this choice, litigants needed a fair degree of confidence that they would persuade the courts if they were to push a case through to its conclusion before they went that far. If they were doubtful of their own powers, they would likely choose only to land a soft blow.[22]

The second aspect of procedural flexibility came after the prosecutor had decided upon a course of action. For if prosecutors got cold feet in the course of planning to land a heavier blow, or defendants in the course of preparing to withstand a heavier blow from others, then they had the option of bailing out—abandoning the prosecution, settling out of court, or leaving the city. The var-

---

observing that the role of writing in Athenian judicial procedure was limited and that this helped keep formalism out of Athenian law: 'Obscure or obsolete expressions are rare in forensic speeches and are normally explained to the jurors in ordinary language'.

19 So also Lanni 2006: 117–118.

20 So Osborne 2010: 171–177 with 202–203. See also Giannadaki in this volume pp. 201–202.

21 On precedent see Lanni 2004, Harris in this volume pp. 44–46.

22 This is the position argued for by Osborne 2010: 171–204. This is not to deny that, as Carey 2004 points out (cf. Johnstone 1999: 7), the way in which offences were defined under different laws meant that the overlap between what could be prosecuted by one route and what by another was not complete.

ious stages of legal procedure—the bringing of charges and counter-charges, the exposure of the case at the *anakrisis*, what happened at an arbitration—gave legal opponents both the chance to assess the nature of the arguments they would face, and to get preliminary reactions likely to indicate how the later trial might go. How plausibly the case made by or against them would succeed in persuading a set of dikasts that the law cited did indeed cover the acts in question would emerge more or less clearly from those pre-trial encounters.[23]

I want to illustrate this claim by examining some of the aborted legal encounters in which Stephanos and Neaira are involved.[24] On Apollodoros' account, Neaira had been bought by Phrynion of Paiania, but she then persuaded Stephanos that Phrynion was abusing her and Stephanos brought her back to Athens and set her up in his own house. Phrynion tried to claim her back as his slave and, when Stephanos asserted her freedom, Phrynion compelled her to post bail before the polemarch ([Dem.] 59.39–40). They took the case to arbitration and the arbitrators compelled Neaira to return property taken from Phrynion and instituted an arrangement where Neaira lived with each man by turns ([Dem.] 59.45–47). So in this first case, Phrynion tries to get access to Neaira by claiming that she is a slave, but drops that case in favour of arbitration. The great advantage of arbitration is that it could decide on a compromise position, rather than simply siding with one or the other of the litigants.[25] So here Phrynion relinquishes his claim of ownership and in return does not entirely lose the possibility of Neaira's company. Had Neaira been Phrynion's slave it is hard to see that Phrynion would have regarded this arrangement as a reasonable alternative to his regaining his property. But in the face of a realisation that his claims that she was his slave were weak, Phrynion used arbitration to get at least something out of Stephanos.

The second set of aborted legal actions involves the marriage of Neaira's daughter, Phano. Stephanos gave Phano in marriage to Phrastor of Aigilia with a dowry of 30 minas ([Dem.] 59.50). On Apollodoros' account, Phrastor found Phano's extravagance hard to bear and threw her out, even though she was pregnant. Stephanos then brought a suit for maintenance (*dikē sitou*) for the return of, or interest on, the dowry, and Phrastor brought a countersuit (*graphē*) for Stephanos' having passed off an alien as if a citizen ([Dem.] 59.52). Phrastor's own deposition suggests the order was the opposite. In any

23 What follows attempts to show that we do indeed have evidence for pre-trial procedures serving a 'winnowing' function, as in modern courts, *contra* Lanni 2006: 36.

24 For a related set of claims, focusing on the various pre-trial actions as a variety of 'dares', see Johnstone 1999: 70–92.

25 Cf. *Ath. Pol.* 53.1 on public arbitrators.

case, Phrastor and Stephanos then reached an out-of-court settlement to drop both cases. Whichever order we think these suits went in, we see an instance when neither party has the confidence that they will make the circumstances fit the terms of the law. Stephanos presumably realised that Phrastor would likely persuade the jury that since Phano was not Stephanos' daughter some deceit had been involved in the marriage (Dem. 44.49, [46.]18 and Hyp. *Athen.* 16 all imply that only fathers, grandfathers and brothers can legitimately betroth a woman, though in practice presumably any *kyrios* did so; Hyp. *Athen.* 16 is precisely concerned with what it means to 'rightly betroth'). Phrastor realised that while he could convince the jury that Phano was not Stephanos' daughter, it was questionable whether he could convince them that she was not an Athenian. Depending on our view of the facts of the case, we will either think that Stephanos decided that he could not persuade the court that the *dikē sitou* covered whatever financial arrangement he had made with Phrastor, or that Phrastor decided that he could not 'stretch' the *graphē* to cover anyone given away by other than her father/grandfather/brother. But in either case we see the stages of the process of bringing a case to court enabling both parties to review their claims and take a view on law's elasticity.

The third set of aborted legal actions concerns Stephanos and Epainetos of Andros ([Dem.]59.64–71). Stephanos makes Epainetos pay 30 minas (that sum again) for having had sex with Neaira's daughter while visiting Stephanos in the country. Epainetos then brings a *graphē* for being wrongly shut up as a *moichos* (seducer), on the grounds that Stephanos' house was a brothel. Stephanos offered to go to arbitration on condition that Epainetos withdrew the suit, and the arbitrators made Epainetos contribute 10 minas to Neaira's daughter's dowry. Again here Epainetos' actions make sense only if he was dubious about his chances of convincing the jury that Phano was a prostitute and that he had indeed been wrongly shut up as a seducer. There might be many reasons for that—including his own status as a non-Athenian—but the importance is that the pre-trial process allows for the parties to reassess their claims.

In discussing Apollodoros' claims, Carey suggests that Apollodoros deliberately refrains from attempting to prove part of his case so as not to draw attention to its weakness, remarking that 'even an Athenian jury might be disinclined to stretch the law to fit Stephanos' alleged conduct'.[26] That sentence seems to me to have the wrong active party. Juries do not themselves 'stretch' the law, they accept or reject the claim that the law was extensive enough to cover the matters in question. The earliest stages of an indictment established

26 Carey 1992: 12.

that there was a *prima facie* case for the activities complained of falling under the law cited. The subsequent pre-trial exchanges allowed both parties to see whether it was likely that they could convince a jury a) that the actions were as they claimed, and b) that those actions were liable under the particular law invoked—or to put it in Steven Johnstone's terms, that the type of criminal meaning attributed to the dispute matched the choice of procedure.[27] If the parties became dubious about their ability to persuade the jury of these two things, they had various options for aborting the action or settling out of court. In the popular jury courts, there were no formal limits on what juries might reckon to be covered by a law—the law simply covered whatever the jury could be persuaded that it covered[28]—but the parties to a potential court case made judgments about whether the jury would in fact reckon a matter covered or not. It was those expectations, put on the line during the pre-trial process, that constituted the limits to the elasticity of the law.

Seen in this way, the law stretched (or contracted) less in relation to the particular terms in which it was framed than in relation to the expectations of the prosecution and defence as to their own and their opponents' persuasiveness. A prosecutor enjoying high regard could render the law much more elastic than a prosecutor regarded with suspicion. From this point of view, Athenian attempts to limit many legal actions to those who could claim to be injured parties—and hence in general to less rather than more experienced speakers—can be seen as indirectly perhaps the most important procedural mechanism for limiting the elasticity of the law.

Bibliography

Carey, C. (1992) *Apollodorus Against Neaira*, Warminster.

Carey, C. (1998) 'The Shape of Athenian Laws', *CQ* 48, 93–109.

Carey, C. (2004) 'Offence and Procedure in Athenian Law', in Harris, E.M. and Rubinstein, L., eds (2004), 111–136.

Gagarin, M. (2008) *Writing Greek law*, Cambridge.

Johnstone, S. (1999) *Disputes and Democracy: The Consequences of Litigation in Ancient Athens*, Austin.

Lanni, A. (2004) 'Arguing from Precedent: Modern Perspectives on Athenian Practice', in Harris, E.M. and Rubinstein, L., eds (2004), 159–171.

27 Johnstone 1999: 7–8.

28 So Lanni 2006: 64–74, distinguishing popular jury courts from the homicide and maritime courts.

Lanni, A. (2006) *Law and Justice in the Courts of Classical Athens*, Cambridge.
Leão, D.F. and Rhodes, P.J. (2015) *The Laws of Solon. A New Edition with Introduction, Translation and Commentary*, London.
Meiggs, R. and Lewis, D.M. (1969) *Greek Historical Inscriptions to the End of the Fifth Century* B.C., Oxford.
Osborne, R. (2010) *Athens and Athenian Democracy*, Cambridge.
Osborne, R. and Rhodes, P.J. (2017) *Greek Historical Inscriptions 478–404* B.C., Oxford.
Rhodes, P.J. (1981) *A Commentary on the Aristotelian* Athenaion Politeia, Oxford.
Rhodes, P.J. and Osborne, R. (2003) *Greek Historical Inscriptions 404–323* B.C., Oxford.
Ruschenbusch, E. (2010) *Solon: Das Gesetzeswerk. Fragmente, Übersetzung und Kommentar*, Stuttgart.
Sunderland, E.R. (1919–1920) 'Verdicts General and Special', *Yale Law Journal* 29, 253–267.
Thayer, James B. (1890) '"Law and Fact" in Jury Trials', *Harvard Law Journal* 4, 147–175.
Todd, S.C. (1993) *The Shape of Athenian Law*, Oxford.
Todd, S.C. (2007) *A Commentary on Lysias, Speeches 1–11*, Oxford.
Wohl, V. (2010) *Law's Cosmos: Juridical Discourse in Athenian Forensic Oratory*, Cambridge.

CHAPTER 3

The Athenian View of an Athenian Trial

Edward M. Harris

Modern scholars who write about Athenian law have many theories about how the Athenian courts made their decisions. One asserts that the courts made *ad hoc* decisions and did not aim at applying legal rules consistently.[1] Another opines that the courts did not attempt to regulate human conduct but simply redistributed honour (*timē*) among citizens.[2] Still another assumes that for the courts the most important issue was not violations of the law but 'one's social identity and reputation in general'.[3] These and other scholars believe that the courts did not pay much attention to the letter of the law when voting about guilt and innocence.[4]

All these views rest mainly on assumptions and assertions, not on a careful study of the forensic speeches of the Attic orators. This chapter examines evidence to which none of these scholars has paid attention: what the Athenians themselves said about the way their courts made their decisions. It is true that for most of the speeches preserved in the corpus, there is no evidence that would permit us to determine if the litigant who delivered the speech was successful when pleading his case before the court. In the few cases for which we do know that outcome, we do not know the reasons why the court voted in the way it did.[5] On the other hand, in the preserved speeches, litigants often men-

1 Lanni 2006. For detailed criticisms see Harris 2009/10b. Lanni's view that the Athenian courts made *ad hoc* judgments is not original; one finds a similar view in Weber 1972: 158. The original essay was published in 1915. Despite his criticisms of Weber, Finley 1985: 101–103 held a similar view.

2 Osborne 2000: 85–86: 'the concern of law being primarily the regulation of relations between citizens rather than the control of human conduct'. For the evidence contradicting this view see Harris 2013a: 138–174, esp. 173–174.

3 Cohen 1995: 92–93. Cf. 186–188, 190–191. For detailed refutation of Cohen's feuding model see Harris 2013a: 60–98 and the brief comments of Rubinstein 2000: 179–180.

4 In addition to those cited in notes 1, 2, and 3 see Christ 1998: 193–224 for this assumption. For the evidence demonstrating that the Athenian courts paid close attention to the precise wording of their laws see Meyer-Laurin 1965, Meinecke 1971 and at greater length Harris 2013a: 166–173, 175–245. Though my own approach some has elements in common with that of Meyer-Laurin, I have major differences when it comes to the issue of open texture and to role of *epieikeia*. See below.

5 There is evidence for the outcome of the trial for the following speeches: Aischin. 1 (conviction

 | DOI:10.1163/9789004377899_005

tion other trials. In some cases, they mention only the verdict, but in others they describe the reasons why they thought the court decided the case the way it did.

Reasons for Citing Previous Trials

Litigants mention trials for several reasons. First, they mention a court's decision to establish a fact relevant to the case before the court. For instance, in his prosecution of Aischines in 343 Demosthenes (19.116) mentions the conviction of Philokrates for treason. Because Aischines was Philokrates' colleague on the embassies that negotiated peace and alliance with Philip in 346, Demosthenes tries to prove Aischines guilty by association. In his reply to Demosthenes' charges, Aischines (2.6) tries to use the evidence of Philokrates' trial in his own favour: if one interprets Philokrates' flight before trial as an admission of guilt, one should view his willingness to stay and stand trial in Athens as proof of his innocence. Aischines (2.14) struck back at Demosthenes by recalling that he spoke in support of Philokrates when the latter was charged with proposing an illegal decree about negotiations with Philip. Aischines does this to undermine Demosthenes' credibility and to cast doubt on his legal charges. Second, speakers may refer to earlier litigation with their opponent to explain the background of the case. In his speech *On the Mysteries* Andokides (1.13, 17, 65–66) mentions several trials to describe the background to the events of 415. In the speech *Against Neaira*, Theomnestos describes two cases brought by Stephanos against Apollodoros to show why he has brought his case against Stephanos' partner and why Apollodoros is speaking as *synēgoros* at the trial ([Dem.] 59.6–10).[6] Third, accusers may mention a prior conviction of the defendant either to impugn his character or to show that he was likely to have committed the crime with which he has been charged. For instance, Aischines (1.113) reminds the court how Timarchos was convicted for embezzlement when serving as *exetastēs*. This evidence demonstrates Timarchos' venality, which indirectly supports Aischines' charge that he squandered his father's estate. Some scholars

of Timarchos); Aischin. 2 (acquittal of Aischines); Aischin. 3 (acquittal of Ktesiphon); Dem. 18 (acquittal of Ktesiphon), Dem. 19 (acquittal of Aischines), Dem. 20 (repeal of Leptines' law—see Harris 2008: 20–21); Dem. 22 (see Dem. 24.8); Dem. 27 and 28 (conviction of Aphobos); Dem. 39 (acquittal of Mantitheos/Boiotos); [Dem.] 49 (conviction of Timotheos—see Plut. *Dem.* 15); Dein. 1 (conviction of Demosthenes); Isa. 11 (victory of Theopompos).

6 Cf. the case brought against Apollodoros by Lykidas to explain the origins of his quarrel with Nikostratos ([Dem.] 53.14–15) and the case brought by Theokrines ([Dem.] 58.1, 30–32, 70).

believe that the Athenian courts had a different standard of relevance when it came to mentioning past convictions than modern courts, but the differences should not be exaggerated. For instance, under the Criminal Justice Act of the United Kingdom enacted in 2003, judges have 'the power to let juries hear about a defendant's previous convictions and other misconduct where relevant to the case'.[7]

Fourth, accusers often recall harsh punishments meted out to offenders in the past to encourage the court to punish the defendant with equal severity (Dem. 21.182; 24.138; Lys. 12.36; 22.16).[8] The argument often runs thus: if you Athenians punished with a harsh penalty an offender who was charged with the same crime, you should do so again in this case. Fifth, a litigant may cite an earlier decision as a precedent when discussing the interpretation of a law.[9] When there is a dispute about the meaning of a law, a litigant may refer to other cases in which the court has clearly followed his interpretation of statute. For instance, Demosthenes (18.114, 120–121, 223–224) in his defence of Ktesiphon cites numerous precedents to prove that his interpretation of two laws about the award of crowns is correct or at least the interpretation that was always followed by the Assembly and by the courts.[10] To justify his interpretation of

7 Partington 2014: 111–112. Rhodes 2004 does not discuss the rules about relevance in modern courts.

8 Rubinstein 2007: 367 mistakenly calls these precedents but see Harris 2013a: 251 with note 14.

9 See Harris 2013a: 246–273.

10 Gagarin (2012: 300–301) claims that the debate about who had the stronger legal arguments in the case against Ktesiphon in 330 is 'futile'. He notes that in the American legal system an appellate court would rule about which side correctly interprets the law, but observes that there was nothing like an appellate court in ancient Athens. By this argument, he claims that there was no way of knowing which verdict in an Athenian court was correct. This may be true about American courts, but Gagarin fails to note that it is possible to determine what the Athenians thought was a correct verdict by examining verdicts in similar cases. In the case of Ktesiphon, Dem. 18.113–121 shows with much evidence that his view of the laws about the award of crowns for officials was the one generally followed while Aischines can cite no precedents. Gagarin also claims that 'Almost all scholars' believe that Aischines has the stronger legal arguments. This may have been true before I published my essay about the topic in 1994a, but has not been true since that date because the majority of scholars now accept my view that Demosthenes has the stronger legal arguments. See for instance, Aviles 2011, Heftner 2012: 30 note 72, Canevaro 2013: 290–295 (with an additional argument in support of my position), and Novotný 2015: 344. One should also mention that Gwatkin 1957 already noted the weakness of Demosthenes' legal argument about the announcement of crowns in the theatre. MacDowell 2009: 388 n. 90 seriously distorts my points and does not take into account the evidence supporting my arguments. For the flaws in MacDowell's opinion see Harris 2013a: 227 n. 42. For detailed refutation of Gagarin 2012 with references to the evidence of inscriptions contradicting his view see Harris 2017b.

the law about deliberate wounding, a litigant in a speech by Lysias (3.40–43) reminds the court that they have followed this interpretation in previous cases. When prosecuting Aischines in 343, Demosthenes (19.277–279) uses the Assembly's conviction of Epikrates as a precedent for his charges against the defendant.[11]

It has been asserted that litigants rarely mention cases in this way and that this is an indication that the courts were not concerned with maintaining consistency in their decisions.[12] This view is untenable for two reasons. First, the alleged rarity of precedents is an illusion. Litigants cite precedents only when they are relevant to the issue in the case, and precedents are only relevant when there is a dispute about the meaning of a law. This rarely occurs in the extant speeches in the corpus of forensic oratory; as in modern courts below the appellate level, most cases concern questions of fact, not law.[13] Second, when there is an issue concerning the interpretation of statute in a forensic speech the litigant either cites a precedent or argues from the intent of the lawgiver.[14] There can be no question that the Athenian courts were concerned with maintaining consistency.[15]

When speakers analyse the reasons for a legal decision, they do not indicate how they discovered it. There is no reason however to doubt that litigants could have spoken with the judges after a trial and discussed why they voted as they did. After all, Athenian judges were not like jurors in the United Kingdom, who are barred by statute from discussing the cases they hear.[16] On the other hand, if the analysis of a court decision by a litigant is only speculation, the analysis must have appeared plausible to the judges who heard the case. A litigant is unlikely to have described the reasons for a court's decision in a way that would not have appeared convincing to his audience. Finally, we do have some official records of court decisions, and these tend to confirm the accounts given by litigants. For instance, Aischines (2.6) says that Philokrates was convicted because he fled Attica before his case came to trial; his account

11 For analysis see Harris 2013a: 260–261.

12 For this assumption see Lanni 2004.

13 See Harris 2013a: 381–387.

14 On the use and role of precedents in Athenian courts see note 9 above.

15 For more evidence showing that the Athenians were concerned about consistency see Canevaro 2013: esp. 160, n. 71 ('Lanni's contention that the Athenians showed little regard for consistency in their legal system is untenable.'). For more evidence about Athens and other Greek *poleis* demonstrating a concern for consistency see Sickinger 2008, endorsed by Rubinstein 2008.

16 For this rule see Partington 2014: 123.

is corroborated by an entry in the records of the *polētai* for the year.[17] Later on in this chapter, I discuss some entries in the naval records that reveal that the courts took extenuating circumstances into account in exactly the way several litigants claimed that they did. On the other hand, there is reason to be sceptical about the accounts given in the fourth century about trials that occurred in the fifth century. For instance, Demosthenes in his *Against Meidias* (21.143–148) reports that Alkibiades was charged with mutilating the Herms; contemporary sources state that the charge against him was parody of the Mysteries (Andok. 1.11; Thuc. 6.28).[18] In *Against Aristokrates* we are told Kimon was charged with overthrowing the democracy (Dem. 23.205); there is no other evidence for this trial. And Lykourgos (*Against Leokrates* 112–115) reports trials whose historicity has been questioned.[19] But even for these trials, the reasons given for the verdicts are similar to those given for contemporary trials.

The Role of the Plaint (*Enklēma*)

Before we examine the reasons litigants give for verdicts, it is necessary to understand the role of the plaint (*enklēma*) in framing the issue about which the judges voted.[20] When an accuser brought a charge, he had to submit to the relevant official a written document called the *enklēma*, which recorded his own name, the name of the defendant, the type of action he was initiating, the charges against the defendant, and the names of those who witnessed the summons. In a private case, the plaintiff indicated the amount of damages he was requesting. If the defendant denied the charges, he submitted a written statement to that effect called an *antigraphē*. In a *diadikasia* the litigant stated the reasons for his claim. The accuser also had to indicate in a brief narrative the illegal actions performed by the defendant. He could not just assert that the defendant had broken the law; he had to show what the defendant had done to violate the substantive part of the law. When describing the actions of the defendant, the accuser also had to follow the language of the substantive part of the statute under which he had initiated his procedure.[21] For instance, in

17 *Agora* XIX, P 26, ll. 455–460. Cf. Hyp. *Eux.* 29–30.

18 For analysis see MacDowell 1990: 358–361; Harris 2008: 136–139 with notes.

19 On these trials see Engels 2008: 165–167.

20 See Harris 2013a: 114–131 and Harris 2013b, which also show that the view of Gagarin 2008: 195 that the Athenians did not maintain records of trials is untenable.

21 Both Thür 2007 and Gagarin 2012: 295–299 in their brief discussions of the plaint miss this important point, which undermines their analysis of the role played by this document.

343 Hypereides brought a charge of treason against Philokrates using the procedure of *eisangelia*. This law applied to three types of offences: 1) attempts to overthrow the democracy, 2) treason (betraying the city, its ships, land or naval forces), and 3) speaking against the best interests of the Athenian people while accepting money (Hyp. *Eux.* 7–8). When he wrote his indictment, he followed the wording of the third offence very carefully.[22]

In a public suit against an illegal decree, the plaint not only stated the charge against the proposer of the decree but also listed the laws that the decree contravened (Aischin. 3.200) and the specific clauses of the decree that were illegal. When Diodoros accused Aristokrates of proposing an illegal decree for Charidemos, he included in the plaint all the laws Aristokrates had violated (Dem. 23.215–218). Litigants in private suits also had to follow the language of the statute. We can see this in a passage from Demosthenes' third speech *Against Aphobos* (Dem. 29.31), in which he uses the term guardianship (*epitropēs*), which is drawn from the name of the legal procedure he followed (*dikē epitropēs*).

> This is the beginning of the *enklēma*: 'Demosthenes makes the following charges against Aphobos. Aphobos has in his possession moneys of mine, received by him in his capacity as guardian (*ap' epitropēs*), as follows: eighty *mnai*, which he received as the marriage-portion of my mother in accordance with the terms of my father's will'.

Even though Athenian law contained nothing like the prescribed phrases of the Roman formulary system, one should not exaggerate the difference between the two systems. When the accuser drew up his plaint, he had to follow the language of the statute. If the plaint did not contain the key words of the relevant statute, the magistrate who received the charge might compel the accuser to add them. When Dionysios used the procedure of *apagōgē* to the Eleven against Agoratos, he charged him with killing his father. For one to use this procedure, however, one had to apprehend the defendant *ep' autophōrō*, that is, in circumstances that made his guilt obvious.[23] To make the plaint Dionysios submitted

---

The heterodox views of Gagarin 2008: 176–224 seriously underestimate the importance of written documents in Athenian legal procedure. The best studies of the role of writing in Athenian law are Maffi 1989, Sickinger 2004, Faraguna 2006, Faraguna 2008, and Pébarthe 2006: 315–344.

22 For the terms of the law see Hyp. *Eux.* 29–30. Cf. Whitehead 2000: 236: Hypereides 'had taken care there to echo the words and phrases of the impeachment law itself.'

23 For the correct translation of the phrase see Harris 2006: 373–390. Wohl 2010: 220 mis-

conform to the language of the statute, the Eleven insisted that he adds the key term *ep' autophōrō* to the charge (Lys. 13.85–87). Otherwise, they would not have accepted the charge.

Finally, the judges swore in their oath that they would vote only about the matters in the indictment, which therefore defined what was relevant to the case and what was not—the Greek term is *exō tou pragmatos* ([Dem.] 45.50):

> You have sworn to judge not about the issues the defendant demands you to decide, but about the (charges of the) prosecution. The nature of the charges must be made clear in plaint. I have brought a charge of false testimony.[24]

According to the *Ath. Pol.* (67.1), litigants in private cases also swore that they would keep to the point, and litigants in public cases probably swore a similar oath.[25] Whatever the case, it is certainly clear that litigants in public cases often accuse their opponents of not keeping to the point, which indicates that this was a requirement also in public cases.[26] There is no reason to believe that the rules of relevance were different in homicide cases or that the Areiopagos had stricter rules of relevance than the other courts.[27] All courts in Athens clearly adhered to the same standard.

This has important implications for our understanding of the Athenian legal system. When the accuser selected a procedure to follow, a *graphē*, a *dikē*, an *eisangelia*, *apogōgē* to the Eleven, or *phasis*, he not only chose a method for getting his dispute into court. He also made a decision about what substantive rule the defendant had violated. Osborne believes that for many offences there were two different procedures leading to different penalties.[28] This view is unconvincing for several reasons. First, it is based on a single passage from Demosthenes *Against Androtion* (22.25–29). As Carey has shown, the information in this passage is both tendentious and unreliable, hardly the kind of evidence one can use to base far-reaching conclusions about the Athenian legal

translates the phrase ('in the act'), which completely undermines her analysis of Lysias' speech *Against Agoratos*.

24 For other citations of this clause see Aischin. 1.154; 1.170; Dem. 22.4, 43, 45; 24.189; 30.9; [32.]13; 37.17; [40.]60; 44.14; 45.50; Isa. 6.51–52; Lykourg. 1.11–13.

25 Cf. Rhodes 2004.

26 For a list of all citations of and allusions to the judicial oath in the Attic orators see Harris 2013a: 353–356.

27 *Pace* Lanni 2006: chapter 4. For a detailed refutation see Harris 2009/10b: 327–328.

28 Osborne 1985.

system.[29] Second, as I showed for the procedures about theft many years ago and Carey has demonstrated for other offences, there were major substantive differences between these procedures.[30] Third, Osborne's approach is based on the flawed assumption that Athenian statutes concerned mostly procedural matters. A recent study of over three hundred laws in literary and epigraphical sources has shown that this assumption is untenable.[31]

Because of the way the plaint was framed, Athenian courts could not make a general decision about the defendant's general character and reputation; the judges had two choices, and only two: they could either accept the accuser's plaint and judge the defendant guilty of the charges in it or reject the charges in the plaint and acquit the defendant. There was no *tertium quid.* They had to decide whether or not the defendant had broken the substantive rule contained in the relevant statute. An arbitrator or board of arbitrators could devise a compromise solution tailored to the particular features of a specific dispute (e.g. [Dem.] 59.69–70). This was impossible for a court with several hundred judges who could not discuss a case and had to choose one of two alternatives. A litigant could also not bring an action to enforce an informal norm; every accusation had to be brought against the violation of a written norm. In fact, magistrates were forbidden from enforcing norms that were not contained in the code of written laws.[32]

It would therefore be a serious mistake to view law serving only as evidence at an Athenian trial, that is, only one means of persuasion among many, which could be used or ignored as the litigant wished.[33] The plaint required the judges to vote on the question, did the defendant violate the law or not? If a litigant wished to persuade the judges, he had to address this question, which meant that he could not ignore the law or just consider it as one piece of evidence among several. Consideration of the substantive rule under which the case was brought was not optional. It was required by the nature of the plaint and the oaths sworn by the judges and litigants.

---

29 Carey 2004: 111–115. Cf. Harris 2008: 179–181.

30 Procedures for theft: Harris 1994b = Harris 2006: 373–390. Other procedures: Carey 2004: 115–130.

31 See Harris 2009/10a = Harris 2013a: 138–174, 359–378.

32 For the prohibition against officials enforcing a law not contained in the written laws see Andok. 1.85, 89 with Canevaro and Harris 2012: 116–119. This evidence is decisive against the claim of Lanni 2009 that the Athenians used the courts to enforce informal norms. Note also that in the accounts of verdicts, those who are convicted are proved to have violated a legal norm, not an informal one.

33 *Pace* Todd 1993: 59–60; Kästle 2012. Cf. the good criticism of Todd by Carey 1996: 34 n. 8.

Reasons for a Just Conviction or Acquittal

We can now turn to the accounts of verdicts in the orators. Let us start with the reasons given for a just conviction or a just acquittal. It should come as no surprise that the standard reason for a just conviction is that the accuser proved the charges in the indictment. For instance, in the speech *On the Estate of Pyrrhos* (Isa. 3.3–4), the speaker says he convicted Xenokles because he proved his charge.

> We brought a charge against his *diamartyria* (that of Xenokles) and brought before you the many who had the audacity to make this declaration. After clearly proving that he had given false testimony, we won a suit for perjury against him.

Aischines (1.173) says that the Athenians put Sokrates to death for educating Kritias—this would indicate that he believed the court accepted the charge in Meletos' indictment that Sokrates corrupted the youth. Demosthenes provides the most elaborate analysis of the reasons for a favourable verdict in his account of his victory in court over his former guardian Aphobos (Dem. 29.29; cf. 44, 59).[34] Conversely, defendants are justly acquitted when they show the charges against them are false (Dem. 24.13–14; Hyp. *Eux.* 35–36). Equally unsurprising is the standard reason for a just acquittal: the accuser failed to prove the charges in the indictment or the defendant successfully refuted the charges in the indictment.

No litigant ever says that a defendant fled Attica because he did not believe that he would get a fair trial. Here the analyses of the litigants differ sometimes from those of the historians. Thucydides (6.27–29, 53, 60–61) implies that Alkibiades escaped and went to Sparta because the charges against him were false, and he believed that he would not receive a fair trial. Xenophon (*Hell.* 1.4.12) reports that many Athenians shared this opinion. By contrast, Aischines and Demosthenes believe that Philokrates' flight before his trial was an implicit confession of guilt.[35]

34 For other examples see Dem. 19.276–279; [Dem.] 53.17–18; [Dem.] 59.91; Dein. 2.12.

35 Compare Nikias' lack of confidence in the Athenian courts (Thuc. 7. 48.3–4).

Reasons for Unjust Verdicts

More interesting are the reasons for unjust verdicts, the abuse of law, one of the themes of this volume. Of course, one must take these stories with a grain of salt. In most cases, the speaker has lost a case and is trying to explain away his defeat in court. In some cases, we have the opponent's speech (e.g. [Dem.] 36), which presents much stronger arguments than the loser's account would have us believe (e.g., [Dem.] 45.6). But this evidence is still important for understanding what factors the Athenians believed had an influence in the minds of the judges. When litigants claim that they or their friends have lost a case unfairly or that their opponents have won unjustly, the most common reason given is that their opponents relied on false testimony. For instance, Theomnestos alleges that Stephanos convicted Apollodoros on a charge of proposing an illegal decree because he brought forward witnesses who falsely testified that Apollodoros was a public debtor ([Dem.] 59.6–8). I have found six other examples of this (Andok. 1.7; [Dem.] 45.5–6; Dem. 47.39; Dem. 54.26–33; Dem. 21.143–148; Isa. 5.7–9).[36] In two other cases, litigants claim that they lost because witnesses they hoped would support them did not show up in court (Dem. 48.22–23; [Dem.] 49.19 [cf. 34, 43–44, 55]). This would also reflect the fact that most cases in Athenian courts were concerned with questions of fact, not questions of law.[37] It is interesting to note that Thucydides (3.82.3) also considers false testimony a major source of injustice at trials during times of *stasis*.

Other reasons given for unjust verdicts relate to procedural violations. For instance, Apollodoros claims that the judges shouted him down after the supporting speaker for Phormion presented his case at a *paragraphē* ([Dem.]. 45.6). This violated his right to a fair trial by depriving him of the chance to present his defence. Apollodoros says that he lost a case because Lykidas did not present him with a summons ([Dem.] 53.14–15). As a result, he did not attend the trial and lost by default. Nikoboulos claims that Pantainetos won his suit for damages against Euergos by making accusations not found in the plaint (Dem. 37.45–48). This meant that Euergos could not present a proper defence and lost. But Nikoboulos' explanation for the verdict is questionable: the judges had good legal grounds for deciding in favour of Pantainetos.[38] It is significant that this is the only occasion when a litigant makes this charge.

36 This evidence undermines the view of Todd 1990 that Athenian judges were not interested in the content of testimony given by witnesses and regarded the main task of a witness to provide support. For detailed criticisms of Todd's view see Rubinstein 2005.

37 On the issues in forensic orations see Harris 2013a: 381–386.

38 Harris 2013a: 213–216.

I have found only one case in which a litigant implies that a defendant was acquitted because of the influence of powerful men. This occurs in the speech *Against Timotheos* in which Apollodoros alleges that his opponent was acquitted because Jason and Alketas spoke for him ([Dem.] 49.9–10). But it is possible that what made a difference was not their influence but the nature of the testimony they gave. And sycophants are another reason given for unjust verdicts: their activity was clearly seen as dysfunctional and undermining the democracy (Hyp. *Eux.* 34; Dem. 37.45–48).[39]

In a speech attributed to Demosthenes (43.7–10), the speaker claims that he lost his claim to an estate at a *diadikasia* because his four opponents collaborated and used the extra time they had to weaken his case. Because he had only one-fourth the time his opponents had, he was at a disadvantage and lost. The most elaborate example of procedural chicanery is the disenfranchisement of Straton described by Demosthenes in his speech *Against Meidias* (21.81–93). I cannot analyse these manoeuvres in detail here: I would only note that Demosthenes' account is rather undermined by the fact that Straton appears to have appealed the verdict of the arbitrators against him and lost. Two speeches of Lysias attribute the unjust verdicts of the Thirty to procedural irregularities. In one case, Kleophon was wrongly convicted because Nikomachos provided the Thirty with a forged law allowing them to join the court (Lys. 30.11–14). Another litigant claims that there was no secret ballot under the Thirty (Lys. 13.36–37).

The explanations *not* given for unjust verdicts are also interesting. Litigants never state that the court gave an unjust verdict because the judges ignored the substantive part of the law or sided with a litigant who distorted or misrepresented the substantive rules contained in a statute. At the trial of Ktesiphon, Demosthenes (18.111) accused Aischines of twisting the laws, but no litigant ever says that his opponent won a case using these tactics. Despite the numerous charges litigants make that their opponents will deceive the court, we never find the language of deceit—words like *apatē* or *paragein* (to lead astray)—used to describe the reasons why a litigant won a lawsuit.[40] Litigants may accuse opponents of misrepresenting the laws, but they never say that judges decided a case based on a mistaken view of the laws. On the contrary, when describing verdicts, litigants give the impression that judges obeyed their oath to decide according to the laws.[41] Nor does any litigant claim that the judges decided to ignore the law because a verdict based on the law would damage

39 On the nature of the sykophant see Harvey 1990 who refutes Osborne 1990. Cf. Harris 2013a: 62–63, 344.

40 On the use of the language of deception in oratory see Kremmydas 2013.

41 On the judicial oath see Harris 2006 and Harris 2013a: 101–137.

the public interest.[42] Another salient point is that litigants almost never blame the judges for unjust verdicts: they blame instead the unscrupulous tactics of other litigants. Here there is a contrast with the attitude of Thucydides, who in some cases blames unjust verdicts on the Athenian people.[43] What this appears to show is that the Athenians generally had confidence in their legal system provided that everyone followed the rules. Or at least they pretended to have confidence when addressing the court because that was the way to make a good impression on the judges.

What Litigants Do Not Consider Important Factors in Legal Decisions

Two words that are conspicuously absent in accounts of verdicts given by litigants are *timē* (honour, respect) and *echthra* (enmity).[44] Some scholars claim that the Athenians viewed their courts as an arena for competition about social prestige or a place where feuds could be pursued in a peaceful manner. The flaw in this approach is that it confuses the possible motives of the litigants who brought charges and the aims of the rules and procedures of Athenian legal institutions. In the language of the New Institutionalism such an approach does not make a crucial distinction between the motives of agents who use an institution and the aims of the institution.[45] For instance, a football player

42 The evidence about verdicts compiled here refutes the unconvincing view of Wallace 2012 that judges ignored the law when it suited the public interest. This is not surprising because litigants always argue that enforcing the law is in the public interest. For a detailed refutation of Wallace's view, see Ismard 2012. At the trial of the generals after Arginousai, the Assembly did ignore the law about the right to a trial in capital cases, but in this case the verdict was later viewed as contrary to the public interest. See Xen. *Hell.* 1.7.6–35 and the discussion in Harris 2013a: 241–243, 340–344.

43 Thuc. 2.65 implies that the verdict against Perikles was unjust because he notes that Perikles was soon re-elected general and criticises the Athenians for being fickle. Thuc. 4.65 also implies that the verdicts against Pythodoros, Sophocles and Eurymedon were unjust by stating that the Athenians had unrealistic expectations at the time. Even though he does not explicitly state that the verdict against Antiphon was unjust, Thuc. 8.68 implies that it was by calling his speech at the trial the finest ever delivered.

44 One should not translate the term *echthra* as 'feud'—this kind of conflict did not occur in Classical Athens (*pace* Cohen [1995]). For detailed analysis of the term and its inapplicability to litigation in Athens see Harris 2013a: 76–98.

45 See for instance North 1990: 4–5: 'Conceptually, what must be clearly differentiated are the rules from the players. The purpose of the rules is to define the way the game is played. But the objective of the team within that set of rule is to win the game—by a combination of skills, strategy, and coordination; by fair means and sometimes by foul means. Modelling

may join a football club and play football because he wants to make money and impress his girlfriend, but that explains nothing about the rules by which football is played and tells us nothing about the institution and the way it works. Even though some accusers (though far from all) were motivated by enmity, one cannot use their motives to analyse the rationale of the legal system. When Athenian judges made their decisions, they did not take sides in a feud or help an ambitious individual to enhance his reputation. They made a decision about guilt and innocence based on their knowledge of the facts and the relevant law. That decision may have had an impact on the reputations of the accuser and defendant, but that was secondary to the main duty of the judges, which was to vote according to the laws and about the issues in the plaint. Enmity (*echthra*) and favour (*eunoia*) had nothing to do with their decision (Dem. 23.96–97; Dem. 57.63).

Finally, litigants hardly ever state that judges made an unjust decision because they allowed emotions to cloud their judgment. The only example is from the speech of Antiphon (5.69–70) *On the Murder of Herodes*, in which the defendant recalls how charges of bribery were brought against the *hellēnotamiai*, who were all condemned to death. All were executed except Sosias, who was set free when evidence confirming their innocence was discovered. The litigant blames the unjust verdict on the anger of the judges and implies that they made their decision without evidence by stating that it was later discovered how the money disappeared. What is important to note, however, is that anger did not cause the judges to ignore the law but to make a decision not based on proven facts.[46] In a similar way, litigants never say that someone's rhetorical performance was the key factor in swaying the judges' opinion.[47]

Litigants also believe that the judges kept to their promise in the Judicial Oath to vote only about the charges in the indictment. When describing the outcomes of trials, litigants always say that the judges did not take public ser-

---

the strategies and skills of the teams as it develops is a separate process from modelling the creation, evolution, and consequences of the rules.' and 'Separating the analysis of the underlying rules from the strategy of the players is a necessary prerequisite to building a theory of institutions'.

46 For the influence of emotions on the court's judgment see the anecdote in Arist. *Rh.* 2.3.13.1380b: the Athenians were angrier with Ergophilos than with Kallisthenes, but they acquitted the former because they had quenched their anger by convicting the latter on the previous day. Cf. Xen. *Hell.* 1.5.19 (the Assembly votes to release a man out of pity).

47 The evidence provided by accounts of verdicts given by litigants calls into question the view of E. Hall 2006: 353–392, esp. 391–392 that what counted most in court was a litigant's performance. For detailed criticism of this view see Harris 2017a.

vice into account and ignored considerations like social status and famous ancestors. One litigant recalls:

> You made no allowance for Timotheos, Athenians, even though he sailed around the Peloponnese and defeated the Lacedaemonians in a sea battle at Kerkyra, and was the son of Konon, who had brought freedom to Greece. Although he took Samos, Methone, Pydna, Potidaia and twenty other cities, you did not allow his public services to be more important than the trial you were conducting or the oaths that control your vote. On the contrary, you set his punishment at a hundred talents because Aristophon said that he had taken money from the Chians and Rhodians.
>
> DEIN. 1.14

Demosthenes (19.273) says that when Epikrates was charged with bribery and other offences in the Assembly, his services in helping to restore the democracy did not prevent him from being convicted.[48] These numerous examples show that the average litigant thought that the judges obeyed their oath to decide only about the charges brought in the indictment and ignored irrelevant matters when making their judgments. This pledge had an influence on the arguments that litigants presented to the court: not one litigant ever argues that a court should ignore the law and acquit him only because he or his supporters have performed liturgies.[49] In fact, one litigant explicitly states that this topic was irrelevant when discussing guilt and innocence (Dem. 54.44). When litigants mention public service, they tend to do it for one of five reasons: 1) public service is directly relevant to the legal charges in the plaint; 2) public service is cited as evidence of good character to show that the defendant is unlikely to have committed the offences with which he has been charged in the plaint; 3) public service is mentioned to prove that someone is wealthy; 4) public service is mentioned to explain some aspect of the narrative; and 5) public service is mentioned to obtain the goodwill of the judges.[50] On the other hand, public service could be mentioned at the *timēsis* phase of a public action as an

48 For other examples of cases in which the defendant was convicted despite an impressive record of public service see Aischin. 3.195; Dem. 21.143–148; 24.133–138; 34.50–51; 54.25; [Dem.] 59.116–117 with Harris 2013a: 127–129. It should come as no surprise that one finds no references to these passages in Lanni 2006 and Lanni 2009.

49 Dem. 21.208 claims that Meidias' supporters will do this, but see Rubinstein 2000: 218–220, who notes that this is probably slander and that no litigant ever states this in his own speech.

50 For a list of mentions of public service in the forensic speeches see Harris 2013a: 387–400.

argument for a milder penalty. For instance, it is clear that Meidias intended to describe his many liturgies at the *timēsis* phase of the trial if he was convicted of *hybris* (Dem. 21.151).[51]

The Role of Extenuating Circumstances

Even though the courts did not pay attention to public service and social status in a private case or during the first phase of a public action, they might take extenuating circumstances or the intent of the defendant into account when determining guilt.[52] This is what Aristotle calls *epieikeia* in the *Nicomachean Ethics* and the *Rhetoric*.[53] Meyer-Laurin, following the lead of Hans-Julius Wolff, denied that Aristotle's discussion of *epieikeia* had anything to do with the way the courts decided cases, but the evidence for the reasons for verdicts in several passages contradicts their view. Deinarchos (1.58–59) reports that the Assembly ordered the Areiopagos to report whether a citizen named Polyeuktos was meeting with exiles in Megara. The Areiopagos investigated and reported to the Assembly that Polyeuktos was indeed meeting with exiles. The Assembly elected public prosecutors and the case against Polyeuktos went to court, but the defendant was acquitted. At the trial Polyeuktos admitted that he did go to Megara to see Nikophanes who was an exile (*apesterēmenos tēs patridos*), but who also happened to be married to his mother.

The charge against Polyeuktos is most likely to have been treason and the procedure *eisangelia*. Deinarchos does not say why Nikophanes was in exile, but the penalty was a serious one and strongly suggests that whatever his actual offence it was one that had threatened public security. Because Nikophanes was regarded as dangerous, any attempt to speak with him and help him might be construed as an attempt to overthrow the democracy, which was one of the offences listed in the *eisangelia* law. But the courts did not look only at Polyeuktos' actions; they also considered his intent in meeting with Nikophanes. The court decided that although Nikophanes was an exile and thus a criminal, Polyeuktos helped him not for the purpose of overthrowing the democracy but for personal reasons. Nikophanes was married to his mother, and Polyeuktos was helping his stepfather not as a co-conspirator but as a relative who had fallen on hard times. One might argue that his actions fit the criteria of treason in the law of *eisangelia*, but he lacked the necessary intent.

51 For the evidence and analysis see Harris 2013a: 131–136.

52 Harris 2013b = Harris 2013a: 274–304.

53 For an analysis of the passages about *epieikeia* in Aristotle see Brunschwig 1996.

For this reason, the court decided to be forgiving (Dein. 1.59: *syngnōmēs*). The court's approach to the case fits one of Aristotle's examples of *epieikeia*: in the *Rhetoric* (1.13.14.1374b) Aristotle says that the person who uses fairness looks not at the action but at the moral intent (*proairesin*). An anecdote recounted by Aristotle in the *Magna Moralia* (1188b30–37) confirms this point that the courts did not just consider the actions of a defendant but also his or her intent. In this case, the Areiopagos took into account the intention of a woman who gave a potion, which she thought would make him love her, when acquitting her on a charge of homicide.

Meyer-Laurin denied that the Athenian courts accepted pleas of necessity, but evidence from official records shows that judges were willing to countenance such arguments as grounds for acquittal.[54] In other cases so far, we have had to rely on the accounts given by orators; here we have an official verdict, which provides confirmation for our analysis. First, some background. Every year the Athenians appointed trierarchs to serve as captains of their triremes. Each trierarch had the duty to return the ship in good repair to the dockyards of the fleet. The supervisors (*epimelētai*) of the fleet in conjunction with a tester (*dokimastēs*) inspected the triremes after their return, classified them as in good shape or not, and reported their findings to the Council. If there was damage to the ship or it was lost, the trierarch could be held financially responsible, and the case was heard before a court, which might impose a penalty of double the value of what was lost. On the other hand, the trierarch could present an excuse (*skēpsis*) and claim that the loss or damage was caused by a storm. If the court accepted his excuse, the trierarch was exonerated. One entry in the records of the supervisors for the year 325/4 states that the trierarchs Euthydikos, the son of Antiphanes of Phegai, and Diphilos, the son of Diopeithes of Sounion, presented such an excuse and were acquitted.[55] They clearly show that the courts accepted pleas of necessity.

Concluding Remarks

To sum up: when an Athenian initiated legal proceedings, he had to describe how the defendant had violated the substantive provisions in a specific statute. At a *diadikasia*, a litigant had to present his request for an estate or other privilege citing the substantive rules that granted him this right. The court had to

54 Meyer-Laurin 1965. Lanni 2006: 50–51 takes a similar position to that of Meyer-Laurin ('the popular courts did not formally recognise' extenuating circumstances).

55 *IG* II[2] 1629, lines 771–780. *Cf.* *IG* II[2] 1631, lines 116–119, 141–143, 148–152.

vote either to accept or to reject the charges in the plaint. It did not make a general decision about the status and reputation of a litigant.[56] Nor did the Athenians view a trial as a way of re-apportioning *timē*[57] or a means of regulating feuds (*echthrai*).[58] In their accounts of verdicts, litigants say that successful accusers won because they convinced the court their charges were valid—successful defendants gained acquittal because they refuted the charges. There are several reasons for unjust verdicts, the main ones being false testimony and procedural violations. Litigants also insist that the courts did not take public service or social status into account when determining guilt; this was only relevant at the *timēsis* phase of a public trial when the judges voted about the penalty. Next, the courts took both intent and extenuating circumstances into account when reaching a decision. Despite all the warnings about crafty speakers and attempts to twist the law, litigants generally assumed that the courts knew the law and upheld their oath to vote according to the laws and only about charges contained in the indictment. This was because the Athenians firmly believed in the rule of law and did their best to implement this ideal. The historians Thucydides and Xenophon were less optimistic about their success in attaining this ideal, but that is the subject of another essay.

Appendix: Cases Mentioned in the Orators

Aischines	
1.34	Timarchos indicts the law appointing one tribe to keep order in the Assembly. Outcome and reason for verdict not known.
1.63	Aristophon threatens Hegesandros with *dokimasia rhētorōn*, but does not bring the case to court.
1.113	Unknown accuser(s) charges Timarchos and two others with receiving bribes as *exetastēs*. Timarchos alone of the three admits taking money, does not address the charges but asks for leniency in the penalty. The court convicts all three but gives Timarchos a smaller penalty. Reason: The court rules Timarchos' confession as an admission of guilt, but takes his willingness to admit his culpability into account when determining the penalty.

56 *Pace* Cohen 1995.

57 *Pace* Osborne 2000.

58 *Pace* Cohen 1995 and Phillips 2008.

(*cont.*)

1.114	Timarchos charges that Philotades is not a citizen. Charge withdrawn.
1.172	Allusion to trial of Aristarchos for murdering Nikodemos. Reason for verdict not given. Cf. Aischin. 2.148, Dein. 1.30, 47; Dem. 21.104.
1.173	Court condemns Sokrates for teaching Kritias, who overthrew the democracy. Verdict: The court clearly thought the charge that Sokrates corrupted the youth was true.
2.6	Philokrates fled Athens and was convicted *in absentia*. Cf., P 26, ll. 455–460. Reason: Aischines argues that the court accepted the charge in the indictment because Philokrates admitted his guilt by fleeing.
2.14	Lykinos accuses Philokrates on a charge of proposing an illegal decree. Lykinos does not receive one-fifth of the votes. Reason for verdict not given.
2.30	Kallisthenes is condemned to death not for the treaty with Philip but for other reasons. Reason for verdict not given.
2.93	The Areiopagos fines Demosthenes for not bringing his charge of wounding against Demomeles to trial. Reason: Areiopagos fines Demosthenes for violating the law.
2.124	Leosthenes is in exile because of *sykophantai*. Reason: Aischines implies the verdict was unjust.
2.148	Nikodemos indicts Demosthenes for desertion, but Demosthenes buys him off.
3.51–52	Three trials involving Demosthenes discussed. One case is withdrawn, no reason for the verdict given in the other two.
3.195	Archinos of Koile convicts Thrasyboulos of Steiria for an illegal decree. Reason for verdict: The court ignores the services of Thrasyboulos.
3.252	Private citizen attempts to sail to Samos and is executed by the Areiopagos on the same day. This may not be a trial but a summary execution during the panic after Chaironeia.
3.252	Allusion to trial of Leokrates, who was acquitted by one vote. Reason for split verdict not given.
Andokides	
1.7	General statement about unjust verdicts resulting from false testimony.
1.13	Polystratos is denounced by Andromachos for parodying the Mysteries and put to death; others flee and are sentenced to death. Reason: Andokides implies that the court accepted the testimony of Andromachos.

(*cont.*)

1.17	The father of Andokides brings an action against Speusippos for proposing an illegal decree. The case is heard by six thousand judges; Speusippos does not get two hundred votes. Reason not given.
1.65–66	Diokleides admits that he committed perjury and is condemned to death. Charge is not known.
Antiphon	
5.69–70	Unknown accusers bring charges of embezzlement against the *hellēnotamiai*. All are condemned to death; all are executed except Sosias. Evidence is later discovered proving their innocence. Reason: The judges acted on anger (presumably without any evidence).
6.35	Speaker brings *eisangelia* before the Council against Philinos, Ampelinos, and the scribe of the *thesmothetai* for embezzlement. The Council condemns them because they are guilty, but the case has not yet reached the court.
Apollodoros	([Dem.] 45, 46, 49, 50, 52, 53, 59)
45.5–6	Apollodoros brings suit for damages against Phormion. Phormion brings a *paragraphē* on the grounds the suit is not admissible and wins case to bar the action. Reason: Phormion provides false documents, Stephanos provides false testimony, and the court refuses to hear his case.
51	Phormion's supporters will claim that the court voted for him on the basis of the release and not Pasion's will.
49.9–10	Kallistratos and Iphikrates prosecute Antimachos (apparently for embezzlement). The court sentences him to death. Reason for verdict not given. Timotheos is acquitted of charge after being deposed from office. Reason: Influence of Jason and Alketas.
49.19. *Cf.* 34, 43–44, 55	Apollodoros loses arbitration. Reason: Witness does not show up to testify.
52.30–31	Kallippos brings suit against Apollodoros and Pasikles for money on deposit in Pasion's bank. The case is submitted to a public arbitrator Lysitheides, who gives judgment for Kallippos. Reason: Lysitheides did not swear the oath and does not feel bound to decide justly.
53.14–15	Lykidas brings *endeixis* against Apollodoros for being a public debtor and gains conviction. Reason: Lykidas does not issue a summons to Apollodoros, who presumably loses because he does not attend the trial.

(*cont.*)

53.17–18	Apollodoros brings case for false summons against Lykidas and wins. The court sets the penalty at one talent. Reason: Apollodoros proves the charges in the indictment.
59.6–8	Stephanos charges Apollodoros with proposing an illegal decree and gains a conviction. The court sets the penalty at one talent. Reason: Stephanos presents false witnesses who claim Apollodoros was a public debtor and makes irrelevant charges.
59.9–10	Stephanos charges Apollodoros with killing a slave woman. Apollodoros is acquitted. Reason: The charges are shown to be false, and Kephisophon and Apollophanes are shown to have hired Stephanos to bring false charges.
59.70	Epainetos brings public charge of false imprisonment against Stephanos. Charges dropped.
59.91	Peitholas the Thessalian and Apollonides the Olynthian are given citizenship. Someone brings a public charge of making an illegal proposal against the proposer. Reason: Peitholas and Apollonides are shown not to be worthy of citizenship.
59.116–117	The court convicts Archias the hierophant for impiety because he did not conduct sacrifices according to ancestral custom. Reason: Archias violated the law about sacrifices for the Haloa. The court ignores his ancestors, his public services, his public office and the pleas of his friends.
Demosthenes	**Private speeches**
27.49–51	Demosthenes brings a private suit against Aphobos for mismanaging his inheritance. The arbitrator rules in his favour. Reason: Aphobos cannot prove that the estate had many debts and that he paid these to the other guardians (he cannot produce witnesses of documents); Aphobos also admits that he paid expenses out of capital and not from revenue, i.e. he mismanaged the finances.
29.2–3, 6–7, 29, 44, 59–60	Demosthenes wins case against Aphobos in court because he proves his charges with witnesses. Reason: Aphobos was proven to have embezzled sums of money and because he did not lease the estate when Demosthenes' father had ordered him to do so.
30.7–8	Aphobos loses case. Reason not given.
[32.]9	Decision of judge in Kephallenia.
[32.]26	Zenothemis brings a private suit for damages against Protos, who does not attend the trial. Reason: The arbitrator decides against Protos because he does not show up.
[33.]13	Parmenon sues Apatourios for violence, and Apatourios sues Parmenon. Case goes before arbitrators.

(*cont.*)

[34.]18–21	Theodotos declines to decide private case as arbitrator because he is a friend of Phormion but does not wish to commit perjury.
[34.]50–51	Unnamed defendant put to death for not turning over securities. Reason: Judges ignore his ancestors who were generals and decide to preserve integrity of the market.
37.45–48	Pantainetos brings suit for damages against Euergos and wins a judgment. Reason: Nikoboulos, the partner of Euergos, claims that Pantainetos made charges before the court that were not contained in the indictment. Because Euergos did not know the charges in advance, he was at a disadvantage. This is *sykophantia* and leads to an unjust decision.
38.23	Nikidas brings a *phasis* against Xenopeithes to compel him to lease an estate and wins. Reason: Nikidas persuades the judges.
38.28	Brief allusion to case against Aisios. No reason given.
39.37. *Cf.* [40.]18	Mantitheos brings suit against Boiotos. Boiotos does not attend trial, and arbitrators give judgment against him. Boiotos later has decision overturned because judgment is given in the wrong name. Reason: Boiotos does not attend trial.
[40.]17	Boiotos loses case because he cannot prove the charges. Reason: Boiotos cannot prove charges.
[40.]32–33	Boiotos brings case against Mantitheos for wounding before Areiopagos and loses. Reason: The doctor Euthydikos testifies that he made the cut on Boiotos' head, i.e., evidence proves charge false.
[40.]34	Mantitheos brings ejectment suit against Boiotos and wins. Reason not given.
43.4	Glaukon and Glaukos claim estate of Hagnias on the basis of a will and testimony of Theopompos but lose case. Reason: The will is shown to be a forgery.
43.7–10. *Cf.* 38–39	Several parties lay claim to estate of Hagnias. Court awards to estate to Theopompos. Reason: Four groups of claimants conspire to have their stories agree; the other claimant has only one-fourth the time to explain his claim and loses. At §§38–39 a different explanation is given that the litigant did not present evidence.
47.28	Speaker brings action to recover naval equipment from Demochares of Paiania and wins case. Reason not given.
47.28	Speaker brings case against Theophemos to recover naval equipment and wins case. Reason: Theophemos offers no defence against the charge.

(*cont.*)

47.39. *Cf.* 45–46	Theophemos brings private suit for assault against the speaker and wins a judgment. Reason: The speaker claims that Theophemos deceived the court by claiming his witnesses committed perjury and that his slave would give true testimony if tortured.
47.42–43	Speaker brings *eisangelia* against Theophemos for delaying the fleet in the Council. The Council awards damages of 25 *drachmas*. Reason: Council finds Theophemos guilty of the charges.
48.22–27	Several claimants claim estate of Komon. Speaker loses his claim. Reason: The speaker claims that he did not know there would be so many claimants. He relied on the support of Olympiodoros, who was absent. The court determined that Olympiodoros did not have public service as an excuse for his absence.
48.31–33	Speaker claims to have an agreement with Olympiodoros about splitting the estate. Reason: Olympiodoros wins because Olympiodoros speaks first and because he deliberately presented a weak case in hopes of splitting the estate.
54.25	Unknown accuser brings charge of deliberate homicide against the father of the priestess of Brauron. The defendant leaves Attica either before the trial or before the verdict. The Areiopagos sentences him to permanent exile *in absentia*. Reason not given, but the speaker, Konon, implies that the verdict was given to encourage bystanders to protect victims of violence.
54.26–33	Ariston brings private suit against Konon. The arbitrator appears to rule against Ariston. Reason: Ariston alleges that Konon delayed his challenge to torture slaves until the last moment and submitted testimony that was either false or irrelevant.
54.39	Bakchios and Aristokrates condemned to death. Charge and reason for verdict not given.
57.8	Euboulides accuses the sister of Lakedaimonios for impiety but does not get one-fifth of the votes. Reason not given.
57.60	Antiphilos loses the deme register of citizens and has ten Halimousians expelled. All appeal to the court, and nine out of ten are reinstated. Reason not given (though the speaker implies they were wrongfully expelled).
[58.]1, 30–32, 70	Theokrines charges the speaker's father with proposing an illegal decree and convicts him. The court imposes a penalty of ten talents. Reason: The speaker claims that the decree was legal, but Theokrines claimed the decree would deprive Charidemos of an estate and distracted the judges.

(*cont.*)

	Public cases
18.103–107	Diondas indicts decree of praise for Demosthenes and does not get one-fifth of the votes. Reason not given.
18.249–250	Demosthenes indicted on several charges (apparently for illegal decrees and at *euthynai*) by Sosikles, Philokrates, Diondas, and Melanthos, and acquitted. Reason: He proved his proposals did not violate the law (ἔννομα—this related to decrees) and that he acted 'justly and honestly' (δικαίως καὶ ἀδωροδοκήτως—this related to *euthynai*), in other words, he disproved the charges in the indictment.
19.116	Hypereides prosecutes Philokrates by *eisangelia*. Reason not given.
19.180	Ergophilos, Kephisodotos, Timomachos, Ergokles, Dionysios and others sentenced to death or to pay large fines (charges not specified). Reason: They damaged the city's interests.
19.241–242, 244, 251, 283, 285	Aischines prosecutes Timarchos. Reason: Demosthenes does not give the reason for the verdict but implies that it was unfair (§ 286).
19.273	Kallias prosecuted at *euthynai* and convicted to a fine of 50 talents. Reason: He was convicted of accepting gifts. The court ignored the public services of Kallias for concluding peace with Persia.
19.276–279	Epikrates condemned to death for misconduct on embassy. Trial in the Assembly. Reasons: 1) As ambassador, he disobeyed orders, 2) he gave false reports to the Assembly, 3) bore false witness against allies, and 4) accepted gifts. These were obviously the charges in the indictment. Court ignores the public service of Epikrates.
19.290	Hegesilaos tried on unknown charge. Verdict unknown. Reason not given.
19.332	Chares was often brought to trial and acquitted. Charges not specified. Reason: Chares was found to act loyally, justly, and in the public interest despite his lack of military success.
20.146	Leodamas brings public suit (*graphē paranomōn*?) against an award made to Chabrias and loses. Reason not given.
21.58	Sannion convicted for desertion. Reason not given.
21.64	Philostratos accuses Chabrias about Oropos. Charge and verdict not given.

(*cont.*)

21.72–75	Euaion convicted for murder (*phonos ek pronoias*). Reason: split verdict with majority voting that he had killed intentionally, the minority taking extenuating circumstances (provocation) into account.
21.81–93	Litigation at public arbitration leads to the disenfranchisement of the arbitrator Straton. Reason: Demosthenes claims Meidias abused legal procedures.
21.103	Euktemon does not bring case and loses right to bring public cases.
21.143–148	Alkibiades convicted for several offences. Reason: Judges paid no attention to ancestors and public service.
21.175–176	Euandros wins maritime suit against Menippos. Reason not given. Menippos brings private suit against Euandros for damages. Reason: Euandros had tried to seize Menippos during the Mysteries.
21.180–181	Ktesikles convicted of *hybris* and put to death. Reason: the judges determined Ktesikles acted with intent to insult and not because he was drunk.
21.182	Pyrrhos executed for serving as judge while in debt to the state. Reason: guilty of violating the law.
21.182	Smikros and Skiton convicted for proposing illegal decrees. Reason: the courts did not take pity on them their children, their friends, their relatives or anyone who appeared on their behalf.
21.218	Aristophanes avoids *probolē* by repaying funds. It is not clear what the charge is or if there was a vote.
22.2–3	See 24.7.
23.104	Autokles put on trial. Charge and verdict not stated.
23.167–168	General convicted and fined five talents. Charge and reason for verdict not stated.
23.205	Athenians convict Themistokles for collaborating with the Persians. Reason: Themistokles is guilty of treason.
23.205	Kimon is charged with subverting the constitution and fined fifty talents. There is no other evidence for this trial, which may have been invented by the speaker.
24.7. *Cf.* 22.2–3	Androtion brings a charge of impiety against Diodoros, who is acquitted. Androtion does not gain one-fifth of the votes. The reason for the decision is not given, but the language implies the charges are false.

(*cont.*)

24.8	Diodoros and Euktemon charge Androtion with several offences—Androtion is acquitted.
24.127	Melanopos is convicted of treason and condemned to pay a fine of three talents.
24.127	Melanopos is convicted of embezzlement and condemned to pay a fine of ten talents.
24.134	Thrasyboulos of Kollytos placed on trial and put in prison. Charge and reason not given.
24.135	Philepsios of Lamptrai and Agyrrhios of Kollytos sentenced to pay fines and spend time in prison. Charges and reason not given.
24.135	Myronides spends time in prison, apparently after being convicted. Charge and reason not given.
24.136	Treasurers of Athena and Other Gods remain in prison until their trial. Charges and verdict not given.
24.136	Men convicted of crimes in the grain trade. Charges and reason for conviction not given.
24.138	Eudemos of Kydathenai put to death for proposing an inexpedient law. Specific charges not given.
24.138	Philip, the son of a ship-captain Philip, sentenced to pay a large fine. Charges and reason not given.
Deinarchos	
1.14	Aristophon indicts Timotheos on charge of accepting gifts (probably at *euthynai*). Timotheos is sentenced to pay a fine of one hundred talents. Reason: Court accepts Aristophon's charges and ignores the public service of Timotheos.
1.23	Court puts Menon the miller to death for keeping a free boy from Pellene in a mill (the charge is probably enslavement). It is not clear who made the charge. Reason: The court accepts the charge.
1.23	The court puts Themistios of Aphidna to death for committing *hybris* against a Rhodian flute-girl during the Eleusinian Mysteries. It is not clear whether the charge is *hybris* or *asebeia*. Reason: The court found Themistios guilty of the charges.
1.23	The court puts Euthymachos to death for putting an Olynthian girl in a brothel. The charge is probably enslavement. Reason: The court accepts the charges. In each of these cases, the court took no account of the victim's foreign status.

(*cont.*)

1.56	The Areiopagos reports one of its members, who is tried for robbing a ferryman of his fare, someone who is tried for claiming the five-*drachma* allowance in the name of an absentee, and a person who is tried for selling the portion distributed to members of Areiopagos at a sacrifice. All are acquitted. Reason: The court finds the punishment proposed too severe for the crimes committed by the defendants.
1.58	The Areiopagos reports Polyeuktos, who is tried on a charge of accompanying exiles to Megara. The charge must be *eisangelia*. He is acquitted. Reason: The court finds nothing wrong in helping his mother's husband who was in difficulties, that is, the defendant lacked treasonable intent in associating with an exile.
1.63	The court sends Charinos into exile for treason. Reason: The court accepts the report of the Areiopagos and its recommendation.
1.94	Demosthenes indicts Kallimedon for associating with exiles for the purpose of revolution. Demosthenes withdraws the indictment.
2.8	Kydimachos condemned to death and flees into exile. Charge and reason for verdict not given.
2.12	Aristogeiton indicted for false statements about the priestess of Artemis Brauronia and her relatives and fined fined talents. The charge is not specified. Reason: The accusers prove that Aristogeiton has lied.
2.24–25	Arthmios of Zelea is condemned by the Assembly for bringing Persian gold to the Peloponnese. It is not clear whether the decision resulted from a trial in the Assembly or was just a decree.
3.17	Same as 1.14.
Hypereides	
Against Philippides 10–11	The judges condemned Philippides twice for proposing illegal decrees. Reason not given.
For Euxenippos 1	Unknown accusers bring *eisangeliai* against Timomachos, Leosthenes, Kallistratos, Philon and Theotimos. Charges are betraying ships, betraying cities or not giving good advice as a speaker. All flee Attica and are convicted *in absentia*. Reason not given.
For Euxenippos 3	Unknown accuser brings *eisangelia* against Diognides for hiring flute-girls at a high price. Verdict not given.
For Euxenippos 3	Unknown accuser brings *eisangelia* against Agasikles of Piraeus for being registered at Halimous. Verdict not given.

(*cont.*)

***For Euxenippos* 12**	Alexandros of Oion prosecutes Polyeuktos. Charge and verdict not given.
***For Euxenippos* 15–18**	Unknown accuser convicts Polyeuktos for proposing an illegal decree. Reason: the decree contains contradictory clauses.
***For Euxenippos* 28**	Hypereides brings *eisangelia* against Aristophon, who is acquitted by two votes. Charge and reason not given.
***For Euxenippos* 28**	Hypereides brings *eisangelia* against Diopeithes of Sphettos. Charge and verdict not given.
***For Euxenippos* 29–30**	Hypereides brings an *eisangelia* against Philokrates for giving bad advice as a public speaker. Philokrates is convicted. Reason: Hypereides has the indictment read out.
***For Euxenippos* 34**	Teisis of Agryle brings an *apographē* against Euthykrates on the grounds it is public property. Teisis does not gain one-fifth of votes and loses right to bring public cases. Reason: Judges do not covet the property of others and reject the slander of a sycophant.
***For Euxenippos* 35**	Lysandros brings *phasis* against Epikrates of Pallene for having his mine go beyond limits. Reason: The judges decide that the mine is within the proper limits, that is, they reject the charge in the indictment. The speaker views this as a vindication of property rights.
***Against Demosthenes* 27**	Unknown accuser accuses Konon of taking Theoric money for his son who was abroad. The court fines him one talent. Reason: The speaker implies he was guilty of the charge.
Isaios	
2.30–31	Private arbitrator decides that the speaker should give what Menekles claims as a free gift. Reason: Decision given to restore good relations between litigants.
3.5–6	Speaker brings private suit for false testimony against Nikodemos and wins case. Reason: The court found his testimony false.
5.7–9	Dikaiogenes claims estate; the court awards it to him. Reason: The speaker claims that Melas the Egyptian and his allies gave false testimony.
5.12	Menexenos, the son of Kephisophon, brings a private action for false testimony against Lykon for testifying that Lykon was the sole heir. Reason: The testimony was false. Proxenos brings a suit for false testimony and wins. Reason: Proxenos proves that the will was forged.
5.17, 19	Speaker indicts Leochares for perjury and wins. Reason: Judges decide Leochares has committed perjury.

(*cont.*)

5.22–23	Speaker brings a private suit for ejectment against Mikion and loses. Reason: Dikaiogenes confirms Mikion's title.
7.7	Apollodoros brings action and recovers estate. Charge and reason not given.
7.7, 10	Apollodoros brings suit against Eupolis for embezzling funds as a guardian and wins. Reason not given.
11.9–10, 17–19, 26	Theopompos, the daughter of Euboulides, and Hagnias' mother lay claim to the estate of Hagnias. The court awards the estate to Theopompos. Reason: Theopompos proves that the statement made by the supporters of Euboulides' daughter in the *antigraphē* is false and that Hagnias' mother is not entitled to the estate because she is not within the legitimate degree of kinship.
12.11–12	Euphiletos brings an action against the demarch and the members of his deme and wins case before the arbitrator. Reason: The arbitrator determines that Euphiletos' opponents are lying.
Isokrates	
16.9	Unknown accusers have Alkibiades banished from Greece. It is not clear whether this is the verdict of a court or a decree of the Assembly.
17.42	Unknown accuser brings a *phasis* against a ship. The speaker has made a loan on the security of the ship and has to give personal security. Outcome not stated.
18.6	Patrokles brings a *phasis* against the speaker for money belonging to the state. The Council hears the case and decides the money belongs to the state. This takes place in 403 under the Ten.
18.22	Unknown accuser indicts Philon of Koile for misconduct on an embassy. Philon claims the prosecution violates the Amnesty and presumably brings a *paragraphē*. The court dismisses the case. Reason: The charges violate the Amnesty.
18.52–53	The brother-in-law of Kallimachos accuses Kratinos of killing a slave. Fourteen witnesses testify for the accuser. Kratinos brings the slave, who is still alive into court. Seven hundred judges vote to acquit Kratinos, not one to convict. Reason: Defendant refutes charge.
Lykourgos	
Against Leokrates 53–54	Unknown accuser brings charge against Autolykos for sending his wife and children abroad after Chaironeia. Punishment not specified. Reason: Autolykos sent people abroad even if they could not fight.

(*cont.*)

Against Leokrates 93	Kallistratos sentenced to death. Later he returns to Athens and supplicates at the altar of the Twelve Gods for a trial. He is condemned and executed. Charges and reason not given.
Against Leokrates 112–115	Unknown accuser brings charge against Phrynichos after his death. The court condemns him, and his bones are cast outside Attica. They also put his defenders Alexikles and Aristarchos to death. The information is suspect, but Lykourgos produces a decree.
Against Leokrates 117	Unknown accuser brings charge against Hipparchos in the Assembly. Hipparchos is condemned to death *in absentia*. Reason: He committed treason.
Lysias	
6.11	Andokides indicts Archippos on a charge of impiety (private?) for desecrating the Herm at his house. Archippos denies charges but settles out of court.
10.1, 22	Lysitheos prosecutes Theomnestos for speaking before Assembly when he has lost the right to do so by throwing away his shield. Theomnestos is acquitted but the speaker implies he was guilty. Reason not given.
10.32	Speaker claims to have accused the Thirty before the Areiopagos. Verdict not known (possibly invented).
12.67	Theramenes accuses Antiphon and Archiptolemos, who are put to death. Reason not given.
13.12	Kleophon is tried (probably for *astrateia*) by political opponents and put to death. The litigant implies the verdict was unjust.
13.36–37	Trials under the Thirty were conducted without a secret ballot and led to unjust convictions.
13.56–57	Menestratos is executed for causing the death of citizens by denouncing them to the Thirty. Litigant implies Menestratos was guilty of the charge.
13.65	Phainippides arrested as a clothes-stealer and put to death. No reason given for verdict, but litigant implies he was guilty.
17.3	Father of the litigant brings a suit for debt against Erasistratos and wins judgment. The narrative implies the debt existed.
17.6	Litigant brings suit against those who occupy his property—defendants use *paragraphē* to have suit dismissed (implies that the defendants cited the terms of the law about *paragraphē*).

(*cont.*)

18.13–15	Litigant complains because the courts vote contradictory verdicts about the confiscation of property. Reason not given.
27.4	Litigant criticises the courts for inconsistency by convicting one man and acquitting another on the same charge when the evidence of witnesses was exactly the same in both cases. No reason for the verdict.
30.11–14	Kleophon was brought into court by his enemies. Nikomachos provided them with a forged law allowing members of the Council to join the court. Litigant implies this led to an unjust verdict.

Bibliography

Aviles, D. (2011) '"Arguing Against the Law": Non-Literal Interpretation in Attic Forensic Oratory', *Dike* 14, 19–42.

Brunschwig, J. (1996) 'Rule and Exception: On the Aristotelian Theory of Equity', in Frede, M., and Striker, G., eds. *Rationality in Greek thought*, Oxford, 115–155.

Canevaro, M. (2013) *The Documents in the Attic Orators: Laws and Decrees in the Public Speeches of the Demosthenic Corpus*, Oxford.

Canevaro, M. and Harris, E.M. (2012) 'The Documents in Andocides' *On the Mysteries*', *CQ* 62, 98–129.

Carey, C. (1996) '*Nomos* in Attic Rhetoric and Oratory', *JHS* 116, 33–46.

Carey, C. (2004) 'Offence and Procedure in Athenian Law', in Harris, E.M. and Rubinstein, L., eds (2004), 111–136.

Christ, M.R. (1998) *The Litigious Athenian*, Baltimore.

Cohen, D. (1995) *Law, Violence, and Community in Classical Athens*, Cambridge.

Engels, J. (2008) *Lykurg: Rede gegen Leokrates*, Darmstadt.

Faraguna, M. (2006) 'Alcibiade, Cratero e gli archivi giudiziari ad Atene', in Faraguna, M. and Vedaldi Iasbez, V., eds (2006) Δύνασθαι διδάσκειν: *Studi in onore di Filippo Cassola*, Trieste, 197–207.

Faraguna, M. (2008) 'Oralità e scrittura nella prassi giudizaria tra V e IV sec. a. C.', in Harris, E.M. and Thür, G., eds (2008) *Symposion 2007: Vorträge zur griechischen und hellenistischen Rechtsgeschichte* (Durham, 2–6 September 2007), Vienna, 63–82.

Finley, M.I. (1985) *Ancient History: Evidence and Models*, London.

Gagarin, M. (2008) *Writing Greek Law*, Cambridge.

Gagarin, M. (2012) 'Law, Politics, and the Question of Relevance in the Case On the Crown', *CA* 31, 293–314.

Gwatkin, W.E. (1957) 'The Legal Arguments in Aischines' *Against Ctesiphon* and Demosthenes' *On The Crown*', *Hesperia* 26, 129–141.

Hall, E. (2006) *The Theatrical Cast of Athens: Interactions Between Ancient Greek Drama and Society*, Oxford.

Harris, E.M. (1994a) 'Law and Oratory', in Worthington, I., ed. (1994), 130–150.

Harris, E.M. (1994b) '"In the Act" or "Red-Handed"'? *Apagoge* to the Eleven and *furtum manifestum*, in Thür, G., ed. (1994) *Symposion 1993: Vorträge zur griechischen und hellenistischen Rechtsgeschichte* (Graz-Andritz, 12–16 September 1993), Cologne, 129–146.

Harris, E.M. (2006) *Democracy and the Rule of Law in Classical Athens: Essays on Law, Society, and Politics*, Cambridge.

Harris, E.M. (2008) *Demosthenes, Speeches 20–22*, Austin. TX.

Harris, E.M. (2009/10a) 'What Are the Laws of Athens About? Substance and Procedure in Athenian Statutes', *Dike* 12/13, 5–67.

Harris, E.M. (2009/10b) Review of Lanni (2006) *Dike* 12/13, 323–331.

Harris, E.M. (2013a) *The Rule of Law in Action in Democratic Athens*, Oxford.

Harris, E.M. (2013b) 'The Plaint in Athenian Law and Legal Procedure', in Faraguna, M. (ed.) (2013) *Archives and Archival Documents in Ancient Societies*, Trieste, 143–162.

Harris, E.M. (2017a) 'How to "Act" in an Athenian Court: Emotions and Forensic Performance', in Papaioannou, S., Serafim, A., and da Vela, B., eds (2017) *The Theatre of Justice: Aspects of Performance in Greco-Roman Oratory and Rhetoric*, Leiden, 223–242.

Harris, E.M. (2017b) *Applying the Law about the Award of Crowns to Magistrates (Aeschin. 3.9–31; Dem. 18.113–117): Epigraphic Evidence for the Legal Arguments at the Trial of Ctesiphon*, ZPE 202, 105–117.

Harvey, D. (1990) 'The Sycophant and Sycophancy: Vexatious Redefinition?', in Cartledge, P., Millett, P., and Todd, S.C., eds (1990) *Nomos: Essays in Athenian Law, Politics and Society*, Cambridge, 103–121.

Heftner, H. (2012) 'Rechts und Verfassungsinstrumente als Mittel der Konfliktbewältigung in der athenischen Demokratie: Stasisgesetze, Ostrakismus und *graphe paranomon*', *Dike* 15, 1–32.

Ismard, P. (2012) 'Le périmètre de la légalité dans l'Athènes classique: réponse à Robert Wallace', in Legras, B. and Thür, G., eds (2012) *Symposion 2011: Vorträge zur griechischen und hellenistischen Rechtsgeschichte* (Paris, 7–10 September 2011), Vienna, 127–134.

Kästle, D. (2012) 'Νόμος μεγίστη βοήθεια: zur Gesetzesargumentation in der attischen Gerichtsrede', *Zeitschrift der Savigny-Stiftung für Rechtsgeschichte* 129, 161–205.

Kremmydas, C. (2013) 'The Discourse of Deception and Characterization in Attic Oratory', *GRBS* 53, 51–89.

Lanni, A. (2004) 'Arguing from Precedent: Modern Perspectives on Athenian Practice', in Harris, E.M. and Rubinstein, L., eds (2004) *The Law and the Courts in Ancient Greece*, London, 159–171.

Lanni, A. (2006) *Law and Justice in the Courts of Classical Athens*, Cambridge.

Lanni, A. (2009) 'Social Norms in the Courts of Ancient Athens', *Journal of Legal Analysis* 1, 691–736.

MacDowell, D.M. (1990) *Demosthenes: Against Meidias*, Oxford.

MacDowell, D.M. (2009) *Demosthenes the Orator*, Oxford.

Maffi, A. (1989) 'Écriture et pratique juridique dans la Grèce classique', in Detienne, M., ed., *Les savoirs de l'écriture en Grèce ancienne*, Lille, 188–210.

Meinecke, J. (1971) 'Gesetzesinterpretation und Gesetzesanwendung im Attischen Zivilprozess', *Revue Internationale des Droits de l'Antiquité* 18, 275–360.

Meyer-Laurin, H. (1965) *Gesetz und Billigkeit im attischen Prozess*, Weimar.

North, D.C. (1990) *Institutions, Institutional Change and Economic Performance*, Cambridge.

Novotný, M. (2015) Review of Harris (2015), *Eirene* 51, 340–347.

Osborne, R. (1985) 'Law in Action in Classical Athens', *JHS* 105, 40–58. (Reprinted in Osborne (2010) 171–204.)

Osborne, R. (1990) 'Vexatious Litigation in Classical Athens: Sykophancy and the Sykophant', in Cartledge, P., Millett, P. and Todd, S.C., eds (1990) *Nomos: Essays in Athenian Law, Politics and Society*, Cambridge, 83–102.

Osborne, R. (2000) 'Religion, Imperial Politics and the Offering of Freedom to Slaves', in Hunter, V. and Edmondson, J., eds (2000) *Law and Social Status in Classical Athens*, Oxford, 75–92.

Partington, M. (2014) *Introduction to the English Legal System, 2014–2015*, Oxford.

Pébarthe, C. (2006) *Cité, démocratie et écriture: histoire de l'alphabétisation d'Athènes à l'époque classique*, Paris.

Phillips, D.D. (2008) *Avengers of Blood: Homicide in Athenian Law and Custom from Draco to Demosthenes*, Stuttgart.

Rhodes, P.J. (2004) 'Keeping to the Point', in: Harris, E.M. and Rubinstein, L., eds (2004) *The Law and the Courts in Ancient Greece*, London, 137–158.

Rubinstein, L. (2000) *Litigation and Cooperation: Supporting Speakers in the Courts of Classical Athens*, Stuttgart.

Rubinstein, L. (2005) 'Main Litigants and Witnesses in the Athenian Courts', in Gagarin, M. and Wallace, R., eds (2005) *Symposion 2001: Vorträge zur griechischen und hellenistischen Rechtsgeschichte* (Evanston, Ill., 5–8 September 2001), Vienna, 99–120.

Rubinstein, L. (2007) 'Arguments from Precedent in Attic Oratory', in Carawan E., ed. (2007) *The Attic Orators*, Oxford, 359–371.

Rubinstein, L. (2008) 'Response to James P. Sickinger', in Harris, E.M. and Thür, G., eds (2008) *Symposion 2007: Vorträge zur griechischen und hellenistischen Rechtsgeschichte* (Durham, 2–6 September 2007), Vienna, 113–124.

Sickinger, J. (2004) 'The Laws of Athens: Publication, Preservation, Consultation', in Harris, E.M. and Rubinstein, L., eds (2004), 93–111.

Sickinger, J. (2008) 'Indeterminacy in Greek Law: Statutory Gaps and Conflicts', in Harris, E.M. and Thür, G., eds (2008) *Symposion 2007: Vorträge zur griechischen und hellenistischen Rechtsgeschichte* (Durham, 2–6 September 2007), Vienna, 99–112.

Todd, S.C. (1990) 'The Purpose of Evidence in Athenian Courts', in Cartledge, P., Millett, P. and Todd, S.C., eds (1990), *Nomos: Essays in Athenian Law, Politics and Society*, Cambridge, 19–39.

Todd, S.C. (1993) *The Shape of Athenian Law*, Oxford.

Thür, G. (2007) 'Das Prinzip der Fairness im attischen Prozess: Gedanken zu *echinos* und *enklema*', in Cantarella, E., ed. (2007), *Symposion 2005: Vorträge zur griechischen und hellenistischen Rechtsgeschichte* (Salerno, 14–18 September 2005), Vienna, 131–158.

Wallace, R.W. (2012) 'When the Athenians Did Not Enforce Their Laws', in Legras, B. and Thür, G., eds (2012) *Symposion 2011: Vorträge zur griechischen und hellenistischen Rechtsgeschichte* (Paris, 7–10 September 2011) Vienna, 115–125.

Weber, M. (1972) *Wirtschaft und Gesellschaft*, 5th ed., ed. J. Winckelmann, Tübingen.

Whitehead, D. (2000) *Hypereides: The Forensic Speeches*, Oxford.

Wohl, V. (2010) *Law's Cosmos: Juridical Discourse in Athenian Forensic Oratory*, Cambridge.

CHAPTER 4

Bridging the Divide between Public and Private: *dikē exoulēs* and Other Hybrids

Chris Carey

The Athenian legal system was built on a binary divide between public and private actions. This divide was of fundamental importance in terms of the right to prosecute, the nature of the judicial procedure, the checks on frivolous litigation and finally on the penology. None of this is new. But the system was more flexible than this simple bifurcation would suggest and the boundaries between public and private were permeable.[1] As will become clear, in framing the laws the Athenians were aware that in some areas at least the interests of the *polis* were best served by raising the stakes for one or other parties to a dispute. I am interested in this chapter in the way the Athenians create hybrids which straddle the procedural and penological divide between public and private action which is at the base of the Athenian administration of justice.

It is a much rehearsed fact that the Athenian system placed a heavy reliance on individual initiative. This fits into the larger endeavour of Athenian democracy to avoid as far as possible the creation of a large central bureaucracy with the financial implications of large fixed overheads and the disadvantages of concentrating power and expertise within a narrow circle.[2] Edward Harris has recently adjusted this picture by rightly drawing attention to the areas where public officials were empowered and often required to investigate and punish.[3] But the fact remains that in the absence of a unitary agency for law enforcement and prosecution for the vast majority of breaches of the law the emphasis was on the individual. This applied not only to the lodging of the prosecution, the investigation and the assembly of witnesses and the presentation of the case in court but also to the execution of judgment. In public cases it was for the state to execute judgment (though even here it could deploy the volunteer to serve this purpose, as in the case of *apographē*[4]). But in private cases it was for the successful plaintiff to implement the court decision. The system

1 Cf. Hansen 1982: 113–120.

2 On the latter see Ober 2008.

3 Harris 2007b.

4 For *apographē* see especially Osborne 1985.

 | DOI:10.1163/9789004377899_006

relied on self-help, that is, individual initiative to redress a wrong or implement a right without recourse to a court or other authority. This is different from the situation in English common law, which leaves little space for self-help[5] by the litigant (in contrast to the array of remedies available through application to the courts)[6] and where there is ready recourse (through a court order) to agents of the court who are authorised to enforce payment or restitution. What interests me here is not the fact of reliance on self-help by the Athenian system but the way self-help operated.

Procedurally it was straightforward for a successful litigant to implement the court's judgment, in that in private cases it was always a matter of money, movables or land. So all that was needed was to obtain entry, access or possession.[7] The individual executing judgment merely turns up and demands possession, payment or access. We can see this in the condensed narrative of Dem. 30.3:

> τοσοῦτον κατεφρονήθην, ὥστ' οὐχὶ μόνον λόγου τυχεῖν οὐκ ἠξιώθην, ἀλλὰ καὶ ἐκ τῆς γῆς, ἣν Ἄφοβος ἐκέκτηθ' ὅτ' ὠφλίσκανέ μοι τὴν δίκην, ὑβριστικῶς ὑπ' αὐτοῦ πάνυ ἐξεβλήθην.
>
> I was viewed with such contempt that not only was I not dignified with an explanation but on top of that I was abusively thrown out of the property which Aphobos owned when he lost his case to me.

The backstory is that Demosthenes has sued his guardian Aphobos for mishandling his estate; he has secured judgment against him and has sought to obtain possession of a farm in part-settlement. However, an associate of Aphobos, Onetor, has asserted that he is the owner of the land and has prevented Demosthenes from taking possession. Evidently therefore the suit could be brought against anyone who contested possession, not just the losing party, a point noted by the lexicographers.[8] It arose from the successful suit but was not confined to the original litigants. However, Demosthenes' narrative also indicates the problems which can arise in a system based on self-help by a private individual. The nature of the self-help was severely circumscribed. It is clear from

---

5 Principally the right of recaption, for which see Macleod and Devenney 2007: 808–809, Gilroy 2014: 319–328, Bridge 2015: 121–122.

6 See www.gov.uk/make-court-claim-for-money/enforce-a-judgment (accessed 26/11/2016).

7 Though the terminology points firmly to property in land as the original focus of the action, there is no reason to doubt Harpocration's statement that it covered other forms of property (καὶ περὶ ἀνδραπόδου δὲ καὶ παντὸς οὗ φησί τις αὐτῷ μετεῖναι).

8 Cf. Harpocration s.v. ἐξούλης: ἐδικάζετο δὲ ἐξούλης καὶ ὁ χρήστης κατέχειν ἐπιχειρῶν κτῆμα τοῦ χρεωστοῦντος καὶ κωλυόμενος ὑπό τινος. 'The case for ejectment was also brought by a creditor

the Demosthenic passage and other instances that the person asserting ownership was not entitled to use force. If he was barred from taking possession, he had to resort to law, specifically the *dikē exoulēs*, the action for ejectment.

Equally and unsurprisingly it seems that the person opposing the assertion of ownership was not legally entitled to use force to prevent the attempted occupation. In Dem. 30 the term used of the act of opposition is *exagein*, 'lead out'. The same verb is used in a papyrus hypothesis of a fragment of Lysias[9] relating to a *dikē exoulēs* and in other passages relating to contested ownership or possession. Its recurrent presence suggests that it is a formalised gesture and the brevity of the mentions in our sources suggests that it was immediately recognisable to a jury.[10] In the case of land the occupant opposes the attempted possession by escorting the claimant from the premises. The term *exagein* also occurs in Dem. 44.32 in a context in which no suggestion is made of the availability of the *dikē exoulēs*.[11] It looks as though it is the normal term for opposition to an attempt to take possession. We are given very little detail but one

---

who is seeking to gain possession of the property of the debtor and is prevented by someone.' Though he is speaking about a specific category, there is no obvious reason to doubt that the broad κωλυόμενος ὑπό τινος would apply across the board.

Cf. Pollux 8.59: ὅταν τις … τὸν νικήσαντα ἃ ἐνίκησεν, ἀλλ' ἢ ἔχοντα ἐκβάλλῃ ἢ σχεῖν κωλύσῃ, ἢ αὐτὸς ὁ ὀφλὼν ἢ ἄλλος ὑπὲρ αὐτοῦ. 'When someone does not allow … the winner [in a suit] [to benefit from] what he won but ejects him when in possession or prevents him from taking possession, whether it is the loser himself or someone on his behalf'.

9 Lys. fr. 175a

πρὸς Ἱπ[πό]μ̣αχ[ον
Ἱπ]π̣όμαχος καταδικα[σάμ]ε̣νος . [c. 12 lit.
..] χωρίον ἐξήγαγ[εν αὐ]τὸν ἐ̣ξ [c. 12 lit.
...] . εσει τῶν πατρῴ[⟨ι⟩ων .] . αιω . [c. 12 lit.
δικά]ζεται·
Hippomachos having won the case …
the land, removed him …
… his inherited property …
is suing

10 Harpocration's entry suggests that resistance need not be formalised or even active. Failure to comply with a judgment suffices: δικάζονται δὲ ἐξούλης κἀπὶ τοῖς ἐπιτιμίοις οἱ μὴ ἀπολαμβάνοντες ἐν τῇ προσηκούσῃ προθεσμίᾳ, ὑπερημέρων γιγνομένων τῶν καταδικασθέντων. 'Actions for ejectment are brought also against people liable to a penalty by those who do not receive payment within the appropriate timescale, when the losers in the suit have not met the deadline'. The point is also made by Dem. 21.44.

11 ἐπειδὴ γὰρ ἐτελεύτησεν ὁ Λεωκράτης καὶ ἡ ταφὴ ἐγένετο αὐτῷ, πορευομένων ἡμῶν εἰς τὰ κτήματα διὰ τὸ ἄπαιδά τε τὸν ἄνδρα καὶ ἄγαμον τετελευτηκέναι, ἐξήγαγε Λεώστρατος οὑτοσὶ φάσκων αὑτοῦ εἶναι. 'When Leokrates died and his burial took place, we proceeded to the property, because he had died childless and unmarried, and Leostratos here removed us, alleging that it was his'.

would suppose that both sides would have witnesses present to protect them against subsequent misrepresentation of their conduct during the encounter when the case came to court.[12] Demosthenes' language in speech 30 suggests that he was subjected to abuse by Onetor. And no doubt the encounter did have the potential to become bruising: in the context of a heated dispute 'leading out' probably did sometimes take a robust form. But despite his outrage his brief references to the act use variants of *exagein*, which suggests that Onetor (rightly or wrongly) simply used standard procedure and that for Demosthenes the *hybris* resides simply in the refusal to accept his claim. He is using *hybris* in its broad sense of behaviour which shows contempt, not of any act of physical abuse, the normal basis in the courts for formal charges of *hybris*.[13]

It is here that the *dikē exoulēs* becomes interesting. If the court finds for the plaintiff—that is, if the court agrees that the plaintiff has been improperly denied access to property adjudicated to him by a court verdict—the person barring access is liable to pay the plaintiff a sum assessed by the court; but he is also liable to pay an equal amount to the state. Thus Harpocration:

> οἱ δὲ ἁλόντες ἐξούλης καὶ τῷ ἑλόντι ἐδίδοσαν ἃ ἀφῃροῦντο αὐτόν, καὶ τῷ δημοσίῳ κατετίθεσαν τὰ τιμηθέντα.
>
> People convicted of ejectment would pay the successful plaintiff the sum they had deprived him of and would pay to the state the sum assessed.[14]

The *dikē exoulēs* thus straddles the line between public and private prosecution. Procedurally this action operates within the private sphere. It is always called *dikē* and it is only open to the victim of the wrong himself. But in terms of penology it operates within the public sphere, that is, in the sphere of the

12 Cf. Isa. 3.19.

13 The definition of *hybris* remains both complicated and contentious. For a brief statement of my own views see Carey 2004: 117–118.

14 Cf. Dem. 21.44 τί γὰρ δή ποτ', ἄν τις ὀφλὼν δίκην μὴ ἐκτίνῃ, οὐκέτ' ἐποίησ' ὁ νόμος τὴν ἐξούλην ἰδίαν, ἀλλὰ προστιμᾶν ἐπέταξε τῷ δημοσίῳ; 'For how is it that if a man who has lost his case fails to pay, the law thereupon is not content with a private suit for ejectment, but directs the imposition of a further fine to the treasury?' (Trans. Murray 1939). The mentions in Harpocration and Demosthenes could be taken to indicate a separate (and potentially different) assessment for the sum due to the state. The issue is clarified by the scholion to Homer *Il.* 21 preserved at *P. Oxy* 221 col. XIV and echoed in the scholia in cod. Genev. 44 (= fr. 36a–b Leão and Rhodes) which indicate that the same sum is awarded to the successful litigant and to the state: ὁπόσου ἂν ἄξιος ᾖ, εἰς δημόσιον ὀφείλειν καὶ τῷ ἰδιώτῃ, ἑκατέρῳ ἴσον.

graphē.[15] Normally in private cases any sum awarded goes to the other party; only in public cases does a financial penalty go to the *polis*. As always with Athenian law, we have to tease jurisprudence from structures and process, since there is no official narrative of legal principles. Only once are we told why the penalty is set like this. Demosthenes claims at one point in his speech against Meidias that the law lays down robust penalties in the *dikē exoulēs* because it contains an element of violence.[16] He is arguing a matter of legal principle there: that the law deals more seriously with any infraction which involves violence. But we need to approach his argument with caution. This is part of Demosthenes' attempt to emphasise the seriousness of Meidias' assault on him. As a general description of the acts which prompt the *dikē exoulēs* it is inaccurate. Like any other face to face legal confrontation, the attempt to physically assert ownership and the rejection of the claim to ownership have the potential to turn ugly. But there is no good reason to believe that the process of formal refusal of claim is inherently or inevitably violent. This is simply an example of Demosthenes' inventive approach to jurisprudence.[17] We are therefore compelled to extrapolate purpose from effect; this is always risky, because laws can have unintended consequences. But it is all we have to go on. The effect of conviction is to make the individual opposing possession a debtor to the state. Like all debtors to the state he is forbidden to exercise his political rights until the debt is repaid; and if he does not pay by the ninth prytany, his debt is doubled.[18] The effect is to raise the stakes for the party resisting without raising them for the party attempting to take possession. The person implementing the court ruling is subject only to the burdens and responsibilities of a private action. The trial follows the rules for the size of juries, the duration of the speeches and procedure for documents.[19] The judicial panel will have 201 or 401 members, not the minimum of 501 for public actions. The amount of time allocated for the trial was less and therefore the demands of presentation reduced. And the waterclock was stopped for the reading of documents, so that depositions and other evidence did not count against the speech time. So (by the standards of the Athenian legal system) it is relatively undemanding. The

15 Dem. 21.44: οὐκέτ' ἐποίησ' ὁ νόμος τὴν ἐξούλην ἰδίαν ('the law no longer treats the ejectment as private').

16 Dem. 21.45: ὅτι πάνθ' ὅσα τις βιαζόμενος πράττει κοίν' ἀδικήματα καὶ κατὰ τῶν ἔξω τοῦ πράγματος ὄντων ἡγεῖθ' ὁ νομοθέτης. 'The answer is that the legislator regarded every deed of violence as a public offence, committed against those also who are not directly concerned'. (Trans. Murray 1939).

17 See on this Giannadaki in this volume pp. 199–203.

18 E.g. Andok. 1.73, Dem. 37.22, [Dem.] 59.7.

19 *Ath. Pol.* 53.3, 67.2–3.

process may not have been risk-free, since there may have been (though we cannot be sure) a penalty for failure.[20] If so, this will have been one-sixth of the sum claimed, not the 1,000 *drachmai* fine and partial *atimia* for conspicuous failure in a public action. In contrast, the defendant, his opponent, is subject to the liabilities arising from conviction in a public action. The person attempting to execute judgment is placed at a significant advantage. The effect is both enabling (to the successful litigant) and punitive (for the person attempting to obstruct). As well as confirming the sum due to the winner in the original trial, it also escalates the risk for the person obstructing in that his civic status is placed in peril, should he fail to pay the sum of money due to the state. This element of additional pressure (and its astuteness—λελογισμένως πάνυ) is noted by the Suda in an otherwise rather garbled entry under ἐξούλης:

> εἰ γὰρ τῷ ἰδιώτῃ διπλάσιον ἐπράττετο, παραιτήσεως ἂν ἐτύγχανε δεόμενος ὁ ἁλοὺς καὶ ἁπλοῦν ἂν ἐξέτινε. νυνὶ δὲ ἀπαραίτητόν ἐστι τὸ δημόσιον.
>
> For if a double penalty were exacted by the individual [i.e. if the successful plaintiff in a *dikē exoulēs* simply received double damages], the person convicted would have begged him off and paid single/simple compensation. As it stands, the exchequer is inexorable.

It is important to bear in mind that the person attempting to take possession has already obtained the approval of an Athenian jury, which represents the sovereign *dēmos*. The two parties do not therefore enter the contest as equals. There is a tacit presumption in favour of the successful litigant attempting to take possession. However, the law does not automatically penalise obstruction. *Exagein* is a neutral act. There is always the possibility that the property seized may exceed what is adjudicated or that the property of third parties (for instance the dowry of a wife, which was never simply absorbed into her husband's estate)[21] will be erroneously or mischievously seized. So obstruction is not itself an offence. Here as elsewhere the system both allows and limits self-help. But the key point for my purposes is the increased risk for the opponent. The court has already found for the plaintiff and the law arms him by adjust-

20 For cases known to involve the *epōbelia* as penalty for prosecutors see Harrison 1971: 183–184. The list is not exclusive and our evidence is patchy; we are not told anywhere if the *dikē exoulēs* was included, though since Athenian law tended to hedge self-help procedures around with sanctions and protections against abuse, it would be surprising if *dikē exoulēs* were risk free.

21 See Harrison 1968: 54, 55–60.

ing the balance of risk. We might speak of contempt of court on the part of the opponent.[22] The principle at work in the *dikē exoulēs* is more elusive. The presence of a fine to the state indicates that the *polis* has an interest in the process beyond merely acting as adjudicator in the resolution of individual disputes. Whether the stimulus is the need to preserve the authority of the courts or the need to make rulings binding and so avoid endless business on the same issues (i.e. to uphold the principle of *res iudicata*),[23] or indeed both, the Athenian system focuses not on the nature of the offence but on the process of ensuring compliance. There is another, and equally important, aspect to the leverage applied by the *polis*: deterrence. Clearly it does not prevent any and all obstruction, since we have attested cases of the *dikē exoulēs*. But it is not meant to. The ratcheting up of the penalty serves to deter cavalier obstruction. In this respect it acts like the penalties for frivolous prosecution. And like the *epōbelia* it operates in direct proportion to the sum at issue (though the multiplier differs). The fine is enough to make someone hesitate before obstructing but is both limited and predictable, since like a number of other aspects of the administration of justice it is linked to the sum at issue. And the greater the greed, the greater the penalty.

It is worth flagging here the efficiency of the process. The Oxford English Dictionary defines efficiency as the quality of 'achieving maximum productivity with minimum wasted effort or expense'. The *dikē exoulēs* still requires litigation, a judicial panel and a further hearing; this is not minimalist. But the existence of the action does limit the scope for resistance. It adjusts penology to apply leverage in order to enforce compliance with court rulings. The state puts its weight behind the party which has convinced the court; but it is not involved directly in implementation, any more than in any other private process. This efficiency has another dimension, drafting: little is needed in the way of wording to add another dimension to the punishment which significantly adjusts the odds.

Although I have focused here on formal adjudication, we should also note that *dikē exoulēs* would probably also be available in cases where a borrower agreed in a contract to waive any legal right to contest liability for a debt. This would agree with the evidence of the contract in [Dem.] 35.13:

---

22 'Contempt of court is where a person who is party to a proceeding in a court of record fails to comply with an order made against him or an undertaking given by him, or where a person, whether party to a proceeding or not, does any act which may tend to hinder the course of justice or show disrespect to the court's authority' (Rapalje and Laurence 1888: i, 276).

23 For the existence of this principle in Athenian law see briefly Harris 2006b: 406.

καὶ ἐάν τι ἐλλείπῃ τοῦ ἀργυρίου, ὃ δεῖ γενέσθαι τοῖς δανείσασι κατὰ τὴν συγγραφήν, παρὰ Ἀρτέμωνος καὶ Ἀπολλοδώρου ἔστω ἡ πρᾶξις τοῖς δανείσασι καὶ ἐκ τῶν τούτων ἁπάντων, καὶ ἐγγείων καὶ ναυτικῶν, πανταχοῦ ὅπου ἂν ὦσι, καθάπερ δίκην ὠφληκότων καὶ ὑπερημέρων ὄντων, καὶ ἑνὶ ἑκατέρῳ τῶν δανεισάντων καὶ ἀμφοτέροις.

If they do not pay within the agreed period, the lenders are to have the right to borrow on the goods or sell them at the price obtaining. If there is any shortfall in the sum due to the lenders under the contract, the lenders both individually and collectively are to have the right to recover it from Artemon and Apollodoros, and from all their possessions everywhere, on land and sea, wherever they may be, as if they had lost a suit at law and were in default on payment.

Liability has been accepted formally. And Athenian contract law stated tersely that agreements made voluntarily were binding.[24] The penalty is agreed and there is no need to for legal action before execution. However, this would not in principle be a separate category of plaintiff or plaint from that discussed above.

There was some debate among ancient scholars about the range of *dikē exoulēs*. Some saw it as simply a means of gaining (access to) any property to which one is entitled. Some saw it as available only where a court had given judgment.[25] Neither is correct. But the confusion probably arises in part because of misunderstanding of cases like Dem. 30 which involve complicated property trails. There is no prior legal action between Demosthenes and Onetor and so it looks as if the *dikē exoulēs* is being brought simply about a claim on a piece of land; but in fact it is the prior dispute with Aphobos which allows for the use of the *dikē exoulēs*. What is clear is that the procedure is limited to specified categories of disputant, who share either a legally established or presumed status of owner. One recurrent category of user is the successful litigant (our starting point) seeking to execute the judgment of a court. This is the case with Demosthenes' suit against Onetor. It is also the case with at least two of the cases in the Lysiac corpus.[26] Another category recognised by modern schol-

24 Dem. 47.77, 56.2, Hyp. *Athen.* 13. This principle could be reinforced by a clause affirming the absolute authority of the contract: [Dem.] 35.13, 39; 56.27, 41.

25 The views appear at the end of Harpocration's compendiary entry: ὅτι δὲ ἐπὶ παντὸς τοῦ ἐκ τῶν ἰδίων ἐκβαλλομένου τάττεται τοὔνομα, καὶ οὐχ ὡς οἴεται Καικίλιος μόνων τῶν ἐκ καταδίκης ὀφειλόντων, καὶ Φρύνιχος ἐν Ποαστρίαις δῆλον ποιεῖ. 'That the term is applied to everyone who is ejected from his private property and not, as Kaikilios supposes, only against those who owe as the result of a verdict against them, Archippos too makes clear in his *Poastriai*.'

26 Lys. fr. 175a cited n. 9 above, also perhaps fr. 297:

ars is the legitimate offspring of a dead man. In some respects, this is effectively a subset of the same category. Isa. 3.62 is clear on this point:

> μηδεὶς οὖν ὑμῶν ἡγείσθω, εἰ ἐνόμιζε γνησίαν εἶναι τὴν ἑαυτοῦ γυναῖκα Ξενοκλῆς, λαχεῖν ἂν ὑπὲρ αὐτῆς τὴν λῆξιν τοῦ κλήρου τοῦ πατρῴου, ἀλλ᾽ ἐβάδιζεν ἂν ἡ γνησία εἰς τὰ ἑαυτῆς πατρῷα καί, εἴ τις αὐτὴν ἀφῃρεῖτο ἢ ἐβιάζετο, ἐξῆγεν ἂν ἐκ τῶν πατρῴων καὶ οὐκ ἂν ἰδίας μόνον δίκας ἔφευγεν ὁ βιαζόμενος, ἀλλὰ καὶ δημοσίᾳ εἰσαγγελθεὶς πρὸς τὸν ἄρχοντα ἐκινδύνευεν ἂν περὶ τοῦ σώματος καὶ τῆς οὐσίας ἁπάσης τῆς ἑαυτοῦ.
>
> So none of you should think that, if Xenokles had thought his wife was legitimate, he would have put in a claim for her father's estate on her behalf. No, the legitimate daughter would have gone to her father's property, and if anyone tried to deprive her or oppose her by force, he would have been ejecting her from her father's property; and the man who opposed her by force would not only have found himself sued on a private charge but would have been the object of a public impeachment before the *archōn* and his life and all his property would have been at risk.

Unlike other claimants to an estate, who have to file a claim, the legitimate offspring of the dead man has the right simply to take possession.[27] His position is in practice the same as that of a claimant who has been awarded the property by a courtroom verdict. The existence of a legitimate heir is sufficient to bar all other claims on an inheritance. This in the fourth century becomes the

---

Ἑ[.]κέτου ἐπιτροπευ̣[θ]έντος ὑπὸ̣ [τοῦ πρεσβυτέρου?
ἀδ̣ελφοῦ καὶ ἐγκαλέ[σα]ντος μ .. [c. 13 lit.
. [. ἀ]πο̣θανόντος δοθ[...]ῃς ... [c. 15 lit.
κληρόνομοι δικασά̣[με]ν̣οι κ[λήρου τοῦ ἐν τῶι
δή]μω⟨ι⟩ καὶ ἑλόντες π̣αρέλαβο̣[ν

'After (?)Hiketes was under the guardianship of his (?older) brother and had sued him ... had died ... his heirs having sued successfully for the property in the deme and taken it over ...'.

We can be more confident about the (now) anonymous case in fr. 308 col ii 3 ff.:

ὑ̣βρισθεὶς ὑπὸ
...............] πεντεκαίδεκα ἔτη δια̣κ̣ρουσθεὶς
.... ἀ]λ̣λὰ μόλις μ̣ε[θ'] ὅρκων ἐπ . [......
.... κατ]αδιαιτήσ̣α̣ν[τ]ος̣ ἐκείνου [.] ..η̣ . [..
...............] π̣ρος .... [.] . [..]ἐξούλης διώκ[ει] ..

'Having been abusively treated by ... and thwarted for fifteen years but finally by means of oaths ..., when he found against him at arbitration ... he is suing for ejectment ...'

27 Isa. 3.59.

main function of the process of *diamartyria*: a witness testifies that an estate cannot be contested because there is a legitimate heir.[28] But with or without a decision in a *diamartyria* there is a legal presumption in his favour, subject only to his ability to demonstrate his lineage if queried. If the heir in these circumstances encounters resistance, he can use the *dikē exoulēs* against anyone who obstructs his exercise of his rights. Again the *dikē exoulēs* serves to allow execution of a legally recognised right.

A further category identified by Pollux (8.59) is the person who has leased a function (such as extraction of minerals) from the state and is prevented from fulfilling the function:

> ἡ δὲ τῆς ἐξούλης δίκη γίνεται, ὅταν τις τὸν ἐκ δημοσίου πριάμενον μὴ ἐᾷ καρποῦσθαι ἃ ἐπρίατο.
>
> The action for ejectment takes place, when someone prevents an individual who has bought a concession from the exchequer from exploiting it.

This may also be the point in a brief clause in Harpocration's entry:

> καὶ ἐπεργασίας δέ τις εἰ εἴργοιτο, δίδωσιν ὁ νόμος δικάζεσθαι πρὸς τὸν εἴργοντα ἐξούλης.
>
> And if anyone were barred from working a concession (?), the law allows him to sue for ejectment against the person obstructing him.

Pollux is supported here by Dem. 37.35, where the speaker (in a *paragraphē*) argues that the fast track *emmēnos* process under the *dikai metallikai* is not available for the opponent:

> οὗτος σαφῶς ὁ νόμος διείρηκεν ὧν εἶναι δίκας προσήκει μεταλλικάς. οὐκοῦν ὁ μὲν νόμος, ἐάν τις ἐξίλλῃ τινὰ τῆς ἐργασίας, ὑπόδικον ποιεῖ· ἐγὼ δ' οὐχ ὅπως αὐτὸς ἐξίλλω, ἀλλ' ὧν τοῦτον ἄλλος ἀπεστέρει, τούτων ἐγκρατῆ κατέστησα καὶ παρέδωκα, καὶ πρατὴρ τούτου δεηθέντος ἐγενόμην.
>
> This law states clearly the actions for which mining suits should be brought. Now if someone ejects another [verb *exillein*] from his workings, the law makes him subject to legal action. But so far from ejecting him, I

28 Cf. Griffith-Williams in this volume.

> gave him control over and restored to him property which someone else was trying to take from him, and I acted as vendor at his earnest entreaty.

Here the reason for allowing the *dikē exoulēs* could be the risk to the lessee, since if he fails to pay his instalments to the exchequer each prytany, he becomes a debtor to the state and his civic rights are put at risk. But equally (and more probably) it may be that the state perceives its own interest to be affected. The mines and any other activity leased to individuals by the *polis* are civic property and the *polis* needs to guarantee its income; and again perhaps to assert its authority. The joint interest (state and individual) is recognised in the hybrid nature of the procedure. But again the *polis* asserts its interest simply by giving the private plaintiff the added benefit of a public penalty if his commitment to the state is imperilled, as well as (at least at this point in the fourth century) use of the more speedy *dikē metallikē* as a mine lessee.

There is a fourth category recognised by Harpocration[29] and Pollux[30] and accepted by modern scholarship, the mortgagee. The sole direct evidence for this appears to be the incident narrated at Isa. 5.22:

> πλὴν γὰρ δυοῖν οἰκιδίοιν ἔξω τείχους καὶ ⟨ἀγροῦ⟩ ἐν Πεδίῳ ἑξήκοντα πλέθρων οὐδὲν κεκομίσμεθα, ἀλλ' οἱ παρὰ τούτου θέμενοι καὶ πριάμενοι· ἡμεῖς δὲ οὐκ ἐξάγομεν· δέδιμεν γὰρ μὴ ὄφλωμεν δίκας. Καὶ γὰρ Μικίωνα, κελεύοντος Δικαιογένους καὶ φάσκοντος ⟨οὐ⟩ βεβαιώσειν, ἐξάγοντες ἐκ τοῦ βαλανείου, ὤφλομεν τετταράκοντα μνᾶς διὰ Δικαιογένην, ὦ ἄνδρες.

> And we've recovered nothing except for two small buildings outside the walls and sixty plethra of land in the Plain but the men who mortgaged and bought it from him have possession. We are not trying to eject them, because we are afraid of losing suits. We tried to eject Mikion from the bath-house when Dikaiogenes urged us to and assured us that he would not guarantee his title, and we were fined forty minas, all on account of Dikaiogenes, gentlemen.
>
> Trans. EDWARDS, adapted

---

29 ἐδικάζετο δὲ ἐξούλης καὶ ὁ χρήστης κατέχειν ἐπιχειρῶν κτῆμα τοῦ χρεωστοῦντος καὶ κωλυόμενος ὑπό τινος. 'The case for ejectment was also brought by a creditor who is seeking to gain possession of the real property of the debtor and is prevented by someone.'

30 καὶ μὴν καὶ εἰ ὁ μὲν ὡς ἐωνημένος ἀμφισβητεῖ κτήματος, ὁ δὲ ὡς ὑποθήκην ἔχων, ἐξούλης ἡ δίκη. 'Furthermore, if one person claims a property as purchaser and the other as in possession as security, the suit is for ejectment.'

I find the narrative here opaque and consequently this is for me the most obscure of all the categories. The context is an inheritance case and the speaker alleges that after agreeing to give up two thirds of the estate the opponent Dikaiogenes is obstructing the speaker's attempts to take possession. I take οἱ παρὰ τούτου θέμενοι καὶ πριάμενοι as a single group of people and καὶ as clarificatory 'those who mortgaged and bought it from him'; so we have a reference not to outright sale but to *prasis epi lysei*,[31] a form of borrowing. Dikaiogenes has borrowed money on the security of a bath-house. On the basis of his promise that he would not act as warrantor for his creditors and confirm their claim on the property, the speaker and his associates escorted the competing claimants from the property and the latter sued for ejectment. Despite his promise Dikaiogenes acted as warrantor for the lenders. They sued our speaker by *dikē exoulēs* and Dikaiogenes' intervention was sufficient to allow the subsequent hearing in court to go against the speaker.[32] The privileging of the plaintiffs in a case like this probably rests on the nature of the transaction. The creditor in *prasis epi lysei* is in some sense the owner of the security until the debt is repaid, though unlike outright sale his ownership is conditional.[33] As with outright sale he can call upon the 'vendor' (the debtor in the case of *prasis epi lysei*) to act as warrantor of his claim to ownership both in dealings with other parties with a potential interest in the property and in any litigation; and he has a legal means available to compel him (in the *dikē bebaiōseōs*).[34] The existence of a ready means of demonstrating title cogently both to potential claimants and to the courts may be an important factor in the privileging of this category of litigant. As with some other con-

31 See e.g. Wyse 1904: 430–431, Harrison 1968: 314. This is confirmed by the wording in § 21, where the speaker indicates what Dikaiogenes should have done:
οὐδὲ γὰρ πρὶν ἡττηθῆναι τὴν δίκην εἶχεν ὧν ἡμεῖς δικαζόμεθα, ἀλλ' οἱ παρὰ τούτου πριάμενοι καὶ θέμενοι, οἷς ἔδει αὐτὸν ἀποδόντα τὴν τιμὴν ἡμῖν τὰ μέρη ἀποδοῦναι.
'Before he lost the case he was not even in possession of the property we are suing him for, but the men who bought it from him and held it on mortgage, whom he should have paid off and then given us our share'.
If this was outright sale, Dikaiogenes had no right simply to buy back the property from the purchasers and it is difficult to believe that any of the audience could take the suggestion seriously. But he could recover property held by creditors against a loan simply by paying off the capital and any outstanding interest.

32 My reading of this passage has benefited from an opportunity to discuss the case with Brenda Griffith-Williams, though her own reconstruction differs and she is not to blame for anything said here.

33 See on this Wyse 1904: 431, 435–437, Harris 2006: 193–206, esp. 178–184, 194.

34 This ought also to mean that the owner by outright sale also has the *dikē exoulēs* at his disposal, a possibility which receives some support from Pollux, cited n. 30 above.

texts of use, a further factor may be the need to deter frivolous disputation, which was a potential hazard in a system with limited means of registering title.

It is difficult to date the procedure precisely. But it can be pushed back at least into the fifth century, since it was mentioned by the comic poet Phrynichos, roughly contemporary with Aristophanes. The Homeric scholia claim that the action featured 'in the fifth *axōn* of Solon',[35] which would take it to the beginning of the sixth century. One has to be suspicious of attribution of laws to Solon, since our sources can be credulous or even indiscriminate. But the precise location in the *axōn* sequence suggests that the ultimate authority may be from the classical period and (unless we have an elegant bluff) well informed. The law as cited by the Homeric scholia does not speak of struck coinage, a phenomenon which postdates Solon, but of values.[36] So there is no reason to rule out on grounds of anachronism. But another linguistic feature does suggest that the law is old. Our sources etymologise the term ἐξούλης from the verb ἐξίλλειν, 'drive out', 'exclude', 'eject'.[37] The verb occurs infrequently (unlike the cognate εἵλω/ἴλλω) and often in the context of the δίκη ἐξούλης. The noun like the verb occurs largely in the context of the legal action either literally or (in later writers) metaphorically. Both noun and verb seem to have largely fallen out of use by the classical period. Athenian laws do not (unlike laws in some modern jurisdictions) espouse an archaising or exclusive terminology but tend to use common polite discourse.[38] The presence of a term which was not in common use indicates that the law is either archaic or early classical, that is, early fifth century at the latest and possibly sixth century. We are badly informed about the state of the lawcode in the sixth century. Even if this was on the *axones*, we cannot be sure that the content of the *axones* was exclusively Solonian. If it belongs to the sixth century, the Athenians were tinkering with the binary division in the legal system (public/private) to create more flexible legal usage

35 Fr. 36a–b Leão and Rhodes 2015: 55–56: ἐκ ε ἄξονος Pap., εννεαξονι cod. Genf. The latter was read as ἐν νε(άτῳ) ἄξονι by Nicole ('the bottom of the *axon*' or 'the bottommost *axōn*'). But Lipsius 1912: 664, 103 rightly presses for ἐν {ν}ε ἄξονι which is equally feasible palaeographically (dittography) and is consistent with the reading in a source which is otherwise (barring graphical errors) identical.

36 ὁπόσου ἂν ἄξιον ᾖ, εἰς δημόσιον ὀφείλειν καὶ τῷ ἰδιώτῃ, ἑκατέρῳ ἴσον. 'If someone ejects a man from what he has won in judgment, he owes its value to the public treasury and the individual, both.'

37 Schol. Hom. *Il.*21.282, Harpocration s.v. ἐξούλης, Paus. Attic. s.v. ἐξούλης δίκη, Lib. *Hyp.* to Dem. 30, Hsch. s.v. ἐξούλης δίκη, *Etym. Mag.* s.v. ἐξούλης, *Lex. Seg.* s.v. ἐξούλης, *Lex. Patm.* s.v. ἐξίλλειν, Souda s.v. ἐξούλης.

38 See on this Willi 2003: 79.

from early on. If it is Solonian, then from the very inception of the public/private dichotomy the Athenians were bridging the divide.[39]

The hybrid nature of *dikē exoulēs* places it at the intersection between the public and private action and calculatedly blurs the boundaries. This is not the only instance of public-private hybridity where a private case results (in cases of conviction) in damages to the plaintiff and an equal fine to the state. Modern scholars have also identified the *dikē exaireseōs* as another such.[40] This is a case arising from an attempt by one person to seize another; it was open to anyone to oppose such a seizure by intervening and posting bail for the person seized. The case then went to the Polemarch. The evidence for the twofold sanction comes from [Dem.] 58.21:

> καί μοι λέγε τόν τε νόμον, ὃς κελεύει τὸ ἥμισυ τοῦ τιμήματος ὀφείλειν τῷ δημοσίῳ ὃς ἂν δόξῃ μὴ δικαίως εἰς τὴν ἐλευθερίαν ἀφελέσθαι, καὶ τὴν τοῦ Κηφισοδώρου μαρτυρίαν.
>
> And please read out the law which bids that a person who is deemed to have improperly intervened to assert freedom is to owe to the exchequer half the sum assessed, and the deposition of Kephisodoros.

In the case of Theokrines (the defendant) the details are missing but we are told that the debt to the state arose (allegedly) from his (and his father's) failure to pay the sum due to the state as a result of his intervention to set free the slave girl of Kephisodoros ([Dem.] 58.19). We are not told why the penalty is doubled (or divided) in this way. One factor may be the presence of self-help. The Athenian system regularly attaches an element of risk to the exercise of self-help; it both empowers and at the same time builds in mechanisms and protections to curb or deter abuse. The possibility of a fine to the state and the resultant risk (depending on the assessment) of temporary *atimia* provides the necessary brake. But the penalty to the state was not needed for this; the effect could have been achieved by multiplying the compensation to the plaintiff and leaving this as an issue between the two parties, as happened in certain kinds of damage.[41] The interest of the *polis* suggests that the case cuts across interest boundaries. At first sight there is no difference between a case like this and

39 Solon did not actually create the public action (see Carey 2013: 19) but in extending it to offences against the individual (*Ath. Pol.* 9.1) he cemented in place the binary classification into public and private actions as the cornerstone of the system.

40 E.g. Lipsius 1912: 641, Harrison 1971: 81.

41 Dem. 21.43.

a case of disputed ownership of a slave or a debt incurred on the security of a slave as property. Each of these would be resolved by a simple private suit with any damages going to the individual. The basis for the addition of a fine to the state may be status. In the event of unjustified intervention there is a combination of infringement of the rights of the owner and contestation of key status categories. The rationale would be different from but comparable with that involving prior court adjudication, in that both cases raise an issue of principle; more is at stake than the rights or wrongs of a particular dispute.

My third instance of public/private hybridity is the *dikē pseudomartyriōn*. Unlike the case of false summonsing, which was a *graphē*,[42] false witnessing is a private case. We have no evidence for a *graphē pseudomartyriōn*. False witnessing is (implicitly) perceived structurally as an infringement of the interests of the opponent, not an offence against the courts or the *polis*. This applies both in public and in private cases and includes surprisingly even major political cases where the substantive charge is one directly affecting the *polis*. The opponent sues for false testimony and any financial penalty imposed on the person who bore witness goes to the individual suing for false testimony. But the penalty for three convictions was loss of civic rights. Again the case is procedurally private, with all that this implies in terms of burdens, risks and responsibilities for the plaintiff. And presumably in the case of a third conviction the plaintiff again receives damages. But the defendant is *de facto* tried on a public charge. As with the *dikē exoulēs* there is a pronounced imbalance of risk. How the penalty is executed is difficult to say. And both share the structural aspect that a private case results in a penalty, in this case a very severe penalty, exacted by the *polis*. Possibly, as with the punishment for homosexual prostitution, the punishment is automatic and the person convicted is expected to abide by the exclusions attached to *atimia*; further action is needed only in the event of infringement of the exclusions and it would come from *ho boulomenos* by way of *endeixis*.[43] Again as with *dikē exoulēs* we are given no explanation for the hybridity. What the penalty does suggest is that at this point the interests of the *polis* are deemed to be affected. Persistent falsehood becomes an offence against the court, the legal system or the *polis*, or all three, and not merely against an individual.[44] The figure of three is to some degree arbitrary—it raises the question: what constitutes persistent falsehood? But the 'three strikes' rule occurs elsewhere in the Athenian courts and three is obviously felt to be a tip-

42 [Dem.] 53.16, *Ath. Pol.* 59.3.

43 See Hansen 1976: 55–90.

44 This receives support from the fact that the other offences known to be subject to the 'three strikes' rule are *graphai* (next note).

ping point at which misconduct is deemed ingrained.[45] There is a perceptible rationale at work. Error is always a possibility, as is misrepresentation by someone prosecuting for false witness; and both can recur. So a threshold of two would be too low. Three begins to establish a pattern. As well as allowing for error, mishap, and misrepresentation the system implicitly tests for intent and justifies the extreme sanction by freeing anyone with two convictions from any obligation to give evidence in court.[46] He is not subject to the process of *klēteusis*, if he refuses either to testify or to take the oath of disclaimer (*exōmosia*) to the effect that he is not in a position to verify the deposition put to him. Though it operates differently in each case, the element of escalation (in that persistence in a line of conduct comes with increased risk) is a feature shared with the *dikē exoulēs*.[47]

The element of escalation seems also to explain the fine to the state in cases of theft with violence. From Dem. 21.44 it seems that conviction involved the payment of a sum to the state equal to that paid to the victim. The element of violence aggravates the original offence and this is reflected in the additional penalty.

The tendency to create hybrids is not confined to the public/private divide. Though space does not allow detailed discussion, another clear instance, this time within the public sphere, may shed light on the underlying dynamic. The *dokimasia rhētorōn* was an action brought against a speaker in the Assembly who for one or more actions has allegedly lost the right to address the people. Its title aligns it with the regular scrutiny of candidates for office. So does the penalty. Most though not all of the acts covered by the procedure would in any case make an Athenian liable to loss of civic rights.[48] The penalty on conviction is simply to confirm ineligibility by depriving the defendant of his rights. So it functions like any *dokimasia* in withholding entitlement, in this case in perpetuity. But structurally the procedure aligns itself with the public action; it is initiated by *ho boulomenos*. There was always a bridge between routine *dokimasia* and litigation. The regular *dokimasia* gave rise to a legal hearing in the case of an objection or rejection.[49] In the case of the *archontes* during the fourth

45 *Graphē paranomōn*: Antiphanes fr. 194 KA, Hyp. *Phil.* 11–12, Dem. 51.12, *graphē pseudoklēteias* Andok. 1.74. *graphē argias* Lys. fr. 40b.

46 Hyp. *Phil.* 12.

47 It is also a feature in appeals, e.g. against withholding or removing citizenship (*Ath. Pol.* 42.1, Libanius *hyp.* Dem. 57), where again the principle seems to be the same. See further on the role of raised stakes in appeals Rhodes 1981: 501–502.

48 Certainly true of desertion, abuse of parents and homosexual prostitution (Aischin. 1.28–29). Whether it applied to squandering one's inheritance (Aischin. 1.30) is far from clear.

49 *Ath. Pol.* 55.4.

century there was an automatic second hearing before a court.[50] The *dokimasia rhētorōn* went a stage further and blended the two in a single process.

The title dates this action to the late fifth century at the earliest, when *rhētōr* becomes a standard term for the politically active individual; it may be later still and date to the restoration of democracy in 403. The action responds to changes in the democratic process, specifically the cultural move from politicians who owe their influence to a combination of military command to one in which influence derives entirely from oratorical and political skill. It acknowledges the structural importance of the public speaker to the democratic process and assimilates him to the formally selected official. But it ingeniously takes account of the fact that the public speaker is not appointed and therefore has no term of office, which rules out *dokimasia* in its regular form and likewise *epicheirotonia*, which requires a designated position which can be prematurely terminated. It is essentially experiential. In this it may be typical of the system in general, in that the Athenians as legislators respond in a flexible and pragmatic way to the exigencies of particular offences. Though we can isolate and even compare the principles at work (at least conjecturally), we appear to have a desire for practical solutions to legal and political needs rather than any rigid template for assimilating actions neatly to an overarching structure. The result, though unsystematic, can be both elegant in its simplicity and very economical, in that relatively minor adjustments to procedure and penology, without the need for complex legislative formulation or administrative support, can have quite radical results.[51]

Bibliography

Bridge, M. (2015) *Personal Property Law*, 4th edn, London.

Carey, C. (2004) 'Offence and Procedure in Athenian Law', in Harris, E.M. and Rubinstein, L., eds, *The Law and the Courts in Ancient Greece*, London, 111–136.

Carey, C. (2013) 'In Search of Drakon', *Cambridge Classical Journal* 59, 1–23.

Gilroy, J.P. (2014) *The Law of Arrest for Merchants and Private Security Personnel*, London.

Hansen, M.H. (1976) *Apagoge, endeixis and ephegesis against kakourgoi, atimoi, and pheugontes: a study in the Athenian administration of justice in the fourth century* BC, Odense.

50 *Ath. Pol.* 55.2.

51 I am grateful to my co-editors for their comments on an early draft.

Hansen, M.H. (1982) '*Atimia* in Consequence of Private Debts?', in Modrzejewski, J. and Liebs, D. eds, *Symposion 1977: Vorträge zur griechischen und hellenistischen Rechtsgeschichte* (Chantilly, 1–4 June 1977), Vienna, 113–120.

Harris, E.M. (2006a) *Democracy and the Rule of Law in Classical Athens: Essays on Law, Society, and Politics*, Cambridge.

Harris, E.M. (2006b) 'The Penalty for Frivolous Prosecution in Athenian Law', in Harris (2006a), 405–422.

Harris, E.M. (2007) 'Who Enforced the Law in Classical Athens?', in Cantarella, E., ed. (2007) *Symposion 2005: Vorträge zur griechischen und hellenistischen Rechtsgeschichte* (Salerno, 14–18 September 2005), Vienna, 159–176.

Harrison, A.R.W. (1968–1971) *The Law of Athens*, 2 vols, Oxford.

Leão, D.F. and Rhodes, P.J. (2015) *The Laws of Solon. A New Edition with Introduction, Translation and Commentary*, London.

Lipsius, J.H. (1905–1915) *Das attische Recht und Rechtsverfahren*, 3 vols, Leipzig.

Macleod, J. and Devenny, J. (2007) *Consumer Sales Law: The Law Relating to Consumer Sales and Financing of Goods*, London.

Murray, A.T., ed. (1939) *Demosthenes V. Private orations XLI–XLIX, with an English translation* (Loeb Classical Library), Cambridge, Ma./London.

Ober, J. (2008) *Democracy and Knowledge*, Princeton.

Osborne, R. (1985) 'Law in Action in Classical Athens', *JHS* 105, 40–58. (Reprinted in Osborne, R. (2010) *Athens and Athenian Democracy*, Cambridge, 171–204.)

Rapalje, S, and Lawrence, R.L. (1888) *A Dictionary of American and English Law*, 2 vols, Jersey City, N.J.

Rhodes, P.J. (1981) *A commentary on the Aristotelian* Athenaion Politeia, Oxford.

Willi, A. (2003) *The Languages of Aristophanes: Aspects of Linguistic Variation in Classical Attic Greek*, Oxford.

Wyse, W. (1904) *The Speeches of Isaeus*. Cambridge.

PART 2

Procedural Manoeuvres

CHAPTER 5

Isaios 6: a Case of Procedural Abuse (and Scholarly Misunderstandings)

Brenda Griffith-Williams

Introduction: the *diamartyria*

Isaios 6, *On the Estate of Philoktemon,* is an important source of information on Athenian inheritance law, including some aspects which are not attested elsewhere, but its significance has often been overlooked or misunderstood by modern scholars. One reason for this is the general tendency, following the example of Wyse (1904), to mistrust Isaios' speeches as a source of Athenian law.[1] The interpretation of Isa. 6, in particular, has also suffered from misconceptions about the facts of the case and the historical background which have led to inaccurate reconstructions of the internal chronology and the legal basis of the case. A complete reappraisal of this complex speech would be beyond the scope of the present volume, but I hope to offer solutions to some of the problems it presents and to suggest some lines of enquiry for further work. The main focus of this chapter is on the procedure followed by Isaios' opponent in the case—in particular, his use of the *diamartyria,* which Isaios repeatedly criticises as unfair.

The *diamartyria* was a formal statement by a witness, used as a procedural device in the Athenian courts to stop a legal action from proceeding on technical grounds without regard to the substantive issues in dispute. The procedure was probably a survival from the archaic period, but its origin and history are obscure.[2] The earliest known references to it are in Isok. 18 *Against Kallimachos* (c. 402 BC) and Lys. 23 *Against Pankleon, showing that he was not a Plataian* (some time before 387 BC). Isok. 18.11 refers to a case which was blocked by a *diamartyria* asserting that it was not admissible because it had already been decided by arbitration (ὡς οὐκ εἰσαγώγιμος ἦν ἡ δίκη διαίτης γεγενημένης). According to Lys. 23.14, testimony was given in a *diamartyria* to the effect that

1 See also Hatzilambrou in this volume.

2 Gernet (1927) remains the authoritative work on the history of the *diamartyria*, which has also been discussed by Wyse 1904: 232–234, Harrison 1971: 124–131, MacDowell 1978: 212–214, and Todd 1993: 135–136.

 | DOI:10.1163/9789004377899_007

Pankleon was not a Plataian (μὴ Πλαταιεὺς εἶναι), with the result that the prosecution against him continued to be heard before the polemarch, who had jurisdiction in cases involving metics.

Later in the fourth century the *diamartyria* was largely replaced by a new procedure, the *paragraphē*, which did not block the progress of an action but reversed the position of prosecutor and defendant.[3] But the *diamartyria* still continued to be used in disputed inheritance cases when a legitimate son wanted to block a rival claim to his father's estate. Legitimate sons, under Athenian law, had an absolute right to inherit a share of their father's estate and were entitled to take possession immediately after the father's death, without formal approval from the court. Among the procedural privileges enjoyed by a legitimate son was the right to testify (or put forward a witness to testify) in a *diamartyria* that the estate was not subject to adjudication by the court.[4] We do not have the original text of any of the *diamartyriai* used in fourth century inheritance claims, but we can infer from the discussion in the speeches that the wording of a typical *diamartyria* would have been along the lines of 'X testifies that the estate of Y is not adjudicable (οὐκ ἔστιν ἐπίδικος ὁ κλῆρος) to Z, because Y left a legitimate son.'[5] The objective was to block any rival claim to the estate from a collateral relative of the deceased, or someone claiming to have been adopted by will, and so make a trial unnecessary. If, nevertheless, the rival claimant still wanted to proceed, his only recourse was to prosecute the witness who had testified in the *diamartyria* for false testimony (*pseudomartyria*). Formally, the issue to be decided in the *dikē pseudomartyriōn* was whether or not the statement made in the *diamartyria* was true, so the outcome did not necessarily determine the substantive dispute.[6] If, on the one hand, the *dikē pseudomartyriōn* was won by the defendant (that is, the truth of the *dia-*

3 For discussion, see Todd 1993: 136–138.

4 Cf. Carey in this volume.

5 We have three speeches for the prosecution (Isa. 3, Isa. 6 and Dem. 44) and one defence speech (Isa. 2) from *dikai pseudomartyriōn* where the original claimant to an estate has prosecuted the witness testifying in a *diamartyria*. In addition, we have some information about the use of the *diamartyria* in inheritance cases from Isa. 5, where the speaker mentions a prosecution for *pseudomartyria* resulting from a *diamartyria* at an earlier stage of the legal proceedings about the estate of Dikaiogenes, and and from Isa. 7, where the speaker says that he could have blocked his opponent's claim to the estate of Apollodoros with a *diamartyria*, but decided not to do so. And there is some further evidence of fourth century *diamartyriai* in the titles of two speeches attributed to Deinarchos: Diamartyria, *claiming that the daughters of Aristophon are not subject to adjudication* (διαμαρτυρία, ὡς οὐκ επίδικοι ⟨αἱ⟩ Ἀριστοφῶντος θυγατέρες, Dein. fr. 60) and Diamartyria *concerning the estate of Euippos against Xares* (διαμαρτυρία περὶ τοῦ Ἐυίππου κλήρου πρὸς Ξάρητα, Dein. fr. 62).

6 See Harrison 1971: 131–132.

martyria was confirmed), then it is clear that the prosecutor lost his claim to the estate. If, on the other hand, the prosecutor won, it appears that he would then have to submit a fresh claim to the estate. At that stage, however, the risk of a further challenge from the defeated opponent was probably not great, so in most cases the outcome of the *dikē pseudomartyriōn* did in practice determine the substantive case.[7]

As other contributors to this volume have pointed out, it can be extremely difficult to distinguish 'abuse' from legitimate use of the law or legal procedure, even in modern jurisdictions where procedural abuse is defined by reference to a fixed code of written rules and where a criminal prosecution or civil claim can fail because the prosecutor or claimant has broken the procedural rules, regardless of the substantive merits of the case. Such a legalistic approach would be meaningless in the context of the Athenian system, which had no fixed procedural rules and no mechanism for determining procedural issues separately from the substance of the case. Although the *archōn* had limited power to decide whether a claim was admissible, he had no power to reject a *diamartyria* because of its origin as a strictly procedural or ritual device.[8] So, if a litigant objected to his opponent's use of the procedure, the final arbiters were the dikasts who heard the *dikē pseudomartyriōn*, when they would have to consider his complaints in relation to the substantive facts of the case. Whatever its originally intended scope, a procedural device such as the *diamartyria* might have evolved over time to fit different circumstances, and it is impossible for us to know what criteria the dikasts would have applied in deciding whether it had been appropriately used in a particular case.

Another possible starting point for a definition of procedural abuse is the proposition that a legal procedure is 'abused' when a litigant adopts it with the deliberate intention of putting his opponent at an unfair disadvantage.[9] It was certainly not uncommon for Athenian litigants to complain that their opponents had followed the 'wrong' procedure, and that is precisely what the speaker of Isa. 6 accuses his opponent of doing. Such allegations are not, of course, objective evidence of procedural abuse, but it is worth considering the possibility that Isaios was not merely making a rhetorical point, as scholars

7 Cf. Todd 1993: 138–139: 'Defeat in *paragraphē* or *diamartyria* was surely so prejudicial to your chances in the original case that you would have dropped your claim or accepted any terms that your opponent was prepared to offer.'

8 *Pace* MacDowell 1978: 212–213: '*Diamartyria* was a formal assertion of a fact by a witness who was in a position to know it. The witness might state, for example, that a man was a member of a certain deme, or the legitimate son of a certain father; and this might enable the magistrate to decide whether he should accept the case or not.'

9 On this cf. Arnaoutoglou in this volume.

such as Wyse and Harrison have assumed,[10] but that his client might really have been disadvantaged by the opponent's choice of procedure.

The Story Told by Isaios' Client

Isaios' client in this case, Chairestratos, has submitted a formal claim (*lēxis*) to the court for the estate of Philoktemon, claiming that Philoktemon, his mother's brother, adopted him by will, and it appears that the estate of Philoktemon's father, Euktemon, is also at issue. Another kinsman, Androkles, has responded with a *diamartyria* asserting that the estate is not subject to adjudication by the court because Euktemon left two legitimate sons by a second wife, and that Philoktemon did not make a valid will. Chairestratos, in turn, has prosecuted Androkles for false testimony in the *diamartyria*, and Isa. 6 (delivered by an unnamed family friend as *synēgoros*) is the prosecution speech in the resulting *dikē pseudomartyriōn*. I shall start with a summary of the factual story told by Isaios to explain the true origin of the claimants put forward by Androkles as Euktemon's legitimate sons; then I consider the historical context and internal chronology of the speech, in order to establish the factual background against which the legal and procedural issues need to be addressed.

Euktemon of Kephisia married a daughter of his fellow demesman, Meixiades. They had three sons (Philoktemon, Hegemon and Ergamenes) and two daughters, one of whom married Phanostratos and the other Chaireas. Phanostratos and his wife had two sons, one of whom (probably the older) was Isaios' client Chairestratos, while Chaireas and his wife had only a daughter. Euktemon lived a happy and prosperous life until, in old age, he was led astray by his infatuation with Alke, a freedwoman and former prostitute who managed a tenement house for him in Piraeus. Euktemon spent more and more time with Alke, until eventually he left his family home and moved in with her permanently. She had two sons, reputedly by a freedman called Dion who had left Athens under a cloud, and she persuaded Euktemon to introduce one of these young men to his phratry as his own son. Philoktemon, by this time the only survivor of Euktemon's three legitimate sons, objected, so the phratry mem-

10 'Androkles had chosen the proper and legal course on the assumption that his wards were legitimate sons of Euktemon. If he had not availed himself of his right, Isaios would have taunted him with a guilty conscience. … Claimants pulled up by a διαμαρτυρία, and compelled to disprove in court a definite allegation before they can proceed with their own case, vent their annoyance in cavils at the procedure of their opponents.' Wyse 1904: 492.

bers refused to admit the candidate and the sacrificial victim (the *koureion*)[11] was removed from the altar. But, after a row with Euktemon in which the old man threatened to re-marry and father more sons, Philoktemon reluctantly gave way, on condition that his younger 'brother' should receive no more than a single farm out of Euktemon's estate. So Euktemon's newly discovered 'son' was duly introduced to the phratry on the agreed terms.

Not long after this Philoktemon set sail on a military campaign, in the course of which he was killed in a naval action off Chios. Euktemon then drew up a written document (or 'will') setting out the terms on which he had introduced Alke's son to his phratry, and deposited the document with a kinsman.[12] His son-in-law Phanostratos was about to set off in his trireme from Mounychia, under the command of the general Timotheos, and the other son-in-law, Chaireas, was there to see him off. Euktemon went there and gave the document in their presence to Pythodoros of Kephisia for safekeeping. Androkles and Antidoros later fell in with Alke in a conspiracy to defraud Euktemon of his property. First they persuaded him to revoke the 'will' in favour of Alke's son and sell the property, so that they could take the proceeds in cash; then he had soon sold further property to the value of more than three talents. After Euktemon died, Androkles and his associates first concealed the news from his wife and daughters,[13] then shut them out of the house until all its contents had been removed.

Historical Background and Internal Chronology

The speech can be dated by the statement at §14 that fifty-two years have elapsed since the departure of the Sicilian expedition in the archonship of Arimnestos (summer 415): the trial must have taken place in 364/3, and the latest possible date is summer 363.[14] This precise reference to a datable historic

11 An Athenian child was normally introduced to his father's phratry by 'a two-stage process of phratry admission, first in infancy at a ceremony known as the *meion*, and second during adolescence at the *koureion*, before he was introduced to his deme at the age of eighteen.' Lambert 1993: 36.

12 The agreement is sometimes referred to as a *grammateion* ('document') and sometimes as a *diathēkē*, which is the word regularly used for 'will' in classical Greek, although it was not a 'will' in the usual Athenian sense.

13 Cf. Lys. 32.7, where a similar allegation is made about Diogeiton's behaviour after the death of his brother Diodotos.

14 Some commentators have taken the reference to the Sicilian expedition as meaning that the speech was delivered in the year 364, but others point out that it could mean either

event is unique in Isaios' speeches. The historical record gives no clue to the date of the naval encounter off Chios in which Philoktemon was killed, and so scholars have focused instead on the dating of the naval campaign on which Phanostratos set off shortly after Philoktemon's death. The expedition was commanded by the general Timotheos, who was instrumental in establishing the Second Athenian Confederacy (378–373) but was subsequently prosecuted and went into exile until 366/5, when he returned and captured Samos. Scholarly discussion focused initially on the period of the Theban war in the 370s, before Timotheos' exile, leading to the conclusion that Philoktemon died at least ten years before Euktemon. On this basis, it was thought that the title given to the speech by the mediaeval copyist must be wrong: the disputed estate was really that of Euktemon, and Chairestratos did not assert his claim to be the adopted son of Philoktemon until after Euktemon's death. There are several factors that might appear to support this view—not least that, in a claim to the estate of Philoktemon, a *diamartyria* asserting that not he but his father had left legitimate sons would look distinctly odd. Moreover, the narrative deals extensively with the alleged conspiracy against Euktemon's estate, and does not identify any specific property as belonging separately to Philoktemon.

Isaios does, nevertheless, consistently put Chairestratos's legal case in terms of a claim to the estate of Philoktemon. He says, for example, that Androkles's *diamartyria* deprived the dikasts of their right to nominate Philoktemon's heir (§4),[15] and in his conclusion the speaker says 'If Philoktemon's estate is adjudicated to my friend …' (τοῦ γὰρ Φιλοκτήμονος κλήρου ἂν μὲν ἐπιδικάσηται ὅδε …, §61). Nor is it easy to reconcile the idea of a ten-year interval between the deaths of Philoktemon and Euktemon with the timescale suggested in the speech. Nearly two years (σχεδὸν δυ' ἔτη, §29) after making his 'will' in favour of Alke's son, Euktemon decided to revoke it. So he destroyed the document and sold off much of his property 'in a very short time' (ἐν πάνυ ὀλίγῳ χρόνῳ, §33), disposing of three talents' worth of property 'hurriedly' after Philoktemon's death (διὰ ταχέων πάνυ τελευτήσαντος Φιλοκτήμονος, §34). For sceptics such as Wyse, any such discrepancies are easily explained as typically Isaian attempts to mislead the court, but a more objective reading would suggest that the supposed ten-year interval creates more problems than it solves. Not least of these is the age of Alke's older son and the date of his introduction into Euktemon's phratry: both Labarbe (1953) and Thompson (1970) have pointed out

365/4 or 364/3, depending on the method of calculation. See, e.g., Roussel 1926: 107: 'D'après l'indication du s. 14, le plaidoyer date de 365/4 ou 364/3 selon que l'on fait entrer dans le calcul l'année de l'archontat d'Arimnestos ou non.'; cf. Wyse 1904: 549.

15 See p. 00 below for a fuller discussion of this passage.

that if he was 'not yet twenty' at the date of the trial (οὔπω ὑπὲρ εἴκοσιν ἔτη, § 14), he would have been too young for the *koureion* ten years earlier. (A sceptic might, of course, assume that Isaios was lying about the boy's age, but it is difficult to see how he could have got away with such a misrepresentation.)[16]

There is, in any event, no need to accept the ten-year interval, in the light of Schweigert's research into the historical background which demonstrated the possibility of a later date for Phanostratos's naval campaign under Timotheos.[17] Phanostratos of Kephisia is named as a trierarch at line 92 of *IG* II^2, 1609, a naval record identified by Schweigert as relating to the first of three cleruchic expeditions to Samos, in 365/4. Suggesting that there could have been a skirmish near Chios during the ten-month siege of Samos, shortly before the departure of the cleruchic expedition, Schweigert concludes: 'Philoktemon, then, was killed in 366/5 near Chios during a sea-battle. Shortly thereafter, Phanostratos, his kinsman, sailed out as trierarch in the cleruchic expedition to Samos (*IG* II^2, 1609, line 92). This would have to be the expedition 'under Timotheos' which is mentioned in Isaios.'[18]

Schweigert's new dating of the campaign led by Timotheos has implications for the interpretation of the speech which have not always been recognised by subsequent scholars.[19] If Euktemon died between two and three years after Philoktemon, and probably only a matter of weeks before Isa. 6 was delivered. It is clearly impossible that a claim to *Euktemon*'s estate could have reached the stage of a trial for *pseudomartyria* in such a short time. On the other hand, it is perfectly plausible that a claim to the estate of *Philoktemon* did not reach that stage until some time between two and three years after he died, allowing time for news of his death to reach Athens and for Chairestratos to submit his claim,[20] as well as for the protracted course of the legal proceedings once they had started. The first step in the legal process, Chairestratos's submission of his

16 Jebb 1876: 346 suggests that the young man was 'really about 27'. Wyse 1904: 100, while conceding that Chairestratos had an interest in presenting his rival as younger than he really was, rightly points out that 'If the claimant was 27, and had not been presented to the deme by Euktemon, it is remarkable that so strong a presumption of illegitimacy was overlooked or omitted by Isaeus.'

17 Schweigert 1940.

18 Schweigert 1940: 198. Schweigert's dating is dismissed as 'impossible' by Davies 1971: 564, on the assumption that the speech was delivered in the year 364; but if the trial date was actually summer 363 (n. 00 above) then the timescale is tight but not impossible.

19 The first to do so were Cobetto Ghiggia 1999 and Naddeo 2008.

20 According to Cobetto Ghiggia 1999: 278 and Naddeo 2008: 27, Chairestratos was unable to submit his claim for the estate immediately after Philoktemon's death because he was himself away from Athens on military service.

lēxis (formal claim), was followed by Androkles' attempt to block the claim with his *diamartyria*, but Chairestratos countered this by prosecuting him for *pseudomartyria*. The *archōn* convened a preliminary hearing (*anakrisis*),[21] at which Chairestratos challenged Androkles to name the mother of the two boys who were purportedly Euktemon's legitimate sons. Androkles could not name her but said she was a Lemnian, and the hearing was adjourned while he sought more detailed information. The case proceeded to trial only after the reconvened hearing at which Androkles identified the woman as Kallippe, daughter of Pistoxenos.

The Process of Litigation

Androkles (as portrayed by Isaios) was clearly an unscrupulous schemer determined to get his hands on both Euktemon's and Philoktemon's property by whatever means possible, legal or illegal.[22] He made three separate legal interventions: first, while Euktemon was still alive, he pretended that the two boys identified in the speech as Alke's sons had been adopted by two of Euktemon's now deceased sons, Philoktemon and Ergamenes. As the self-proclaimed guardians of the two children, Androkles and Antidoros applied to the *archōn* for permission to lease the property of the 'orphans', but their fraud was exposed by members of the family before the procedure could be completed. Secondly, after Chairestratos had submitted his claim to Philoktemon's estate, Androkles tried to block it with his *diamartyria* claiming that Euktemon had left legitimate sons. Finally, after Euktemon's death, Androkles claimed one of his daughters (the widow of Chaireas) as *epiklēros*, together with a share of the estate (one-fifth, according to the manuscripts).[23] Isaios ridicules these interventions as being inconsistent with one another: the boys cannot be simultaneously Euktemon's sons and the sons of Philoktemon and Ergamenes, and if Euktemon left legitimate sons, his daughter cannot be an *epiklēros*.[24]

---

21 For the *anakrisis* see Kremmydas in this volume.

22 Cf. Cobetto Ghiggia 1999: 277: 'Non si può negare che il comportamento di Androcle sia ai limiti della legalità o forse ben oltre …'.

23 See appendix to this chapter pp. 107–108.

24 Isaios' most recent editor, Cobetto Ghiggia (who accepts that the estate claimed by Chairestratos was that of Philoktemon, and that Philoktemon died not long before Euktemon) offers an alternative interpretation. Androkles succeeded, in Chairestratos's absence from Athens, in having Alce's sons posthumously adopted by Philoktemon, and they are accordingly named in the *diamartyria* as Philoktemon's legitimate sons. Androkles, according to this theory, has used the *diamartyria* legitimately, and Chairestratos has no chance of suc-

Let us turn now to Androkles' *diamartyria*. The text is not preserved, but the contents emerge from the speaker's discussion: Androkles has testified, first, that the estate is not subject to adjudication (μὴ ἐπίδικον εἶναι τὸν κλῆρον, § 4); secondly, that Chairestratos' opponent in the litigation is a legitimate son of Euktemon (ὑὸν εἶναι γνήσιον Εὐκτήμονος τοῦτον, § 10; μεμαρτύρηκε δ' Εὐκτήμονος ὗον εἶναι γνήσιον, § 46); thirdly, that Philoktemon did not leave a will (γέγραπται ὡς οὐκ ἔδωκεν οὐδὲ διέθετο Φιλοκτήμων, § 62); and finally, that Philoktemon died childless (τελευτῆσαι ἄπαιδα Φιλοκτήμονα, § 63). So, if Isaios was citing the *diamartyria* accurately, as it appears that he was, the wording was certainly unusual. The basic point is the procedural one, that the estate was not subject to adjudication, and that needs to be supported by the 'factual' statement about the existence of legitimate sons, but the additional substantive assertion that Philoktemon died childless without leaving a will is not relevant to the procedural issue of admissibility. Some modern scholars have found this juxtaposition of apparently separate issues puzzling, but have not sought to explain it or seriously questioned the legitimacy of the procedure.[25] In fact, it is impossible to know for sure on what grounds (if any) an Athenian court would have considered a *diamartyria* unacceptable, especially given that the *archōn* had no discretion to reject it, but a closer look at Isaios' argumentation may help to throw some light on the problem.

Isaios makes three specific objections to Androkles' use of the *diamartyria*, which is first mentioned in the introduction to the speech:

> Φιλοκτήμων γὰρ ὁ Κηφισεὺς φίλος ἦν Χαιρεστράτῳ τουτῳι δοὺς δὲ τὰ ἑαυτοῦ καὶ ὑὸν αὐτὸν ποιησάμενος ἐτελεύτησε. λαχόντος δὲ τοῦ Χαιρεστράτου κατὰ τὸν νόμον τοῦ κλήρου, ἐξὸν αμφισβητῆσαι Ἀθηναίων τῷ βουλομένῳ καὶ εὐθυδικίᾳ

ceeding in his claim to testamentary adoption unless he can prove that the boys were not eligible for adoption because they were illegitimate. (Cobetto Ghiggia 2012: 227–231). Even if it could be reconciled with the wording of the *diamartyria*, which, according to Isaios, named the boys as sons of Euktemon, Cobetto Ghiggia's ingenious hypothesis is, in my view, ultimately flawed because a posthumous adoption would not have been permissible if there had been a valid adoption by will. (On the circumstances in which a posthumous adoption would have been accepted as valid, see Griffith-Williams 2013: 203–205.)

25 'The juxtaposition of two distinct and independent issues is confusing. The substance of a διαμαρτυρία was a protest founded on the existence of sons. To sustain such an objection Androkles had to prove the legitimacy of the alleged sons, but was not obliged to show that Philoktemon had not made a will.' Wyse 1904: 486–487; cf. Roussel 1926: 105: '… [Androclès] attestait à la fois qu'il existait des fils légitimes d'Euktémon, et que Philoktémon n'avait pas fait de testament. On comprend mal comment ces deux faits distincts étaient confondus dans une même procédure dont l'effet ordinaire se fonde uniquement sur l'existence d'héritiers de plein droit.'

> εἰσελθόντι εἰς ὑμᾶς, εἰ φαίνοιτο δικαιότερα λέγων, ἔχειν τὸν κλῆρον, διεμαρτύρησεν Ἀνδροκλῆς οὑτοσὶ μὴ ἐπίδικον εἶναι τὸν κλῆρον, ἀποστερῶν τοῦτον τῆς ἀμφισβητήσεως καὶ ὑμᾶς τοῦ κυρίους γενέσθαι ὅντινα δεῖ κληρονόμον καταστήσασθαι τῶν Φιλοκτήμονος· καὶ ἐν μιᾷ ψήφῳ καὶ ἑνὶ ἀγῶνι οἴεται ἀδελφοὺς καταστήσειν ἐκείνῳ τοὺς οὐδὲν προσήκοντας, καὶ τὸν κλῆρον ἀνεπίδικον ἕξειν αὐτός, καὶ τῆς ἀδελφῆς τῆς ἐκείνου κύριος γενήσεσθαι, καὶ τὴν διαθήκην ἄκυρον ποιήσειν.
>
> For Philoktemon of Kephisia was a friend of Chairestratos here, and when he died he had given him his property and adopted him as his son. But when Chairestratos claimed the estate, in accordance with the law, although it was permissible for any Athenian who wished to come before you in a *euthydikia* and contest the estate, and, if he appeared to have the better case, to obtain it, Androkles here testified in a *diamartyria* that the estate was not subject to adjudication, trying to deprive my friend of the opportunity to contest it and you of determining who should be established as Philoktemon's heir. And with a single vote and in a single contest he thinks he can establish people who had no relationship to Philoktemon as his brothers, and get the estate himself without an adjudication, and become *kyrios* of Philoktemon's sister, and annul the will.
>
> §§3–5

This passage is crucial to our understanding of the legal basis of the speech, but its significance has not always been properly recognised by translators and commentators. The first point to note is that the estate (*klēros*) claimed by Chairestratos is, from the context, clearly that of Philoktemon.[26] The second is the speaker's criticism of Androkles' choice of procedure: he should have proceeded by way of a 'direct trial' (*euthydikia*) not a *diamartyria*, but that is a point not clearly conveyed by the two most recent published translations of Isaios' speeches into English. Both Forster (1927) and Edwards (2007) take the accusative absolute ἐξὸν αμφισβητῆσαι in the second sentence of the Greek text as causal, as in Forster's version: '*Since* it is lawful for any Athenian who wishes to do so to bring a direct action [*euthydikia*] before you ... Androkles here put

26 Wyse 1904 ad loc. reveals both his bias against Isaios and the prevailing scholarly consensus about the historical background to the speech: 'This is a disingenuous narrative. ... What Athenian judge listening to these artful paragraphs could have suspected that Philoktemon had been dead at least 10 years, and that Chairestratos only applied to the archon after the death of Euktemon?'

in a protestation [*diamartyria*] …'[27] But this misses the point of the antithesis between *euthydikia* and *diamartyria*, giving the impression that Androkles has followed the correct procedure, when in fact Isaios intended the opposite. So the meaning must be concessive, as Jones (1779) and various continental European translators have recognised.[28] Nevertheless, despite the clear implication that Androkles *ought* to have brought a direct action, there is in fact nothing in Isaios' wording to suggest that it was in fact compulsory to follow one procedure rather than the other: *exon* (rather than *deon*) denotes an option, not a duty, so the passage might be interpreted merely as a rhetorical criticism of Androkles for clever procedural manoeuvring, rather than strictly legal abuse.

Later, in the context of his accusation that Androkles has acted inconsistently, Isaios points out that the statement in the *diamartyria* that the two boys put forward by Androkles were legitimate sons of Euktemon is not only untrue, but also contradicts a previous claim by Androkles in which he asserted that the boys had been adopted by Euktemon's deceased sons. This, then, is his second specific objection:

> καὶ εἰς τοῦτο ἀναιδείας ἥκουσιν, ὥστ' εὐθυδικίᾳ μὲν οὐκ ἐτόλμησαν εἰσελθεῖν, ἀλλὰ διεμαρτύρουν ὡς ὑπὲρ γνησίων …
>
> And they are so shameless that they did not dare to appear in a *euthydikia*, but have testified in the *diamartyria* as if it were a case of legitimate sons.[29]
>
> § 43

The third is that by using the *diamartyria* Androkles has exposed Chairestratos to unnecessary risk: if the court decides that the estate is subject to adjudica-

27 Cf. Edwards 2007: 101: 'But any Athenian who wished could make a claim, enter a direct action (*euthydikia*) before you … Androcles here thus made a declaration that the estate was not adjudicable …'.

28 '… when, therefore, Chairestratos claimed his succession in due form (at which time any Athenian had a right to set up an adverse claim in a direct course of law, …) this Androkles, instead of bringing a fair and regular action, entered a protestation that the estate was not liable to controversy, intending to prevent my friend from supporting his claim …' Jones 1779: 56; cf. Dareste 1898: 107–108, Caccialanza 1901: 322, Roussel 1926: 109, and Cobetto Ghiggia 2012: 227.

29 Cf. Isa. 7.3, where the speaker says that he could have blocked his opponent's claim with a *diamartyria*, but preferred to argue his case in a *euthydikia* so that they could not accuse him of being unwilling to come to trial. This suggests that the *diadikasia*/*euthydikia* contrast may have been used, in appropriate circumstances, as a rhetorical ploy.

tion, and Chairestratos wins the *dikē pseudomartyriōn*, Androkles will still be able to make another claim to the same property:

> τουτὶ γὰρ αὐτοῖς ἡ διαμαρτυρία δύναται, ἵν' ὁ κίνδυνος τοῖσδε μὲν ᾖ περὶ πάντων, οὗτοι δὲ κἂν νῦν διαμάρτωσι τοῦ ἀγῶνος, δόξῃ δὲ ὁ κλῆρος ἐπίδικος εἶναι, ἀντιγραψάμενοι δὶς περὶ τῶν αὐτῶν ἀγωνίζωνται.
>
> For this is the effect of [Androkles's] *diamartyria*, that all the risk falls on [Chairestratos], and that even if he loses the case and the estate is held to be subject to adjudication, he may claim again and contest the same estate twice.
>
> §52

Conclusion

Isaios' main contention in this case is that the factual statements made by Androkles in his *diamartyria* are untrue. Thus, according to Isaios, Androkles' two protégés are *not* legitimate sons of Euktemon, but Philoktemon *did* leave a will in which he adopted his nephew Chairestratos as his heir. Isaios is, nevertheless, unable to deny that Euktemon introduced one of the boys to his phratry as his son—a fact which is highly damaging to his case—so it is not surprising that he devotes most of the speech to a counternarrative designed to refute Androkles' version of the story. But in addition to that, and despite acknowledging that Androkles would have been perfectly within his rights to contest the estate in a *euthydikia*, he repeatedly argues that Androkles' choice of procedure has put Chairestratos at an unfair disadvantage.

In fact, according to Isaios' account, Androkles has conflated his claim to Philoktemon's estate with what ought to have been a separate claim to the estate of Euktemon. In other words, he has made it impossible for the dikasts to vote separately on two distinct issues: whether Euktemon had left legitimate sons, and whether Philoktemon had adopted a son. To understand why this was unfair to Chairestratos, we need to consider his position in the family (both as Philoktemon's adopted son and as a natural, legitimate son of Euktemon's daughter) and its significance under Athenian inheritance law, where the principle of male precedence favoured descendants through a male line over those through a female line.

Chairestratos had started the proceedings by formally claiming the estate of Philoktemon, and, if his claim had been opposed in the proper way, all he would have had to prove was that his adoption by Philoktemon was legally valid. If he was successful, that, in turn, would entitle him to at least a share of Euktemon's estate, as, *de jure*, Euktemon's grandson through a male line. (If Androkles' protégés succeeded in proving that they were Euktemon's legitimate sons, they would have had to share Euktemon's estate with Chairestratos. If they failed, Chairestratos would have been entitled to the whole estate.) On the other hand, even if Chairestratos failed in his claim to have been adopted by Philoktemon, he would still have been entitled to claim a share in Euktemon's estate as his grandson through a female line—provided he could successfully defeat any claim that Euktemon had left legitimate sons.

Androkles had certainly taken a risk by proceeding as he did: if Chairestratos won the *dikē pseudomartyriōn* (that is, if his status as Philoktemon's adopted son was confirmed, and at the same time it was found that Euktemon did not leave legitimate sons), then he would have succeeded both to the estate of Philoktemon (as his adopted son) and to that of Euktemon (as his only surviving descendant through a male line). But Androkles, relying on his evidence about the phratry introduction, must have had strong hopes of winning. If he did, and his two protégés were recognised as Euktemon's legitimate sons, then they would have shared both Euktemon's estate (as his sons) and Philoktemon's (as his legitimate half-brothers). Chairestratos, in that case, would get nothing: he would not be recognised as Philoktemon's adopted son, and, as the son of Euktemon's daughter, he would have no claim to even a share of either his grandfather's or his uncle's estate.

I conclude, then, that, if Isaios' account of the proceedings is accurate (and even if we allow for an element of rhetorical exaggeration in his criticisms of Androkles), this case does represent an example of procedural abuse; but it shows that the concept of such abuse in the Athenian courts can only be understood in relation to the particular facts of the case, not by reference to an abstract, rule-based definition of the correct procedure.

Appendix: Isa. 6.46

Ἔτι δὲ καὶ τοῦ μάρτυρος αὐτου σκέψασθε τὴν τόλμαν καὶ ἀναίδειαν, ὅστις εἴληχε μὲν αὐτῷ τῆς θυγατρὸς τῆς Εὐκτήμονος ὡς οὔσης ἐπικλήρου, καὶ αὐτοῦ τοῦ κλήρου τοῦ Εὐκτήμονος πέμπτου μέρους ὡς ἐπιδίκου ὄντος, μεμαρτύρηκε δ' Εὐκτήμονος ὑὸν εἶναι γνήσιον.

Furthermore, consider the effrontery and shamelessness of the actual witness, who has claimed for himself the daughter of Euktemon, alleging that she is an heiress, and that a fifth of Euktemon's estate should be adjudicated to her, but has also testified that Euktemon has a legitimate son.

Modern editors and translators (Dareste 1898, Caccialanza 1901, Wyse 1904, Roussel 1926, Forster 1927, Edwards 2007, Cobbetto Ghiggia 2012) have been unable to explain why Androkles claimed one-fifth of the estate as the share belonging to one of Euktemon's daughters; so, although none has been able to suggest a credible alternative reading, all agree that the words πέμπτου μέρους are corrupt. Isaios' eighteenth century translator, William Jones (1779), accepted the text as it stands, taking it as an indication that if Euktemon had died leaving no descendants through a male line, his estate would have been divided *per capita* (and not *per stirpes*)[30] among all his surviving descendants: one-fifth each to his two daughters and three grandchildren (the daughter of Chaireas and the two sons of Phanostratos, i.e. Chairestratos and his brother). This interpretation gained some currency in the nineteenth century, with scholars such as Bunsen[31] and Schoemann[32] explaining that, if an *epiklēros* was claimed by her father's next of kin and divorced from her existing husband, it would be unfair to deprive her children from the first marriage of a share in their grandfather's estate. The idea has, however, been discredited by more recent scholars as being inconsistent with the rules of the epiklerate.[33] In fact, we know very little about the detailed operation of the epiklerate, especially when the woman in question was already married (or widowed) and had adult offspring, and our evidence of distribution *per stirpes* under Athenian law is not sufficient to warrant the assumption that it was a fixed rule. A full discussion of the issue is beyond the scope of this chapter, but it deserves further consideration as part of a wider re-appraisal of Athenian inheritance law.

Bibliography

Caccialanza, F.P. (1901) *Le orazione di Iseo*, Rome.
Caillemer, E. (1879) *Le droit de succession légitime à Athènes*, Paris.
Cobetto Ghiggia, P. (1999) *L'adozione ad Atene in epoca classica*, Alessandria.
Cobetto Ghiggia, P. (2012) *Iseo: Orazioni*, Alessandria.
Dareste, R. (1898) *Les plaidoyers d'Isée*, Paris.

30 Literally 'by branch'. When a dead person's estate is divided *per stirpes*, one share goes to each branch of the family, rather than to each individual as in a *per capita* division. So, in the example of Euktemon's family, distribution *per stirpes* would have given half of the estate to each of his daughters, then each of the halves would have been further subdivided among each daughter's surviving children when she died.

31 Cited approvingly by Moy 1876: 214, n. 1.

32 Cited dismissively by Caillemer 1879: 53–54.

33 See, e.g., Wyse 1904: 533–534.

Davies, J.K. (1971) *Athenian Propertied Families: 600–300 B.C.*, Oxford.
Edwards, M.J. (2007) *Isaeus*. Austin.
Forster. E.S. (1927) *Isaeus*, Cambridge, Ma.
Gernet, L. (1955) 'La diamartyrie procédure archaïque du droit athénien' in Gernet, L. (1955) *Droit et société dans la Grèce ancienne*, Paris, 83–102. (Originally published 1927.)
Griffith-Williams, B. (2013) *A Commentary on Selected Speeches of Isaios*, Leiden.
Harrison, A.R.W. (1968–1971) *The Law of Athens*, 2 vols, Oxford.
Jebb, R.C. (1876) *The Attic Orators from Antiphon to Isaeos*, vol. 2, London.
Jones, W. (1779) *The Speeches of Isaeus in Causes Concerning the Law of Succession to Property at Athens*, London.
Lambert, S. (1993) *The Phratries of Attica*, Ann Arbor, Mich.
MacDowell, D.M. (1978) *The Law in Classical Athens*, London.
Moy, L. (1876) *Étude sur les plaidoyers d'Isée*, Paris.
Naddeo, C. (2008) 'Nota a Iseo VI: per una nuova cronologia (§§1 e 27)', in C. Talamo, ed. (2008) *Saggi di commento a teste greci e latini*, Napoli, 17–30.
Roussel, P. (1926) *Isée: Discours*, Paris.
Schweigert, E. (1940) 'The Athenian Cleruchy on Samos', *AJP* 61, 194–198.
Todd, S.C. (1993) *The Shape of Athenian Law*, Oxford.
Wyse, W. (1904) *The Speeches of Isaeus*. Cambridge.

CHAPTER 6

Anakrisis and the Framing of Strategies of Argumentation in Athenian Public Trials

Christos Kremmydas

Anakrisis: a Little-Known Pre-trial Stage

The legal term *anakrisis* has been translated as 'previous examination of parties concerned in a suit' (*LSJ* ii), 'inquiry, examination' (*LSJ* iii), 'Vorprüfung'[1] and 'Vorverhandlung'.[2] In 1930 Bonner and Smith described it as 'an informal interrogation'.[3] More recently, MacDowell called it 'preliminary inquiry', while Todd and Lanni render it as 'preliminary hearing'.[4]

In the Athenian adversarial system, the pre-trial stage of *anakrisis* seems to have represented an inquisitorial element: the magistrate asked the two parties a number of specific questions while the litigants could also direct questions at each other. Although this question and answer session probably did not seek to arrive at the truth, it still sought to clarify important legal and procedural issues before the case could proceed any further.

In fifth-century prose the verb *anakrinō*/*anakrinomai* is used rarely with reference to interrogations in connection with criminal offences and, although one has to wait until the fourth century for attestations of the term *anakrisis* and its cognates as *termini technici*, these early attestations may echo a broader understanding of what the procedure involved.[5] Its historical origins are not known but it is not unlikely that it may represent a relic from an early period (possibly pre-Solonian) of the Athenian administration of justice

1 Lipsius 1905: 54–55.

2 Lämmli 1938: 72.

3 Bonner and Smith 1930: 292. They raise a number of issues about the nature and objective of this interrogation, which I shall return to later in this chapter.

4 MacDowell 1978: 240, Todd 1993: 360, Lanni 2006: 36.

5 Thuc. 1.95 (interrogation of King Pausanias by the Spartans), Antiph. 2.1.9 (where the participle ἀνακρινόμενος is use in conjunction with ἐξελεγχόμενος), 2.3.2, Andok. 1.101 (an example of Andokides' fictitious *anakrisis*-interrogation in the hands of Epichares if he had been arrested by the Thirty); cf. Lykourg. 1. 112 which describes the *anakrisis* of Archippos' accomplices in 411.

 | DOI:10.1163/9789004377899_008

when a single judge or *archōn* was responsible for the conduct of the trial and for delivering the verdict.[6]

We know very little about the *anakrisis* and the paucity of evidence prevents scholars from reconstructing it fully. A number of issues are still being contested among scholars: *inter alia* its significance for court proceedings, its objective, and whether evidence not presented before the magistrate at the *anakrisis* could be ushered in later, at the trial itself.

Some scholars, like Dorjahn, maintain that it was not a significant stage in the trial proceedings: 'some scholars seem to find it difficult to reconcile themselves to the thought that the anakrisis was a relatively insignificant and circumscribed thing in the fifth and fourth century.'[7]

In this chapter I first distinguish the *anakrisis* from other pre-trial stages in the Athenian justice system. I then proceed to give an overview of this pre-trial stage, examine what it involved and consider its objective within the Athenian administration of justice. Finally, I explore how information gathered by the litigants at the *anakrisis* informed and shaped their strategies of argumentation at the trial itself and conclude with an evaluation of its significance.

Pre-trial Proceedings in Athens: Arbitration (*diaita*) and *anakrisis*

Any Athenian could initiate legal proceedings by summoning the defendant to appear before a magistrate and submitting a plaint (called *enklēma* in private actions, *graphē* in public ones) to the magistrate. The defendant had to submit his own written response to the plaint (called *antigraphē*).[8] On the appointed day, both litigants appeared before the magistrate and responded to questions put to them by the magistrate himself or exchanged between them.

But the *anakrisis* is not the only pre-trial stage in the Athenian administration of justice that involved an examination by an *archōn* or a third, independent party (appointed by the two parties or the state) of the cases put forward by the parties to a dispute. It is well established that the character of the case determined what pre-trial stages took place.

Homicide trials were preceded by the so-called *prodikasiai*, a stage that involved three 'pre-trials' before the *basileus*, who was tasked with deciding

---

6 See Bonner and Smith 1930: 283 and MacDowell 1978: 240.

7 Dorjahn 1941: 182.

8 For a detailed account of the initiation of proceedings, see Harrison 1971: 85–94, Lipsius 1905: 829–844, Lämmli 1938: 74–128 and Harris 2013: 156–157.

whether the case should proceed to court or not.[9] While we do not know much else about what the *prodikasiai* involved, it is assumed that the litigants would have delivered speeches before the *basileus*.[10]

In private cases where a small amount (up to ten *drachmai*) was at stake, the two parties had to go through an arbitration stage (*diaita*), where both parties appeared before a mutually acceptable arbitrator(s) in the hope that the dispute might be resolved out of court. Private cases involving sums greater than ten *drachmai* were referred by the Forty to a public arbitrator appointed by the state (all Athenians over the age of fifty-nine had to serve as arbitrators). Only if arbitration was unsuccessful did the matter proceed to a full trial before a court. In cases where the arbitrator's verdict was rejected by the two parties, any evidence presented up until the arbitration was sealed in a clay jar (*echinos*) and no new evidence could be brought in when the case was brought to the *dikastērion*.[11] Conversely, most public cases and those private cases going before specific magistrates, e.g. the *archōn* or the *basileus*, did not have to go through *diaita*; the litigants proceeded to an *anakrisis* before the magistrate.

Although it would be wrong to minimise the differences between private and public procedures, and between the proceedings at the *diaita* and the *anakrisis*, it appears that the Athenian administration of justice sought to apply the principle of fairness by giving the two parties an opportunity to demonstrate the evidence they were going to use to support their respective cases (especially if the *diaita* proved unsuccessful, as a means of avoiding a court hearing) in advance of the trial proper.[12] This also suggests that the two parties might have also been familiar with each other's key arguments and evidence. Be that as it may, one should also examine the role played by the written plaint in relation to what went on in the *anakrisis*.

---

9 See Antiph. 6.42 with MacDowell 1963: 36–37, 1978, 118, and Phillips 2008: 74–76.

10 MacDowell 1978: 118 questions the rationale of having three *prodikasiai*, instead of just one.

11 The prohibition of introducing new evidence not previously presented up until the stage of *anakrisis* is called by German scholars *Neuerungsverbot*; see also *Ath. Pol.* 53.2 (and n. 29 below). On the dropping of cases at the *anakrisis* see Harrison 1971: 104–105, Harris 2006: 412–414.

12 Bonner and Smith 1930: I, 284 caution against blurring between the *diaita* and the *anakrisis* ('the *Ath. Pol.*'s description of arbitration cannot be transferred to the *anakrisis*'). On the principle of fairness in Athenian legal procedure in general, see Thür 2008: 51–73.

The *enklēma* and the *graphē*

In the fourth century, a period of increasing reliance on written evidence, the plaint would have played an increasingly important role in setting out the boundaries of the legal case to be tried in the court. It would have listed the names of the plaintiff and the defendant, the charges, and even the penalty proposed. In addition, it would have highlighted the law broken by the defendant. In private cases, it would have also included information about the key facts to be proved by the plaintiff. Harris argues that the plaint could be both very detailed and extensive, effectively laying out the structure of the prosecution's arguments and key written evidence.[13] But not all plaints would have been long and detailed; some would have been confined to the absolutely minimum legal information required and strategic considerations might have affected how much information was provided in it. It is not unlikely that it would have included only a key clause(s) from a relevant law, while the laws in their entirety were appended in separate documents brought to the magistrate during the *anakrisis* and, once the magistrate decided that the case should proceed to a trial, displayed in front of the monument of the Eponymous Heroes.

The plaint made the defendant aware of the charges laid against him while the plaintiff sought to ground these charges in specific laws. Thus both parties benefited from the existence of the plaint: on the one hand, by making public the charges and any supporting evidence, the plaintiff made it easier for the defendant to prepare his defence, his arguments, and supporting evidence. The defendant's own *antigraphē* laid out his counter-arguments and this gave the prosecutor an insight into the strategy of the defence. Equally importantly, the plaint also gave the magistrate the opportunity to look into the legal merits of the case and take a decision regarding its admissibility (*to eisagōgimon*).

However, to what extent did the plaint determine what was said at the *anakrisis* and at the trial proper? And if the plaint contained the blueprint for cases presented by the parties, how important were proceedings at the *anakrisis*? Furthermore, to what extent could the three-way exchange between plaintiff, defendant, and magistrate affect the rhetorical strategies adopted at the trial itself?

13 Harris 2013: 161.

Questions and Answers at the *anakrisis*

Gerhard Thür has called the *anakrisis* the 'dialectic segment' and the court hearing itself the 'rhetorical segment of the trial'.[14] By 'dialectic' Thür probably denotes briefer exchanges between the parties (and the *archōn*) compared to the more detailed analysis of the parties' respective cases with a view to persuading an audience of judges (*dikastai*), Thür's 'rhetorical segment'. A closer examination of the kind of exchanges involved at the *anakrisis* is necessary at this stage.

While the main legal charge(s) would have been made known as soon as the prosecutor had lodged his *graphē* or *enklēma* with the *archōn* and then at the summons, the *anakrisis* would have shed further light on the supporting evidence and even the basic outline of the strategies of argumentation that the two parties were going to follow. The magistrate would ask the two parties certain questions (more on which below) and the litigants themselves could also direct questions at one another. All the questions would be based on the charges made and any other information provided by the plaint.

A rare piece of evidence representing what might have gone on at the *anakrisis* comes from Isaios' speech *On the Estate of Philoktemon*, a speech delivered in a *dikē pseudomartyriōn*, which arose out of a dispute about a will. The speech is delivered by an unknown *synēgoros* ('supporting speaker')[15] who supports Chairestratos' claim that he had been adopted by his maternal uncle Philoktemon and through him inherited the estate of Philoktemon's father, Euktemon. Androkles, a kinsman of Euktemon, had blocked Chairestratos' claim with a *diamartyria*[16] testifying that the latter had left two legitimate sons from a marriage to a woman called Kallippe who were therefore entitled to Euktemon's[17] inheritance (and ultimately to Philoktemon's estate, too, as his legitimate half-brothers). Chairestratos brought a *dikē pseudomartyriōn* against Androkles. In the following passage the speaker is trying to prove that Androkles' attempt to pass off the two male children as legitimate children of Euktemon was based on flimsy evidence. In order to prove that, he goes back to the exchanges that took place at the *anakrisis*, where Androkles and his associate Antidoros claimed

14 Thür 2008: 55.

15 His name is not attested. Edwards 2007: 97 follows Davies 1971: 564 in suggesting that it might have been Aristomenes.

16 On the *diamartyria* in Isa. 6, cf. Griffith-Williams in this volume.

17 There is some ambiguity as to which estate was being disputed (e.g. 6.3–4, 56; 38 states that father and son had performed liturgies jointly). It is possible, as suggested by Davies 1971: 563 that the properties of Euktemon and Philoktemon had not been divided.

that the mother of Euktemon's alleged sons was a woman from Lemnos and thus an Athenian as the daughter of a cleruch. This claim apparently led to an adjournment that would enable them to find out more about the identity of this woman.

> Ὅτε γὰρ αἱ ἀνακρίσεις ἦσαν πρὸς τῷ ἄρχοντι καὶ οὗτοι παρακατέβαλον ὡς ὑπὲρ γνησίων τῶνδ' Εὐκτήμονος ὄντων, ἐρωτώμενοι ὑφ' ἡμῶν τίς εἴη αὐτῶν μήτηρ καὶ ὅτου θυγάτηρ, οὐκ εἶχον ἀποδεῖξαι, διαμαρτυρομένων ἡμῶν καὶ τοῦ ἄρχοντος κελεύοντος ἀποκρίνασθαι κατὰ τὸν νόμον. ⟨Καίτοι δεινόν⟩, ὦ ἄνδρες, ἀμφισβητεῖν μὲν ὡς ὑπὲρ γνησίων καὶ διαμαρτυρεῖν, μητέρα δὲ ἥτις ἦν μὴ ἔχειν ἀποδεῖξαι μηδὲ προσήκοντα αὐτοῖς μηδένα. Ἀλλὰ τότε μὲν Λημνίαν σκηψάμενοι ταύτην, ἀναβολὴν ἐποιήσαντο. Τὸ δ' ὕστερον ἥκοντες εἰς τὴν ἀνάκρισιν, πρὶν καί τινα ἐρέσθαι, εὐθὺς ἔλεγον ὅτι Καλλίππη μήτηρ, αὕτη δ' εἴη Πιστοξένου θυγάτηρ, ὡς ἐξαρκέσον εἰ ὄνομα μόνον πορίσαιντο τὸν Πιστόξενον. Ἐρομένων δ' ἡμῶν ὅστις εἴη καὶ εἰ ζῇ ἢ μή, ἐν Σικελίᾳ ἔφασαν ἀποθανεῖν στρατευόμενον, καταλιπόντα ταύτην θυγατέρα παρὰ τῷ Εὐκτήμονι, ἐξ ἐπιτροπευομένης δὲ τούτῳ γενέσθαι, πρᾶγμα πλάττοντες ἀναιδείᾳ ὑπερβάλλον καὶ οὐδὲ γενόμενον, ὡς ἐγὼ ὑμῖν ἀποφανῶ ἐκ τούτων πρῶτον ὧν αὐτοὶ ἀπεκρίναντο.
>
> When the preliminary hearings were taking place before the *archōn* and they had paid the court-deposit regarding their claim that these boys were legitimate sons of Euktemon, we asked them who was their mother and who her father was and they could not provide any names, even though we protested and the *archōn* ordered them to respond in accordance with the law. And it was certainly strange, gentlemen, that they had claimed that they (*sc.* the two boys) were legitimate sons and made a sworn deposition but could not provide the names of their mother or those of any relatives. At that time, they alleged that she was a Lemnian woman and obtained an adjournment. Later, when they returned to the preliminary hearing, even before anyone asked them, they immediately stated that Kallippe was their mother and that she was the daughter of Pistoxenos, as though the mere mention of the name Pistoxenos was going to suffice. And when we asked who he was and whether he was alive or not, they replied that he had been killed in Sicily during an expedition and had left this daughter at Euktemon's house. The latter apparently had the children by her while she was his ward—a made up story totally shameless and untrue, as I am going to prove to you from the very first responses they had given.
>
> ISA. 6.12–13

This passage suggests that the *archōn* did have an active role and could press a party to respond to a question ('in accordance with the law') that they might be tempted to duck (or might be unable to answer). The speaker is seeking to present the ignorance on the part of Androkles and Antidoros as part of a wider attempt to deceive the court through an improbable story (note 'a made up story totally shameless and untrue') which was presented to the court after the adjournment. The woman's name was Kallippe and her father's name was Pistoxenos who had died in Sicily. It is obvious that the important issue of the woman's paternity was not going to go away after the adjournment, hence the speaker's comment that the opponents stated the facts even though no one asked them. However, it is striking that the *archōn's* role is minimised in this second 'phase'. Both the mention of his intervention before the adjournment and his apparent silence at the resumption of the *anakrisis* are rhetorically significant as they help to demonstrate the weakness of the opponent's case.

In another passage from Isaios' speech *On the Estate of Aristarchos* the speaker alleges that at the *anakrisis* he had been compelled to add to his claim (προσγράψασθαι) at the *anakrisis* that his mother was Aristarchos' sister when in fact she was originally his aunt:[18]

> Ἠνάγκασμαι μὲν οὖν, ὦ ἄνδρες, διὰ τὸ μὴ δύνασθαι δίκην παρ' αὐτῶν λαβεῖν, τὴν μητέρα τὴν ἐμὴν ἐν τῇ ἀνακρίσει Ἀριστάρχου εἶναι ἀδελφὴν προσγράψασθαι· οὐ μὴν διὰ τοῦτο ὑμῖν ἡ διάγνωσις ἧττον περὶ αὐτῶν εὐκρινὴς γενήσεται, [ἀλλ'] ἐκ τῶν νόμων σκοποῦσιν εἰ τὰ ἑαυτοῦ δέδωκε τούτῳ Ἀρίσταρχος ἢ τὰ μηδὲν προσήκοντα.
>
> So, men of the jury, because I could not obtain justice from them, I have been forced to add to my claim at the preliminary hearing that my mother was a sister of Aristarchos. This will not, however, make your decision any easier as you consider whether Aristarchos bequeathed the estate to my opponent in accordance with the laws when it was his own or when he had no entitlement to it.
>
> ISA. 10.2

The speaker is at pains to argue that this 'addition' to his claim, which he appears to be uncomfortable about, should not compromise his overall rhetorical and legal position at the trial. However, given the placement of this state-

18 This might have been part of a written statement submitted at the *anakrisis* which he was compelled to amend to reflect his mother's relationship to Aristarchos junior after the latter's adoption by Aristarchos senior.

ment at the start of his speech, it is probably meant to address a weakness in his case.[19] In any case, this passage does suggest that at the *anakrisis* there was room for rhetorical manoeuvring, and that concessions could be made as a result of the triangular 'dialectical' process between the two parties and the magistrate. In inheritance cases, as exemplified in the two earlier passages from Isaios, the exact relationships between individuals and the reconstruction of the family tree would have been central not only to the questions and answers at the *anakrisis* but also of paramount importance to the course of the trial itself. But what kinds of questions did the *anakrisis* broach in other types of trials?

It is reasonable to assume that the questions would have been tailored to the type of suit and the legal issues at stake in each case. However, in the absence of conclusive evidence, we can only conjecture what questions the *archōn* and the litigants may have asked each other at an *anakrisis* preceding e.g. a *graphē paranomōn* or an *eisangelia*. Quite a lot would have depended on the wording of the charges in the *graphē* and their refutation in the *antigraphē*. The plaintiff would have probably needed to expound the procedural and substantive grounds for bringing the *graphē*, while the defendant would have had to refute the plaintiff's charges. Bonner and Smith reconstruct a series of questions that might have been asked at the *anakrisis* and I adapt them to a *graphē paranomōn or nomon mē epitēdeion theinai*:[20]

i) Was the plaintiff eligible to appear in court?
ii) Was the defendant qualified to answer the charge or the claim?
iii) Were the documents (*graphē* and *antigraphē*) properly drawn?
iv) Was the matter at issue actionable?
v) Was the proper form of action chosen?
vi) Did the magistrate have jurisdiction in the case?
vii) Was the action brought at the proper time according to the law?

However, such a reconstruction is, at best, sketchy. Certain questions, such as iv) and v) would have required more than yes or no answers or even a rudimentary exchange between the parties. The legal basis of the charges included in the plaint would also need to be discussed, too, so that the magistrate could reach a decision as to whether the matter should be referred to a law-court. It is likely that the question of the admissibility or inadmissibility of a *graphē*

19 Griffith-Williams 2013: 213–214 notes that the speaker is vague as to who compelled him to make this concession and argues that either the magistrate did not accept his original claim, or his opponent deceived him into changing his claim; alternatively, the speaker himself might have chosen to alter this key aspect of his claim.

20 Bonner and Smith 1930: I, 289.

((*mē*) *eisagōgimon einai tēn graphēn*: (μή) εἰσαγώγιμον εἶναι τὴν γραφήν) would have been contested even during the *anakrisis* as it could give rise to a *paragraphē* before the trial itself could commence.[21] But even where the magistrate's decision to admit a suit was not contested giving rise to a *paragraphē*, this did not actually stop litigants from raising the issue of inadmissibility during the trial.[22] The discussion of this issue at the *anakrisis* would have acted as a prelude to the more elaborate legal argumentation presented at the trial itself.

In Apollodoros' speech *Against Nikostratos* ([Dem.] 53.22–23), the speaker argues that at the first *anakrisis* his opponents had offered to hand over their slaves to him to be tortured (*proklēsis eis basanon*). Their alleged intention was to use the slave testimony extracted through torture as evidence at the trial itself. The speaker states that he declined the challenge because Arethousios' slaves belonged to the state (and were thus 'public') because their master was a state-debtor and therefore they could not be subjected to torture ([Dem.] 53.24). According to the speaker, this would have been both illegal and procedurally wrong. This passage, too, shows that the *anakrisis* was not a mere Question and Answer session between the two parties and the *archōn*; rhetorical strategy could be rehearsed and the two parties could attempt to learn more about or even influence each other's strategy at the trial. It also suggests that it was possible to use evidence (in this case the slave testimony resulting from their torture) that had not been presented at the *anakrisis* at the trial.

The Objective of the *anakrisis*

Modern scholars agree that the main objective of the *anakrisis* was to determine the admissibility of the suit and the framing of the charge. Harrison avers that 'the object of the exercise was to determine first whether there was an issue to be put to a dikastery (whether the case was εἰσαγώγιμος), and second

21 The question of admissibility of a suit might have been broached (but not fully discussed) already at the summons where the two parties appeared before the magistrage and agreed on a date for the *anakrisis*. It has to be noted at this point that our evidence for *paragraphai* relates to private actions but it cannot be ruled out that it was also used in connection with public cases which were considered to be inadmissible (a point also made by Todd 1993: 137). Further on *paragraphē* see Harrison 1971: 106–124, Todd 1993: 136–138, and Isager-Hansen 1975: 123–132.

22 It is theoretically possible for a suit to be dropped at the *anakrisis* due to the defendant's objection to the procedure followed before he could launch a *paragraphē*.

how exactly the question was to be framed. Some, if not all, of these questions must have arisen at the preliminary stage when the plaintiff made his first approach to the magistrate'.[23] MacDowell suggests, further, that this questioning '… would give each of them a clearer idea of what the other was alleging and what were the exact points in dispute, and it would help them to decide how it would be best to present their arguments in the trial and what supporting evidence would be needed'.[24]

MacDowell touches on two important and related issues here, both pointing to the rhetorical dimension of this preliminary stage: first, the question of what evidence was adduced at the *anakrisis* relative to the trial itself and, second, the extent to which the proceedings at the *anakrisis* helped shape the litigants' rhetorical strategy at the trial. I shall give a brief overview of the first issue before proceeding to a longer discussion of the second. It will become apparent that both issues relate to the principle of fairness that undergirded this preliminary stage of Athenian legal proceedings.

In *Das Attische Recht und Rechtsverfahren* Lipsius stressed the notion of the *Neuerungsverbot*,[25] namely that the plaintiff should make available all the relevant evidence at the *anakrisis* and could not introduce any new material at the trial.[26] Lämmli tried to modify this view, by arguing that the prohibition to introduce new material only affected cases that had first gone through official, public arbitration, therefore it did not apply to cases that had first gone through *anakrisis*.[27] In a similar vein, Bonner and Smith also argued that the fact that in our extant forensic speeches litigants often express uncertainty as to what their opponents would say in their speech suggests that all the evidence is unlikely to have been submitted at the *anakrisis*: 'There was no restriction on producing evidence for the first time at the trial'.[28] Thür, however, refutes the views of both Lämmli and Bonner and Smith and argues that the *Neuerungsverbot* also applied to the *anakrisis* but notes that such a prohibition would have been 'valid for *written records*, which were read out by the clerk to the court'. He goes on to stress that 'the virtual staged performance and rhetorical tricks just mentioned could not have been prevented by the *echinoi*'.[29] Thür tries to explain away passages implying that new arguments were introduced, sug-

23 Harrison 1971: 96–97.
24 MacDowell 1978: 241.
25 See definition in n. 11 above.
26 Lipsius 1905: 55.
27 Lämmli 1938: 75–128.
28 Bonner and Smith 1930: I, 286 (286–291 for further discussion).
29 Thür 2008: 58–64: in order to prove that *Neuerungsverbot* applied to the *anakrisis*, too,

gesting that they were not based on new written evidence. Whether one concurs or disagrees with Thür, it is worth exploring further whether familiarity with the range of documents available in support of a litigant's case as presented at the *anakrisis* affected the rhetorical strategy adopted during the trial itself.

There is no doubt that there were no restrictions on the introduction of new arguments during the trial that had not been used at the *anakrisis*. Even though the written *graphē* would have outlined the formal charges thus theoretically at least limiting the range of arguments to be used, it is more than likely that prosecutors (more so than defendants) would have employed arguments at the trial that would not necessarily have been presented at the *anakrisis* (e.g. different interpretations of laws). The opposition could always seek to undermine such arguments by claiming that they were irrelevant to the charges stated at the *anakrisis*. However, since there was no way of forestalling the use of such arguments, this could represent a tactical advantage that could make a difference in terms of the outcome of the trial. In sum, the exchanges between the litigants and the *archōn* at the *anakrisis* and the rudimentary argumentation presented in support of the charges effectively demonstrated which arguments were effective and how much room there was for the introduction of further arguments during the trial that could cause 'surprises' and were likely to wrongfoot the opponent (and his supporting speakers).

Both Lämmli and Thür discuss passages where the litigants appear to complain that they have been surprised by the use of certain pieces of evidence but, as Thür suggests, this may be a 'feigned surprise', a rhetorical ploy in the speaker's overall rhetorical strategy. I agree that although the written plaint and the discussion of the charges at the *anakrisis* does provide a footprint for the rhetorical strategy during the trial, we need to allow more room for rhetorical manoeuvring both at the *anakrisis* and during the court hearing. It is not possible, of course, to identify the range of arguments used at the *anakrisis* because they are not always identified as such but it is likely that litigants might try to wrongfoot or confuse their opponents by introducing new, previously unrehearsed arguments during the trial. This is the stage where rhetorical skill and strategy would have made a difference in terms of the outcome of the trial.

---

he points to the inscription on the lid of an *echinos* which states ἐξ ἀνακρίσεως ('from the *anakrisis*'; see Boegehold 1982) and to the 'structural similarity' of the obligatory *diaita* and the *anakrisis*.

Shaping Arguments and Strategies of Argumentation

On the face of it, it would seem that the Question and Answer session at the *anakrisis* operated on a principle of equity and fairness seeking to create a level playing field between the two litigants.[30] Having been made aware of the documents that each other were going to base their charges (and the refutation thereof) on and key arguments they were going to use, both litigants would be better placed to prepare their respective cases, for the plaintiff and the defendant respectively.[31] It is likely that the *anakrisis* would have favoured the plaintiff as the side speaking first at the trial, since it would have provided them with a better understanding of how the defence were likely to argue in response to their argumentation, but the defendant would have also been aware of arguments that the prosecution were likely to muster. Still, the prosecution might have had an opportunity to introduce 'pre-emptive strikes', namely new arguments not advanced before the magistrate at the *anakrisis*. Conversely, the defendant would have probably been resigned to refuting allegations made by the prosecutor both at the *anakrisis* and the trial itself. The speaker of Hypereides' *For Lykophron* (supporting speech in an *eisangelia*) puts it as follows:

> ἀλλ' οἶμαι, ὦ ἄνδρες δικασταί, πολλὰ πλεονεκτοῦσιν ἐν τοῖς ἀγῶσιν οἱ κατήγοροι τῶν φευγόντων· οἱ μὲν γὰρ διὰ τὸ ἀκίνδυνον αὐτοῖς εἶναι τὸν ἀγῶνα ῥᾳδίως ὅ τι ἂν βούλωνται λέγουσι καὶ καταψεύδονται, οἱ δὲ κρινόμενοι διὰ τὸν φόβον πολλὰ καὶ τῶν πεπραγμένων αὐτοῖς εἰπεῖν ἐπιλανθάνονται. ἔπειτα οἱ μὲν ἐπειδὰν πρότερον λόγον λάβωσιν, οὐ μόνον ἃ ἔχουσιν αὐτοὶ δίκαια περὶ τοῦ πράγματος λέγουσιν, ἀλλὰ συσκευάσαντες λοιδορίας ψευδεῖς κατὰ τῶν κρινομένων ἐξιστᾶσιν τῆς ἀπολογίας· ὥστε συμβαίνειν αὐτοῖς δυοῖν τὸ ἕτερον, ἢ περὶ τῶν ἔξωθεν διαβολῶν ἀπολογουμένοις τῆς περὶ τοῦ πράγματος ἀπολογίας ἀπολελεῖφθαι, ἢ μεμνημένοις τῶν προκατηγορηθέντων, οἴησιν καταλείπειν παρὰ τοῖς δικασταῖς ὅτι ἀληθῆ ἐστιν τὰ εἰρημένα. πρὸς δὲ τούτοις τούς τε μέλλοντας βοηθεῖν τοῖς φεύγουσιν προδιαβάλλουσι καὶ αὐτοῦ τοῦ κρινομένου τὴν ἀπολογίαν διαστρέφουσιν …[32]

30 As argued by Thür 2008: 51–53, *passim*.

31 The question remains whether the parties had to disclose all arguments (legal and paralegal?) or just the bare minimum. And did the clause *kata ton nomon* (see above) imply that there was the possibility of compulsion?

32 On how the defence should respond to the charges and what diversionary tactics Demosthenes is likely to use in his supporting speech for Ktesiphon see Aischin. 3.205–206; note also Aischines' exhortation to the *dikastai* (§206): … καὶ μὴ ἐᾶτε αὐτὸν ἔξω τοῦ παρανόμου

> But in my view, men of the jury, the prosecutors in a trial have many advantages over the defendants. It is easy for the former to say whatever they wish and lie as much as they want because they run no risk. On the other hand, the men who are on trial even forget to mention many of the things they have done because they are afraid. Moreover, because prosecutors speak first, they not only mention their just claims in the case, but they also invent unfounded slanders against the accused and force them to change their defence. Defendants thus have two options: either they defend themselves against the extraneous slanders and fail to make an adequate defence on the main issue, or they forget the accusations just made and leave the jury with the impression that they are true. What is more, the prosecution create prejudice against those who intend to help the defendants and distort the accused's own defence ...
>
> HYP. *Lyk.* 8–10

The speaker paints a sinister picture of Athenian legal process, where the plaintiffs have the upper hand over the defendants and are able to introduce extraneous and false allegations thus distorting the legal process by distracting the defence from the key charges at issue in the trial. He draws a stark contrast between 'legitimate claims' (δίκαια περὶ τοῦ πράγματος) and invented 'baseless slanders' (λοιδορίας ψευδεῖς). The former probably represents what was included in the plaint and discussed at the *anakrisis*, and what ought to be debated in the court hearing, too. The latter, conversely, reflects the rhetoric of the lawcourt, where the plaintiffs might have been able to develop accusations irrelevant to the charges included in the plaint. This may well be an exaggeration of the rhetorical advantage enjoyed by the plaintiffs who spoke first during the trial, but it may still suggest that the *anakrisis* was not achieving one of its intended objectives, namely the creation of a level playing field between the two litigants. The principle of fairness aimed for by the *anakrisis* could thus be adulterated to some extent. And if the courts could tolerate the introduction of slanders and extraneous allegations (see the passage above), they must have also heard arguments not relating to the charges as stated in the plaint and enunciated at the *anakrisis*. But can such new arguments be identified in the extant speeches delivered in Athenian public trials?

περιίστασθαι, ἀλλ' ἐγκαθήμενοι καὶ ἐνεδρεύοντες ἐν τῇ ἀκροάσει, εἰσελαύνετε αὐτὸν εἰς τοὺς τοῦ παρανόμου λόγους, καὶ τὰς εκτροπὰς αὐτοῦ τῶν λόγων ἐπιτηρεῖτε. ('... and do not let him move to issues outside the question of illegality, but watch and lie in wait for him as you listen and drive him into the discussion of the question of illegality and look for any digressions in his speech').

Due to the scarcity of references to the *anakrisis* in the surviving speeches of the Attic orators, it is difficult to distinguish between arguments that derived from the *anakrisis* and new arguments that found their way into the speeches through other means (e.g. Agora gossip, intelligence gathered through friends and associates).[33] This is further complicated by the fact that, when it comes to public cases in particular, arguments originally made at the *anakrisis* are likely to have been divided between teams of speakers (main speaker and *synēgoroi*) at the trial. What have come down to us through the extant speeches of the Attic orators are just some of the arguments that might have been used by a prosecution or defence team. Due to the complications of the endeavour, it is preferable to focus on anticipated arguments and arguments that purport to be anticipated, as they might shed light on how arguments rehearsed at the *anakrisis* could be used rhetorically at the trial itself.

There are, in my view, three types of anticipated arguments in extant public speeches and their identification or non-identification with the stage of the *anakrisis* may be significant from a rhetorical perspective: i) arguments clearly identified as having been brought up at the *anakrisis*; ii) those that may have been rehearsed at the *anakrisis* but are not clearly flagged up as such; iii) those arrived at through mere conjecture (or fabrication) by the speaker. The second type is the most difficult to identify. The use of the adverbs τάχα and ἴσως in the *formulae* used to introduce argument anticipation or pseudo-anticipation (e.g. οὗτος ἴσως ἐρεῖ … 'he (*sc.* my opponent) may say …'), but also the use of the third-person singular or plural when quoting an argument of the opposition (φησίν/φασίν: he/they argue …) may be flagging up arguments of the third type, arguments not necessarily brought up by the opponent at the *anakrisis* but still mentioned by the speaker for reasons to do with his rhetorical strategy.

A key question, of course, is why a speaker would want to identify an argument as one that was brought up at the *anakrisis* or, conversely, why they would want to conceal the fact that it had first been broached at the *anakrisis*? It is possible that this was a means of highlighting controversial arguments advanced by the opposition. By suggesting that an argument had already been addressed at the *anakrisis*, the speaker probably indicated that it had lost much of its effectiveness and could thus be refuted emphatically. Conversely, not identifying arguments as originating from the *anakrisis* may indicate the fact that the speaker was dealing with a strong argument or an objection that had been raised at the *anakrisis* and needed to be dealt with and refuted. Alternatively,

33 On anticipation of arguments see Dorjahn 1935: 274–295.

if the argument in question had nothing to do with the *anakrisis*, it might represent an attempt on the part of the plaintiff to wrongfoot the defendant by pretending to address an argument that they were never going to raise anyway.

The passage below exemplifies the second category of anticipated arguments and may go back to the *anakrisis* although this is not explicitly flagged up. The insinuation that the argument is deceptive (ἀπάγων ὑμᾶς ἀπὸ τούτων; '... Leptines may try to carry you away from these considerations ...') is intended to weaken further what might be a strong argument for the defence:[34]

> Τάχα τοίνυν ἴσως ἐκεῖνο λέγειν ἂν ἐπιχειρήσειε Λεπτίνης, ἀπάγων ὑμᾶς ἀπὸ τούτων, ὡς αἱ λῃτουργίαι νῦν μὲν εἰς πένητας ἀνθρώπους ἔρχονται, ἐκ δὲ τοῦ νόμου τούτου λῃτουργήσουσιν οἱ πλουσιώτατοι.
>
> Now, Leptines may perhaps try to carry you away from these considerations by using this argument, namely that the liturgies now fall on poor people, whereas through this law they will be performed by the richest.[35]
>
> DEM. 20.18

As far as their content is concerned, arguments likely to originate in the *anakrisis* (types i, ii above) seem to focus primarily on questions of procedure and the phrasing of laws as well as on key legal arguments, all issues at the heart of the *anakrisis*.

Anticipation of Arguments, Their Character, and the *anakrisis*

i *Arguments about Procedure*

Anticipated arguments that derive (or are likely to derive) from the *anakrisis* seem to focus primarily on aspects of procedure, an issue at the heart of proceedings at the *anakrisis* and relevant to the key question of admissibility. In the the speech *Against Leptines*, Demosthenes is seeking to persuade the *dikastai* that Apsephion's alternative proposal should replace Leptines' law if the latter were to be repealed as a result of the trial. He has this draft law read out to the *dikastai* and expounds its merits. It is in this context that he anticipates

34 The fact that he devotes six sections (18–23) to the refutation of this argument suggests its perceived importance.

35 Cf. also Dem. 22.5–8.

potential objections on the part of Leptines' team as to the illegality of this suggested procedure. It is then that he recalls an objection originally put forward by Leptines at the *anakrisis* and makes a rather clumsy attempt at undermining it:[36]

> … ἃ δὲ πρὸς τοῖς θεσμοθέταις ἔλεγεν, ταῦτ' ἴσως λέγων παράγειν ὑμᾶς ζητήσει. ἔφη γὰρ ἐξαπάτης εἵνεκα παραγεγράφθαι τοῦτον τὸν νόμον, ἐὰν δ' ὃν αὐτὸς ἔθηκεν λυθῇ, τοῦτον οὐ τεθήσεσθαι. ἐγὼ δ', ὅτι μὲν τῇ ὑμετέρᾳ ψήφῳ τοῦ τούτου νόμου λυθέντος τὸν παρεισενεχθέντα κύριον εἶναι σαφῶς ὁ παλαιὸς κελεύει νόμος, καθ' ὃν οἱ θεσμοθέται τοῦτον ὑμῖν παρέγραψαν, ἐάσω, ἵνα μὴ περὶ τούτου τις ἀντιλέγῃ μοι, ἀλλ' ἐπ' ἐκεῖν' εἶμι. ὅταν ταῦτα λέγῃ δήπου, ὁμολογεῖ μὲν εἶναι βελτίω καὶ δικαιότερον τόνδε τὸν νόμον οὗ τέθεικεν αὐτός, ὑπὲρ δὲ τοῦ πῶς τεθήσεται ποιεῖται τὸν λόγον.
>
> As for what he told the *thesmothetai*, he may say the same things trying to mislead you. For he argued that our law had been deceptively introduced as a replacement and will not be enacted if the law he passed were to be repealed. As for me, in order to avoid any objections, I will omit the fact that the old law, according to which the *thesmothetai* allowed us to introduce this replacement law, clearly orders that as soon as his law is repealed, the one that has been introduced as a replacement should be enacted, and will move to my next point. When he is saying these things he admits, I presume, that our law is better and fairer than his own but turns the discussion to how the law should be enacted.
>
> DEM. 20.98–99

Leptines' objection was a justified one, as Apsephion and his *synēgoroi* were pushing for the automatic replacement of the repealed law by a new one; this was not warranted by the law on *nomothesia*. Demosthenes felt that this was one of his weak points and thus likely to be attacked by Leptines and preempted such an attack by arguing that his opponent is a pedant who cares more about procedure than about the substance of the law. As far as our understanding of the *anakrisis* is concerned, this passage suggests that, although Leptines' side had justified objections regarding the legality of the procedure of replacing Leptines' law with a new law as proposed by the prosecution team, the magistrates did not intervene to stop this because it was not part of their jurisdiction. Nevertheless, the argument supporting the prosecution's proposal was put to

36 See Kremmydas 2012 ad loc.

the *dikastai* to consider and by addressing the defence's objections, first aired at the *anakrisis*, Demosthenes hopes to weaken their potential effect on the audience when the defence team take the *bēma*.

In Demosthenes' *Against Androtion*, a supporting speech in public prosecution for having proposed an illegal proposal—*graphē paranomōn*, the speaker (Diodoros) refutes a key argument advanced by Androtion, namely that the allegations of prostitution made against him should not have been made in the current trial (22.21). Instead, they should have formed the subject of a separate suit. This, according to Androtion's objection, would have exposed the prosecutor to risk, had he failed to persuade one-fifth of the *dikastai* of the guilt of his opponent.[37] This passage sheds precious light on how the rhetorical strategies at the trial interacted with what had been said at the *anakrisis*. We can see, for instance, how the defendant castigates the sneaking of a new legal argument about prostitution into a public case of *graphē paranomōn*. He claims that this tactic is defamatory and slanderous (βλασφημία, λοιδορία) thus recalling the defence tactic also employed by the speaker in Hypereides' *For Lykophron*: anything not brought up at the *anakrisis* or included in the plaint is labelled λοιδορία ('slander') and thus should not be brought up in the lawcourt. But Diodoros goes on to respond to Androtion's key objection and touching on the issue of legal procedure, which is likely to have been raised at the *anakrisis*:

> ὅταν δ' ὅτι πρὸς τοὺς θεσμοθέτας προσῆκεν ἐπαγγέλλειν ἡμῖν, ἐκεῖνο ὑπολαμβάνετε, ὅτι καὶ τοῦτο ποιήσομεν καὶ νῦν προσηκόντως περὶ τοῦ [24] νόμου λέγομεν.
>
> And when he argues we should have brought a charge before the *thesmothetai*, consider this point that we will also do this, but now we are discussing the law in the appropriate manner.
>
> DEM. 22.23

He pledges (22–24) that they (the prosecution team) are going to bring a separate prosecution against Androtion at an unspecified time in the future and defends the relevance of making the allegation of prostitution in the context of the current *graphē paranomōn*.[38] It appears then that the defence can make a point that seems to be about the procedure and the relevance of new charges brought up in court.

---

37 I.e. the penalty for frivolous prosecution (1,000 *drachmai*); see Harris 1999.

38 Cf. the 'pledge' made by Demosthenes at Dem. 20.9 with Kremmydas 2012 ad loc.

Earlier in the same speech (22.5), Diodoros had addressed another key legal argument that is likely to have featured at the *anakrisis*. Androtion's honorific decree had not gone through *probouleusis*, the preliminary vetting by the Council. The decree's proposer had maintained the legality of the process he followed: he had defended the absence of a *probouleuma* on the grounds that the law allowed the *dēmos* to award the *Boulē* honours without a *probouleuma*, as long as the Council was deemed to have conducted its affairs in a worthy manner. Androtion is also expected to argue that there was a strong precedent for such an award:

> Ἔστι γὰρ εἷς μὲν ὃν οἴεται τεχνικῶς ἔχειν αὐτῷ λόγος περὶ τοῦ ἀπροβουλεύτου. νόμος ἐστί, φησίν, ἐὰν ἀξίως ἡ βουλὴ δοκῇ βουλεῦσαι δωρειᾶς, διδόναι τὸν δῆμον τὴν δωρειὰν αὐτῇ. ταῦτ' ἐπήρετο, φησίν, ὁ ἐπιστάτης, διεχειροτόνησεν ὁ δῆμος, ἔδοξεν. οὐδὲν δεῖ, φησί, προβουλεύματος ἐνταῦθα· κατὰ γὰρ νόμον ἦν τὰ γιγνόμενα ... [6] φησὶ τοίνυν τοῦτον ἁπάσας τὸν τρόπον εἰληφέναι τὰς βουλάς, ὅσαι πώποτ' ἔχουσι παρ' ὑμῶν δωρειάν, καὶ οὐδὲ μιᾷ γεγενῆσθαι προβούλευμα πώποτε.
>
> For, he has one argument, which he thinks is clever, namely regarding his failure to obtain a preliminary decree from the Council. 'There is a law' he argues 'that if the Council appears to deserve an award for performing its duties, the Assembly may grant the award'. He argues that 'the president asked the question, the Assembly cast its vote, and the motion was passed. 'There is no need', he argues, 'for a preliminary decree in this case. For everything was done in accordance with the law'.' [6] Now, then, he argues that all the Councils that have ever received an award from you have received it in this way and there was never a preliminary motion passed for even one of them.
>
> DEM. 22.5–6

These two arguments come across as too central to the opposition's case for them not to have been broached at the *anakrisis*. Once again, the issue of procedure is central to the argumentation of the defence and this is something that goes back to the exchanges at the *anakrisis*. This occasion would have given the prosecution team the chance to identify the defendant's strongest argument and thus anticipate and refute it at the trial.[39]

---

39 Cf. anticipation of argument about the charge of *aprobouleuton* at Dem. 23.92–93.

ii *Arguments about Law or the (Wording of) Legal Arguments*

Another passage from the speech *Against Leptines* seems to raise an important legal point about the wording of Leptines' law:

> … καὶ παρανομίας δόξαν αἰσχίστην τῇ πόλει καταλείπει. ἴστε γὰρ δήπου τοῦθ' ὅτι τῶν τὰ δεινόταθ' ἡμᾶς ἀδικούντων ἓν ἑκάστῳ τίμημ' ὑπάρχει διὰ τὸν νόμον, ὃς διαρρήδην λέγει 'μηδὲ [ὡς χρὴ] τίμημ' ὑπάρχειν ἐπὶ κρίσει πλέον ἢ ἕν, ὁπότερον ἂν τὸ δικαστήριον τιμήσῃ, παθεῖν ἢ ἀποτεῖσαι· ἀμφότερα δὲ μὴ ἐξέστω.' ἀλλ' οὐχ οὗτος ἐχρήσατο τούτῳ τῷ μέτρῳ, ἀλλ' ἐάν τις ἀπαιτήσῃ χάριν ὑμᾶς, 'ἄτιμος ἔστω' φησὶ 'καὶ ἡ οὐσία δημοσία ἔστω.' δύο τιμήματα ταῦτα. 'εἶναι δὲ καὶ ἐνδείξεις καὶ ἀπαγωγάς· ἐὰν δ' ἁλῷ, ἔνοχος ἔστω τῷ νόμῳ ὃς κεῖται, ἐάν τις ὀφείλων ἄρχῃ τῷ δημοσίῳ.' θάνατον λέγει· τοῦτο γὰρ ἐστ' ἐπ' ἐκείνῳ τοὐπιτίμιον. οὐκοῦν τρία τιμήματα ταῦτα. πῶς οὖν οὐ σχέτλιον καὶ δεινόν, ὦ ἄνδρες Ἀθηναῖοι, εἰ χαλεπώτερον εἶναι παρ' ὑμῖν δόξει χάριν εὖ ποιήσαντ' ἀπαιτεῖν ἢ τὰ δεινότατ' ἐργαζόμενον ληφθῆναι;
>
> … but also because it leaves the city with a most disgraceful reputation of illegality. For you know, of course, that there is one penalty for each one of those who commit the most horrible offences in accordance with the law which states explicitly: 'at a trial there should be no more than a single penalty, either corporal or financial, whichever the court decides to impose; it should not be both'. But this man has not used this measure, but instead, if anyone requests a favour of you, he is saying 'he should be stripped of his honours' and 'his property should be confiscated'. These are two penalties. 'There should also be denunciations and summary arrests. And if he gets convicted he should be guilty according to the law which concerns magistrates serving while in debt to the state'. In other words, the death penalty; for this is the penalty for this offence. Therefore, these are three penalties. So, is it not detestable and terrible, men of Athens, if it will become more difficult in our city to request a gift for a benefaction than to be caught committing the worst offences?
>
> DEM. 20.155–156

Could this legal argument about the phrasing of the law have been brought up during the *anakrisis*? The possibility cannot be ruled out but it is interesting that Demosthenes does not go on to have the clause of the law he quotes ('μηδὲ ὡς χρὴ τίμημ' ὑπάρχειν ἐπὶ κρίσει πλέον ἢ ἕν, ὁπότερον ἂν τὸ δικαστήριον τιμήσῃ, παθεῖν ἢ ἀποτεῖσαι: ἀμφότερα δὲ μὴ ἐξέστω'.) read out to the *dikastai*. This suggests that the law in question had not been included in the *graphē*. It is therefore more likely that Demosthenes' legal argument would have been more effective in the context of the trial proper than at the *anakrisis*. It would have wrongfooted the defence by causing them to spend valuable time on its refutation.

Another anticipation of a legal argument, likely to have been brought up at the *anakrisis* occurs in Aischines, *Against Timarchos* 160. Aischines devotes space to the refutation of the opposition's argument that the allegation of prostitution cannot be substantiated unless a written contract is produced. This is a key argument of the defence, which seeks to refute the charge of prostitution on the basis of absence of evidence, thus implying that the charge is unfounded. And a little later (§166) after making a legal argument about prostitution by contract he comments that Demosthenes was going to try diversionary tactics and, crucially, would abuse the law of the *polis*, once again alluding to well-known defence strategies:

> Ἀλλ' ὅμως οὕτω σαφῶς τούτων διωρισμένων, πολλαὶ παρεμβολαὶ λόγων ὑπὸ Δημοσθένους εὑρεθήσονται. Καὶ ταῖς μὲν ὑπὲρ τοῦ πράγματος κακοηθείαις λεγομέναις ἧττον ἄν τις ἀγανακτήσειεν· ἃ δὲ ἔξωθεν ἐπεισάξεται λυμαινόμενος τὰ τῆς πόλεως δίκαια, ἐπὶ τούτοις ἄξιόν ἐστιν ὀργισθῆναι.
>
> Yet, although these issues have been defined so clearly, Demosthenes will discover many diversionary arguments. And the wickedness of his statements regarding the main issue might not arouse so much resentment. But the irrelevant arguments he will introduce to the detriment of the city's system of justice deserve your anger.
>
> AISCHIN. 1.166

Conclusion

It is unlikely that the *anakrisis* would have revealed the full detail of the rhetorical strategies that the litigants were likely to employ at the trial. After all, it did not give both parties ample time and space to develop any strategies in full. The presentation of relevant documents in support of the charges and key arguments about procedure, the wording, and the substance of the charges would have dominated this Question and Answer session between the litigants. After all, its main objective was to persuade the magistrate to admit the charge and set a date for a trial, not an audience of *dikastai*. Yet the awareness of such key arguments and the way they were likely to be framed would have still proved invaluable to the litigants as they prepared their strategies of argumentation for the trial and would have gauged their respective strengths and weaknesses. It also enabled them to anticipate and refute arguments of the opposition and introduce new arguments that the opposition would not expect. Associating arguments with the *anakrisis* (whether the arguments had been rehearsed at the *anakrisis* or not) was a rhetorical tactic of attracting attention to the speaker's refutation of such arguments and thus implicitly characterising them as controversial, weak and unconvincing. But both parties and especially the plaintiff were also better placed to introduce new arguments that were likely to confuse, wrongfoot the opponent. And while the plaint itself would have represented a legal foot-print on which to base argumentation at the trial, the *anakrisis* would have provided the parties with vital intelligence in terms of the ways in which arguments were likely to be received by the dikastic audience. Alongside the plaint, it would have provided parties with a basic road-map, which litigants could follow as they prepared their strategies of argumentation ahead of the trial.[40]

Bibliography

Boegehold, A.L. (1982) 'A Lid with a *Dipinto*', *Hesperia Supplements* 19, 1–6.

Bonner, R.J. and Smith, G. (1930–1938) *The Administration of Justice from Homer to Aristotle* (2 vols), Chicago.

Davies, J.K. (1971) *Athenian Propertied Families: 600–300 B.C.*, Oxford.

Dorjahn, A.P. (1935) 'Anticipation of Arguments in Athenian Courts', *TAPA* 66, 274–295.

Dorjahn, A.P. (1941) 'On the Athenian *anakrisis*', *CP* 36, 182–185.

Edwards, M.J. (2007) *Isaeus*. Austin.

Griffith-Williams, B. (2013) *A Commentary on Selected Speeches of Isaios*, Leiden.

Harris, E.M. (1999) 'The Penalty for Frivolous Prosecution in Athenian Law', *Dike* 2, 123–142.

Harris, E.M. (2006) *Democracy and the Rule of Law in Classical Athens: Essays on Law, Society, and Politics*, Cambridge.

Harris, E.M. (2013) 'The Plaint in Athenian Law and Legal Procedure', in Faraguna, M., ed. (2013) *Archives and Archival Documents in Ancient Societies*, Trieste, 143–162.

Harrison, A.R.W. (1968–1971) *The Law of Athens*, 2 vols, Oxford.

Isager, S. and Hansen, M.H. (1975) *Aspects of Athenian Society in the Fourth Century B.C.*, Odense.

40 I am grateful to the editors for their invitation to contribute to this volume and for their insightful comments on an earlier version of this chapter.

Kremmydas, C. (2012) *A commentary on Demosthenes'* Against Leptines, Oxford.

Lämmli, F. (1938) *Das attische Prozessverfahren und ihre Wirkung auf die Gerichtsrede*, Paderborn.

Lanni, A. (2006) *Law and Justice in the Courts of Classical Athens*, Cambridge.

Lipsius, J.H. (1905–1915) *Das attische Recht und Rechtsverfahren*, 3 vols, Leipzig.

MacDowell, D.M. (1963) *Athenian Homicide Law in the Age of the Orators*, Manchester.

MacDowell, D.M. (1978) *The Law in Classical Athens*, London.

Phillips, D.D. (2008) *Avengers of Blood: Homicide in Athenian Law and Custom from Draco to Demosthenes*, Stuttgart.

Thür, G. (2008) 'The Principle of Fairness in Athenian Legal Procedure: Thoughts on the *echinos and enklema*', *Dike* 11, 51–73.

Todd, S.C. (1993) *The Shape of Athenian Law*, Oxford.

CHAPTER 7

The Postponement of the Trial by Jury in Athens: the Timing of the *graphē paranomōn*

László Horváth

In this chapter I examine the phenomenon of the postponement or adjournment of the trial in the so-called *graphē paranomōn* lawsuits. The best known classical example is the Crown lawsuit (that is, Aischines' prosecution of Ktesiphon for the proposal of an award to Demosthenes) where the trial by jury followed the indictment laid by Aischines in 336 BC, six years later, in 330 BC.[1] The same phenomenon can also be observed in the Diondas case concerning Hypereides, where four years passed between the indictment and the trial.[2]

In both cases, the background of current internal politics can be more or less reconstructed, but we are not told the legal basis of the postponement. The authors of the major works and papers dealing with the *graphē paranomōn* and the similar *graphē nomon mē epitēdeion theinai*, such as Lipsius, Gerner, Wolff, Hansen, MacDowell and Yunis—just to mention the most significant contributions—acknowledge this deficiency in our sources and at the same time they try to modify the standpoint of *non liquet* with *testimonia* borrowed from other types of lawsuits.[3] The question of the penalties in connection with dropping a *graphē*—which is also related to the phenomenon of postponement—has been discussed by Wallace and particularly by Harris more recently.[4] Although the new data from the Diondas speech can only supplement their statements, I think it can also help us to elaborate our present picture of the phenomenon to some extent.[5]

In the case of the *graphē paranomōn*, after the discussion of the proposed decrees or after the declaration on oath (*hypōmosia*) of intention to prosecute,

1 Wankel 1976: 20; Lipsius 1905–1915: 903.

2 Horváth 2008: 27 ff.

3 Cf. Gerner 1949: 1281 ff.; Wolff 1970; Hansen 1987: 63 ff. particularly 64, n. 11.; Hansen 1974; MacDowell 1990: 327 f.; Yunis 2001: 11.

4 Harris 1999b: 123 ff.; Wallace 2006: 57 ff.; Harris 1999a: 67 ff. Most recently: cf. Sato's chapter in this volume.

5 I have already partially discussed the question in an earlier paper focusing on various issues connected to the new Hypereides text: Horváth 2009: 187 ff. Here, I have carried out a more thorough analysis of the phenomenon with new elements.

 | DOI:10.1163/9789004377899_009

the prosecutor laid the indictment before the *thesmothetai*, who determined the date of the trial.[6] The effect in either case was to suspend the proposed decree. The decree was not implemented before the judgment of the jury. The legal procedure could be postponed in two phases: through the postponement of the introduction of the indictment and by interfering with the determination of the date of the trial.

One can find only one—partly debated—example for the first possibility, i.e. for the postponement of the indictment.[7] In the Crown speech, Demosthenes describes how his political opponents tried to impede the reform of the trierarchy initiated by Demosthenes, more specifically with its proposal. The leaders of the *symmoriai* wanted to bribe Demosthenes so that he would let the case fade away after they took their oath (*hypōmosia*) which had the effect of suspending the proposed decree or law until the decision of the jury:

> ἔθηκα νόμον καθ' ὃν τοὺς μὲν τὰ δίκαια ποιεῖν ἠνάγκασα, τοὺς πλουσίους, τοὺς δὲ πένητας ἔπαυσ' ἀδικουμένους, τῇ πόλει δ' ὅπερ ἦν χρησιμώτατον, ἐν καιρῷ γίγνεσθαι τὰς παρασκευὰς ἐποίησα. καὶ γραφεὶς τὸν ἀγῶνα τοῦτον εἰς ὑμᾶς εἰσῆλθον καὶ ἀπέφυγον, καὶ τὸ μέρος τῶν ψήφων ὁ διώκων οὐκ ἔλαβεν. καίτοι πόσα χρήματα τοὺς ἡγεμόνας τῶν συμμοριῶν ἢ τοὺς δευτέρους καὶ τρίτους οἴεσθέ μοι διδόναι, ὥστε μάλιστα μὲν μὴ θεῖναι τὸν νόμον τοῦτον, εἰ δὲ μή, καταβάλλοντ' ἐᾶν ἐν ὑπωμοσίᾳ; τοσαῦτ', ὦ ἄνδρες Ἀθηναῖοι, ὅσ' ὀκνήσαιμ' ἂν πρὸς ὑμᾶς εἰπεῖν.

> I proposed a law through which I compelled some, the rich, to assume their fair burden, stopped the unjust treatment of the poor, and brought about what the city most needed—armed forces ready for action. I was indicted, came before you to stand trial on this issue, and was acquitted, the prosecutor failing to win even his minimum share of the votes. Yet how much money do you think I was offered by the heads of the symmories, as well as by the citizens in the second and third ranks, to refrain from bringing the law forward or, failing that, to let it drop in the event of an indictment? So much, Athenians, that I hesitate to tell you.
>
> DEM. 18.102–104[8]

6 About the procedure see Lipsius 1905–1915: 901 ff.; and Hansen 1999: 205 ff.

7 It is impossible to decide whether this was a *graphē paranomōn* or whether it offers the only example of a *hypōmosia* in a *graphē nomon mē epitēdeion theinai*. Cf. Wankel 1976: 565 ff. and 558 ff.; and Lipsius 1905–1915: 389, n. 55–57.

8 Trans. Yunis 2005, with slight adaptation.

There is no need for the trial. The proposer could simply let his proposal rest in response to the declaration of intention to prosecute by *graphē paranomōn*: καταβάλλοντ' ἐὰν ἐν ὑπωμοσίᾳ. However, Demosthenes submitted a further independent proposal so that he could appear before the court with his original proposal—thus he demanded an immediate trial with a decree (ψήφισμα καθ' ὃ εἰσῆλθον τὴν γραφήν).[9] This was the only way in which he could force a decision on the legality of his proposal and ensure that it could take effect and with it his reform of the trierarchic system. Since no other source is available for this phenomenon, Lipsius was right to conclude that with all probability no legislation controlled the introduction of the indictment into the court after the *hypōmosia*. The case of Demosthenes shows that the admission to court could be forced, but equally the case could be left to fade away for ever.[10] There was only one thing that could pressure the Athenian citizen acting as volunteer prosecutor who took the oath, the *hypōmosia*: if he wanted to prosecute the proponent in person, he had to lay the indictment within a year, otherwise only the law or decree could be prosecuted, while the author was not punished, as personal liability expired after that interval of time.[11]

---

9 Dem. 18.105. Cf. Yunis 2001: 172: 'The nature of this decree can only be guessed at: it may have been moved by D. or an associate to force a judicial decision on the proposed law and thus remove it from the legal limbo created by *hypōmosia*. The short time, in which D.'s law was proposed, indicted, enacted, and implemented, all in the summer and fall of 340, suggests that D. pressed the issue hard'. Also Lipsius 1905–1915: 389, n. 57 clearly gives the interpretation that in chapter 105 Demosthenes does not refer to the original law, but to a further decree forcing the legal action. Similarly, Wankel 1976: 572. The law and the *psēphisma* are regarded as identical by Atkinson 1939: 107ff. particularly 119; and by de Laix 1973: particularly 57f., who follows this latter interpretation.

10 Lipsius 1905–1915: 395: 'Aus demselben Beispiele ist auch klar ersichtlich, wie der Zweck der Hypomosie lediglich der war, die Beschlussfassung über ein Gesetz oder Psephisma oder wenigstens ihr Inkrafttreten bis zur gerichtlichen Entscheidung zu verhindern und wie es also durchaus nicht immer im Interesse derer, die die Hypomosie einlegten, gelegen war, ihr die Anklage folgen zu lassen, wozu sie in dem Falle des Demosthenes, wie gezeigt, durch besonderen Volksbeschluss gezwungen werden mussten. Je gefährlicher somit die Waffe war, die den Gegnern einer Maßnahme in die Hand gegeben war, um so näher liegt es zu vermuten, dass die Gesetzgebung Vorkehrungen getroffen hatte, um für Maßregeln von besonderer Dringlichkeit die Suspensivkraft der Hypomosie einzuschränken. Da hierauf aber nicht die geringste Spur in unserer Überlieferung hinweist, so müssen wir glauben, dass man eine ausreichende Schutzwehr gegen solchen Missbrauch des Instituts in der Gefahr erblickt hat, der sein Urheber sich aussetzte. Wurde auf sofortige Erreichung jenes Zweckes kein Gewicht gelegt, so wird die Hypomosie keine Anwendung gefunden haben. Der Einbringung der Klage aber selbst bedurfte es, um für ein Psephisma den Antragsteller auch über die Dauer eines Jahres hinaus verantwortlich zu machen'.

11 For a concise summary of the procedure of the *graphē paranomōn* see Gerner 1949: 1286ff.; and Hansen 1999: 205ff.

The second possible phase of the delay could be realised in the adjournment of the trial in court. As is usual in the analysis of the *graphē paranomōn*, we need to rely on data from other analogous types of lawsuit. This is true for instance for the attested penalties (fine and partial, then complete (?) *atimia*) which have previously been discussed in detail.[12] However, for our purposes, in a wider context it is not the kind of penalty imposed that is interesting. It would be more important to know at which stage of the legal procedure the prosecutor or the person taking the initial *hypōmosia* of indictment was liable to this penalty. (This deadline is not usually indicated clearly in the secondary literature, which speaks only of liability.) A fragment from Theophrastos' *Laws*—corroborating the much debated passages of the orators—clearly states that the prosecutor was liable to a penalty only if he did not take the case to resolution *after* laying the indictment:

> πρόστιμον ἔκειτο τῷ μὴ μεταλαβόντι τὸ πέμπτον μέρος τῶν ψήφων, ὡς Θεόφραστος ἐν πέμπτῳ περὶ νόμων· ἐν δὲ τοῖς δημοσίοις ἀγῶσιν ἐζημιοῦντο χιλίαις καὶ πρόσεστί τις ἀτιμία, ὥστε μὴ ἐξεῖναι μήτε γράψασθαι παρανόμων μήτε φαίνειν μήτε ἐφηγεῖσθαι· ἐὰν δέ τις γραψάμενος μὴ ἐπεξέλθῃ, ὁμοίως· περὶ δὲ τῆς εἰσαγγελίας, ἐάν τις μὴ μεταλάβῃ τὸ πέμπτον μέρος τῶν ψήφων, οἱ δικασταὶ τιμῶσιν.[13]
>
> A fine was applicable for the man who did not obtain the one-fifth of the votes, as Theophrastos (says) in his fifth (book) of *On Laws*; in the public trials they were fined with one thousand *drachmai* and additionally disfranchisement, so that it was not possible either to introduce a *graphē paranomōn*, or a *phasis* or *ephēgēsis*. If one does not proceed (with the case), having introduced a *graphē*, the same applies. As far as *eisangelia* is concerned, if one does not obtain the one-fifth of the votes, the dikasts will determine a penalty.

12 N. 4, above, and cf. MacDowell 1990: 327 f.

13 *Lex. Rhet. Cant.* s.v. πρόστιμον = Theophr. fr. 636c (Forthenbaugh et al.) puts it similarly in Lysias' speech against Antigenes: ἃς δεῖ ἀποτίνειν ἐάν τις μὴ ἐπεξέλθῃ γραψάμενος. Carey 2007: fr. 19.; *Lex. Rhet. Cant.* s.v. ἐπιτίμιον, cf. Wallace 2006: 64. The procedure is plausibly explained by Harris 1999b: 136: 'This must mean that when the parties met at the *anakrisis*, the prosecutor informed the magistrate that he wished to cancel the indictment, thus formally ending the procedure. This in turn indicates that the prosecutor could 'follow through' (ἐπεξελθεῖν) on his charge by either of two means: he could bring the case to trial, or alternatively he could withdraw his charge at the *anakrisis*. What the prosecutor could not do was simply to let the case drop after making his initial indictment as Theokrines and Euktemon did. He had to 'follow through' in one way or another. If he did not, he was in violation of the law and subject to a fine and loss of the right to prosecute'.

Thus the aorist participle γραψάμενος clearly indicates that the liability to a penalty was in effect from the moment when the prosecutor laid the indictment officially, if he did not then conduct the lawsuit in accordance with the valid regulations. This statement can be corroborated by a passage from Demosthenes' speech *Against Meidias*, where Demosthenes states that Meidias attempted to discredit him by hiring a sykophant to prosecute him, but in the end the prosecutor did not follow up the charge, and consequently he was subject to partial loss of his citizenship rights:

> ὅτι μὲν δὴ λιποταξίου γραφὴν κατεσκεύασεν κατ' ἐμοῦ καὶ τὸν τοῦτο ποιήσοντ' ἐμισθώσατο, τὸν μιαρὸν καὶ λίαν εὐχερῆ, τὸν κονιορτὸν Εὐκτήμονα, ἐάσω. καὶ γὰρ οὔτ' ἀνεκρίνατο ταύτην ὁ συκοφάντης ἐκεῖνος, οὔθ' οὗτος οὐδενὸς εἵνεκ' αὐτὸν ἐμισθώσατο πλὴν ἵν' ἐκκέοιτο πρὸ τῶν ἐπωνύμων καὶ πάντες ὁρῷεν 'Εὐκτήμων Λουσιεὺς ἐγράψατο Δημοσθένην Παιανιέα λιποταξίου'· καί μοι δοκεῖ κἂν προσγράψαι τοῦθ' ἡδέως, εἴ πως ἐνῆν, ὅτι Μειδίου μισθωσαμένου γέγραπται. ἀλλ' ἐῶ τοῦτο· ἐφ' ᾗ γὰρ ἐκεῖνος ἠτίμωκεν αὑτὸν οὐκ ἐπεξελθών, οὐδεμιᾶς ἔγωγ' ἔτι προσδέομαι δίκης, ἀλλ' ἱκανὴν ἔχω.
>
> Now, I shall say nothing of the fact that he procured a prosecution for desertion against me, and hired the man to do that, that over-pliable scoundrel 'dusty' Euktemon. That sycophant didn't even proceed to the preliminary inquiry in the case, nor did Meidias hire him for any purpose except to get posted up in front of the eponymous heroes for all to see 'Euktemon of Lousia prosecuted Demosthenes of Paiania for desertion'—and I think he would gladly have had added, if it had somehow been possible, that Meidias hired him to prosecute! But I say nothing about that; for a prosecution for which the man has disfranchised himself by not proceeding, I need no further compensation, I have sufficient.
>
> DEM. 21.103[14]

In some types of lawsuit, it was prescribed by law that the jury should deliver judgment within thirty days, but this rule cannot be regarded as universal. Thus in the case of the *graphē paranomōn*, we can only assume that the *thesmothetai* were supposed to designate a date for the trial within thirty days after the indictment.[15] The opposing litigants could reach agreement before or during

14 Trans. MacDowell 1990.

15 Dem. 21.47 and Dem. 24.63; [Dem.] 42.13 (where the postponement of trials by mutual agreement is also discussed): πολλάκις γὰρ ἔν τε τοῖς νόμοις γεγραμμένης τριακοστῆς ἡμέρας ἑτέραν ἡμῖν αὐτοῖς συγχωρήσαντες ἐθέμεθα, παρά τε ταῖς ἀρχαῖς ἁπάσαις καὶ δίκας καὶ

the *anakrisis* also in *graphē paranomōn* lawsuits. According to the speaker of Dem. 58, his opponent Theokrines, when acting as prosecutor in previous cases, reached an agreement with the defendants for a small sum of money so that he could end the legal procedure without incurring any penalty:

> ὅτι δὲ πολλὰς ἑτέρας προσκαλεσάμενος καὶ γραψάμενος καθυφεῖκεν, καὶ μικρὸν ἀργύριον λαμβάνων ἀπαλλάττεται, τοὺς δόντας ὑμῖν αὐτοὺς καλῶ, ἵνα μὴ πιστεύητε αὐτῷ λέγοντι ὡς αὐτὸς φυλάττει τοὺς παράνομα γράφοντας.
>
> But to prove that he has indicted many people and then dropped the case, agreeing to settle for a small sum, I shall call before you the very people who paid him, so that you will not believe him when he claims that he is the one who watches out for those who propose illegal measures.
>
> [DEM.] 58.34

The speaker calls Demosthenes and Hypereides, who were among the victims, as witnesses of Theokrines' malpractice:

> λέγε δὴ καὶ τὰς τῶν ἄλλων ἐφεξῆς τὰς τοιαύτας μαρτυρίας, καὶ τὴν Ὑπερείδου καὶ Δημοσθένους. τοῦτο γάρ ἐστιν ὑπερβολή, τὸ παρ' ὧν οὐδ' ἂν εἷς ἀξιώσαι λαβεῖν, τοῦτον παρὰ τούτων ἥδιστα λαμβάνειν πωλοῦντα τὰς γραφάς.
>
> Read, also, the other depositions of a similar kind in sequence, including those of Hypereides and Demosthenes. For this is beyond everything, that he gladly sells indictments to get money from men from whom no-one else would think of asking for it.
>
> [DEM.] 58.35

The speaker also discusses the most common and most trivial excuses supported with a *hypōmosia*:[16]

κρίσεις ἀναβάλλονται τοῖς ἀντιδίκοις οἱ ἄρχοντες συγχωρησάντων ἐκείνων ἀλλήλοις. 'For often, although the thirtieth day is set down in the laws, we fix upon another by mutual agreement; and in all the offices the magistrates put off trials and judgments for the litigants, when these have come to a mutual agreement'. (Trans. Murray 1939 adjusted) See Lipsius 1905–1915: 901ff.; and Gerner 1949: 1287.

16 The ὑπωμοσία which could suspend a proposal or a decree and could also delay proceedings is described in the *Lex. Rhet. Cant.* (s.v.) most concisely: ὑπωμοσία. δύο σημαίνει τροπὰς ἡ λέξις μίαν μὲν ὅταν τις γράψηται νόμον παρανόμων ἢ καὶ αὐτὸς εἰσηγήσηται, ἔπειτα καταγνοὺς αὐτοῦ ἐξομόσηται παραλελογίσθαι· ὑπωμοσία δὲ λέγεται, ὅτι ὀμνύοντες ἀφίενται μήτε ἀργυρίῳ πεισθῆναι μήτε καταχαρίσασθαι τὴν σιγήν. μνημονεύει τοῦ τρόπου τούτου καὶ Δημοσθένης ἐν τῷ

> πῶς; οὐδὲν καινὸν διαπραξάμενος, ἀλλ' ὅπερ ἕτεροί τινες τῶν ὁμοίων τούτῳ. τὸν μὲν Δημοσθένην τις ὑπωμόσατο καλουμένης τῆς γραφῆς ὡς νοσοῦντα, τὸν περιιόντα καὶ λοιδορούμενον Αἰσχίνην τοῦτον δ' οὗτος τὸν ἐχθρὸν εἴασεν, καὶ οὔτε τότε ἀνθυπωμόσατο οὔθ' ὕστερον ἐπήγγελκεν.
>
> How? Not by doing anything new, but just what others like him have done. When the indictment was called, someone declared in a *hypomosia* that Demosthenes was ill—the same Demosthenes who was going around abusing Aischines. So he let this enemy of his off, and neither opposed the *hypōmosia* at the time nor subsequently called the case for trial.
>
> [DEM.] 58.43

Thus a litigant could excuse himself from attending the trial by stating under oath that he was ill. It is not necessarily rhetorical exaggeration to claim that this could happen even if it was known to everybody that the defendant was as sound as a bell. One of the most popular excuses (i.e. 'I have gone abroad') has even become a proverb, an item in lexicographical works: we can read in Hesychius' lexicon and in the works of other lexicographers the following: Ἴμβριος καὶ Λήμνιος· οἱ τὰς διαίτας ὑποφεύγοντες ἐσκήπτοντο ἐν Λήμνῳ ἢ ἐν Ἴμβρῳ εἶναι.—'Imbrian and Lemnian: the persons postponing the trial made an excuse by saying that they were on Lemnos or Imbros'.[17] And the 'most beautiful' one: καλλίστη ἀναβολή Dem. 48.23–26, an excellent ground for postponement was when the defendant was abroad on military service: δημοσίᾳ ἀποδημοῦντος στρατευομένου.[18] In the background of the eventual postponements we might conclude that resuming the postponed trial was probably not the function of the state officials, but rather that of the prosecutor. With all probability, as suggested by Lipsius, this is the right interpretation of the closing clause of the above quoted passage Dem. 48.43: οὔθ' ὕστερον ἐπήγγελκεν—'nor did he subsequently call the case for trial'.[19]

Finally, let us see how Hypereides' *Diondas* speech can add to our present knowledge about the issue of postponement of *graphai*, and, more specifi-

περὶ στεφάνου. κατὰ μίμησιν δέ ἐστι τὸ ὑπερτίθεσθαι δίκην προφάσει χρώμενον ἢ ἀποδημίᾳ ἢ νόσῳ ἢ ἄλλῳ τινὶ τῶν παραπλησίων μεθ' ὅρκου, καὶ τὸ ποιεῖν τοῦτο ὑπόμνυσθαι λέγουσιν. ἑτέρως οὖν λέγεται πάλιν, ὡς ἔφαμεν, ἀπωμοσία, ὅταν τις κρινόμενος σκήπτηται τὸ μὴ εὐκαιρεῖν πρὸς τὴν δίκην, ἀνθυπομνύηται δὲ ὁ ἀντίδικος, καὶ περὶ αὐτοῦ προδικάζωνται. Cf. Thür 1998.

17 Hsch. s.v. Ἴμβριος.

18 Dem. 48.23–26.

19 Lipsius 1905–1915: 903.

cally, the *graphē paranomōn*. In all probability Diondas attacked Hypereides' decree in praise of Demosthenes immediately after the defeat at Chaironeia. The decree was proposed before the battle, but the trial took place four years later. The statements concerning Diondas in the speech suggest that the postponement of *graphai* cases was not a rare phenomenon in the legal practice of Athens. A prosecutor could even have several legal cases in progress at the same time. Hypereides claims the following:

> ἢ πάλιν, ἐπειδὰν Διώνδας ἐπὶ τῶν δικαστηρίων σεμνύνηται λέγων ὅτι πεντήκον(τα) γραφὰς ἐγράψατο, εἰ δέ τις αὐτὸν ἐρωτήσαι· 'ἔστιν οὖν ἥντινα τούτων ᾕρηκας;', οὐδεμίαν φανήσεται.
>
> Or again (*sc.* who would not be pained) when Diondas puffs himself up in the lawcourts saying that he brought fifty indictments, and someone asks him: 'Is there any one of them you've won?', it will be evident that there isn't one.
>
> 174v 27 ff.[20]

Even if Diondas delivered many of the fifty indictments by means of the procedure of *eisangelia* (where the prosecutor was protected by the absence of a penalty for failure to obtain one-fifth of the votes cast),[21] one can hardly believe that he could retain his political position after losing *all* the cases.[22] But Hypereides claims that he won none of the cases! However, the terminology is not completely clear; Hypereides even seems to be calculatedly obscure in using the expressions *graphesthai*, *apopherein*, *agōna agōnizesthai* and *haireō*, and it is possible that there were fifty suits, very few of which got to court. We should interpret Hypereides' definition of 'sykophant' accordingly: ἔστι γὰρ συκοφάντου μὲν τὸ πολλοὺς ποιῆσαι ἀγῶνας, πολίτου δὲ δικαίου τὸ ἐξελέγχειν τοὺς ἐν τοῖς δικαστηρίοις. 'It is the job of the sykophant to initiate many cases and of the good citizen to refute those that get to court.' (175v 1ff.) The orator thus clearly distinguishes between the cases initiated and those that got to court. This implies that not all the cases initiated by Diondas, the hardened sykophant, got to court (the sykophant 'by profession'—as Hypereides

20 Translations from the Diondas speech are by Carey et al. 2008.

21 In *eisangelia* lawsuits no penalty was imposed for the cancellation of an indictment: Harris 1999b: 135. n. 35; and Hansen 1974: 30 f. See also Volonaki in this volume.

22 Moreover, 145r 7 ff. of our speech clearly indicates that Diondas' favourite type of prosecution was the *graphē paranomōn*, although the orator in all probability blends Diondas' private and public actions to impress his audience.

tries to present Diondas—raises money by blackmailing with the *threat* of a prosecution). Losing all the cases is naturally not the same as winning none of them. (Furthermore, it is also important to what extent and how many times the accuser loses: Diondas could fail to obtain one-fifth of the votes twice at most.) The orator combines or confuses two different situations. Diondas thus did not lose fifty times; instead, many of the fifty cases he had initiated could have been still in progress.[23]

The above interpretation of Hypereides' statements strongly suggests that Demosthenes' and Aischines' 'Crown case' was not at all exceptional; there were certain circumstances and legal possibilities through which any legal case, even a *graphē paranomōn*, could be postponed for years after the indictment. In the Diondas case, the postponement could be explained by one of the common

23 Although Hypereides intends to deliberately combine the concepts (175v 1ff.): 'And you? Although the law forbids anybody under 30 years to attend law courts, you are still under 25 and you have laid twice as many indictments, in addition, all in the service of others'. (σὺ δὲ τοῦ νόμου ἀπαγορεύοντος μηδένα προσιέαι πρὸς τὰ δικαστήρια πρὶν ἂν τριάκοντα ἔτη γένηται, πρὶν πέντε καὶ εἴκοσι ἔτη σοι γενέσθαι, διπλασίας αὐτῶν γραφὰς ἀπενήνοχας, καὶ ταῦτα ἑτέροις ὑπηρετῶν)—the grown-up Diondas had the right to lay indictments and to attend the law courts as accuser. The age limit of 30 years was valid for judges (*Ath. Pol.* 63.3: δικάζειν δ' ἔξεστιν τοῖς ὑπὲρ λ ἔτη γεγονόσιν, ὅσοι αὐτῶν μὴ ὀφείλουσιν τῷ δημοσίῳ ἢ ἄτιμοί εἰσιν). On the other hand, all adult Athenian citizens had the right to prosecute. The age of majority and the practice of the related personal rights were attained theoretically at the age of 18, but in practice—because of the obligatory military service—at the age of 20. (Cf. Hansen 1999: 88f.; and Rhodes 1981: 702f.) Thus Diondas laid an average of ten indictments per year. Also in other passages, Hypereides uses the forms of the verb ὑπηρετέω for the servile representation of anti-Athenian interests, to the service of the enemy (cf. Hyp. *Eux.* 29, 39). Similarly, Demosthenes e.g. 18.138 in connection with Aischines, cf. Wankel 1976: 750. Besides, the expression ὑπηρέτης δημόσιος appears in the *Ath. Pol.* as a *terminus technicus* meaning 'public servant', which clearly indicates the pejorative character of the word used (cf. Dem. 18.261; and *Ath. Pol.* 50.2; 65.4). In Athens, not only were political hirelings employed, but friends who shared political views could also help each other. Timarchos instead of Demosthenes attempted to attack Aischines in connection with the legation to Philip. Political factions employed and advanced a competent person who gave his name to the given case not necessarily because of financial considerations, but in accordance with the inner 'division of labour'. In her analysis of the *synēgoria*, Lene Rubinstein rightly emphasises that rich citizens or well-known politicians could safely attend the lawcourts as co-accusers standing behind, then next to, other accusers, proposers: '… wealthy citizens who wished to demonstrate their skills and political clout in a public action would be able to do so, but without running the risk of having their wings clipped as a result of the partial *atimia* that would be imposed on *ho grapsamenos* for gaining less than the required 20% of the vote'. (Rubinstein 2000: 203) Cf. Harvey 1990: 103ff. Hypereides describes this phenomenon in connection with Diondas (175v 7ff.): 'Since with their own names—to avoid coming into prominence—they do not dare lay an indictment, but they perfectly exploit your unscrupulous nature'.

suppositions also known to us from other sources. Some public *vis maior* could also emerge (cf. the text of the *hybris* law of debated authenticity:[24] Dem. 21.47. οἱ δὲ θεσμοθέται εἰσαγόντων εἰς τὴν ἡλιαίαν τριάκοντα ἡμερῶν ἀφ' ἧς ἂν γραφῇ, ἐὰν μή τι δημόσιον κωλύῃ, εἰ δὲ μή, ὅταν ᾖ πρῶτον οἷόν τε. 'and the *thesmothetai* shall bring the case before the court within thirty days from the date of the indictment, unless some public business prevents, in which case it shall be brought on the earliest possible date'); or the parties could mutually agree to come to court later.[25] However, it is most probable that Diondas as prosecutor used the *kallistē anabolē* of military service. Hypereides claims (174r 18) that Diondas 'would have abandoned his actions against' him (ἀπολιπὼν ἂν τοὺς κατ' ἐμοῦ ἀγῶνας), if Philip's campaign had taken place against the Persians where Diondas enlisted with the support of the people.

The prevalence of such postponements can also be detected in the fact that Hypereides means to suggest that Diondas—disregarding the earlier court decisions—attacks the anti-Macedonian politicians with new *graphē paranomōn* prosecutions again and again. However, lines 174r 26ff. reveal that he could have started numerous private actions which undoubtedly had a political function as well, yet in their case different rules were valid regarding the procedure. 'However, I'll leave the others aside, but his father actually begs at the preliminary hearing that he stops them'.[26] If we accept the picture drawn by Hypereides, in several cases Diondas's father managed to achieve exactly the postponement of the trial.

The first postponement of the *graphē paranomōn* started against Hypereides (which was in effect until the prosecutor thought that the hour had come to resume the procedure in 334 BC) could be justified because, after laying the indictment, Diondas, as a volunteer supported by the state, applied for military service. In Demosthenes' Crown case a similar reason can be suspected to which the prosecutor Aischines could refer so that he would not have to call the case for trial after Philip's sudden death. The suddenness of the postponement might also be indicated by the fact that Demosthenes in his extant defence

24 See Canevaro 2013: 230–231.

25 [Dem.] 42.13: πολλάκις γὰρ ἔν τε τοῖς νόμοις γεγραμμένης τριακοστῆς ἡμέρας ἑτέραν ἡμῖν αὐτοῖς συγχωρήσαντες ἐθέμεθα, παρά τε ταῖς ἀρχαῖς ἁπάσαις καὶ δίκας καὶ κρίσεις ἀναβάλλονται τοῖς ἀντιδίκοις οἱ ἄρχοντες συγχωρησάντων ἐκείνων ἀλλήλοις. The passage deals with private lawsuits. The postponement was valid until one of the parties cancelled the agreement. Cf. MacDowell 1990: 266f.

26 ὁ δὲ πατὴρ αὐτοῦ ἐπὶ ἁπάντων τῶν ἀγώνων καὶ πρὸς ταῖς ἀνακρίσεσιν δεῖται αὐτοὺς παύσασθαι. Cf. Lipsius 1905–1915: 829ff.; Harrison 1971: 94ff. esp. 103ff.; and Thür 1977, 76f.; Thür 2005: 146ff. esp. 156ff.

speech does not discuss the events between 336 and 330 BC in detail; thus his speech could have been completed by the time of the postponement.

Returning to the main question of this chapter, we might be right to infer on the basis of the analysis of the 'Diondas phenomenon' that a large number of indictments were not eventually tried before a jury. The extant forensic speeches which relate to legal cases which went to trial and were resolved by a *dikastērion* need to be set against the fact that our surviving speeches represent only a fraction of the litigation in Athens.[27]

This can also explain the much debated statement of Aristophon, who—according to previous interpretations—boasted of having being acquitted 75 times in his life in *graphē paranomōn* lawsuits:

> Ἐτόλμα δ' ἐν ὑμῖν ποτε σεμνύνεσθαι Ἀριστοφῶν ἐκεῖνος ὁ Ἀζηνιεὺς λέγων ὅτι γραφὰς παρανόμων ἀπέφυγεν ἑβδομήκοντα καὶ πέντε. Ἀλλ' οὐχὶ Κέφαλος ὁ παλαιὸς ἐκεῖνος, ὁ δοκῶν δημοτικώτατος γεγονέναι, οὐχ οὕτως, ἀλλ' ἐπὶ τοῖς ἐναντίοις ἐφιλοτιμεῖτο, λέγων ὅτι πλεῖστα πάντων γεγραφὼς ψηφίσματα, οὐδεμίαν πώποτε γραφὴν πέφευγε παρανόμων, καλῶς οἶμαι σεμνυνόμενος. Ἐγράφοντο γὰρ ἀλλήλους παρανόμων οὐ μόνον οἱ διαπολιτευόμενοι, ἀλλὰ καὶ οἱ φίλοι τοὺς φίλους, εἴ τι ἐξαμαρτάνοιεν εἰς τὴν πόλιν.
>
> The celebrated Aristophon of Azenia once dared to boast in court that he had been acquitted seventy-five times on indictments for illegal legislation. This was not the way, though, with the famous Kephalos of old, who was considered outstandingly loyal to the people; in fact, his source of pride was the opposite, for he claimed that, though he had proposed more decrees than anyone, he had never been indicted for illegal legislation; this was a worthy boast in my view. For indictments for illegality were brought not just by active politicians against each other, but by friends against friends, if they committed any offence against the city.
>
> AISCHIN. 3.194[28]

We have little by way of data about the number of indictments and defence speeches in connection with the characters of political life in Athens, as Hansen

27 Harris 1999b: 140 suggests that the legal system could have markedly supported the cancellation of indictments and the anticipatory agreements, otherwise a vast number of trials would have burdened the lawcourts which—in the case of public lawsuits—had sessions lasting a whole day and often 501 judges were paid daily allowances.

28 Trans. Carey 2000.

rightly warns us.[29] In connection with Aristophon's case, nevertheless, Oost and Whitehead agree that 75 is a rounded number meaning 'immense' and it should not be taken seriously. Although Aristophon was politically active for an exceptionally long time, there is no space for so many lawsuits in his career.[30]

As the 'Diondas phenomenon' well illustrates, lawsuits could be postponed for a long time after the indictment without the case being called for trial, and they could even 'fade away' for ever. All this can also support Aischines' description of Aristophon's boastful claim (Hypereides uses the same verb—*semnynesthai*, 'to boast'—in connection with Diondas): Ἐτόλμα δ' ἐν ὑμῖν ποτε σεμνύνεσθαι Ἀριστοφῶν ἐκεῖνος ὁ Ἀζηνιεὺς λέγων ὅτι γραφὰς παρανόμων ἀπέφυγεν ἑβδομήκοντα καὶ πέντε. If we do not interpret the expression *apephugen* in its usual stricter sense, as a legal *terminus technicus* ('he has been acquitted'), but in a wider sense ('he has escaped'), Aristophon only boasted of the fact that 75 indictments had been laid against him and he had not been found guilty in any of these lawsuits. Thus we have no ground to question his statement even if we know that 75 trials could not fit even his long life, and he could not have defended himself successfully in so many cases.[31]

29 'We possess no fewer than thirty-five examples of its use in the period 403–322, and that is a very large number if one thinks how limited our sources are. ... Aristophon, on his own admission, according to Aischines, had been acquitted in no less than seventy-five prosecutions for proposing unconstitutional decrees in the course of a political career of more than half a century (Aischin. 3.194) ... The natural conclusion is that seventy-five is an excessively large number of prosecutions of a single political leader and probably an exaggeration on Aischines' part, but that it was a notable exception for a political leader to escape altogether from exposure to a *graphē paranomōn*. Demosthenes says that in the period after the defeat at Chaeroneia he had to defend himself almost daily against people trying to accuse him of proposing unconstitutional decrees and attack him for political crimes and maladministration (Dem. 18.250). The vast majority of Athenian political leaders must, at least once and often more than once in their careers, have been sent before the courts to defend the proposals they had made in the Assembly; and there is nothing against supposing that the jurors must have judged a *graphē paranomōn* something like one every month.' Hansen 1999: 208 f.

30 Oost 1977: 238 ff.; and Whitehead 1986: 313 ff.

31 This chapter was supported by National Research, Development and Innovation Office—NKFIH NN 124539.

Bibliography

Atkinson, K.M.T. (1939) 'Athenian Legislative Procedure and Revision of Laws', *Bulletin of the John Rylands Library* 23, 107–150.

Canevaro, M. (2013) *The Documents in the Attic Orators: Laws and Decrees in the Public Speeches of the Demosthenic Corpus*, Oxford.

Carey, C., (2000) *Aeschines*, Austin.

Carey, C. (2007) *Lysiae orationes cum fragmentis*, Oxford.

Carey, C., et al. (2008) 'Fragments of Hypereides' *Against Diondas* from the Archimedes palimpsest', ZPE 165, 1–19.

de Laix, R.A. (1973) *Probouleusis at Athens: A Study of Political Decision-Making*, Berkeley, Cal.

Gerner, E. (1949) '*Paranomon graphe*', in PWRE 18/2/2, K. Ziegler, col. 1281–1293, Stuttgart.

Hansen, M.H. (1974) *The Sovereignty of the People's Court in the Fourth Century BC and the Public Action Against Unconstitutional Proposals*, Odense.

Hansen, M.H. (1987) '*Graphe paranomon* Against *psephismata* Not Yet Passed by the *ekklesia*', C&M 38, 63–73.

Hansen, M.H. (1999) *The Athenian Democracy in the Age of Demosthenes*, London.

Harris, E.M. (1999a) 'A Response to Robert Wallace', *Dike* 2, 67–72.

Harris, E.M. (1999b) 'The Penalty for Frivolous Prosecution in Athenian Law', *Dike* 2, 123–142.

Harrison, A.R.W. (1968–1971) *The Law of Athens*, 2 vols, Oxford.

Harvey, D. (1990) 'The Sycophant and Sycophancy: Vexatious Redefinition?', in Cartledge, P., Millett, P. and Todd, S.C., eds (1990) *Nomos: Essays in Athenian Law, Politics and Society*, Cambridge, 103–121.

Horváth, L. (2008) 'Dating Hyperides' *Against Diondas*', ZPE 166, 27–36.

Horváth, L. (2009) 'Hyperidea', BICS 52, 187–222.

Lipsius, J.H. (1905–1915) *Das attische Recht und Rechtsverfahren*, 3 vols, Leipzig.

MacDowell, D.M., (1990) *Demosthenes: Against Meidias*, Oxford.

Murray, A.T., (1939) *Demosthenes V. Private orations XLI–XLIX, with an English translation* (Loeb Classical Library), Cambridge, Ma./London.

Oost, S.I. (1977) 'Two Notes on Aristophon of Azenia', CP 72, 238–242.

Rhodes, P.J. (1981) *A Commentary on the Aristotelian* Athenaion Politeia, Oxford.

Rubinstein, L. (2000) *Litigation and Cooperation: Supporting Speakers in the Courts of Classical Athens*, Stuttgart.

Thür, G. (1977) *Beweisführung vor den Schwurgerichtshöfen Athens: die* Proklesis *zur* Basanos, Vienna.

Thür, G. (1998) 'Hypomosia', in Cancik, H. and Schneider, H., eds (1998) *Die Neue Pauly*, vol. 5, Stuttgart, 815.

Thür, G. (2005) 'The role of the witness in Athenian law', in Gagarin, M. and Cohen, E. eds (2005) *The Cambridge companion to ancient Greek law*, Cambridge, 146–169.

Wallace, R.W. (2006) 'Withdrawing *graphai* in Ancient Athens: A Case Study in 'Sycophancy' and Legal Idiosyncrasies', in Thür, G. and Rupprecht, H.-A., eds (2006) *Symposion 2003: Vorträge zur griechischen und hellenistischen Rechtsgeschichte* (Rauischholzhausen, 30 September–3 October 2003) Vienna, 57–66.

Wankel, H. (1976) *Demosthenes, Rede für Ktesiphon über den Kranz*, Heidelberg.

Whitehead, D. (1986) 'The Political Career of Aristophon', *CP* 81, 313–319.

Wolff, H.J. (1970) *'Normenkontrolle' und Gesetzesbegriff in der athenischen Demokratie: Untersuchungen zur graphe paranomon*, Heidelberg. (Sitzungsberichte der Heidelberger Akademie der Wissenschaften, philosophische-historische Klasse 2.)

Yunis, H. (2001) *Demosthenes: On the Crown*, Cambridge.

Yunis, H. (2005) *Demosthenes, Speeches 18 and 19*, Austin.

CHAPTER 8

Use and Abuse of Legal Procedures to Impede the Legal Process

Noboru Sato

1 Introduction

Many studies have approached Athenian legal practices and the social functions of the Athenian judicial system from the perspective of dispute settlement: for example, the extent to which a plaintiff could choose a specific type of lawsuit from among various alternatives, considering the risks and prospects of success, or the degree to which the courts were regarded as the appropriate arena for pursuing feuds with a prosecutor's personal enemies.[1] However, the legal procedures available after the official initiation of a legal case but before the beginning of the trial in court, such as *hypōmosia* and *paragraphē*, have remained largely unexamined in terms of the litigants' perspective, despite the fact that Athenian litigants in the fourth century BC seem to have used these procedures strategically from time to time. To obtain a larger view of the nature of dispute settlement practices in classical Athens, it is necessary to investigate the strategies that were available to litigants during the preliminary stage of a court case, namely before the beginning of the trial in court. This study examines how various procedures were used and abused during this preliminary stage in order to impede legal proceedings, and suggests that the stage that followed the filing of a case could be used not merely as inactive waiting time but rather as a period during which strategic negotiations between the disputants could be conducted.[2]

1 Osborne 1985 triggered debates on the flexibility of the legal procedures that were available in the Athenian judicial system (cf. Todd 1993; Harris 2000; Carey 2004; Osborne 2010: 200–204). Cohen 1991; Cohen 1995 argues that the courts of law were another arena for pursuing private enmities, which provoked various responses (e.g. Harris 1994; Christ 1998, esp. 160–192).

2 Recent important works on the preliminary stage before a trial came into court include, e.g. Hunter 1994: 55–66 (arbitration); Scafuro 1997, esp. 31–42, 117–141, 393–399 (arbitration); Johnstone 1999 (dare or *proklēsis*).

 | DOI:10.1163/9789004377899_010

2 Ways and Means of Postponing a Case

2.1 *Private and Public Arbitration and* anakrisis

Athenian litigants used various means during the preliminary stage of trials to impede the progress of legal proceedings. First, private arbitrations provided litigants with opportunities to delay the legal process. Since a matter could be handed over to private arbitrators even after the official initiation of a *dikē*,[3] unsurprisingly some litigants tried to impede or evade trial in court by delaying their private arbitrations. Hegesandros is said to have gained a distinct advantage by delaying such a private arbitration. In 361/0 BC or slightly earlier, Pittalakos, a public slave, brought a *dikē* against Hegesandros for his insolent treatment of Pittalakos.[4] The defendant claimed that the plaintiff was his private slave and attempted to enslave him for his personal use only. One Glaukon of Cholargos, however, sought to have Pittalakos freed through *aphairēsis eis eleutherian*. Hegesandros, in turn, initiated a *dikē exaireseōs* against Glaukon, but the matter was subsequently handed over to Diopeithes of Sounion for arbitration. According to Aischines, this arbitrator, who was a fellow demesman and an old friend of Hegesandros, evaded his duty for a long time and this delay worked to Hegesandros' advantage. While the hearing was repeatedly postponed, Hegesandros began to speak in the Assembly and his brother Hegesippos regularly made public speeches, which eventually discouraged Pittalakos from continuing with the case. When Mantitheos and his half-brother 'Boiotos' brought *dikai* against each other in the middle of the fourth century BC, they submitted their claims to Solon of Erchia for arbitration; however, according to Mantitheos, Boiotos evaded the arbitration for such a long time that the arbitrator died and they filed their cases afresh.[5] It is uncertain for how long the hearing was delayed in this particular case, but arbitration was obviously regarded as a typical mechanism for delaying and/or evading legal proceedings.

Public arbitration, which was instituted for the majority of private cases, could likewise be postponed. According to Demosthenes, on the day of the public arbitration for the *dikē kakēgorias* against Meidias, their public arbitrator, Straton (presumably, though Demosthenes does not say, at Meidias' request) asked Demosthenes to adjourn the arbitration for a while, and subsequently to

---

3 Scafuro 1997: 38, 396–397 shows that, among the extant cases, most private arbitrations were offered after legal action had begun.

4 Aischin. 1.62–64. For details of the affair concerning Pittalakos and the relevant legal procedures, see Fisher 2001: 199–201; Scafuro 1997: 400–401.

5 [Dem.] 40.16, 19, 30.

postpone it until the next day.[6] In this case, since the plaintiff refused to agree to an adjournment and the defendant did not appear, Straton could not postpone the arbitration and pronounced his verdict against Meidias. This incident suggests that a public arbitrator could postpone a hearing with the consent of the contending parties.[7] It is not entirely certain why Straton sought postponement, but it seems that it was possible for a litigant (as Meidias here) to delay legal proceedings by urging or putting pressure on his public arbitrator to postpone the arbitration process. After the public arbitration, Straton was prosecuted and disfranchised by Meidias. This incident suggests that a public arbitrator was subject to the risk of being prosecuted and had good reason to attempt to delay the arbitration at the request of a litigant, especially a powerful litigant like Meidias.[8] The arbitration mentioned in Isa. 12.11, which may have been a public arbitration for a private suit, was suspended for two years.[9] In this case, it is uncertain what caused the delay. In Dem. 54, Konon is said to have attempted to delay the completion of a public arbitration. According to Ariston, the speaker of this oration, Konon protracted the proceedings beyond midnight by various means such as refusing to read aloud the depositions or to provide copies, introducing irrelevant depositions, and issuing a challenge (*proklēsis*), in order to 'delay and to prevent the evidence urns (*echinoi*) from being sealed (ἐπὶ διακρούσει καὶ τῷ μὴ σημανθῆναι τοὺς ἐχίνους)', i.e. in order to delay the completion of the arbitration.[10] Although it is not explicitly mentioned, the speaker does not seem to imply that Konon attempted to postpone the arbitration until the next day, but that he intended to delay the progress of the meeting and to provide a false witness at the last moment of the public arbitration.

Litigants could also postpone legal proceedings during the course of the *anakrisis*, the preliminary hearing by presiding magistrates.[11] At the *anakrisis* concerning the estate of Philoktemon, son of Euktemon, in the 360s BC, Androkles, who had entered the declaration (*diamartyria*)[12] that Euktemon had left two legitimate sons, was asked to state the names of their mother

6 Dem. 21.84.

7 This rule may have been applied to the adjournment of an *anakrisis*, as well. See Kremmydas and Horváth in this volume.

8 On the other hand, if a public arbitrator postponed the arbitration against the will of one of the contending parties, he could have been prosecuted, too. Straton therefore needed to obtain Demosthenes' consent.

9 Rubinstein 2000: 61 n. 99.

10 Dem. 54.26–29.

11 On *anakrisis*, see Kremmydas in this volume.

12 On *diamartyria*, and more specifically on Isa. 6, see Griffith-Williams in this volume.

and her father.[13] Since he could not answer the question, Androkles secured an adjournment by alleging that the mother was a Lemnian. He presumably asked the *archōn* to postpone the hearing in order to gather information about her from Lemnos. He may have temporised in order to fabricate the details of her background, as Androkles' opponent perhaps wanted to imply.[14] In any case, the request for postponement was granted, and after a short time, the disputants returned to the *anakrisis*, at which Androkles immediately revealed that their mother was Kallippe, daughter of Pistoxenos.

2.2 Hypōmosiai

Athenian litigants could request to adjourn the legal proceedings by having someone swear an oath of *hypōmosia* on their behalf, either because of illness or military service abroad.[15] It is likely that any legal case, either *graphē* or *dikē*, could be postponed through this procedure, with the exception of a few special cases, such as *eisangelia*.[16] It appears that the formal purpose of instituting this oath was not to drag out legal proceedings, but to remove any disadvantages resulting from inability to attend owing to illness or military service by suspending the legal process temporarily.

However, litigants who asked someone to swear a *hypōmosia* on their behalf were often suspected of delaying or even avoiding the trial without any legitimate reasons for doing so. In 343/2 BC, Kallistratos tried to suspend a trial regarding Komon's estate by swearing a *hypōmosia* for his brother-in-law, Olympiodoros, as the latter was called for military service in Akarnania.[17] Later, at a different trial, Kallistratos confessed that he and Olympiodoros were completely unprepared for the sudden and unexpected appearance of so many other claimants to Komon's estate, and that they had consequently sought a way to postpone it for the time being. The other claimants, however, swore a counter-oath (*antōmosia*) and persuaded the dikasts that Olympiodoros was absent not because of his public duty but merely to avoid the trial. This episode shows that a *hypōmosia* was often correctly regarded as a delaying tactic that could be abused by litigants. At the trial concerning his half-brother's name, Mantitheos claimed that when he filed the case against 'Boiotos', the defendant

13 Isa. 6.12–13. See also Wyse 1904: 498–499.

14 Isa. 6.13.

15 Harp. s.v. *hypōmosia*; Pollux 8.81; Dem. 48.25; [58.]43; Thalheim 1914; Thür 1998; Harrison 1971: 155 f.; Horváth in this volume.

16 *Graphē*: Dem. [58.]43; *dikē*: Dem. 21.84; 39.37; not applicable to *eisangelia*: Hyp. *Eux*. 7. Cf. Volonaki in this volume. See also Horváth in this volume on the reasons for justifying the postponement.

17 Dem. 48.23–25.

applied for a postponement of the trial through a *hypōmosia*, but eventually, 'when there was no longer room for evasion' (ἐπεὶ οὐκέτ' ἐνῆν αὐτῷ διακρούσασθαι), Boiotos let the arbitrator give judgment against him by default and moved a *mē ousa* (non-suit) in order to have the case regarding the name of 'Boiotos' reopened.[18] The plaintiff seemed to imply that Boiotos was trying to use the *hypōmosia* to evade, and not just to postpone, the trial. According to Demosthenes, on the day of the public arbitration for the *dikē kakēgorias* against Meidias, 'all the legal procedures, *hypōmosiai* and *paragraphai*, had been already exhausted, and there was nothing left any more' (πάντα δ' ἤδη διεξεληλύθει ταῦτα τἀκ τῶν νόμων, ὑπωμοσίαι καὶ παραγραφαί, καὶ οὐδὲν ἔτ' ἦν ὑπόλοιπον). As noted above, Straton, their public arbitrator, asked Demosthenes to adjourn the arbitration for the time being, and subsequently, to postpone it until the next day.[19] In this example *hypōmosia* is considered to be one of the ways of delaying public arbitration, and the following passage seems to imply that a *hypōmosia* could be used to postpone or even avoid trial by a litigant without legally acceptable reasons for doing so. Demosthenes himself is said to have abused the *hypōmosia*. When prosecuted by Theokrines for an illegal proposal, Demosthenes had someone swear a *hypōmosia* for him on grounds of illness, but the prosecutor neither made a counter-oath against him nor prosecuted him later, even though he was going around slandering Aischines.[20] In this case, Theokrines was accused of abusing the *hypōmosia*—i.e. not resuming but suspending the trial indefinitely—to discharge Demosthenes from the public prosecution, which was legally not allowed to be withdrawn. This trick is described as 'nothing new' (οὐδὲν καινὸν), which suggests that dropping a *graphē de facto* through a *hypōmosia* was more or less common, although it is not possible to gauge accurately how often such a trick was used.

2.3 Paragraphai

Demetrios of Phaleron reported that 'some defendants who had a weak case and feared an unfavourable verdict by the public arbitrators stalled for time and provided whatever excuse seemed reasonable, first by using a *paragraphē*, and next by a *hypōmosia* on the basis of illness or being abroad for military service' (ἐνίους δὲ ἀσθενὲς τὸ δίκαιον ἔχοντας καὶ δεδοικότας τὴν καταδίαιταν χρόνους ἐμβάλλειν καὶ σκήψεις οἵας δοκεῖν εἶναι εὐλόγους, καὶ τὸ μὲν πρῶτον παραγράφεσθαι, εἶτα ὑπόμνυσθαι νόσον ἢ ἀποδημίαν).[21] Here, *paragraphē* is counted, along with

18 Dem. 39.37.

19 Dem. 21.84.

20 [Dem.] 58.43.

21 *Lex. Rhet. Cantab.*, s.v. Μὴ οὖσα δίκη.

hypōmosia, as a common means for a litigant with a weak case to delay legal proceedings. In fact, *paragraphē* combined with *hypōmosia* also appears in Attic orations. As seen above, when accusing Meidias of trying to avoid a public arbitration, Demosthenes mentioned this combination as a legally admissible way of adjourning further legal proceedings.[22] The same combination appears in the Demosthenic oration 47. In the middle of the fourth century BC, the unnamed speaker of this oration had a quarrel with Theophemos about recovering equipment for a trireme, and their dispute developed into a fistfight. When the speaker brought a *dikē aikeias* against Theophemos, the latter also filed a case against the speaker over the same fight. The speaker said, 'I did not resort either to *paragraphē* or to *hypōmosia*, because those measures had placed me at a disadvantage in a former suit' (οὐ παραγραφομένου ἐμοῦ οὐδ' ὑπομνυμένου διὰ τὸ καὶ πρότερόν ποτε ἐφ' ἑτέρας δίκης ταῦτά με βλάψαι).[23] In contrast, his opponent, Theophemos, used these measures at the public arbitration for the case against him.[24] In this case, the speaker did not accuse the opponent of delaying tactics; rather, because of the *paragraphē* and *hypōmosia*, the case against the speaker came to court first and Theophemos won, while the case against Theophemos was suspended.

There is a controversy regarding the nature of these *paragraphai*. It has been suggested that the term may also have been used to designate a procedural means of adjourning legal proceedings, similar to the *hypōmosia*, even that the term may have referred to the written text of the *hypōmosia*. However, since nothing in these contexts bars the usual sense of *paragraphē* in classical Athens, as a special plea to block a case as inadmissible on specific legal grounds, the term may simply carry this normal meaning. After analysing the relevant evidence (i.e. Dem. 21.84; 47.47; *Lex. Cant.*, s.v. Μὴ οὖσα δίκη; Pollux 8.60; Scholion on Dem. 21.84), MacDowell argues that a *paragraphē* coupled with a *hypōmosia* should be regarded as a procedure separate from the oath for postponement, i.e. *hypōmosia*. Although his argument does not necessarily prove that a *paragraphē* was always a special plea to bar an action, there seems no strong reason for denying that it has its usual meaning, as MacDowell suggests.[25]

In fact, the *paragraphē* to bar an action in itself seems to have been used to delay further legal proceedings. In the Demosthenic oration *For Phormion* the speaker explains that the reason why Phormion, the defendant, entered a *para-*

22 Dem. 21.84.
23 Dem. 47.39.
24 Dem. 47.45.
25 MacDowell 1990: 306–307.

graphē, a special plea to bar an action, was to effectuate a discharge from the business, and the speaker denies that Phormion's intention was to 'gain time by putting off the trial' (οὐχ ἵν' ἐκκρούοντες χρόνους ἐμποιῶμεν).[26] This excuse seems to support the belief that a special plea to bar an action was regarded as a delaying tactic.

However, it is not certain how a litigant could delay the original case by means of a *paragraphē*, as there is much uncertainty about the details of the procedure. Scholars have especially discussed the procedure that followed after a *paragraphē* was unsuccessful, namely whether it was followed by a second hearing regarding the original issue, and if it was, whether that second hearing took place on the same day as the *paragraphē* or later.[27] If there was a fresh hearing regarding the original issue on a later day, as MacDowell claims on the basis of [Dem.] 36.2, the defendant in the original case could have gained time after the *paragraphē* trial. However, this remains speculative, and even if it were the case, such a means of delaying the case would have had serious disadvantages. The losing party in a *paragraphē* case had to pay the penalty of *epōbelia*, one-sixth of the amount of money or value of the property in dispute.[28] Moreover, it is likely that defeat in a *paragraphē* would have seriously affected the reopened original case, since litigants at a *paragraphē* trial normally discussed not only technical aspects of legality concerning the original prosecution but also its substantive issues.

However, the defendant in the original case could obviously prolong the period prior to the *paragraphē* trial, at least. When Chrysippos prosecuted Phormion, the defendant entered a *paragraphē* to bar the action. When the case was about to come to court (μελλούσης δὲ τῆς δίκης εἰσιέναι εἰς τὸ δικαστήριον), the disputants submitted the case to a private arbitrator.[29] In other words, the *paragraphē* trial was adjourned after the preliminary procedures were already or almost completed. A litigant, therefore, could delay a *paragraphē* trial by using private arbitration. Subsequently, following the instructions of the arbitrator, the *paragraphē* case of Chrysippos and Phormion came to court the next year ([34.]17). At this *paragraphē* trial, Chrysippos gave tes-

26 [Dem.] 36.2.

27 Wolff 1966 argues that, if a trial of *paragraphē* was unsuccessful, it was followed by a separate hearing of the original issue. However, he thinks that the trial of substance could have taken place on the same day, before the same judges (84–85). MacDowell 1978: 215 argues that a hearing of the original issue took place a later day. No contemporary text explicitly shows what happened after a *paragraphē* trial. Carawan 2011 argues that there would have been no second stage.

28 Isok. 18.35, 37.

29 [Dem.] 34.18.

timony about this private arbitration (§ 21), which means that a preliminary hearing, at which the disputants placed their testimonies, was held again after the arbitration. In this instance, the case clearly came to court much later than it would have done without the *paragraphē*. Although a litigant who entered a *paragraphē* ran the risk of defeat and incurring *epōbelia*, he had the chance to avoid the serious disadvantages of defeat in the *paragraphē* by strengthening his weak points or negotiating with the plaintiff for an out-of-court settlement during the prolonged period before the *paragraphē* trial took place. Although we have no explicit evidence, *hypōmosia* may have been used for delaying *paragraphē* trials, in a similar way to how private arbitration was used by Phormion.

3 Reasons for Impeding the Legal Process

Thus far, it has been demonstrated that Athenian litigants made use of various legal procedures from time to time to impede the commencement of a trial in court. To understand the nature of this preliminary stage that followed after the filing of a case, it is useful to investigate the reasons for which Athenian litigants impeded legal proceedings.

One obvious reason for an Athenian litigant to use delaying tactics is to rectify any weaknesses in his case and gain the advantage over his opponent. A prolonged preliminary stage could provide a litigant with more opportunities to obtain additional information, witnesses and *synēgoroi*, so that he could present a better argument in court or revise his strategy to gain ascendancy over his opponent. As mentioned above, Kallistratos admitted that he and Olympiodoros tried to postpone a *diadikasia* trial with a *hypōmosia* to deal with a situation that they were completely unprepared for, so that they 'could make preparation for the trial at leisure' (ὥστε παρασκευάσασθαι ἡμᾶς καθ' ἡσυχίαν πρὸς τὸν ἀγῶνα).[30] It is not clear what they would have done exactly, if an adjournment had been allowed. However, at least they could have developed a new strategy to overcome the difficulty. As in this instance, from time to time, litigants would have faced difficulties resulting from unexpected situations or insufficient preparation. Sositheos explained that the reason why he had a large number of depositions read out in court was to avoid the same difficulty he had previously encountered due to a lack of preparation (Dem. 43.47). In order to resolve a similar problem, Androkles, as mentioned above, made use of the adjournment of an *anakrisis* and gathered, or possibly fabricated, additional

30 Dem. 48.23–25.

information so that he could provide it at the next hearing (Isa. 6.12–13). Moreover, if these litigants had felt a need to rectify their weaknesses, they might have tried to use the time that would have resulted from the delays to gather information, especially from in and around the Agora.[31]

Athenian litigants could have expected not only chances to gather more information but also (at least in public actions) a shift in public opinion or in the citizens' sentiments during the period of delay. They may have tried to manipulate their fellow citizens' opinion by spreading rumours or taking similar actions.[32] In the case of Hegesandros, as seen above, he and his brother made public speeches in the Assembly while the arbitration between Hegesandros and Glaukon was suspended (Aischin. 1.62–64). In other words, Hegesandros and his brother displayed and established their social status and credibility before the case came to court. In high profile cases such as this, defendants could expect the dikasts to have forgotten the event in question by the time the trial would begin; as it might have been an event that angered the jurors, it would therefore have been unfavourable to the defendant if the trial had gone to court immediately.[33] Demosthenes lamented that the wealthy, like Meidias, were given whatever date they wanted for trial and that their wrongdoings were 'stale and cold' (ἕωλα … καὶ ψύχρ') by the time the case reached court (21.112). On the other hand, prosecutors, at least in *graphē paranomōn*, could wait for a good occasion before bringing the case to court once they had brought in an indictment.[34] It is well known that Aischines brought a *graphē paranomōn* against Ktesiphon, but the case came to court only six years later in 330 BC. Diondas brought an indictment against Assembly's proposal in 338 BC, but the trial did not take place until four years later. While no ancient source explicitly tells us how or why they delayed these trials, it is generally agreed that they chose a time which might give them a better prospect of persuading the dikasts to vote against their opponents.[35]

If a defendant filed a counter-suit against his opponent and succeeded in delaying the case that had been brought against him, as Theophemos did (Dem. 47.39–45), he could use the counter-suit as a test case, especially when both

31 E.g. Aischin. 1.94; Lys. 23.6. On the circulation of news in Athenian society, see Lewis 1996: 9–23; Hunter 1994: esp. 96–117.

32 E.g. Dem. 21.104; 24.15.

33 E.g. Aischin. 3.221; Dem. 21.112.

34 In contrast, a prosecutor of *graphē paranomōn* had to bring an indictment within a one-year of time limit (*prothesmia*). On this point, see Giannadaki 2014.

35 On the possible means to delay a public case, see Horváth in this volume. On the possible reasons for suspending the prosecution, see Harris 1995: 138–142; Rhodes 2009: 226; Horváth 2014: 35–45; Horváth in this volume.

cases concerned the same matter. If the plaintiff in the counter-suit won the case, he must have been in an advantageous position either for contesting the other case as defendant or for conducting negotiations for an out-of-court settlement. Even if he lost the case, the plaintiff was still in a position to contest the original suit.[36] In this case, it is likely that he would have chosen to negotiate with his opponent towards reconciliation. While this strategy may have been advantageous if successful, it may have been difficult to achieve, since it does not seem to have been easy for a litigant to make his opponent agree to delay only the original case brought against him.

Another possible reason for impeding legal proceedings would be to evade trial through an out-of-court settlement. Gathering information and choosing the right timing may have contributed not only to the improvement of a litigant's position in the faceoff in court but also to their successful negotiation with their opponents regarding out-of-court settlements. In fact, Pittalakos eventually dropped his case after coming to realise his opponent's sociopolitical strength during the period of delay. Realising the potential for adverse developments and/or merely the inconvenience of continuing the legal process, plaintiffs might prefer an out-of-court settlement to a trial, although this was not necessarily a satisfactory solution for both parties. If a defendant, his friends or his relatives had enough time to negotiate with the plaintiff, the plaintiff might have been persuaded to avoid the trial. Menekles and his adopted son eventually decided to withdraw their *dikē* against Menekles' brother after a lengthy and unfriendly negotiation with the defendant, although it is not certain whether they delayed the legal process for the negotiation.[37] Apollodoros seems to have dropped a *graphē hybreōs* against Phormion because while the case was delayed, affectionate appeals were advanced by Apollodoros' mother on behalf of her second husband Phormion.[38] It is true that a prosecutor would be fined at least 1,000 *drachmai*, in certain circumstances at least, if he dropped a *graphē*.[39] Apollodoros may just have paid the penalty. However, it was also possible for a prosecutor to drop his public case

36 That is not to say there were no risks associated with launching a countersuit: the plaintiff in a counter prosecution needed to pay the fees for the countersuit as well as those for the case against him. He was also liable to the *epōbelia* (see above p. 152). Moreover, he was likely to be less prepared in general than an 'ordinary' plaintiff.

37 Isa. 2.29–30.

38 [Dem.] 45.4. Apollodoros offers no reason for the delay. Nor does he clearly mention what happened with the *graphē* after they were reconciled, but he seems to have dropped the case at some point.

39 On dropping *graphai*, see Harris 1999; Harris 2005; MacDowell 1990: 327–328; Rubinstein 2000: 198–212; Wallace 2006: 57–66; Sato 2015.

de facto by leaving it suspended with a *hypōmosia*, an oath for postponement, indefinitely, because he presumably had the right to resume it. As mentioned above, Theokrines is said to have used this tactic to, in effect, drop the *graphē paranomōn* against Demosthenes, when they were secretly reconciled. In this case, the *hypōmosia* was abused not only to achieve a postponement but also an out-of-court settlement. Presumably, not only verbal negotiation but also monetary compensation, or bribery in public cases, worked well as a means of persuading a plaintiff to drop a case.[40]

4 Importance of Negotiations

In order to achieve the goals of these delaying strategies, the mutual consent of the disputants was quite important. Mutual agreement between the contending parties was required for the postponement of a public arbitration, as demonstrated by the case of Demosthenes and Meidias.[41] The procedures for private arbitration likewise required the disputants' consent and negotiation.[42] The choice of arbitrator and that of the hearing date were made by mutual agreement. If the disputants decided upon a different day from the one prescribed by law, any trial or judgment would be postponed. A litigant in the fourth century BC said, 'even when the thirtieth day is prescribed by law, we quite often set a different day by mutual consent; and at any office the officials postpone trials and judgments for the contending parties, when they have reached an agreement' (πολλάκις γὰρ ἔν τε τοῖς νόμοις γεγραμμένης τριακοστῆς ἡμέρας ἑτέραν ἡμῖν αὐτοῖς συγχωρήσαντες ἐθέμεθα, παρά τε ταῖς ἀρχαῖς ἁπάσαις καὶ δίκας καὶ κρίσεις ἀναβάλλονται τοῖς ἀντιδίκοις οἱ ἄρχοντες συγχωρησάντων ἐκείνων ἀλλήλοις).[43] Although the speaker was probably exaggerating,[44] it is also likely that this rule was applied to most private cases. In theory, therefore, a litigant could considerably delay the legal process further by persuading his opponent to do so.[45] In order to suspend legal procedures by swearing a *hypō-*

40 Numerous passages suggesting the use of bribery to secure the abandonment of a trial are found in the extant Attic orations, e.g. Lys. 6.11–12; 20.7, 10, 15; 25.3, 26; 27.14–15; Aischin. 2.93, 148; 3.52; Dem. 18.102–103; 21.3, 39, 215–216; [25.]47, 49–50; [Dem.] 58. 6, 8, 12–13, 32, 33, 35. Monetary compensations: e.g. [Dem.] 36.14–17; 38.4; Isok. 18.7.

41 Dem. 21.84.

42 Scafuro 1997: esp. 31–42, 117–141, 393–399; Hunter 1994: 55–66.

43 [Dem.] 42.13. Moreover, private agreements between two parties before witnesses were highly respected ([Dem.] 42.12; 47.77; 56.2; Dein. 3.4; Hyp. *Athen.* 13).

44 E.g. *eisangelia* allowed no procedural delay (Hyp. *Eux.* 7).

45 Even after a private arbitration was delayed for a long time, a plaintiff could file the same

mosia, an oath for postponement, it was necessary to secure the opponent's consent. Otherwise, an *antōmosia*, a counter-oath, could prevent the delay of the procedures.[46] If, on the other hand, both parties agreed, the prosecutor would not resume the suspended trial for as long as they chose; the trial could even be suspended indefinitely. It is true that the use of some means of delay required no mutual consent. For example, the prosecutor of a *graphē paranomōn* could presumably suspend his case without the defendant's consent[47] after the indictment was brought. *Paragraphē* as a special plea to bar an action does not seem to have required the agreement of the plaintiff, either. However, as in the case of Chrysippos ([Dem.] 34.17), a defendant could ask his prosecutor to submit their case to a private arbitrator after entering a *paragraphē*. Presumably, he could also have adjourned a *paragraphē* trial with a *hypōmosia*. As argued above, if a defendant brought a *paragraphē* and delayed it through a private arbitration or a *hypōmosia*, he could gather information and/or conduct negotiations with the plaintiff in the original case before the *paragraphē* trial would come to court, and through this, he could avoid the risk of defeat and the penalty of *epōbelia*. Therefore, negotiations with the opponent could have played an important role even when a defendant tried to delay legal proceedings through a *paragraphē*.

These strategies could not possibly be implemented in the absence of a plaintiff's readiness for negotiation. Some plaintiffs may have wanted to defeat their opponents in public. However, the extant Attic orations reveal that a number of plaintiffs offered to entrust their cases to private arbitrators after they themselves had formally initiated *dikai*.[48] It is true that, when consider-

case afresh (e.g. [Dem.] 40.16, 19, 30). As for a public arbitration, *Ath. Pol.* 53.5 reports that each public arbitrator had to complete all cases that were allotted to him. This could mean either that a public arbitrator was required to finish all of his arbitrations within his year of service, or that it was obligatory for him to complete all the assigned cases by himself even after the end of the year. See Whitehead 2002: 76–79. Isa. 12.11 reports that an arbitrator held a case for two years, but that may have been exceptional rather than normal. Even if public arbitrators were legally allowed to do their jobs beyond the end of an *archōn* year, some of them may have preferred to complete their cases within the year and thus have avoided delaying an arbitration beyond the year's end.

46 Dem. 48.25; [58.]43. In the inheritance case concerning Komon's estate, since the *antōmosia* against Olympiodoros' *hypōmosia* was approved by the juries, his claim was dismissed (Dem. 48.26). It is not certain what happed after an *antōmosia* was approved in other types of trials.

47 For the options available to a defendant to compel his opponent to proceed to trial see Horváth in this volume.

48 E.g. [Dem.] 36.14–17; [Dem.] 52.14–45, 30; Isa. 2.28–30. But the request for arbitration was not infrequently made by defendants (e.g. Isa. 5.31–33; [Dem.] 34.18–21; Lys. fr. 20. 44, 45

ing Attic orators' rhetoric, the initiative for out-of-court settlements described in forensic orations should not be taken literally; but they at least suggest that a noteworthy number of plaintiffs were, either willingly or reluctantly, ready to negotiate with their defendants. Needless to say, negotiations were neither always successful nor necessarily satisfactory for both parties. The contending parties must have probed their opponents' intentions and must have chosen tactics that were suitable to the situation in which each of them was placed. Therefore, the period that followed after the filing of a case, but before the case came to court, seems to have been a stage for strategic negotiations between the two parties.

5 Developing Strategies

This section provides a summary of the historical development of delaying strategies. Athenian litigants presumably used their delaying tactics in accordance with newly instituted legal procedures. Among the above-mentioned procedures, *paragraphē*, a special plea to bar an action, was instituted in 401/0 BC or slightly earlier, and subsequently, its scope was extended to cover a much wider range of cases.[49] Therefore, the tactic of delaying legal proceedings through a *paragraphē* must have been developed during the fourth century BC.

Hypōmosia, an oath for postponement of legal proceedings, coupled with *antōmosia*, may also have been formally instituted in the fourth century BC. This type of *hypōmosia* is attested only in the fourth century BC (Dem. 21.84; 39.37; 47.39; Dem. 48.25; [58.]43; Hyp. *Eux.* 7; fr. 202).[50] Xenophon used the same term to describe the situation in 406 BC, but that was not an oath to postpone legal proceedings but rather an oath to express strong objection to a decree passed in the Assembly (Xen. *Hell.* 1.7.34). The oath for postponement of legal proceedings, therefore, may have been formally instituted along with other

(Baiter and Sauppe); cf. Dem. 21.119), including those who brought a countersuit against the plaintiff of the original case ([Dem.] 59.65–71; cf. Andok. 1.122). Cf. Scafuro 1997: 396–398.

49 Isager and Hansen 1973: 123–124; Todd 1993: 136–137; Whitehead 2002.

50 Harrison 1971: 155–156; Sato 2010 shows that no *hypōmosia* for postponement is attested in the fifth century BC. I also argue that the *hypōmosia* mentioned in Dem. 18.103 is possibly an oath for postponing legal procedures, not one for initiating a *graphē nomon mē epitēdeion theinai*. If so, all *hypōmosiai* attested in the extant Attic orations were oaths for postponement (Dem. 18.103; 21.84; 39.37; 47.39; Dem. 48.25; [58.]43; Hyp. *Eux.* 7; fr. 202). *Hypōmosia* as an oath to express strong objection to a decree in the Assembly is also attested in the fourth century BC, but only in comedy (Ar. *Plut.* 725).

legal procedures after the restoration of the Athenian democracy.[51] However, like any *argumentum e silentio*, this is impossible to prove.

Although the precise date is uncertain, public arbitration could have been instituted in 400/399 BC, or perhaps slightly earlier, and the first official arbitrators could have taken office in 399/8 BC.[52] When using delaying tactics, Athenian litigants in private cases seem to have been conscious of the importance of public arbitration. In fact, Attic orations attest that some litigants used delaying tactics before a public arbitrator gave his verdict.[53] Demetrios of Phaleron also suggests that delaying tactics, such as a *paragraphē* and a *hypōmosia*, were used by litigants with a weak case in order to impede the legal procedure before public arbitration took place.[54]

It is true that a public arbitrator's verdict was not binding. However, an unfavourable verdict at a public arbitration could leave a negative impression with the jurors in a court case. In fact, in court cases, many litigants referred to the favourable verdicts they secured at their public arbitrations.[55] For this reason, litigants must have wanted to make sufficient preparations to avoid an adverse verdict. Moreover, the disputants were required to place all their evidence into two separate urns, *echinoi*, after the arbitrator's verdict was given, and once they were sealed, no new evidence could be submitted (*Ath. Pol.* 53.2–4).[56] Therefore, it is reasonable to believe that Athenian litigants would have tried to delay the public arbitration and to gather more information, witnesses and *synēgoroi* during the delay, in order to either win the trial in court or to make advantageous negotiations.

It is beyond the scope of this chapter to investigate what types of delaying tactics existed, if any, before the end of the fifth century BC. However, in the fourth century BC, the Athenians presumably developed delaying strategies—in conjunction with the developments of the judicial system, including public arbitration, *paragraphē*, and possibly *hypōmosia*—to facilitate negotiations for settling disputes both through a trial in a court of law and through out-of-court settlements.

---

51 On the development of Athenian judicial procedures in the fourth century, see e.g. Rhodes 1995; Thür 1995.

52 MacDowell 1971; Scafuro 1997: 391; Whitehead 2002: 89.

53 E.g. Dem. 21.84; 39.37; 47.45. Cf. Dem. 54.26–29.

54 *Lex. Rhet. Cantab.*, s.v. Μὴ οὖσα δίκη.

55 E.g. Dem. 21.83–87; 39.37; [40.]17.

56 On public arbitration in general, see Gernet 1934; Harrell 1936; Ruschenbusch 1989; Rhodes 1981: 587–596; Todd 1993: 128–130. On the nature of evidence put in the *echinoi*, see Thür 2007.

Conclusion

In order to delay legal proceedings, Athenian litigants used and abused various procedures, such as *hypōmosia* or *paragraphē*, after their cases were filed. In some cases, delaying tactics may have helped them to win at trial in court, but in a presumably noteworthy number of cases, those tactics were used to give them the opportunity to negotiate a private settlement. Moreover, most delaying tactics required mutual agreement between the contending parties. For Athenian litigants, therefore, the period between the filing of a case and the beginning of a trial constituted an important stage for strategic negotiations concerning dispute settlements. The Athenians devised delaying and negotiating tactics in accordance with the judicial system that was developed in the fourth century BC. In other words, not only the judicial system but also the culture of dispute settlement was developed in Athens in the fourth century BC.[57]

Bibliography

Carawan, E. (2011) '*Paragraphê* and the Merits', *GRBS* 51, 254–295.

Carey, C. (2004) 'Offence and Procedure in Athenian Law', in Harris, E.M. and Rubinstein, L., eds (2004) *The Law and the Courts in Ancient Greece*, London, 111–136.

Christ, M.R. (1998) *The Litigious Athenian*, Baltimore.

Cohen, D. (1991) *Law, Sexuality and Society: The Enforcement of Morals in Classical Athens*, Cambridge.

Cohen, D. (1995) *Law, Violence, and Community in Classical Athens*, Cambridge.

Eder, W., ed. (1995) *Die athenische Demokratie im 4. Jahrhundert v. Chr.: Vollendung oder Verfall einer Verfassungsform?* Stuttgart.

Fisher, N. (2001) *Aeschines, Against Timarchos*, Oxford.

Gernet, L. (1934) 'L'institution des arbitres publics a Athènes', *Revue des Ètudes Grecques* 52, 389–414.

Giannadaki, I. (2014) 'The Time Limit (*prothesmia*) in the *graphe paranomon*', *Dike* 17, 15–34.

Harrell, H.C. (1936) *Public Arbitration in Athenian Law*, Columbia, Mo.

Harris, E.M. (1994) 'Law and Oratory', in Worthington, I., ed. (1994) *Persuasion: Greek Rhetoric in Action*, London, 130–150.

Harris, E.M. (1995) *Aeschines and Athenian Politics*, Oxford.

57 I am grateful to Prof. P.J. Rhodes, Prof. H. van Wees, Prof. H. Bowden, the editors of this volume and the participants of the International Conference 'Use and Abuse of Law in Athenian Courts' for their useful comments. I also would like to thank Enago (www.enago.jp) for the English language review.

Harris, E.M. (1999) 'The Penalty for Frivolous Prosecution in Athenian Law', *Dike* 2, 123–142.

Harris, E.M. (2000) 'Open Texture in Athenian Law', *Dike* 3, 27–79.

Harris, E.M. (2005) 'Feuding or the Rule of Law? The Nature of Litigation in Classical Athens. An Essay in Legal Sociology', in Gagarin, M. and Wallace, R., eds (2005) *Symposion 2001: Vorträge zur griechischen und hellenistischen Rechtsgeschichte* (Evanston, Ill., 5–8 September 2001) Vienna 125–142. (Reprinted in Harris, E.M. (2006) *Democracy and the Rule of Law in Classical Athens: Essays on Law, Society, and Politics*, Cambridge, 405–422.)

Harrison, A.R.W. (1968–1971) *The Law of Athens*, 2 vols, Oxford.

Horváth, L. (2014) *Der 'Neue Hypereides': Textedition, Studien und Erläuterungen*, Berlin.

Hunter, V. (1994) *Policing Athens: Social Control in the Attic Lawsuits, 420–320 B.C.*, Princeton.

Isager, S. and Hansen, M.H. (1975) *Aspects of Athenian Society in the Fourth Century B.C.*, Odense.

Johnstone, S. (1999) *Disputes and Democracy: The Consequences of Litigation in Ancient Athens*, Austin.

Lewis, S. (1996) *News and Society in the Greek Polis*, London.

MacDowell, D.M. (1971) 'The Chronology of Athenian Speeches and Legal Innovations in 401–398 B.C.', *Revue Internationale des Droits de l'Antiquité* 18, 267–273.

MacDowell, D.M. (1978) *The Law in Classical Athens*, London.

MacDowell, D.M. (1990) *Demosthenes: Against Meidias*, Oxford.

Osborne, R. (1985) 'Law in Action in Classical Athens', *JHS* 105, 40–58. (Reprinted in Osborne (2010) 171–204.)

Osborne, R. (2010) *Athens and Athenian Democracy*, Cambridge.

Rhodes, P.J. (1981) *A Commentary on the Aristotelian* Athenaion Politeia, Oxford.

Rhodes, P.J. (1995) 'Judicial Procedure in Fourth-Century Athens', in Eder, W., ed. (1995), 303–319.

Rhodes, P.J. (2009) 'Hyperides' *Against Diondas*: Two Problems', *BICS* 52, 223–228.

Rubinstein, L. (2000) *Litigation and Cooperation: Supporting Speakers in the Courts of Classical Athens*, Stuttgart.

Ruschenbusch, E. (1989) 'Drei Beiträge zur öffentlichen Diaita in Athen', in Fernandez Nieto, F.J. ed., (1989) *Symposion 1982: Vorträge zur griechischen und hellenistischen Rechtsgeschichte (Santander, 1–4 September 1982)*, Cologne, 31–40.

Sato, N. (2010) '*Hypomosia*: an interpretation of Demosthenes 18.103', in Oshiba, Y. and Koike, N., eds (2010) *For the future of classics: Festschrift in honour of Prof. K. Itsumi*, Tokyo, 311–322. (In Japanese)

Sato, N. (2015) 'Out-of-Court Settlement and Public Opinion in Democratic Athens', *Kodai* 16, 43–55.

Scafuro, A. (1997) *The Forensic Stage: Settling Disputes in Graeco-Roman New Comedy*, Cambridge.

Thalheim, T. (1914) 'Ὑπωμοσία' in Kroll, W., ed., *Paulys Realencyclopädie der classischen Altertumswissenschaft* IX-1, Stuttgart, 337–338.
Thür, G. (1995) 'Die athenischen Geschworenengerichte—eine Sackgasse?', in Eder, W. ed. (1995), 321–331.
Thür, G. (1998) 'Hypomosia', in Cancik, H. and Schneider, H., eds (1998) *Die Neue Pauly*, vol. 5, Stuttgart, 815.
Thür, G. (2007) 'Das Prinzip der Fairness im attischen Prozess: Gedanken zu *echinos* und *enklema*', in Cantarella, E., ed. (2007) *Symposion 2005: Vorträge zur griechischen und hellenistischen Rechtsgeschichte* (Salerno, 14–18 September 2005), Vienna, 131–158.
Todd, S.C. (1993) *The Shape of Athenian Law*, Oxford.
Wallace, R.W. (2006) 'Withdrawing *graphai* in Ancient Athens: A Case Study in 'Sycophancy' and Legal Idiosyncrasies', in Thür, G. and Rupprecht, H.-A., eds (2006) *Symposion 2003: Vorträge zur griechischen und hellenistischen Rechtsgeschichte* (Rauischholzhausen, 30 September–3 October 2003), Vienna, 57–66.
Whitehead, D. (2002) 'Athenian Laws and Lawsuits in the Late Fifth Century B.C.', *Museum Helveticum* 59, 71–96.
Wolff, H.J. (1966) *Die attische* paragraphe, Weimar.
Wyse, W. (1904) *The Speeches of Isaeus*. Cambridge.

PART 3

The Rhetoric of Law

CHAPTER 9

Clauses out of Context: Partial Citation of Statutes in Attic Forensic Oratory

Lene Rubinstein

> οὕτω τοίνυν περιφανῶς παράνομα γεγραφώς, παραταχθεὶς μετὰ Δημοσθένους ἐποίσει τέχνας τοῖς νόμοις· ἃς ἐγὼ δηλώσω καὶ προερῶ ὑμῖν, ἵνα μὴ λάθητε ἐξαπατηθέντες. οὗτοι γάρ, ὡς μὲν οὐκ ἀπαγορεύουσιν οἱ νόμοι τὸν ὑπὸ τοῦ δήμου στεφανούμενον μὴ κηρύττειν ἔξω τῆς ἐκκλησίας, οὐχ ἕξουσι λέγειν, οἴσουσι δὲ εἰς τὴν ἀπολογίαν τὸν Διονυσιακὸν νόμον, καὶ χρήσονται τοῦ νόμου μέρει τινὶ κλέπτοντες τὴν ἀκρόασιν ὑμῶν, καὶ παρέξονται νόμον οὐδὲν προσήκοντα τῇδε τῇ γραφῇ …
>
> Since he has so blatantly proposed something unlawful and has been lined up next to Demosthenes, he will apply cunning tricks to the laws. What they are, I shall reveal and inform you about in advance, so that you won't be deceived unawares. Now, these men cannot produce any arguments to the effect that the laws do not forbid that the person crowned by the *dēmos* should be proclaimed anywhere except in the Assembly. However, they will adduce in their defence the law on the Dionysia, and, deceiving your ears, they will use a part (μέρει τινὶ) of the law, and they will produce a law that is not in any way relevant to the present legal action (*graphē*) …
>
> AISCHIN. 3.35

This passage, delivered in a *graphē paranomōn* (public trial against an illegal decree) against Ktesiphon, contains one of the most explicit comments on how partial citation of a law can be deployed as a method of deception. Aischines' claim is that by citing a clause of another law in isolation, suppressing its original statutory context, Ktesiphon will try to demonstrate the legality of a particular clause in his own decree, one of the clauses that had been singled out as unconstitutional by Aischines in his formal writ that was forming the basis of his *graphē*.[1]

1 On the contents and layout of the writ which formed the basis of Aischines' legal action, see

 | DOI:10.1163/9789004377899_011

To a modern observer, it may seem obvious that the interpretation of a statute requires the consideration of the text in its entirety. When we engage with a law or a decree preserved on stone, we naturally approach the text with the view that our interpretation of an individual clause should be informed not only by the clause itself, but also by the clauses that have preceded it as well as by those which follow. If read in isolation from its context, the wording of a single clause may permit a range of interpretations that are much broader and thus potentially quite different from those envisaged by the persons who originally drafted the enactment.[2] But however trivial such an observation may seem to us, the evidence of the Attic orators suggests that partial citation of statutes was much less controversial, and that the same may have been true of the kind of creative interpretation to which this tactic could give rise.

The starting point of the present chapter will be Aischines' admonition to the court that partial citation of specific statutes could be used as a way of misinforming the judges as to what the laws actually said and meant. To what extent did it reflect a more widespread concern that even the actual words of a genuine enactment might be twisted and interpreted in a way that distorted the enactment's meaning and applicability? And if partial citation of statutes could be perceived as a method by which the laws might be misrepresented and misapplied—that is, 'abused'—it needs to be asked why complaints about the practice are not found more frequently in surviving Attic oratory.

That Aischines' complaint was not an entirely eccentric one may be suggested by Demosthenes' counterattack in the published version of his speech. In a highly charged *apostrophē*, he responds to Aischines' point as follows:

> ἀκούεις, Αἰσχίνη, τοῦ νόμου λέγοντος σαφῶς, 'πλὴν ἐάν τινας ὁ δῆμος ἢ ἡ βουλὴ ψηφίσηται· τούτους δ' ἀναγορευέτω.' τί οὖν, ὦ ταλαίπωρε, συκοφαντεῖς; τί λόγους πλάττεις; τί σαυτὸν οὐκ ἐλλεβορίζεις ἐπὶ τούτοις; ἀλλ' οὐδ' αἰσχύνει φθόνου δίκην εἰσάγων, οὐκ ἀδικήματος οὐδενός, καὶ νόμους μεταποιῶν, τῶν δ' ἀφαιρῶν μέρη, οὓς ὅλους δίκαιον ἦν ἀναγιγνώσκεσθαι τοῖς γ' ὀμωμοκόσιν κατὰ τοὺς νόμους ψηφιεῖσθαι;
>
> Do you hear, Aischines, the law which says clearly 'except if the Assembly or the Council vote for them. Let the herald proclaim these'. Then why, you miserable man, do you play the sykophant? Why are you fabricating

Aischin. 3.200. For a recent general discussion of the writ as a basis for Athenian trials, see Harris 2013.

2 On this problem in relation to enactments that have survived in the epigraphical corpus, see Rubinstein 2008.

> tales? Why are you not bringing yourself to your senses on these matters by taking a dose of hellebore? No, you are not ashamed of taking a legal action to court, not for any crime, but a legal action for envy, or of refashioning the laws or of removing parts of some of them, which it would be just to have read out in their entirety for the benefit of those who have sworn to vote in accordance with the laws.
>
> DEM. 18.121

What is interesting here is that Demosthenes does not explicitly defend the practice of citing clauses out of context; instead, he accuses Aischines of employing the very same tactic, leading to a similar kind of distortion. Taken together, the two passages suggest that both speakers were expecting that at least some members of their audience might be aware of the kind of manipulation that could be achieved through partial citation.

It seems certain that it was not in itself unlawful to submit only parts of statutes for recital by the court attendant. In his commentary on Dem. 18.121, Wankel (1976: 653) has drawn attention to Dem. 23.88 as explicit evidence that confirms the legality of the practice. Here the speaker prefaces the recitation by the court attendant of a number of decrees as follows:

> λέγε τὰ ψηφίσματα ταυτί. ἀλλ' ἵνα μὴ μακρὸν ὑμῖν ἀκούειν ᾖ, ἐξ ἑκάστου τῶν ψηφισμάτων αὐτὸ τοῦτ' ἐξείλεκται περὶ οὗ τούτου κατηγορῶ. λέγε.
>
> Recite these decrees. But in order that you should not have to listen for long, this very matter on the basis of which I am prosecuting my opponent has been excerpted from the decrees. Recite.
>
> DEM. 23.88

Carey (1994: 101–102) has suggested that a similar tactic was deployed in Lys. 1.28, where the speaker may have submitted only part of the law on adultery for recitation by the court attendant. Other passages, including the celebrated lecture on Athenian legislation offered in Lys. 10.15–21, provide further evidence that the practice was in keeping with Athenian court etiquette and convention.[3] But here, as is also the case with for example the numerous short quotations of statutes incorporated into Apollodoros' second speech against

3 On these sections of Lys. 10, see Hillgruber 1988: 66–80 and Todd 2007: 677–685. Although only three of the six brief citations are preceded by explicit instructions to the court attendant, it is most likely that all were read out by him, interspersed with the speaker's own interpretations.

Stephanos ([Dem.] 46), it is an open question whether what we now read is the same text as the judges originally heard. Even when a good case can be made for the authenticity of a particular clause, it cannot be ruled out that the law originally submitted for recitation by the court attendant has been abridged not by the litigant himself or his speechwriter, but by a later editor, who chose to include only the words which would make the litigant's line of argument intelligible to a reading audience.

It complicates matters even further that the term *nomos* itself sometimes seems to be used by litigants to refer to a single clause of a law, rather than to the piece of legislation in its entirety. Thus in Isa. 7.21–22, what appear to be two clauses from the same law on intestate succession are read out separately, each under its own heading as a separate *nomos*, by the court attendant.[4] This ambiguity means that we cannot always tell if a litigant, when using the plural *nomoi* in his own text, is referring to several different laws or to several clauses of the same law.

Yet, despite the uncertainty that surrounds the length and type of citations that were originally read out by the court attendant in specific cases, it is clear that partial citations of laws were an important part of the logographer's toolkit. For, as is well known, law texts, quoted directly or paraphrased by the litigants themselves, often formed an important part of their legal argumentation. There was evidently no expectation that such quotations should be accompanied by a formal reading of the clauses by the court attendant. In his article on the use of *nomoi* in the speeches of Isaios, Edwards (2008) observes that is surprisingly rare for Isaios' clients to ask for *nomoi* to be formally recited; indeed, it is far more frequently the case that the litigants cite or paraphrase parts of laws in their own voice, as an integral part of their own addresses. With the exception of some, but not all, of the speeches delivered in *graphai paranomōn* and in *graphai nomon mē epitēdeion theinai* (public suits for introducing illegal decrees/unsuitable laws), the pattern identified by Edwards is replicated across the corpus.[5]

Edwards also draws attention to a number of individual instances where litigants use such partial citations as the basis for legal interpretations that may be open to question, at least when seen from a modern perspective. In addi-

4 See Edwards 2008: 48 and Wyse 1904: 564–565. See also Gagarin 2008: 192 with n. 40 on this terminological ambiguity in the context of Dem. 23.

5 See Rubinstein 2008: 122 n. 23 for quotations or paraphrases of specific statutes in forensic speeches delivered by litigants who do not appear to have submitted any laws for recitation by the court attendant. For an overview of such integrated citations in the corpus of forensic oratory as a whole, see the list of legal citations in Harris 2009/10: 42–61, Appendix 2.

tion to the examples in Isaios' speeches, there are several other instances where litigants explore the interpretative potential of partial citations incorporated directly into their own speeches, of which the best known and most frequently discussed can be found in Hypereides' speech against Athenogenes.[6] Another striking example of the tactic is found deployed in Dem. 24 *Against Timokrates for the proposal of an unsuitable law*, where, as demonstrated by Mossé (2004: 97–100), the speaker Diodoros bases his argumentative strategy on what are clearly selective quotations of the law under attack.[7]

Here I shall confine myself to just one example found in Dem. 44 *Against Leochares*. The speech was delivered by the plaintiff in a private action for false testimony, a *dikē pseudomartyriōn*. The defendant Leochares, who claimed to be the adopted son of the long dead Archiades, had attempted to block an inheritance procedure concerning Archiades' estate by asserting in a *diamartyria* the existence of a legitimate (*gnēsios*) son. In 44.49 the plaintiff cites, in his own voice, a single line from the law relating to betrothals as proof that the term *gnēsios*, which apparently was the term used in the defendant's *diamartyria*, was applicable only to biological offspring but not to adopted sons, and consequently not to Leochares himself:

> οὑτοσὶ τοίνυν διαμεμαρτύρηκεν τοὺς οὐκ ὄντας εἶναι, καὶ γέγραφεν ἐν τῇ διαμαρτυρίᾳ 'ὄντων παίδων', ἕνα φάσκων αὑτὸν εἶναι. ἀλλὰ μὴν 'γνησίων' γ' ὅταν λέγῃ καὶ 'κυρίως κατὰ τὸν θεσμόν', παρακρούεται παρὰ τοὺς νόμους. τὸ μὲν γὰρ γνήσιόν ἐστιν, ὅταν ᾖ γόνῳ γεγονός· καὶ ὁ νόμος ταῦτα μαρτυρεῖ λέγων, 'ἣν ἂν ἐγγυήσῃ πατὴρ ἢ ἀδελφὸς ἢ πάππος, ἐκ ταύτης εἶναι παῖδας γνησίους.' τὸ δὲ 'κυρίως' κατὰ τῶν ποιήσεων ὁ νομοθέτης ἔλαβεν, ὑπολαμβάνων δεῖν, ὅταν τις ὢν ἄπαις καὶ κύριος τῶν ἑαυτοῦ ποιήσηται υἱόν, ταῦτα κύρια εἶναι.

> Well, then, my opponent here has asserted in his *diamartyria* the existence of non-existing sons, and he has written in his diamartyria 'because there are children', claiming that he himself is one such child. Yet, surely when he says 'legitimate' (*gnēsioi*) and 'validly according to the ordinance', he is engaging in deceit in violation of the laws. For the term 'legit-

6 The bibliography on this speech, and on the strategies of legal interpretation adopted by the speaker, is vast. For recent discussions see Phillips 2009, Aviles 2011: 26–34, Kästle 2012a: 191–204, Thür 2013. See also Gagarin pp. 24–26, Arnaoutoglou pp. 190–191, and Giannadaki p. 209 n. 48.

7 See Canevaro 2013: 113–121 for a detailed discussion of the text of Timokrates' law, purportedly read out by the court attendant in 24.39–40 and again in 24.71, where the court attendant is stopped by the speaker halfway through the text, as well as of the selective quotations from it in the course of the speech itself.

> imate' applies when a child is born of one's body. And the law testifies to this when it says: 'From a woman whom her father or brother or grandfather has pledged in marriage, from her there shall be legitimate children'. And the term 'validly' the lawgiver understood in relation to adoptions, considering that when a man who is childless and authorised to dispose of his property adopts a son, this should be 'valid'.[8]
>
> [DEM.] 44.48–49

In her comment on the passage, Scafuro (2011: 208) observes that the speaker's partial citation of the law on betrothal permits him to interpret its contents to mean that only those children who were born from a betrothed woman were *gnēsioi*. This, in turn, allows the speaker to convey the impression that the law served to distinguish between natural children and adopted children, with only the former being *gnēsioi*.[9] But as she points out, the paraphrase of the same law offered by Apollodoros in [Dem.] 46.19, following immediately after a recital of the law by the court attendant, shows that that the law also contained a clause pertaining to the betrothal of women who had no surviving male relatives belonging to the prescribed categories. This clause makes it clear that the emphasis of the law in its entirety was on betrothal and on who was authorised to betroth a woman in marriage; it was not at all concerned with any distinction between natural and adopted children (and as Scafuro emphasises, according to Athenian law only those who were born from betrothed women were eligible for adoption in the first place).

Although the speaker's creative application of the law in his attack on Leochares' *diamartyria* might not have been irretrievably damaged if he had included this clause, it would almost certainly have weakened its persuasive force. It would have revealed the intended, original emphasis of the law text quoted by the speaker and raised doubts as to the law's applicability to a case concerning the standing of a posthumously adopted son.

As mentioned above, the remarks in Aischin. 3.35 and Dem. 18.121 may be taken to suggest that there was an awareness among the Athenians generally that partial citation could be deployed as a way of manipulating the laws, and it is not inconceivable that this awareness extended also to the partial citation of statutes that were incorporated directly into the litigants' own speeches. Yet, given that this latter practice was so widespread, it must be asked why we do not hear more complaints about it in surviving forensic oratory. Surely, if partial

8 For a slightly different interpretation of the speaker's reasoning and rhetorical tactic, see Meinecke 1971: 299–302.

9 Cf., e.g., Gernet 1957: 145.

citation was recognised by the Athenians as a method of distortion or 'abuse' of the laws, we should expect more objections to the practice than we actually find?

There are several possible answers to that question, in my view complementary rather than mutually exclusive. The first part of the explanation may be related to the question of *ēthos*, a relation that has been discussed in some detail by Carey (1996) and de Brauw (2001/2). It has often been observed that litigants (and their logographers) had to strike a careful balance between demonstrating their own knowledge of and adherence to the city's laws on the one hand, and, on the other, avoiding the kind of sophisticated legal interpretation that might suggest excessive familiarity with the courtroom and the process of litigation.[10] A specific and detailed attack on the opponent's interpretation of a particular statute or clause had the potential to hit the speaker like a boomerang: by exposing his opponent's cleverness in manipulating the text of the law, the speaker might inadvertently be drawing attention to his own cleverness in the process.

Another part of the explanation may well be that a litigant who objected too explicitly to a statutory interpretation produced by his opponent might inadvertently draw the judges' attention to the ambiguity of the statute itself. As has frequently been observed, a litigant who engages in legal interpretation of a particular law in order to demonstrate its applicability to his own case needs to represent his own reading of its wording as authoritative—that is, as the only interpretation possible.[11] Discussing the opponent's handling of a particular statute, even if only to dismiss it, might constitute a disadvantage from a rhetorical point of view and, at worst, might even be construed by the judges as an attempt to argue against the law itself. By contrast, representing the statute itself as a) unambiguous and transparent and b) entirely in keeping with the speaker's own position may normally have been considered a far safer option.

Yet these considerations only take us so far in explaining the absence of objections to the opponents' partial citations. First, as far as *ēthos* is concerned, it is important not to generalise too far. As is well known, the (allegedly) simple-minded farmer's son Epikrates, for whom Hypereides wrote the speech *Against Athenogenes*, did explain his obvious familiarity with legislation that he claimed was of relevance to his case, citing his fear of his formidable opponent and the scale of his own financial plight as the reason why he had had to

10 The bibliography on this topic is vast. For references to previous literature see the recent discussion of Kästle 2012.

11 See e.g. Carey 1996: 44–45, Johnstone 1999: 23–24, Sickinger 2007: 290–296, Kästle 2012: 174–175.

study the laws 'day and night'.[12] In the particular context of the Athenogenes case, it is easy to see why Epikrates had to include this explanation in order not to undermine the very convincing character created by his logographer: much of his case hangs on his ability successfully to represent himself as a naive man of the countryside, unfamiliar with the ways of the city and its courts as well as with the wiles of experienced businessmen such as Athenogenes.

Epikrates' explanation is frequently represented as a standard means by which a litigant might counter the suspicion that he was overly litigious; yet, there are few parallels in the surviving corpus of Attic forensic oratory (indeed, the most explicit parallel to Epikrates' apology for his detailed research into the law, Dem. 54.17, is likewise voiced by a litigant who claims to be unfamiliar with the courts). The reason may well be that not all litigants felt the need to hide or apologise for their own extensive knowledge of their city's legislation or for their own ability to engage in quite sophisticated legal interpretation. Just as the general *topos* of inexperience is conspicuous by its absence in speeches written and delivered *in propria persona* by men who were well-known on Athens' political stage, so it is unsurprising that seasoned political figures would see no need to apologise for being well versed in the city's laws and their application.[13] In fact, some of them even flaunt their expertise, as does for example Hypereides in his discussion of the *nomos eisangeltikos* in his defence of Euxenippos.[14]

As for the danger that a systematic discussion and refutation of the opponent's interpretation of a particular law might undermine the litigant's own authoritative reading, it needs to be borne in mind that several litigants were in fact prepared to run this risk. Such refutations are found in several speeches: in addition to the attacks on the opponent's use of the law on *homologia* in Hyp. *Against Athenogenes*, the law on *kakēgoria* in Lys. 10.12–13 and the discussion of the *nomos eisangeltikos* in Hyp. *For Euxenippos* 1–10 and 28–31, we find them also in e.g. Antiph. 5.9–10 (on the opponent's application of the *nomos tōn*

12 Hyp. *Athen.* 13.

13 I have argued elsewhere (Powell, Rubinstein, and Kremmydas 2013: 2) that the *topos* of inexperience is found predominantly in speeches where the speakers' claims appear to be believable, whereas it is largely absent from public prosecution speeches. Several of the speakers who plead inexperience appear to be young (Lys. 17.1, 18.1, Dem. 27.1, 29.1, 44.4, [52.]1–2, 54.1, and [Dem.] 58.1–3), which may well have added plausibility to their claims. As for Theomnestos, nominally the prosecutor of Neaira, it is interesting to note that his plea of inexperience ([Dem.] 59.15) is immediately followed by his stepping down from the *bēma* and handing over to his *synēgoros*, who, he says, is older and has more legal experience (καὶ γὰρ πρεσβύτερός ἐστιν ἢ ἐγώ, καὶ ἐμπειροτέρως ἔχει τῶν νόμων …).

14 For this speech see Volonaki in this volume p. 296, 307 f.

kakourgōn), Lys. 6.9–10 (on the opponent's claims relating to the decree of Isotimides; cf. Andok. 1.71), Lys. 13.85–87 (on the clause *ep' autophōrō* in the writ), Lys. 13.88–90 (on the opponent's appeal to the reconciliation agreement), Lys. 14.4–8 (on the opponent's interpretation of the law on desertion), Isa. 11.1–4 (on the opponent's interpretation of the law on succession) and Dem. 22.8–11 (on the opponent's interpretation of the law forbidding awards to outgoing councillors, if the council had not had the requisite number of triremes constructed).

This brings us, then, to the third part of the explanation, which has to do with the way Athenian legal procedures operated, and, crucially, with the type of information that was made available to litigants (and their logographers) in advance of the trial, typically during the preliminary hearing (*anakrisis*) and public arbitration where applicable. A successful anticipation and refutation of the opponent's statutory interpretation would depend on prior knowledge of what laws the opponent intended to apply to his case.

It is a thorny question whether or not the opposing litigants were required to disclose in advance all the documents, including transcripts of laws, that they intended to use during the trial itself. There is no doubt that the litigants were required to submit all their documents when the trial was preceded by a public arbitration, and that they were prohibited from introducing further documents during the hearing-in-chief. However, some uncertainty surrounds the question whether this also applied in connection with those legal actions (including public actions of various kinds) in which the *anakrisis* was the only preliminary stage.

It has recently been argued[15] that the rule which pertained to trials preceded by arbitration applied also in connection with the *anakrisis*, that is, it would have applied to most Athenian legal procedures. If this is correct, it means that litigants, whatever the type of legal action, had to reveal to their opponent all the law texts that they wanted to have the court attendant read out during the course of the trial.[16] That would of course provide an opportunity for the opponent to predict and counter any sharp practices, including the kind of partial citation that might facilitate a creative interpretation of the words of the law itself.

If Thür's reconstruction is right (and it must be noted that the debate is still ongoing), this may well account for the attested examples provided above

15 By Thür 2008.

16 I find Thür's reconstruction of the *anakrisis* perfectly plausible when applied to ordinary *graphai* and *dikai*. However, many questions remain in regard to other types of public legal action, not least those which were introduced through the Assembly, the Council of 500 or the Areiopagos, such as some types of *eisangelia* and *apophasis*. On the *anakrisis* see also Kremmydas in this volume.

of litigants who directly challenged their opponents' interpretation of particular laws. On the other hand, the extant examples of litigants' anticipating their opponents' legal interpretations do not presuppose that the litigants were required fully to disclose their *atechnoi pisteis* in advance of the trial. Common to most of the passages listed above is that they focus on laws that had either formed the basis of the legal action itself or else been submitted as documentation by the prosecutor or defendant in order to substantiate their claims and counterclaims. Among the former are the *nomos tōn kakourgōn* in Antiph. 5 and Lys. 13, the law on military obligations in Lys. 14, the law on *kakēgoria* in Lys. 10, and the *nomos eisangeltikos* in Hyp. *For Euxenippos*. Among the latter are, of course, chiefly the laws submitted in connection with *graphai paranomōn* and *graphai nomon mē epitedeion theinai* and included in the prosecutor's writ, but also, for example, the law on intestate succession discussed and interpreted by Theopompos in Isa. 11.1–4. While the prosecutor had brought his action as a case of *kakōsis orphanou*, it is clear from Isa. 11.1 that he had deployed the inheritance law in order to substantiate his claim that the orphan's interests had indeed been harmed, and it is the prosecutor's interpretation and application of this law that is challenged directly by the defendant. And a similar use of a law pertaining to *epiklēroi* had almost certainly been made by Pantainetos in his *dikē metallikē* against the speaker of Dem. 37.[17]

However, as Thür has emphasised, such a rule would have applied to documents and documents *only*. It would not have applied to the laws or parts of laws that a litigant chose to integrate into his speech and deliver in his own voice. A litigant who opted for this tactic would not have been under any obligation to tip his hand in advance; he could freely hurl his quotations and paraphrases at his opponent in the courtroom. And it is precisely in connection with such integrated quotations that we find some of the most conspicuous examples of partial citations. It is striking, for example, that Epikrates does not ask the court attendant to read out even a single one of the partially cited laws on which he is basing his attack on Athenogenes' application of the law on *homologia* (Hyp. *Athen.* 13–22). Unless Athenogenes had got wind of the speaker's strategy through the various Athenian channels of gossip, there was no way that he or his advisers would have been in a position to prepare a detailed counterattack directed at Epikrates' creative use of these statutes. The widespread use of this strategy in the surviving speeches may, then, account in part for the relatively low frequency of specific complaints about the kind of distortion that could be achieved through the citation of individual clauses out of context.

17 As argued by Thür 2008: 63–64.

However, the choice to deploy the strategy may nevertheless have been a delicate one, for there were undoubtedly also considerable advantages connected with having one's laws read out formally by the court attendant. One advantage is a purely practical one of time, at least in private actions, where we know for certain that the water clock was stopped while laws were read out (*Ath. Pol.* 67.3). Thus, a litigant like Apollodoros, who padded his second speech against Stephanos for false testimony ([Dem.] 46) with no fewer than ten formal recitations of *nomoi* in the space of a mere 28 paragraphs, would have ended up being visible on the *bēma* for rather longer than the allocation provided to him by the water clock.

Another advantage is a less concrete one of performance, authority, and authenticity. Demosthenes prefaces the formal recitation of the law on *hybris* with the words:

> ἀνάγνωθι δ' αὐτόν μοι τὸν τῆς ὕβρεως νόμον· οὐδὲν γὰρ οἷον ἀκούειν αὐτοῦ τοῦ νόμου.
>
> But read me the actual law of *hybris*, for nothing is like hearing the law itself.
>
> DEM. 21.46

This may reflect not only an attempt on the part of Demosthenes to use the law as a way of attacking Meidias' character,[18] but also his expectation that his audience would have recognised and responded more favourably to 'the real thing' than to a quotation or paraphrase.[19] For the authority of an integrated citation or paraphrase undoubtedly rested, to a significant degree, on the credibility of the litigant himself. By contrast, a text, read out in the formal voice of the court attendant, would have been endowed with an authority of its own. And all the more so, if the Athenian law that prescribed the death penalty for 'producing a non-existing law'—as paraphrased by the speaker of Dem. 26.24—applied only when the laws had been submitted as written documents: just as the risk to the witness in the form of the *dikē pseudomartyriōn* could add weight to the witness statement itself, so the risk surrounding the written submission of a law text may well have added to the persuasive force of the law's words themselves. Regrettably, there is no evidence that will throw further light on the scope of

18 As has been argued by De Brauw 2001/2: 166–168.

19 Cf. also the phrase *ex autōn tōn nomōn* in Isa. 8.30 with the comment by Griffith-Williams 2013: 134–135.

the law referred to in Dem. 26.24 or, for that matter, the reliability of the wording of the speaker's paraphrase (it must be noted that the speaker does not have the law text read out by the court attendant!). Unless new evidence comes to light, the question must therefore remain open.

It must be emphasised, however, that the choice between the two, integration or recitation, was not always a clear-cut one. An adept litigant like Aischines could devise his speech so as to have his cake and eat it, especially if he was involved in the type of action that would permit a lengthy address. In his speech against Timarchos Aischines has a law on *hetairēsis* read out early in his speech, a move which would have lent significant authority to his rendering of the law in the preceding paragraphs (1.19–20). He reverts to the law, 140 paragraphs later, in order to counter his opponent's interpretation of what actually constitutes *hetairēsis*. Only this time his reference to the law is not accompanied by a formal reading. What is notable about this later reference is that Aischines uses it to assert what the laws do *not* include with rather less emphasis on what the laws do in fact prescribe:

> ἐὰν δ' ἐπιχειρῶσι λέγειν ὡς οὐχ ἡταίρηκεν ὅστις μὴ κατὰ συγγραφὰς ἐμισθώθη, καὶ γραμματεῖον καὶ μάρτυρας ἀξιῶσί με τούτων παρασχέσθαι, πρῶτον μὲν τοὺς περὶ τῆς ἑταιρήσεως νόμους μέμνησθε, ἐν οἷς οὐδαμοῦ μνείαν ὁ νομοθέτης περὶ συνθηκῶν πεποίηται. οὐ γάρ, εἰ κατὰ γραμματεῖόν τις ἑαυτὸν κατήσχυνε, τοῦτ' ἐξήτασεν, ἀλλὰ παντελῶς, ὅπως ἂν ἡ πρᾶξις γένηται, τὸν πράξαντα κελεύει μὴ μετέχειν τῶν τῆς πόλεως κοινῶν. Εἰκότως· ὅστις γὰρ νέος ὢν ἀπέστη δι' αἰσχρὰς ἡδονὰς τῆς εἰς τὰ καλὰ φιλοτιμίας, τοῦτον οὐκ ᾠήθη δεῖν πρεσβύτερον γενόμενον ἐπίτιμον εἶναι.
>
> If they try to say that the man who has not been hired out according to a contract has not engaged in prostitution, and if they ask me to provide a document and witnesses to this, then you must first remember the laws on prostitution, in which the lawgiver has made no mention of contracts anywhere. He did not ask if someone had brought shame on himself according to a written contract; he categorically prescribes that the man who has done this shall not have a share in the public life of the city, no matter what way the act has taken place. And with good reason. For if a man, while young, turns his back on noble ambition for the sake of sordid pleasure, the lawgiver did not think that this man, once he has become older, should be in possession of his political entitlements as a citizen.
>
> AISCHIN. 1.160

It is of course possible that the audience would have been sufficiently familiar with the relevant laws to feel able to accept Aischines' claim about what the law does not say. However, the separation in time between the formal recitation and the present paraphrase would have made it considerably more difficult for the judges to assess the validity of Aischines' paraphrase on the basis of the exact wording of the law.[20]

A further indication that Aischines was aware of the strategic potential of such an approach is his use of the law on *proagōgeia* ('procuring'). Again, he refers twice in his speech to what appears to be the same law 170 paragraphs apart, in 1.14 and 1.184. In the first passage his paraphrase of the law on *proagōgeia* occurs alongside paraphrases of several other laws. Most of his paraphrases in this part of the speech are accompanied by a formal recitation of the texts by the court attendant; however, the law on *proagōgeia* is not among them. When Aischines returns to the law at a much later stage of his address, it highly likely that at least some among his audience would have found it difficult to remember at this point whether or not they had in fact heard an authoritative version of the law at the beginning of the speech. The very fact that his unsupported paraphrase was first 'sneaked in' among several other paraphrases that were accompanied by formal recitation may have lent greater authority to Aischines' second paraphrase in his peroration at a point where the emotional temperature of his appeal was clearly rising.

Moreover, it is striking that the use that Aischines makes of the law as well as the intentions he ascribes to the lawgiver differ considerably between the two passages. In 1.14, he represents the purpose of the law as that of 'protecting our children'. In 1.184, by contrast, the law has nothing to do with child protection; instead, the reason why the lawgiver has prescribed the death penalty in this law is allegedly that:

> ὅτι τῶν ἐξαμαρτάνειν ἐπιθυμούντων ὀκνούντων καὶ αἰσχυνομένων ἀλλήλοις ἐντυγχάνειν, αὐτοὶ τὴν αὑτῶν ἀναίδειαν παρασχόντες ἐπὶ μισθῷ τὸ πρᾶγμα εἰς διάπειραν καὶ λόγον κατέστησαν.
>
> while those who desire to commit such a crime hesitate and feel shame at meeting with one another, the procurers themselves offer their own shamelessness for a fee and bring the matter to the test and to negotiation.
>
> AISCHIN. 1.184

20 This general point that litigants could engage in selective quotation and rewording of law texts integrated into their own speeches only 'when the actual quotations (*sc.* read out by the court attendant) were at a safe distance' is made convincingly by Canevaro 2013: 28–31.

To what extent would Aischines' audience have been aware of the potential for distortion that was offered by his strategies as exemplified by these four passages? And to what extent would they have regarded his skilful combination, at different points in his speech, of formal recitation and his own citation of individual clauses in isolation as a kind of 'abuse' of the laws? This is extremely difficult to tell. As argued earlier, because partial citations of laws in the litigants' own voices were difficult to predict and counter by their opponents, we should not expect to find objections to the practice voiced all that frequently. In this respect, absence of evidence is not evidence of absence.

On the other hand, it is clear that the citation of laws, integrated into the litigant's own speeches and unaccompanied by formal recitations of the laws themselves, was an integral part of Athenian court practice. This, in turn, may suggest that the level of tolerance of this practice, and perhaps also of the creative interpretations that it could permit, was quite high.

The fact that a large number of litigants, especially those who were engaged in private actions, display a preference for integrated paraphrases and quotations of law texts rather than formal recitation by the court attendant also adds a further dimension to the debate on the classification of statutes as 'artless' or 'artful' means of persuasion (*pisteis*). It has often been noted that even fourth-century theorists disagree on this point.[21] In his *Rhetoric* 1375a22–24, Aristotle includes laws along with contracts, witness statements, oaths and evidentiary torture in his list of 'artless' (*atechnoi*) means of persuasion.[22] But laws do not figure on the corresponding list of *epithetoi pisteis* (the 'opinion', *doxa*, of the speaker, witnesses, evidentiary torture, and oaths) in the *Rhetorica ad Alexandrum* 7.2–3 or in this author's systematic discussion of them in 14.8–17.2.

The uncertainty surrounding the classification of *nomoi* as either artful or artless *pisteis* may be due not only to the fact that laws probably required more supporting, 'artful' argumentation than most other types of documentary evidence in order for them to work effectively as part of the speaker's presentation of his case. It may also reflect the variety in the employment of laws in Athenian trials: some litigants preferred to submit their law texts along with other documents to be read out by the court attendant (often commenting on the content of such laws), other litigants preferred to treat and present law texts,

21 See above all Mirhady 1991 with Carey 1996: 33; for further discussion, see Kästle 2012: 176–181.

22 It must be noted that even Aristotle himself is inconsistent, in that he does not include *nomoi* in a similar list (albeit clearly not an exhaustive one) in 1355b35–40. However, there is general agreement that Aristotle's list is broadly coterminous with the kind of documentation that would normally be submitted for recitation by the court attendant.

to all intents and purposes, as *entechnoi pisteis*, by incorporating them in their speeches without having them read out by the court attendant. The drawback of the latter strategy was that the text itself may have lost some force in terms of its authority and authenticity. The advantage was that the litigant would have more scope for subtle alteration of its wording and for presenting precisely the part of the text that would permit him to interpret it in such a way that it lent the strongest possible support to his case. Some litigants (in fact the majority) submitted some of their law texts as documents while integrating (parts of) other law texts into their speeches without formal recitation. And, finally, many litigants preferred to combine the two strategies, presenting the same laws as documents and as integrated paraphrases at different stages of their speeches, as we see it done in Aischin. *Against Timarchos*.

The fact that each individual litigant had a choice as to whether to use a particular law text as a citation by the clerk or incorporate legal provisions in the text of the speech potentially makes a significant difference to the reliability of his paraphrase of the text and to his interpretation of its contents. Thus, each time we discuss the meaning and possible application of individual Athenian statutes attested in the Attic Orators, we need to make sure that we note when we are dealing with one or the other.

Bibliography

Aviles, D. (2011) '"Arguing Against the Law": Non-Literal Interpretation in Attic Forensic Oratory', *Dike* 14, 19–42.

Canevaro, M. (2013) *The Documents in the Attic Orators: Laws and Decrees in the Public Speeches of the Demosthenic Corpus*, Oxford.

Carey, C. (1994) '"Artless" Proofs in Aristotle and the Orators', *BICS* 39, 95–106.

Carey, C. (1996) '*Nomos* in Attic Rhetoric and Oratory', *JHS* 116, 33–46.

De Brauw, M. (2002) '"Listen to the Laws Themselves": Citations of Law and Portrayal of Character in Attic Oratory', *CJ* 97, 161–176.

Edwards, M.J. (2008) 'Isaeus and the Athenian Inheritance Laws', in Harris, E.M. and Thür, G., eds (2008) *Symposion 2007: Vorträge zur griechischen und hellenistischen Rechtsgeschichte* (Durham, 2–6 September 2007) Vienna, 41–54 (with a response by S.C. Todd, 55–62).

Gagarin, M. (2008) *Writing Greek Law*, Cambridge.

Gernet, L. (1957) *Démosthène. Plaidoyers civils: discours XXXIX–XLVIII*. Paris.

Griffith-Williams, B. (2013) *A Commentary on Selected Speeches of Isaios*, Leiden.

Harris, E.M. (2009/10) 'What Are the Laws of Athens About? Substance and Procedure in Athenian Statutes', *Dike* 12/13, 5–67.

Harris, E.M. (2013) 'The Plaint in Athenian Law and Legal Procedure', in Faraguna, M., ed. (2013) *Archives and Archival Documents in Ancient Societies*, Trieste, 143–162.

Hillgruber, M. (1988) *Die zehnte Rede des Lysias: Einleitung, Text und Kommentar mit einem Anhang über die Gesetzesinterpretationen bei den attischen Rednern*, Berlin.

Johnstone, S. (1999) *Disputes and Democracy: The Consequences of Litigation in Ancient Athens*, Austin.

Kästle, D. (2012) 'Νόμος μεγίστη βοήθεια: zur Gesetzesargumentation in der attischen Gerichtsrede', *Zeitschrift der Savigny-Stiftung für Rechtsgeschichte* 129, 161–205.

Meinecke, J. (1971) 'Gesetzesinterpretation und Gesetzesanwendung im Attischen Zivilprozess', *Revue Internationale des Droits de l'Antiquité* 18, 275–360.

Mirhady, D. (1991) 'Non-Technical *pisteis* in Aristotle and Anaximenes', *AJP* 112, 5–28.

Mossé, C. (2004) 'Les citations de lois dans les plaidoyers des orateurs attiques', in C. Darbo-Peschanski, ed. (2004) *La citation dans l'antiquité*, Grenoble, 95–108.

Phillips, D.D. (2009) 'Hypereides 3 and the Athenian Law of Contracts', *TAPA* 139, 89–122.

Powell, J.G.F., Rubinstein, L. and Kremmydas, C. (2013) 'Introduction', in Kremmydas, C., Powell, J.G.F., and Rubinstein, L. eds (2013) *Profession and Performance: Aspects of Oratory in the Greco-Roman World* (*BICS supplement* 123), London, 1–14.

Rubinstein, L. (2007) 'Arguments from Precedent in Attic Oratory', in Carawan E., ed. (2007) *The Attic Orators*, Oxford, 359–371.

Rubinstein, L. (2008) 'Response to James P. Sickinger', in Harris, E.M. and Thür, G., eds (2008) *Symposion 2007: Vorträge zur griechischen und hellenistischen Rechtsgeschichte* (Durham, 2–6 September 2007) Vienna, 113–124.

Scafuro, A.C. (2011) *Demosthenes, speeches 39–49*, Austin.

Sickinger, J. (2007) 'Rhetoric and the Law', in Worthington, I., ed. (2007) *A Companion to Greek Rhetoric*, Oxford, 286–302.

Thür, G. (2008) 'The Principle of Fairness in Athenian Legal Procedure: Thoughts on the *echinos* and *enklema*', *Dike* 11, 51–73.

Thür, G. (2013) 'The Statute on *homologein* in Hyperides' Speech *Against Athenogenes*', *Dike* 16, 1–10.

Todd, S.C. (2007) *A Commentary on Lysias, Speeches 1–11*, Oxford.

Wankel, H. (1976) *Demosthenes, Rede für Ktesiphon über den Kranz*, Heidelberg.

Wyse, W. (1904) *The Speeches of Isaeus*. Cambridge.

CHAPTER 10

Twisting the Law in Ancient Athens

Ilias Arnaoutoglou

In the fourth paragraph of Isaios' speech *On the estate of Hagnias* (Περὶ τοῦ Ἁγνίου κλήρου), composed in mid fourth century and delivered in a case of denunciation for maltreating orphans (*eisangelia kakoseōs orphanōn*), Theopompos, the speaker, provides an enviable performance. He directs the clerk to take and read the laws, while with an assertive and sarcastic tone he demands the presence of his opponent (in fact, the co-guardian of his orphan nephew) at the podium.

> ἀναβιβασάμενος οὖν αὐτὸν ἐναντίον ὑμῶν ἐρωτήσω τὰ ἐν τοῖς νόμοις ὑπαναγιγνώσκων οὕτως γὰρ εἴσεσθε εἰ προσήκει τῷ παιδὶ τῶν Ἁγνίου χρημάτων ἢ μή. λαβὲ οὖν αὐτοῖς τοὺς νόμους· σὺ δ' ἀνάβηθι δεῦρο, ἐπειδὴ δεινὸς εἶ διαβάλλειν καὶ τοὺς νόμους διαστρέφειν. σὺ δ' ἀναγίγνωσκε. NOMOI. ἐπίσχες. ἐρωτήσω σέ. ἀδελφός ἐσθ' ὁ παῖς Ἁγνίου ⟨ἢ⟩ ἀδελφιδοῦς ἐξ ἀδελφοῦ ἢ ἐξ ἀδελφῆς γεγονώς, ἢ ἀνεψιός, ἢ ἐξ ἀνεψιοῦ πρὸς μητρὸς ἢ πρὸς πατρός; τί τούτων τῶν ὀνομάτων, οἷς ὁ νόμος τὴν ἀγχιστείαν δίδωσι;

> I intend, therefore, to make him stand up before you and to interrogate him, reading out the text of the law. You will thus learn whether, or no, the child has any right to the fortune of Hagnias. (*To the clerk*): Please take these laws; (*To his opponent*) and you, come up here, since you are so clever at misrepresenting and distorting the laws. (*To the clerk*): Read on. LAWS. Stop. (*To his opponent*): I wish to question you. Is the child a brother of Hagnias, or a nephew, the son of a brother or sister, or a cousin, or the child of a cousin on his mother's or his father's side? Which of these titles, which are regarded by the law as constituting kinship, does he possess?

Theopompos uses vitriolic terms, calling his opponent a sykophant and someone who eagerly distorts the laws. In this way he sets the pieces, like a skilful director, for the 'answer my question' game and at the same time establishes his dominance.[1]

1 The speaker ascribes to his opponent δεινότης that is a special ability, a skill that implies particular preoccupation with laws (also in Lys. 10.13), Edwards 2008: 41. This is consonant with the *ēthos* projected in most speeches, litigants depicting themselves as amateurs in law, Christ

 | DOI:10.1163/9789004377899_012

The accusation of slander (διαβάλλειν) is clear[2] but what exactly does 'you are skilful at distorting the laws' (διαστρέφειν τοὺς νόμους) mean? Does it involve irregular quoting of law with convenient additions and omissions and/or twisting the meaning of key (legal) terms of the rules? It is worth noting that the term διαστρέφειν, although not often attested in Athenian lawcourt speeches,[3] can be associated with the archaic opposition between straight (εὐθεία) and crooked (σκολιά) judgment (δίκη). It is probably one of the means that produce crooked judgments, agents of which are, of course, the litigants themselves, and those who compose the speeches for them, *logographoi* (speech writers).[4] A second observation concerns the integrity of the quoted law. In those rare cases in which the law cited is genuine and not an unhappy concoction of a later scribe, there is no evidence that any litigant has falsified the text. We do not know whether falsifying the text of a statute was equated to citing a non-existent law and therefore fell within the prohibition reported in Dem. 26.24.[5] In this case, since there was no *ex-officio* prosecution, the opponent should have raised the alarm.

An answer to the above brings forward, perhaps unavoidably, an enquiry into the meaning of the emblematic phrase 'use and abuse of law'. Were there similar fundamental concepts in classical Athens and if so, how did they operate in the idiosyncratic Athenian legal framework?

1998: 165–166. In Dem. 57.5, the speaker accuses his opponent that he knows the laws all too well and brings an unjust accusation with the purpose of accruing a material advantage, πλεονεκτικῶς; see also Hyp. *Eux.* 13, Carey 1996: 41 and Christ 1998: 203–208. Litigants accused of abusing the law are portrayed in the speeches of their opponents as bad citizens, see Christ 1998 and 2006. Predictably, a characteristic of a good litigant is obedience to the statutes. For the financial aspects of Theopompos' dealings see Davies 2002. For the content of *kakōsis* see the brief discussion in Rubinstein 2009: 151 n. 8.

2 For *diabolē* see Vögelin 1943, Carey 2004.

3 Διαστρέφειν was probably the standard term in fourth-century Athens, see Dem. 10.75; 18.140; 24.210; *Exordia* 46.2; Hyp. *Lyk.* 10; fr. 95; Demades, fr. 79.2 (De Falco) For synonyms see Dein. fr. 9.3 (Konomis) (apud Harp. *s. v.* κλιμάζῃ); see also Pollux 3.155, Phot. *Lexicon* s.v. κλιμακίζειν (= κ 783), and Suda s.v. κλιμακίζειν.

4 See also the etymology of the name of the main hero in Ar. *Nub.*, Strepsiades (the Twister). For a late attestation see Dio Chrys. 76.3–4 and Schol. Anonymi in Arist. *Rh.* 23.823 for the role of *diabolē* in producing crooked judgments.

5 Carey 1996: 36–37. In some cases, a litigant is accused of falsifying laws, Isok. 18.11, of altering (proposed) laws in the assembly, Dein. 1.42 and in Dem. 18.121. Death penalty for citing a non-existent law, Dem. 26.24 and the case reported in Lykourg. 1.63–67.

The Legal Context

For an understanding of διαστρέφειν it is necessary to recall the salient features of the classical Athenian legal system: (i) its oral context: arguments, documents,[6] depositions and laws were read to a panel of at least two hundred men (*dikastai*); (ii) the ambivalent position of law in the ideology of the Athenian *dikastai*;[7] (iii) the 'open texture' of the legal provisions, that is laws are framed in general terms attempting to regulate a large number of possible cases and circumstances;[8] (iv) the nature of the classical Athenian administration of justice; it was not based on a court hierarchy and therefore did not recognise any right of appeal against the verdicts of the popular courts—the only procedure resembling modern appeal was the possibility of challenging the decision of a magistrate in front of a popular court; and (v) laws are treated during the hearing in court as pieces of evidence. According to the oath sworn by the *dikastai*, it was their duty to decide a case according to the laws;[9] therefore, the modern civil law principle of *jura novit curia* (i.e. the lawcourt knows the laws) obviously did not apply. The *locus classicus* for laws as pieces of evidence is the passage in Aristotle's *Rhetoric* 1375a–b where they are included among the 'artless proofs'.[10] Aristotle puts forward an instrumental approach to laws, i.e.

6 Canevaro 2013, 27–32.

7 Even if law enjoyed the respect of *dikastai* and a special place among evidence, its written character and the need for interpretation raised eyebrows in some quarters. This is perhaps the reason why in one case law transubstantiates into a witness, [Dem.] 33.27, and in another into a supporting speaker for Aischines (3.37). Athenian juries seem to have had a more ambivalent stance to laws and their interpretation than mere eulogy but I cannot share Christ's 1998 interpretation that the ambivalence is due to the limited literacy prevalent among the *dikastai*. Even if they could comfortably read, their effective role as an audience with no right to ask, clarify or discuss, limited their ability to intervene in the process unfolded in front of them.

8 For the open texture see Harris 2000 and 2006; they are superseded now by the extensive and detailed treatment in Harris 2013a: 175–245. For the effects and side effects of oral performance see Wolff 1968 [repr. 2007]: 105].

9 The Heliastic oath provided that *dikastai* will vote in accordance with the laws and decrees of the *polis*, only about matters pertaining to the charge, to listen to both sides impartially, and to judge following their *dikaiotatē gnōmē*, Harris 2006a and 2013a: 101–137.

10 Arist. *Rh.* 1375a–b. Note that the quality of laws as *atechnoi pisteis* should not conceal their normative aspect, embodiment of the will of the *dēmos*. In this respect, there is a significant difference between *nomoi* and the rest of *atechnoi pisteis*. Litigants could prosecute witnesses for false testimony, but they could not turn against the legal interpretation of their opponent. Witnesses' testimonies are used to establish facts, laws were used to demonstrate the legitimacy, the superiority and the prevalence of one's claim. Therefore,

exalting their power in cases where it is expedient for the speaker and undermining their applicability in cases where laws do not serve the speaker's case.[11] Despite that manichaeistic advice, I will argue that Athenians displayed a much more nuanced, varied and intelligent approach to laws in law courts.[12] This is partly due to the nature of laws as normative texts; while other means of proof (e.g. witnesses) certify facts, the invocation of laws in the plaint and in the speech shapes the dispute (or at least aspects of it) in such a way that the *dikastai* could decide with a yes or no.[13] Digging out, presenting and having the text of a law read is one thing; spelling out the content, explaining particular terms, and the reason it applies to the case under consideration, in a convincing manner, is an altogether different business. The need to interpret legal provisions is artfully expressed in Aristotle's *Rhetoric* 1354a21–b16; in a statute there is a holistic approach aiming to regulate most if not all the possible aspects of a problem, while the decision of a law court, by applying the law to a set of facts, individualises the legal rule. Applying a rule to specific circumstances requires it to be interpreted and argued for by the speaker(s).[14] Usually logographers and litigants devoted a substantial part of their speech to raising any legal questions and putting forward claims; characteristic in this respect is the programmatic statement made by Aischin. 1.8 arguing that he is going to prove his case by comparing Timarchos' actions with the text of the laws. Quite often we encounter very modern snippets of legal reasoning, as for example in Isa. 4.14–16; the speaker summarises the law on the validity of the testament and then argues:

> Ἀλλὰ μὴν καὶ ὁ νόμος, ὦ ἄνδρες, οὐκ ἐάν τις διαθῆται μόνον, κυρίας εἶναι κελεύει τὰς διαθήκας, ἀλλὰ ἐὰν εὖ φρονῶν. Σκεπτέον δὲ ὑμῖν πρῶτον μὲν εἰ ἐποιήσατο τὰς διαθήκας, ἔπειτα εἰ μὴ παρανοῶν διέθετο.
>
> Again, gentlemen, the law commands that a testament in order to be valid must not merely include the wishes of the testator but the testator must be in his right senses. You ought, therefore, to scrutinise, first,

nomos was a rather peculiar kind of *atechnos pistis*. See the concise analysis of the passage in Gagarin 2014: 22–28 and Mirhady 2015: 242.

11 See Mirhady 1990 and 1991; Carey 1996.

12 Similar assessment in Carey 1994: 96; Carey 1996: 46.

13 Especially for the role of the plaint see Harris 2013b.

14 Exactly this process of interpretation was thought to be fraught with contesting claims, Christ 1998: 198. Gagarin 2014: 28–29.

whether the deceased drafted a will and, secondly, whether he was in his right mind at the time.[15]

Definitions

The concept of abuse requires an authoritative voice to expound what constitutes admissible use of law. In modern jurisdictions this is accomplished through guidelines, regulations, laws, the decisions of higher courts and through jurisprudence.[16] In classical Athens there were no similar mechanisms (or preoccupations). In any hearing at the law courts we can only have: (a) invocation of at least two different and possibly conflicting legal rules by the litigants, and/or (b) *prima facie* competing interpretations of a single legal act.[17] In this context, there is ample room and motive for (mis)representation, (mis)interpretation, and manipulation of rules. However, the available space was limited (to what extent we can only guess) by i) the principle of keeping to the point (explicitly, at least, in the Areiopagos)[18] and thus the avoidance of presenting irrelevant evidence and ii) by the prevailing social (due to lack of a mechanism to elaborate and refine legal concepts, like the Roman *iurispru-*

15 I cannot share Yunis' 2005: 208 sweeping assertion of the non-legal use of legal texts in the orators; law court speeches provide ample evidence of legal interpretation of key legal terms by the speakers. It is an altogether different question whether this use is dictated by the rhetorical aims of the orator; see Wolff 1968.

16 For the principle of prohibition of abuse of rights, i.e. law must not be used to allow or cause harm, in civil law jurisdictions and especially EU, see Lenaerts 2010.

17 See Sickinger 2008: 101–102 and Carey 1996: 38 who argues that this strategy is also prescribed by Aristotle but in fact due to the procedural orientation of Greek laws there was less scope for exploiting internal inconsistencies within a law. However, the procedural orientation provided fertile ground to cases of abuses of procedure and anyway did not stop Aischines and Demosthenes from arguing about the place where honours are to be proclaimed. Questions concerning the authority a litigant's legal interpretation could carry and how it was legitimised and made attractive remain outside the scope of this contribution. See also Harris 2013a: 180.

18 See Rhodes 2006 with Dem. 57.66, [Dem.] 45.50, Aischin. 1.154; cf. Yunis 2005: 194–195. See also Lanni 2012: 129–130 about the publicity of legal proceedings as inhibiting wild exaggerations. *Dikastai* had at least a rudimentary grasp of legal rules and concepts and were not ignorant of laws. They have had at least a grip on the legal environment in which they were active; their sources of acquaintance with law included family, neighbours, networks of friends, associates in various groups, business partners, participation in assemblies, courts, activities as mediators, arbitrators, and exercise of *polis* magistracies. For the legal vocabulary as technical language see Willi 2003: 72–79.

dentes) understanding and therefore knowledge of key legal terms. For example, most (if not all) of the *dikastai* listening to Isaios' speeches understood the content of legal terms such as testament, adoption, or *epiklēros* and probably knew the core elements of intestate succession.[19] Therefore, where do we locate the thin red line between legitimate and improper usage of legal texts? Is it legitimate to speak of 'abuse' of law in a symbolic battle of arguments, especially as in almost every case of invoking a law (substantive or procedural) there was the potential for it to be turned into a case of 'abuse' of law by the opponent? Take for example the estate of Nikostratos, a mercenary who died abroad, whose property, in the first quarter of the fourth century, was claimed at least five times (Isa. 4.8–10).[20] What is noteworthy is the bewildering variety of legal reasons (no shortage of ingenuity and legal acumen there). Were the claimants 'abusing' the law? I do not think so. What they actually did was to bring forward a false factual basis on which they enshrine a perfectly legal claim. This may be regarded as an abuse of the legal system and procedures, or an instrumental use of legal provisions.[21]

If 'use' and 'abuse' pertain essentially to the interpretation of a legal rule then, instead of treating them as two diametrically opposed notions, it might be more fruitful to consider them as parts of a spectrum, of an interpretative continuum, defined at one end by the absolute respect for the text of the law and at the other end by the desire to win the case. It stretches from mere (sometimes selective) quotation and paraphrase to interpretation of the law cited with the aid of arguments *ex contrario*, *ex maiore ad minore* (or *vice versa*), by analogy, by contraction or expansion of the meaning of a legal term, to concealment and 'adulteration' of parts of a law. Therefore, one could define use of law as the invocation of legal provisions in order to circumscribe litigants' actions, to construct their arguments (i.e. justify, support or further their claims) and counter-argue against his opponent's claims, and as abuse of law any treatment of legal rules by a litigant so as to confer an (unfair?) advantage to his case.

19 Reference to a principle of Athenian inheritance law as being common knowledge, Isa. 3.58–59 and Isa. 7.19. Christ 1998 refers to it as a sense of justice, τὸ δίκαιον, τὰ δίκαια. Harris 2004: 261 speaks about the customary understanding of a given statute; this is also behind the community norms of Christ 1998: 196.

20 *Demosthenes* claimed that he was N.'s nephew, *Telephos* claimed that N. donated (bequeathed?) his property, *Ameiniades* tried to have recognised as a son of N. a three-year old boy and himself as a guardian, *Pyrrhos* of Lamptrai claimed that N. has consecrated his property to Athena and left him the usufruct, *Ktesias* of Besa and *Kranaos* initially claimed that N. owed them a sum of money and later that N. was their freedman.

21 I wish to thank the editors for drawing my attention to the subtleties of this passage.

The first opportunity a litigant had to spot any sign of 'abuse' of law was at the preliminary hearing (*anakrisis*).[22] If Isa. 6.12–13[23] is a safe guide to go by, at this stage there was an enquiry by the magistrate into the claims of the plaintiff and the counter-arguments of the defendant. There is no evidence that the magistrate conducting the *anakrisis* could assess the legal implications of the litigants' arguments. This was a task entrusted to the litigants themselves who could use the procedures of *diamartyria* and *paragraphē*, among others, to attack what they thought as abuses of law.[24]

Uses of Law

Most often laws were used in order to support the central claim and advance the arguments of the speaker, In Isa. 2.1–2 the speaker claims that the adoption was performed *kata tous nomous* and in 19–20 he elaborates on the motives of the adoption and their agreement with the legal requirements—something that his opponents probably argued strongly against—, especially the term εὖ φρονῶν and the influence of a woman, οὐδὲ τῇ γυναικὶ πεισθείς. Isaios refers several times to the law about claiming an inheritance (e.g. Isa. 6.3) or the privilege enjoyed by patrilineal over matrilineal relatives in the order of intestate succession (e.g. Isa. 11.17).[25] Laws may be used to illustrate the violation of law by the opponent, as in Isa. 1.26 where the speaker (a kinsman of Kleonymos) argues

22 For the *anakrisis* see Kremmydas' discussion in this volume. As far as procedure is concerned, I believe that we cannot speak of abuse of procedure when the legal provision itself provides more than one way to proceed (Dem. 22.26) for which see Carey 2004. Sometimes, diversionary tactics may rely on rather tenuous interpretation of legal rules. In this respect sykophancy (i.e. malicious prosecution) may involve abuse of legal provisions but this has to remain outside the scope of this article; see Menander's quip: 'The laws are a splendid thing; but a man who looks too closely at the laws is clearly a sykophant': fr. 545 K–T with Christ 1998: 48–70. On enmity and sykophancy see now Kucharski 2012 and Alwine 2015.

23 See also Harris 2000: 76; 2013a: 210–211.

24 See the *echinos*-lid published in *SEG* 32.329 (a different restoration in *SEG* 36.296) in which an objection (*diamartyria*) was submitted at the stage of the preliminary hearing (*anakrisis*). Cases brought in front of arbitrators, despite the almost certain presentation of diverging interpretations (see Lys. 10.6), were concluded by a mutually acceptable settlement. For *diamartyria*, see Griffith-Williams in this volume.

25 See Carey 1996: 45. Sometimes arguments may border on pure sophistry and legal naivety as in [Dem.] 46.15 Apollodoros attempts to transpose and combine the effects of adoption with naturalization, since in both cases the same term is used, *poiēsis*. Cf. Harrison 1968: 86, n. 2.

that his opponents are trying to persuade the court to reach a verdict against the laws, but he does not specify which law. Since the main point of disagreement is a will, one may assume that the law on testaments is meant. But the law on testaments is not of any particular value in deciding the case, because Kleonymos' will was lawfully drafted and deposited; it was never amended as was his intention (if we are to believe the speaker's side of the story).[26] Law could be employed in order to discount the opponent's arguments; in Dem. 57.30–32 the opponent of the speaker challenged the personal status of the speaker claiming that his mother earned her living by selling ribbons in the market. The speaker answers by invoking a law attributed to Solon, according to which only Athenians were allowed to do business in the Agora.[27] Laws also served to legitimise the use of a particular legal procedure,[28] to underline any dealings of the opponent(s) with the law, accusations, convictions, or even pending trials in order to taint his reputation[29] and to depict the speaker as a law-abiding, moderate citizen.

The most usual techniques of introducing a law were:

1. *to paraphrase it*: in Isa. 3.42 the speaker paraphrases the law on testament and *epiklēroi* and in § 74 the law on the marriage of an *epiklēros*. In Isa. 3.68–69 the speaker paraphrases the law on testament and in order to describe the female descendant uses the term θηλείας (παῖδας), female children, (see also Dem. 43.51) equated in the next sentence to θυγάτηρ (daughter) and in the next period to γνησία θυγάτηρ (legitimate daughter). This observation may seem trivial but (i) there is a difference between female children and legitimate daughters, at least in legal parlance, and (ii) it illustrates very vividly the liberty of the speaker to use interchangeable terms, socially recognisable and acceptable. Whether paraphrasing involves a concealed interpretation, effectively suggesting an answer to the legal question put to the *dikastai*, is a matter for a further thorough investigation.[30]

---

26 In Aischin. 3.11 the speaker paraphrases the law about crowning so that it will be contrasted with the tactics of certain citizens. Aischines praises the lawgiver who did not allow the crowning of a magistrate unless he has submitted an account of his activity and of the financial dealings involved. The text of a statute can be presented to contrast the illegality of a proposed decree just as Aischines did in 3.32–35, to demonstrate that Deinarchos' opponent has violated it. See also Carey 1996: 45, Sickinger 2008: 101.

27 See Isa. 6.28 with Carey 1996: 45. For anticipation of opponents' arguments in other venues than the preliminary hearing, see Dorjahn 1935.

28 Dem. 24.32, 34–38; [32.]1; [33.]2–3; [35.]3; 43.7, 15–16; [59].66.

29 See Dem. 55.1–2, 31–32, Carey 1996: 34, de Brauw 2002, Lanni 2009: 699.

30 See the case study on Isaios' speeches by Edwards 2008: 46–47 and Hatzilambrou in this

2. *to explain it*: interpretation could start as a simple explanation of (legal) terms such as λυμαίνεσθαι and ἀποινᾶν in Dem. 23.33:

> 'λυμαίνεσθαι δὲ' φησὶ 'μή, μηδὲ ἀποινᾶν.' ταῦτα δ' ἐστὶν τί; τὸ μὲν δὴ μὴ λυμαίνεσθαι γνώριμον οἶδ' ὅτι πᾶσιν μὴ μαστιγοῦν, μὴ δεῖν, μὴ τὰ τοιαῦτα ποιεῖν λέγει, τὸ δὲ μηδ' ἀποινᾶν μὴ χρήματα πράττεσθαι: τὰ γὰρ χρήματ' ἄποιν' ὠνόμαζον οἱ παλαιοί.

> 'Not to maltreat', it says, 'or to amerce'. What does it mean? Everyone understands that not to maltreat means that there is to be no flogging, no binding nor anything like that, while not to amerce means not to extort blood-money, for the ancients called fining amercement.[31]

Or it could involve explanation of obscure terms, such as ἀνδροφόνος, ποδοκάκη, δρασκάζειν, στάσιμον in Lys. 10.6–10, 16–19.[32] In Isa. 3.45–49 the speaker implicitly provides an interpretation of the term *kakōsis epiklērou. Kakōsis* could be considered as any demeaning behaviour towards an *epiklēros*, such as being given in marriage without dowry, i.e. as a courtesan. In the field of public law, Aischin. 3.13–14 invokes a law in support of his interpretation of the word *archē* (magistrates).[33]

3. *to contrast the spirit vs letter of the law*: the most eloquent example of recourse to the spirit of the regulation is found in Lys. 10.6–10. The speaker attacks the interpretation offered by Theomnestos on the breadth of the regulatory framework for slander. It is not a particular word that is banned but also similar expressions to the same effect, not mentioned in the law.[34]

4. *to employ arguments* e contrario: In Isa. 10.2 the speaker refers to the law on testaments and the free disposal of one's property but hurriedly complements this with an interpretation *e contrario*:

> ὁ γὰρ νόμος κελεύει τὰ μὲν ἑαυτοῦ διαθέσθαι ὅτῳ ἂν ἐθέλῃ, τῶν δὲ ἀλλοτρίων οὐδένα κύριον πεποίηκε.

---

volume. Also Aischin. 1.9–11, 13–14, 17–20, 28–32; Aischin. 3.11 and 26 (meaning of *archē*) with Harris 2013a: 227–228.

31 Similarly, in Lys. 14.6 and Isa. 7.20.

32 See Biscardi 1970; Hillgruber 1988; Harris 2000: 56–57; Todd 2007: 634–635; Kästle 2012.

33 For a sober assessment of the arguments in the case of Ktesiphon see Harris 2000.

34 See Arist. *Rh.* 1397a7–11 and Todd 2007: 631–637.

> The law ordains that one can dispose of his property to whoever he wishes, but he does not have the authority to dispose of other people's belongings.

In this way, the speaker demonstrates that the contested inheritance did not belong to his adversary but to the speaker's mother.[35]

5. *to employ arguments by analogy*: in Isa. 1.39–40 the speaker argues by analogy that had their grandfather died intestate, or had Kleonymos left any under-age daughters, it would have been his and his brothers' duty to take care of the old man or to marry (or to give away in marriage) the surviving daughters. The speaker's point is clear: as a close relative he had certain duties and in the same way, he had a claim on Kleonymos' property, despite the existence of a disputed testament.[36] Apollodoros in [Dem.] 59.116–117 provides as parallel the case of Archias the hierophant who was condemned for sacrilege, and argues that Neaira should suffer the same penalty.
6. *to employ arguments* ex minore ad maiore: in Dem. 23.76 Euthykles claims that since we punish objects that cause death, we should also punish individuals like Aristokrates who propose illegal decrees. In another speech from the Demosthenic corpus, Dem. 20.9 the speaker in order to prove that Leptines' law is inexpedient argues that, since lying in the Agora (e.g. when concluding a contract) is prohibited, which would inflict minimal damage on the wider community, the same rule should apply to public affairs and therefore to Leptines' law which will cause much greater damage to the city, since it will be perceived as deception of Athens' benefactors.
7. *to narrow down the meaning of a term*: Hypereides in his speech *Against Athenogenes* 13–17 provides us with a very rich passage (although not representative) on legal interpretation. It contains several laws presented in an abridged form and interpreted. Hypereides' client launches a two-pronged attack on Athenogenes: he challenges the validity of the concluded agreement (nullity of volition due to deceit) and he cites parallel cases to support a contracted version of the binding force of agreements. The aim of the speaker is to interpret the rule ὅσα ἂν ἕτερος ἑτέρῳ ὁμολογήσῃ κύρια εἶναι by introducing a qualification of ὅσα; not *any* agreement can be valid but only a fair one, τὰ δίκαια. In order to prove his point, the speaker had studied the laws, night and day (something unusual for a

---

35 Griffith-Williams 2013: 214 notes that the truism will have had some persuasive force.

36 See also Lys. 6.17; Isa. 8.31; Dem. 20.89–90; Lykourg. 1.53; Hyp. *Eux.* 14–17; Hyp. *Diond.* 145r.

speaker to admit, cf. Dem. 18.111) and he invokes (i) the law about ἀψευδεῖν in the market place; Athenogenes has concealed debts on the transferred property, (ii) that the law on concealed natural defects of the thing sold requires restitution; the question is whether this rule applied to debts of slaves, and (iii) provides a rather disappointing argument about the term δίκαια (lawful) in the law on marriage and on testament.[37]

8. *to refer to the presumed will of the legislator*:[38] litigants may use the authority of a lawgiver (in Athens, it is mainly Solon) to support their legal interpretation. In Isa. 2.13 the speaker invokes and interprets the law on testamentary adoption with a reference to the intention of the lawgiver:

> ὁ γὰρ νομοθέτης, ὦ ἄνδρες, διὰ τοῦτο τὸν νόμον ἔθηκεν οὕτως ὁρῶν μόνην ταύτην καταφυγὴν οὖσαν τῆς ἐρημίας καὶ παραψυχὴν τοῦ βίου τοῖς ἄπαισι τῶν ἀνθρώπων, τὸ ἐξεῖναι ποιήσασθαι ὅντινα ἂν βούλωνται.
>
> The legislator, gentlemen, introduced the law for this reason, because he saw that the possibility to adopt anyone they wished, was the only refuge to loneliness and the only comfort in life for childless individuals.

Beyond Mere Interpretation ...

Sometimes, treatment of a legal rule turns out to be a little more drastic; let me start with what I believe is a classic case of being economical with the truth.[39]

---

37 See Christ 1998: 203–204, 221–223, Johnstone 1999: 28–30, Harris 2000: 48–54; Whitehead 2000, Aviles 2011, Harris 2013a: 198–205 and Mirhady 2015: 238–240. Thür 2013 has argued that the statute on *homologein* pertains to procedure and not to contracts, cf. Gagliardi 2014, 2015. Similarly, Theomnestos in Lys. 10 had argued, according to his opponent, for a contracted interpretation of the legal terms defining slander. See on this Giannadaki and Gagarin in this volume.

38 Christ 1998: 196, Johnstone 1999: 27, Yunis 2005: 202–208, Lanni 2006: 69 and Rubinstein 2009: 155–156. See also Dem. 48.56; [Dem.] 58.11 and Aischin. 1.7 (Solon).

39 Isa. 1.17. In the passage there is no direct reference to laws; instead the speaker claims that his lawful right to intestate succession as nearest of kin prevails over any other (similar) right. The argument is correct, provided that the deceased has not drafted a will, and that's exactly his opponents' claim. It is evident, therefore, that the speaker is not simply economical with the truth (Kleonymos had drafted a will!) but he tacitly misrepresents a fundamental principle of Athenian inheritance law. It was suggested to me that this interpretation is excessive; however, the speaker does not distinguish between intestate and testamentary succession: ἡγοῦμαι μὲν τοίνυν, ὦ ἄνδρες, πᾶσι τοῖς τῶν κλήρων ἀμφισβητοῦσιν

Isa. 10.9–10 refers to testamentary adoption as the only valid form of adoption; this is a gross misrepresentation of adoption law since there was also the possibility of a posthumous or an *inter vivos* adoption.[40] Similar interventions fall into recognisable patterns.

1. *Manipulation of key elements of a legal rule*: in the dispute about the property of Kleonymos (Isa. 1), the speaker in paragraphs 42–43 admonishes the *dikastai* to accept his version of events and allocate the inheritance to him. In order to succeed he has to put the validity of Kleonymos' testament into doubt on the ground that πρὸς δὲ τούτοις ἐνθυμήθητε ὅτι αὐτὰς ἔλυσε μὲν Κλεώνυμος εὖ φρονῶν, διέθετο δὲ ὀργισθεὶς καὶ οὐκ ὀρθῶς βουλευόμενος. ('on top of that remember that while Kleonymos revoked (his testament) in his right mind, he made it when he was angered and not in his right mind'). The speaker claims, masterfully associating εὖ φρονῶν with the annulment of a testament, that Kleonymos was angry (ὀργισθεὶς) with the speaker when he drafted his will (implying that it was perhaps void?) and when they were reconciled Kleonymos wanted to cancel it but he was unsuccessful. At this point there is an inaccuracy in the account; the speaker presents the case as if Kleonymos had cancelled the will, ἔλυσεν, while we know that he did not, a development blamed on the opponents.[41] In Dem. 20.155–156 the prosecutor argues that Leptines' law violated the principle of one penalty for each offence, while later he counts *atimia* and confiscation as two different penalties. However, there are many cases where concurrent penalties are provided by Athenian law, the most obvious being Eukrates' law on the protection of democracy.[42]

---

and in the end of the period concludes περίεργον εἶναι τοὺς ἄλλους λόγους λέγειν. I do not include selective quotation of laws in this category (as Carey 1994: 102 suggests for Lys. 1), since there is no quotation. See also Dem. 24.191 warning about selective quotation. See Harrison 1968: 85 n. 1, Edwards 2008: 43, and Rubinstein 1993: 16.

40 See Griffith-Williams 2012: 150 for the rhetorical needs served by such 'generalized statements of principle', and Griffith-Williams 2013: 225: 'The structure of the speaker's argument is syllogistic: his major (and highly misleading) premise is that an adoption is always carried out in accordance with the testamentary dispositions of an adopter …'.

41 See Edwards 2008: 49, arguing that in Isa. 1 and Isa. 9 the speakers dispute the validity of wills on moral grounds. But at least in Isa. 1 there is no morality involved. Similar loose interpretation of the term εὖ φρονῶν in Isa. 6.7–9. See also Harris 2013a: 194–195.

42 See Kremmydas 2012: 436–437. The only explanation for such a statement I can suggest is that perhaps law courts, when no statutory penalty was provided, are usually imposing one of the two categories of penalties. Statutory penalties did not fall within this restriction, see *SEG* 12.87, 16–22 (337/6 BC), also Dem. 21.43. Similar usage of laws in Andok. 1.99 with Canevaro and Harris 2012: 124 and Dem. 24 with Canevaro 2013: 74–75 and 148.

2. *Abuse of procedure*:[43] in Isa. 3.60 the speaker points out a contradiction that implies abuse of procedure. In particular, his opponents claimed that Pyrrhos had a daughter who, following Pyrrhos' death, became the sole heiress of his property (*epiklēros*). A legitimate heir or heiress could take hold of the inheritance without any judicial authorisation or confirmation (*embateusis*). Instead, the speaker's opponents chose to launch the procedure of *epidikasia*, that is a procedure aimed at establishing who among the claimants had the strongest claim to the inheritance.[44]
3. '*Adulteration*': In Isa. 7.1 the speaker introduces his argument with a seemingly paradoxical assertion; for an adoption *inter vivos* he uses a word reminiscent of the clause εὖ φρονῶν, probably influenced by (or deliberately hinting at) the wording of the law on testamentary adoption. MacDowell 1978: 101 accepts the testimony of Isaios about the extension of the criteria for a valid will to adoption. I would agree to the extent that this applied where adoption was performed through a will; however, if adoption was performed *inter vivos* there was no mechanism to challenge that declaration. Isaios' argument is a particularly crafty way to adulterate a rule, since quite a well-known element from a similar institution is inserted, one that passes for being self-evident or even natural in an oral context.[45]

---

43 In Isa. 5.31–33 the speaker narrates the diversionary tactics of his opponents. Diversionary tactics as in the case of Antiphon 6, when the speaker claims that his opponents launched the prosecution for a *bouleusis phonou* once they have learnt that he was ready to act on an *eisangelia* process against them may constitute abuse of procedure. There is a case of real conspiracy to alienate Euktemon's property reported in Isa. 6.35–37. It involved manipulation of legal procedures in an attempt to safeguard the enjoyment of Euktemon's property by the pretenders. It was averted at the last moment. Procedural abuse referred to in Hyp. *Lyk*. 12: αὐτὸς δὲ ὑπερπηδήσας ἅπαντας τοὺς νόμους εἰσαγγελίαν δέδωκας ὑπὲρ ὧν γραφαὶ πρὸς τοὺς θεσμοθέτας ἐκ τῶν νόμων εἰσίν ('but you override all the laws yourself, by presenting an impeachment in a case where the laws require a public charge before the *thesmothetai*').

44 This procedural diversion may be due to the fragile status of the sole heiress; she was expected to marry the closest kin from the paternal side, and there may have been several contestants if the property was significant.

45 εἴ τις αὐτὸς ζῶν καὶ εὖ φρονῶν ἐποιήσατο καὶ ἐπὶ τὰ ἱερὰ ἀγαγὼν εἰς τοὺς συγγενεῖς ἀπέδειξε ('if anyone himself, alive and in his right mind, adopted and having led the adopted to the shrines presented him to the relatives'); cf. Rubinstein 1993: 17, Griffith-Williams 2013: 43 and Hatzilambrou in this volume accepting that any adoption required the element of the adopter's sanity. In the same speech (§ 20), Thrasyllos is trying to adulterate the law on intestate succession by applying the principle that males are preferred to female relatives in cases of inheritance of distant relatives to the degree of cousins, while the same does not apply for the paternal property or that of a brother, Edwards 2008: 49. Probable inspiration for such an interpretation is the law reported in Dem. 43.51 and the close proximity of the male preference clause to the succession of cousins. The same strategy is employed

In [Dem.] 59.16–17 Apollodoros, having cited a law about marriage, usually deemed genuine, inserts in his explanation the term *paidopoieisthai*; this may have gone down well with the *dikastai* since procreation was thought of as the main purpose of marriage.[46]

Conclusion

This overview of usages of law does not aim to list exhaustively all similar cases, but rather to draw attention to the variety of 'contemporary' ways in which litigants could make a text of 'superior' authority serve their needs.[47] Despite the Aristotelian injunctions about the instrumental uses of legal texts in litigation, Athenians showed a remarkable versatility in employing legal texts or vague references to laws not only to counter their opponents' claims, but also to provide adequate ground for their own. A legal text was used to blacken the integrity of the opponent, it was paraphrased, interpreted (using different techniques), it was enriched with social conventions masked as legal requirements. It is this malleability of the legal text that the term διαστρέφειν encompasses. At the end of the day, the thin red line between use and 'abuse' was indeed so thin that perhaps it did not matter at all, since the final pronouncement rested in the hands of the Athenian *dikastai*, who were not qualified lawyers.[48] In a legal system with no Court of Appeal or Supreme Court, no professional

in Isa. 3.80 where instead of *gamēlia* there is a dinner on the occasion of the Thesmophoria festival and in Isa. 3.8, in which behind a series of questions posed by the speaker lies the presumption that a marriage must be accompanied by the provision of a dowry, proportional to the estate of the bride's father. What underlies this kind of argument is the conviction that providing a dowry is part and parcel of a marriage. Along similar lines the argumentation about witnesses to providing the dowry in Isa. 3.28. In paragraphs 52–53, οἱ δὲ νόμοι περὶ ἁπάντων διορίζουσι τούτων, need not refer to a law regulating dowries as envisaged by Edwards (2008: 48); the passage concerns besides the small amount of the dowry, the false ascription of Phile as niece of Nikodemos, the omission to lodge an *eisangelia* for *kakōsis epiklērou*. Isa. 3.11: καίτοι ὅπου κοινὴν αὐτοὶ ὡμολογήκασιν εἶναι τοῦ βουλομένου τὴν γυναῖκα, πῶς ἂν εἰκότως ἡ αὐτὴ γυνὴ ἐγγυητὴ δόξειεν εἶναι; there was no legal impediment to marrying a κοινὴ τῷ βουλομένῳ γυνή, if she was an Athenian. The speaker amplifies implicitly the legal requirements, implying that a prostitute cannot marry. Similarly, in Isa. 1.17 (addition of *philia* in the intestate succession order) and Dem. 48.56.

46 On the genuineness of the law, Kapparis 1999: 198.

47 Similar assessment in Frost 1992: 111, 116.

48 The omnipotence of the verdict reached by *dikastai* is rhetorically underlined in Lys. 15.4: εὖ εἰδότες ὅτι, ὅπως ἂν ὑμεῖς νυνὶ περὶ αὐτῶν γνῶτε, οὕτω καὶ τὸν ἄλλον χρόνον ἡ πόλις αὐτοῖς χρήσεται.

jurists and lawyers, no clear rules of binding precedent, litigants argued their case and positioned themselves in an advantageous spot, closer to the perceived opinions of the *dikastai*. If juries tended to side with interpretations reaffirming the *status quo* and against any novel interpretation of laws—the sample of verdicts is too small and we should remain circumspect,[49] then cases of 'abusive' interpretation would have been difficult to establish. It was, then, the decision of Athenian *dikastai* that approved and established interpretations of legal rules and a sense of security and continuity.

Bibliography

Alwine, A.T. (2015) *Enmity and Feuding in Classical Athens*, Austin.

Aviles, D. (2011) '"Arguing Against the Law": Non-Literal Interpretation in Attic Forensic Oratory', *Dike* 14, 19–42.

Biscardi, A. (1970) 'La "gnome dikaiotate" et l'interprétation des lois dans la Grèce ancienne', *Revue Internationale des Droits de l'Antiquité* 17, 219–232.

Canevaro, M. (2013) *The Documents in the Attic Orators: Laws and Decrees in the Public Speeches of the Demosthenic Corpus*, Oxford.

Canevaro, M. and Harris, E.M. (2012) 'The Documents in Andocides' *On the Mysteries*', CQ 62, 98–129.

Carey, C. (1994) '"Artless" Proofs in Aristotle and the Orators', BICS 39, 95–106.

Carey, C. (1996) '*Nomos* in Attic Rhetoric and Oratory', JHS 116, 33–46.

Carey, C. (2004) 'Offence and Procedure in Athenian Law', in Harris, E.M. and Rubinstein, L., eds (2004) *The Law and the Courts in Ancient Greece*, London, 111–136.

Christ, M.R. (1998) *The Litigious Athenian*, Baltimore.

Christ, M.R. (2006) *The Bad Citizen in Classical Athens*, Cambridge.

Davies, J.K. (2002) 'The Strategies of Mr. Theopompos' in Cartledge, P., Cohen, E. and Foxhall, L., eds (2002) *Money, Labour and Land. Approaches to the Economics of Ancient Greece*, London, 200–208.

de Brauw, M. (2002) '"Listen to the Laws Themselves": Citations of Law and Portrayal of Character in Attic Oratory', CJ 97, 161–176.

Dorjahn, A.P. (1935) 'Anticipation of Arguments in Athenian Courts', TAPA 66, 274–295.

Edwards, M.J. (2008) 'Isaeus and the Athenian Inheritance Laws', in Harris, E.M. and Thür, G., eds (2008) *Symposion 2007: Vorträge zur griechischen und hellenistischen Rechtsgeschichte* (Durham, 2–6 September 2007) Vienna, 41–54 (with a response by S.C. Todd, 55–62).

49 Harris 2000 and 2013a: 213–245.

Frost, M. (1992) 'Greco-Roman Legal Analysis: The Topics of Invention', *St. John's Law Review* 66, 107–128.

Gagarin, M. (2014) '*Eikos* Arguments in Athenian Forensic Oratory' in Wohl, V., ed. (2014), *Probabilities, Hypotheticals, and Counterfactuals in Ancient Greek Thought*, Cambridge, 15–29.

Griffith-Williams, B. (2012) '*Oikos*, Family Feuds and Funerals: Argumentation and Evidence in Athenian Inheritance Disputes', *CQ* 62, 145–162.

Griffith-Williams, B. (2013) *A Commentary on Selected Speeches of Isaios*, Leiden.

Harris, E.M. (2000) 'Open Texture in Athenian Law', *Dike* 3, 27–79.

Harris, E.M. (2004) 'More Thoughts on Open Texture in Athenian Law', in: Leão, D., Fialho, M. and Rossetti, L., eds., *Nomos: estudos sobre direito e sociedade na antiguidade clássica*, Coimbra, 241–262.

Harris, E.M. (2006) *Democracy and the Rule of Law in Classical Athens: Essays on Law, Society, and Politics*, Cambridge.

Harris, E.M. (2013a) *The Rule of Law in Action in Democratic Athens*, Oxford.

Harris, E.M. (2013b) 'The Plaint in Athenian Law and Legal Procedure', in Faraguna, M., ed. (2013) *Archives and Archival Documents in Ancient Societies*, Trieste, 143–162.

Harrison, A.R.W. (1968–1971) *The Law of Athens*, 2 vols, Oxford.

Hillgruber, M. (1988) *Die zehnte Rede des Lysias: Einleitung, Text und Kommentar mit einem Anhang über die Gesetzesinterpretationen bei den attischen Rednern*, Berlin.

Johnstone, S. (1999) *Disputes and Democracy: The Consequences of Litigation in Ancient Athens*, Austin, TX.

Kapparis, K. (1999) *Apollodoros 'Against Neaira'* [*D*. 59], Berlin.

Kästle, D.J. (2012) 'Recht und Rhetorik in der Rede gegen Theomnestos (Lysias or. 10)', *Rheinisches Museum für Philologie* 155, 1–40.

Kremmydas, C. (2012) *A commentary on Demosthenes'* Against Leptines, Oxford.

Kucharski, J. (2012) 'Vindictive Prosecution in Classical Athens: On Some Recent Theories', *GRBS* 52, 167–197.

Lanni, A. (2006) *Law and Justice in the Courts of Classical Athens*, Cambridge.

Lanni, A. (2009) 'Social Norms in the Courts of Ancient Athens', *Journal of Legal Analysis* 1, 691–736.

Lanni, A. (2012) 'Publicity and the Courts of Classical Athens', *Yale Journal of Law and Humanities* 24, 119–135.

Lenaerts, A. (2010) 'The General Principle of the Prohibition of Abuse of Rights: A Critical Position on Its Role in a Codified European Contract Law', *European Review of Private Law* 18, 1121–1154.

Mirhady, D. (1990) 'Aristotle on the Rhetoric of Law', *GRBS* 31, 393–410.

Mirhady, D. (1991) 'Non-Technical *pisteis* in Aristotle and Anaximenes', *AJP* 112, 5–28.

Mirhady, D. (2015) 'Knowing the Law and Deciding Justice: Lay Expertise in the Democratic Athenian Courts', *Comparative Legal History* 3, 231–244.

Rhodes, P.J. (2006) 'The Reforms and Laws of Solon: An Optimistic View', in Blok, J.H. and Lardinois, A.P.M.H., eds (2006) *Solon of Athens: New Historical and Philological Approaches*, Leiden. 261–275.

Rubinstein, L. (1993) *Adoption in IV. Century Athens*, Copenhagen.

Rubinstein, L. (2009) 'Legal Argumentation in Hypereides *Against Timandros*', BICS 52, 149–159.

Sickinger, J. (2008) 'Indeterminacy in Greek Law: Statutory Gaps and Conflicts', in Harris, E.M. and Thür, G., eds (2008) *Symposion 2007: Vorträge zur griechischen und hellenistischen Rechtsgeschichte* (Durham, 2–6 September 2007) Vienna, 99–112 (with a response by L. Rubinstein, 113–124).

Thür, G. (2013) 'The Statute on *homologein* in Hyperides' Speech *Against Athenogenes*', *Dike* 16, 1–10.

Todd, S.C. (2007) *A Commentary on Lysias, Speeches 1–11*, Oxford.

Vögelin, W. (1943) *Die Diabole bei Lysias*, Basle.

Whitehead, D. (2000) *Hypereides: The Forensic Speeches*, Oxford.

Willi, A. (2003) *The Languages of Aristophanes: Aspects of Linguistic Variation in Classical Attic Greek*, Oxford.

Wolff, H.J. (1968) *Demosthenes als Advokat*, Berlin. (Translated as 'Demosthenes as Advocate: The Functions and Methods of Legal Consultants in Classical Athens', with an epilogue by G. Thür, in Carawan, E., ed. (2007) *The Attic orators*, Oxford, 91–115.)

Yunis, H. (2005) 'The Rhetoric of Law in Fourth-Century Athens', in Gagarin, M. and Cohen, D., eds (2005) *The Cambridge Companion to Ancient Greek Law*, Cambridge, 191–208.

CHAPTER 11

(Re)constructing the Athenian Legal System

Ifigeneia Giannadaki

Introduction

Athenian law had no formal legal theory; no unified code of laws, reasoned judgments or system of precedent, such as we find in modern legal systems. For us Athenian law is untidy and it was never fully systematised, despite repeated attempts to tidy up the legislative process.[1] Unlike modern legal systems, where there is a unified law code (civil law systems) or formalised jurisprudence based on the principle of precedent (common law systems),[2] in Athenian law courts citation and interpretation of the laws came from the litigants themselves and were inevitably partisan: litigants manipulate and sometimes distort the law in the interest of persuasively presenting their case. My interest here however is not in the room for exploitation of individual laws but in the presentation of the architectonics of the system as a whole. In the orators, law acquires its own narrative as part of the rhetoric of the speech, analogous to the narrative of the facts surrounding a case. This rhetoric manifests itself through the shaping of competing and complementing rationalisations of the Athenian legal system designed to advance litigants' rhetorical argumentation. In effect this strategy amounts to the creation of a story of law.[3] This subject has been recently touched upon by Victoria Wohl,[4] who sets the essential frame in her elegant and articulate reading of forensic legal narratives; this chapter attempts to build on and extend Wohl's discussion, with particular reference to the speech *Against Androtion* (which is not discussed in Wohl's study). My

1 There were repeated attempts to systematise the numerous laws in 411 and 403, but the fruits of these efforts hardly give the picture of a complete and unified law code. See Gagarin 2008: 74–75, 181–185; Lanni 2006: 37; Thomas 1995: 71, 74; Thomas 1989: 37; Sickinger 1999: 114–118, 160–169, Todd 1993: 57–58, 299. For laws on the legislative process see Canevaro in this volume.

2 See Lanni 2006: 117–118: cultural and moral values may have played a role in achieving some sort of consistency in the Athenian courts rather than legal knowledge and jurisprudence in the modern sense, which was alien to the amateur system of the administration of justice in ancient Athens. Wohl 2010: 26–32 (law as source of authority in classical Athens); compare, e.g., Harris 2013 for a different approach.

3 Cf. Scheppele 1989: 2073–2098.

4 Wohl 2010.

 | DOI:10.1163/9789004377899_013

examination of the reconstruction of the law in Dem. 22 in comparison with alternative and competing accounts seeks to show the dynamics of such rhetorical representations of the system as a coherent and unified 'law code'. I also compare (in part 3) the rhetorical reconstructions of the system with the advice of contemporary rhetoricians about the manipulation of law.

Dem. 22 was written for Diodoros' prosecution of Androtion through *graphē paranomōn* for a decree, which proposed the grant of honours to the outgoing Council of 356 BC. Although such cases involve legal technicalities and a litigant would be normally expected to collate and cite old and new legislation, through the reading of laws/legal clauses by the clerk of the court, in order to prove the infringement,[5] there is no such treatment of the law in this speech.[6] Instead, the four legal objections raised by Diodoros are incorporated into the narrative—cited and commented on by the litigant himself.[7] Of the legal objections raised in the speech, the treatment of Androtion's alleged prostitution by Demosthenes will be the starting point and main focus of the present analysis.

1 The (Re)construction of a Coherent and Cohesive Legal System

Procedural (In)flexibility of the Athenian Legal System

Diodoros offers very briefly the clause from the law regulating the sexual conduct of citizens, according to which, if a man prostituted himself, he was banned from public speaking.[8] Androtion has allegedly breached the relevant law by proposing decrees despite being a former prostitute.[9] However, Androtion is expected to claim that, had Diodoros evidence against him for prostitution, he should have chosen the most appropriate procedure, the *graphē hetairēseōs* (public case for prostitution), rather than dragging in the allegation in the *graphē paranomōn*—and thus have him punished for that very offence.[10] In an evasive riposte Diodoros presents an elegant and seductive depiction of a legal system which is flexible enough to allow for various types

5 E.g. Dem. 23.22, Aischin. 3.15, 32; Dem. 18.106, 120–121; Dem. 20.92.

6 See also Sundahl 2000: 117 Table 1. Diodoros in Dem. 22 is alone in not having statutes read out: there are six laws in Aischin. 3; two laws in Dem. 18, eleven laws in Dem. 23.

7 One cannot exclude the possibility that certain legal objections have been already presented to the audience by previous supporting speaker(s) or Euktemon himself, given that this is a deuterology (cf. Dem. 22.1). Rubinstein 2000: 135–136.

8 Dem. 22.24.

9 Dem. 22.21. The prostitution law is also found in Aischin. 1.19–20.

10 He also briskly alludes to another procedure, the *dokimasia rhētorōn*, scrutiny of public speakers as another option against the prostitution charge, but he suppresses the fact

of actions for the same offence, accompanied by a rationalisation of the procedural flexibility, providing an analysis of the intent of the legislator who consciously allowed for this feature.[11]

The flexibility according to this model consists in the possibility of choosing a legal action to prosecute an offence on the basis of an estimation of the risk, the prospects of success, and the nature of the penalty which the prosecutor would incur in a *graphē* in case of acquittal of the defendant, or failure to secure one-fifth of the votes of the *dikastai*:

> δεῖν δ' ᾤετο μηδέν' ἀποστερεῖσθαι τοῦ δίκης τυχεῖν, ὡς ἕκαστος δύναται. πῶς οὖν ἔσται τοῦτο; ἐὰν πολλὰς ὁδοὺς δῷ διὰ τῶν νόμων ἐπὶ τοὺς ἠδικηκότας οἷον τῆς κλοπῆς. ἔρρωσαι καὶ σαυτῷ πιστεύεις· ἄπαγε· ἐν χιλίαις δ' ὁ κίνδυνος. ἀσθενέστερος εἶ· τοῖς ἄρχουσιν ἐφηγοῦ· τοῦτο ποιήσουσιν ἐκεῖνοι. φοβεῖ καὶ [27] τοῦτο· γράφου. καταμέμφει σεαυτὸν καὶ πένης ὢν οὐκ ἂν ἔχοις χιλίας ἐκτεῖσαι· δικάζου κλοπῆς πρὸς διαιτητὴν καὶ οὐ κινδυνεύσεις. [οὐδέτερον βούλει τούτων· γράφου. κατοκνεῖς καὶ τοῦτο· ἐφηγοῦ.] τούτων οὐδέν ἐστι ταὐτό. τῆς ἀσεβείας κατὰ ταὔτ' ἔστ' ἀπάγειν, γράφεσθαι, δικάζεσθαι πρὸς Εὐμολπίδας, φαίνειν πρὸς τὸν βασιλέα. **περὶ τῶν ἄλλων ἁπάντων τὸν αὐτὸν τρόπον σχεδόν.**
>
> DEM. 22.26–27

> He thought that no one should be deprived of the right to obtain justice in a way suited to his level of ability. How then will this come about? If he creates many legal procedures for proceeding against offenders, as, for example, in the case of theft. You are strong and confident in your own ability: arrest him and risk a fine of 1,000 *drachmas*. You are weaker: lead the magistrates to him, and they will do it. You are also afraid of this: bring a public charge. [27] You do not feel confident, and since you are poor, you would not be able to pay the fine of 1,000 *drachmas*; bring a private action before the arbitrator, and you will run no risk. None of these procedures is the same. The situation is the same with cases of impiety: someone can make an arrest, bring a public charge, bring a private charge before the Eumolpidai, or make a denunciation to the King. **And it is more or less the same for all other procedures.**
>
> Trans. HARRIS 2008

---

that this procedure is available specifically for politicians, those addressing the Assembly/Council, not all citizens. For *dokimasia rhētorōn* see MacDowell 2005: 79–88.

11 Dem. 22.25. For the intent of the legislator in such reconstructions of the system see part 2 below.

This neatly-structured system is not a meticulous presentation of the Athenian legal system, but a selective distillation. For his rhetorical purposes Demosthenes blurs and obscures the circumstances of detection of a given offence and the identity of the prosecutor by suppressing the substantive distinctions between the various offences he mentions to achieve persuasion.[12] He presents the range of procedures available in cases of theft (*klopē*) and impiety (*asebeia*) and the narrative follows a hierarchical arrangement of actions on the basis of the skill and confidence of the victim:[13] riskier and more complex procedures are lodged by the most confident and articulate speakers, while less risky and demanding procedures are specifically designed to correspond to the abilities of the less physically competent and intellectually confident speakers. Thus Demosthenes evades the need for an argument relying on the *substance* of law to counter Androtion's anticipated riposte by creating a *coherent reconstruction of the legal system* to justify the choice of the *graphē paranomōn* instead of a *graphē hetairēseōs* as a result of the 'open texture' of Athenian law.[14] Although his starting point is offences of theft and impiety, he extends the application of his model to *almost* (σχεδόν) every offence. This systematisation, especially the tight hierarchy—although a substantial oversimplification—adds considerable plausibility to his argument.

Diodoros' reconstruction of a procedurally flexible system finds its counterpart in a competing rationalisation and reconstruction in Hypereides' speech *For Euxenippos*, where he challenges the employment of *eisangelia* (impeachement)[15] against Euxenippos on the ground that the latter was not a *rhētōr* (public speaker), against whom the procedure would be normally employed for high crimes against the city (Hyp. *Eux.* 7–8), but an *idiōtēs* (private individual). Accordingly, Hypereides offers a reconstruction of the legal system which calculatedly restricts the room for *eisangelia*: on this 'foreclosing model'

12 See Carey 2004: 111–136 who subjects this model to scrutiny and shows that Diodoros' model needs modification. See also Osborne in this volume.

13 Cf. Dem. 24.113: a certain degree of flexibility in punishing theft in the night: death, wounding, or *apagōgē* (summary arrest). The legal remedies are arranged from the most severe to the least severe. Cf. also Dem. 21.25–29: Demosthenes anticipates and pre-empts Meidias' argument that Demosthenes should not have brought a *probolē* against Meidias, but a private case (i.e. *dikē blabēs*), or a *graphē hybreōs* if he really thought that Meidias had committed *hybris*.

14 On the 'open texture' (cf. Hart 1994: 135–136) of Athenian law see Osborne 1985: esp. 42–44; updated in his 2010: 202 study; cf. Harris (2008: 179n. 44; cf. 2013a: 175–212), also Carey 1998: 98 n. 18 and in more detail in Carey 2004: 111–136 for the modification of Osborne's model. For a thorough discussion of the passage see Giannadaki (forthcoming).

15 Hyp. *Eux.* 5–6.

of the system, it is the *nature of the offence*, not the *ability of the prosecutor*, that determines the choice of procedure. It is striking that he indulges in an oversimplification similar to Androtion's about the operation of the *entire* system, not just the offences covered by the *eisangelia* law: τὸν αὐτὸν δὲ τρόπον καὶ ἐπὶ τῶν ἄλλων ἀδικημάτων ἁπάντων καὶ νόμους καὶ ἀρχὰς καὶ δικαστήρια τὰ προσήκοντα ἑκάστοις αὐτῶν ἀπέδοτε, 'Similarly, to deal with every other offence you have established laws, offices, and courts appropriate to each' (§ 6; cf. Dem. 22.27 cited on p. 200).[16] But where Demosthenes maximises the diversity of procedures, Hypereides minimises it. He, therefore, suggests that the prosecutor[17] has improperly applied the law of *eisangelia* and classed a private individual as a public speaker.[18] The striking resemblance in tone and style of the two passages may indicate that Hypereides was aware of this mode of argument in Dem. 22.[19] The existence of these competing rationalisations of the legal system, as procedurally flexible on the one hand, and tightly structured and inflexible on the other, does not necessarily invalidate either of them, but it manifestly shows the rhetorical function of such juridical narratives which reconstruct the system according to the purposes they serve: Diodoros from the perspective of the prosecution—anticipating the defence's argument and preempting it—Hypereides' from the perspective of the defence, challenging the suitability of the procedure employed by the prosecution.[20] What the two competing models share is a persuasive but reductive representation of the untidy legal system as logically, coherently, and tightly fixed, adapted to their rhetorical strategies on each occasion. Although law as a *substantive rule* is weak in Diodoros' case, the rhetoric of law that surrounds the specific legal issue of

16 The phrasing of the conclusion here is remarkably similar to that of Demosthenes' sweeping exaggeration. Cf. Hyp. *Athen.* 17 for a distortive presentation of a series of laws with similar phrasing (see n. 48 below).

17 Hypereides offers evidence for the treatment of the legal issue from the prosecution's angle, too, and it is remarkable that the prosecutor appears well aware of the legal narrative the defendant will adopt, i.e. to challenge the application of the law of *eisangelia* against a private individual (*idiōtēs*) and Hypereides' narrative suggests that the exactly opposite line has been taken by Polyeuktos, the prosecutor: opening up the application of *eisangelia* not only to those who qualify to be described as *rhētōres*, but for those who would be described as *idiōtai*. Polyeuktos' line of argument appears to be remarkably similar to that of Diodoros. Cf. Hyp. *Eux.* 4, cf. § 9.

18 Hyp. *Eux.* 13, 27–28, 29, 30. Cf. Gagarin pp. 29–30 and Volonaki 307–312 in this volume.

19 Thus Rubinstein 2000: 224. This may well be the case, but as this chapter suggests this type of rhetorical reasoning may have not been unusual in the fourth century.

20 Cf. Dem. 21.25–26 for a similar justification of the choice of procedure which gives an insight about the employment of such rhetorical arguments both from the perspective of the prosecution and the anticipated response by the defence.

prostitution skilfully compensates for the weak legal grounds to prove Androtion's infringement. Similarly, Hypereides exploits the legal status and notion of *rhētōr* to deny its application in the case of Euxenippos who (he claims) would not qualify as such, and accordingly, would not be liable for the prosecution by *eisangelia*.

The Procedural (In)flexibility of the System and the 'Genealogy of Law':[21] Dem. 54

Judicial narratives such as the competing reconstructions of Diodoros and Hypereides are not confined to political (or public) trials, such as the ones we have examined so far. Demosthenes in a private speech, *Against Konon* (Dem. 54), offers another sophisticated reconstruction of the system—a story about the 'genealogy' of the law dealing with violence.[22] More specifically, this is a case of battery (*dikē aikeias*) brought against Konon who had allegedly beaten and verbally abused Ariston. Ariston, in his attempt to effectively pre-empt Konon's defence—who is expected to laugh the whole matter off as a trivial private issue within the limits of socially acceptable behaviour—offers a tight model of the system according to which every act of violence is punished through a specific procedure and the law does not allow pleas on the ground of mitigating circumstances (Dem. 54.17–19).

More precisely, this tight system of laws regulating a number of procedures available against acts of violence is presented in hierarchical order—in *inverted hierarchy*, compared to the legal narrative of Diodoros—ranging from the less serious offence, the verbal abuse (*loidoria*), to the most serious, homicide (*phonou*).[23] In Ariston's reconstruction of the genealogy of law violence exists before and outside the law, which was created at a certain stage to prevent a cycle of escalation and it is designed to exclude the existence of socially understandable violent behaviour (of the sort Konon will argue for, cf. §§14, 35).[24] Also, for every type of violence there is a corresponding procedure to stop the aggressor from committing a more serious offence (*loidorias*,

---

21 This terminology is aptly used by Wohl 2010: 76 in her study of the speech from which it is borrowed. My focus here is specifically on the reconstruction of the legal system offered by Ariston.

22 Cf. also Isok. 20.8–9 who takes a similar view about the escalation of violence and its potential severe consequences for the offender.

23 Dem. 54.18; cf. Dem. 22.26–27 (p. 200 above).

24 Dem. 54.17 προείδοντο, §19 προεώραται. This is essentially the narrative we find in Aesch *Eum*. 490–496, 540–545 and Orestes' trial has been seen as the rejection of any further private 'vendetta' and the introduction of legal and civic justice; see Allen 2000: 20, 22,

plēgas, traumata, thanaton). Consequently, where *Against Androtion* sees procedural diversity as almost complete freedom for the prosecutor, here diversity is seen as foreclosing options, and *Against Konon* has more in common with *Euxenippos* than with the *Against Androtion*. Thus Konon's attempt to present his serious act of violence as socially acceptable gang activity,[25] and his pleas for acquittal on that basis, look absurd set against this neatly-structured system.

Simultaneously, Dem. 54 offers an excellent example of the reconstruction of the Athenian legal system envisaged as a *flexible* one, in a similar fashion that Diodoros envisages it in *Against Androtion*. In his proem, Ariston acknowledges a certain degree of flexibility in the selection of an appropriate procedure to prosecute the violent act suffered by him (§1): the offence was so serious (we are told) that it was qualified for prosecution by *apagōgē* and *graphē hybreōs*, but he opted for the *dikē* as he did not want to take upon himself a greater task than he could bear (§1 παραινούντων μὴ μείζω πράγματ' ἢ δυνήσομαι φέρειν ἐπάγεσθαι) and he wanted to avoid appearing over-ambitious for his age. His first reason about the selection of the procedure is significant, as it is in direct correspondence with the ability of the prosecutor, the criterion for selecting a procedure in Diodoros' shaping of the system (cf. Dem. 22.26 ὡς ἕκαστος δύναται, cited above p. 200). Ariston's reconstruction of the legal system serves his rhetorical purpose to justify the employment of a less risky procedure against Konon. And in that respect, the procedural flexibility he envisages is close to the conceptualisation of the system by Diodoros in Dem. 22, though Diodoros posits a higher degree of flexibility. Ariston's justification of the less risky procedure in the scale of actions aims at portraying himself as a young and inexperienced man,[26] who wisely followed the advice of his friends and family to act in accord with his personal circumstances and ability. His legal narrative (only two public procedures are mentioned: *apagōgē lōpodytōn, graphē hybreōs*, §1) to explain his rationale behind the selection of the *dikē aikaias* is less elaborate compared to the later reconstruction of the system to address forms of violence (§18).[27]

Sommerstein 1989: 19–25, 182–183. For the idea that law stops the escalation of violence cf. Dem. 21.75–76.

25 This is presumably why the speech is addressed as a prosecution against Konon rather than his son. He himself is expected to allege that both Ariston and his sons belong to street-gangs (cf. Dem. 54.16): the *dikastai* would be more likely to accept the line of argument that one cannot stop young men fighting.

26 This legal narrative serves as a means of constructing the *ēthos* of the litigants: see Carey 1996: esp. 36–37, 44.

27 If we believe Ariston's narrative of the events leading to beating and his subsequent critical health condition (§§8–9, 11–12) the employment of *apagōgē* would be in action highly

But here the system is (conveniently) diverse enough to allow the prosecutor to select an appropriate procedure in accord with his personal circumstances and ability, and he effectively chooses a less demanding action down the scale, despite the fact that the degree of violence is consistently described in more severe terms, as *hybris* (bullying).[28] Ariston is eager to establish his peaceable nature and abstinence from any form of aggression not only by refusing to respond with violence to Konon, but also by opting for a less severe procedure to obtain justice for such a serious offence on the legal sphere.[29]

The procedural flexibility envisaged in the proem and the neatness and fixity of the Athenian legal system as it appears later in the speech might reasonably appear as contradictory *prima facie*. Demosthenes himself appears to be conscious of the risk of inconsistency and thereby he skilfully introduces the model of fixity though the employment of reported speech and Ariston's 'second-hand' knowledge of the respective laws.[30] Ariston denied being a legal expert from the outset, and the sophisticated juridical narrative of the 'genealogy of law' features as a result of his inevitable close study of the laws to be able to seek justice (§ 17). But careful comparison of the two passages reveals that these two principles, flexibility and fixity, envisaged for the legal system are not necessarily contradictory and the audience would not have been expected to find these two 'competing' reconstructions as incompatible, or Demosthenes would not have juxtaposed these reconstructions in the same speech. The initial flexibility of procedure, on the one hand, and the structural neatness and tightness of the system, on the other hand, are designed to serve different rhetorical needs of the prosecution: to pre-empt the defence and justify the chosen procedure by the prosecutor, respectively. In fact, the points made are rather complementary in that the system is flexible enough to allow for the victim of a violent act to choose from a number of suitable procedures for the offence, but at the

unlikely on this occasion given Ariston's condition, but what matters for his purposes is the availability of this procedure to deal with the offence of violence.

28 Cf. Dem. 54.1, 4, 10, 11, 13, 15, 16, 17, 20, 24 (reading of the law by the clerk), 25, 28, 33, 37. Ariston exploits the rhetoric of *hybris* to highlight the severity of the offence and this rhetoric is exploited in Dem. 22 too: e.g. Dem. 22.47, 55, 56, 68.

29 As Carey and Reid 1985: 76 note, the choice of procedure in the present case as presented by Ariston supresses other aspects he may have well taken into account, i.e. penalties attached in *apagōgē* and *graphē* in failing to obtain the one-fifth of the votes, and damages awarded to the plaintiff in private cases, unlike public cases (any fine was payable to the state). The financial risks are explicit in Dem. 22, but suppressed in Dem. 54.

30 Dem. 54.18: [the laws] φασίν/ἀκούω/οἶμαι. I would like to thank Stephen Todd for drawing my attention to this passage. The narrative hovers between a heuristic and a systematic reading (cf. Carey and Reid 1985: 89).

same time it is characterised by firmness, completeness and correspondence of offence and procedure at each level, to ensure that no offender can escape unpunished. The legal system offers a comprehensive number of laws tightly-structured and exhaustive (so the prosecution goes) to ensure their effectiveness (§ 21).

Suppressing the Availability of Legal Procedure(S): Lys. 1

Lys. 1 (*dikē phonou*), the defence speech of Euphiletos on a charge of killing Eratosthenes, who was caught in the act of illicit sex with Euphiletos' wife (*moicheia*), offers another example of a juridical narrative in contrast with Diodoros' model on procedural flexibility. Euphiletos alleges that the killing of Eratosthenes was not a matter of choice, but *the* sanction prescribed by the homicide law for dealing with *moichoi* (seducers).[31] Euphiletos excerpts a clause for justifiable homicide from the homicide law from the stele of Areiopagos, which *authorises* (but does not prescribe) killing in such cases. The law can be safely identified, by Euphiletos' commentary, with the law preserved in Dem. 23.53 and attributed to Drakon.[32] Comparison between the Lysianic and Demosthenic versions shows a certain degree of manipulation of the law by Lysias, in the form of additions and suppression of details to reinforce his rhetorical interpretation: killing was the only legal remedy against the seduction of Euphiletos' wife. Most notably, the homicide law (Dem. 23.53) does not explicitly mention the offence of *moicheia* but Euphiletos inserts the relevant terms (§ 30, τῇ ἑαυτοῦ μοιχὸν λαβών), misrepresenting the law as explicitly authorising lawful homicide in cases of *moichoi*. At the same time, the Demosthenic version of the law appears to include other types of female relatives which are not mentioned in the 'commentary' of Euphiletos, whose selective presentation of the content of the law is designed to offer a solid legal provision which exactly corresponds to his own circumstances. Thus he emphasises the explicit provision about *non-conviction* for killing of a seducer (§ 30, διαρρήδην

---

31 Lys. 1.30. There is a long-lasting debate about *moicheia* (which I take to cover cases of illicit sex with female relatives other than a man's wife; hence I translate 'seduction', cf. Gagarin in this volume, p. 20, n. 10). For the debate see Carey 1995: 405–417 (*moicheia* as 'seduction'); *pace* Cohen 1991: 407–417 (who views *moicheia* as 'adultery', linked to marriage). Cf. Todd 2007: 46–49, Leão and Rhodes 2016: 44 (with references). On the debate whether the Athenians regarded *moicheia* as a worse crime than rape see Harris 1990: 370–377 (= 2006: 283–296), exposing the sophistry of Euphiletos' argument.

32 Todd 2007: 126–127; Canevaro 2013: 65, 69. The law in the Demosthenic version is discussed by Leão and Rhodes 2015: 30–31, cf. 43–44. They consider the provision on lawful homicide with relation to *moicheia* as possibly a clause already found in the homicide law of Drakon (p. 43).

εἴρηται τούτου μὴ καταγιγνώσκειν φόνον, 'it is explicitly decreed not to convict a man for murder'), but the Demosthenic version reads τούτων ἕνεκα μὴ φεύγειν κτείναντα, 'he shall not *be exiled* (or *be put on trial*) *as a homicide* for these things'.[33]

Euphiletos' restrictive model also tacitly suppresses the range of procedures available, as we learn from other sources: that is, to hold the *moichos* to ransom[34]—a possibility never directly addressed in the speech, only briskly mentioned by the speaker in passing;[35] *graphē moicheias*, as we learn from the *Ath. Pol.* 59.3–4;[36] and physical abuse.[37] Euphiletos was not *obliged* to kill, as he would have us believe. The penalty on conviction in a *graphē moicheias* is not known, but the possibility that this included financial compensation erodes the neat distinction between *moicheia* and rape which Lysias creates through the comparison of the two offences, insisting on the more serious character of *moicheia*. This is presumably why he distorts the relevant provision from the homicide law rather than citing the law(s) prescribing the various remedies against the act of *moicheia*.[38] Had he done so, his suppression of the legal actions available would have exposed his distortive legal narrative. This manipulative and reductive legal narrative comes in stark contrast with the flexible model offered by Diodoros, and Lys. 1 is closer to Hypereides' reconstruction of the system, though in an extreme form: the killing of a seducer is presented as the *only* available course of action to punish seduction.[39]

---

33 Dem. 23.53. Cf. *Ath. Pol.* 57.3 which also summarises the clause about seduction. However, the Demosthenic passage 23.53 is not unproblematic itself in terms of its wording: the phrase referring to lawful homicide for seduction has been translated 'is not to flee into exile' (e.g. Canevaro 2013: 64), or 'put into exile', Todd 2007: 127 (who also notes 'put on trial' as a possible interpretation). In terms of authenticity Canevaro 2013 considers the clause in question 'fairly acceptable'.

34 Lys. 1.25, 29.

35 There is an allusion to it in §19 and it is remarkable that the possibility is placed by the speaker in the mouth of Eratosthenes, and it is explicitly contrasted with Euphiletos' own obedience to the law.

36 *Ath. Pol.* 59.3. We also have fragments of Hypereides' *For Lykophron*, a case where an *eisangelia* (333 BC) was used against an alleged *moichos*, apparently on the pretext that his actions had undermined the basis of civil order (Todd 1993: 278). The normal procedure for this offence was a *graphē* (*moicheias*) as the defendant is arguing, not *eisangelia*; cf. Hyp. *Eux.* 1–3. Cf. *Ath. Pol.* 59.3 for *thesmothetai* accepting *graphai moicheias*.

37 Lys. 1.48, Ar. *Nub.* 1083 and Todd 2007: 50, Cantarella 2005: 243–244, Carey 1993: 53–55.

38 See Carey 1995: 410. Harris 1990 (= 2006: 283–296): 370–377.

39 Cf. Lys. 1.25–26; see further Carey 1995: 410–412; Carey 1998: 96.

The 'Biography' of Law and the Neat and Cohesive 'Law Code': Aischin. 1

Another coherent and cohesive rhetorical reconstruction envisaging a coherent Athenian legal system, which complements Diodoros' reconstruction, comes from Aischines' *Against Timarchos*. Timarchos is charged with being ineligible to address the Assembly as a former prostitute, in a 'scrutiny of public speakers' (*dokimasia rhētorōn*). Aischines, dealing with a weak legal case and in the absence of solid evidence to support Timarchos' alleged prostitution, presents the *wider legal frame* of the case, by offering an extended legal narrative (Aischin. 1.6–36) about the laws regulating the conduct of citizens throughout their lives to preserve decency and morality (Aischin. 1.7–8). This legal narrative is arranged by citation of the laws on *sōphrosynē* (moderation/self-control) in the order in which the laws had been (allegedly) created, which also corresponds to the lifetime of those the laws apply to—children, young boys, adult citizens, private individuals and public speakers[40]—not only to give the impression of the existence of a cohesive and *unified* 'law code', but also to illustrate rhetorically the *continuous* violation of *all the laws* by Timarchos.[41] This law code is artificially, but artfully, attributed to a single legislator, Solon, although most likely some of the laws were more recent.[42] This sophisticated rhetorical narrative[43] serves as the foundation for the contrast between the 'model citizen' as envisaged by the 'Solonian' laws and Timarchos' overly shameful life, which effectively disqualified him from being a public speaker. Not all the laws discussed are strictly relevant to the case at hand,[44] or accurately interpreted by Aischines.[45] But his narrative reshapes the legal system as a series of laws, neatly devised and gradually developed to form a unified

40 Aischin. 1.6–36: laws regulating the *sōphrosynē* (moderation/self-control) of citizens throughout their lives: boys and their conduct at school; teachers' conduct (*didaskaloi*); *nomoi* prescribing penalties for guardians who hire out boys as prostitutes; laws against procurers with the most severe penalties for those procuring a free boy or woman; the law of *hybris* (bullying). Cf. de Brauw 2002: esp. 171–172. Aischin. 1.19–21 on prostitution law; Aischin. 1.22–23 and 34ff. on law regarding the *eukosmia* (orderly conduct) of the public speakers.

41 Aischin. 1.8, 36.

42 Aischin. 1.7 πρῶτον μὲν … /ἔπειτα δεύτερον … /τρίτον δ' ἐφεξῆς … cf. Aischines' line of argument to follow exactly the arrangement of the laws in the law code regulating the behaviour of children, youths, other ages (private individuals and *rhētores*). For the chronology of the laws cf. Fisher 2001: 129–130.

43 Cf. Ford 1999: 243–244.

44 Aischines himself is aware of this: Aischin. 1.39–40. Cf. Wooten 1988: 42.

45 See Dover 1978: 27–28 (repr. 2016: 27–28).

law code, attributed to a single legislator, Solon.[46] The prostitution laws which are the most relevant to Timarchos' case, are presented only as a part of the series of these laws regulating the morality of the citizens.[47] The effectiveness of this model lies in the presentation of prostitution as *one case* in a series of law violations, which are never presented as a whole. But this cumulative effect of illegal actions creates a powerful image of Timarchos' shameful life. The charge of prostitution is never proved, but Timarchos was manifestly convicted. The outcome of the trial may be indicative for the effectiveness of this reconstruction of the system, given that it comprises the central part of the legal narrative of the speech and shapes its entire content.[48]

2 The 'Intent of the Legislator' in the (Re)constructions of the Legal System

There is another feature of the manipulation of the system which becomes a recurrent diegetic element in Diodoros' narrative in Dem. 22: the exploitation of arguments based on the intent of the legislator. The intent of the legislator is cursorily treated in Arist. *Rh.* 1.13.17, and Aristotle links such arguments with the idea of lenient treatment (*epieikeia*), which he recommends in cases not explicitly covered by the law. The *Rhetoric to Alexander* (*Rh. Al.* 36.24–25) offers advice on how to turn an unfavourable legal interpretation to its opposite, by

46 Aischines' presentation of a system as neatly structured is close to Ariston's representation of a neat system regulating procedure in acts of violence (verbal and physical).

47 Aischin. 1.28–29.

48 Lack of space prevents detailed discussion of another projection of a consistent 'code of laws', in Hypereides' *Against Athenogenes*. Hypereides' legal narrative reconstructs the universal principle of 'fairness'/'legitimacy' (*dikaion*, §13) to argue that this principle is applicable to the law regulating agreements. But the wording of the law, to the best of our knowledge, ὅσα ἂν ἕτερος ἑτέρῳ ὁμολογήσῃ, κύρια εἶναι, 'all agreements made by one man with another are to be binding/valid', takes no interest in qualifying the content of the agreement, i.e. the *accuracy* of the terms and conditions, which would be presumably on the involved parties to examine (only here is *dikaion* mentioned as part of the law: cf. [Dem.] 42.12, 47.77, 56.2). Not only does he rely on analogy, as argued by recent studies (see Phillips 2009: 93, Whitehead 2000) but also he manipulates the shaping force of the analogy to make a bigger claim about the system and the legal frame within which the contract law should be interpreted to best serve his legally weak case. The law only recognises the *binding* character of an agreement (*kyria*). Interestingly, the intent of the lawgiver is presented in the form of personification of the laws (cf. §§13, 14, 15, 16, 17), along the lines the inexperienced Ariston is presenting the legislator's intent (cf. also pp. 203–206) and the name of Solon finds its way in this narrative too (cf. discussion in part 2). I intend to discuss the reconstruction of law in this narrative elsewhere.

offering arguments relying on the intent of the legislator, particularly in cases where the laws are ambiguous. The treatment of the intent of the legislators by the rhetoricians is rather simplistic compared to the elaborate treatment of the intent (and morality) of the legislator in Attic oratory, but it is undeniable that rhetoricians do understand the potential of manipulation relying on the intent of the legislator.

Rhetorical appeals to the intent of the legislator, and especially Solon, have been discussed in more generic terms by Thomas (1994) who explores the image of the legislator in the ideology of the democracy, and earlier by Hansen (1989) who discusses the fourth-century popular ideology about Solon and 'Solonian democracy', which reaches the extreme of the ascription of demonstrably later laws to him.[49] The approach to the subject in the present study is rather different: it examines appeals to the intent of the legislator as a constant diegetic element in the elaborate reconstructions of the system by Diodoros and other litigants in the competing and complementing narratives examined. Study of arguments based on the intent of the legislator in these legal narratives illustrate some nuanced uses of such arguments, which enhance the elaborate, but artificial reconstructions of the legal system. Solon is made the representative of the speaker's/orator's *own* interpretation and depiction of the legal system in its entirety, and the manifestly fictional nature of the legislator both enables and validates the somewhat contradictory reconstructions of the system. Although there was never any record of the debates which led to the creation of any given law, and therefore reconstructions relying on the intent of the legislator are necessarily subjective and conjectural, litigants articulate elegant rationalisations behind the laws they discuss in a tone of authority. Diodoros emphatically presents his *own* reconstruction of the Athenian legal system as Solon's conscious creation. He credits the design of the system to the *original* and 'democratic'[50] intent of the legislator and his legal narrative is framed (§§ 25, 30) by appeals to the legislator's mind at each stage of his legisla-

49 Thomas 1994: 119–133. Hansen 1989: 71–99 for the fourth-century popular perception of Solon and 'Solonian democracy'. Cf. also Lanni 2004: 168; Yunis 2005: 201–208 associates such arguments with the advancement of the democratic ideology. Harris 2013: esp. 250, 266 interprets this strategy as an indication that the Athenian system aimed at achieving consistency. Johnstone 1999: 25–33. On Solon and the figure of the lawgivers in the orators see Carey 2015: 110–128.

50 On the nature of 'democratic', legal reforms of Solon cf. *Ath. Pol.* 9.1 with Rhodes 1981: 159. Carey 2004: 131 takes a positive view in the presentation of procedural flexibility as a democratic development of the system. See also Carey 2015: 113–114 on Solon's reception as a democrat. Along similar lines Osborne 2010: 203; *pace*, e.g., Harris and Rubinstein 2004: 10–11.

tive acts.[51] Such arguments are also employed in the speech, not only to make capital of the authority and prestige of the legislator, but also as a means of constructing *ēthos* and portraying the parties involved in this high-profile public case in political terms. Democratic Solon is consistently contrasted with the oligarchic Androtion, whose alleged prostitution is described as a threat to the democratic constitution.[52] This antithesis is a recurrent theme, which gradually develops and climaxes towards the end of the speech.[53] In Dem. 22 the intent of the legislator, his authority, and his morality are interwoven to underpin the seductive reconstruction of the system by Diodoros.

Aischines' biography of law and his conceptualisation of the tightly-structured legal system is likewise emphatically attributed to Solon, and the focus is again sustained on the legislator's intent during the gradual development of the system.[54] All the laws cited in this narrative are mentioned in order to demonstrate Solon's rationale in legislating, regardless of their time of enactment and the original intent behind each law.[55] The notion of the χρήσιμος ('useful', §11) citizen is the key-term in this narrative as Timarchos consistently shows a character diametrically opposed to the ideal citizen that Solon's laws systematically envisage[56] and his statue on Salamis exemplifies.[57] The intent of the *single* legislator is profound in this legal narrative and offers coherence and fixity to the 'law code' as reconstructed by Aischines. Just like Diodoros, Aischines has created an elegant reconstruction of the system, which now acquires 'Solonian authority' as a *whole*.

The intent of the legislator is employed in a similar way in private cases. Ariston in Dem. 54 attributes his reconstruction of the 'genealogy of law' to the

51 Dem. 22.25 ᾔδει, §26 ᾤετο, §30 ἑώρα/ἡγεῖτο βαρύ, §31 ᾔδει γάρ, ᾔδει … /οὔκουν ἐνόμιζεν.

52 Dem. 22.30–32.

53 Dem. 22.30, 31, 32, and 37. Cf. also towards the end: 22.47–50, 22.53–55, 22.68–69; cf. also Giannadaki (forthcoming); Carey 2015: 122–123. cf. Thomas 1994: 132, 'the lawgiver is appealed to, discussed, interpreted, to such an extent that he has a character and authority in his own right'.

54 He ascribes his genealogy of law to Solon (Aischin. 3.6), but he also mentions Drakon and 'other legislators'. Carey 2015: 117–118 notes also the introduction of the name of Drakon in order for Aischines to stress the severity of the laws on decency. Cf. other appeals to Solon's own decency 1.25, and his laws regulating women's decency 1.183.

55 Some of them cannot be attributed to Solon (see Fisher 2001: 37–38, 129, 138), but what is crucial for this legal narrative is the unity of the laws (single legislator and rationale in all laws) and the authority of the legislator which strengthen the rhetorical reconstruction of the system.

56 Aesch. 1.6 πρόνοιαν, §22 ἐσκέψατο, §23 κελεύει, §24 οὐκ ἠγνόει οἶμαι ὁ νομοθέτης/βουλόμενος, διδάσκει, §27 συνιδών.

57 Aischin. 1.25.

legislator: although there is no specific legislator named, the 'legislator's' rationale is expressed by the personification of the laws, which think, foresee, and prevent escalation of violence.[58] Ariston's avoidance of an explicit reference to a named legislator in the manner of Aischin. 1 and Dem. 22 is consistent with his youth and inexperience and the private character of the trial, which render some elements of deliberate 'unsophistication'. Therefore, in his case, it is not Solon, by name, who is credited with the genealogy of the law, but the personified laws framing vividly the narrative in a ring composition (Dem. 54.17, 20).

Along the same lines, Euphiletos makes an appeal to the intent of the legislator through a misleading comparison between seduction and rape to advance his line of argument. *His* commentary on the law gives an insight into the alleged intent of the legislator (Lys. 1.31–34), who is credited with the establishment of this severe penalty against seducers. As with Ariston, the legislator is not discussed by name,[59] which is compatible with Lysias' characterisation of the rather naïve Euphiletos, but his reconstruction of the intent of the legislator is impressive (if misleading) in its detail. Thus the intent of the legislator shows nuanced applications in these legal reconstructions according to the nature of the case (private *vs* public/political, legal experience), or the character of the respective litigant, but in all accounts such arguments enable and simultaneously validate these competing reconstructions of the law. 'Solonian', or perhaps more accurately, contemporary 'Athenian', and to some degree, 'democratic' rationale can be traced in such reconstructions (especially in Dem. 22 and arguably in the opening of Dem. 54). Ultimately, Solon becomes the representative of the litigants' interpretations of the system as a whole. Recurrence of such use of the intent of the legislator in these complementing and competing (to some extend) narratives may well suggest that the name of Solon was appealing to the *dikastai* to challenge these representations of the system as non-Solonian.[60]

58 Cf. Dem. 54.17–19: [the laws] προείδοντο, φασί, τὴν ἐκ τοῦ νόμου δίκην ἀναμένῃ. The personification of the laws suggests an implicit reference to the legislator, who introduced these laws to put a stop to the escalation of violence. Compare Wohl's 2010: 76 rather different reading of this narrative which offers 'a cosmogonic myth in which the law is both the divine creator … and the entity newly created …'.

59 It is worth noting that earlier orators, such as Lysias, tend to be much more reluctant to identify Solon by name than do the later ones, and especially when they discuss legislative intention. Later orators also discuss the legislator and his intent in a more confident tone. Cf. Todd 2007: 337, 448 with n. 12.

60 Along the same lines, cf. Carey's (2015: 127–128) conclusions with reference to Solon in the Attic orators, in general. Cf. also Hansen (n. 49 above).

3 The Use of Law in the (Re)constructions of the Legal System *vs* Treatment of Law by the Rhetoricians

Having examined a number of narratives which reshape the Athenian legal system, having as reference point *Against Androtion*, it is beneficial for this analysis to examine the approaches to law of the contemporary rhetoricians, Aristotle[61] and the author of *Rhetoric to Alexander*,[62] from a comparative perspective, and to determine how far the actual practice of the orators is reflected in/draws on contemporary rhetorical theory. For Aristotle, laws are included in his category of *atechnoi pisteis*, 'artless proofs', which are defined as those 'which have not been furnished by ourselves but were already in existence' (1.1.2). Anaximenes' treatment of laws is less systematic than Aristotle's;[63] although he does not explicitly include laws in his discussion of the *epithetoi pisteis*, 'supplementary proofs' (which seem to correspond to Aristotle's 'artless proofs'),[64] laws must be seen under that category.[65] Both rhetorical handbooks suggest ways of manipulating law from the perspective of the prosecutor and the defendant, although they both perceive the laws as 'artless'/'supplementary' means of persuasion (i.e. law has an external existence, whereas syllogisms exist only as constructed by the orator's artfulness). Aristotle (*Rh.* 1.15.3–12) offers a range of ways of exploiting the law depending on whether it is favourable for one's case or not: if law is unfavourable for a litigant's case he is advised to resort to arguments based on 'universal law' (law recognised by most/all communities) and equity, as more in line with justice (*Rh.* 1.15.4–5); he suggests making capital of the dikastic oath as either offering room to the *dikastai* not to abide rigorously by the written laws (*Rh.* 1.15.6). Alternatively, where law is favourable for the litigant's case, Aristotle suggests an argument along the lines that the oath's clause for the *dikastai* 'to decide to the best of his judgment' does not

61 *Rh.* 1.15.1–12.

62 Anaximen. *Rh. Al.* 5.7. This work is generally attributed to Anaximenes (e.g. Chiron 2007: 90) and I henceforth refer to him as the author of *Rhetoric to Alexander* for convenience.

63 Anaximen. *Rh. Al.* 36.20–23.

64 Carey 1994: 95–96 for the almost exact identical distinction of the *pisteis* in the two and their treatment of 'artless' proofs.

65 The way Anaximenes treats law and its use in *Rh. Al.* reveals that he understands laws in the same way that he understands the function of other types of *pisteis* he classifies as *epithetoi* (see Carey 1996: 36, Sickinger 2007: 290). *Pace* Mirhady 1991: 10 ff. who suggests that 'law' in Aristotle's schema corresponds to 'opinions of the speakers' in Anaximenes' account and that they both reflect the *enklēma*, the 'statement of claim'. This *pistis* is not, however, discussed in association with facts in *Rh. Al.*, which suggests that Mirhady's reconstruction is difficult to accept.

justify them in deciding against the law (*Rh.* 1.15.12). He also offers advice in cases where the law is equivocal: the litigant has to stress the interpretation which advances his case, as if fitting to justice and expediency (*Rh.* 1.15.10–11). If the law is obsolete, then Aristotle advises to argue against the law (*Rh.* 1.15.12).

Anaximenes suggests emphasis on justice and expediency of the laws that favour the litigant's case and discredit the laws employed by the opponent (*Rh. Al.* 36.20). If the law is unfavourable, the litigant is advised to stress that the *dikastai* do not decide on matters of law, but only on matters of fact, having sworn to cast their votes according to the existing laws (*Rh. Al.* 36.21). Another line of argument he suggests is arguing that the law unfavourable to the litigant's case appears to be detrimental and therefore enforcing that law is essentially an illegality. As a result, the *dikastai* will not violate the law if they disregard this allegedly detrimental law, but they will appear as legislators themselves, ultimately benefitting the city (*Rh. Al.* 36.22–23). Anaximenes also advises exploitation of the ambiguities of the law in favour of one's case (*Rh. Al.* 36.24). Finally, in support of one's case, which is weak on legal grounds, he advises appeal for pardon (*Rh. Al.* 36.35–36).

Despite the general 'mismatch' between the strategies suggested by the rhetoricians and actual Athenian practice (more broadly),[66] both rhetorical treatises share an awareness of the 'artful' use of laws by suggesting manipulative tactics to underline the significance of a law if favourable to one's case, or to undermine the law if it is unfavourable, which is what matter for our purposes. Both rhetoricians are aware of manipulative modes and provide advice on how a litigant can reinforce his argument and discredit the line of argument of the opponent by using such manipulative modes, some of which find application in contemporary Attic oratory.

However, my analysis of the competing and complementary reconstructions of the legal corpus as a whole—drawing on both in private and public, prosecution and defence speeches—suggests that litigants *in action* exploit the laws in a much more nuanced way than the rhetoricians would advise. In stark contrast with the formulaic treatment of the law in the rhetoricians, in oratory law is artfully used in a variety of flexible and seductive (if often inaccurate) legal narratives which move beyond the discussion of the *substance* of *individual* laws to the *structure* and philosophy of the Athenian legal system as a whole (including the rationale and motivation of the lawgiver), as coherent, cohesive, planned and highly systematised, offering legal narratives, which are designed to meet the rhetorical needs of each case.

66 See Carey 1996: 33–46.

Conclusion

The speeches examined reveal a complex rhetorical use of laws by the litigants as a vehicle to make claims about the *whole* system, beyond the artful use of individual laws found in the orators, as eloquently discussed in other chapters in this volume; furthermore, the sophistication of such reconstructions goes beyond the conceptualisation of laws by contemporary rhetoricians. However, this is *not* to say that rhetoric surpassed law in the Athenian courts: law becomes a vital element of rhetoric in practice, but a case was always introduced on the basis of a legal breach and legal proceedings could not be initiated without legal foundation of the case.

The presentation of a coherent, vivid, and superficially cogent narrative of the legal frame within which the trial is taking place, by a careful strategy of simplifying and even distorting its complexities, becomes a very appealing mode of argumentation. Comparison of the competing and complementary rhetorical reconstructions of the system of the sort we have been discussing shows a complex use of the law and the intent of the lawgiver to create and enhance the narratives. A system in which there was no collective verdict or binding precedent, such as in modern legal systems, seems to acquire something like its own concept of 'jurisprudence' at the level of the rhetoric of law. More impressively, it acquires different co-existing models of conceptualisation of law, even credited to a single legislator, Solon. But as Rubinstein has remarked, in a similar context, differentiated modes of rhetorical argumentation of such kind 'may well reflect the flexibility on an ideological level',[67] which allowed the exploitation of this type of 'legal' reasoning, and in fact, competing rationalisations may not have seemed as contradictory as they may seem to us in a system which never developed formal legal doctrines.

Bibliography

Allen, D.S. (2000) *The World of Prometheus: The Politics of Punishing in Democratic Athens*, Princeton.

Canevaro, M. (2013) *The Documents in the Attic Orators: Laws and Decrees in the Public Speeches of the Demosthenic Corpus*, Oxford.

Cantarella, E. (2005) 'Gender, Sexuality, and Law' in Gagarin, M. and Cohen, E., eds (2005) *The Cambridge Companion to Ancient Greek Law*, Cambridge, 236–253.

67 Rubinstein 2000: 224–225.

Carey, C. (1993) 'The Return of the Radish, or Just When You Thought It Was Safe to Go Back into the Kitchen', *Liverpool Classical Monthly* 18, 53–55.

Carey, C. (1994) '"Artless" Proofs in Aristotle and the Orators', *BICS* 39, 95–106.

Carey, C. (1995) 'Rape and Adultery in Athenian Law', *CQ* 45, 407–417.

Carey, C. (1996) '*Nomos* in Attic Rhetoric and Oratory', *JHS* 116, 33–46.

Carey, C. (1998) 'The Shape of Athenian Laws', *CQ* 48, 93–109.

Carey, C. (2004) 'Offence and Procedure in Athenian Law', in Harris, E.M. and Rubinstein, L., eds (2004) *The Law and the Courts in Ancient Greece*, London, 111–136.

Carey, C. (2015) 'Solon in the Orators', in Nagy, G. and Noussia-Fantuzzi, M., eds (2015) *Solon in the Making: The Early Reception in the Fifth and Fourth Centuries*, Berlin, 110–128.

Carey, C. and Reid, R. (1985) *Demosthenes: Selected Private Speeches*, Cambridge.

Chiron, P. (2007) 'The Rhetoric to Alexander' in Worthington, I., ed. (2007) *A Companion to Greek Rhetoric*, Oxford, 90–106.

Cohen, D. (1991) *Law, Sexuality and Society: The Enforcement of Morals in Classical Athens*, Cambridge.

de Brauw, M. (2002) '"Listen to the Laws Themselves": Citations of Law and Portrayal of Character in Attic Oratory', *CJ* 97, 161–176.

Dover, K.J. (1978) *Greek Homosexuality*, Harvard (Reprinted in 2016, Bloomsbury Publishing).

Fisher, N. (2001) *Aeschines, Against Timarchos*, Oxford.

Ford, A. (1999) 'Reading Homer from the Rostrum: Poems and Laws in Aeschines' *Against Timarchus*', in Goldhill, S. and Osborne, R., eds, *Performance culture and Athenian democracy*, Cambridge, 231–256.

Gagarin, M. (2008) *Writing Greek Law*, Cambridge.

Giannadaki, I. (forthcoming) *A Commentary on Demosthenes' Speech* Against Androtion, Oxford.

Hansen, M.H. (1989) 'Solonian Democracy in Fourth-Century Athens', *C&M* 40, 71–99.

Harris, E.M. (1990) 'Did the Athenians Regard Seduction as a Worse Crime than Rape?' *CQ* 40, 370–377. (Reprinted in 2006, *Democracy and the Rule of Law in Classical Athens: Essays on Law, Society, and Politics*, Cambridge.)

Harris, E.M. (2008) *Demosthenes, Speeches 20–22*, Austin.

Harris, E.M. (2013) *The Rule of Law in Action in Democratic Athens*, Oxford.

Harris, E.M. and Rubinstein, L. eds (2004) *The Law and the Courts in Ancient Greece*, London.

Hart, H.L.A. (1994) *The Concept of Law*, Oxford.

Johnstone, S. (1999) *Disputes and Democracy: The Consequences of Litigation in Ancient Athens*, Austin.

Lanni, A. (2004) 'Arguing from Precedent: Modern Perspectives on Athenian Practice', in Harris and Rubinstein, eds (2004) *The Law and the Courts in Ancient Greece*, London, 159–171.

Lanni, A. (2006) *Law and Justice in the Courts of Classical Athens*, Cambridge.

Leão, D.F. and Rhodes, P.J. (2016) *The Laws of Solon. A New Edition with Introduction, Translation and Commentary*, London.

MacDowell, D.M. (2005) 'The Athenian Procedure of *dokimasia* of Orators', in Gagarin, M. and Wallace, R., eds (2005) *Symposion 2001: Vorträge zur griechischen und hellenistischen Rechtsgeschichte (Evanston, Ill., 5–8 September 2001) Vienna*, 79–88.

Mirhady, D. (1991) 'Non-Technical *pisteis* in Aristotle and Anaximenes', *AJP* 112, 5–28.

Osborne, R. (1985) 'Law in Action in Classical Athens', *JHS* 105, 40–58. (Reprinted in Osborne (2010) 171–204.)

Osborne, R. (2010) *Athens and Athenian Democracy*, Cambridge.

Phillips, D.D. (2009) 'Hypereides 3 and the Athenian Law of Contracts', *TAPA* 139, 89–122.

Rhodes, P.J. (1981) *A Commentary on the Aristotelian* Athenaion Politeia, Oxford.

Rubinstein, L. (2000) *Litigation and Cooperation: Supporting Speakers in the Courts of Classical Athens*, Stuttgart.

Scheppele, K. (1989) 'Legal Story Telling', *Michigan Law Review* 87, 2073–2098.

Sickinger, J. (1999) *Public Records and Archives in Classical Athens*, Chapel Hill, N.C.

Sickinger, J. (2007) 'Rhetoric and the Law', in Worthington, I., ed. (2007) *A Companion to Greek Rhetoric*, Oxford, 286–302.

Sommerstein, A.H., ed. (1989) *Eumenides*, Cambridge.

Sundahl, M. (2000) 'The Use of Statutes in the Seven Extant *graphe paranomon* and *graphe nomon me epitedeion theinai* Speeches'. Diss., Brown University.

Thomas, R. (1989) *Oral Tradition and Written Record in Classical Athens*, Cambridge.

Thomas, R. (1994) 'Law and Lawgiver in the Athenian Democracy' in Osborne, R. and Hornblower, S., eds (1994) *Ritual, Finance, Politics: Athenian Democratic Accounts Presented to David Lewis*, Oxford, 119–134.

Thomas, R. (1995) '"Written in Stone": Liberty, Equality, Orality and the Codification of Law', *BICS* 40, 59–74.

Todd, S.C. (1993) *The Shape of Athenian Law*, Oxford.

Todd, S.C. (2007) *A Commentary on Lysias, Speeches 1–11*, Oxford.

Whitehead, D. (2000) *Hypereides: The Forensic Speeches*, Oxford.

Wohl, V. (2010) *Law's Cosmos: Juridical Discourse in Athenian Forensic Oratory*, Cambridge.

Wooten, C.W. (1988) 'Clarity and Obscurity in the Speeches of Aeschines', *AJP* 59, 40–43.

Yunis, H. (2005) 'The Rhetoric of Law in Fourth-Century Athens', in Gagarin, M. and Cohen, D., eds (2005) *The Cambridge Companion to Ancient Greek Law*, Cambridge, 191–208.

CHAPTER 12

Liturgies and the Rhetoric of Law in Fourth-Century Athens: a Case Study on an *antidosis* ([Dem.] 42)

Kostas Apostolakis

Introduction

The assignment and performance of liturgies and *eisphorai* (war levies) often resulted in litigation. In such disputes elite Athenian citizens sometimes contested on matters concerning the financing and the performance of a particular liturgy.[1] As one would expect, appeal to and argument from the law is a crucial factor in such trials. The speakers therefore support their points by citing appropriate statutes. Whereas the citation of non-existent laws was forbidden on penalty of death, it was always possible to paraphrase a law with minor additions, subtractions and imperceptible modifications.[2] This practice allows litigants to assert that the opponent twists (*diastrephei*, Isa. 11.4) or alters (*metapoiei*, Dem. 18.121) the laws.[3] In particular, disputes concerning property and financial matters lend themselves to versatile uses of law. A good example is complicated procedures like *antidoseis*, which provide various steps and legal provisions, susceptible to different interpretations.

It is well known that, especially during the course of the fourth century, a common practice for affluent Athenians was to conceal their wealth in order to avoid undertaking liturgies.[4] When a liturgy was assigned to a citizen, he had the right to challenge somebody else either to exchange properties or to be charged with the liturgy if he believed that the other citizen was richer than himself. This complicated and controversial procedure was called *antidosis*. On the basis of evidence from texts and inscriptions, it seems that, while exchange of properties was theoretically possible, in practice it was unlikely in the fourth century. Despite being difficult to apply, the procedure was entirely

1 Dem. 51 *On the Trierarchic Crown*; [Dem.] 47 *Against Euergos and Mnesiboulos*; [Dem.] 42 *Against Phainippos*; Dem. 50 *Against Polykles*. See MacDowell 2009: 127–151.

2 See Rubinstein in this volume.

3 See Arnaoutoglou in this volume.

4 See Christ 1990.

 | DOI:10.1163/9789004377899_014

in keeping with the tendency of the Athenian system to pass on responsibility for raising public funds to citizens themselves, thus transforming what was essentially a public taxation issue into one settled between private individuals. The state only intervened to appoint the individual responsible for undertaking the liturgy in cases where the interested parties were incapable of finding a solution. Therefore, rather than meaning 'exchange', it seems that the *antidosis* procedure activates a comparison of properties.[5]

The sole surviving speech written and delivered at the judicial stage of an *antidosis* is [Dem.] 42 *Against Phainippos in the matter of an exchange of properties*, dated to around 328 B.C. Of 1,200 wealthy Athenians liable to *eisphora*, the 300 wealthiest had to pay in advance the total amount for all *eispherontes*, which they then claimed back from the other contributors. Those 300 citizens were called *proeispherontes* and the relevant liturgy was known as *proeisphora*.[6] The speaker, a lessee of public mines, is charged with the liturgy of *proeisphora* and claims that he is no longer financially able to undertake this particular liturgy, because his involvement in mining operations turned out to be disastrous (§ 3). Accordingly, he challenges the landowner Phainippos as a substitute.[7] *Antidosis* included an initial quasi-judicial stage, which was conducted without the intervention of public authorities. However, this stage presupposed a well-intentioned cooperation between the challenger and the challengee, which was in fact very unlikely.[8] If this attempt proved unsuccessful, the procedure was transferred to the judicial field. Phainippos did indeed pretend to follow the legal proceedings; he allowed the challenger to inspect his estate, record all the material contained in it and confirm that the estate was not mortgaged (§§ 5–6). But later on he obstructed the procedure in every possible way (§§ 8–9). After that, a special trial called *diadikasia* was initiated and at this judicial stage of *antidosis* this speech was delivered.[9]

The rhetorical uses of law in the speech *Against Phainippos*, within the legal framework of *antidosis* procedure, are the subject of this chapter. Since *antidosis* is inevitably associated with the private and public economy, my analysis

5 For a review of the older bibliography on *antidosis* see Goligher 1907: 514–515. For the recent bibliography see Gabrielsen 1987: 8–9; Christ 1990: 161; Apostolakis 2009: 13–18.

6 For the *proeisphora* see de Ste Croix 1953: 30–70; Thomsen 1964: 220–226; MacDowell 1986: 448; Wallace 1989: 483–484.

7 See Apostolakis 2009.

8 See Christ 1990: 167, who notes that the *antidosis* procedure was often vulnerable to abuses and manipulations by litigants.

9 *Diadikasia*, 'judgment (contested) between', was a special procedure, in which neither plaintiff nor defendant existed, but both parties were rival claimants. See Todd 1993: 119–120, 228–229.

also treats relevant issues, such as conditions and laws governing the lease and operation of the mines at Laurion, and family law issues, such as adoption and the disposal of a dowry.

1 Ἀποφαίνειν *vs* ἀποκρύπτεσθαι in the *antidosis* Law

1.1 *Interweaving Law and Character*

A keystone of *antidosis* law is the provision that both parties should give a true and honest inventory of their property (§ 18 ὀρθῶς καὶ δικαίως ἀποφαίνειν τὴν οὐσίαν) and the antithesis 'declare' *vs* 'conceal' (*apophainein vs apokryptesthai*) pervades the entire speech. The challenger argues that he has declared (*apophainei*) all his property, even that which is exempt by law; Phainippos conceals (*apokryptetai*) whatever would support an impression of wealth on the one hand, and reveals (*apophainei*) debts that do not exist on the other.

As expected, the laws which govern the *antidosis* procedure are always at the centre of the speech, and the relevant rhetoric of law is almost ubiquitous.[10] The speaker refers to these laws in one way or another no fewer than twenty times: either by citing or paraphrasing clauses of the *antidosis* law, or by stressing his adherence to the law, in contradistinction to the opponent's violations. In the last sentence of the prologue, he argues that the *antidosis* law, ascribed, like many other Athenian laws, to Solon (§ 1), provides for the *antidosis* procedure to be held every year, given that it is unusual for most citizens to enjoy unbroken prosperity:

> διὰ τοῦτο γὰρ οἱ νόμοι καθ' ἕκαστον ἔτος ποιοῦσιν τὰς ἀντιδόσεις, ὅτι τὸ διευτυχεῖν συνεχῶς τῇ οὐσίᾳ οὐ πολλοῖς τῶν πολιτῶν διαμένειν εἴθισται (§ 4).
>
> For it is on this account that the laws initiate exchanges every year: it is not the norm for many of our citizens to enjoy a continuous and unbroken course of prosperity.
>
> [DEM.] 42.4

Here the *topos*—the purpose of law (i.e. the legislator's intention)—is properly applied to the challenger's case, since the law is supposed to provide a fair

10 See Harris 1994: 133, who notes the frequency of legal citations, and argues that 'litigants attempted as much as possible to base their arguments on the actual text of the laws relevant to their cases'. Cf. de Brauw 2002: 162.

assignment of financial burdens within the liturgical class, to offer relief to citizens like him and to suggest a rotation of liturgies.

Since the dispute was transferred to the law court, the *antidosis* procedure had been formally completed.[11] The only thing which the jurors had to decide was which of the two was wealthier and therefore liable to perform the particular liturgy of *proeisphora*. In order to reach a verdict, however, the jurors had to compare the properties of the two opposing sides. They had to rely upon documents, witnesses and assertions which were not always easy to follow. Therefore, the pre-history of the dispute seems to have been important for the jurors, because it provided them with the entire context and particular aspects of the case under discussion. Moreover, a latent but decisive parameter was the character of the litigants; in cases where a fair declaration of properties was crucial, qualities such as trustworthiness and compliance with the law were very much appreciated; on the other hand, any violation of the law and any attempt to conceal property items and downgrade property was liable to cause disapproval and suspicion.[12] Therefore, it was a matter of strategic value to litigants and/or logographers to include such information in their speeches.

The section consisting of §§10–16, which is devoted to the demonstration of Phainippos' violations of the *antidosis* procedure, is very indicative of the rhetoric which contextualises the laws cited in this speech. The challenger not only cites laws associated with *antidosis*, but also applies the rhetoric of law at both the beginning and the end of the section. Phainippos repeatedly violated specific rules of *antidosis*, which are under the protection of the jurors (§10). More specifically, although according to the *antidosis* law the inventories should be declared within three days of taking the corresponding oath (§12), Phainippos himself asked the speaker to arrange a settlement meeting and to put off the declaration of the property for just a few days (§11).[13] The challenger accepted this request, in order to facilitate the procedure and not give the impression of a litigious man; he is presenting himself as μέτριος, 'moderate', and ἀπράγμων, 'not meddlesome, someone who avoids troubles, i.e. litigation'.[14] But Phainippos neither appeared at the meeting nor gave his opponent any

11 See MacDowell 1978: 103, 106; Gabrielsen 1987: 24–29; Lanni 2006: 65–66; Apostolakis 2009: 52–56.

12 As Carey 1994: 26–45, points out, the ethical proofs were not limited to proems, as the rhetorical handbooks say, but were spread in all parts of a speech. See also de Brauw 2002: 162.

13 For the delaying procedure cf. Sato in this volume.

14 [Dem.] 42.12 ἡγησάμενος δ' ἐγὼ καὶ μετρίου καὶ ἀπράγμονος εἶναι πολίτου μὴ εὐθὺς ἐπὶ κεφαλὴν εἰς τὸ δικαστήριον βαδίζειν, ἐπείσθην (τί γὰρ δεῖ μακρολογεῖν;) τὴν μὲν σύνοδον περὶ τῶν διαλύσεων τῇ ὀγδόῃ φθίνοντος τοῦ βοηδρομιῶνος μηνὸς ὁμολογῆσαι ποιήσασθαι ...

inventory (§ 12), and he has, therefore, broken two laws, the first referring to the inventory deadline, and the second declaring that mutual agreements stipulated in the presence of witnesses are binding. But the challenger himself accepted the request to put off the meeting, so there is no formal charge of violation of this law.

1.2 *Revealing the Opponent's Duplicity*

The challenger uses the wording of the law as a starting point in order to proceed to a moral evaluation of himself and his opponent. The formulation of *antidosis* law demands a proper and fair declaration of property (§ 11 ὀρθῶς καὶ δικαίως ἀποφαίνειν τὴν οὐσίαν; cf. § 18). According to the speaker, however, Phainippos has repeatedly violated the law, by removing (ἀποκρύπτεσθαι) the products from his stores from the very beginning of the procedure (§ 23):

> ἀποκρύπτεσθαι γὰρ καὶ διαδύεσθαι καὶ πάντα ποιεῖν ἐξ ὧν μὴ λῃτουργήσεις τουτοισὶ μεμάθηκας.
>
> … for you've learned how to conceal and to dodge and to do anything to escape carrying out a liturgy for your fellow citizen here.

However, his conduct as a citizen in the past, which is not *stricto sensu* connected with the proceedings, is revealing of his attitude. More specifically, the speaker describes Phainippos as φιλότιμος, a man with public ambitions (§ 24):

> ἓν μόνον ἄν τις ἔχοι δεῖξαι τουτονὶ Φαίνιππον πεφιλοτιμημένον εἰς ὑμᾶς, ἄνδρες δικασταί· ἱπποτρόφος ἀγαθός ἐστιν καὶ φιλότιμος, ἅτε νέος καὶ πλούσιος καὶ ἰσχυρὸς ὤν. τί τούτου μέγα σημεῖον; ἀποδόμενος τὸν πολεμιστήριον ἵππον καταβέβηκεν ἀπὸ τῶν ἵππων, καὶ ἀντ' ἐκείνου ὄχημ' αὑτῷ τηλικοῦτος ὢν ἐώνηται, ἵνα μὴ πεζῇ πορεύηται· τοσαύτης οὗτος τρυφῆς ἐστι μεστός.
>
> There is one thing only, men of the jury, in which anyone could show that Phainippos here has been eager to gain public honour: he is an excellent and ambitious horse-breeder, inasmuch as he is young and rich and strong. What's a proof of this? Having sold his war-horse, he has stepped down from his horses, and as a replacement for that—at his age—he has bought a chariot for himself so he need not travel on foot! Such a delicate man!

Traditionally, *philotimia* ('love of honour') was associated with expenditures and offerings to the state.[15] In the course of the speech, it appears that the sole field in which Phainippos has demonstrated this virtue is horse breeding (*hippotrophia*). Even there, however, he demonstrated his selfish attitude when he sold his war horse and bought a vehicle, for his own convenience and luxury. This act is indicative of his political *ēthos*. Moreover, this time the wording of the *antidosis* law ἀποφαίνειν τὴν οὐσίαν is indirectly associated not only with the morals, but also with the very name of the challengee. *Phainippos hippotrophos*, literally 'a horse breeder who shows his horse', (ὁ φαίνων τὸν ἵππον), the token of his class and family tradition (being a son of Kallippos), sold his war horse—in other words, put it out of sight—depriving his city and his fellow citizens of his cavalry services, and bought a vehicle, for his own comfort! This suggests that, according to the challenger, Phainippos appears to contradict his own name, since in his case the components 'show' and 'horse' cannot be combined (like the Aristophanic hero Φειδιππίδης in the *Nubes*, where *pheidō* 'thrift' and *hippos* 'horse' also present a comic internal contradiction).[16] Calling a person by antonyms is a kind of irony (*eirōneia*) and finds its proper place, according to the rhetoricians, in vituperations like the passage at issue.[17] The latent connotation of this passage is that Phainippos followed the same practice in the *antidosis* procedure. As the description of his removing products from his stores indicates, he systematically turns his property from visible (*phanera ousia*) into invisible (*aphanēs ousia*) in order to downgrade it in case of an exchange in an *antidosis*. Instead of *philotimia*, he demonstrates his indulgence and luxury.[18] It is important that the formulation of *antidosis* law is the starting point for an attack on the opponent's *ēthos* (in particular, *argumentum ad hominem*).

---

15 On *philotimia* see Whitehead 1983: 55–74; Sinclair 1988: 61–65.

16 See Kanavou 2011: 73.

17 Cf. e.g. Anaximen. *Rh. Al.* 35.19.

18 Ar. *Nub.* 14–16 ὁ δὲ κόμην ἔχων/ ἱππάζεταί τε καὶ ξυνωρικεύεται/ ὀνειροπολεῖ θ' ἵππους. Cf. also Dem. 18.320, where Demosthenes speaks sarcastically of Aischines. Phainippos' flamboyant manner, not unlike that of *hippotrophos* Pheidippides, the comic hero of Aristophanes, is comparable with Meidias' lavish behaviour, Dem. 21.133 ἐπ' ἀστράβης ὀχούμενος ἀργυρᾶς. For this type of *diabolē* see Ober 1989: 207–208.

2 Rhetorical Uses of Law

2.1 *Adding to the Text of the Law*

According to the challenger, Phainippos has also violated the law which declares that mutual covenants shall be binding (§ 12):

> ἕτερον δὲ τὸν κελεύοντα κυρίας εἶναι τὰς πρὸς ἀλλήλους ὁμολογίας, ἃς ἂν ἐναντίον ποιήσωνται μαρτύρων …
>
> and the other stating that mutual agreements—which are made in the presence of witnesses—shall be binding.

It seems that the appropriate action for breaching such an agreement was the *dikē blabēs*.[19] The paraphrase used by the speaker includes the provision that such covenants should be attested by witnesses. However, in the remaining sources this provision does not exist.[20] It has been suggested that the crucial information of our passage is the reference to witnesses, who testify that the agreement under discussion did exist.[21] It seems that the law itself did not include such a provision, but that it was an implicit and expected assumption and common practice, which was followed in similar cases or transactions.[22] Rather, the challenger incorporates this addition in the law, in order to exploit it later, where he calls upon the secretary to read the relevant depositions. It is worth noting that he is careful to do this in a paraphrase, not a citation of the law itself (§ 16 λέγε τῶν ἀρτίως εἰρημένων τὰς μαρτυρίας καὶ τοὺς νόμους; 'read the depositions concerning the statements I have just now made and also the laws').[23]

Between paraphrasing and citing the two laws, the speaker uses once more the rhetoric of 'the law's voice', by emphasising the interdependence of jurors and law (§ 15):

---

19 Cf. Dem. 48 *Against Olympiodoros*; see Scafuro 2011: 115 n. 44.

20 Cf. Dem. 47.77 τὸν νόμον ὃν κελεύει κύρια εἶναι ὅ τι ἂν ἕτερος ἑτέρῳ ὁμολογήσῃ; [56.]2 τοῖς νόμοις τοῖς ὑμετέροις οἵ κελεύουσι, ὅσα ἄν τις ἑκὼν ἕτερος ἑτέρῳ ὁμολογήσῃ κύρια εἶναι; Hyp. *Athen.* 13 ὅσα ἂν ἕτερος ἑτέρῳ ὁμολογήσῃ κύρια εἶναι; Dein. 3.4 καὶ ὁ μὲν κοινὸς τῆς πόλεως νόμος, ἐάν τις εἰς ἕνα τινὰ τῶν πολιτῶν ὁμολογήσας τι παραβῇ, τοῦτον ἔνοχον εἶναι κελεύει τῷ ἀδικεῖν; Pl. *Symp.* 196c2–3 ἃ δ' ἂν ἑκὼν ἑκόντι ὁμολογήσῃ, φασὶν 'οἱ πόλεως βασιλῆς νόμοι' δίκαια εἶναι; Arist. *Rh.* 1375b9–10 οἷον ἐνίοτε ὁ μὲν κελεύει κύρια εἶναι ἅττ' ἂν συνθῶνται, ὁ δ' ἀπαγορεύει μὴ συντίθεσθαι παρὰ τὸν νόμον. See MacDowell 1978: 140; Carawan 2007: 321–342.

21 See MacDowell 1978: 140; Carawan 2007: 321–342.

22 See Pringsheim 1950: 17–85.

23 There is a similar case in [Dem.] 59.17, where παιδοποιεῖσθαι seems to be an addition by the speaker. See Arnaoutoglou in this volume p. 194.

χρὴ δ', ὦ ἄνδρες δικασταί, μὴ τοῖς ἰσχυροτέραν νομίζουσι τῶν νόμων τὴν αὑτῶν βδελυρίαν εἶναι, πλέον τούτοις τοῦ δικαίου νέμειν (εἰ δὲ μή, πολλοὺς ποιήσετε τοὺς καταγελῶντας τῶν ἐν τοῖς νόμοις δικαίων γεγραμμένων), ἀλλ' ἐκείνοις βοηθεῖν, οἵτινες ἂν τὴν τῶν νόμων φωνὴν ὑμετέραν εἶναι νομίζωσι, καὶ τὴν ἡμέραν ταύτην, τὴν εἰς τὸ δικαστήριον, ὑπὲρ τῶν ἠδικημένων εἶναι [νομίζωσιν], μὴ τῶν ἠδικηκότων.

But, judges, you shouldn't grant more to those who think their shamelessness is above the law—otherwise you will encourage many men to mock the just provisions of the laws: instead, you should help those who think that the voice of the law is your voice and that the appointed day is for the benefit of those who have been subjected to wrongs, not for those who have committed them![24]

Here again the laws assume an anthropomorphic dimension, and the jurors are presented as their mouthpiece. And, most importantly, the speaker, by setting this rhetoric at a central point of his argumentation, claims an authoritative interpretation of the law's voice throughout the speech.

2.2 *Interpreting 'Grey Areas'*

However, as the reactions of the other party indicate, the laws cited by the speaker may be interpreted in a different way. An interesting example, which has perplexed modern scholars, is the passage where the challenger initially claims that his mining operations should be excluded from the list for *antidosis*, since they are public property, and cites the relevant law (§ 18):

ὑμεῖς δ' ἴστε, ὦ ἄνδρες δικασταί (ὑμεῖς γὰρ ἔθεσθε) τὸν νόμον, ὃς διαρρήδην οὕτω λέγει, 'τοὺς δ' ἀντιδιδόντας ἀλλήλοις, ὅταν ὀμόσαντες ἀποφαίνωσι τὴν οὐσίαν, προσομνύειν τόνδε τὸν ὅρκον "ἀποφαίνω τὴν οὐσίαν τὴν ἐμαυτοῦ ὀρθῶς καὶ δικαίως, πλὴν τῶν ἐν τοῖς ἔργοις τοῖς ἀργυρείοις, ὅσα οἱ νόμοι ἀτελῆ πεποιήκασι."'

But you know the law, judges (for you enacted it), which explicitly says this, 'and men who are engaged in an exchange with one another, whenever they declare their property under oath, are to swear an additional

24 Cf. [Dem.] 33.33 μάρτυρά μοι φημι τὸν νόμον εἶναι; [Dem.] 34.4 οἱ μὲν οὖν νόμοι, καθ' οὓς ὑμεῖς δικασταὶ κάθησθε, οὐχ οὕτως λέγουσιν; [Dem.] 59.88; In Dem. 21.223–225 the interdependence between laws and jurors is stressed. See Svenbro 1993: 28–30, 109–122, 172–174; Yunis 2005: 191–208.

> oath, "I am declaring my property accurately and lawfully, except for shares in the silver mines, all of which the laws have made exempt from taxes."'

The challenger first introduces the law with the reminder that the particular beneficial provision for the mine lessees was enacted by the jury, acting as both jurors and legislators,[25] and then calls upon the secretary to read out the law verbatim (μᾶλλον δὲ λέγε τὸν νόμον αὐτόν). This law is to the speaker's advantage, since it exempts his mining operations from the list submitted in *antidosis*. But, quite unexpectedly, the challenger renounces his rights and offers to surrender to his opponent all his property, including his operations in mine works, on condition that the challengee will hand over the estate and return all the assets removed from the storehouses of the property.[26]

This is a strange rhetorical manoeuvre. Some scholars believe that the law allowing this exception relating to mines had either never existed or was obsolete, because such a law would encourage many rich citizens to lease mines in order to avoid liturgies.[27] This suggestion would be supported by Phainippos' counter-prosecution (*antigraphē*) against the challenger, on the ground that the latter did not include his mine operations in the inventory (§17 ἀλλ' ὅμως ἐμὲ ἀντεγράψατο Φαίνιππος μὴ δικαίως ἀποφαίνειν τὴν οὐσίαν, 'but nevertheless Phainippos introduced a counter-prosecution against me that I had not declared justly my property)'. However, it seems unnecessary and risky for the speaker to invoke and cite a non-existent law, since this could entail even a death sentence (cf. Dem. 26.24). Rather, it seems that the purpose of the particular law in force was to attract new mine investors to Laurion, as indicated by the corresponding provision concerning the *isoteleia* (equal liability to taxation) offered to metics involved in mines, described as an effective measure by Xenophon in his *On Ways and Means* 4.29–31 (ca 355/4 B.C.): παρέχει γοῦν (ἡ πόλις) ἐπὶ ἰσοτελείᾳ καὶ τῶν ξένων τῷ βουλομένῳ ἐργάζεσθαι ἐν τοῖς μετάλλοις ('and so the city allows for equality in tax for both resident

25 It is interesting that the jurors are said to have legislated the particular law themselves, so they are familiar with its content. This may be theoretically true, since in the fourth century the νομοθέται (legislators) were selected by the jurors, though in the second half of the century this was not obligatory; see MacDowell 1975: 62–74; Rhodes 1985: 55–60. On the other hand, the Athenian jurors as *ekklēsiastai* participated in any case in the resolution-making process.

26 [Dem.] 42.19.

27 See especially Boeckh 1828: 489–491, who believes that, since mine investors like Phainippos were not property owners but lessees of a state property, mines were excluded from the property transferred by *antidosis*.

aliens and for those who are willing to work in the mines').[28] Possibly this measure was designed to avoid disfranchising holders of mining concessions, who would be at risk if they were unable to pay their instalments. However, since the author of this work does not mention such a law, but proposes other solutions to problems connected with mining operations, e.g. that the state should offer each tribe an equal number of slaves, it seems that this law was introduced soon after 355/4 and was quite recent when this speech was delivered.

As we can see, the challenger first ascribes the beneficial law to the jurors themselves and then lays out the law, noting that it is cited verbatim (*diarrhēdēn*). In fact, the law which is cited is that obliging the opponents in an *antidosis* to swear an oath concerning a fair declaration of their properties, whereas the law excepting mining operations from *antidosis* is incorporated in the wording of the oath. It seems, therefore, that the vague phrase ἐν τοῖς ἔργοις is not the exact wording of the initial exception law, but a convenient paraphrase. This paraphrase suggests that the law exempts from the *antidosis* both the underground mine operations and the surface ore-processing installations, called *ergastēria*. It is achieved through the vagueness created by the relative clause ὅσα οἱ νόμοι ἀτελῆ πεποιήκασιν, which could be mean either 'with the exception of silver mines, all of which the laws except' or 'with the exception of those in silver mines, which the laws exempt'.[29] But it is almost certain that the workshops were considered private property, since they could be sold and made invisible (ἀφανῆ) by individual citizens, in order to avoid liturgies, or be sold along with slaves as private belongings. This is indicative of the behaviour of Timarchos, who allegedly sold off two such workshops in order to avoid liturgies.[30]

It seems, therefore, that the challenger profits from the relative vagueness of the law and presents an obligation as an ultimate concession to an avid oppo-

---

28 See Hopper 1953: 25, who connects this immunity law with Euboulos' reformative measures; Apostolakis 2007: 105.

29 [Dem.] 42.18 πλὴν τῶν ἐν τοῖς ἔργοις τοῖς ἀργυρείοις ὅσα οἱ νόμοι ἀτελῆ πεποιήκασι.

30 Aischin. 1.101 Φοβηθεὶς γὰρ τὰς λητουργίας ἀπέδοτο ἃ ἦν αὐτῷ κτήματα … χωρίον Κηφισιᾶσιν, ἕτερον ἀγρὸν Ἀμφιτροπῆσιν, ἐργαστήρια δύο ἐν τοῖς ἀργυρείοις, ἓν μὲν ἐν Αὐλῶνι, ἕτερον δ'ἐπὶ Θρασύλλῳ; cf. Isa. 3.22 Ξενοκλῆς τοίνυν Βήσαζε μὲν ἰὼν εἰς τὸ ἐργαστήριον τὸ ἡμέτερον εἰς τὰ ἔργα, οὐχ ἡγήσατο δεῖν τοῖς ἀπὸ τοῦ αὐτομάτου ἐκεῖ ἐντυχοῦσι μάρτυσι χρῆσθαι περὶ τῆς ἐξαγωγῆς; Dem. 37.5 πρατὴρ μὲν δὴ τοῦ ἐργαστηρίου καὶ τῶν ἀνδραπόδων ὁ Μνησικλῆς ἡμῖν γίγνεται (καὶ γὰρ ἐώνητ' ἐκεῖνος αὐτὰ τούτῳ παρὰ Τηλεμάχου τοῦ πρότερον κεκτημένου). See Ste Croix 1953: 33 n. 13; Gabrielsen 1987: 18; Apostolakis 2009: 47–48, 141–142. For *aphanēs* and *phanera ousia* see further Engen 2011: esp. 99–102. Carmichael 1997: 261–270 (liturgy avoidance). Cohen 1992: 191–207.

nent. If that suspicion stands, then the original article would be clearer than the version cited by the challenger. And that is why the challenger suddenly changes his mind on this issue and why he does not allow the clerk to read out the whole text of the law. Instead, by giving up his supposed legal advantages, he attempts to appear as an equitable (*epieikēs*) citizen, who is ready to sacrifice his own interests and avoid litigiousness.[31]

A further opportunity for the challenger to present himself as a fair and law-abiding citizen, while simultaneously accusing Phainippos of deceiving the jurors, is the contrary practices they followed concerning the dowry of their widowed mothers. More specifically, Phainippos declares his mother's dowry in the inventory as a debt, which should be excluded from the *antidosis* procedure (§ 27):

> ἐπίσχες. αὕτη ἐστίν, ὦ ἄνδρες δικασταί, ἡ Ἀριστονόη τοῦ Φιλοστράτου θυγάτηρ, μήτηρ δὲ τουτουί. ταύτῃ χρέως φησὶν ὀφείλεσθαι Φαίνιππος τὴν προῖκα, ἧς οἱ νόμοι κύριον τοῦτον ποιοῦσιν, ψευδόμενος καὶ οὐ δικαίως χρώμενος τῇ ἀποφάσει.
>
> Stop reading. This Aristonoe, judges, is the daughter of Philostratos and the mother of this fellow. He says that a debt is owed to her, the dowry—of which the laws make him proprietor; he lies and manipulates the declaration unjustly.

In contrast, the challenger reckons his mother's dowry as his property and includes it in his inventory for the *antidosis*; moreover, he paraphrases the relevant law, which appears to make the son the owner of his mother's dowry if she is living with him, on the condition that the mother 'has a share' in her son's property before and after *antidosis*; in addition, in a sarcastic address, the challenger argues that his opponent is deceiving the jurors by applying a misleading interpretation of the law (§ 27):

> διὰ τί γὰρ ἐγώ, Φαίνιππε, μενούσης μοι τῆς μητρὸς ἐν τῷ οἴκῳ καὶ ζώσης καὶ προῖκα ἐπενεγκαμένης, οὐκ ἀπογράφω τὴν προῖκα χρέως αὐτῇ, οὐδὲ παρακρούομαι τοὺς δικαστάς, ἀλλ' ἐῶ μετέχειν τῶν ἐμαυτοῦ τὴν μητέρα, ἄν τε τὴν Φαινίππου ἄν τε τὴν ἐμαυτοῦ ἔχω οὐσίαν; ὅτι οἱ νόμοι ταῦτα κελεύουσιν, ὦ βέλτιστε· σὺ δὲ πάντα ποιεῖς παρὰ τοὺς νόμους.

31 Cf. Dem. 44.8; 56.14. See Carey 1996: 40–41.

> For why is it, Phainippos, that while my mother dwells in my house and is alive and has brought a dowry along with her, I don't list the dowry as a debt owed to her and I don't try to lead the judges astray, but I allow my mother to have a share of my property, whether I am to have Phainippos'—or my own? Why? Because the laws require this, my good fellow. But you do everything contrary to the laws.

Phainippos is said to be deceiving the jurors (παρακρούεσθαι τοὺς δικαστάς).[32] But what is his deceitful action? Obviously it concerns his attempt to count his mother's dowry as a debt and accordingly to exclude it from the property liable to *antidosis*. It has been suggested by L. Foxhall that the dowry of a widow could be included in her son's property, if she was living with him, but not the property of the wife whose husband was still alive.[33] Accordingly, she suspects that Phainippos does not make clear that Aristonoe is his mother rather than his wife, and therefore deceives the jurors. But this explanation does not seem very convincing to me. We might expect, for instance, that the challenger would submit his opponent to a thorough examination and invoke witnesses, in order to demonstrate more explicitly that Phainippos is untrustworthy and deceitful. A good parallel is found in Isaios' *On the Estate of Hagnias*. The context is also that of inheritance matters, and the crucial question is whether a boy belongs to the degree of kinship prescribed in law entitling him to Hagnias' property. The speaker brings his opponent up before the jurors and questions him, while reading out the law clause by clause, in order to demonstrate that his opponent is slandering him and twisting the laws (τοὺς νόμους διαστρέφειν).[34]

It seems that the circumstances of the litigant's widowed mother were different. The challenger argues that his mother lives in his house. This would

---

32 *Parakrouesthai* (used 42 times in the *Corpus Demosthenicum*) seems to be a favourite verb for Demosthenes; in the sense of misinterpreting the law it is also used in family context, cf. Dem. 44.49 (cited below); cf. 43.39 παρακρουόμενοι τοὺς δικαστάς. An interesting use of παρακρούεσθαι occurs in Dem. 44.49, where the speaker accuses his opponent of misleading the jurors, but in fact he himself is modifying the sense of 'legitimate children' in order to exclude the adopted children from the inheritance, ἀλλὰ μὴν 'γνησίων' γ' ὅταν λέγῃ καὶ 'κυρίως κατὰ τὸν θεσμόν', παρακρούεται παρὰ τοὺς νόμους; See Scafuro 2011: 208, who notes that adopted children were legitimate, provided that they were born of two Athenian citizens.

33 Foxhall 1989: 41–42. On dowry see also Griffith-Williams 2013: 112–113, Cox 1998: 115.

34 Isa. 11.4–5 Λαβὲ οὖν αὐτοῖς τοὺς νόμους· σὺ δ' ἀνάβηθι δεῦρο, ἐπειδὴ δεινὸς εἶ διαβάλλειν καὶ τοὺς νόμους διαστρέφειν. σὺ δ' ἀναγίγνωσκε. Ἐπίσχες. ἐρωτήσω σέ. ἀδελφός ἐσθ' ὁ παῖς Ἁγνίου, ⟨ἢ⟩ ἀδελφιδοῦς ἐξ ἀδελφοῦ ἢ ἐξ ἀδελφῆς γεγονώς, ἢ ἀνεψιός, ἢ ἐξ ἀνεψιοῦ πρὸς μητρὸς ἢ πρὸς πατρός; τί τούτων τῶν ὀνομάτων, οἷς ὁ νόμος τὴν ἀγχιστείαν δίδωσι; cf. Arnaoutoglou in this volume.

mean that the dowry had returned with her, and therefore it would be the property of the speaker, who was thus obliged to include it in the inventory for *antidosis*. On the contrary, when Kallippos, Phainippos' father, died, his widow Aristonoe opted to return to her paternal house, and Phainippos was adopted by Philostratos, his maternal grandfather. Obviously, Aristonoe was the only daughter of Philostratos, so if Philostratos died, she would become an *epiklēros*. In that case, Aristonoe's dowry would be suspended, perhaps in the case of a second marriage. Therefore, Phainippos' choice not to include his mother's dowry in the inventory, which was prepared for the *antidosis* procedure, might suggest that some form of ownership by Aristonoe was possible. It is indicative that in [Dem.] 45.28 Pasion is said to have bequeathed to his wife Archippe as dowry for her second marriage,[35] female slaves, gold jewellery and a *synoikia*, 'a multiple dwelling-house'.[36]

However, the crucial point is that the law cited by the challenger does indeed refer to ownership, but does not specify what should happen concerning the maternal dowry in case of an *antidosis*. This vagueness allows the two litigants to follow opposite practices and support their different interpretation of law with arguments appropriate to their cases. More specifically, Phainippos considered the maternal dowry as a loan which potentially should be returned to her paternal *oikos*, on the analogy of what happened in the event of a divorce,[37] and therefore not to include it in the inventory given in *antidosis* procedure. On the other hand, the challenger seems to consider the dowry not as a loan, but as a gift which does not create an obligation,[38] and accordingly he counts the dowry in his inventory. This choice gives him the rhetorical advantage of arguing that he honestly declares all his property as a law-abiding citizen, and at the same time to consider the subtraction of Aristonoe's dowry from the inventory an action compatible with Phainippos' systematic concealment of property and an indication of his untrustworthiness and selfishness.

35 Cf. [Dem.] 36.8; Cohen 2002: 111.

36 Besides, women's involvement in financial matters seems to be supported by a fragmentary *horos*-inscription (Fine 1951: no 28), where a woman appears to be one of the lenders in a real-estate financing. See Harris 1992: 311, who, on the condition that the proposed restoration of the text of the inscription is correct, notes: 'this *horos* demonstrates that women's role in financial matters was potentially much more extensive than the evidence of Athenian law would lead us to assume'.

37 *Cf. IG* II^2 2722 ὅρος χωρίου πεπραμένου ἐπὶ λύσει Εὐθυδίκῃ προικός: See Harris 1993: 90–91; Apostolakis 2009: 164; Phillips 2013: 172.

38 See Harris 1993: 90.

Conclusions

The rhetoric of law is a dominant feature in the speech *Against Phainippos*. Apart from stereotyped uses, the speech offers interesting examples of a subtler use of law: introductory notes and comments accompany these citations, often associated with artistic proofs, *ēthos*, in particular. Throughout the speech, the speaker supports his case with inventiveness and versatility by either citing, or paraphrasing or commenting upon laws and legal provisions. He especially exploits legal provisions which appear susceptible to partial interpretations. He also makes additions which supposedly interpret laws or make them more specific. Moreover, he systematically combines the wording of the law with the portrayal of character. It is to be expected that in litigation, where complicated and ambivalent financial issues are dealt with, trustworthiness is crucial. In addition, he extends this practice to laws concerning family issues associated with the *antidosis* procedure, like the dowry of a widowed mother. The speech indicates that one and the same law could be presented and interpreted in a different way and leave more room for rhetoric and speculation. The speech *Against Phainippos* offers a sample which may be indicative of the uses of law in forensic disputes concerning liturgies, and the *antidosis* procedure in particular, in fourth-century Athens.[39]

Bibliography

Apostolakis, K. (2007) 'The Rhetoric of an *antidosis*: [D.] 42 Against Phaenippus', *Ἀριάδνη* 12, 93–112.

Apostolakis, K. (2009) *Δημοσθένους Πρὸς Φαίνιππον περὶ ἀντιδόσεως*, Athens.

Boeckh, A. (1828) *The Public Economy of Athens*, book 4, London.

Carawan, E. (2007) 'Oral "Agreement", Written Contract, and the Bonds of Law at Athens', in Cooper, C., ed. (2007) *Politics of Orality*, Leiden, 321–342.

Carey, C. (1994) 'Rhetorical Means of Persuasion', in Worthington, I., ed. (1994) *Persuasion: Greek Rhetoric in Action*, London, 26–45.

Carey, C. (1996) '*Nomos* in Attic Rhetoric and Oratory', *JHS* 116, 33–46.

Carmichael, C.M. (1997) 'Public Munificence for Private Benefit: Liturgies in Classical Athens', *Economic Inquiry* 35, 261–270.

Christ, M.R. (1990) 'Liturgy Avoidance and *antidosis* in Classical Athens', *TAPA* 120, 147–169.

---

39 I would like to thank Chris Carey, Ifigeneia Giannadaki, Brenda Griffith-Williams and Ilias Arnaoutoglou for their valuable comments on earlier versions of this chapter.

Cohen, E.E. (1992) *Athenian Economy and Society*, Princeton.

Cohen, E.E. (2002) 'An Unprofitable Masculinity', in Cartledge, P., Cohen, E. and Foxhall, L., eds (2002) *Money, Labour and Land. Approaches to the Economics of Ancient Greece*, London, 100–112.

Cox, C.A. (1998) *Household Interests: Property, Marriage Strategies, and Family Dynamics in Ancient Athens*, Princeton.

de Brauw, M. (2002) '"Listen to the Laws Themselves": Citations of Law and Portrayal of Character in Attic Oratory', *CJ* 97, 161–176.

de Ste Croix, G.E.M. (1953) 'Demosthenes' τίμημα and the Athenian *eisphora* in the Fourth Century B.C.', *C&M* 14, 30–70.

Engen, D.T. (2011) 'Democracy, Knowledge, and the Hidden Economy of Athens', *The Journal of Economic Asymmetries* 8, 93–106.

Fine, J.V.A. (1951) *Horoi: studies in mortgage, real security and land tenure in ancient Athens* (Vol. 9). American school of classical studies at Athens.

Foxhall, L. (1989) 'Household, Gender and Property in Classical Athens', *CQ* 39, 22–44.

Gabrielsen, V. (1987) 'The Antidosis Procedure in Classical Athens', *C&M* 38, 7–38.

Goligher, W.A. (1907) 'Studies in Attic Law II: The *antidosis*', *Hermathena* 14, 481–515.

Griffith-Williams, B. (2013) *A Commentary on Selected Speeches of Isaios*, Leiden.

Harris, E.M. (1992) 'Women and Lending in Classical Athens: A *horos* Re-examined', *Phoenix* 4, 309–321.

Harris, E.M. (1993) '*Apotimema*: Athenian Terminology for Real Security in Leases and Dowry Agreements', *CQ* 43, 73–95.

Harris, E.M. (1994) 'Law and Oratory', in Worthington, I., ed. (1994) *Persuasion: Greek Rhetoric in Action*, London, 130–150.

Hopper, R.J. (1953) 'The Attic Silver Mines in the Fourth Century B.C.', *Annual of the British School at Athens* 48, 200–254.

Kanavou, N. (2011) *Aristophanes' Comedy of Names: A Study of Speaking Names in Aristophanes*, Berlin.

Lanni, A. (2006) *Law and Justice in the Courts of Classical Athens*, Cambridge.

MacDowell, D.M. (1975) 'Law-Making at Athens in the Fourth Century B.C.', *JHS* 95, 62–67.

MacDowell, D.M. (1978) *The Law in Classical Athens*, London.

MacDowell, D.M. (1986) 'The Law of Periandros about Symmories', *CQ* 36, 438–449.

MacDowell, D.M. (2009) *Demosthenes the Orator*, Oxford.

Ober, J. (1989) *Mass and Elite in Democratic Athens*, Princeton.

Phillips, D.D. (2013) *The Law of Ancient Athens*, Ann Arbor, Mich.

Pringsheim, E. (1950) *The Greek Law of Sale*, Weimar.

Rhodes, P.J. (1985) 'Nomothesia in Fourth-Century Athens', *CQ* 35, 55–60.

Scafuro, A.C. (2011) *Demosthenes, speeches 39–49*, Austin.

Sinclair, R.K. (1988) *Democracy and Participation in Athens*, Cambridge.

Svenbro, J. (1993) *Phrasikleia: an Anthropology of Reading in Ancient Greece* (trans. J. Lloyd), Ithaca, N.Y.

Thomsen, R. (1964) *Eisphora: A Study of Direct Taxation in Ancient Athens*, Copenhagen.

Todd, S.C. (1993) *The Shape of Athenian Law*, Oxford.

Wallace, R.W. (1989) 'The Athenian *proeispherontes*', *Hesperia* 58, 473–490.

Whitehead, D. (1983) 'Competitive Outlay and Community Profit: φιλοτιμία in Democratic Athens', *C&M* 34, 55–74.

Yunis, H. (2005) 'The Rhetoric of Law in Fourth-Century Athens', in Gagarin, M. and Cohen, D., eds (2005), 191–208.

CHAPTER 13

Jurisdiction and Jurisprudence: the Topography of Law in Demosthenes 23 *Against Aristokrates*

Victoria Wohl

Demosthenes 23 *Against Aristokrates* is a *graphē paranomōn*. It challenges the legality of a decree proposed in 352 BC by Aristokrates to grant physical protection to a certain Charidemos, agent of the Thracian king Kersobleptes, by stipulating that 'if any person kills Charidemos he shall be liable to seizure (*agōgimos*) from the allied territory and if anyone prevents this, whether city or individual, they shall be excluded from the treaty (*ekspondos*)' (§§16, 91).[1] Harvey Yunis (1988) has argued that in *graphai paranomōn* legal and political pleas are complementary and mutually supporting, as speakers work to convince the jurors that the suspect decree is against both the law (*paranomon*) and the city's interests (*asymphoron*). *Against Aristokrates* is no exception. The speech begins by foregrounding the political: at stake in the case, Demosthenes tells the jurors in the proem, is not just the fate of Charidemos but Athens' control over the entire Chersonese (§1). But the bulk of the speech is devoted to judicial, not political arguments, with a detailed analysis of the many laws—'too many to list them all' (§63)—transgressed by Aristokrates' decree.[2]

My chapter explores the complex symbiosis of law and politics in this speech. I argue that Demosthenes here uses the laws to smooth over problems of jurisdiction raised by the speech's politics. Aristokrates' decree extends Athenian law to Thrace and deploys it as an instrument of intervention in

1 The decree had been approved by the Council but not yet by the Assembly. See Hansen 1974: 52 on the political power wielded by the courts in such cases. The speech is delivered by a man named Euthykles (*pace* Sealey 1993: 131), otherwise unknown to us. We do not know the verdict in this case, but Aristokrates' responsibility for the decree had lapsed by the time the trial was completed, and the affair seems not to have harmed Charidemos' political fortunes.

2 Papillon (1998: 23–25) notes the foregrounding of the 'deliberative' in this proem. He divides the speech into three sections: a juridical (§§22–99), deliberative (§§100–143), and epideictic (§§144–195) proof. This sort of tripartite division was not uncommon in *graphai paranomōn*: cf. Lykourg. fr. 91 and Yunis 1988: 370–373. But here the ethical arguments concerning Charidemos' unworthiness that Papillon identifies with epideictic oratory (§144 ff.) seem to me essentially a continuation of the political, with *ēthos* used primarily to establish a pattern of political activity.

 | DOI:10.1163/9789004377899_015

Thracian internal politics. The assumptions about and implications for interstate relations are not explored overtly in the political sections of the speech. Instead, they are addressed obliquely in the course of the legal plea. That section (§§22–64) deploys a spatial rhetoric that equates law with legal procedure and localises that procedure within clear spatial limits: a well-defined (*hōrismenos*) law is one that respects borders (*horoi*). The speech's famous tour of the Athenian courts (§§65–81) is the most conspicuous example of this spatial rhetoric, as the law is embodied in the physical space of its procedural enactment. Demosthenes uses the laws not only, as one might expect, to demonstrate the illegality of the *paranomōn* decree, but also to articulate a spatial logic of law that roots *dikē* in the physical topography of Athens itself. That same logic allows him to represent the Chersonese as an extension of the *polis*, a monument to Athenian justice not unlike the court buildings (§§207–208). The speech thus uses the law to draw distant politics near and to evade difficult questions of jurisdiction by bringing Thrace within the proximate physical boundaries of Athenian jurisprudence.

The politics behind this case are complicated. After the death of king Kotys, Thrace was divided between three rival kings. Charidemos, the subject of this decree, is the agent and general of one of these kings, Kersobleptes, whom he is apparently trying to help obtain sole supremacy. Charidemos, a native of Oreos in Euboea, had been granted Athenian citizenship and awarded a crown several years earlier for furthering Athenian interests in Thrace. Aristokrates' decree protecting Charidemos rests on the assumption that it was to Athens' advantage to have all of Thrace united under Kersobleptes, and that Charidemos was the man to make it happen. Demosthenes argues against this that neither Kersobleptes nor Charidemos has Athens' best interests at heart and Athens would be better served by maintaining an equilibrium among the three kings and thereby keeping the whole region weak (§§100–195). Behind all this lurks the growing threat of Philip in this strategically and economically important region.[3]

One can imagine the issues of sovereignty this situation would raise for us simply by replacing Athens with the US and Thrace with Iraq. Aristokrates' decree essentially proposes propping up a local strongman, the 'faithless barbarian' (*barbaros kai apistos*, §135) Kersobleptes, who, Demosthenes predicts, will be emboldened by this decree to become a tyrant toward his people (§§141–143) and a danger to Athens (§§135–140). Demosthenes' objection to

3 On the historical background see Sealey 1993: 102–136 and on the Athenians' ambivalent view of Thrace, Sears 2013.

the decree is not principled but pragmatic: the political section of the speech is concerned not with *to dikaion* but with *to sympheron*, and what is *sympheron* not for the Thracians, obviously, but for the Athenians. Athens' advantage, he argues, lies in destabilising the entire region (§§102–103). Questions of sovereignty and the limits of Athenian intervention in the politics of independent Greek states are never broached by either side. No more are the questions of legal jurisdiction involved in actually implementing this decree, which would make Charidemos' imagined assassin, who may or may not be an Athenian citizen, subject to summary arrest anywhere in the allied territory and would penalise any state that harboured him.[4] Neither the proposer nor the prosecutor of the decree seems to feel any discomfort at extending the reach of Athenian law beyond Athens' borders or at using the law as a means of interceding in the political affairs of an autonomous Greek kingdom.

The speech's lack of overt interest in issues of political sovereignty or legal jurisdiction seems not to be exceptional. 'International law' is an undertheorised area in ancient Greek history, as Polly Low has shown, undertheorised both by modern scholars and by the Greeks themselves.[5] In general, though, it seems that the Greeks felt less acutely than we do today the tension between autonomy and intervention. One reason the tension did not arise—or one way it was mitigated if it did arise—was the extension of internal ethical and legal principles to foreign relations.[6] Thus as Low and others have argued, the extension of *philia*, with its imperative to help friends, to foreign relations not only justifies but in some cases demands intervention.[7] Likewise, Athenian legal concepts like *dikē* and *nomos* are extended beyond the sphere in which they could actually be adjudicated and enforced, and function as informal regulatory ideals in negotiations between states.[8]

4 It was not uncommon for Athenian decrees to honour non-Athenians by stipulating that anyone who killed them should be punished as if he had killed an Athenian citizen: see e.g., *IG* I³ 57.9–12, II² 32.9–14, 226.35–50; and further references in de Ste Croix 1961: 275–276, Sealey 1983: 281, n. 17. This is not the situation here for, as Demosthenes notes (§89), Charidemos has already been made a citizen, so the protection granted by Aristokrates' decree is an additional, and undeserved, honour. MacDowell 1990: 201 notes that the novelty of Aristokrates' decree from a legal standpoint is the extension of *apagōgē*, which normally applied only to homicides encountered in the public spaces of Athens (§80), to the entire allied territory.

5 Low 2007: 7–32, 78–83. Cf. Hunt 2010: 13–15, 220–226.

6 On sovereignty and intervention: Low 2007: 187–199; *contra* Hunt 2010: 94–96. On the extension of internal ideals to external relations: Low 2007: 83–102, 129–174; Hunt 2010: 108–133. Davies 1994: 60–65 questions whether there was a concept of sovereignty in our sense in ancient Greece.

7 Low 2007: 33–76; Mitchell 1997, Mitchell 1998: 22–40 (and 134–147 particularly in connection to Thrace); Hunt 2010: 186–192.

8 Low 2007: 94–102.

Demosthenes 23 can be seen as an instance of this rhetorical smoothing over of the discontinuities between *polis* law and interstate law. But its rhetorical strategy is rather different from the examples mentioned above: instead of extending internal principles of legality to foreign states and thus expanding the ideational, if not literal, jurisdiction of Athenian law, this speech defines that jurisdiction narrowly, identifying the theoretical borders of the law with the geographical borders of Attica; it then rhetorically situates Thrace within those borders. Thrace becomes part of the territory of Athens, not only subject to its laws but in fact, as we shall see, a monument to them. In this way the speech extends Athenian jurisdiction precisely by limiting it, as the laws used to prove the illegality of Aristokrates' decree simultaneously legitimate its interventionist politics.

The core of the legal plea in this speech, as in most *graphai paranomōn*, is the *paragraphesthai*, the side-by-side reading of the decree with the established laws. Demosthenes begins by comparing Aristokrates' decree to Drakon's homicide laws.[9] His primary charge in this section is that because it does not explicitly specify a procedure for trial and sentencing, Aristokrates' decree intends to eliminate the jury trial, and thus goes against all of the established procedures of jurisprudence. The first law is read: 'The Council on the Areiopagos is to judge cases of murder and intentional wounding and arson and poisoning, if someone kills in giving it' (*ean tis apokteinēi dous*, § 22). The final clause, 'if someone kills in giving it', is obviously intended to differentiate fatal from non-fatal poisoning,[10] but Demosthenes tendentiously generalises it to all murder, and interprets this law as if it were the founding mandate for the procedure of *krisis*, trial by jury. The law does not assume someone is guilty of murder, but says 'if he kills', which is what the Areiopagos must determine. 'If someone kills' is just words (*onomata*): it is the trial that converts it into a crime (*adikēmata*, § 26). The trial is the necessary suture between the law's protasis and apodosis, between the supposed crime and its punishment. Aristokrates' decree, by contrast, jumps from *onoma* to *adikēma*: it presupposes the contents of the protasis ('if any person kills Charidemos') and proceeds straight to the apodosis ('he shall be liable to seizure'), shamefully omitting the trial.[11]

---

9 See Gagarin 1981 on Drakon's homicide law: he posits that Demosthenes is here quoting from a *stēlē* on the Areiopagos which contained the original law of Drakon as well as subsequent amendments (§§ 26–29). Carawan 1998: 88–98 examines the authenticity of the Drakonian laws in this speech.

10 Cf. *Ath. Pol.* 57.3: 'Trials for homicide and wounding, if someone kills or wounds intentionally, are tried in the Areiopagos, as well as trials for poisoning, if someone kills by giving the poison, and arson.'

11 A related argument is developed at §§ 29–30 (cf. § 36). The law stipulates that it is lawful

This argument rests on several sleights of hand. First, Demosthenes holds this decree to a standard of explicitness and completeness more appropriate to a law than a decree: because decrees were subordinate to written laws (according to a law that Demosthenes himself later cites, § 87) they presumably had to follow established legal procedures, and could take those procedures as read even if they didn't spell them out in full detail.[12] By the logic of Demosthenes' argument, every decree would have to include the text of all the relevant laws—a real nightmare for the scribe. Second, Demosthenes interprets *agōgimos* as summary execution, not as a legal process. The precise meaning of this term is disputed, as we shall see, but if we understand it as meaning 'led back to Athens for trial', not 'led away for execution' then Aristokrates' decree is unremarkable. But even if we take *agōgimos* as a punishment rather than a procedure, as Demosthenes wishes us to do, the omission of the latter is not extraordinary. Although the procedural bent of Greek law is well known, not all written laws mention the trial specifically: they omit it presumably not because they licensed proceeding directly from accusation to condemnation but because they took for granted the procedural steps in between.[13]

So legally the argument seems dubious. Rhetorically, though, it is effective in insisting that Aristokrates' decree aims to eliminate the trial and jump from a presumption of guilt to a punishment imposed on the spot. By doing so, he argues, Aristokrates' decree 'bypasses the court defined by the law (*parabas to diōrismenon ek tou nomou dikastērion*) and hands [the presumed assassin] over to his accusers without a trial to do whatever they want to him, when it is not even clear if he is guilty' (§ 27). The omission of the trial is figured in concrete topographical terms. The trial is embodied in the physical court (*dikastērion*) defined (*diōrismenon*) by the law. *Diorizein*, a key term in the speech, represents the law's precision in terms of clearly demarcated boundaries (*horoi*), both lit-

---

to kill murderers under certain conditions. Demosthenes takes the term 'murderers' (*tous androphonous*) to imply that there has already been a trial and conviction; if the law reads 'if someone kills', on the other hand, that means that a verdict has not yet been rendered. In the former case, the lawmaker stipulates a punishment; in the latter, the jury. Again the judicial procedure is interpolated into the written text of the law, 'for the trial is intermediate between the accusation and the conviction' (*meson gar estin aitias kai elenchou krisis*, § 36).

12 He treats the decree as if it were a law at § 86, for instance. Laws must apply equally to all Athenians; decrees must conform to the laws; this decree, in applying only to Charidemos, goes against the law. But such specificity was one difference between *psēphismata* and *nomoi*. On the distinction see Hansen 1978.

13 Aristokrates' decree follows the standard formula for *nomoi*: if someone commits X crime, let him be subject to juridical procedure Y. See Todd 1993: 64–67, Carey 1998. In the cases cited by the latter, some specify the trial, some do not.

eral and figurative.[14] In this phrase, legality is vested in legal procedure, which in turn is located in a specific concrete space that Aristokrates' decree literally transgresses (*parabas*).

The spatial idiom is elaborated in the argument that follows. Bypassing the court and its procedures, Aristokrates' decree allows the captor to take Charidemos' presumptive killer anywhere and do anything he wants to him there: torture him, abuse him, extort money. Again this claim is suspect: the decree does not spell out precisely what *agōgimos* means, but it probably intends for the killer to be led back to Athens for trial; to pretend that it is an invitation to torture or summarily execute the suspect is tendentious at best.[15] But Demosthenes interprets the decree's imprecise language by way of an antithesis between the courts and the captor's own home, which he figures as the scene of criminal abuse (§§31, 32). A second law is read allowing a murderer taken within Athenian territory to be killed or arrested in accordance with the laws of Solon, but not to be tortured (§28). Demosthenes interprets this as meaning that a murderer is to be led to the *thesmothetai*. 'And what is the difference between this and taking him to one's own house?' he asks. 'The man who takes a murderer to the *thesmothetai* gives authority over the criminal to the laws, whereas a man who takes him to his own home gives that authority to himself. The former is to pay the penalty as the law commands; the latter as the captor wishes. Obviously there is a great difference between the laws having authority over the punishment and the enemy having it' (§32). Again, the authority of the laws lies in correct legal procedure, which is symbolised by the physical place of its enactment: leading a suspect to the *thesmothetai* affirms the justice of the law; taking him home is a different matter altogether.

In the same vein, the vagueness of *agōgimos* is read as an invitation to arrest the suspect anywhere, not just within Athenian territory, as the law specifies (§§34–36). Drakon's law defined (*diōrisen*) not only how a murderer is to be punished but also where: he may be killed only if taken within the *hēmedapē*, by which Demosthenes understands the fatherland of the victim (§34). But Aristokrates' decree allows him to be seized anywhere within the entire allied

---

14 Forms of the verb appear seven times in Dem. 23, more than in any other speech. Its nine occurrences of forms of *horos* are equalled only by Dem. 31 *Against Onetor II*, which deals with the removal of mortgage markers (*horoi*) from a property. That speech, however, does not deploy the verb *diorizein*, nor use *horos* in a metaphorical sense. *Dikastērion* denoted both the empanelled *dikastai* and the physical place where they sat: see Boegehold 1995: 4.

15 The word may indicate that the individual is subject to *apagōgē*, summary arrest (Thür 1991: 67); but even *apagōgē* entailed a jury trial if the suspect maintained his innocence. The scholiast notes Demosthenes' exploitation of the decree's ambiguous terminology: see Whiston 1868: 400 ad 16, MacDowell 1990: 201, Sealey 1993: 131.

territory (*pantachothen*, §§ 34–35, *pantachou*, § 38). This lack of spatial delimitation contravenes not just the letter of the law, but also the spirit of legality entailed by its clear definition (*diōrisen* is used twice in § 34) and the jurisdictional boundaries that it justly places upon itself. The law's justice lies in its own limits: in its establishment of its own clear *horoi* and its restriction of its own jurisdiction to those *horoi*.

The laws' spatial self-limitation defines not only their legality, but also their equity. In the next section Demosthenes turns to the law that enables convicted homicides to go into permanent exile, presumably to avoid the pollution of encountering the family of the victim. This 'most carefully and lawfully defined' provision (*eulabōs diōrise kai nomimōs*, § 37), puts a geographical limit on the law itself: the law will not pursue a homicide beyond the boundaries of Athens.[16] This is presented as a question of jurisdiction: if we kill Athenians who have gone into exile elsewhere, others will kill those in exile here (§ 38). But it is also a question of the law's piety, justice, and mercy, for the lawmaker knew that 'it is not right to kill him anywhere' (*kteinein de ouk' hosion pantachou*, § 38). Exile, as Demosthenes represents it, is the only refuge of the hapless murderer. Throughout this section, the putative murderer is referred to as 'unfortunate' (*atychousin*, §§ 39, 42), as if every murderer were guilty of involuntary manslaughter, the result of some regrettable accident that he leaves to the jurors to imagine for themselves. Indeed, he suggests, such a misfortune could befall any one of them, inasmuch as no man can foresee his fate (*tychēs*, § 42). A most humane and excellent law (*nomos anthrōpinōs kai kalōs keimenos*, § 44) allows these poor souls to go into self-imposed exile and in this way places a clear *horos* (§ 46) on their prosecution, without which 'the punishment of misfortunes would be without bounds' (*aperantoi*, § 39). This *horos* is simultaneously the literal geographical boundary of the *polis* (§ 46) and the theoretical limit the law places on its own prosecutorial reach.[17] Its voluntary self-limitation is an expression of the law's philanthropic mercy (*anthrōpinōs*, §§ 44, 70, 82), 'a boon of forgiveness' (*to tēs sungnōmēs ōphelimon*, § 42) it extends to the poor remorseful killer. Aristokrates' decree, by contrast,

16 On the provision for exile, see MacDowell 1963: 113–115, 117–122; Gagarin 1981: 58–61, 120–124. The spatial limit on retribution also provides a temporal limit, as endless retribution is forestalled by placing a physical border between the murderer and the victim's family.

17 This boundary is concretely marked in the law by the frontier-markets (*agorai ephoriai*) and the games and Amphictyonic sacrifices which brought together people from both sides; Demosthenes explicates this point at some length, §§ 39–41. Since the law indicts not only anyone who kills a homicide in legal exile but also anyone who allows him to be killed, the jurors would be guilty, if (by passing this decree) they allow Charidemos' killer to be killed, of breaking their own law (§ 43).

acknowledges no limits. 'What boundary (*horon*) have you left in this text, since the law clearly forbids pursuing a man beyond the borders, but you allow him to be seized from anywhere' (*pantachothen*, § 48)? Aristokrates would drag the poor unfortunate manslaughterer back to the fatherland of his unintended victim, 'confounding all human decency' (*syncheis t'anthrōpina*, § 49).

In this first section of the legal argument, then, 'law' is equated with legal procedure and that legal procedure is insistently spatialised, its *horoi* both defined and defended by the *nomoi* themselves. It is worth noting that the Drakonian *nomoi* Demosthenes cites have virtually nothing to do with the case at hand: they deal with Athenians killing other Athenian citizens who have been found guilty of homicide in an Athenian court and have gone into voluntary exile from Athens. The presumptive assassin of Charidemos may or may not be an Athenian citizen; he is abroad not in legal exile after a homicide conviction but, presumably, because he lives in Thrace.[18] Demosthenes does not address the larger questions of jurisdiction raised by the decree. Did Athenian law extend beyond its own geographical boundaries, and when it did operate beyond those boundaries, what legal bounds were there upon it? In short, what are the *horoi*, physical and theoretical, that define Athenian law and what happens when the law crosses those limits?

Instead of addressing those issues of jurisdiction, the speech deploys a spatial metaphor that associates the law's very legality with its self-limitation, that defines the law by its boundaries and makes those boundaries coterminous with the geographical boundaries of Attica. Aristokrates' law is *paranomon* because it goes beyond (*para*) the limits, both literal and metaphorical, of the law and transgresses the *horos* of a *eu hōrismenos nomos*. So Demosthenes closes this section by reading the law against overturning or altering Drakon's laws and concludes: 'what else is it than to alter the law if one applies penalties outside of the appointed court (*dikastēriōn*) and the boundaries (*horōn*) of prohibited places' and robs individuals of the right to a fair trial (§ 62)?

The speech's spatial rhetoric reaches a crescendo in its famous tour of Athenian homicide courts.[19] These monuments to Athenian *nomos* and *eunomia* are

---

18 Cf. §§ 57–59 on the difficulty of foreseeing the exact circumstances covered and entailed by the decree: since no one can know the future, Demosthenes is free to imagine Charidemos, emboldened by this decree, returning to Athens, where he could steal other men's property and rape their wives without fear of reprisal, since the man who killed him would be subject to the decree.

19 On the five homicide courts, see *Ath. Pol.* 57.2–4, Paus. 1.28; MacDowell 1963: 39–89, Sealey 1983, Boegehold 1995: 43–50 (with *testimonia* at 121–150), Carawan 1998: 84–125. Compare the similar argument from civic topography at Aischin. 3.183–187, on which see Hobden 2007: 495–498 (my thanks to Lene Rubinstein for the reference).

the city's glory, a treasure which Charidemos—so little interested in the gift of Athenian citizenship that he doesn't even make his home there (§ 126)—fails to appreciate (§§ 64–65). They are also touchstones of legality by which to judge Aristokrates' decree. The extended survey of these five courts is coordinated with the previous section's reading of the laws: all the judicial provisions and procedures Aristokrates' decree omits 'have been assigned by the laws to five courts' (§ 63). 'Perhaps one might say that all these courts are worthless and unjustly founded, while his decree is just and good. On the contrary, I know of no more dreadful decree ever proposed before you, while of all the courts that exist among men, none will be found that are more holy and just (*semnoteron oute dikaioteron*) than these' (§ 64). As Demosthenes moves from one to the next, each tribunal becomes a physical instantiation of the laws tried there. In breaking those laws, Aristokrates transgresses the court itself: it will be up to the jurors either to dismantle the courts or to reject the decree.[20]

The laws protected by the five courts are not only themselves well-defined (*dioristhenta*, § 73; *horisantes*, § 74; *diorizousi*, § 74) but they also show the same just self-limitation Demosthenes emphasised in the previous section. He begins with the Areiopagos, the most unique and holy of courts (*idiōtaton pantōn kai semnotaton*, § 65), a tribunal conspicuous not only for its divine origins, mythic prestige and infallible judgment, but also for allowing the defendant to flee after the first speech (§ 69). This provision was established because those who established this court 'whoever they were, whether heroes or gods, did not go after misfortunes but humanely lightened them, as much as they rightly could' (§ 70). The jurisdictional boundaries and boundedness that Demosthenes reads out of the laws in the *paragraphesthai* are now attributed to the Areiopagos' divine founders and located within the tribunal where they are tried. Likewise, the Palladion is praised for its precise forensic procedure—the very procedure Aristokrates' decree omits—and for allowing the exile of those convicted of involuntary manslaughter (§ 71). Next is the Delphinion: in this tribunal, which heard cases of justified homicide, is vested the most fundamental principle of jurisprudence, the *horos* between justifiable and unjustifiable homicide (*horisantes, diorizousi*, § 74). The very boundary between just and unjust, the difference that grounds the law, is located within this court, and confounded by Aristokrates' decree, which, in failing to specify that the

20 Note the hendiadys of court and laws: Aristokrates' decree is written 'against this court [the Areiopagos] and its written laws (*nomoi*) and unwritten conventions (*nomima*)' (§ 70); 'he confounds the court at the Palladion, transgressing its laws (*nomoi*)' (§ 71); 'these two courts, so ancient and august, and their usages (*nomimoi*) handed down through all time, he has shamelessly overleapt' (§ 73, cf. § 81).

murder of Charidemos be unjustified, 'has transgressed this third court and its provisions' (*triton touti dikastērion kai ta toutou nomima parabebēkōs phainei*, § 75).

Fourth is the Prytaneion. This is more of a stretch for his argument, since here were tried murders caused by inanimate objects. But if even a rock or a piece of wood 'which is inanimate and without sense' cannot be charged without a trial, he gamely argues, 'then surely it is terrible and impious to make a man liable to arrest without a trial or verdict ... a human being who shares the same nature as us' (§ 76). Legal procedure, as was hinted in the previous section, is the source of law's humanity, its acknowledgment of the human nature of its defendants. Finally, he reaches the mysterious tribunal in Phreatto, which heard cases involving those who committed voluntary murder while in exile for involuntary murder.[21] With this court, the legal question is explicitly spatial: how can the law grant such a man due process without committing the impiety of recalling a murderer to the homeland of his victim? The solution to this spatial and legal conundrum is physically embodied in this court, which literally straddles this difficult jurisprudential boundary: the jurors sit on Attic soil, but the defendant is on a boat just off shore and makes his defence from there (§ 78). This description of the jurors on land and the accused at sea offers a clear mental image of the spatial boundaries that have been the theme throughout this speech, and reinforces the speech's close association both of law with the geographical boundaries of Athens and of legality with the law's respect for those boundaries.

With this image of law at the limits, the tour of courts is complete, but Demosthenes adds an odd supplement (§ 80). In addition to these five courts there is also a procedure for instances where the other procedures have not been followed for any reason. This is the *apagōgē*, which provides the legal basis for his interpretation of the term *agōgimos*.[22] If someone sees the killer 'going around the temples and the market place, it is permitted to lead him away (*apagein*) to the jail (*desmōtērion*), but not to his house or wherever he wishes', as Aristokrates allows (§ 80). Again procedure is imagined in spatial terms, and justice is localised in the prison, as opposed to the extra-legal and illegal space of the arrester's home—'or wherever he wishes': the lack of a specific judicial location in itself is a breach of the logic of law, as this speech has so carefully mapped it. So Demosthenes concludes: Aristokrates' decree would

21 There are no known instances of a trial in this court and, as MacDowell 1963: 84 notes, Aristotle's description at *Pol.* 1300b28 implies that he had never known it to sit.

22 On the *apagōgē*, a form of summary arrest, see MacDowell 1963: 130–140, Harrison 1971: 222–229, Hansen 1976, Todd 1993: 117–118.

mean 'the end of these procedures (*nomimois*) and the dissolution of these courts (*dikastēriois*), which the gods themselves established and humans have used continually ever since' (§ 81).

Through the spatial rhetoric of the legal plea, then, the law is defined as bounded, and its boundaries are defined as coterminous with those of Athens. What is the relation between this Athenian topography of law and the speech's larger political project, between the rhetoric of proximity in the judicial plea and the politics-at-a-distance of the speech's deliberative plea? This pointedly localised jurisdiction of the law obviously supports Demosthenes' argument against Aristokrates' decree: if Athenian law stops—indeed, stops itself—at the borders of the *polis*, Athens would seem to have no business legislating the arrest of the killer of Charidemos in Thrace or wherever he may be, nor the diplomatic censure of any foreign individuals or states that offered him protection. In fact, this speech's localisation of law would seem to militate against interventionist politics in general. It would seem to work in the opposite direction from the common metaphorical extension of *philia* to external affairs. If that rhetorical operation has the effect of subjecting foreign relations to internal standards of ethical action, the spatialisation of law here suggests that Athens is just and lawful precisely to the extent that it respects its own limits. But in fact Demosthenes' politics, as we see them in this speech and throughout his deliberative oratory,[23] are no less interventionist than those of Aristokrates' decree: he just advocates different interventions. The rhetoric of the speech's legal argument would seem to vitiate its political argument, delegitimising in advance its detailed claims about Athens' interests in Thrace and how best to achieve them.

The speech's solution to this seeming disjunction between the legal and the political is not to extend Athenian law beyond its boundaries but instead to bring Thrace within the physical space of Athenian justice. After a mind-numbingly detailed discussion of the foreign policy background—alliances made and broken, the complex negotiations among the Thracian kings and the reactions, official and unofficial, of Philip and of Athens—Demosthenes turns to the political consequences of rewarding someone like Charidemos. He berates the jurors for failing to punish those who harm them, and compares them to their glorious ancestors (§ 204). In the past, he says, the *polis* was glorious and well-off, and no man was above the masses.

23 Papillon 1998: 91–104 shows the consistency of Demosthenes' position in this speech and his political speeches.

τεκμήριον δέ· τὴν Θεμιστοκλέους μὲν οἰκίαν καὶ τὴν Μιλτιάδου καὶ τῶν τότε λαμπρῶν, εἴ τις ἄρ' ὑμῶν οἶδεν ὁποία ποτ' ἐστίν, ὁρᾷ τῶν πολλῶν οὐδὲν σεμνοτέραν οὖσαν, τὰ δὲ τῆς πόλεως οἰκοδομήματα καὶ κατασκευάσματα τηλικαῦτα καὶ τοιαῦθ' ὥστε μηδενὶ τῶν ἐπιγιγνομένων ὑπερβολὴν λελεῖφθαι, προπύλαια ταῦτα, νεώσοικοι, στοαί, Πειραιεύς, τἄλλ' οἷς κατεσκευασμένην ὁρᾶτε τὴν πόλιν. νῦν δ' ἰδίᾳ μὲν ἑκάστῳ τῶν τὰ κοινὰ πραττόντων τοσαύτη περιουσία [ἐστὶν] ὥστε τινὲς μὲν αὐτῶν πολλῶν δημοσίων οἰκοδομημάτων σεμνοτέρας τὰς ἰδίας κατεσκευάκασιν οἰκίας, γῆν δ' ἔνιοι πλείω πάντων ὑμῶν τῶν ἐν τῷ δικαστηρίῳ συνεώνηνται· δημοσίᾳ δ' ὑμεῖς ἃ μὲν οἰκοδομεῖτε καὶ κονιᾶτε, ὡς μικρὰ καὶ γλίσχρα, αἰσχύνη λέγειν. ἀλλ' ἔχετ' εἰπεῖν ὅ τι κοινῇ κτησάμενοι καταλείψετε, ὥσπερ ἐκεῖνοι Χερρόνησον, Ἀμφίπολιν, δόξαν ἔργων καλῶν;[24]

§§ 207–208

Here is the proof: if any of you knows what sort of house Themistokles and Miltiades lived in, or any of the men who were famous at the time, he sees that it is no grander than those of the majority, but the public buildings and structures were such as to leave their descendants no chance of surpassing them: these gateways and shipyards and colonnades and the Piraeus and all the other structures with which, as you see, the city is built up. But today every public figure has such a surplus of wealth that some of them have constructed private homes that are more grand than public buildings, and some have bought up more property than all of you here in the courtroom together. Meanwhile, it is a shame to say how poor and paltry are the public buildings you build and whitewash. Can you say what you have acquired in common and will leave to your descendants as they left the Chersonese and Amphipolis to you, the glory of their noble deeds?

The passage offers a number of familiar themes: the current generation is failing to live up to the glorious legacy of its forefathers; the orators and politicians who used to be servants of the people are now their masters (§ 209). The city's magnificence and power have fallen into disrepair as individuals are enriched at the public's expense. But what is remarkable, in light of the spatial rhetoric we have been tracing throughout the speech, is the way Demosthenes concretises the comparison between the shabby present and the glorious past in the built environment of the city. Demosthenes invites the jurors to look around

24 Demosthenes repeats this section nearly verbatim at 13.29 and 3.25–26, 29. In both passages the emphasis is likewise on the balance between public and private and the contrast between past and present. See MacDowell 2009: 227–229 on the relative dating and rhetorical overlap among the speeches.

them or to cast their mind's eye over the familiar topography of the city. With its shipyards and Piraeus, the survey has a military cast, but it complements the survey of courts earlier in the speech. Athens' traditional democratic *ēthos*, its political power, and imperial wealth, are all inscribed in its physical monuments, no less than are its just and venerable laws.

Among those monuments Demosthenes includes, astonishingly, Thrace: 'Can you say what you have acquired in common and will leave to your descendants as they left the Chersonese and Amphipolis to you, the glory of their noble deeds?' Thrace becomes part of the topography of Athens, a physically far-flung but symbolically central edifice in Athens' ideological landscape. This geographically improbable move is made through a daring syllogism: our ancestors left us many glorious monuments; our ancestors left us the Chersonese and Amphipolis, which we have squandered just as we have let those monuments fall into disrepair. Demosthenes denounces the fact that now powerful individuals 'enjoy the inheritance (*klēronomousi*) of your glory and prosperity, while you get no benefit from it at all' (§ 210). Literal and figurative become hard to disentangle as Thrace is represented as the Athenians' *klēros*, an inheritance both physical and ideological left to them by their powerful forefathers, along with those other glorious bequests, the *stoas* and shipyards and Piraeus, but also the Areiopagos and Palladion and Delphinion and, one might suppose, the Heliaia where the jurors themselves sat to hear this case.[25] Through the metaphor of the ancestral bequest and the compressed syllogistic logic of this passage, Thrace itself becomes one of those glorious buildings, now sadly left to rot while Aristokrates slaves to ornament the marble mansions of Charidemos and his ilk.

Taking his evidence from the jurors' immediate physical surroundings, Demosthenes constructs his argument out of literal marble and mortar: the stones of Athens speak. The city is enlisted as Demosthenes' *synēgoros* in a case that simultaneously advocates jurisprudential boundaries and interventionist politics. It manages this balancing act by drawing Thrace within the narrow limits of Athenian law; not only subject to that law, it becomes another embodiment of it, another physical instantiation of Athenian justice like the five tribunals. Demosthenes thus extends the jurisdiction of Athenian law precisely by limiting it. By localising law in the physical environment of Athens and imagining Thrace as part of that environment, he erases any jurisdictional issues that might arise from the distant Thracian politics that the decree and the speech against it both likewise pursue.

25 On the possible identification of this building, see Boegehold 1995: 3–4 (with the *testimonia* at 168–171), 11–12, 93, 150–152.

The political and the legal thus are complementary and mutually supporting in this speech, not only at the superficial level at which *to dikaion* and *to sympheron* are always one and the same, but at the deeper level of the speech's basic rhetorical architecture. Through its spatial rhetoric, the speech not only prosecutes a *paranomon* decree but performatively enacts the jurisprudential logic of the *graphē paranomōn*: fixing *nomos* within space, it situates Aristokrates' decree beyond (*para*) it, on the far side of legality. In so doing it simultaneously localises the law and, paradoxically, deterritorialises it, for it tries Aristokrates not only in the Heliaia, where *graphai paranomōn* were heard, but in all the courts of Athens at once. Encompassing the entire judicial landscape of Attica within its rhetorical *horoi*, *Against Aristokrates*—a speech famous already in antiquity for its 'distinctness' (*eukrineia*), its clear argumentative organisation and well-articulated logical boundaries[26]—itself defines the space of legality. In one and the same gesture, it exiles Aristokrates and Charidemos from this jurisdiction and locates distant Thrace at its very centre. Through his rhetorical use—and perhaps abuse—of the laws, Demosthenes thus maps an imaginative topography of Athenian jurisprudence that provides the foundation for the entire edifice of his foreign policy, a policy he frequently pursued in and through the courts of Athens.

Bibliography

Boegehold, A.L. (1995) *The Lawcourts at Athens: Sites, Buildings, Equipment, Procedure, and Testimonia*, Princeton.

Carawan, E. (1998) *Rhetoric and the Law of Draco*, Oxford.

Carey, C. (1998) 'The Shape of Athenian Laws', CQ 48, 93–109.

Davies, J.K. (1994) 'On the Non-Usability of the Concept of "Sovereignty" in an Ancient Greek Context', in Aigner Foresti, L. Barzanò, A. et al., eds, *Federazioni e federalismo nell' Europa antica*, Milan.

de Ste Croix, G.E.M. (1961) 'Notes on Jurisdiction in the Athenian Empire II', CQ 11, 268–280.

Gagarin, M. (1981) *Drakon and Early Athenian Homicide Law*, New Haven.

Hansen, M.H. (1974) *The Sovereignty of the People's Court in the Fourth Century* BC *and the Public Action Against Unconstitutional Proposals*, Odense.

26 It was so praised by Hermogenes *On Types of Style* 1.4, who characterises *eukrineia* as 'the definition of the whole' (*to kat'athroisin hōrismenon*, 1.4.87). See Papillon 1998: 77–82.

Hansen, M.H. (1976) *Apagoge, endeixis and ephegesis Against kakourgoi, atimoi, and pheugontes: A Study in the Athenian Administration of Justice in the Fourth Century BC*, Odense.

Hansen, M.H. (1978) '*Nomos* and *psephisma* in Fourth-Century Athens', GRBS 19, 315–330.

Harrison, A.R.W. (1968–1971) *The Law of Athens*, 2 vols, Oxford.

Hobden, F. (2007) 'Imagining Past and Present: A Rhetorical Strategy in Aeschines 3, *Against Ctesiphon*', CQ 57, 490–501.

Hunt, P. (2010) *War, Peace, and Alliance in Demosthenes' Athens*, Cambridge.

Low, P. (2007) *Interstate Relations in Classical Greece: Morality and Power*, Cambridge.

MacDowell, D.M. (1963) *Athenian Homicide Law in the Age of the Orators*, Manchester.

MacDowell, D.M., ed. (1990) *Demosthenes: Against Meidias*, Oxford.

MacDowell, D.M. (2009) *Demosthenes the Orator*, Oxford.

Mitchell, L.G. (1997) 'φιλία, εὔνοια and Greek Interstate Relations', *Antichthon* 31, 28–44.

Mitchell, L.G. (1998) *Greeks Bearing Gifts: The Public Use of Private Relationships in the Greek World, 435–323 BC*, Cambridge.

Papillon, T.L. (1998) *Rhetorical Studies in the Aristocratea of Demosthenes*, New York.

Sealey, R. (1983) 'The Athenian Courts for Homicide', CP 78, 275–296.

Sealey, R. (1993) *Demosthenes and His Time: A Study in Defeat*, New York.

Sears, M.A. (2013) *Athens, Thrace, and the Shaping of Athenian Leadership*, Cambridge.

Thür, G. (1991) 'The Jurisdiction of the Areopagos in Homicide Cases', in Gagarin, M., ed. (1991) *Symposion 1990: Vorträge zur griechischen und hellenistischen Rechtsgeschichte* (Pacific Grove, Cal., 24–26 September 1990), Cologne, 53–72.

Todd, S.C. (1993) *The Shape of Athenian Law*, Oxford.

Whiston, R. (1868) *Demosthenes, with an English Commentary*, vol. II, London.

Yunis, H. (1988) 'Law, Politics and the *graphē paranomōn* in Fourth-Century Athens', GRBS 29, 361–382.

CHAPTER 14

'Theft' as a Metaphor for the Abuse of Legal Process at Athens

S.C. Todd

I

Most of the chapters in this book are devoted to the space offered by the Athenian legal system for creative interpretation of substantive law and manipulation of legal procedures. Much of the discussion is focused on how litigants use the wording of laws to their own advantage, and how they depict the various stages and aspects of the litigation process. However, there is more to the flexibility of law than statute and procedure; legal language too has its elements of flexibility. A well-known example of this is the way in which speakers in trials for physical violence routinely deploy the language of *hybris* (aggravated assault) in speeches that relate formally to the lesser charge of *aikeia* (battery). In the present chapter, I explore a specific aspect of the elasticity of legal language, viz. the use of technical or quasi-technical terminology as metaphor to exploit procedural ambiguity, taking as the starting-point for my case-study a puzzling but not often discussed passage in the *Rhetoric to Alexander*, a treatise generally attributed to the fourth-century rhetorical theorist Anaximenes of Lampsakos. As the last of a series of points about witness testimony (*martyria*), we are told that:

> ἔστι δὲ καὶ κλέπτειν τὴν μαρτυρίαν τρόπῳ τοιῷδε· μαρτύρησόν μοι, ὦ Λυσικλῆς· μὰ τοὺς θεοὺς οὔκουν ἔγωγε· κωλύοντος γὰρ ἐμοῦ ταῦτα ἔπραξεν οὗτος. καὶ διὰ τούτου ἐν ἀποφάσει ψευδομαρτυρήσας ψευδομαρτυρίου δίκην οὐχ ὑφέξει. τοιγαροῦν ὅταν μὲν ἡμἰν συμφέρῃ κλέπτειν τὴν μαρτυρίαν, οὕτως αὐτῇ χρησόμεθα· ἐὰν δὲ οἱ ἐναντίοι τοιοῦτόν τι ποιήσωσιν, ἐμφανιοῦμεν τὴν κακοποιίαν αὐτῶν καὶ συγγραψαμένους μαρτυρεῖν κελεύσομεν.
>
> It is also possible to steal (vb. *kleptō*) the testimony, in the following way: 'Testify for me, Lysikles.' 'By the gods I will not, for it was (despite) my seeking to prevent it that this man did these things.' And in this way, having testified falsely in his refusal, he will not be liable to a prosecution for false testimony. So then, whenever it is in our interests to steal the testi-

 | DOI:10.1163/9789004377899_016

> mony, we will use it like this. But if the opponents should do something of this sort, we will publicise their malpractice and bid them submit their evidence in writing.[1]
>
> *Rh. Al.*, 1432a4–11 =15.7–8

The passage is clearly describing some form of procedural trickery, though the precise nature of the trick is not fully explained. One of the difficulties in interpretation is the possibility that it might allude to a real and presumably notorious incident, and hence a complex back-story known to the audience but lost to us. But the general tendency in Anaximenes is to use invented examples rather than real ones,[2] and it may therefore be best to interpret the interlocutor's name simply as narrative colour,[3] and to reconstruct the passage without hypothesising such a shared back-story. Whitehead (2007: 72), in the only detailed discussion of the passage known to me, envisages as background a prosecutor having suborned a witness who had previously promised to testify for the defendant, with the conversation here representing the defence calling on the witness in court to testify as agreed and the latter refusing; he glosses the theft metaphor as being 'to steal [the services of the witness] (from those who had been intending to rely on it)'. Whitehead is however evidently concerned by Lysikles' use of the third person ('this man' rather than 'you'), because of its implication that the first speaker cannot be the defendant himself but must be some form of advocate speaking on his behalf.[4] On this basis, and perhaps also for other reasons, it may be better to follow the alternative interpretation suggested albeit in less detail by the Budé editor Chiron,[5] who renders the participial clause in the third sentence as 'having given false testimony under cover of a refusal (to testify)':[6] what Chiron has in mind here is evidently a chal-

1 For the interlocutor's name, cf. n. 3 below.

2 Cope 1867: 414–415 indeed presents this an all but universal contrast with Aristotle's *Rhetoric*, i.e. that the examples quoted by the latter are real ones.

3 It is perhaps worth noting that the two branches of Anaximenes' manuscript tradition offer different versions of the name: 'Kallikles' is accepted by some editors, e.g. Fuhrmann in the 1966 Teubner and Rackham in the 1937 Loeb, but the Budé editor (Chiron 2002: 153 n. 343) gives reasons for preferring 'Lysikles', a reading which is accepted also in Mirhady's revised 2011 Loeb.

4 'Testify for me', on this reading, would have to be a loose usage for 'on my client's side of the dispute'.

5 Chiron's reading may also make better sense of the suggestion at 15.8 that opponents who attempt this trick should be challenged to submit their evidence in writing (i.e. presumably ahead of the trial), though it may be unwise to put too much emphasis on this.

6 Chiron 2002: 75: 'après avoir fait un faux témoignage sous couvert d'un refus de témoigner' (cf. index p. 214 s.v. ἀπόφασις, where he repeats but bracketing the final two words).

lenge issued in court not by the defence but by the prosecutor, addressed to a potential witness who (as a result presumably of prior collusion) has agreed to refuse the challenge but to word this refusal (itself given under pretence of reluctance) in terms which constitute a clear assertion of the defendant's guilt.

On this second interpretation, the question of who has stolen what from whom is more difficult to analyse, because the prosecutor is no longer envisaged as taking away something that the defendant could reasonably regard as being his (viz., the support of Lysikles as 'his' witness, as on Whitehead's reading), but rather is represented as creating for himself, out of nothing, something that has the persuasive appearance of being a witness testimony but without the reality and its accompanying risks (in that because Lysikles has not taken the stand as a witness, he cannot subsequently be prosecuted by *dikē pseudomartyriōn* for false testimony). It is perhaps not surprising therefore that translators have generally shied away from using the language of theft for this passage: Rackham in the first Loeb edition renders the two usages of the verb with the phrase 'get evidence (or 'procure it') by a trick'; Mirhady in the more recent Loeb edition uses the phrase 'sneak in witness (or 'the witness') testimony'; while Chiron in the Budé speaks of 'giving surreptitious testimony' ('porter un témoignage subreptice'/'témoigner subrepticement').[7]

Among the virtues of Whitehead's 2007 paper is precisely that he explores both the force and the prevalence of the metaphor. Indeed, his paper focuses on a discussion of no fewer than six passages in the fourth-century rhetorical theorists (three each in the *Rhetoric to Alexander* and in Aristotle's *Rhetoric*) that include what he describes as 'figurative uses of the verb *kleptein* which relate to rhetorical modes of deception'.[8] In part, this is a caution against the authority of the LSJ lexicon, which offers a range of meanings for the verb, viz. '(I) *steal* …, (II) *cozen, cheat* …, (III) *conceal, keep secret* …, (IV) *do secretly* or *treacherously* …'—the danger being that translations which adopt a secondary meaning risk assuming that the metaphorical sense of theft will have escaped the attention of the original audience.[9]

---

7 Rackham 1937: 345; Mirhady 2011: 539, 541; Chiron 2002: 75, 77, though his index at p. 233 does offer the more literal gloss 'Dans l'expression κλέπτειν τὴν μαρτυρίαν, témoigner à la dérobée, subrepticement'.

8 Quotation from Whitehead 2007: 70. In addition to the passage quoted at n.1 above, the other five are as follows: Anaximen. *Rh. Al.*, 1.17 = 1422b1–8; [35.]3–4 = 1440b20–24; Arist., *Rh.*, 3.2.5 = 1404b24–25; 3.2.10 = 1405a28–30; and 3.7.10 = 1408b4–8.

9 Words can of course lose their metaphorical sense over time, as has largely happened with the

The primary focus of Whitehead's paper is on the force of the metaphor in the rhetorical theorists, and he does not discuss the Athenian orators themselves in detail beyond citing some passages mainly as parallels.[10] The aim of the present chapter, by contrast, is to consider the use of the metaphor specifically within the Athenian orators.[11] The question of translation will be addressed only briefly (§ II), because the underlying methodological issues in this regard have been well explored by Whitehead. Issues of frequency and distribution will receive more attention (§ III), partly because to my knowledge they have not previously been pointed out, and also because there are readings of individual passages which seem worth exploring: in particular, such an approach may contribute to our understanding of some of the rhetorical strategies adopted by Aischines in the notoriously problematic dispute on the Crown.[12] My most significant contribution, however, will be to suggest an explanation (§ IV) of why the metaphor of theft may have been particularly attractive specifically to the orators (so much so, indeed, that they routinely use it in contexts where translators do not):[13] since my proposed explanation is linked to juridical as well as linguistic considerations about the vocabulary of theft-offences at Athens, this final section of the paper will open with a contextualising discussion of Athenian theft law; and as a concluding footnote (in the spirit of recent calls for research publications to articulate how they open up new connections and new possibilities) it will close with some suggestions for future research.[14]

English noun 'stealth': pointed out by Whitehead 1988: 49, but he rightly insists that this process should not be assumed. For the continuing significance of supposedly 'dead' metaphors within a conceptual/ cognitive reading, in that conventional language can nevertheless continue to influence patterns of thought, see Lakoff & Turner 1989: 128–131.

10 Passages [j]-[m] in my appendix are cited by Whitehead 2007: 74–75 as evidence that the metaphor could be used repeatedly in a single speech, plus passages [a], [c], and [e] for specific points.

11 Indeed, the only passage from the rhetorical theorists discussed in the present chapter is the one quoted at n.1 above, which is included precisely because of the specific problems of interpretation.

12 Aischin. 3 *Against Ktesiphon*, discussed at pp. 256–258 below.

13 I should emphasise that I am not trying to argue that the metaphorical use of *kleptō* is unprecedented. Indeed, from Homer onwards we find it either with a direct object in the sense of stealing away somebody's wits (*noos*, at Hom., *Il.*, 14.217 and Hes., *Theog.*, 613), or alternatively with a dative to denote the use of cleverness or similar (*noos* at Hom., *Il.*, 1.132, *boulai* at Pind., *Pyth.*, 3.29, *mythoi* at Pind., *Nem.*, 7.23). My claim is, rather, that the orators use this metaphor with distinctive and interesting dynamics.

14 It is perhaps worth remarking, by way of research context, that the study of metaphors of any type in the Athenian orators is a neglected field. Both Roschatt 1866 and Radfield 1901 are really more collection than analysis, the former with some odd categorisation of topics

II

Assembled for convenience in an appendix to the present chapter are a total of fourteen 'theft' passages (all using *kleptō* or its cognates) gathered from the forensic speeches of the orators. The majority are unquestionably metaphorical: there are a couple which could be classified as literal in that they allege the illicit pre-trial removal of court documents,[15] and which are included partly because they contain no suggestion that such behaviour would ever give rise to an actual prosecution for theft, but also because of a possible continuity with a further passage that deals with the allegedly illicit pre-trial removal of a human informant.[16] About half of the appendix passages relate to behaviour attributed to the opponent during the trial itself, typically his actual or expected strategies of argument,[17] with others referring to actual or hypothetical behaviour during previous court proceedings or the legal preparations for the present trial,[18] and a couple to previous behaviour by the opponent or a third party which may have given rise to litigation (passages [d], [n]). In the majority of the passages, the language of theft is used to describe behaviour attributed the opponent or his close allies.[19] Given the normally pejorative connotations of *kleptō* and its cognates, we may not be surprised that none of these texts from the orators attribute their metaphorical thefts either to the speaker or to those with whom he wishes to be associated, and that all of them regard the action so labelled as being transgressive. But it is worth emphasising the contrast not only with the opening quotation at the start of this chapter (where Anaximenes is being

---

(*kleptō* at p. 26 in a chapter dealing with commerce, industry and everyday life), and the latter focusing specifically on personified abstracts as subjects of verbs. The recent study by Brock 2013 is vastly more sophisticated in its analysis of the uses and implications of the metaphors discussed, but focuses primarily on political images rather than (as in my chapter) on those with a source domain in law and especially legal procedure. See further at n.59 below.

15 Passages [f] = [Dem.] 32.27 and [h] = [Dem.] 46.25 in my appendix.

16 Passage [a] = Antiph. 5.38, discussed in more detail at p. 259 below.

17 Passages [c] = Lys. 26.3, [e] = Dem. 29.5, [i] = Aischin. 2.57, [j] = Aischin. 3.35, [k] = Aischin. 3.99, [l] = Aischin. 3.142, and [m] = Aischin. 3.200.

18 Passages [a] = Antiph. 5.38, [b] = Lys. 20.7, [f] = [Dem.] 32.27, [h] =[Dem.] 46.58, and probably [g] = [Dem.] 45.58: for the context of the final passage in this list, see further pp. 258–259 below.

19 The exceptions are passages [a] = Antiph. 5.38 (a hypothetical generalisation about the behaviour of defendants in other cases), [b] = Lys. 20.7 (again a generalisation, this time about collusion by previous prosecutors), and [f] = [Dem.] 32.27 (the actions of a defendant in a prior case from which the speaker seeks to be dissociated); passage [n] = Hyp. fr. 134 is uncertain because fragmentary.

deliberately frank in a way that a speaker facing a lawcourt could probably not afford to be), but also with the use of theft language in some other contexts, most notably warfare.[20]

The translations offered in this chapter are my own, and (for reasons similar to those given by Whitehead 2007: 71) are deliberately literal especially as regards the terminology of theft: in particular, I have used some form of 'steal' for compound verbs even where this is not the form preferred e.g. by *LSJ*.[21] In general, my translations are intended as a deliberate contrast to a tendency at least in published translations into English for at least some of these passages to use non-theft language such as 'cheat' or 'conceal' or 'deceive':[22] the very fact that translators have so often not retained the theft metaphor may be significant, because it invites speculation as to why such language is so much more common in the Greek text than is comfortable to the modern ear.

As a final comment on translation, it is worth noting that twelve of the fourteen appendix passages use the verb form *kleptō* or its compounds,[23] with only

---

20 It is worth emphasising here the moral neutrality of Anaximenes' discussion (text at n.1 above), which precisely envisages this action as a good trick when played by oneself but a trick to be challenged (cf. his use of κακοποιίαν, 'malpractice') if played by the opponents. For possible comparisons elsewhere, see Whitehead on e.g. Euripides' use of language being described as 'well stolen' (Arist. *Rh.* 3.2.5 = 1404b24–25, at 2007: 73), and on the metaphor of theft in warfare as an 'inescapably ambivalent concept' (Whitehead 1988: 50–52). By contrast, the nearest in the orators to a morally neutral view of theft is Isok. 12.214, which acknowledges but rejects such a view, by pointing out that the Spartans regard it as socially appropriate behaviour for their young men but emphasising that 'other [Greeks] consider common criminals and those who steal as the basest of slaves' (οἱ μὲν γὰρ ἄλλοι τοὺς κακουργοῦντας καὶ κλέπτοντας πονηροτάτους τῶν οἰκετῶν νομίζουσιν).

21 See next but one n.

22 E.g. in Aischines alone, 'cheat' is preferred by Adams 1919 for passages [j] = 3.35, [l] = 3.142, [m] = 3.200; 'conceal' by Carey 2000 for passage [l]; 'deceive' by Carey for passages [j], [m], and by both Adams and Carey for passage [k] = 3.99, with 'deceit' and 'deception' used respectively by Adams and by Carey for passage [i] = 2.57. Of non-English translations, a similar pattern is certainly found in the Budé edition, where Martin 1927–1928 translates as 'duper' (passage [j]), 'abuser' (passages [k], [m]), 'user de phrases trompeuses' (passage [l]), and 'dénaturer un fait capital' (passage [i]). Cf. Whitehead's point about the dangers of translation in the rhetorical theorists, at p. 251 above.

23 Seven uses of the uncompounded verb (passages [a] = Antiph. 5.38, [f] = [Dem.] 32.27, [h] = [Dem.] 46.25, [j] = Aischin. 3.35, [k] = Aischin. 3.99, [l] = Aischin. 3.142, [m] = Aischin. 3.200); three of the compound *ekkleptō* (passages [b] = Lys. 20.7, [d] = Dem. 24.87, [n] = Hyp. fr. 134) and two of the compound *diakleptō* (passages [c] = Lys. 26.3, [e] = Dem. 29.5). We would expect the first of these compounds to carry the sense 'steal away'; and I have used 'persistently steal' for the second compound (*LSJ s.v. diakleptō* I offers '*steal at different times*').

one example of the agent noun *kleptēs* ('thief', passage [i] = Aischin. 2.57) and one instance of the action noun *klopē* ('theft', passage [g] = [Dem.] 45.58). To give some sense of the horizon, a *TLG* search of the orators reveals 48 instances of the simple verb *kleptō*, with a variety of compound verbs occurring on a further 8 occasions, as compared with 35 uses of the agent noun *kleptēs* and 24 of the action noun *klopē* (albeit the latter includes 4 examples citing titles of lost speeches). What this implies is that whereas metaphorical use of the nouns is relatively rare, for the verb it is significantly more common (more than 1:7 for the simple verb), and indeed for compound forms of the verb it predominates (5:8).[24]

III

In terms of distribution, we may note at the outset that the frequency with which the language of theft is used (i.e. the totality of *kleptō* plus compounds plus *kleptēs* plus *klopē* as above, including non-metaphorical as well as metaphorical usages) varies considerably between speeches. Particularly notable is the prevalence of such language in several public speeches which deal with political cases: of the total of 110 examples summarised in the preceding paragraph, no fewer than 25 are found in a single albeit fairly long such speech (Dem. 24 *Against Timokrates*), with the next most frequent being 7 uses each in Dem. 22 *Against Androtion* and in Aischin. 3 *Against Ktesiphon*. The frequency in these two Demosthenic speeches is not in itself surprising, given that Dem. 24 in particular (and perhaps by extension Dem. 22, a slightly earlier speech, but dealing with events at the same time and involving one of the same opponents) focuses on alleged attempts by Androtion and his fellow-envoys to retain personal ownership of war-booty from a trireme which had been captured during their diplomatic mission, and which Demosthenes is arguing should be regarded as public property.[25] Against this background, it is convenient to present the opponents as serial misappropriators of state property, so it is perhaps unsurprising that there is a good deal of language here

24 The only literal usages of compound verb forms in the orators are Dem. 27.12 (*diakleptō*), Isa. 11.44 (*parakleptō*), and Antiph. 6.35 (*synkleptō*).

25 There are indeed significant overlapping passages in the two speeches, which include 4 appearances of this terminology: πολλὰ τῶν ὑμετέρων κέκλοφεν at Dem. 22.65 = Dem. 24.161, τὰ παρὰ τῶν συμμάχων κλέπτοντες at Dem. 22.65 = Dem. 24.172, ἱεροσυλίᾳ καὶ ἀσεβείᾳ καὶ κλοπῇ ... ἔνοχος at Dem. 22.69 = Dem. 24.177, and κλέπτης ὢν ἐφωρῶ at Dem. 22.71 = Dem. 24.179.

about the opponents being those who steal (i.e. embezzle) public funds. But it should be noted that the pattern of metaphorical usage does not necessarily correlate with the literal: only one passage from either of these Demosthenic speeches appears in the appendix (passage [d] = Dem. 24.87).

The pattern of theft language in Aischin. 3, by contrast, shows a much higher prevalence of metaphorical usage: of the 7 occasions where such language appears in the speech, no fewer than 4 appear in my appendix as being metaphorical (passages [j]-[m]): it is indeed the only speech in the corpus with more than one appendix passage. To understand what is going on here, it may be worth setting this speech in a wider context, by contrasting the case in which was delivered, viz. the Crown trial of 330 BC (in which Aischin. 3 prosecuted Ktesiphon for proposing an honorific decree for Demosthenes, and Dem. 18 was the main speech in Ktesiphon's defence) with the earlier Embassy trial of 343 BC (in which Dem. 19 prosecuted Aischin. 2 for treason allegedly committed during their term as fellow-ambassadors to Philip). In both these trials, the language of theft is significantly more frequent in the prosecution than in the defence speech (from the first trial there are 3 examples in Dem. 19 *versus* 1 in Aischin. 2; from the second, 7 examples in Aischin. 3 and none in Dem. 18). We may not be surprised to find Demosthenes using such language in the first case given his allegations that supporters of Philip have been motivated by bribes, though we should perhaps note that Aischines' sole use in his Embassy defence is not an attempt directly to deny such allegations but a suggestion (passage [i] = Aischin. 2.57) that Demosthenes' failure properly to consult public records constitutes a metaphorical theft (as if the documentary evidence is somehow being stolen from the public consciousness?). In general, it seems that such language is something that defendants may find it better to pass over in silence rather than risk responding to.[26]

In the Crown case, by contrast, I have noted elsewhere with reference to other patterns of linguistic usage that Aischines' strategy seems to have been 'an inversion of the narrative from the previous trial, i.e. claiming that there was corruption but that it is Demosthenes who had acted corruptly'.[27] With that in mind, we may note that the first two (both non-metaphorical) uses of theft in Aischin. 3 occur in the same section of text within sixty words of each other, as generalising statements set in the context of a purported explanation of why the law had been changed to make illegal the proposing of honours to

26 Only three passages in the appendix are from defence speeches, passages [a] = Antiph. 5.38 and [b] = Lys. 20.7 being the others alongside passage [i].

27 Todd 2009: 172, arguing on the basis of frequency-tables in these four speeches for terms like *dōrodokeō* (take bribes), *exapataō* (deceive) and *prodidōmi* (betray).

those who, like Demosthenes, had not yet undergone their *euthynai* (judicial scrutiny of accounts on demitting public office): Aischines claims that 'very many of those liable to *euthynai* were [previously] escaping conviction in the law-courts despite being proved red-handed to be thieves of public funds', and he goes on to suggest that the reason for these improper acquittals was the jurors' embarrassment at seeing the same person both honoured at the festivals and then 'coming out of the lawcourt a short while later convicted of theft on the basis of his *euthynai*'.[28] Only the last of the three non-metaphorical usages is directed explicitly at Demosthenes, with the allegation that he had been 'stealing the military fund'.[29] By that stage, we have already had three of the four metaphorical uses (passages [j]-[l] = §§ 35, 99, 142), with only one to follow (passage [m] = § 200); it is worth noting that the first and fourth of these are alleged formally against Demosthenes' supporters (generic supporters presumably including Ktesiphon at passage [j], Ktesiphon specifically at passage [m]), with only the second and third of them being directed explicitly against Demosthenes (passages [k]-[l]).

One way of reading the unusual frequency of metaphorical uses of 'theft' in Aischin. 3 might be to link this to a recent proposal to read the speech as part of a Platonic culture war, noting in particular the suggestion that one of the things attacked in Dem. 18 is Aischines' use of 'methods for producing images, symbols, models, and allegories, that Plato elaborates in the *Republic*' (among them perhaps the use of metaphors).[30] But the exceptional pattern of distribution of metaphorical vis-à-vis non-metaphorical uses as analysed in the previous paragraph, and in particular the delay in applying a non-metaphorical use specifically to Demosthenes himself, may suggest another explanation: a tentativeness on Aischines' part in putting forward a view which he evidently expects at least some of the audience to regard as counter-intuitive, viz. the allegation of personal financial corruption. Rather than make the charge immediately and directly, it is I suggest safer for him to begin with general comments about theft by public officials and the difficulty of dealing with it, and then to use the language of theft repeatedly but in metaphorical ways which link it with the argumentative strategies adopted initially by Demosthenes' supporters and

28 Aischin. 3.10: πολλοὶ γὰρ πάνυ τῶν ὑπευθύνων, ἐπ' αὐτοφώρῳ **κλέπται** τῶν δημοσίων χρημάτων ὄντες ἐξελεγχόμενοι, διεφύγγανον ἐκ τῶν δικαστηρίων … ὁ δὲ αὐτὸς ἀνὴρ μικρὸν ἐπισχὼν ἔξεισιν ἐκ τοῦ δικαστηρίου **κλοπῆς** ἕνεκα τὰς εὐθύνας ὠφληκώς.

29 Aischin. 3.146: τὰ στρατιωτικὰ χρήματα **κλέπτων**. It is not in context clear whether the allegation is one of embezzlement or of wasted expenditure, but Peter Liddel suggests to me a possible link with Philochorus' statement that Demosthenes had in 339/8 proposed to transfer money to the stratiotic fund (*FGrH* 328 F 56a = Dion. Hal. *To Ammaeus*, 1.11.741f.).

30 Allen 2013: 96–106, quotation at p. 105.

then with Demosthenes himself, before presenting the charge in a more personal and direct form but one which even then is ambiguous in its reference.[31]

In terms of the distribution of types of metaphor, it has already been noted (at p. 253 above) that about half the passages in the appendix relate to the opponent's behaviour in court and typically his argumentative strategies, with another significant group referring either to previous court proceedings or to the legal preparations for the present trial. Many of those in the first group have been analysed in the immediately preceding discussion of Aischin. 3, but it may be worth a few words here on the second group. Several of these passages (as has again been noted) relate to the illicit removal of documents. Passage [f] = [Dem.] 32.27 refers to the actions of a third party whom the speaker is trying to portray as irrelevant to the present case (presumably because the opponent is trying to link the speaker to this misappropriation of documents), and is correspondingly vague about the nature of the documents in question, but we are left to infer that they have something to do with the case. More explicit and more direct is passage [h] = [Dem.] 46.25, which claims that what Stephanos has stolen was 'witness testimonies that are truthful' (i.e. in contrast to his own alleged readiness to give false testimony). Most interesting, however, is the peculiarly obscure passage [g] = [Dem.] 45.58, precisely because this is set within a context which appears to support the claim in passage [h] about Stephanos and documents. The background to passage [g] is a narrative developed very gradually at [Dem.] 45.57–59: we are told first that a witness testimony was missing but without saying how or by whom;[32] then the responsibility for this is provisionally attributed but initially in the wrong direction and using language that suggests impropriety but not specifically theft;[33] this is immediately modified by the claim that information subsequently available has redirected responsibility directly to Stephanos, using language that is suggestive of theft but indirectly;[34] then comes a challenge which again hints indi-

31 See last-but-one n.

32 [Dem.] 45.57: ταύτην (*sc.* μαρτυρίαν) οὐχ ηὗρον ἐνοῦσαν ἐν τῷ ἐχίνῳ. 'I did not find it in the *echinos*' (jar used for the documents presented by the litigants at arbitration to be stored under seal by the court).

33 [Dem.] 45.58: τὴν ἀρχὴν ἠδικηκέναι με καὶ τὸν ἐχῖνον κεκινηκέναι '(I imagined) that the magistrate had wronged me and had meddled with (lit. 'moved') the *echinos*'.

34 [Dem.] 45.58: νῦν δ' ἀφ' ὧν ὕστερον πέπυσμαι, πρὸς αὐτῷ τῷ διαιτητῇ Στέφανον τουτονὶ αὐτὴν ὑφῃρημένον εὑρίσκω, πρὸς μαρτυρίαν τιν' ἵν' ἐξορκώσαιμι, ἀναστάντος ἐμοῦ 'but now, from what I have learned subsequently, I find that Stephanos here had filched it away (*hyphaireomai*, not *kleptō*) in the very presence of the arbitrator, when I got up to put (another witness) on oath for his testimony'.

rectly at theft;[35] it is only after this that the language of theft is explicitly used, not with direct reference to the disappearance of the witness testimony but in an obscure phrase about the type of behaviour one might expect from the sort of man who is happy who be described as 'thief (*kleptēs*) of the misfortunes of others' (passage [g]). Scholars continue to debate the meaning of this phrase;[36] it is however worth noting the indirectness with which it is introduced, and the failure to use *kleptō* terminology (in contrast to passage [h]) to describe the alleged abstraction of the document.

While it is easy to envisage a legal document as the object of theft,[37] it is from our perspective more of an imaginative leap to think in these terms about a person who might give evidence. It may in this context be significant that the hypothetical informants in passage [a] = Antiph. 5.38 are envisaged as presenting the type of denunciation (*mēnysis*) that is normally brought by slaves, and that the real informant whose evidence Antiphon is seeking to undermine here is evidently a slave also. There is some indication that the prosecution had purchased him for the purpose of obtaining evidence under torture—i.e. presumably purchased from a third party—before unilaterally putting him to death (Antiph. 5.47, cf. 5.31–37); and the use of the theft metaphor here may therefore represent an attempt to underline the alleged impropriety in their having acquired ownership for this purpose, by implicitly associating their action with the behaviour of kidnappers who intend to kill their victim.[38] But once the idea of stealing a person is accepted, it is a fairly easy step to passage [b] = Lys. 20.7, in which allegedly guilty citizen defendants are envisaged as being somehow the rightful property of the court, from which collusive prosecutors have therefore stolen their acquittal.

---

35 [Dem.] 45.59: πρόκλησιν ὑμῖν ἀναγνώσεται, ἐξ ἧς τούτους τ' ἐπιορκοῦντας ἐπ' αὐτοφώρῳ λήψεσθε, καὶ τοῦτον ὁμοίως ὑφῃρημένον τὴν μαρτυρίαν εἴσεσθε '(the clerk) will read to you a challenge, on the basis of which you will catch these men in the act (*sc.* of perjuring themselves), and you will similarly know that this man did filch the testimony'. For *hyphaireomai*, see previous n.; the phrase *ep' autophōrō* ('in the act') is associated with the procedure of *apagōgē*, which is irrelevant to perjury but available against *kakourgoi* (common criminals), including certain categories of thief.

36 See most recently Scafuro 2011: 256 n. 116.

37 Though there is (as noted at p. 253 above) no suggestion that this would ever form the subject of legal proceedings for theft.

38 By contrast, the language of theft is not used (or at least, not used with reference to the allegation of having caused the alleged slave to disappear) in either of the speeches in which litigants dispute whether a potential source of evidence is a slave and hence available for torture or an ex-slave and hence exempt from torture, viz. Isok. 17 and Dem. 29 (passage [e] = Dem. 29.5 relates not to the stealing of a person but to stealing the truth); this may be because there is no suggestion of improper acquisition of ownership.

IV

Theft in modern jurisdictions tends to be a juridically complex concept. In English law the reasons for this are partly contingent and historical, in that the absence until 1968 of a Theft Act[39] led to a system in which different forms of offence were developed over time to criminalise particular forms of perceived misbehaviour. But there are also conceptual distinctions: for instance, English law has traditionally distinguished larceny (taking with intent permanently to deprive) from burglary (characterised by unlawful entry to property) from robbery (characterised by force or the threat of force) from offences involving deceit (e.g. fraud, esp. by misrepresentation) or breach of trust (e.g. embezzlement).

Athenian law had a variety of terminology to deal with offences that we might classify as theft, but the extent to which these represented conceptual distinctions is less clear. One of the problems here, as has often been noted, is that we have no surviving speeches dealing directly with cases of theft, as opposed to those in which allegations are made e.g. that the opponent has stolen public money. But it is notable that there seems to be no technical vocabulary to distinguish what we would classify as fraud or embezzlement. Some attempt has been made by scholars to establish a systematic distinction between *kleptō* meaning 'take away' and *apostereō* meaning 'withhold, misappropriate',[40] but it is not clear that such distinctions are in practice consistently maintained (Dem. 27.12 for instance uses both *diakleptō* and *apostereō* to denote the actions of the guardians left by his father, who are presumably to be regarded as having taken possession legitimately of what was willingly granted to them),[41] and it is not clear that there is a separate legal action which would e.g. cover all cases of misappropriation.[42]

39 Ormerod and Williams 2007: 1.

40 E.g. Cohen 1983: 13–14.

41 For the frequent use of *apostereō* in inheritance speeches to accuse an opponent of 'stealing' property that the speaker claims should have been his, see Griffith-Williams 2013: 107–108, with refs.

42 Cohen 1983: 14 n. 13 cites Wolff 1957: 49 n. 57 = 1968: 508–509 n. 57 for the proposition that the withholding of money would for Athenian law be a matter of *blabē* rather than *klopē*, but Wolff's discussion here is very brief and does not offer examples. There is certainly no hint in our sources of a *dikē aposterēseōs* (i.e. that would putatively cover all cases of misappropriation), though there is some evidence for separate actions being available against maladministration by guardians (the *dikē epitropēs*, as well as the *graphē/eisangelia kakōseōs*) and possibly an action for return of moneys deposited (*dikē parakatathēkēs*).

As another form of possible classification, we hear of a range of terms for those who appear to have been identified collectively as *kakourgoi* (common criminals) and as such liable to being punished potentially without trial by means of *apagōgē* (summary arrest). The conventional lists of such offenders include not just *kleptai* (thieves) themselves but various more specific descriptions of thieves, including but not restricted to *ballantiotomoi* ('cut-purses'), *lōpodytai* ('clothes stealers'), and *toichōrychoi* ('those who burrow through walls'), as well as certain other categories of offenders who are clearly not thieves.[43] But it is not clear whether what is going on here is a conceptual classification, or simply a list of those who might typically be caught in aggravating circumstances, since the underlying requirement for *apagōgē* to take place was that the offender had to be caught *ep' autophōrō* ('in the act', though there is some dispute as to precisely what this meant).[44]

One striking feature of the Athenian law of theft which is generally accepted by scholars, however, is that it seems to have been capable of prosecution through a variety of legal procedures. This at any rate is the implication of a notorious passage in which Demosthenes purports to explain Solon's plan of granting multiple ways in which a victim could seek legal redress, depending on his self-confidence and financial resources.

> πῶς οὖν ἔσται τοῦτο; ἐὰν πολλὰς ὁδοὺς δῷ διὰ τῶν νόμων ἐπὶ τοὺς ἠδικηκότας οἷον τῆς κλοπῆς. ἔρρωσαι καὶ σαυτῷ πιστεύεις· ἄπαγε· ἐν χιλίαις δ' ὁ κίνδυνος. ἀσθενέστερος εἶ· τοῖς ἄρχουσιν ἐφηγοῦ· τοῦτο ποιήσουσιν ἐκεῖνοι. φοβεῖ καὶ τοῦτο· γράφου. καταμέμφει σεαυτὸν καὶ πένης ὢν οὐκ ἂν ἔχοις χιλίας ἐκτεῖσαι· δικάζου κλοπῆς πρὸς διαιτητὴν καὶ οὐ κινδυνεύσεις.

> … How will this come into being? If he grants many routes through the laws against wrongdoers, as in the case of theft (*klopē*). You are strong and have confidence in yourself? Use *apagōgē* (summary arrest), but the risk is 1,000 *drachmas*. You are relatively weak? Bring an *ephēgēsis* to the *archontes*, and they will do this themselves. You are afraid even of this? Bring a *graphē*. You distrust yourself, and as a poor man you

43 References and discussion in Hansen 1976: 36–53.

44 I am not convinced by the argument of Cohen 1983: 52–61, cf. 48–49 that 'flagrance' should be regarded as an objective criterion for aggravated theft, for the reason proposed by MacDowell 1984: 230, viz. that this is better regarded as a quality of the evidence than as a quality of the offence.

> would not be able to pay 1,000 *drachmas*? Bring a *dikē klopēs* before the arbitrator and you run no risk.[45]
>
> DEM. 22.26–27

On the face of it, this passage would seem to imply the existence of both a *dikē* and a *graphē klopēs*,[46] and it is hard to escape the inference that both these forms of action specifically for *klopē* were available in at least some circumstances, though Demosthenes' failure to mention the *ep' autophōrō* requirement for *apagōgē* should make us pause before over-interpreting his silence and e.g. inferring that the *graphē klopēs* was available for use against every type of theft.

Klopē was unusual and possibly unique in being the subject both of a *graphē* and of a *dikē* at Athens, whereas the law normally permitted either one or other of these types of procedure against a named offence, but not both. One of the differences between *dikē* and *graphē* tends to be that the latter is available for offences against the community or cases where there is no identifiable individual victim,[47] and on this basis a long-standing and plausible suggestion has been that the *graphē klopēs* might have been available primarily in the most obvious category of such circumstances, viz. the theft of public or sacred funds (which would not necessarily rule out the possibility that the *graphē* procedure might also have been available in certain aggravated categories of private theft, though it would not require it).[48] But if this is the case, then it would have interesting implications for our present enquiry.

One of the features of *kleptō* as a metaphor, I suggest, may be that it is capable of conjuring up images both of a private offence against the speaker (a relatively minor matter, in Demosthenes' terms, cf. n. 45 above), but also and

45 For the debate over the passage, see Carey 2004, with reference at p. 112 n. 2 to previous discussions e.g. by Osborne and by Harris. See also Giannadaki p. 200 (this vol.).

46 For the distinction between *dikē* (private prosecution, i.e. broadly speaking one that could be brought only by the aggrieved party) and *graphē* (public prosecution, i.e. that could be brought by anybody), with a list of the best-attested procedures under each such heading, see Todd 1993: 102–105 and 105–109. For hybridities between public and private procedures, see Carey in this volume.

47 For discussion of this and other possible differences, see Todd 1993: 109–112.

48 Lipsius (1905–1915.ii: 438, cf. 399–401) argues for the *graphē klopēs* being available in cases of aggravated private theft (1905–1915.ii: 438), as well as for theft of public or sacred property (1905–1915.ii: 399–401), while Harrison (1968–1971.ii: 15 with n. 8) appears to believe in a *graphē klopēs* certainly for theft of public property; by contrast, Cohen rejects a *graphē* for theft of private property (1983: 47–48), tentatively accepts a *graphē* for theft of sacred property (1983: 100–101), and regards a *graphē* for theft of public property as unproven (1983: 51).

much more seriously of the theft of public or sacred funds as an offence against the community or its gods. The advantage of the procedural ambiguity, in other words, is that the jury can be encouraged to think of both forms of procedure without the orator having to specify which one he has in mind,[49] not least because of a secondary feature of the language of theft, which is that although this offence requires there to be a victim (whether individual or collective), nevertheless the victim does not necessarily have to be named. There is a contrast here with the language of deceit, for which orators repeatedly use the verb *exapataō*,[50] in ways that have the potential to conjure up the concept of *apatē tou dēmou* (deceiving the people), which itself seems to have been one of the offences covered by the procedure of *eisangelia* (impeachment) and punishable by death.[51] It is not the case that *exapataō* is absent from the Athenian orators: indeed, a TLG search reveals its presence as a verb on 259 occasions, i.e. much more commonly than *kleptō*, let alone than *kleptō* used metaphorically.[52] But *exapataō* expects to be used with a person as the direct object, and the object in a law-court speech will naturally be the jurors as representatives of the Athenian *polis*: indeed, out of 170 uses of the active verb in the orators, no fewer than 48 in the law-court speeches have *hymas* (ὑμᾶς: 'you', accus. pl.) not simply as the object but tied into a single phrase.[53] In other words, for an Athenian orator to use the language of 'deceive' risks appearing to commit oneself to the proposition that the opponent is guilty of 'deceiving the *dēmos*',[54] and as such is a traitor worthy of death:[55] in at least some cases, this may be asking a lot for a not necessarily sympathetic audience to swallow.

---

49 Hence perhaps the fact that the appendix passages include a balance of private litigation (e.g. cases of false witness arising out of inheritance in Dem. 29 [passage e] and [Dem.] 45–46 [passages g-h], as well as a maritime contract *paragraphē* in [Dem.] 32 [passage e]), as well as a slightly greater number of public cases.

50 For a detailed study, see Kremmydas 2013.

51 ἐάν τις τὸν δῆμον ὑποσχόμενος ἐξαπατήσῃ (if anybody makes promises and deceives the *dēmos*) apparently in the wording of the *eisangelia* law: [Dem.] 49.67. Punishment of death for deceiving the *dēmos*: Dem. 20.100, 135.

52 For the comparable TLG figures for *klepto* and cognates, see p. 255 above.

53 i.e. either as neighbouring words or else separated simply by a particle or by a verb on which the infinitive form of ἐξαπατάω depends. In terms of word order, there is a broadly even distribution of ἐξαπατάω + ὑμᾶς (found on 27 occasions) vis-à-vis ὑμᾶς + ἐξαπατάω (found on 21), though Demosthenes has perhaps a slight preference for the former and Lysias for the latter. The figures in this footnote relate only to law-court oratory: there are a further 8 examples in non-forensic speeches.

54 The fact that English does not have these connotations may help explain cases of *kleptō* where translators have found it most natural to render the theft metaphor with the language of deceit: cf. n. 22 above.

55 It is notable that *apatē* and its cognates are found only rarely in proximity to language

By contrast, it is part of the linguistic logic of *kleptō* that it can be used absolutely ('he is a thief', i.e. without a direct object); and that even where a grammatical object is expressed, this will be the thing stolen, not the victim.[56] In this context, it is notable how many of the appendix passages do not specify the victim of the metaphorical theft, even in cases where it is natural for translators to do so.[57] This applies even in cases where there is no grammatical necessity. In three of the four appendix examples from Aischin. 3, for instance, the grammatical object is *akroasis* ('steal the hearing', or as we might say, 'steal the ears': passages [j], [k], [m]). But whereas translators have tended (as is natural in English) to render this by specifying whose hearing,[58] the Greek does so on only one occasion (passage [j]), in a passage aimed formally not at Demosthenes but at his unnamed supporters and with its reference formally limited to the interpretation of a point of law underlying the current trial, on which most scholars think that Aischines is on stronger ground than would be implied by the outcome (a humiliating failure to obtain 20% of the votes).

Metaphorical theft in the Athenian orators therefore becomes not so much a victimless but a victim-ambivalent crime. The point of not specifying the victim, particularly in a legal system where *klopē* may be thought of both as a public and as a private offence, could be precisely that it permits the litigant to allege something that on one level is a fairly minor transgression ('my opponent has put me at a disadvantage by misappropriating something on which I had a right to rely'), but which on another level can hint at something much

---

about false witness (for which the penalty was simply a fine), despite the fact that both allegations are separately very frequent: the exceptions tend to be cases where there either is or has been high-profile public litigation (as in Dem. 47, with seven examples); apart from this, the only other examples of proximity are at Isa. 4.17 (hypothetical, rather than referring to the present case), Isa. 5.8 (unusual in naming a third party as having concocted the allegedly false evidence), and [Dem.] 46.25 (evidently seeking to up the stakes with the claim that the opponent's mis-use of legal procedure could give rise to a *graphē*). See however Kremmydas (2013: 84–85) for additional cases of *apatē* vocabulary in *dikai pseudomartyriōn* but without proximity of language.

56 Contrast *apostereō*, which typically takes an accusative of the victim and a genitive of the object, i.e. deprive a person of a thing (*LSJ s.v.* I.2).

57 We may note again here the absence of a separate category of fraud (p. 260 above), which allows the language of theft a broader range and offers a bridge to the use of theft language to describe various kinds of cheating.

58 Passage [j] = Aischin. 3.35: κλέπτοντες τὴν ἀκρόασιν ὑμῶν, lit. '(supporters) stealing your hearing', cf. Adams 1919 (Loeb) 'cheating your ears' and Carey 2000 (Texas) 'to deceive your ears'. Passage [k] = Aischin. 3.99: κλέπτων τὴν ἀκρόασιν, lit. '(Demosthenes) stealing the hearing', cf. Adams 1919 'deceiving your ears' and Carey 2000 'deceiving his hearers'. Passage [m] = Aischin. 3.200: κλέπτεις τὴν ἀκρόασιν, lit. 'you (Ktesiphon) are stealing the hearing', cf. Adams 1919 'you cheat the ears of the jury', Carey 2000 'you are deceiving your audience'.

more serious ('he has stolen public property, i.e. from the jury or from the court system or from the polis at large').[59] It is, I suggest, the flexible and ambiguous nature of the offence which explains the utility of the metaphor.[60]

Appendix: List of Metaphorical 'Theft' Passages in Athenian Orators

For reasons noted at p. 254 above I have translated fairly literally, so as to permit retention of the vocabulary of 'steal' or 'theft'.

[a] Antiph. 5.38: καὶ οἱ μὲν ἄλλοι καθ' ὧν ἂν μηνύῃ τις, οὗτοι **κλέπτουσι** τοὺς μηνύοντας κᾆτ' ἀφανίζουσιν· αὐτοὶ δὲ οὗτοι οἱ ἀπάγοντες καὶ ζητοῦντες τὸ πρᾶγμα τὸν κατ' ἐμοῦ μηνυτὴν ἠφάνισαν. (Seeking to undermine the evidence of a slave who has evidently been tortured and put to death by the prosecution unilaterally, rather than on the basis of agreement to torture a slave belonging to one or other litigant.) 'And the others, those against whom somebody makes a denunciation, [are the ones who] **steal** those making the denunciation and subsequently eliminate them; but these men have themselves carried out the arrest, investigated the case, and eliminated the one who was an informer against me.'

[b] Lys. 20.7: καὶ τοὺς μὲν ἀδικοῦντας οἱ κατήγοροι **ἐκκλέπτουσιν**, ἀργύριον λαμβάνοντες. (Part of a catalogue of events in which the wrong people have allegedly been blamed for the first oligarchy.) 'And the prosecutors are **stealing away** those who are guilty, in return for bribes'.

[c] Lys. 26.3: καὶ νυνὶ αὐτὸν ἀκούω μὲν ὑπὲρ τῶν αὐτοῦ κατηγορουμένων διὰ βραχέων ἀπολογήσεσθαι, ἐπισύροντα τὰ πράγματα καὶ **διακλέπτοντα** τῇ ἀπολογίᾳ

59 The argument of this chapter has been the need to take seriously the legal metaphors in legal sources (following the lead of Whitehead 2007), with attention to their procedural as well as linguistic implications. As noted at n. 14 above, metaphors in the Athenian orators have received surprisingly little critical attention, though several of those collected if not discussed by Roschatt 1886 and Radfield 1901 would seem to merit further discussion: e.g. perhaps the metaphorical uses of *diadikasia* (Roschatt 1886: 1), *martyreō* (Radfield 1901:41–42), or *parakatathēkē* (Roschatt 1886: 22–23, cf. brief discussion in Brock 2013: 27–28). Other possibilities suggested to me by Chris Carey include the use of *epiklēros* at Lys. 24.14, and the notions of violence associated with the allegation of illegal intrusion into the citizen body (e.g. *biazomai* at [Dem.] 59.28).

60 My thanks are due to the editors of this volume for the invitation to contribute, and for extensive feedback; to David Whitehead for discussion of Anaximenes; to Lene Rubinstein for hospitality, and for a conference-paper which drew my attention to appendix passage [j], albeit using it for a different purpose; and to David Langslow, Peter Liddel, and Robin Osborne, for additional advice on a range of issues including presentation and structure.

τὴν κατηγορίαν. 'And now I hear that he will defend himself only briefly over the things charged against him, slurring over the facts and **persistently stealing** the charge in his defence.'

[d] Dem. 24.87: ἀλλὰ τὸν καιρὸν ἐν ᾧ τὸν ἠδικηκότ' ἐνῆν παρόντα λαβεῖν **ἐκκλέψας**, τοὔνομα μὲν τῆς τιμωρίας ἔλιπεν τοῖς ἀδικουμένοις ὑμῖν. (Attacking a proposal by Timokrates which extended the period for repayment of debts to the state). 'But after **stealing away**[61] [from you] the time in which it was possible to catch the wrongdoer when present, he left for you, the people who were being wronged, [merely] the name of vengeance.'

[e] Dem. 29.5: **διακλέπτοντα** τοῖς ἑαυτοῦ λόγοις τὴν ἀλήθειαν τῶν πεπραγμένων. (Attacking Aphobos' claims about the status of Demosthenes' father's former slave Milyas.) '**persistently stealing** the truth of the events with his own words.'

[f] [Dem.] 32.27: ἢ εἰ γράμματ' **ἔκλεπτεν**; εἰ ὑπανέῳγεν; (A list of allegations made by Zenothemis against Protos but irrelevant to the present case.) 'Or if he **stole** documents? Or if he secretly opened them?'

[g] [Dem.] 45.58: καίτοι ὅστις, ὦ ἄνδρες Ἀθηναῖοι, κακῶν ἀλλοτρίων **κλέπτης** ὑπέμεινεν ὀνομασθῆναι, τί ἂν ἡγεῖσθε ποιῆσαι τοῦτον ὑπὲρ αὑτοῦ; (A particularly obscure passage, cf. at pp. 258–259 above.) 'And yet, men of Athens, [in the case of] a man who can stand to be described as **thief** of the misfortunes of others, what do you imagine such a man would do on his own behalf?'

[h] [Dem.] 46.25: τὰ ψευδῆ μὲν αὐτὸς μαρτυρῶν ἑτοίμως, **κλέπτων** δὲ τὰς ἀληθεῖς μαρτυρίας, ἐξαπατῶν δὲ τοὺς δικαστάς (Part of a sequence of alleged procedural abuses by Stephanos.) 'being eager yourself to testify falsely, stealing witness testimonies that are truthful, deceiving the jurors'

[i] Aischin. 2.57: σκέψασθε δὴ πράγματος μεγάλου **κλοπὴν** καὶ δεινὴν ἀναισχυντίαν ἀνθρώπου. (A comment on Demosthenes' alleged failure properly to consult public records.) 'You see the fellow's **theft** in a matter of great importance, and his appalling shamelessness.'

[j] Aischin. 3.35: οἴσουσι δὲ εἰς τὴν ἀπολογίαν τὸν Διονυσιακὸν νόμον, καὶ χρήσονται τοῦ νόμου μέρει τινὶ **κλέπτοντες** τὴν ἀκρόασιν ὑμῶν. '(Demosthenes' supporters) will produce the Dionysiac law for the defence, and will use [only] a particular part of that law, **stealing** your hearing.'

[k] Aischin. 3.99: καὶ ὧν τὰ σώματα οὐχ ἑώρακε, τούτων τὰ ὀνόματα λέγει, **κλέπτων** τὴν ἀκρόασιν καὶ μιμούμενος τοὺς τἀληθῆ λέγοντας. (Unlike other braggarts, who make vague promises, Demosthenes has the audacity to be

61 For the translation, see n.23 above.

specific.) 'And he gives the names of people that he has not personally seen, **stealing** the hearing and mimicking those who speak the truth.'

[l] Aischin. 3.142: γράψας ἐν τῷ ψηφίσματι, ἐάν τις ἀφιστῆται πόλις ἀπὸ Θηβαίων, βοηθεῖν Ἀθηναίους Βοιωτοῖς τοῖς ἐν Θήβαις, τοῖς ὀνόμασι **κλέπτων** καὶ μεταφέρων τὰ πράγματα, ὥσπερ εἴωθεν. (Demosthenes' allegedly misleading decree for the Thebans.) 'Having written in his decree that "if any city secedes from Thebes, the Athenians are to assist the Boiotians in Thebes"—**stealing** with words and distorting the situation, as he is accustomed to do.'

[m] Aischin. 3.200: ὅταν δ' ὑπερπηδήσας τὴν δικαίαν ἀπολογίαν παρακαλῇς κακοῦργον ἄνθρωπον καὶ τεχνίτην λόγων, **κλέπτεις** τὴν ἀκρόασιν, βλάπτεις τὴν πόλιν, καταλύεις τὴν δημοκρατίαν. (A challenge to Ktesiphon to do without the support of a speech from Demosthenes.) 'But when you jump over the defence based on justice and call to your aid a man who is a common criminal and a word-smith, you are **stealing** the hearing, damaging the *polis*, and destroying the democracy.'

[n] Hyp. fr. 134 (Harp. s.v. συμμορία, etc.): ἐπειδὴ δὲ ταῦτα κατιδὼν Δημοσθένης νόμον ἔθηκε τοὺς τ' τριηραρχεῖν καὶ βαρεῖαι γεγόνασιν αἱ τριηραρχίαι, νῦν ὁ Φορμίων αὑτὸν **ἐκκλέπτει**. 'But when Demosthenes saw this, and brought in a law that the Three Hundred should serve as trierarchs, and trierarchies became a burden, Phormion now **steals** himself away.'

Bibliography

Adams, C.D. (1919) *The Speeches of Aeschines, with an English Translation* (Loeb Classical Library), Cambridge, MA/London.

Allen, D.S. (2013) *Why Plato Wrote*, Chichester.

Brock, R. (2013) *Greek Political Imagery from Homer to Aristotle*, London.

Carey, C., (2000) *Aeschines*, Austin.

Carey, C. (2004) 'Offence and Procedure in Athenian Law', in Harris, E.M. and Rubinstein, L., eds (2004) *The Law and the Courts in Ancient Greece*, London, 111–136.

Chiron, P. (2002) *Pseudo-Aristote, Rhétorique à Alexandre*, Paris.

Cohen, D. (1983) *Theft in Athenian Law*, Munich.

Cope, E.M. (1867) *An Introduction to Aristotle's* Rhetoric, *with Analysis, Notes and Appendices*, London and Cambridge.

Fuhrmann, M. (1966) *Anaximenis Ars Rhetorica, quae vulgo fertur Aristotelis ad Alexandrum*, Leipzig.

Griffith-Williams, B. (2013) *A Commentary on Selected Speeches of Isaios*, Leiden.

Hansen, M.H. (1976) *Apagoge, Endeixis and Ephegesis against kakourgoi, atimoi, and pheugontes: A Study in the Athenian Administration of Justice in the Fourth Century* BC, Odense.

Harrison, A.R.W. (1968–1971) *The Law of Athens*, 2 vols, Oxford.

Kremmydas, C. (2013) 'The Discourse of Deception and Characterization in Attic Oratory', GRBS 53, 51–89.

Lakoff, G. and Turner, M. (1989) *More than Cool Reason: A Field Guide to Poetic Metaphor*, Chicago.

Lipsius, J.H. (1905–1915) *Das attische Recht und Rechtsverfahren*, 3 vols, Leipzig.

MacDowell, D.M. (1984) Review of Cohen (1983), CR 34, 229–231.

Martin, V. (1927–1928) *Discours: Eschine*, Paris.

Mirhady, D.C. (2011), in R. Mayhew & D.C. Mirhady, *Aristotle*, vol. 16: *Problems, books xxii–xxxviii*, ed. and trans. R. Mayhew, and *Rhetorica ad Alexandrum*, ed. and trans. D.C. Mirhady, Cambridge, Ma.

Ormerod, D. & Williams, D.H. (2007) *Smith's Law of Theft*, 9th ed., Oxford.

Rackham, H. (1937), in W.S. Hett & H. Rackham, *Aristotle, vol. 16: Problems, Books xxii–xxxviii*, trans. W.S. Hett, and *Rhetorica ad Alexandrum*, trans. H. Rackham, Cambridge, Ma.

Radfield, R.S. (1901) 'Personification and the Use of Abstract Subjects in the Attic Orators and in Thucydides'. Diss., Johns Hopkins, Baltimore.

Roschatt, A. (1886) *Die Metaphern bei den attischen Rednern*, Straubing.

Scafuro, A.C. (2011) *Demosthenes, speeches 39–49*, Austin.

Todd, S.C. (1993) *The Shape of Athenian Law*, Oxford.

Todd, S.C. (2009) 'Hypereides *Against Diondas*, Demosthenes *On the Crown*, and the Rhetoric of Political Failure', BICS 52, 161–174.

Whitehead, D. (1988) 'ΚΛΟΠΗ ΠΟΛΕΜΟΥ: "theft" in ancient Greek warfare', *C&M* 39, 43–53.

Whitehead, D. (2007), '"Theft" in Greek Oratory', CQ 57, 70–76.

Wolff, H.J. (1957) 'Die Grundlagen des griechischen Vertragsrechts', *Zeitschrift der Savigny-Stiftung für Rechtsgeschichte, romanistische Abteilung*, 74, 26–72. (Reprinted in Berneker, E. ed. (1968) *Zur griechischen Rechtsgeschichte*, Darmstadt, 483–533.)

PART 4

Specific Areas of Law

CHAPTER 15

Laws against Laws: the Athenian Ideology of Legislation

Mirko Canevaro

Introduction

A seminal moment of the heated debate on the reconstruction of Athenian fourth-century *nomothesia* was the publication in 1975 of MacDowell's 'Law-Making at Athens in the Fourth Century B.C.'.[1] MacDowell analysed systematically all the extant evidence and proposed an articulation of fourth-century *nomothesia* in separate procedures all in turn supplemented at various points throughout the fourth century. His conclusions have not ultimately withstood scrutiny, but his focus on reconstructing precisely the relevant procedures and institutions has been upheld in later studies by Hansen, Rhodes, Piérart and myself.[2] Among MacDowell's contentions, one that was immediately, and rightly, criticised by Hansen and Rhodes is that the statements at Dem. 20.91–92 describe a New Legislation Law that replaced an Old one: Demosthenes states that as long as the Athenians observed the original Solonian laws on *nomothesia* they did not enact new laws, but when powerful politicians made it possible for themselves to pass laws whenever and however they wanted, contradictions started arising among the laws, and laws no longer differed from decrees, and often were more recent than the decrees.[3] Diodoros at Dem. 24.142 makes similar remarks and complains that *rhētores* legislate almost every month, repeal the laws of Solon and replace them with their own.

Both Hansen and Rhodes pointed out that these passages, rather than describing a specific law, blame malpractices and procedural infractions that are allegedly current when politicians without scruples enact new legislation. In Rhodes' words, '*Lept.* and *Tim.* are only two years apart, and the irregular-

1 MacDowell 1975. Before MacDowell, particularly influential works were Schöll 1886, Kahrstedt 1938, Atkinson 1939.

2 Hansen 1979–1980; Hansen 1985; Rhodes 1985; Rhodes 2003; Piérart 2000; Canevaro 2013b; 2015; 2016.

3 MacDowell 1975: 65, 73 and *passim*; cf. also MacDowell 2009: 156–166. *Contra* Hansen 1979–1980: 88–95, Rhodes 1985: 56, Canevaro 2013a: 241.

 | DOI:10.1163/9789004377899_017

ities which Demosthenes alleges in them are very similar'. Both Leptines and Timokrates 'failed to comply with a *palaios nomos* which requires action at a specified time, advance publicity for the new proposal, and concurrent repeal of any law with which the new proposal conflicts'.[4] Moreover, the claims made in these passages (Dem. 20.91–92; 24.142) are exaggerated and largely unjustified: Demosthenes claims that with the old law on legislation the Athenians did not enact new laws, yet we have epigraphical evidence of laws enacted before 355.[5] He claims that clever politicians enact laws whenever and however they want, yet Leptines' law had in fact been enacted by the *nomothetai* according to the *palaios nomos*, as Demosthenes admits at 20.94,[6] and Leptines' law was repealed at the trial, which is evidence that if the appropriate procedure was not followed, the infractions were later sanctioned in court.[7] As for the charges found in these passages (Dem. 20.91–92; 24.142) that *nomoi* are indistinguishable from *psēphismata*, and that the Athenians legislated too much, Hansen has convincingly shown that the distinction (procedural and substantive) between laws and decrees was upheld all the way down to 322, and the evidence shows that decrees were much more frequently enacted than laws.[8]

If the statements at Dem. 20.91–92 and 24.142 are not descriptions of actual institutional arrangements, they must be read as rhetorical statements about current illegal practices, statements to which the orator expected the audience to respond sympathetically, because they reflected shared attitudes to the law, inscribed into an ideology of legislation that could be successfully exploited in court. This line of enquiry has been less popular among scholars than strictly institutional and legal reconstructions, but a few works have attempted to tackle it: Hansen's, Thomas' and Wohl's discussions have isolated important features of fourth-century discourse on legislation, and highlighted the reliance on the figure of the lawgiver, Solon, in order to confer authority to the laws on the basis of their antiquity. They have also argued that, even in the fourth century, in order to be acceptable, innovations in the laws had to be

4 Rhodes 1985: 56. See also Hansen 1979–1980: 88–95.

5 Fourth-century laws in chronological order are *SEG* 26.72; Stroud 1998; Agora Excavations, inv. no. I 7495 (unpublished); *IG* II^2 140; *IG* II^2 244; *IG* II^3 1 320; *IG* II^3 1 447; *IG* II^3 1 445. Cf. also Clinton 2005–2008: no 138; 2008: 116; *SEG* 52.104. The first five are earlier than these speeches. The document at Dem. 24.63 preserves a law earlier than these speeches, and should be reliable; see Canevaro 2013a: 151–157.

6 This law is referred to as παλαιός νόμος at Dem. 20.89.

7 Cf. Harris 2008: 20–21 and Kremmydas 2012: 58–69.

8 Cf. Hansen 1978, 1979–1980 (*pace* e.g. Banfi 2012: 59–69, who takes instead Demosthenes' criticisms at face value).

described as a return to the *patrioi nomoi*.[9] These features seem to be evidence of a conservative ideology of legislation, which relies on the antiquity of the laws and on the authority of Solon the lawgiver as the foundations of the legal system,[10] which is ideally characterised by absolute fixity and permanence, and refuses, and is threatened by, any change. Such an ideology of legislation seems to be in complete opposition to any recognition of popular sovereignty, and Thomas has gone so far as to describe it as 'non-democratic' and 'somewhat Spartan'.[11]

Of course, if we accept such a description of the fourth-century ideology of legislation, we need also to accept that the discourse of legislation was fundamentally divorced from, and antithetical to, the contemporary procedures and institutions for enacting new laws and changing the existing ones. I have reconstructed the relevant procedures elsewhere,[12] and here is not the place to repeat my arguments. It will suffice to say that the evidence shows clearly that these procedures were aimed at safeguarding the coherence of the laws and their place as separate from matters of day-to-day administration. Laws were marked as higher rules that must be scrutinised more carefully and extensively, and enacted in a different and more complex manner. At the same time, the fourth-century procedures of *nomothesia* are very clear and effective rules of change that formally allow the *dēmos* to introduce new laws and change the existing ones, and provide a venue for it, relying on democratic institutions like the popular lawcourts to secure their implementation. Moreover, they show a concern with publicity and accountability that is very democratic in tone.[13]

This procedure and its underlying concerns are inconsistent with the discourse of legislation as it has been reconstructed in recent studies,[14] with the focus of this discourse on the immutability and permanence of the laws and its apparent mistrust for popular sovereignty. Yet such a discrepancy is difficult to account for, and we should expect it to hamper the workings of legislation, to make laws liable to accusations of illegality, and to give rise to widespread mistrust for their provisions. We should expect legislative institutions that so radically contradict the shared ideology of legislation to be ultimately unworkable, and to undergo significant changes throughout the fourth century. Yet

9 Hansen 1989; Thomas 1994; Wohl 2010: 287–301. Cf. Johnstone 1999: 25–33.

10 Cf. Giannadaki in this volume pp. 208–211.

11 Thomas 1994: 124, 128–131, 32.

12 Canevaro 2013b.

13 See in particular Canevaro 2015 and Canevaro 2013a: 158–160. Cf. Sickinger 2008.

14 See the references at n. 9.

this is not the case. Hansen has shown that throughout the fourth century the procedural and substantive distinctions between *nomoi* and *psēphismata* were carefully respected, and general permanent rules were invariably enacted by the *nomothetai* as laws.[15] He has also shown that laws preserved on stone are significantly fewer than decrees (we have now ten laws, published or unpublished, and ca. 550–600 decrees from the fourth century).[16] On the other hand, these laws on stone, and several more attested in the literary record, show that legal change happened, and new legislation was regularly enacted. Dem. 24.142, a passage in which Diodoros accuses the Athenians of legislating too much, states that the Athenians summoned *nomothetai* almost once a prytany, that is, almost ten times a year. If we halve this figure to allow for rhetorical exaggeration, we are still left with five sessions of *nomothetai* a year, each probably dealing with several proposed laws. Yet despite the regular enactment of new legislation, the orators invariably show great respect for the laws, and often state that the laws are the foundation of anything good happening to the city (e.g. Lykourg. 1.4, [Dem.] 25.20–24; Dem. 24.5). We never find any argument which resembles Aristotle's suggestion at *Rh.* 1.15.1375a5 that, when the law does not support one's case, one should oppose the law of nature to the laws of the city and criticise them because they change too often.[17] The laws of Athens, within the boundaries of legal discourse and public life, command universal respect throughout the fourth century, and legal change has no negative effect on their authority. Moreover, no serious dysfunction in the procedure of *nomothesia* emerges from the epigraphical record—the procedures worked steadily for around eighty years, securing the distinction between *nomoi* and *psēphismata*, and were repealed only in 322 with the Macedonian domination. The only change appears to be the institution of special commissioners (Dem. 20.91) elected to inspect the existing laws and find contradictions at some point in the fourth century.[18] This addition, rather than witnessing the instability of the system, shows that the only reform deemed necessary was one whose purpose was to reinforce the checks against inconsistent laws which were already built into the original *nomothesia* procedure.

---

15 Hansen 1978, 1979: with the reform of the late-fifth century, *nomoi* were general permanent rules enacted by the *nomothetai*, while *psēphismata* were *ad hoc* decisions whose application was limited in time, enacted by the Assembly or the Council (cf. Canevaro 2015, section 6).

16 Lambert 2012: 57, n. 31.

17 Cf. Carey 1996: 36–38; Harris 2006: 162–164.

18 Aischin. 3.38–39 attributes the same task to the *thesmothetai*, see MacDowell 1975: 72, Rhodes 1985: 60, Hansen 1985: 356.

It is then difficult to believe that the discourse about legislation exploited in the courts could be so antagonistic to the principles underpinning the actual legislative institutions. Recent work in institutional analysis, and in particular what have been termed 'ideational historical institutionalism' and 'discursive institutionalism', has stressed the importance of shared and coherent institutional ideologies for the success and duration of an institution.[19] My purpose in this chapter is to reassess what the orators (and more specifically Demosthenes) have to say about legal change and its consequences, and explain, from an ideological point of view, the stability of the legislative procedures throughout the fourth century. The two main texts I will analyse are Demosthenes' *Against Timokrates* and *Against Leptines*, both speeches written for *graphai nomon mē epitēdeion theinai* and whose purpose was to repeal laws enacted through *nomothesia*.

What Makes a Law Non-*epitēdeios*? Ideological Justifications for *nomothesia* Norms

Diodoros in the *Against Timokrates* goes systematically about the task of demonstrating that the law of Timokrates is not *epitēdeios*. This law allowed public debtors condemned to the additional penalty of imprisonment until they paid back their debts to avoid prison if they could provide sureties. Diodoros claims that it was enacted with the specific aim of saving Androtion, Glauketes and Melanopos from prison. At §§15–16 Diodoros anticipates two of the main issues he will discuss: when the law was passed, and the fact that it was enacted avoiding publicity, almost secretively. In the next few paragraphs he goes into more detail about the arrangement of his argument against the law, and therefore about its illegalities. He announces at §§17–18 that he will speak first of the laws that permit *graphai nomon mē epitēdeion theinai*, that is about the laws setting the rules for passing new legislation, and then he will discuss merits and problems of the law of Timokrates itself. In Diodoros' summary, the law on legislation provides a precise timescale for the enactment of new laws, publicity for the proposed laws in front of the monument of the Eponymous Heroes, it prescribes that laws should apply to all citizens equally, and that any existing laws that contradict it must first be repealed. Diodoros mentions that there are also other provisions, but these are the main ones. Timokrates has allegedly sinned in all these respects, and therefore Diodoros will have to pro-

19 *Cf.* e.g. Smith 2008; Lieberman 2002; Schmidt 2008; Schmidt 2010; Schmidt 2011.

ceed systematically and discuss his infractions one by one. First, Timokrates has not respected the correct times to enact legislation, thus his legislation was not enacted according to the correct procedures. Second, he has failed to give his proposal adequate publicity. The next two infractions are substantive: third, the law of Timokrates fails to apply equally to all Athenians, and fourth, it contradicts existing laws that Timokrates has failed to repeal.

At § 19 Diodoros announces that he will deal systematically with all these aspects. From § 20 to 31 the topic is procedure; from § 32 to 38 the law forbidding the enactment of a new law that contradicts existing ones without repealing them first; from § 39 to 67, after the speaker has the law of Timokrates read out, we find a series of contradictory statutes read and discussed (among these, at § 59, Diodoros discusses the law about *leges ad hominem*). Following this long discussion of the grounds on which the law of Timokrates is illegal, Demosthenes argues that it is also harmful for the city.[20] The arrangement of the speech, at least in its first part, follows closely the issues covered by the laws on *nomothesia*: procedures (that distinguish the enactment of laws from that of *psēphismata*), publicity, and contradictory statutes. The accusation, as should be expected, is grounded on a close reading of the relevant laws. The accuser had to quote in the plaint the laws on which he founded his prosecution, as well as those that contradicted the law he wanted to repeal.[21] Yet Diodoros' legal argument is not drily adherent to the technicalities of the relevant laws, but rather full of ideologically charged statements that justify the provisions of these laws, and damn the law of Timokrates. These statements draw a nuanced picture of an ideology of legal change that is consistent with the relevant Athenian institutions and underpins them.

Diodoros paraphrases the law on *nomothesia* at § 24 after the secretary reads it out,[22] and then at § 27 has the decree of Epikrates that summons the *nomo-*

20 Quass 1971: 27, Rubinstein 2000: 42–43, n. 48 and Kremmydas 2012: 49 all correctly show that arguments about illegality and expediency were equally relevant to both *graphai nomon mē epitēdeion theinai* and *graphai paranomōn*, regardless of the names of the procedures. *Contra* Wolff 1970: 13–14, 60–64 argues that only legal arguments were relevant, whereas Hansen 1974: 71–72, 1987: 71–72 believes that political arguments were sufficient, without a real need to prove the illegality. According to Yunis 1988: 364–370 both lines of argument were essential for winning. The evidence of the speeches for both *graphai nomon mē epitēdeion theinai* and *graphai paranomōn* shows that identifying inconsistencies in the new law or decree with existing laws and with the spirit of the laws was essential, and legal arguments came always first in these speeches (see Wolff 1970: 13–14, 60–64). Moreover, the inclusion of the inconsistent laws in the plaint was compulsory in *graphai paranomōn*, and presumably also in *graphai nomon mē epitēdeion theinai*.

21 Aischin. 3.200 with Harris 2013: 121–122.

22 Canevaro 2013a: 139–150 for Demosthenes' account of the law.

thetai read out to show that it infringes upon all the rules just read and discussed.[23] The list of these infringements at § 26 is instructive: proposals for new laws must be published before the monument of the Eponymous Heroes for everyone to see and make up their mind,[24] yet Timokrates has not published his proposal, nor has he allowed the Athenians the chance to consider it. Moreover, he did not respect the 'times prescribed' by the law (τῶν τεταγμένων χρόνων).[25] The main issues with the law of Timokrates, on the procedural side, are the lack of publicity for the proposal, and the failure to enact it following the correct timetable specified by the law on *nomothesia*. These are not just technical objections. The rationale of the relevant provisions is important and stressed by Diodoros. Advance publicity is key because 'if [someone] notices anything against your interests, he may point it out and speak against it at his convenience' (κἂν ἀσύμφορον ὑμῖν κατίδῃ τι, φράσῃ καὶ κατὰ σχολὴν ἀντείπῃ; cf. Dem. 20.94 ἵν' ἕκαστος ὑμῶν ἀκούσας πολλάκις καὶ κατὰ σχολὴν σκεψάμενος, ἂν ᾖ καὶ δίκαια καὶ συμφέροντα, ταῦτα νομοθετῇ; 'so that each of you may hear the laws many times and have a chance to study them at leisure and enact those that were just and in the public interest'). And respecting the prescribed timescale is key to allowing the people enough time to examine the proposals and if necessary to oppose them. In fact, Diodoros (§ 36–37) lists the advocates of the old laws, the advance publicity for proposals, the time before the enactment, and the possibility of bringing *graphai nomon mē epitēdeion theinai* as the key checks to guarantee that no bad legislation (that is, contradicting other laws) is enacted. In the *Against Leptines* Demosthenes stresses repeatedly that he and Phormion abided by the correct procedures, and contrasts their behaviour with Leptines' failure to respect the rules of *nomothesia*. In this case, Demosthenes does not go into detail about Leptines' infractions, presumably because Leptines, unlike Timokrates, had indeed followed the correct procedures, as Demosthenes has to admit at § 94.[26] Demosthenes therefore makes general arguments about the importance of these procedures, giving the impression that Leptines has not followed them without having to provide evidence for it:

> οὐ γὰρ ᾤετο δεῖν ὁ Σόλων, ὁ τοῦτον τὸν τρόπον προστάξας νομοθετεῖν, τοὺς μὲν θεσμοθέτας τοὺς ἐπὶ τοὺς νόμους κληρουμένους δὶς δοκιμασθέντας ἄρχειν, ἔν τε

23 The document found in the speech which purports to be the decree of Epikrates is an unreliable later forgery; see Canevaro 2013a: 104–112.

24 On the use and significance of the expression 'for everyone to see', which usually (as in this case) refers to publicity of temporary records, cf. Hedrick 2000: 331–333.

25 On this timescale see Canevaro 2013a: 146–147.

26 See Canevaro 2016: 44.

> τῇ βουλῇ καὶ παρ' ὑμῖν ἐν τῷ δικαστηρίῳ, τοὺς δὲ νόμους αὐτούς, καθ' οὓς καὶ τούτοις ἄρχειν καὶ πᾶσι τοῖς ἄλλοις πολιτεύεσθαι προσήκει, ἐπὶ καιροῦ τεθέντας, ὅπως ἔτυχον, μὴ δοκιμασθέντας κυρίους εἶναι.
>
> Solon, who set up this method of enacting laws, did not think it right for the *thesmothetai*, who are chosen by lot to administer the laws, to take office after two examinations, in the Council and before you in court, but for the laws themselves, which these men and all citizens are obliged to follow in their public actions, to be passed haphazardly and go into effect without having been examined.
>
> DEM. 20.90

To sum up, a law, in order to be *epitēdeios*, must be different from a decree, must undergo multiple checks, must not be enacted on the spur of the moment and in haste, and, in order to make sure that this is the case, following the correct procedure is essential. A new law is good if it is enacted following scrupulously the procedure of *nomothesia*, while it is doomed to be non-*epitēdeios* if enacted in defiance of it.

The other key issue for a new law is its consistency with the existing laws, the topic of the whole section Dem. 24.32–67. Diodoros states that in addition to not respecting the set times and not giving advance publicity to his proposal, Timokrates committed another violation: introducing his law in violation of all the existing laws. At § 33 the relevant law, prescribing that one must repeal all contradictory laws before enacting a new one and threatening a *graphē nomon mē epitēdeion theinai* if one fails to do so, is read out, and afterwards Diodoros explains in detail the rationale and the qualities of these provisions (§ 34–35):[27] because the judges have sworn to vote in accordance with the laws, if there existed contradictory laws, favouring both litigants, that are equally valid, it would be impossible for them to honour their oath. A similar rationale is given at Dem. 20.93, where Demosthenes states that 'contradictory laws are repealed so that there is one law on each matter, so that private individuals, who would be at a disadvantage in comparison to people who are familiar with all the laws, do not get confused, but points of law are the same for all to read as well as simple and clear to understand' (λύοντα τοὺς ἐναντίους, ἵν' εἷς ᾖ περὶ τῶν ὄντων ἑκάστου νόμος, καὶ μὴ τοὺς ἰδιώτας αὐτὸ τοῦτο ταράττῃ καὶ

27 The speaker asks the *grammateus* to read out the law, but the document found in the speech is a later insertion, and a forgery; see Canevaro 2013a: 102–104. My summary of the law that the *grammateus* actually read out depends on the summary of the orator.

ποιῇ τῶν ἅπαντας εἰδότων τοὺς νόμους ἔλαττον ἔχειν, ἀλλὰ πᾶσιν ᾖ ταὔτ' ἀναγνῶναι καὶ μαθεῖν ἁπλᾶ καὶ σαφῆ τὰ δίκαια). Such a rationale is not just generically flagged up in trials concerning the enactment of new laws, as a requirement to be upheld in enacting new laws. The coherence of the legal system and consistency of the laws is in fact affirmed and rhetorically exploited elsewhere, in speeches that are not concerned with the enactment or repeal of new laws, and informs the interpretation and presentation of statutes relevant to a variety of cases.[28]

At Dem. 24.39 Diodoros has the law of Timokrates read out, and then discusses a series of seven laws that allegedly contradict it yet have not been repealed by Timokrates.[29] The section is interspersed with statements about how inconsistent Timokrates' law is with these statutes: 'Consider then how much the law that this man enacted is contrary to this law' (§ 44, τούτῳ μέντοι τῷ νόμῳ σκέψασθ' ὡς ἐναντίος ἐστὶν ὃν οὗτος τέθηκεν); 'Timokrates immediately begins his law by contradicting this rule' (§ 55, Τιμοκράτης τοίνυν [...] εὐθὺς ἀρχόμενος τοῦ νόμου τἀναντί' ἔθηκε τούτοις); 'Anyone could cite many excellent laws, all of which the law enacted by this man contradicts' (§ 61, πολλοὺς δ' ἄν τις ἔχοι νόμους ἔτι καὶ καλῶς ἔχοντας δεικνύναι, οἷς πᾶσιν ἐναντίος ἐστὶν ὃν οὗτος τέθηκεν). Some of the laws presented by Demosthenes as contradictory in fact are not, and the arguments of Diodoros are clearly unacceptable. To give only one example, the law at § 50 forbids convicted wrongdoers to make any supplication in the Council or the Assembly, and anyone else to make supplications on their behalf. Diodoros explains the alleged intent of the lawgiver: as the Athenians are too gentle and would be moved by the misfortunes of convicted wrongdoers to accept their supplications and cancel their debts, the lawgiver passed a law that forbade such supplications. As begging, that is, making a supplication, is better than giving orders, and enacting a law equates to giving orders,

28 E.g. Aischin. 3.37–40 argues that, because there are procedures in place to ensure that inconsistent laws are spotted and blocked, it is impossible for two contradictory laws about the awarding of crowns to be valid at the same time, and therefore one law quoted by Demosthenes in support of his case must be irrelevant to the present case. Regardless of whether Aischines is correct, or is pushing the coherence of the laws too far, the fact that he can make such an argument, and consider it effective, shows that the judges expected the laws to be coherent because of the existence of the procedures of *nomothesia*. See Sickinger 2008 on the practice of eliminating disagreements among statutes, e.g. destroying contradictory inscriptions (*pace* Lanni 2006: 115–148), which must have reinforced these expectations, and Harris 2013: 246–273 on the use of precedents to inform consistent interpretation of statutes. Johnstone 1999: 28–29 and Wohl 2010: 287–292 also stress that fourth-century Athenians saw their laws as a coherent and rational whole.

29 Cf. on this section of the speech Canevaro 2013a: 113–156.

then *a fortiori* Timokrates has ordered through his law to save Androtion, a convicted wrongdoer, when the law would not even allow begging on his behalf. The argument is specious, because the law is concerned specifically with supplications, not with enacting new laws.[30] On the other hand, some of the other laws discussed do contradict Timokrates' law: at § 63 Diodoros quotes another law of Timokrates that prescribes that if someone, following an *eisangelia*, is condemned to pay a fine, he must stay in prison until the fine is paid. The law of Timokrates indicted by Diodoros allows instead anyone to escape prison if he offers sureties for his debt. These laws are not only contradictory, but they have both been enacted by Timokrates, who has therefore contradicted himself.[31]

It is interesting, however, that Demosthenes/Diodoros should choose to mention a series of statutes as contradictory, despite the fact that many of his arguments can be proved wrong, while he could as easily have stuck to one or two that are actually inconsistent, and this would have sufficed to prove that Timokrates had failed to repeal the contradictory laws. The reason for such a list is that the orators understand the importance of the coherence of the laws on two levels: one level is that of actual contradictory provisions with specific statutes, the other, that of consistency with the overall aims and spirit of the laws, that is with the legal system as a whole. Because of this, proving that the indicted law contradicts specific provisions of other laws is as important as proving that it contradicts and virtually invalidates all the laws of the city, and their spirit and overall aim. Demosthenes, in his two speeches against laws, makes such claims very often. At Dem. 24.1 Diodoros states that Timokrates has enacted a law *para pantas tous nomous* (against all the laws); and at § 5, that the judges have to decide 'whether all the other laws that you have enacted against men who harm the state are to be repealed while this one is to remain valid, or this one is to be repealed while the others are to remain valid' (πότερον δεῖ τοὺς μὲν ἄλλους νόμους, οὓς ἐπὶ τοῖς ἀδικοῦσι τὴν πόλιν ὑμεῖς ἀνεγράψατε, ἀκύρους εἶναι, τόνδε δὲ κύριον, ἢ τοὐναντίον τοῦτον μὲν λῦσαι, κατὰ χώραν δὲ μένειν τοὺς ἄλλους ἐᾶν). At § 38, just before the law of Timokrates is read out and contrasted with seven contradictory statutes, Diodoros states: '[Timokrates] has introduced a law that contradicts, one might say, all those now valid. He did not read out anything, repeal anything …' (νόμον εἰσήνεγκεν ἅπασιν ἐναντίον, ὡς ἔπος εἰπεῖν, τοῖς οὖσιν, οὐ παραναγνούς, οὐ λύσας …). At § 61 he reiterates that 'Anyone could cite many excellent laws, all of which the law enacted by this man contradicts

30 Canevaro 2013a: 133–135.

31 Canevaro 2013a: 152.

[...] it will be liable to the charge even if it contradicts just one of the existing laws' (πολλοὺς δ' ἄν τις ἔχοι νόμους ἔτι καὶ καλῶς ἔχοντας δεικνύναι, οἷς πᾶσιν ἐναντίος ἐστὶν ὃν οὗτος τέθηκεν [...] ὑμῖν δ' ὁμοίως ἔνοχος φανεῖται τῇ γραφῇ, καὶ εἰ ἑνὶ τῶν ὄντων νόμων ἐναντίος ἐστίν). Demosthenes is aware that some of his examples are weak, and stresses that one single contradictory statute would be enough, but the impression he is seeking to give is clear: the whole legal system is at odds with Timokrates' law. At § 66 Diodoros summarises this point: 'I think it is clear to all of you that he has enacted his law in violation both of these laws and of those discussed earlier, in fact, I could almost say in violation of all the laws of the city' (ὅτι μὲν τοίνυν καὶ παρὰ τούτους τοὺς νόμους καὶ παρὰ τοὺς προειρημένους, καὶ μικροῦ δέω παρὰ πάντας εἰπεῖν τοὺς ὄντας ἐν τῇ πόλει, τέθηκε τὸν νόμον, οἶμαι δῆλον ἅπασιν ὑμῖν εἶναι).[32]

As a bad law is one that contradicts all the laws, it can destroy the city and its entire legal system. This is why Diodoros, later in the speech, after all the contradictions have been pointed out, can ask the judges whether the law of Timokrates is in fact a law or *anomia*, that is, the absence of laws (§ 152).[33] He states that 'the law subverts the entire *politeia*, destroys political activity and deprives the city of many incentives for *philotimia*' (§ 91, ὅλην συγχεῖ τὴν πολιτείαν καὶ καταλύει πάντα τὰ πράγμαθ' ὁ νόμος, καὶ πολλὰς φιλοτιμίας περιαιρεῖται τῆς πόλεως). Diodoros goes so far as to represent at §§ 155–156 the very enactment of the law of Timokrates as a ruse to destroy all the existing laws. He attributes a similar argument to Solon himself, in an anachronistic re-enactment of a *graphē nomon mē epitēdeion theinai* brought by the ancient lawgiver (§§ 213–214). Cf. also the following passage:

> δεῖν δὴ τοὺς δικαστὰς πολλῷ μᾶλλον, εἴ τις ὃ τῆς πόλεώς ἐστι νόμισμα, τοῦτο διαφθείρει καὶ παράσημον εἰσφέρει, μισεῖν καὶ κολάζειν, ἢ εἴ τις ἐκεῖν' ὃ τῶν ἰδιωτῶν ἐστιν. προσθεῖναι δὲ τεκμήριον τοῦ καὶ μεῖζον εἶναι τἀδίκημα, τὸ τοὺς

32 These passages show very clearly (*pace* Lanni 2009) that the *graphē nomon mē epitēdeion theinai* is not exclusively or primarily concerned with securing the correctness of democratic procedure. The implication is rather that a bad law substantively contradicts the spirit of the laws of the city (and has been enacted only thanks to procedural infractions), and this must be shown by pointing to contradictions with individual statutes. The correctness of democratic procedure is only one of the aspects protected through safeguarding the integrity of the laws of the city.

33 *Pace* Wohl 2010: 292–301, who reads the reference to *anomia* as a hidden admission that the *nomothesia* procedure is intrinsically unstable and that any change to the laws can endanger the unity and coherence of the laws. It is only the introduction of a bad law, without following the correct procedures, that endangers the system; cf. Canevaro 2012: 442–443.

> νόμους διαφθείρειν ἢ τὸ ἀργύριον, ὅτι ἀργυρίῳ μὲν πολλαὶ τῶν πόλεων καὶ φανερῶς πρὸς χαλκὸν καὶ μόλυβδον κεκραμένῳ χρώμεναι σῴζονται καὶ οὐδ' ὁτιοῦν παρὰ τοῦτο πάσχουσιν, νόμοις δὲ πονηροῖς χρώμενοι καὶ διαφθείρεσθαι τοὺς ὄντας ἐῶντες οὐδένες πώποτ' ἐσώθησαν.
>
> Thus if someone debases the currency of the city and introduces a counterfeit coin, the judges ought to despise and punish him much more than if someone debased the currency of private citizens. He added, to prove that corrupting the laws is a worse crime than counterfeiting money, that although many cities clearly using coins mixed with bronze and lead have survived and suffered no harm at all, none of those that use bad laws and allow the destruction of existing laws has ever survived.
>
> DEM. 20.167

But stressing that a new law contradicts the existing laws is not the only method of proving that a law is inconsistent with the laws of the city. An orator can just as effectively argue that it contradicts the spirit and the aims of the existing laws.[34] Such arguments rely on an understanding of the laws as a coherent whole, predicated both, as we have seen, on the existence of procedures to avoid contradictions, and on the unifying figure of the lawgiver. The lawgiver is often identified with Solon, but his identity sometimes fades, much as it does in modern codes and legal interpretation, into an abstract figure which guarantees the coherence of the system.[35] This strategy is only sparsely used in the *Against Timokrates*, at the end of which (§ 211) Diodoros points out that Drakon's and Solon's greatest contribution to the greatness of Athens is that they συμφέροντας ἔθηκαν καὶ καλῶς ἔχοντας νόμους ('they enacted laws that were useful and good'). Is it surely just therefore that the judges should vote serious punishments τοῖς ὑπεναντίως τιθεῖσιν ἐκείνοις ('for those who enact laws that contradict theirs')? And elsewhere, at §§ 103 and 106, Diodoros laments that Timokrates is a lawgiver very much unlike Solon.

---

34 This aspect is key, and Wolff 1970: 45–67 correctly identifies as a distinctive category of arguments stressing that the law contradicts general principles extrapolated from other statutes. *Contra* Sundahl 2000, 2009: 493–502 notes that this kind of argument is rare when the *grammateus* reads out an actual law. But the actual reading of the contradictory statute was necessary when the point was a formal contradiction. Contradiction of general principles could be discussed on a more general level without the law being read out in full.

35 The importance of the figure of Solon and 'the lawgiver' as the foundation of the coherence of the laws is stressed by Johnstone 1999: 29. See also Giannadaki in this volume pp. 208–211.

In the *Against Leptines* this strategy is exploited fully: at §§13–14 Demosthenes states that the *ēthos* of every new law must conform to that of the city, and as the *ēthos* of a law reflects that of the man who enacts it, the *ēthos* of the man himself must be consistent with that of the city. He illustrates at §§11–12 the *ēthos* of the city by narrating an episode, and later at §§102–104 by commenting on some of its oldest laws, those on wills and on defamation, which he attributes to Solon. This *ēthos* is then contrasted at §105–108 with those of the Spartans and of the Thebans, which are different and yet consistent within themselves and with their laws and customs. At §153 again Demosthenes urges the Athenians not to allow a law that is completely at odds with the *ēthos* of the city, and whose author seems to be moved by envy and spite, to stay valid. One should also point out that, seen within this framework, the frequent appeals to the intent of the lawgiver (e.g. Hyp. *Athen.* 13–22; Dem. 18.6, 22.8–11, 25, 30, [36.]27, [58.]11; Lykourg. 1.9; Lys. 31.27; Isa. 2.13), which have been extensively studied by other scholars, seem to be less conservative, and have more to do with the preservation and argumentative exploitation of the inner consistency of the laws of the city.[36] The laws of the city are coherent among themselves in their provisions and in their spirit and overall aims, as every new legislator has to conform to the *ēthos* of the city, which is in turn defined by its laws, most of which were originally enacted by Solon. Thus Solon's *ēthos* and intentions provide reliable guidance on interpreting and enacting laws, as abiding by the correct procedures of *nomothesia* has made sure that that the original *ēthos* is preserved and reproduced with every new law. The choice of the adjective used to define laws that should be discarded in the formal definition of a public charge against a law, *epitēdeios*, is of course not casual. The general meaning of this adjective is 'fit or adapted for [something]' (*LSJ s.v.* ἐπιτήδειος). It marks something that is appropriate, suitable. A law that is *epitēdeios* is not just a law

36 Thomas 1994: 121–128 argues that such references are evidence of the Athenians' reactionary attitudes to legislation, and that they constitute extra-legal arguments (pp. 130–132; see also Hillgruber 1988: 107–119). On the contrary, as shown by Johnstone 1999: 25–33, they aim to guide legal interpretations of particular laws on the basis of the coherence and rationality of the legal system, predicated on the aims, the *ēthos* of the original lawgiver. They therefore provide the orator with the chance to argue for non-literal interpretations of laws, or for interpretations based on principles from different laws (see Wolff 1970: 45–67). Schreiner 1913: 12–60 argued that they were shorthand for the revised code of the last decade of the fifth century, while Ruschenbusch 1966 saw them chiefly as references to the laws of the *axones*. Hansen 1989: 79–80 has shown that this is usually true only for private law, criminal law and more rarely for the administration of justice. He also argues (pp. 80–82) that the audience was meant to believe in the Solonian origin of these laws, but see below pp. 289–290.

that is generically useful, or good. It is a law that is fit to be an Athenian law, that fulfils the necessary criteria—it must be fit to be a coherent part of laws of the city, it must be suitable, and accord to their spirit and their purpose.[37]

Is Legal Innovation Legitimate?

When it comes to legal change and new laws, the Athenians seem to have stuck to an ideology that defined good laws as ones that were enacted following the correct procedures, that is, abiding by the prescribed times and giving proposals advance publicity. If these rules were respected, new laws would not be enacted in haste, they would be substantively different from decrees, and most importantly they would contradict neither particular existing laws nor the overall spirit of the laws. Following the correct procedures ensured that the *ēthos* of the new laws (and therefore the *ēthos* of the proposer) was consistent with the *ēthos* of the city and of the existing laws. We have seen, however, at the beginning of this chapter, that sometimes new laws were met with more radical criticism than that described here, and were criticised apparently for the very fact that they were new, that they represented legal change. Such statements suggest that criticism of new legislation could be more conservative, and predicated on the immutability of the laws and on their antiquity. Such a view would make all new legislation fundamentally illegitimate.[38] In the last part of this chapter I will therefore try to qualify the statements of Dem. 20.91–92 and 24.142 in the light of the principles I have identified, and finally to highlight significantly different approaches to legal change found in the orators, to show that nothing in the fourth-century Athenian ideology of legislation was fundamentally undemocratic, and the principles it fostered were not antagonistic to those embodied in the *nomothesia* procedure.

Dem. 20.91–92 and 24.142 at first sight seem to be unequivocally conservative and critical of legal change *per se*. Demosthenes at 20.90 discusses the 'old law' about legislation, enacted by Solon, which set multiple checks for new laws and made sure that to enact a law one had first to repeal contradictory ones. These checks were put in place so that laws could not be 'passed haphazardly and go into effect without having been examined'. This 'old law' is actually the fourth-century law on *nomothesia*, which is attributed to Solon as

37 See also Kremmydas 2012: 58–61, Wohl 2010: 293, n. 17.

38 This view is expressed most prominently by Thomas 1994: particularly 128–130; see also Wohl 2010: 292–301. The passages discussed below are taken at face value also by Kahrstedt 1938: 12–18; Harrison 1955: 26–35; Ehrenberg 1960: 57.

many other recent laws are in the orators.[39] At §§ 91–92 Demosthenes goes on to claim that τέως τὸν τρόπον τοῦτον ἐνομοθέτουν ('until they enacted legislation in this way'), they kept to the existing laws and did not enact others. Demosthenes seems to be unequivocally referring longingly to a time when people followed the correct rules of change and, ironically, as a result did not change the laws at all. But is this what he is actually aiming for? If we keep reading, the picture becomes more complicated, yet at the same time more familiar after the previous analysis: at some point powerful politicians conspired to make it possible for themselves to pass laws ὅταν τις βούληται καὶ ὃν ἂν τύχῃ τρόπον ('whenever they wanted in any possible way'). As soon as Demosthenes stops painting, as a counterpoint for a present in which bad laws are enacted, a fabulous past in which, allegedly, laws were never changed, the problems with the laws passed by the powerful politicians become recognisable. They do not follow the set times and the correct procedures. And what is the result of this? Again, Demosthenes' answer is familiar: 'the number of laws that contradicted each other became so large that you have been for a long time appointing men to correct the contradictions' (τοσοῦτοι μὲν οἱ ἐναντίοι σφίσιν αὐτοῖς εἰσὶ νόμοι, ὥστε χειροτονεῖθ' ὑμεῖς τοὺς διαλέξοντας τοὺς ἐναντίους ἐπὶ πάμπολυν ἤδη χρόνον). And moreover 'the laws do not differ at all from decrees' (§ 92, ψηφισμάτων δ' οὐδ' ὁτιοῦν διαφέρουσιν οἱ νόμοι). So, despite the exaggerated picture of a past completely antithetical to the present, what Demosthenes is accusing present politicians of doing is not of passing laws at all, but of passing them without following the correct times and procedures, with the result that they enact contradictory laws that do not respect the key requirement of being general permanent rules, and that therefore resemble decrees. Demosthenes paints an extreme counterpoint to current practices in order to stress how negative current practices are, not to propose that the Athenians should not legislate at all.

At Dem. 24.139–142 we find a similar argument. Diodoros recalls the laws of the Locrians, which allow a citizen to propose a new law only with a noose around his neck. If the law is accepted, the proposer walks away, but if not, the noose is drawn tight.[40] As a result, Diodoros says, 'they do not dare to pass new laws, but strictly adhere to the long established laws' (καὶ γάρ τοι καινοὺς μὲν οὐ τολμῶσι τίθεσθαι, τοῖς δὲ πάλαι κειμένοις ἀκριβῶς χρῶνται). Only once did a citizen dare to pass a law, confident that his case was so fair that he could not lose. Again, this statement seems to suggest that a desirable situation is one in which no new laws are ever passed, yet once again this example is a polemical counter-

39 See Hansen 1979–1980: 88–95, Rhodes 1985: 56, Canevaro 2013a: 241.

40 Polyb. 12.16 attributes this law to Zaleukos.

point to current practices by bad legislators, rather than a positive proposition of how the city should administer itself. First of all, the example given comes from outside Athens, and Demosthenes himself (20.105–111), explains that the customs and laws of other cities can be good, but are suited to the characters and constitutions of the other cities, and cannot be uncritically transferred elsewhere. It is interesting to reconstruct what the argument of Leptines might have been in that context: according to Demosthenes' account, he argued that in other well-administered cities like Sparta nobody is ever granted honours, whereas in Athens the honours are excessive, and sometimes individuals who do not deserve it are beneficiaries of *ateleia*. The extreme case of *poleis* where no honours are allowed is used to make the point not that Athens should grant no honours, but only that it should cancel *ateleia*. Extreme examples are used to show that practices completely opposite to the Athenian ones are possible and successfully followed elsewhere (in time or space), but their actual purpose is hardly ever to suggest that the Athenians should adopt the same extreme practices described. The actual aim of an orator is usually more modest: to cancel one honour, or, in the *Against Timokrates*, to enact laws more carefully and follow the correct procedures.

After the Locrian example, in fact, Diodoros goes on to describe the Athenian situation, and unsurprisingly the fault, once again, of the Athenian *rhētores* is not simply that ὅσοι μῆνες μικροῦ δέουσι νομοθετεῖν ('they legislate almost every month'), but that they enact laws τὰ αὑτοῖς συμφέροντα ('for their own benefit', 24.142). They legislate too much, but this is an issue because of the kind of laws they enact, which are not meant to benefit the *polis* and apply to all Athenians alike, but rather to benefit themselves. And as they enact these unsuitable laws for their own profit, they repeal Solon's laws. Yet once again the phrasing is not that simple: the passage does not say that repealing the laws of Solon οὓς οἱ πρόγονοι ἔθεντο is unacceptable without qualification. First, the passage makes clear that the problem is repealing the laws of Solon to replace them with bad laws drafted for the benefit of dishonest *rhētores*. And second, the laws of Solon are not simply good laws, they are good because πάλαι δεδοκιμασμένους. The perfect with the adverb πάλαι ('long ago') stresses that their antiquity guarantees their worth because they have been repeatedly tested (δεδοκιμασμένους) and have proved their expediency. In Dem. 20 and 24 the references to the antiquity of a law often have this pragmatic justification of their authority: at Dem. 24.24 Diodoros praises the laws about *nomothesia* because they have been in force for a long time, so they have often proved that they are beneficial to the Athenians, and no one would want to criticise them; at Dem. 24.34 the law about repealing contradictory laws before enacting a new one is excellent not simply because it is old, but because it is just and defends the people's interests. And at Dem.

20.118 Demosthenes goes so far as to state that it is the duty of the judges, sanctioned by their oath, to give judgment in accordance with the laws, not those of the Spartans or the Thebans, and not even those of their earliest ancestors, but those those that are valid at the time.

To sum up, even these passages, which have been interpreted as suggesting a more extremely conservative view of legislation, one which altogether questions the legitimacy of legal change, upon closer reading prove to be more nuanced, and certainly not undemocratic. In fact, they show the very same concerns with procedural observance, distinction between *nomoi* and *psēphismata*, and coherence of the laws that we have observed in the previous section, and that are embodied in the procedure of *nomothesia*. And, moreover, one should keep in mind that these passages are all found in speeches delivered for the purpose of repealing a law recently enacted. It is not surprising that they should indulge in strong arguments against the enactment of these laws. It is likely that our picture would be significantly different if we could read speeches in defence of a new law, or speeches that actually propose its approval to the *nomothetai*. Regrettably, no such speech is extant. Yet a few passages about enacting new laws in the *Against Leptines*, the *Against Timokrates*, and Aischines' *Against Timarchos* shed some light on Athenian public discourse about legislation, and balance out some of the most conservative statements we have discussed. They suggest that enacting laws is a viable and perfectly acceptable option, that there is nothing fundamentally wrong with it, as long as the correct procedures are followed and the requirements are upheld.

The *Against Timokrates* is completely concerned with showing how illegitimate the enactment of Timokrates' law is, yet even in this context a couple of passages show that enacting laws is not a problem *per se*. At § 44 Diodoros discusses a law which contradicts the law of Timokrates, and concludes with the apostrophe: 'Timokrates, you should either have not proposed this law or repealed that one, rather than throw everything into confusion just to suit your wishes' (καίτοι χρῆν σ', ὦ Τιμόκρατες, ἢ τοῦτον μὴ γράφειν ἢ ἐκεῖνον λύειν, οὐχ, ἵν' ὃ βούλει σὺ γένηται, πάντα τὰ πράγματα συνταράξαι). As long as the laws of the city are consistent, enacting a new law is a perfectly acceptable option, but doing so without repealing the contradictory laws is not. At § 29 Diodoros points out that Timokrates had the *nomothetai* summoned with the excuse of the budget and the Panathenaea, and the object of his blame is the fact that no law was actually introduced about these matters. Once again, legislating is perfectly acceptable, and there is nothing wrong in summoning the *nomothetai*, as long as one legislates on the matters about which they are summoned. More interestingly, at §§ 144–147 Diodoros allows us to see how Timokrates may have justified his law, and the argument Diodoros foresees he might employ is based on the very same principle that underscores many arguments against new laws: Timokrates will justify his law by quoting and discussing a law that orders that no Athenian must be sent to prison, claiming that his own law is consistent with it (φήσειν ἀκόλουθον αὐτῷ τεθηκέναι, 24.144). The distinguishing factor between a good and a bad law, whether the speaker is accusing or defending the law, is its coherence with the laws in force in the city.

The *Against Leptines* is even more instructive about attitudes towards enacting new laws, because it not only argues for repealing the law of Leptines, but also advocates the enactment of a replacement law.[41] At the very beginning of the speech (§ 4) Demosthenes argues that if one believed that Leptines' reasons for enacting his law (the Athenians are often deceived) were justified, then it would also be justified to deprive the people completely of their sovereignty, as the people are often deceived on many matters. The speaker observes that the Athenians would never pass such a law, and should rather pass one that punishes those who deceive the people. The alternative to enacting a bad law is enacting a good one, not refusing to enact any. And at § 23 Demosthenes suggests that if Leptines were right and the Athenians really had difficulties in finding enough liturgists, they should reform the system and administer it through *symmoriai*, as they do with *eisphora* and trierarchies. Again, the solution to an issue is good legislation, which is evidently an acceptable option. At § 88 Demosthenes introduces the topic of the replacement law proposed by him and Phormion. He is careful to show that the law is fair and does not order anything shameful, and then proceeds to show in the next paragraphs that they are proposing it according to the correct procedures, and are contextually repealing the law of Leptines that is contradictory. The new law proposed is defended by appealing to the same principles used to attack the laws of Leptines and Timokrates. The discourse about legislation seems to be consistent with the principles underpinning *nomothesia*, and can be used both against and in favour of a law. At §§ 100–101 Demosthenes even anticipates that Leptines and his supporters will accuse him of using the replacement law as a ruse, and having in fact no intention to enact it. Apparently accusing somebody of not enacting a new law was in appropriate circumstances a viable argumentative strategy, and Demosthenes counters the accusation by urging his opponents to enact the law themselves, if they are so keen.

In fourth-century Athens, procedures and ideas about legislation matched and reinforced each other, and ultimately legislation was considered to be the

---

41 See Canevaro 2016 for a reconstruction of the legal case and the procedure. See Kremmydas 2012: 45–55 for an overview of previous interpretations.

remit of the people as much as enacting the decrees in the Assembly or passing judgments in court. As Aischines states very clearly (1.177–178), the Athenians are responsible for making the best laws, and their laws are good because of how the Athenians comport themselves when enacting them: they take into account the principles of justice and the public good and do not enact them for dishonest profit or enmity.

When the authority of Solon is invoked as the foundation of the laws, this is because his legislative action is the blueprint on which all Athenian legislation is (or should be) modelled, reproduced by the Athenian people every time new legislation is enacted. One of the most interesting pieces of evidence for the Athenian reliance, even in the fourth century, on the authority of the lawgiver rather than on popular sovereignty, Aischin. 1.5–37,[42] after a long list of ancient laws, significantly ends with a new law, consistent in spirit and intent with these, and therefore no less authoritative. In this section Aischines discusses Solonian laws that show how the concern for decency is central to the laws of Athens. At the beginning of the section Aischines states 'My belief is that whenever we enact laws, we should be concerned with how to make laws that are good and advantageous for our *politeia*' (§ 6, προσήκειν δὲ ἔγωγε νομίζω, ὅταν μὲν νομοθετῶμεν, τοῦθ' ἡμᾶς σκοπεῖν, ὅπως καλῶς ἔχοντας καὶ συμφέροντας νόμους τῇ πολιτείᾳ θησόμεθα). Before even mentioning Drakon and Solon, the author of the laws in Athens is identified as the Athenian people, who should enact good and advantageous laws. And finally, after discussing a series of ancient laws concerned with decency, Aischines at §§ 33–34 concludes by mentioning a new law, which gives a different tribe the task of presiding over the platform at each Assembly meeting and policing decorum. He claims that this law was proposed following the observation of Timarchos' shameless behaviour at the *bēma*, and that its provisions, spirit and aims are perfectly consistent with those of the laws of Solon discussed in the previous section. This law, according to Aischines, deserves a place next to the ancient laws he has just discussed, despite having been indicted through a *graphē nomon mē epitēdeion theinai* by Timarchos and other speakers of the same sort (it was in fact retained, as we learn from Aischin. 3.4).

This passage, like the others mentioned above, is evidence that there is in Athenian public and legal discourse about legislation no prejudice against legal change and the enactment of new statutes. Enacting a new law is always a viable option, as it is well within the prerogatives of the Athenian people. There are however rules. These rules make sure that laws are not passed in

42 Cf. the discussion of Thomas 1994: 123.

haste, without regard for the distinction between *nomoi* and *psēphismata*, and most importantly that they do not contradict other statutes, and are consistent with the overall aims and *ēthos* of the legal system. The ideas about legislation expressed and exploited in the extant speeches against inexpedient laws, as well as in other speeches of the orators, are hardly evidence of undemocratic attitudes to legislation. They form a complex texture of interconnected ideological tenets and argumentative options that manages to reinforce and underpin the relevant procedures, recognising popular sovereignty while at the same time grounding the internal rationality and coherence of the legal system in the original *ēthos* of the ancient lawgiver, which is perpetuated through abiding by the *nomothesia* procedures.

Bibliography

Atkinson, K.M.T. (1939) 'Athenian Legislative Procedure and Revision of Laws', *Bulletin of the John Rylands Library* 23, 107–150.

Banfi, A. (2012) 'Qualche considerazione intorno al controllo di legittimità ad Atene', in Legras, B. and Thür, G., eds (2012) *Symposion 2011: Vorträge zur griechischen und hellenistischen Rechtsgeschichte* (Paris, 7–10 September 2011) Vienna, 49–76.

Canevaro, M. (2013a) *The Documents in the Attic Orators: Laws and Decrees in the Public Speeches of the Demosthenic Corpus*, Oxford.

Canevaro, M. (2013b) 'Nomothesia in Classical Athens: What Sources Should We Believe?', CQ 63, 1–22.

Canevaro, M. (2015) 'Making and Changing Laws in Ancient Athens' in Harris, E.M. and Canevaro, M., eds, *Oxford Handbook of Ancient Greek Law, Oxford Handbooks Online* (http://www.oxfordhandbooks.com/view/10.1093/oxfordhb/9780199599257.001.0001/oxfordhb-9780199599257-e-4).

Canevaro, M. (2016) 'The Procedure of Demosthenes' *Against Leptines*: How to Repeal (and Replace) an Existing Law', JHS 136, 39–58.

Carey, C. (1996) '*Nomos* in Attic Rhetoric and Oratory', JHS 116, 33–46.

Clinton, K. (2005–2008) *Eleusis, the Inscriptions on Stone: Documents of the Sanctuary of the Two Goddesses and Public Documents of the Deme*, Athens.

Ehrenberg, V. (1960) *The Greek State*, Oxford.

Hansen, M.H. (1974) *The Sovereignty of the People's Court in the Fourth Century BC and the Public Action Against Unconstitutional Proposals*, Odense.

Hansen, M.H. (1978) '*Nomos* and *psephisma* in Fourth-Century Athens', GRBS 19, 315–330.

Hansen, M.H. (1979–1980) 'Athenian *nomothesia* in the Fourth Century B.C. and Demosthenes' Speech Against Leptines', C&M 32, 87–104.

Hansen, M.H. (1985) 'Athenian *nomothesia*', GRBS 26, 345–371.

Hansen, M.H. (1987) '*Graphe paranomon* Against *psephismata* Not Yet Passed by the *ekklesia*', C&M 38, 63–73.

Hansen, M.H. (1989) 'Solonian Democracy in Fourth-Century Athens', C&M 40, 71–99.

Harris, E. M (2006) 'The Rule of Law in Athenian Democracy: Reflections on the Judicial Oath', *Dike* 9, 157–181

Harris, E.M. (2013) *The Rule of Law in Action in Democratic Athens*, Oxford.

Harris, E.M. (2008) *Demosthenes, Speeches 20–22*, Austin.

Harrison, A.R.W. (1955) 'Law-Making at Athens at the End of the Fifth Century B.C.', *JHS* 75, 26–35.

Hedrick, C.W. (2000) 'For Anyone Who Wishes to See', *Ancient World* 31, 127–135.

Hillgruber, M. (1988) *Die zehnte Rede des Lysias: Einleitung, Text und Kommentar mit einem Anhang über die Gesetzesinterpretationen bei den attischen Rednern*, Berlin.

Johnstone, S. (1999) *Disputes and Democracy: The Consequences of Litigation in Ancient Athens*, Austin, TX.

Kahrstedt, U. (1938) 'Die Nomotheten und die Legislative in Athen', *Klio* 31, 1–25.

Kremmydas, C. (2012) *A commentary on Demosthenes'* Against Leptines, Oxford.

Lambert, S. (2012) *Inscribed Athenian Laws and Decrees, 352/1–322/1 BC*, Leiden.

Lanni, A. (2006) *Law and Justice in the Courts of Classical Athens*, Cambridge.

Lanni, A. (2009) 'Judicial Review and the Athenian Constitution', in Hansen, M.H., ed. (2009) *Démocratie athénienne—démocratie moderne: tradition et influences*, Geneva, 235–276.

Lieberman, R.C. (2002) 'Ideas, Institutions, and Political Order: Explaining Political Change', *American Political Science Review* 96, 697–712.

MacDowell, D.M. (1975) 'Law-Making at Athens in the Fourth Century B.C.', *JHS* 95, 62–67.

MacDowell, D.M. (2009) *Demosthenes the Orator*, Oxford.

Piérart, M. (2000) 'Qui étaient les nomothètes à l'époque de Démosthène?', in E. Lévy, ed. (2000) *La codification des lois dans l'antiquité*, Paris, 229–256.

Quass, F. (1971) Nomos *und* psephisma: *Untersuchung zum griechischen Staatsrecht*, Munich.

Rhodes, P.J. (1985) 'Nomothesia in Fourth-Century Athens', CQ 35, 55–60.

Rhodes, P.J. (2003) 'Sessions of *Nomothetai* in fourth-century Athens', CQ 53, 124–129.

Rubinstein, L. (2000) *Litigation and Cooperation: Supporting Speakers in the Courts of Classical Athens*, Stuttgart.

Ruschenbusch, E. (1966) *Solones Nomoi: die Fragmente des solonischen Gesetzwerkes mit einer Text-und Überlieferungsgeschichte*, Wiesbaden.

Schmidt, V.A. (2008) 'Discursive Institutionalism: The Explanatory Power of Ideas and Discourse', *Annual Review of Political Science* 11, 303–326.

Schmidt, V.A. (2010) 'Taking Ideas and Discourse Seriously: Explaining Change Through Discursive Institutionalism as the Fourth "New Institutionalism"', *European Political Science Review* 2, 1–25.

Schmidt, V.A. (2011) 'Speaking of Change: Why Discourse Is Key to the Dynamics of Policy Transformation', *Critical Policy Studies* 5, 106–126.

Schöll, R. (1886) 'Über attische Gesetzgebung', *Sitzungsberichte der bayerischen Akademie der Wissenschaften, philosophisch-historische Klasse*, 83–139.

Schreiner, J. (1913) *De corpore iuris Atheniensium*, Bonn.

Sickinger, J. (2008) 'Indeterminacy in Greek Law: Statutory Gaps and Conflicts', in Harris, E.M. and Thür, G., eds (2008) *Symposion 2007: Vorträge zur griechischen und hellenistischen Rechtsgeschichte* (Durham, 2–6 September 2007), Vienna, 99–112 (with a response by L. Rubinstein, 113–124).

Smith, R.M. (2008) 'Historical Institutionalism and the Study of Law' in Whittington, K.E., Kelemen, R.D. and Caldeira, G.A., eds (2008) *The Oxford Handbook of Law and Politics*, Oxford, 46–59.

Stroud, R.S. (1998) *The Athenian Grain-Tax Law of 374/3 B.C.*, Princeton.

Sundahl, M. (2000) 'The Use of Statutes in the Seven Extant *graphe paranomon* and *graphe nomon me epitedeion theinai* Speeches'. Diss., Brown University.

Sundahl, M. (2009) 'The Living Constitution of Ancient Athens: a Comparative Perspective on the Originalism Debate', *The John Marshall Law Review* 42, 463–504.

Thomas, R. (1994) 'Law and Lawgiver in the Athenian Democracy' in Osborne, R. and Hornblower, S., eds (1994) *Ritual, Finance, Politics: Athenian Democratic Accounts Presented to David Lewis*, Oxford, 119–134.

Wohl, V. (2010) *Law's Cosmos: Juridical Discourse in Athenian Forensic Oratory*, Cambridge.

Wolff, H.J. (1970) *'Normenkontrolle' und Gesetzesbegriff in der athenischen Demokratie: Untersuchungen zur graphe paranomon*, Heidelberg. (Sitzungsberichte der Heidelberger Akademie der Wissenschaften, philosophische-historische Klasse 2.)

Yunis, H. (1988) 'Law, Politics and the *graphē paranomōn* in Fourth-Century Athens', GRBS 29, 361–382.

CHAPTER 16

Abuse of the *eisangelia* in the Latter Half of the Fourth Century BC

Eleni Volonaki

Introduction: the Procedure and Its History

Eisangelia[1] was a public procedure, which was directed mainly against offences committed by public officials (either generals who had betrayed the Athenian forces or *rhētores* who deceived the Athenian *dēmos* after bribery), but could also be used against any citizen who attempted to overthrow the democracy.[2] The *eisangelia* was a democratic institution most probably introduced by Kleisthenes in 507; it could be initiated at the first stage either before the Council or before the Assembly, and at the second stage it was brought to the court. The Council had the power to inflict a fine of up to 500 *drachmas*, so when the punishment would exceed this amount the case would be heard in court. The Assembly, after accepting the charge of the *eisangelia* and ordering the Council to draw up a *probouleuma* regulating the charge, the procedure and the sentence, and finally passing the proposal, could either hear the case at a third meeting of the Assembly or refer the case to the court. The Council dealt with *eisangeliai* against public officials and citizens performing a public service (*Ath. Pol.* 8.4, 25.3–4), whereas the Assembly dealt with *eisangeliai* against private citizens, politicians and public officials (Hyp. *Eux.* 7–10).

Eisangelia could be initiated at any time of year without any time limitation, a fact that facilitated prosecutions against officials, particularly if the prosecutors did not wish to wait until the end of their office, when they would officially account for their administration in their *euthynai*. Moreover, *eisangelia* was not subject, as were other public procedures, to the time limitation of five years, a fact shown in the case of Leokrates, which was brought to court by Lykourgos in 330 BC, eight years after the alleged act of treason by fleeing from Athens

1 The term is often translated as 'impeachment', but to avoid ambiguity the Greek word is retained throughout this chapter.

2 For a basic and full account of the *eisangelia* procedure as well as the known *eisangelia* cases from the oratorical speeches, see Hansen 1975. Cf. also Harrison 1971: 51–59, MacDowell 1978: 28–29, 179–185, Todd 1993: 114.

 | DOI:10.1163/9789004377899_018

(338 BC).[3] Moreover, in an *eisangelia* the prosecutor did not face any risk, in contrast to other public cases (*graphai*), in which he was subject to a fine of 1,000 *drachmai* if he failed to secure one-fifth of the jurors' votes. Evidently, the main difference between other types of *graphai* and *eisangeliai* was that in the latter the charge had already been accepted by either the Council or the Athenian Assembly before it went to court, a control process that may explain the exemption from fine for the prosecutor of an *eisangelia*.

Nevertheless, the fact that *eisangeliai* were *azēmioi* (i.e. not subject to a penalty) until 333 BC indicates that it did offer an advantage for the prosecutor, since between 333 and 330 BC the law changed and assimilated the procedure of *eisangelia* to the conditions authorised for all other public procedures. The particular change, as well as further adjustments in matters of legislation, the form and use of *eisangelia* that occurred after the mid-fourth century in Athens, may be associated with the possible abuse of the procedure. In the present chapter, we will focus on the regulation of the *eisangelia* after the defeat of the Athenians in the battle of Chaironeia in 338 BC, in connection with the extraordinary measures voted by the Athenians at the time, in fear of Philip and Macedonian supremacy, reflecting thus the Athenians' anxiety about the threat of tyranny. Furthermore, this study explores the argumentation presented in court, in particular as derived from Lykourgos' speech *Against Leokrates* and Hypereides' speeches *For Lykophron* and *For Euxenippos*, concerning the improper use of *eisangelia* and the allegedly common abuse of the procedure. As will be shown, there seems to be a tendency to stretch the law concerning the *eisangelia*, the so-called *eisangeltikos nomos*, to cover extraordinary crimes against the state which should not have been subsumed to the specific procedure. Concerning the term of the law: 'any citizen who tried to overthrow the democracy', the charges presented in court after 338 BC were apparently extended to a remarkable degree.[4]

The specific clause in the law on *eisangelia* dealing with crimes against the constitution actually replaced all previous legislation against tyranny and overthrow of the democracy, which dates back to Drakon's time.[5] Drakon's law was supplemented by Demophantos' law, which is preserved at Andok. 1.96–98, prescribing the crimes subject to *eisangelia*.[6] According to Demophantos' law,

3 Another public legal procedure, the *apagōgē phonou*, was also exempt from any time-limit, as can be seen in Lys. 13.83.

4 Todd 1993: 114.

5 Todd 1993: 103–128.

6 There are some issues, concerning firstly the authenticity of the document cited in Andokides' speech as Demophantos' law, secondly the nature of the document (whether it is a decree

anyone who suppressed democracy or held public office after its suppression or attempted to become a tyrant or helped to install tyranny was to be treated as a public enemy, and all Athenians were expected to take an oath that such a man 'shall be killed with impunity'.

The law is datable to the first prytany of 410/09.[7] The text quoted in Andokides' speech reaffirms an ancient law, which most probably had not been invoked to prevent the tyranny of the Four Hundred in 411, and therefore required the Athenians to take an oath to observe it. The term τυραννεῖν in the text of the oath (§ 97, καὶ ἐάν τις τυραννεῖν ἐπαναστῇ ἢ τὸν τύραννον συγκαταστήσῃ) may indicate that Demophantos took over an outdated reference to tyranny from a previous law, but it could simply have derived from the common accusation of tyranny widely mentioned in the late fifth century.[8] The wording of the oath is very similar to that of the law quoted in *Ath. Pol.* 16.10: ἐάν τινες τυραννεῖν ἐπανιστῶνται [ἐπὶ τυραννίδι] ἢ συγκαθιστῇ τὴν τυραννίδα, ἄτιμον εἶναι καὶ αὐτὸν καὶ γένος ('if any persons rise in insurrection in order to govern tyrannically, or if any person assists in establishing the tyranny, he himself and his family shall be disfranchised').[9]

The *stēlē* upon which Demophantos' law was inscribed still existed in the fourth century BC and Demosthenes refers to this *stēlē* in his speech *Against Leptines*, which was delivered in 355/4 BC (Dem. 20.159). Demosthenes mentions both the inscription and the oath concerning the gratitude owed to anyone who suffered in defence of the constitution. It appears that the Athenians were committed to the oath prescribed by Demophantos' law and wished to recognise defenders of the democracy as benefactors of the city.

Lykourgos, in his prosecution against Leokrates which will be fully analysed below, also mentions Demophantos' law as prescribing that a person who aspired to tyranny or attempted to overthrow the constitution or betray the city should be put to death (Lykourg. 1.124–125). Subsequently, Lykourgos cites the decree, including the oath taken, and for his own purposes he stresses death as the inevitable punishment of a traitor, and impunity for the citizen who would dare to kill the traitor (§ 126). Lykourgos, however, states three times

---

proposed by Demophantos or a Solonian law), and finally the revision of the Solonian law that occurred after the restoration of the democracy in 403 BC. For a detailed discussion, cf. Canevaro and Harris 2012: 119–225.

7 As Edwards 1995: 181 argues with comparison to ML 84.

8 Cf. MacDowell 1962: 136 with Thuc. 6.53.3, 60.1; Ar. *Vesp.* 417, 464, 488; *Av.* 1074; *Thesm.* 338, 1143; *Lys.* 619, 630.

9 For a review of the evidence for measures against attempts to overthrow the democracy or set up a tyranny, cf. Ostwald 1955: 103–128 and Rhodes 1981: 220–222.

(1.125, 126, 127) that Demophantos' decree applied to those who killed both those who had attempted to set up a tyranny and those who had attempted to betray the city. However, the oath in the inserted document in Andok. 1 does not include traitors.[10] Moreover, it is striking that Lykourgos makes use of Demophantos' law at this point of the speech, towards the end of his prosecution, in his attempt to persuade the jurors to condemn Leokrates to death. He takes it for granted that Leokrates is a traitor to the constitution, a charge that has supposedly been well established through a variety of examples of traitors in the past, who had been punished by the whole of the city, but not substantiated by any decree prescribing that Leokrates' flight could be considered an act of treason.

Demophantos' law had obviously preserved the spirit of the original law of Drakon and must have been popular among the Athenians throughout the fourth century BC. Lykourgos prefers to cite Demophantos' law rather than that of Eukrates, which had been introduced in 336 BC, a few years before Leokrates' trial, and which prohibited the Areopagites from holding office or sitting in council in the event of the democracy being overthrown. Eukrates' law reflected the anti-tyrannical mood of the Athenians due to their fear of Philip and Macedonian military superiority in general. Both in Demophantos' and in Eukrates' law it is made clear that the rebel who attempts to overthrow the democracy or impose tyranny loses all right to the protection of the law and may be killed with impunity.

The *eisangeltikos nomos* was most probably introduced after 336. It was almost certainly in place by 330 BC, since it is cited in the speech delivered by Hypereides at Euxenippos' trial (between 330 and 324):[11]

> ὑπὲρ τίνων οὖν οἴεσθε δεῖν τὰς εἰσαγγελίας γίγνεσθαι; τοῦτ' ἤδη καθ' ἕκαστον ἐν τῷ νόμῳ ἐγράψατε, ἵνα μὴ ἀγνοῇ μηδείς: 'ἐάν τις,' φησί, 'τὸν δῆμον τὸν Ἀθηναίων καταλύῃ:'—εἰκότως, ὦ ἄνδρες δικασταί: ἡ γὰρ τοιαύτη αἰτία οὐ παραδέχεται

10 Based on the content of the oath, its contradiction of the content of Demophantos' law, its wording and its structure, Canevaro and Harris 2012: 124 argue that neither the oath nor Demophantos' law as a whole should be taken as an authentic document.

11 Various dates have been suggested by scholars, as for example 411/10 immediately after the fall of the Four Hundred, 403 after the restoration of the democracy and in connection with the republication of all Athenian laws, after 336 when Eucrates' law on treason and *eisangelia* was introduced; for a review of these suggestions, cf. Ostwald 1955: 127. Given that the *eisangeltikos nomos* was based on and combined all preceding decrees and laws on *eisangelia* as used and extended to cases of treason in the second half of the fourth century BC, the latter date would seem more likely.

> σκῆψιν οὐδεμίαν οὐδενὸς οὐδ' ὑπωμοσίαν, ἀλλὰ τὴν ταχίστην αὐτὴν δεῖ εἶναι ἐν τῷ δικαστηρίῳ:—[ἢ 'συνίῃ ποι ἐπὶ καταλύσει τοῦ δήμου ἢ ἑταιρικὸν συναγάγῃ, ἢ ἐάν τις πόλιν τινὰ προδῷ ἢ ναῦς ἢ πεζὴν ἢ ναυτικὴν στρατιάν, ἢ ῥήτωρ ὢν μὴ λέγῃ τὰ ἄριστα τῷ δήμῳ τῷ Ἀθηναίων χρήματα λαμβάνων': τὰ μὲν ἄνω τοῦ νόμου κατὰ πάντων τῶν πολιτῶν γράψαντες (ἐκ πάντων γὰρ καὶ τἀδικήματα ταῦτα γένοιτ' ἄν), τὸ δὲ τελευταῖον τοῦ νόμου κατ' αὐτῶν τῶν ῥητόρων, παρ' οἷς ἔστιν καὶ τὸ γράφειν τὰ ψηφίσματα.
>
> So in what circumstances do you think *eisangeliai* should arise? You have already specified this in detail in the law, to leave nobody in doubt. 'If anyone', it says, 'seeks to overthrow the Athenian people.' Naturally, men of the jury: such a charge allows no procedural delay whatsoever, not even an affidavit for postponement, but must be heard in the jurycourt as soon as possible. 'Or if he gets together anywhere with a view to overthrow of the people, or assembles an association; or if anyone betrays a city or ships or an army or fleet; or says things, as a *rhētōr*, not in the best interests of the Athenian people and takes money for doing so'.
>
> HYP. *Eux.* 7–8[12]

The law refers explicitly to the *eisangelia* procedure, and the offences subject to it include firstly the attempt to overthrow the democracy or conspiracy against the constitution, but also additional charges such as treason, acceptance of bribes by *rhētores* to speak against the public interest, deceiving the *dēmos* by giving false promises, and finally offences relevant to treason, such as damage to naval facilities or trading, arson of public buildings or documents, and acts of sacrilege. The *eisangeltikos nomos* presents similarities with clauses in earlier legislation concerning attempts to overthrow or conspiracies against the constitution of the democracy, such as Demophantos' decree and Eukrates' law, but it seems likely that we are dealing with a distinct law which coexists with a number of earlier laws dealing with specific offences. The evidence from the attested *eisangeliai* in the Assembly during the period from 493 until 324 shows that there was a change after 360/50,[13] and no *eisangelia* was heard by the Assembly after that date, but all *eisangeliai* in the Assembly were referred immediately to court.[14] Further modifications to the orig-

---

12 The translation of all texts from Hypereides' speeches is by Whitehead 2000 with a few adjustments.

13 Hansen 1975: 51–53.

14 Cf. Dem. 24.63. The reference in Timokrates' law to the γραμματεύς κατά πρυτανείαν, who is not attested before 363, proves that the *nomos eisangeltikos* was revised at some time

inal *eisangeltikos nomos* must have occurred after the middle of the fourth century BC, as reflected in the introduction of the provision that the prosecutor of an *eisangelia* was subject to a fine of 1,000 *drachmai*, after 333 BC. The amendment to the *eisangeltikos nomos* resulted in strengthening the powers of the court and reducing the powers of the Assembly, while the powers of the Areiopagos were considerably extended in the second half of the fourth century.[15]

The Impact of the Defeat at Chaironeia

The Athenians took extraordinary measures after the defeat at Chaironeia in order to secure the protection of their city and of the women and the children in it. The authority of the Areiopagos was exceptionally increased to the same end. Lykourgos in his speech *Against Leokrates* refers to a decree, according to which the Council of the Areiopagos could seize and execute men who had fled from their country after the battle of Chaironeia and had abandoned it to the enemy:

> ... ἡ μὲν γὰρ ἐν Ἀρείῳ πάγῳ βουλή (καὶ μηδείς μοι θορυβήσῃ: ταύτην γὰρ ὑπολαμβάνω μεγίστην τότε γενέσθαι τῇ πόλει σωτηρίαν τοὺς φυγόντας τὴν πατρίδα καὶ ἐγκαταλιπόντας τότε τοῖς πολεμίοις λαβοῦσα ἀπέκτεινε. ... ἀλλὰ μὴν Αὐτολύκου μὲν ὑμεῖς κατεψηφίσασθε, μείναντος μὲν αὐτοῦ ἐν τοῖς κινδύνοις, ἔχοντος δ' αἰτίαν τοὺς υἱεῖς καὶ τὴν γυναῖκα ὑπεκθέσθαι, καὶ ἐτιμωρήσασθε ...
>
> The council of the Areiopagos;—No one, please, interrupt me; that council was, in my opinion, the greatest reason for the survival of the city at the time) arrested and executed men who at that time fled their country and abandoned it to the enemy. (...) Moreover you condemned and

during the decade 363–354; cf. Hansen 1975: 54. Hansen suggests a date around 355 and associates the modification of the law with the relevant institutions to the division of powers between the Assembly and the court. The first institution was the limitation of the number of extraordinary assemblies and the second institution was the introduction of the procedure called *apophasis*, which also involved charges of treason and bribery of public speakers. Both institutions were introduced in 350 BC. Furthermore, Hansen suggests that the *eisangeltikos nomos* had a Solonian origin, since all the powers exercised by the court in the fourth century were believed to be Solonian in origin.

15 Cf. Lykourg. 1.55–56.

> punished Autolykos for secretly sending his wife and sons away, even though he himself remained here to face danger.
>
> LYKOURG. 1.52–54[16]

From this passage, it appears that the Areiopagos took the initiative not only in arresting deserters from the city but also in condemning them to death. Such a power was both suspect and contentious, as can be inferred from Lykourgos' request not to be interrupted (μηδείς μοι θορυβήσῃ). The Areiopagos' executions were a punishment beyond its jurisdiction, which occasioned outrage both at the time and even at its mention in 330 BC at Leokrates' trial.[17] The Athenian Assembly had also prescribed by decree that the women and children should be brought inside the walls, and that the generals should appoint guards to protect the Athenian citizens and other residents at Athens. Under these circumstances the scope of the offences subject to *eisangeliai* was extended or allowed space for legal argumentation in court.

Lykourgos, who was politically prominent in Athens in the period 338 until 326 BC, played a significant role either as a prosecutor or as a *synēgoros* in *eisangeliai*.[18] Lykourgos had denounced Autolykos in 338 BC for the flight of his wife and sons from Attica after the defeat at Chaironeia and most probably after the vote of the relevant decree forbidding the citizens to flee from Athens. The procedure was an *eisangelia* and the trial resulted in the condemnation of Autolykos to death.[19]

Autolykos was condemned to death on the basis of a decree made after the battle of Chaironeia forbidding citizens and their families to flee from the city of Athens. There is no evidence about the date of this decree; but Autolykos was obviously subject to punishment because his action followed the enactment of the decree. In the same year (338 BC) Lykourgos denounced Lysik-

16 The translation of passages from Lykourgos' *Against Leokrates* derives from Harris 2001 (in Worthington/ Cooper/ Harris 2001) with some adjustments.

17 Further on the Areiopagos' abuse of authority after the defeat in Chaironeia, cf. Sullivan 2003: 130–134.

18 As Plutarch mentions (*X orat.* 843d), Lykourgos accused and had several persons convicted as guilty, and even condemned them to death and his successful prosecution against Diphilos contributed to the amount of 160 talents for the treasury. Immediately after the battle of Chaironeia, in 338 BC, he prosecuted Autolykos, based on both decrees passed by the Athenians, for treason, on the grounds that he had secretly sent his wife and sons away and the trial resulted in his condemnation to death; Hansen 1975: no 113. Lykourgos also denounced Lysikles for his role as a general in the battle and succeeded in having him condemned to death Hansen 1975: no 112.

19 Hansen 1975: no 113.

les for his role as a general at the battle of Chaironeia and brought him to court by an *eisangelia*; he was also convicted as responsible for the Athenians' defeat.[20] The cases of both Autolykos and Lysikles were closely related to the defeat at Chaironeia, after which the Athenians were devastated, and the charge of treason would have been an easy one to invoke for any kind of misconduct.

The Prosecution of Lykophron

A few years later, in 333 BC, Lykourgos acted as a *synēgoros* in the prosecution against Lykophron, which was an *eisangelia* with the accusation of treason, even though the actual offence was adultery; Hypereides had composed the speech in defence of Lykophron.

The prosecutor is Ariston, who maintains that Lykophron has had an affair with an Athenian woman who was married first to an unknown Athenian and, after his death, to Charripus. In particular, the indictment seems to involve Lykophron's attempt to persuade the woman to avoid physical contact with Charippos:

> ἄξιον δ' ἐστίν, ὦ ἄνδρες δικασταί, κἀκεῖθεν ἐξετάσαι τὸ πρᾶγμα, ἀφ' ὧν ἐν τῷ δήμῳ τὸ πρῶτον αὐτοὶ εὐθὺς ᾐτιάσαντο. ἐμοὶ γὰρ οἱ οἰκεῖοι ἀπέστειλαν γράψαντες τήν τε εἰσαγγελίαν καὶ τὰς αἰτίας ἃς ἐν τῇ ἐκκλησίᾳ ᾐτιάσαντό με, ὅτε τὴν εἰσαγγελίαν ἐδίδοσαν, ἐν αἷς ἦν γεγραμμένον ὅτι Λυκοῦργος λέγει, φάσκων τῶν οἰκείων ἀκηκοέναι, ὡς ἐγὼ παρακολουθῶν, ὅτε Χάριππος ἐγάμει τὴν γυναῖκα, παρεκελευόμην αὐτῇ ὅπως μὴ πλησιάσει Χαρίππῳ ἀλλὰ διαφυλάξει αὐτήν.
>
> In examining the affair, men of the jury, an appropriate starting-point is what these men originally accused me of, before the people. My family, you see, wrote to me with an account both of the eisangelia *and of the charges they brought against me in the Assembly when they submitted the* eisangelia. *Amongst these was a record of a statement by Lykourgos. He claimed to have heard from the family that, during Charippos' wedding to the woman, I tagged along and tried to persuade her not to be intimate with Charippos, but to be on her guard against him.*
>
> HYP. *Lyk.* 3

20 Hansen 1975: no 112.

Although Lykophron refers later to many accusations, all of them false, on the prosecution side, it is clear that the alleged crime attributed to him is *moicheia*. This is emphatically repeated in a form of a rhetorical question, where Lykophron suggests that it would have been senseless for Charippos to marry a woman who had sworn to be true to her lover:

> τὸ δὲ κεφάλαιον ἁπάντων, ὡς καὶ μικρῷ πρότερον εἶπον, εἰς τοῦτο ἀναισθησίας ὁ Χάριππος, ὡς ἔοικεν, ἦλθεν, ὥστε πρότερον μέν, ὥς φασιν, τῆς γυναικὸς προλεγούσης ὅτι συνομωμοκυῖα εἴη πρὸς ἐμέ, πάλιν δὲ ἀκούων ἐμοῦ παρακελευμένου αὐτῇ ὅπως ἐμμείνειεν τοῖς ὅρκοις οἷς ὤμοσεν, ἐλάμβανε τὴν γυναῖκα; καὶ ταῦτα δοκεῖ ἂν ὑμῖν ἢ Ὀρέστης ἐκεῖνος ὁ μαινόμενος ποιῆσαι ἢ Μαργίτης ὁ πάντων ἀβελτερώτατος;
>
> And to cap it all, as I said a short while ago: had Charippos become so obtuse, apparently, as to have married the woman, when first she had said beforehand—*they claim—that she had pledged herself to me, and later he had heard me urging her to abide by the oaths which she had sworn?* Do you think that either Orestes the madman would have done that, or Margites, the biggest fool of all?
>
> HYP. *Lyk.* 7

In order to strengthen his argument that the prosecutor is lying, Hypereides draws on the common topos that 'prosecuting is better than defending' (Hyp. *Lyk.* 8). The phrase, however, 'prosecuting in the trial entails no risk' (διὰ τὸ ἀκίνδυνον) seems to refer particularly to the *eisangelia*, and so implies an abuse of the procedure due to the risk-free privilege.[21] In order to undermine further the *eisangelia* procedure used for the specific case, Lykophron ridicules the false accusations and argues that he is innocent on the grounds that adultery is a practice which no man can begin after fifty (Hyp. *Lyk.* 15).

Lykophron protests that it is not in an *eisangelia* that he should be defending himself. He maintains that the charges against him are charges 'concerning matters where the laws prescribe public actions before the thesmothetai' (Hyp. *Lyk.* 12). An obvious alternative would be a *graphē moicheias*. The second point of the defence concerning the propriety of the procedure is to present Lykophron as a private person, an *idiōtēs*, rather than a public figure, against whom an *eisangelia* should not be initiated, as presented in §§16–

21 For a parallel implication in the *topos*, 'prosecution is risk-free in eisangelias', cf. Isa. 3.47, where it is explained in procedural terms—fines, deposits, fees; cf. Whitehead 2000: 124.

20. However, Lykophron's personal record reveals that he had been honoured for his *andragathia* on eight occasions.[22] Evidently, his socio-economic status was high, since he was a *hippeus*. Although Hypereides' defence strategy was based on the argument that Lykophron was a private rather than a public person, he proudly mentions his tenure of two elective military posts: *phylarchos* of his tribe and *hipparchos* in Lemnos. In § 20 the term 'private individual' (*idiōtēs*) is qualified as 'unaccustomed to speaking'. He is an inexperienced speaker because he has avoided involvement in litigation or an active role in the Assembly. His office-holding, as phylarch and hipparch, does not weaken this claim, but still the question whether he can be considered an *idiōtēs* remains open. Any Athenian citizen was subject to an *eisangelia*, if he could be charged with an attempt to overthrow the democracy. According to Hansen 'this crime committed against a free-born Athenian woman is interpreted as an infringement of the law as such and, accordingly, as an infringement of the democratic constitution, which is based on the law'.[23] Hypereides' claim is designed to stress the unsuitability of the *eisangelia* firstly on the grounds of the offence, which is adultery and not treason, and secondly on the grounds of the offender who is not a public speaker but a simple Athenian citizen.

The allegation of *moicheia* had obviously and most probably exceptionally been accepted as the basis for a charge of treason by the Athenian Assembly. One possible explanation might have been that Lykourgos, who was influential at the time and heavily involved in the prosecution of *eisangeliai*, played a significant role in persuading the Assembly to accept adultery as treason. It may have been his prestige and his decisive defence for the protection of the city from traitors and threatening offenders that had secured the Athenians' approval. It is likely that the prosecution of Lykophron served as a test case for Lykourgos' efforts to transform the *eisangelia* procedure 'into a quasi-catch-all remedy for un-Athenian-activities'.[24]

The fact that arguments on the suitability of the procedure are raised in court may reflect the novelty of the presentation of charges that would not normally have been considered to be subject to the *eisangeltikos nomos*. It appears to be rather a matter of interpretation of the scope of the law than an issue of legislation extending the range of the process. One might expect that the

22 (i) By the entire cavalry corps, (ii) and by his colleagues in office, (iii–iv) three times by the citizen-body in Hephaistia, (v–viii) and as many times again by the one in Myrine; cf. Whitehead 2000: 138 ff.

23 Hansen 1975: no 119.

24 Phillips 2006: 393. For an analysis of Lykophron's case of *eisangelia*, ibid 375–394.

jury would be unwilling to agree with the prosecution that exile, execution and prohibition of burial in the city would be appropriate for a seducer, whose enemies had waited for three years to press charges against him.[25] Unfortunately, the result is not known and we can only make assumptions. If, however, Hypereides had won the case he would have mentioned it later in his defence for Euxenippos where he mentions various *eisangeliai* based on minor offences irrelevant to the *eisangeltikos nomos*. Finally, the use of *eisangelia* to prosecute a case of alleged treason indicates that at the time *eisangelia* was widely used as a potent weapon against 'enemies' of the city, reflecting a moralising agenda at the time due to the political instability and vulnerable security of the city of Athens.

The Prosecution of Leokrates

In 330 BC, eight years after the battle of Chaironeia, Lykourgos prosecuted Leokrates in an *eisangelia* based on the charge of treason:

> εὔχομαι γὰρ τῇ Ἀθηνᾷ καὶ τοῖς ἄλλοις θεοῖς καὶ τοῖς ἥρωσι τοῖς κατὰ τὴν πόλιν καὶ τὴν χώραν ἱδρυμένοις, εἰ μὲν εἰσήγγελκα Λεωκράτη δικαίως καὶ κρίνω τὸν προδόντ' αὐτῶν καὶ τοὺς νεὼς καὶ τὰ ἕδη καὶ τὰ τεμένη καὶ τὰς ἐν τοῖς νόμοις τιμὰς καὶ θυσίας τὰς ὑπὸ τῶν ὑμετέρων προγόνων παραδεδομένας …
>
> This is my prayer to Athena and those other gods and heroes whose statues stand throughout our city and countryside—if the *eisangelia* I have brought against Leokrates is just and if I have brought this man to court because he has betrayed the temples, shrines and precincts of the gods as well as the honours granted by the laws and the sacrificial rites handed down by your ancestors …
>
> LYKOURG. 1.1

Lykourgos defines treason as desertion of the city and the temples, as well as breach of the ancestral traditions. In particular, Leokrates' assumed treason is, according to Lykourgos, the violation of the decree made by the Athenians immediately after the defeat at the battle of Chaironeia in order to protect their city:

25 Colin 1934: 120.

> γεγενημένης γὰρ τῆς ἐν Χαιρωνείᾳ μάχης, καὶ συνδραμόντων ἁπάντων ὑμῶν εἰς τὴν ἐκκλησίαν, ἐψηφίσατο ὁ δῆμος παῖδας μὲν καὶ γυναῖκας ἐκ τῶν ἀγρῶν εἰς τὰ τείχη κατακομίζειν, τοὺς δὲ στρατηγοὺς τάττειν εἰς τὰς φυλακὰς τῶν Ἀθηναίων καὶ τῶν ἄλλων τῶν οἰκούντων Ἀθήνησι, καθ' ὅ τι ἂν αὐτοῖς δοκῇ. Λεωκράτης δὲ τούτων οὐδενὸς φροντίσας …
>
> After the battle at Chaironeia was over, all of you ran to meet in the Assembly, and the people decreed that the women and children should be brought from the countryside inside the walls and that the generals should appoint any Athenians or other residents at Athens for guard duty in whatever way they saw fit. Leokrates paid no attention at all to these decisions.
>
> LYKOURG. 1.16

The question is whether Leokrates can be accused of violating any of the decrees passed after the battle of Chaironeia. In the trial of Leokrates, Lykourgos may be effectively applying Autolykos' case as a precedent to persuade the jurors to convict Leokrates.[26] However, there seems to have been no law or decree in place at the time forbidding Leokrates' flight.[27] The most likely assumption is that these special terms were enacted and validated after Leokrates had left the city, because otherwise Lykourgos would have emphasised this fact, as he clearly mentions that Autolykos had smuggled his family out of Athens in violation of the decree. Due to the technical difficulty of charging Leokrates for the breach of this legislative measure, Lykourgos attempts to extend the definition of treason, an offence included in the *eisangeltikos nomos*. The definition of offences subject to an *eisangelia* seems to have expanded and included further different crimes in the second half of the fourth century BC. Lykourgos cites definitions and explanations of such crimes when he accuses Leokrates of many offences, reflecting a rhetorical exaggeration rather than a legislative reform:

> … ἔνοχον ὄντα Λεωκράτην ἔστιν ἰδεῖν, **προδοσίας** μὲν ὅτι τὴν πόλιν ἐγκαταλιπὼν τοῖς πολεμίοις ὑποχείριον ἐποίησε, **δήμου δὲ καταλύσεως** ὅτι οὐχ ὑπέμεινε τὸν ὑπὲρ τῆς ἐλευθερίας κίνδυνον, **ἀσεβείας** δ' ὅτι τοῦ τὰ τεμένη τέμνεσθαι καὶ τοὺς νεὼς κατασκάπτεσθαι τὸ καθ' ἑαυτὸν γέγονεν αἴτιος, **τοκέων δὲ κακώσεως** τὰ μνημεῖα αὐτῶν ἀφανίζων καὶ τῶν νομίμων ἀποστερῶν, **λιποταξίου** δὲ καὶ **ἀστρατείας** οὐ παρασχὼν τὸ σῶμα τάξαι τοῖς στρατηγοῖς.

26 Usher 1999: 327 indicates that Autolykos' case was different from that of Leokrates.

27 Usher 1999: 324.

> Leokrates is guilty of every one of these crimes: **treason**, since he left the city and surrendered it to the enemy; **overthrowing the democracy**, because he did not face danger in defence of freedom; **impiety**, because he is guilty of doing all he could to ravage the sacred precincts and destroy the temples; **mistreatment of parents** by destroying their tombs and robbing them of their ancestral rites; and **desertion** and **cowardice**, for refusing to report to the generals for duty.
>
> LYKOURG. 1.147

It is remarkable how many charges are rhetorically emphasised and subsumed in the main accusation of treason; Lykourgos is accused of treason and consequently charged for the same cause with the overthrow of the democracy, impiety, mistreatment of his parents, desertion and refusal to serve. It is also striking, as we shall see below, that these alleged offences, as they are defined by Lykourgos here, were also invoked for the use of the *eisangelia* after the battle of Chaironeia (338 BC).

Lykourgos' interpretation of flight from the city of Athens as the basis for an *eisangelia* seems to have been used for the first time in the trial of Leokrates:

> … ἀλλὰ διὰ τὸ μήτ' ἐν τοῖς πρότερον χρόνοις γεγενῆσθαι τοιοῦτον μηδὲν μήτ' ἐν τοῖς μέλλουσιν ἐπίδοξον εἶναι γενήσεσθαι. διὸ καὶ μάλιστ', ὦ ἄνδρες, δεῖ ὑμᾶς γενέσθαι μὴ μόνον τοῦ νῦν ἀδικήματος δικαστάς, ἀλλὰ καὶ νομοθέτας. (…) ἀναγκαῖον τὴν ὑμετέραν κρίσιν καταλείπεσθαι παράδειγμα τοῖς ἐπιγιγνομένοις.
>
> … but because no such crime occurred in earlier times, as no one at the time expected it would happen in the future. As a result, gentlemen, you must above all act not only as judges for this crime but also as legislators. (…) your verdict must be left as a precedent for your successors.
>
> LYKOURG. 1.9

The rhetorical *hyperbolē* that the jurors set a legal precedent with their vote in a court case is a common *topos* in oratorical speeches, which aims to prejudice the jurors and influence their decision. In general, arguments from consequence with reference to the effects of the jurors' verdicts are very frequent in forensic oratory.[28] In reality, however, it was impossible for the jurors to make their verdicts consistent with previous verdicts by other jurors in different court

---

28 E.g. Lys. 1.48–49, 12.99–100, 13.92–97, 30.32–34.

cases. There was no legal requirement for the jurors to comply with previous decisions, even if there was a relevant connection between the cases.[29]

The additional force of Lykourgos' argument, here, is that he asks the jurors to become *nomothetai*, judging a case supposedly for the first time and thus setting a legal precedent to be followed by future juries, and, as it appears, the prosecutor creates the legal basis for his prosecution within the court case.[30] Moreover, the use of the argument reflects an awareness that the prosecutor is stretching the definition of treason to an unusual and perhaps unprecedented degree. The *eisangelia* does not seem to be legally the most appropriate procedure in Leokrates' case, since his flight was not forbidden by law at the time, but most probably it was silently accepted and brought to court.

The result of Leokrates' case is known to us from Aischines *Against Ktesiphon*:

> ἕτερος δ' ἐκπλεύσας ἰδιώτης εἰς Ῥόδον, ὅτι τὸν φόβον ἀνάνδρως ἤνεγκε, πρώην ποτὲ εἰσηγγέλθη, καὶ ἴσαι αἱ ψῆφοι αὐτῷ ἐγένοντο: εἰ δὲ μία ψῆφος μετέπεσεν, ὑπερώριστ' ἄν.
>
> Another private citizen, who sailed away to Rhodes, was only recently prosecuted, as a coward in the face of danger. The vote of the jury was a tie, and if a single vote had been changed, he would have gone into exile.
> AISCHIN. 3.252

According to Aischines, Leokrates was acquitted because the votes were equal; in particular ὅτι τὸν φόβον ἀνάνδρως ἤνεγκε. It is undoubtedly remarkable that Lykourgos actually managed to persuade such a large number of jurors to accept the *eisangelia* in order to prosecute Leokrates for treason, merely because he had left the city of Athens at a crucial time without being required by law to stay in the city. On the other hand, an equally large part of the jury was not convinced that such an interpretation of treason as flight from the city could be valid; therefore, they could only understand Leokrates' alleged offence as acting from fear and cowardice. The verdict in the specific case suggests that there was a real difference in Athenian public opinion on the appropriate scope of the *eisangelia*.

29 For a different view, see Harris in this volume.

30 Further on 'the rhetoric of consistency and prospective precedent in the extant speeches' and Lykourgos' consequentialist argument, cf. Lanni 1999: 41–44.

The Prosecution of Euxenippos

At some point between 330 and 324 BC, most probably after the trial of Leokrates, who had been charged with treason on the grounds that he had fled from Athens immediately after the battle of Chaironeia and was eventually acquitted, Euxenippos was charged with deceit of the *dēmos* after bribery, even though he himself was not a *rhētōr*; Lykourgos participated in the *eisangelia* against Euxenippos and Hypereides had composed his speech *For Euxenippos* in his defence. As will be shown, Euxenippos' case constituted again an exceptional use of *eisangelia.*

Euxenippos and two unnamed fellow-citizens had been given the task of sleeping overnight in the sanctuary of the god Amphiaraos at Oropos, so as to discover, through what the god told them in their sleep, whether a particular tract of land in Oropos belonged to him or could be allocated to two of the ten Athenian tribes, Acamantis and Hippothoöntis (§§15–18). Euxenippos had a dream which he announced before the Assembly, but it was considered that the meaning of the dream was not fully clear. Polyeuktos proposed a decree that the land should be returned to the god and that the other eight tribes should compensate Hippothoöntis and Acamantis for their loss. The decree was defeated, and Polyeuktos was convicted in court for proposing an illegal decree but only fined 25 *drachmai.* However, he was not dissuaded, and with the support of Lykourgos, who would speak at the trial, he brought an *eisangelia* against Euxenippos with the allegation of aceepting bribes from both tribes in order to report his dream (§§30, 39, cf. 15). Furthermore, Euxenippos was charged with being pro-Macedonian (§§19–26) and, finally, with various offences irrelevant to the case (§31).

The evident aim of the prosecution was to deepen the significance of Euxenippos' action so that it would seem a crime which threatened the security of the democracy.[31] As the defendant in an *eisangelia*, Euxenippos obviously risked conviction if the jury took the view that his conduct had breached any provision of the *nomos eisangeltikos.* Thus one of Hypereides' lines of defence is that no such breach has occurred. But the central thrust of his argument is that Euxenippos is an *idiōtēs* (§§3, 9, 11, 13, 27–30), whereas the section in the *nomos eisangeltikos* which deals with bribery concerns only *rhētōres* (§§1–2, 4–10, 27–30, 38–39).

It is striking that Hypereides begins his defence of Euxenippos by arguing that the *eisangeliai* made at the present time are different from the *eisangeliai*

31 Curtis 1970: 31–32.

that used to be made in earlier times. He mentions five 'previous' *eisangeliai*, apparently from the late 360s,[32] which all involved cases against generals and dealt with major crimes; the speaker shows amazement at the extraordinary use of the specific procedure in current cases and emphasises the fact that none of the charges described in more recent cases had anything to do with the *eisangeltikos nomos*:

> ἀλλ' ἔγωγε, ὦ ἄνδρες δικασταί, ὅπερ καὶ πρὸς τοὺς παρακαθημένους ἀρτίως ἔλεγον, θαυμάζω εἰ μὴ προσίστανται ἤδη ὑμῖν αἱ τοιαῦται εἰσαγγελίαι. τὸ μὲν γὰρ πρότερον εἰσηγγέλλοντο παρ' ὑμῖν Τιμόμαχος καὶ Λεωσθένης καὶ Καλλίστρατος καὶ Φίλων ὁ ἐξ Ἀναίων καὶ Θεότιμος ὁ Σηστὸν ἀπολέσας καὶ ἕτεροι τοιοῦτοι: καὶ οἱ μὲν αὐτῶν ναῦς αἰτίαν ἔχοντες προδοῦναι, οἱ δὲ πόλεις Ἀθηναίων, ὁ δὲ ῥήτωρ ὢν λέγειν μὴ τὰ ἄριστα τῷ δήμῳ. καὶ οὔτε τούτων πέντε ὄντων οὐδεὶς ὑπέμεινε τὸν ἀγῶνα, ἀλλ' αὐτοὶ ᾤχοντο φεύγοντες ἐκ τῆς πόλεως, οὔτ' ἄλλοι πολλοὶ τῶν εἰσαγγελλομένων, ἀλλ' ἦν σπάνιον ἰδεῖν ἀπ' εἰσαγγελίας τινὰ κρινόμενον ὑπακούσαντα εἰς τὸ δικαστήριον: οὕτως ὑπὲρ μεγάλων ἀδικημάτων καὶ περιφανῶν αἱ εἰσαγγελίαι τότε ἦσαν. νυνὶ δὲ τὸ γιγνόμενον ἐν τῇ πόλει πάνυ καταγέλαστόν ἐστιν. Διογνίδης μὲν καὶ Ἀντίδωρος ὁ μέτοικος εἰσαγγέλλονται ὡς **πλέονος** μισθοῦντες τὰς αὐλητρίδας ἢ ὁ νόμος κελεύει, Ἀγασικλῆς δ' ὁ ἐκ Πειραιέως ὅτι εἰς Ἁλιμουσίους ἐνεγράφη, Εὐξένιππος δ' ὑπὲρ τῶν ἐνυπνίων ὧν φησιν ἑωρακέναι: ὧν οὐδεμία δήπου τῶν αἰτιῶν τούτων οὐδὲν κοινωνεῖ τῷ εἰσαγγελτικῷ νόμῳ.

Well, personally, men of the jury, as I was just saying to those seated nearby, I am amazed that by now *eisangeliai* like this do not sicken you. Previously, those prosecuted in *eisangeliai* were Timomachos and Leosthenes and Kallistratos, and Philon from Anaia and Theotimos who lost Sestos, and others of that sort; some of them accused of betraying ships, others Athenian cities—and one of saying things, as a speaker, not in the best interests of the people. None of these five awaited their trial:

---

32 The five *eisangelia* cases were the following: the case against Timomachos, a general in 361/0, who is charged with treason, embezzlement and with having ordered Kallippos to convey Kallistratos, his relative, from Methone to Thasos on board an Athenian trireme (cf. Dem. 19.180, Aischin. 1.56); the case against Leosthenes a general in 362/1, who is charged with treason (cf. Aischinin. 2.124); Kallistratos, charged with 'having been bribed to make proposals in the Assembly contrary to the interests of the people' and acquitted in the Oropos case (Plut. *Dem.* 5) but convicted and sentenced to death in a later case (Lykourg. 1.93); Philon, a *bouleutēs* in 335/4 and most probably a general, but nothing further is known about him (Hansen 1975: no 89); Theotimos who lost Sestos (Hansen 1975: no 94), a general in 361/0 or 360/59. Cf. Whitehead 2000: 172–174.

> they left, fleeing the polis of their own accord. Many others who were facing *eisangelia* did the same; it was a rarity to see a defendant in an *eisangelia* obediently appearing before the jurycourt. Such were *eisangeliai* then: they dealt with major crimes, *causes célèbres*. But what is happening now in the polis is totally ridiculous. It is Diognides and Antidoros the metic who are accused of hiring out pipers for more than the law prescribes; and Agasikles from Piraeus because he was registered as a demesman of Halimous, and Euxenippos on account of the dreams he says he had. Not one of these charges, of course, has anything to do with the *eisangeltikos nomos*.
>
> HYP. *Eux.* 1–3

Although the force of the comparison between previous and more recent *eisangeliai* is largely rhetorical, it does seem to reflect a real change in the use of the procedure and a certain attitude of the Athenians to it. The present practice in the city is described as absurd, *katagelaston*, which implies that prosecutors do not bring *eisangeliai* on serious charges any more. In particular, the cases mentioned are the *eisangeliai* against Diognides, presumably a citizen and doubtless a pimp but not otherwise known, and Antidoros the metic, not otherwise known, who were both accused of hiring out girl pipers for more than the law prescribed.[33] The *eisangelia* against Agasikles from Piraeus, who was accused either of being a citizen falsely enrolled in the wrong deme or an alien usurping the rights of citizenship, had a successful outcome for the defendant and Agasikles was listed as a Halimousian. Even though the charge was a serious one, it would more appropriately have been addressed by a *graphē xenias*, an indication that *eisangelia* superseded the use of other public procedures covering a wide range of offences related to or interpreted under the label of 'treason'. The lack of seriousness emphasised by Hypereides in this effective rhetorical contrast between past and present *eisangeliai* may also imply the trivialisation of the procedure dealing with charges irrelevant to the law.

Hypereides, when quoting the *eisangeltikos nomos* in § 8, draws a contrast between the two sections of the law: its 'opening provisions' (τὰ μὲν ἄνω τοῦ

33 According to *Ath. Pol.* 50.2 it fell to the ten *astynomoi* in office each year to see that female pipers (*aulētrides*), harpists (*psaltriai*), and lyre-players (*kitharistriai*) were not hired out for more than 2 *drachmas*. The concern was keeping the sex trade within bounds. Hansen 1975: nos 122–123 understands Hypereides as meaning that Diognides and Antidoros were the defendants in separate trials of a comparable kind, and suggests that the offence was perhaps 'interpreted as an infringement of the law as such, and, accordingly, as an attempt to overthow the democracy'. For an interpretation of the ridiculous current *eisangeliai*, cf. Whitehead 2000: 177–181.

νόμου) include everything from 'if anyone seeks to overthrow the Athenian people' to 'if anyone betrays a city or ships or an army or fleet'. For the purposes of the defence strategy all this is 'applicable to all citizens'. The 'last part' of the law (τὸ δὲ τελευταῖον τοῦ νόμου) was 'or says things, as a *rhētōr* (ῥήτωρ ὢν), not in the best interests of the Athenian people and takes money for doing so'; this part was not apparently intended to apply to a man like Euxenippos.[34]

Another point connected with Hypereides' argument that Euxenippos was not a *rhētōr*, otherwise this would be common knowledge for all the Athenians, is presented in § 22:

> εἰ γὰρ ταῦτα ἦν ἀληθῆ ἃ κατηγορεῖς, οὐκ ἂν σὺ μόνος ᾔδεις, ἀλλὰ καὶ οἱ ἄλλοι πάντες οἱ ἐν τῇ πόλει: ὥσπερ καὶ περὶ τῶν ἄλλων ὅσοι τι ὑπὲρ ἐκείνων ἢ λέγουσιν ἢ πράττουσιν, οὐ μόνον αὐτοί, ἀλλὰ καὶ οἱ ἄλλοι Ἀθηναῖοι ἴσασι καὶ τὰ παιδία τὰ ἐκ τῶν διδασκαλείων καὶ τῶν ῥητόρων τοὺς παρ' ἐκείνων μισθαρνοῦντας καὶ τῶν ἄλλων τοὺς ξενίζοντας τοὺς ἐκεῖθεν ἥκοντας καὶ ὑποδεχομένους καὶ εἰς τὰς ὁδοὺς ὑπαντῶντας ὅταν προσίωσι: καὶ οὐδαμοῦ ὄψει οὐδὲ παρ' ἑνὶ τούτων Εὐξένιππον καταριθμούμενον.
>
> For if these accusations of yours were true, not only you but everyone else in the *polis* would know it. Just as with the others who either speak or act in the Macedonians' interests at all, not only do they themselves know but so does the rest of Athens, even the children coming out of the schools: they know which of the speakers are on their payroll and who else plays host to Macedonian visitors, both entertaining them and going out into the streets to meet them when they arrive.
>
> HYP. *Eux.* 22

Hypereides uses the 'common knowledge' topos referring to children to add plausibility by presenting his allegation as self-evident. To stress further the point that Euxenippos is an *idiōtēs* and not a *rhētōr*, Hypereides presents himself as an experienced prosecutor in *eisangelia* cases and suggests that an *eisangelia* for bribery of public speakers is 'just' only if it involves an orator who makes proposals against the best interests of the people, and this specific clause 'against the best interests of the people' should have been written in the *eisangelia* (Hyp. *Eux.* 28–30). Furthermore, the contrast Hypereides draws stems ultimately from the fact that Philokrates and the others had put

34 Whitehead 2000: 189.

their words on record as proposers of the decree. Euxenippos, on the other hand, had merely made, as requested, a verbal report on his experiences at the Amphiaraon.[35]

The same line of argumentation, that the prosecution against Euxenippos contravenes the law on *eisangelia* since he is not a *rhētōr*, is emphasised towards the end of Hypereides' speech, when he encourages the jurors to save the defendant from an unjust prosecution:

> τούτους μὲν οὖν ἴσως οὐ ῥᾴδιόν ἐστι κωλῦσαι ταῦτα πράττειν: ὑμεῖς δέ, ὦ ἄνδρες δικασταί, ὥσπερ καὶ ἄλλους πολλοὺς σεσώκατε τῶν πολιτῶν ἀδίκως εἰς ἀγῶνας καταστάντας, οὕτω καὶ Εὐξενίππῳ βοηθήσατε, καὶ μὴ περιίδητε αὐτὸν ἐπὶ πράγματι οὐδενὸς ἀξίῳ καὶ εἰσαγγελίᾳ τοιαύτῃ, ᾗ οὐ μόνον οὐκ ἔνοχός ἐστιν, ἀλλὰ καὶ αὐτὴ παρὰ τοὺς νόμους ἐστὶν εἰσηγγελμένη, καὶ πρὸς τούτοις ὑπ' αὐτοῦ τοῦ κατηγόρου τρόπον τινὰ ἀπολελυμένη.
>
> So: where they are concerned, perhaps it is not easy to stop this behaviour. You though, men of the jury, just as you have saved many other citizens unjustly brought to trial, should help Euxenippos too. Do not desert him over a trivial matter, and in such an *eisangelia*. Not merely is he innocent of it, but the *eisangelia* itself has been couched in defiance of the laws, and besides, it has in a way been destroyed by the prosecutor himself.
>
> HYP. *Eux.* 38

The *eisangelia* as described here is one of the intrinsically 'trivial' ones ridiculed in § 3. According to the defence, the framing of the procedure has violated the laws, but obviously according to the prosecutor Euxenippos has spoken publicly and has received bribes (Hyp. *Eux.* 39). Hypereides rhetorically focuses on the fact that those who allegedly bribed Euxenippos are outside the city and it is they who should be punished instead of him; however, he implicitly admits that Euxenippos did take bribes. Thus, the emphasis is mainly placed upon the contrast between an *idiōtēs* and a *rhētōr*, undermining the facts that Euxenippos had received bribes and that he had made an announcement before the Athenian Assembly.

Hypereides emphatically stresses that he has never yet, in his life, prosecuted an *idiōtēs*. On the contrary, he appears to be on their side. In both defences for Lykophron and Euxenippos his line of argumentation was established upon the claim that the defendants were not public persons or speakers but sim-

35 Whitehead 2000: 236.

ply private citizens, *idiōtai*. The fact that he repeatedly grounds his defence in these two *eisangeliai* upon such a claim may indicate that the Athenian people and the jurors would be expected to understand and accept the validity of using the procedure for charges such as these against politicians, generals and public officials, but not private citizens, presumably because the vast majority of *eisangeliai* attested and known to us, until the latter half of the fourth century, did involve cases of generals or public officials. Moreover, the emphasis on such a line of argumentation may reflect a transformation in relations between the private citizens and the public speakers and in effect between the *dēmos* and the authorities. Since, however, Euxenippos took on a public duty and also addressed the Assembly, it could be argued that he was covered by the law. Hypereides is applying a rigid distinction between public and private which might not have been universally accepted.

A final case of *eisangelia* initiated by Lykourgos was his prosecution against Menesaichmus for impiety in 325/24 BC, where he successfully convicted the defendant.[36] As a whole, it appears that Lykourgos set the example by actively participating himself in prosecutions of various *eisangelia* cases after the defeat at Chaironeia, involving the offences prescribed by the *eisangeltikos nomos* but attributing a complementary definition and interpretation to them.

Conclusion

As has been shown, there is obviously a tendency to extend the scope of the *eisangelia* in the period after Chaironeia for political, constitutional and moral purposes. There was an anxiety to secure the democracy and protect the constitution and the city against any attempt at overthrow or destruction. Prominent political figures of the period, such as Lykourgos and Hypereides, played a significant role either as prosecutors or as *synēgoroi* in a number of *eisangeliai* against politicians or private citizens (*idiōtai*). In the context of the extraordinary legislative measures that were taken immediately after the defeat at Chaironeia, *eisangelia* was initially used against officials who were charged with being responsible for the military destruction and desertion of the city, such as Autolycus and Lysicles, but it was later extended to cover offences that were not explicitly proscribed by the *eisangeltikos nomos*, such as the accusations of *moicheia* against Lykophron and the flight from the city of Athens against Leokrates.

36 Hansen 1975: no 126.

The latter two charges are of special interest concerning the use of *eisangelia* towards the end of the fourth century BC. Both allegations of adultery and flight were exceptionally brought to court by *eisangelia* to be accepted as the basis for a charge of treason by the Athenian Assembly. Lykourgos, who was heavily involved in the prosecution of *eisangeliai* at this point, attempted to persuade the Assembly to accept the specific charges of adultery and flight as treason. It was a matter of interpretation of the scope of the law rather than an issue of legislation extending the range of the process.

Lykourgos' public prestige and influence were used to secure the jurors' approval, appealing to the Athenians' ancestral morality and the political stability of the Athenian constitution.[37] It is unlikely that the jury would be willing to agree with the prosecution that exile, execution and prohibition of burial in the city would be appropriate for a seducer (*moichos*), but given that the result of the trial against Lykophron is not known, we can only make assumptions. We do know, however, the result of the prosecution against Leokrates which ended with the acquittal of the defendant, by only one vote.

Lykourgos employs a variety of rhetorical strategies and techniques in order to persuade the jurors that Leokrates' flight from the city of Athens should be seen as treason, though it had not broken a law. He even invites them to act as legislators and set their conviction of the defendant as a precedent for similar cases in the future. As it seems, Athenian public opinion was different from that of Lykourgos, since the jurors only accepted the allegation of cowardice.

Despite the rhetorical efforts of the orators to offer new interpretations of the scope of the *eisangeltikos nomos*, the Athenians probably expected that *eisangelia* should involve serious crimes against the constitution or the safety of the city rather than accusations of minor offences. Hypereides' rhetorical claims about the number of ridiculous accusations in cases of *eisangelia* brought in the same period, such as the hiring of girl pipers for more than the law prescribed and the registration of a metic as a demesman, seem to reflect a real change in the use of the procedure. Moreover, the element of ridicule used to undermine also the accusation against Euxenippos on account of the dreams he said he had reflects a certain attitude of the Athenians to this use of the procedure; they would obviously have agreed that cases of *eisangeliai* should involve only serious offences, even though non-serious allegations had presented a novel approach to the court on the scope of the law of *eisangelia*.

37 For Lykourgos' vision of reconstructing the civic and political ideals of fifth century Athens, cf. Hanink 2014: 1–22.

On balance, the attitude of the Athenians towards the *eisangeltikos nomos* was different from the interpretation offered by orators in court and was most probably consistent with the use of the procedure in the fifth and early fourth century BC; as has been shown, it was not always so easy to get through to the majority of the people that a wide interpretation of the offences prescribed by the *eisangeltikos nomos* could be enforced to cover any kind of a public figure's misconduct.

Bibliography

Canevaro, M. and Harris, E.M. (2012) 'The Documents in Andocides' *On the Mysteries*', CQ 62, 98–129.

Colin, G. (1934) *Le Discours d'Hypéride contre Démosthène sur l'argent d'Harpale*, Paris.

Curtis, T.B. (1970) *The Judicial Oratory of Hypereides*, Chapel Hill, N.C.

Edwards, M. (1995) *Greek Orators 4: Andocides*, Warminster.

Hanink, J. (2014) *Lycurgan Athens and the Making of Classical Tragedy*, Cambridge.

Hansen, M.H. (1975) *Eisangelia: The Sovereignty of the People's Court in Athens in the Fourth Century BC and the Impeachment of Generals and Politicians*. Odense.

Harrison, A.R.W. (1968–1971) *The Law of Athens*, 2 vols, Oxford.

Lanni, A. (1999) 'Precedent and Legal Reasoning in Ancient Athenian Courts: A Noble Lie?' *American Journal of Legal History* 43, 27–51.

MacDowell, D.M. (1962) *Andocides On the Mysteries*, Oxford.

MacDowell, D.M. (1978) *The Law in Classical Athens*, London.

Ostwald, M. (1955) 'The Athenian Legislation Against Tyranny and Subversion', TAPA 86, 103–128.

Phillips, D.D. (2006) 'Why Was Lykophron Prosecuted by *eisangelia*?', GRBS 46, 375–394.

Rhodes, P.J. (1981) *A Commentary on the Aristotelian* Athenaion Politeia, Oxford.

Sullivan, J. (2003) 'Demosthenes' Areopagus Legislation: Yet Again' CQ 53, 130–134.

Todd, S.C. (1993) *The Shape of Athenian Law*, Oxford.

Usher, S. (1999) *Greek Oratory: Tradition and Originality*, Oxford.

Whitehead, D. (2000) *Hypereides: The Forensic Speeches*, Oxford.

Worthington, I., Cooper, C.R. and Harris, E.M. (2001) *Dinarchus, Hyperides, and Lycurgus*. Austin.

CHAPTER 17

Athenian Homicide Law and the Model Penal Code

David D. Phillips

1 Offence Elements and Culpability under the Model Penal Code

In 1962, the American Law Institute promulgated the Model Penal Code (MPC), in order to encourage the reform of American criminal law.[1] The general principles of the Code (MPC §2.02(2): Appendix 1) include a partition of three objective elements of an offence—conduct, circumstance, and result—and, for each element, the designation of four levels of culpability: purposeful, knowing, reckless, and negligent. This chapter argues that corresponding—though not identical—distinctions operated to varying degrees in Athenian homicide law, litigation, and legal thought from Drakon to Aristotle—whose treatment is closest to that of the MPC (Appendix 2)—and that these distinctions can accordingly serve as valuable interpretative tools in an analysis of the use, abuse, and critique of the law in the Athenian courts and beyond.

My application of the MPC categories to Athens involves one certain and one potential departure from the terms of the Code. (1) The MPC includes apparently conflicting definitions of 'conduct', no definition of 'circumstance' or 'result', and inconsistent definition of culpability levels with regard to different offence elements.[2] I apply the definitions of culpability as to result to all three elements. Thus the difference between purpose and knowledge is that purpose requires the 'conscious object' of the actor, while knowledge requires either actual knowledge or practical certainty. The difference between recklessness and negligence is that a reckless actor 'consciously disregards a substantial ... risk', whereas a negligent actor should be aware of the risk but is not. (2) Owing to the nature of Athenian legal procedure, I include within 'circumstance' things that the MPC might treat as continuing conduct. In the case of Lys. 1, for example, a prosecutor operating under the MPC could try Euphiletos simultaneously on multiple charges, including assault, kidnapping, felonious restraint, and false imprisonment,[3] in addition to homicide. But under the

1 Citations of the MPC are from American Law Institute 1985.
2 Robinson 1997: 150–153, 219–220.
3 MPC §§211.1; 212.1; 212.2; 212.3.

 | DOI:10.1163/9789004377899_019

Athenian system of discrete actions for discrete offences,[4] Euphiletos was tried by *dikē phonou* for homicide, and so the prosecution's allegation of purposeful entrapment by Euphiletos is circumstantial to the charged offence.

2 Conduct, Circumstance, Result, and Volition in Athenian Homicide Law

Drakon's homicide law divides killings into two volitional categories: intentional (*hekōn*, *hekousios*, or *ek pronoias*) and unintentional (*akōn*, *akousios*, or *ou/mē ek pronoias*).[5] The terms denoting positive intent correspond to purpose or knowledge under the MPC; the terms denoting negative intent correspond to recklessness, negligence, or faultlessness.[6] In the age of the orators, on the view adopted here, a killing qualified as intentional if the killer intended his conduct and the result of harm (not necessarily death).[7] Drakon, in fact, tacitly posits that conduct, circumstance, and result may be separate issues involving varying levels of intent. The general definition of liability at the beginning of Drakon's law (*IG* I³ 104.11–13) equates two forms of conduct that produce the same result:

> [δ]ικάζεν δὲ τὸς βασιλέας αἴτιο[ν] φόνο ἒ [τὸν αὐτόχερ κτέναντ'] ἒ [β]ολεύσαντα …
>
> The *basileis* shall judge him guilty of homicide whether he killed with his own hand or conspired to kill …[8]

Circumstance affects liability in at least three cases.

---

4 See, e.g., Dem. 37.33; Lykourg. 1.147.

5 On the equivalences of the respective positive and negative terms see Dem. 23.50; Loomis 1972; Gagarin 1981: 30–37; Phillips 2008: 59 with n. 4; *contra* Cantarella 1976: 84–111; Carawan 1998: 38–41.

6 Strictly speaking, in the MPC 'knowing' is a term of neutral intent, positive intent being denoted by the term 'purposeful' (MPC § 1.13(12)).

7 Loomis 1972; Phillips 2013: 45–46; *contra* Carawan 1998: 223–225; Pepe 2012: 87–128.

8 While reconstructions of the clause following the first ἤ vary in specifics (my restoration is from Phillips 2008: 41 n. 25; cf., e.g., Wolff 1946: 73; Gagarin 1981: xiv–xv; Pepe 2012: 32), the prevailing view is that the lacuna made reference to own-hand killing (cf. Antiph. 6.16; Andok. 1.94). The later (Solonian?) Areopagite jurisdiction law (Dem. 23.22 (*lex*); *Ath. Pol.* 57.3) distinguishes between conduct and result with regard to poisoning: the Areiopagos tries cases of poisoning if a person kills by giving poison—ἐάν τις ἀποκτείνει (result) δούς (conduct).

(1) The killing of a killer in exile is prohibited, whereas an exiled killer caught in trespass is fair game:

> ἐὰν δ]έ [τ]ις τὸ[ν ἀν]δρ[οφόνον κτένει ἒ αἴτιος ἐ̂ι φόνο, ἀπεχόμενον ἀγορᾶ]ς ἐφορί[α]ς κ̣[α]ὶ [ἄθλον καὶ *h*ιερôν Ἀμφικτυονικôν, *h*όσπερ τὸν Ἀθεν]αῖον κ̣[τέ-να]ν̣[τα, ἐν τοῖς αὐτοῖς ἐνέχεσθαι· διαγιγνόσκεν δὲ τὸς] ἐ[φ]έτα[ς]. … τὸς δ' ἀνδροφόνος ἐξε̂ναι ἀποκτένεν ἐν] τε̂ι ἐμεδ[απε̂ι καὶ ἀπάγεν …
>
> And if a person kills the killer or is responsible for his killing, when the killer has stayed away from the border-market, games, and Amphictyonic rites, he shall be bound by the same terms as the killer of an Athenian; the *ephetai* shall decide the case. … And it shall be permitted to kill or arrest killers in our land …
>
> *IG* I^3 104.26–31 = DEM. 23.37 (*lex*) + DEM. 23.28, *lex*

(2) Deadly force is permitted in immediate self-defence against robbery:

> κα[ὶ ἐὰν φέροντα ἒ ἄγοντα βίαι ἀδίκος εὐθὺς] ἀμυνόμενος κτέ[ν]ει, ν[εποινὲ τεθνάναι …
>
> And if in immediate self-defence he kills someone carrying or leading away [his property] forcibly and without justification, the death shall be uncompensated.[9]
>
> *IG* I^3 104.37–38 = DEM. 23.60, *lex*

(3) Immediately before this clause, the formula for starting a fight without justification (ἄρχειν χειρῶν ἀδίκων) occurs at least once, and probably twice, and is followed by a provision that "the *ephetai* shall decide the case":

> …^{39} … ἄρχον]τα χερōν ἀ[δίκον …^{30} … χερ]ōν ἀδίκον κτέ[νει …^{7} …]σ […^{19} … διαγιγνόσκ]εν δὲ τὸς ἐ[φέτ]ας …
>
> … starting a fight without justification … a fight without justification, he kills … the *ephetai* shall decide the case …
>
> *IG* I^3 104.33–36

9 In his discussion of this clause (§60), Demosthenes emphasises both its circumstantial nature (ἐφ' οἷς ἔξεστι κτεῖναι … ἐφ' οἷς ἐξεῖναι κτείνειν) and its implications for the killer's volition (τῷ … προσγράψαι τὸ 'εὐθὺς' ἀφεῖλε τὸν τοῦ βουλεύσασθαί τι κακὸν χρόνον).

The most economical reconstruction of these lines, and the most plausible given its position in the law, is that Drakon granted to the victim of an ordinary attack the same right of lethal response as he granted to the victim of special attack by the robber or highwayman (Dem. 23.53: *infra*), probably with the qualification, as against the robber, that the responder act in immediate self-defence (εὐθὺς ἀμυνόμενος). The *ephetai* were to decide whether the decedent had initiated the fight and whether the defendant's response was immediate; if so, the defendant was absolved of liability.[10] In all these cases, the killer is presumed to be knowing as to circumstance: he knows whether his victim is in violation of his exile; he knows that he is being robbed; he knows that his assailant threw the first punch.

Additional cases occur in laws attributed to Drakon in Demosthenes 23.

(4) One of these laws protects killers in exile:

> ἐάν τίς τινα τῶν ἀνδροφόνων τῶν ἐξεληλυθότων, ὧν τὰ χρήματα ἐπίτιμα, πέρα ὅρου ἐλαύνῃ ἢ φέρῃ ἢ ἄγῃ, τὰ ἴσα ὀφείλειν ὅσα περ ἂν ἐν τῇ ἡμεδαπῇ δράσῃ.
>
> If, beyond the border, a person drives, carries, or leads [the person and/or property of] one of the killers who have left the country and whose property is unconfiscated, he shall owe the same amount as if he committed the act in our land.
>
> § 44, *lex*

This law implies that the killer may not be forcibly repatriated (§ 49). No one may create the circumstance of the killer's trespass; thus the killing of a trespassing killer is permitted to the actor who is knowing, but not purposeful, as to circumstance.

(5) Another law immunises the person who denounces a trespassing killer and so causes his death:

10 Cf. Stroud 1968: 56. Gagarin 1978: 119 notes the parallel constructions at lines 13 and 29. On this reconstruction, the substantive right of response was the same against ordinary and specific attack, but the procedure differed: Drakon declares the responder to specific attack immune from liability (νηποινεὶ τεθνάναι, Dem. 23.60; μὴ φεύγειν κτείναντα, Dem. 23.53) but mandates trial of the responder to ordinary attack (διαγιγνώσκειν ... τοὺς ἐφέτας).

> φόνου δὲ δίκας μὴ εἶναι μηδαμοῦ κατὰ τῶν τοὺς φεύγοντας ἐνδεικνύντων, ἐάν τις κατίῃ ὅποι μὴ ἔξεστιν.
>
> There shall be no *dikai phonou* anywhere against those who denounce exiles, if one of them returns where he is not allowed.
>
> § 51, *lex*

Thus, in this circumstance, permissible *bouleusis* mirrors permissible *autocheir* killing.

(6) Most conceptually complex are the clauses on lawful homicide preserved at § 53:

> ἐάν τις ἀποκτείνῃ ἐν ἄθλοις ἄκων, ἢ ἐν ὁδῷ καθελὼν ἢ ἐν πολέμῳ ἀγνοήσας, ἢ ἐπὶ δάμαρτι ἢ ἐπὶ μητρὶ ἢ ἐπὶ ἀδελφῇ ἢ ἐπὶ θυγατρί, ἢ ἐπὶ παλλακῇ ἣν ἂν ἐπὶ ἐλευθέροις παισὶν ἔχῃ, τούτων ἕνεκα μὴ φεύγειν κτείναντα.
>
> If a person kills unintentionally in the games, or having come upon a highwayman on the road, or in war without recognising his victim, or [finding his victim] upon his consort, mother, sister, daughter, or concubine whom he keeps for the procreation of free children, for these acts he shall not stand trial as a killer.
>
> § 53, *lex*

While the foundation of all these cases is circumstantial,[11] the treatment of circumstance, as well as conduct and result, varies.[12] The friendly-fire killer is as a rule purposeful as to conduct and result, and at least knowing as to general circumstance (ἐν πολέμῳ), but he makes an unintentional error as to specific circumstance (his victim's identity). The killer ἐν ἄθλοις ἄκων, in the standard case envisioned by Demosthenes—competition combat sports (§ 54)—is purposeful as to conduct and circumstance, and as to the result of harm: the boxer, wrestler, or pancratiast punches, kicks, throws, or chokes with the conscious

11 As understood by Demosthenes (διδόντος τοῦ νόμου σαφῶς οὑτωσὶ καὶ λέγοντος ἐφ' οἷς ἐξεῖναι κτεῖναι, § 53 *infra*). Cf. Pl. *Leg.* 874b–d: ὧν δὲ ἐφ' οἷς τε ὀρθῶς ἂν καθαρὸς εἴη (*sc.* ὁ ἀποκτείνας); Arist. *Eth. Nic.* 1111a11 ff.: ἐν οἷς ἡ πρᾶξις.

12 The law does not qualify the intent of the killer of a highwayman or a *moichos*, who thus may be *hekōn* (up to purposeful) as to conduct and result, and by default assumption is knowing as to circumstance.

object of causing harm. He can only be ἄκων as to the result of death; and the difficulty in practice will have been distinguishing intent to harm from intent to kill.[13]

3 Conduct, Circumstance, Result, and Volition in Forensic Argument, Actual and Hypothetical, and Beyond

1 *Isolating Circumstance: Lysias 1*

In Lys. 1, Euphiletos proffers several laws, including the Drakonian provisions on lawful homicide (§ 30), in support of his affirmative defence that since he caught Eratosthenes ἐπί his wife,[14] he was obligated to kill him. Euphiletos does not dispute his purpose as to conduct and result; circumstance alone is the deciding factor. The prosecution contends that Euphiletos was purposeful as to circumstance, since he created it by luring Eratosthenes to his house and dragging him in (§§ 37, 27). Euphiletos maintains that he was merely knowing as to circumstance: he dismissed his dinner companion, then was informed that Eratosthenes was in the house, whereupon he immediately gathered a posse without knowing which intended members were at home, and then, at the first reasonable opportunity, he apprehended Eratosthenes in the act.

As a fallback position, Euphiletos suggests that even entrapment would have been justified:

> κατηγοροῦσι γάρ μου ὡς ἐγὼ τὴν θεράπαιναν ἐν ἐκείνῃ τῇ ἡμέρᾳ μετελθεῖν ἐκέλευσα τὸν νεανίσκον. ἐγὼ δέ, ὦ ἄνδρες, δίκαιον μὲν ἂν ποιεῖν ἡγούμην ᾡτινιοῦν τρόπῳ τὸν τὴν γυναῖκα τὴν ἐμὴν διαφθείραντα λαμβάνων.
>
> They accuse me of ordering my slave on that day to fetch the young man. But for my part, gentlemen, I would think I was acting justly in catching by any means whatsoever the man who had corrupted my wife.
>
> § 37

13 In Demosthenes' view, the lawgiver 'looked not to what happened (τὸ συμβάν: bare conduct and/or result, without regard for the actor's intent, as shown by what follows) but to the purpose (διάνοιαν) of the actor', which is 'to defeat a living opponent, not to kill' (§ 54). On these events see Miller 2004: 46–60.

14 While I have translated the preposition in Drakon's law *supra* as 'upon', 'on' or 'with' would be equally correct. The sense is 'in immediate carnal proximity to or contact with, *in flagranti* with.' As Pepe 2012: 221 observes, Lysias and Euphiletos perceived no conflict between the law's 'upon his consort' (ἐπὶ δάμαρτι) and Euphiletos' discovery of Eratosthenes 'lying next to [his] wife' (κατακείμενον παρὰ τῇ γυναικί, § 24).

Significantly, though, this represents the limit of his abuse of the law. He misrepresents Drakon's law as a mandate, rather than a licence, to kill; he falsely alleges that the laws unanimously treat seduction as a more serious offence than rape.[15] But the argument for the validity of entrapment is explicitly his own, as marked by the emphatic ἐγὼ δέ and the hesitant (and hypothetical) ἄν … ἡγούμην.[16] And this qualification is made even though, in all probability, the provisions on lawful homicide contained no prohibition on entrapment.[17] Euphiletos, who elsewhere blatantly misinterprets the letter of the law, here shies from violating its understood spirit: where he could interpret Drakon's silence as to the manner of capture as a legal argument in his favour, he demurs.

2 *Refining Result in Self-Defence (and Elsewhere)*

Distinguishing intent to harm from intent to kill will frequently have been crucial in cases of ordinary self-defence. Here, in the Classical period, the Drakonian doctrine of unlimited force that authorised lethal response to ordinary attack confronted a rival doctrine of reasonable force.[18] Euaion responded to a single blow by killing his assailant, Boiotos, and at trial was convicted by a margin of only one vote (Dem. 21.71, 73–75). Demosthenes posits that 'those who voted to convict did so *not because he defended himself, but because he did so in such a way as to kill*, while those who voted to acquit granted even this excess of vengeance' to the victim of hybris (τοὺς μὲν καταγνόντας αὐτοῦ μὴ ὅτι ἠμύνατο, διὰ τοῦτο καταψηφίσασθαι, ἀλλ' ὅτι τοῦτον τὸν τρόπον ὥστε καὶ ἀποκτεῖναι, τοὺς δ' ἀπογνόντας καὶ ταύτην τὴν ὑπερβολὴν τῆς τιμωρίας τῷ γε τὸ σῶμα ὑβρισμένῳ δεδωκέναι, §75). All Demosthenes tells us about Euaion's defence is that he made no plea for pity or sympathy. In fact, Euaion will certainly have argued that since Boiotos struck the first blow, he was entitled, under Drakon's law and others,[19] to respond; and in all probability he will have argued that he did not intend to kill Boiotos, especially since they were friends (§§71, 73). Likewise, if, as alleged by the speaker of Isaios 9, Thoudippos mortally injured his brother Euthykrates

15 Harris 1990.

16 Cf. Todd 2007: 138 with n. 98.

17 We have no positive evidence for such a prohibition, and if one existed, Euphiletos would presumably not contradict it, however cautiously. (It is, of course, possible that Euphiletos would omit such a prohibition in the clauses he had the court clerk read out, but then he would unnecessarily expose himself to impeachment on that point by the prosecution.)

18 For the survival of the former cf. Antiph. 4.2.2–3 (*infra*); Sophocles *OT* 270–272, 810 with Dawe 1982: 17; Dover 1994: 184.

19 Such as the law governing the *dikē aikeias*: Dem. 23.50; Dem. 47.40 *et alibi*.

in a boundary dispute (Isa. 9.17, 19),[20] one of the factors impelling the relatives not to prosecute will have been the presumption that Thoudippos intended to harm his brother but not to kill him.

This argument from *philia*, however, was not available in the default self-defence case represented in Antiphon's *Third Tetralogy*. The defendant argues, up to a point, essentially as Demosthenes represents the minority interpretation of the Euaion case. The victim started the fight and so got what was coming to him; the defendant did no wrong in responding with his bare hands, and would have done no wrong even had he used a weapon:

> ἄρχων γὰρ χειρῶν ἀδίκων … οὐχ αὑτῷ μόνον τῆς συμφορᾶς ἀλλὰ καὶ ἐμοὶ τοῦ ἐγκλήματος αἴτιος γέγονεν. … τὸν γὰρ ἄρξαντα τῆς πληγῆς, εἰ μὲν σιδήρῳ ἢ λίθῳ ἢ ξύλῳ ἠμυνάμην αὐτόν, ἠδίκουν μὲν οὐδ' οὕτως—οὐ γὰρ ταὐτὰ ἀλλὰ μείζονα καὶ πλείονα δίκαιοι οἱ ἄρχοντες ἀντιπάσχειν εἰσί—· ταῖς δὲ χερσὶ τυπτόμενος ὑπ' αὐτοῦ, ταῖς χερσὶν ἅπερ ἔπασχον ἀντιδρῶν, πότερα ἠδίκουν;
>
> By starting the fight without justification … he became responsible not only for his own misfortune but also for the charge against me. … He struck the first blow; if I had defended myself with a blade, rock, or club, even then I would be guilty of no wrong, since aggressors deserve to suffer not the same as they inflict but worse and more. But in fact, he was striking me with his hands, and I retaliated with my hands for the beating I was taking; did I do wrong?
>
> ANTIPH. 4.2.1–2

But the homicide law of the *Tetralogies* differs from that of Athens in forbidding both just and unjust killing, and thereby rendering every killer liable: intentional killers suffer death (4.1.7), unintentional killers suffer exile; there is no such thing as a lawful killing.[21] The defendant in the *Third Tetralogy*

20 On this passage see Wyse 1904: 636–638; Phillips 2008: 90–96, 102–104; Griffith-Williams 2013: 172–175.

21 Cf. 3.2.9, 3.3.7. *Pace* Gagarin 1997: 151–152, 'just' and 'unjust' do not correspond to 'unintentional' and 'intentional' respectively. In Antiph. 4, the defendant argues that had he (rather than the doctor) caused the victim's death, the killing would have been both intentional (as charged in the instant case: 4.1.6) and just (4.2.3: *infra*). In this case the defendant would be liable, since Antiphon's hypothetical homicide law forbids just as well as unjust killing. *Non obstat* 4.4.7 (τῷ μὲν γὰρ ἄρξαντι πανταχοῦ μεγάλα ἐπιτίμια ἐπίκειται, τῷ δὲ ἀμυνομένῳ οὐδαμοῦ οὐδὲν ἐπιτίμιον γέγραπται); see Dittenberger 1897: 5–6, 1905: 455–456. Nor are we dealing with multiple laws (*pace* Decleva Caizzi 1969: 23).

must therefore argue that he did not kill; the decedent's death was caused by his doctor's incompetence:

> Εἶεν· ἐρεῖ δὲ 'ἀλλ' ὁ νόμος εἴργων μήτε δικαίως μήτε ἀδίκως ἀποκτείνειν ἔνοχον τοῦ φόνου τοῖς ἐπιτιμίοις ἀποφαίνει σε ὄντα· ὁ γὰρ ἀνὴρ τέθνηκεν.' ἐγὼ δὲ δεύτερον καὶ τρίτον οὐκ ἀποκτεῖναί φημι. εἰ μὲν γὰρ ὑπὸ τῶν πληγῶν ὁ ἀνὴρ παραχρῆμα ἀπέθανεν, ὑπ' ἐμοῦ μὲν δικαίως δ' ἂν ἐτεθνήκει—οὐ γὰρ ταὐτὰ ἀλλὰ μείζονα καὶ πλείονα οἱ ἄρξαντες δίκαιοι ἀντιπάσχειν εἰσί—νῦν δὲ πολλαῖς ἡμέραις ὕστερον μοχθηρῷ ἰατρῷ ἐπιτρεφθεὶς διὰ τὴν τοῦ ἰατροῦ μοχθηρίαν καὶ οὐ διὰ τὰς πληγὰς ἀπέθανε.
>
> Well, [the prosecutor] will say, 'But the law prohibiting both just and unjust killing declares you liable to the penalties for homicide, since the man is dead.' But I say, for the second and third time, that I did not kill. If the man had died immediately from the blows, he would have died at my hands, and justly, since aggressors deserve to suffer not the same as they inflict but worse and more. In fact, though, many days later, having been entrusted to an incompetent doctor, he died on account of the doctor's incompetence, not on account of the blows.
>
> ANTIPH. 4.2.3–4

Accordingly, it is left to the prosecution to concede what any defendant in an actual *dikē phonou* would have argued; namely, that the defendant did not intend the death of his victim:

> ὁ μὲν γὰρ ἐξ ὧν ἔδρασεν ἐκεῖνος διαφθαρείς, οὐ τῇ ἑαυτοῦ ἁμαρτίᾳ ἀλλὰ τῇ τοῦ πατάξαντος χρησάμενος ἀπέθανεν· ὁ δὲ μείζω ὧν ἤθελε πράξας, τῇ ἑαυτοῦ ἀτυχίᾳ ὃν οὐκ ἤθελεν ἀπέκτεινεν.
>
> [The victim] was killed as a result of what that man did and died not by his own error but by that of the man who hit him; [the defendant] did more than he wanted, and by his own misfortune killed a man whom he did not want to kill.[22]
>
> ANTIPH. 4.3.4

The contrast between this admission against interests by the prosecution and the defendant's emphasis on justification to the exclusion of remorse informs

---

22 The defence picks this up in its second speech (4.4.4).

Antiphon's decision to have the defendant abscond before his second speech. This decision is an implied critique of the defendant's argument:[23] even in the *Tetralogies*, simply arguing that the victim 'had it coming', without distinguishing intended conduct (and result) from unintended result, is unlikely to succeed.

Outside the realm of self-defence, intent to harm is clearly distinct from intent to kill in the *dikē phonou* that Euthyphron plans to bring against his father (Pl. *Euthphr.* 4c3–e3). A labourer at the family farm on Naxos killed a slave; Euthyphron's father bound the killer and threw him into a ditch pending a ruling by one of the *exēgētai* in Athens; before the ruling arrived, the killer perished of hunger, cold, and his bonds. Euthyphron's father is purposeful as to harm: you do not fetter a person and throw him into a ditch for the duration of a round trip to Athens, and expect him to remain unscathed. Euthyphron contends that his father was reckless as to death: he was aware of the risk but did not care.[24] But this is contradicted by Euthyphron's own narrative. A person who is scrupulous enough to send to the *exēgētai* actively desires that his prisoner live, which excludes any degree of culpability above negligence. Euthyphron's father would not want to flout the authority of the *exēgētai* by permitting the prisoner to die in his custody, which might render him liable for a homicide that he has essentially advertised in advance. So he was at most negligent as to the prisoner's death. Thus, as in the self-defence cases, the argument 'I meant to harm him, but not to kill him' will have figured prominently in Euthyphron's father's defence, and he has a stronger argument against intent as to death than does the default self-defence killer, who cannot avail himself of the argument from *philia*.

3 *The Problem of Complex Liability: Antiph. 3 and 4*

The problem of complex liability in cases of self-defence—to what extent are the killer and victim respectively responsible?—becomes even more acute when the prosecution concedes that the defendant possessed no positive intent to harm, let alone kill, as in Antiphon's *Second Tetralogy*. During practice in the gymnasium, a youth threw his javelin, which accidentally struck and immediately killed a boy who ran into the line of fire. Prosecution and defence stipulate that the thrower threw purposely and within the designated area, the victim ran purposely, and neither actor intended a result of harm, much less death.

---

23 Cf. Gagarin 2002: 130; Pepe 2012: 206.

24 Εἰ καὶ ἀποθάνοι (4d2–3) indicates the relative remoteness of the chance of death (which Euthyphron's father consciously disregarded) in comparison to the certainty of harm.

Since the affirmative excuse defence of killing ἐν ἄθλοις ἄκων does not exist in the *Tetralogies*,[25] the defence must argue, as in the *Third Tetralogy*, that the thrower did not kill; rather, the victim killed himself:

> τὸ γὰρ μειράκιον οὐχ ὕβρει οὐδὲ ἀκολασίᾳ, ἀλλὰ μελετῶν μετὰ τῶν ἡλίκων ἀκοντίζειν ἐν τῷ γυμνασίῳ, ἔβαλε μέν, οὐκ ἀπέκτεινε δὲ οὐδένα κατά γε τὴν ἀλήθειαν ὧν ἔπραξεν …
>
> The youth, not out of *hybris* or lack of self-control, but practising javelin-throwing with his agemates in the gymnasium, threw, but he did not kill anyone, according to the truth of what he did …
>
> ANTIPH. 3.2.3

Consequently, the dispute concerns the identification of the relevant conduct and the relevant circumstance. The actor whose conduct produced the result is liable for that result:

> θέλω δὲ μὴ πρότερον ἐπ' ἄλλον λόγον ὁρμῆσαι ἢ τὸ ἔργον ἔτι φανερώτερον καταστῆσαι ὁποτέρου αὐτῶν ἐστί. τὸ μὲν μειράκιον οὐδενὸς μᾶλλον τῶν συμμελετώντων ἐστὶ τοῦ σκοποῦ ἁμαρτόν, οὐδὲ τῶν ἐπικαλουμένων τι διὰ τὴν αὑτοῦ ἁμαρτίαν δέδρακεν· ὁ δὲ παῖς οὐ ταὐτὰ τοῖς συνθεωμένοις δρῶν, ἀλλ' εἰς τὴν ὁδὸν τοῦ ἀκοντίου ὑπελθών, σαφῶς δηλοῦται παρὰ τὴν αὑτοῦ ἁμαρτίαν περισσοτέροις ἀτυχήμασι τῶν ἀτρεμιζόντων περιπεσών.
>
> I do not want to advance to another argument before establishing even more clearly to which of them the act belongs. The youth did not miss the target any more than any of the others who were practising with him, and he did not do any of the things he is charged with through his own error. The boy, though, did not do the same as his fellow spectators but ran into the path of the javelin, and so is clearly shown to have incurred by his own error greater misfortunes than those who stood still.
>
> ANTIPH. 3.4.5; cf. 3.2.8

The prosecution identifies the conduct as the thrower's javelin cast and the circumstance—the *status quo ante*, however minimally *ante*—as the victim's run:

25 This is one of the issues Antiphon expects his (Athenian) readers to argue about; cf. Plut. *Per.* 36.5. His success is demonstrated by the modern debate over whether under Athenian law trial would occur at the Delphinion (the venue for defendants who asserted a lawful-

ὁ μὲν γὰρ ἐν τούτῳ τῷ καιρῷ καλούμενος ὑπὸ τοῦ παιδοτρίβου, ὃς ὑπεδέχετο τοῖς ἀκοντίζουσι τὰ ἀκόντια ἀναιρεῖσθαι, διὰ τὴν τοῦ βαλόντος ἀκολασίαν πολεμίῳ τῷ τούτου βέλει περιπεσών, οὐδὲν οὐδ' εἰς ἕν' ἁμαρτών, ἀθλίως ἀπέθανε· ὁ δὲ περὶ τὸν τῆς ἀναιρέσεως καιρὸν πλημμελήσας ... ἑκὼν μὲν οὐκ ἀπέκτεινε, μᾶλλον δὲ ἑκὼν ἢ οὔτε ἔβαλεν οὔτε ἀπέκτεινεν.

[The victim] was called at that moment by the trainer, who was in charge of recovering the javelins for the throwers. On account of the thrower's lack of self-control, he met with his hostile missile; having committed no error against anyone, he died wretchedly. The thrower, however, made a mistake regarding the moment of recovery ...; he did not kill intentionally, but it is better to say that he killed intentionally than that he neither threw nor killed.

ANTIPH. 3.3.6

The thrower was thus at least negligent, but no more than reckless, as to circumstance: his lack of self-control manifested in a culpable mistake as to the time of recovery. The defence, by contrast, argues that the circumstance was that at least one javelin was in the air, and the conduct was the victim's subsequent (however immediately subsequent) run:

τοῦ δὲ παιδὸς ὑπὸ τὴν τοῦ ἀκοντίου φορὰν ὑποδραμόντος καὶ τὸ σῶμα προστήσαντος, ... ὁ δὲ ὑπὸ τὸ ἀκόντιον ὑπελθὼν ἐβλήθη, καὶ τὴν αἰτίαν οὐχ ἡμέτερον οὖσαν προσέβαλεν ἡμῖν. διὰ δὲ τὴν ὑποδρομὴν βληθέντος τοῦ παιδός, τὸ μὲν μειράκιον οὐ δικαίως ἐπικαλεῖται, οὐδένα γὰρ ἔβαλε τῶν ἀπὸ τοῦ σκοποῦ ἀφεστώτων· ὁ δὲ παῖς εἴπερ ἑστὼς φανερὸς ὑμῖν ἐστι μὴ βληθείς, ἑκουσίως ⟨δ'⟩ ὑπὸ τὴν φορὰν τοῦ ἀκοντίου ὑπελθών, ἔτι σαφεστέρως δηλοῦται διὰ τὴν αὑτοῦ ἁμαρτίαν ἀποθανών ...

Because the boy ran under the path of the javelin and put his body in front of it, ... he was hit because he ran under the javelin; and he has hit us with

homicide defence: Dem. 23.74; *Ath. Pol.* 57.3; so, apparently, Daube 1969: 169–170; cf. Glotz 1904: 506–507 n. 7; Decleva Caizzi 1969: 212) or the Palladion (the default venue for unintentional homicide: Dem. 23.71–73; *Ath. Pol.* 57.3; so MacDowell 1963: 74; Gagarin 1997: 144). Antiphon invites a similar debate in the *Third Tetralogy*: in favour of the Areiopagos is, e.g., Gagarin 1978: 117–118; in favour of the Delphinion, e.g., MacDowell 1963: 75, 1990: 292–293. Demosthenes gives no indication as to the venue of the trial of Euaion, which is likewise variously identified (Areiopagos: Gagarin 1978: 117–118; Delphinion: MacDowell 1990: 292–293).

> the responsibility, which is not ours. Since the boy was hit on account of his running under, the youth is not justly charged, since he hit none of those who were standing away from the target. As for the boy, if it is clear to you that he was hit not while standing still but having intentionally gone under the path of the javelin, then he is shown even more clearly to have died through his own error …
>
> ANTIPH. 3.2.4–5

> ἔστι δὲ οὐδὲ τὸ ἁμάρτημα τοῦ παιδὸς μόνον, ἀλλὰ καὶ ἡ ἀφυλαξία. ὁ μὲν γὰρ οὐδένα ὁρῶν διατρέχοντα πῶς ἂν ἐφυλάξατο μηδένα βαλεῖν; ὁ δ' ἰδὼν τοὺς ἀκοντίζοντας εὐπετῶς ἂν ἐφυλάξατο μὴ βληθῆναι· ἐξῆν γὰρ αὐτῷ ἀτρέμα ἑστάναι.

> And it is not just the error that belongs to the boy, but the lack of care as well. How could the thrower, seeing no one running across, have taken care not to hit anyone? But the boy, seeing the people throwing javelins, could easily have taken care not to get hit: he could have stood still.
>
> ANTIPH. 3.4.7

The victim, by his lack of care (ἀφυλαξία), was probably reckless, but at least negligent, as to circumstance.[26] Intent as to circumstance determines intent as to result: as one actor or the other was negligent or reckless as to circumstance, so was he negligent or reckless as to the victim's death.

At the end of his second speech, the prosecutor proposes that the error and the resulting death belong to the thrower and victim jointly; the thrower must pay for his partial responsibility:

> ὡς δὲ οὐδὲ τῆς ἁμαρτίας οὐδὲ τοῦ ἀκουσίως ἀποκτεῖναι … ἀπολύεται, ἀλλὰ κοινὰ ἀμφότερα ταῦτα ἀμφοῖν αὐτοῖν ἐστι, δηλώσω. εἴπερ ὁ παῖς διὰ τὸ ὑπὸ τὴν φορὰν τοῦ ἀκοντίου ὑπελθεῖν καὶ μὴ ἀτρέμας ἑστάναι φονεὺς αὐτὸς αὑτοῦ δίκαιος εἶναί ἐστιν, οὐδὲ τὸ μειράκιον καθαρὸν τῆς αἰτίας ἐστίν, ἀλλ' εἴπερ τούτου μὴ ἀκοντίζοντος ἀλλ' ἀτρέμα ἑστῶτος ἀπέθανεν ὁ παῖς. ἐξ ἀμφοῖν δὲ τοῦ φόνου γενομένου, … ὁ δὲ συλλήπτωρ καὶ κοινωνὸς … τῆς ἁμαρτίας γενόμενος

26 Probably reckless, on the reading of ἀφυλαξία as subjective ('the boy *saw the people throwing* and *could easily have taken care* not to get hit' by standing still); cf. Maschke 1926: 77–78. If his ἀφυλαξία is objective (from the standpoint of a reasonable actor but not of the victim), he is negligent. The victim is knowing as to general circumstance (people are throwing javelins) but reckless (or negligent) as to specific circumstance (the thrower has thrown his javelin and he is running into its path).

> πῶς δίκαιος ἀζήμιος ἀποφυγεῖν ἐστιν; ἐκ δὲ τῆς αὐτῶν τῶν ἀπολογουμένων ἀπολογίας μετόχου τοῦ μειρακίου τοῦ φόνου ὄντος, οὐκ ἂν δικαίως οὐδὲ ὁσίως ἀπολύοιτε αὐτόν.
>
> I shall demonstrate that … he is absolved neither of the error nor of the unintentional killing, but that both these things belong jointly to the two of them. If the boy, because he went under the path of the javelin and did not stand still, is rightly considered his own killer, then the youth is not clear of responsibility either; that would be the case only if he was not throwing but standing still when the boy died. Since the homicide occurred as a result of both of them, … how does the one who was an accomplice and partner in the error deserve to escape unpunished? Since from the argument of the defence itself the youth is a participant in the homicide, you could not justly or piously acquit him.
>
> ANTIPH. 3.3.10–11

Contrast with the first prosecution speech (Antiph. 3.3.6: *supra*) indicates that this constitutes a secondary line of attack designed to persuade jurors who remain unconvinced of the thrower's full responsibility.[27] But the defence rejects joint liability, as it must. Since every killing produces liability, the thrower cannot be a participant in the victim's death; the act (ἔργον, 3.4.5), the lack of care (ἀφυλαξία, 3.4.7), and the result (πάθος, 3.4.10) all belong to the victim alone:

> ὡς δ' οὐδενὸς μᾶλλον τῶν συνακοντιζόντων μέτοχός ἐστι τοῦ φόνου, διδάξω. εἰ γὰρ διὰ τὸ τοῦτον ἀκοντίζειν ὁ παῖς ἀπέθανε, πάντες ἂν οἱ συμμελετῶντες συμπράκτορες εἴησαν τῆς αἰτίας· οὗτοι γὰρ οὐ διὰ τὸ μὴ ἀκοντίζειν οὐκ ἔβαλον αὐτόν, ἀλλὰ διὰ τὸ μηδενὶ ὑπὸ τὸ ἀκόντιον ὑπελθεῖν· ὁ δὲ νεανίσκος οὐδὲν περισσὸν τούτων ἁμαρτών, ὁμοίως τούτοις οὐκ ἂν ἔβαλεν αὐτὸν ἀτρέμα σὺν τοῖς θεωμένοις ἑστῶτα. (…) μεμνημένοι τοῦ πάθους ὅτι διὰ τὸν ὑπὸ τὴν φορὰν τοῦ ἀκοντίου ὑπελθόντα ἐγένετο, ἀπολύετε ἡμᾶς· οὐ γὰρ αἴτιοι τοῦ φόνου ἐσμέν.
>
> I will show that he is no more a participant in the homicide than his fellow javelin-throwers. If the boy died because he threw, all those practising with him would be sharers in the responsibility: they failed to hit him not because they did not throw but because he did not run under any of their javelins. The young man no more committed an error than they did; just

27 Cf. Gagarin 1997: 156.

> like them, he would not have hit the boy if he had stood still with the spectators. (…) Remember that the unfortunate incident occurred because of the one who went under the path of the javelin, and acquit us, since we are not responsible for the killing.
>
> ANTIPH. 3.4.6–10

In an actual Athenian *dikē phonou*, the defendant in the *Third Tetralogy* could proffer the legal argument that he killed in lawful self-defence. Accordingly, his argument on the facts could differ as well: he would not have to deny any involvement in the death. By comparison, the defence in the *Second Tetralogy* would have the legal argument that the javelin-thrower killed ἐν ἄθλοις ἄκων, but the argument on the facts would have to remain essentially the same. The Athenian *dikē phonou*, like that of the *Tetralogies*, is a fixed-penalty lawsuit (*atimētos agōn*). The defendant is either guilty and liable or innocent and not liable. For the defence in the *Second Tetralogy* to concede partial responsibility would be just as harmful in an Athenian court as it is in the *Second Tetralogy*: the defence would have nothing to gain and everything to lose. In the Second and Third Tetralogies, Antiphon poses problems of complex liability that are just as intractable in Athenian law as they are in the law of the *Tetralogies*. In both cases, the most reasonable and impartial interpretation of the facts admits of no equitable legal solution in either system. Partial responsibility by the javelin-thrower in the *Second Tetralogy* cannot result in partial liability. He is either convicted and sentenced to exile, just as if he were fully responsible, or acquitted and absolved, just as if he bore no responsibility.[28] The central *aporia* of the *Second Tetralogy* is exactly this: how does one meaningfully apportion liability in a system where economy of liability is impossible?

A similar problem defines the *Third Tetralogy*. Here Antiphon draws special attention to the most reasonable interpretation of the facts, at 4.3.4 (*supra*): the defendant intended to harm but not to kill, μείζω ὧν ἤθελε πράξας—a phrase marked for emphasis both by the coincidence of the end of a dactylic hexameter with the end of a phrase, and by the occurrence of hiatus.[29] This is the crux of the problem: at what point does lethal response to attack make the responder liable for intentional homicide, just as the attacker would have been had

28 Under Athenian law, account of this might be taken by the victim's relatives, who possessed the right to pardon by unanimous consent, and thus controlled—at their sole discretion—the duration of the unintentional killer's exile (*IG* I³ 104.13–19). The *Tetralogies* appear to feature a similar rule: the father of the javelin-thrower assumes that in the case of a conviction he will be deprived of his son for the rest of his life (3.2.10).

29 On hiatus in Antiphon see Pearson 1978: 136–138, cited by Gagarin 1997: 32.

he killed the responder, even though the attacker created the circumstance by initiating the assault and the responder did not intend to kill? In the *Second Tetralogy*, we have independent proximate causes of death—the thrower's throw and the victim's run—with the thrower and victim not knowingly acting in concert. In the *Third Tetralogy*, ignoring the role of the doctor, we have a chain of causes in which the proximate cause, response to attack by the killer, depends fully upon the ultimate cause, initiation of attack by the victim. In both cases, Antiphon has the prosecution advance a compromise position in fact for which, in Athens as well as in the *Tetralogies*, there is no corresponding compromise in law: even if the respective defendants are partially responsible, there is no way to hold them partially responsible. In his forensic speeches *On the Killing of Herodes* and *On the Chorus Boy*, the latter delivered by the defendant in an actual *dikê phonou*, Antiphon offers this encomium of the homicide laws of Athens:

> καὶ τοὺς μὲν νόμους οἳ κεῖνται περὶ τῶν τοιούτων πάντες ἂν ἐπαινέσειαν κάλλιστα νόμων κεῖσθαι καὶ ὁσιώτατα. ὑπάρχει μὲν γὰρ αὐτοῖς ἀρχαιοτάτοις εἶναι ἐν τῇ γῇ ταύτῃ, ἔπειτα τοὺς αὐτοὺς αἰεὶ περὶ τῶν αὐτῶν, ὅπερ μέγιστον σημεῖον νόμων καλῶς κειμένων· ὁ χρόνος γὰρ καὶ ἡ ἐμπειρία τὰ μὴ καλῶς ἔχοντα διδάσκει τοὺς ἀνθρώπους.
>
> All would praise the laws established for such matters as the finest and most hallowed of laws. For they are the oldest in this land, and moreover they have always been the same regarding the same things, which is the greatest indication of well-enacted laws, since time and experience teach men what is not right.
>
> ANTIPH. 6.2; nearly verbatim at 5.14

But the Second and Third Tetralogies constitute a powerful critique of the inflexibility of these same laws, whose very antiquity and sacrosanctity militate against reform that might accommodate developing thought concerning complex liability.[30] Thus the criticism of Athenian homicide law that would be developed more fully and explicitly in the next century by Plato and Aristotle begins with the first of the Attic orators.[31]

---

30 Cf. Sealey 1984: 76; Carawan 1993: 268.

31 I would like to thank Christopher Carey and Ifigeneia Giannadaki, the organisers of the conference from which this volume derives, for inviting me to present my work at University College London; these two scholars, together with their co-editor, Brenda Griffith-

Appendix 1

Model Penal Code § 2.02(2). Kinds of Culpability Defined.

(a) *Purposely*
A person acts purposely with respect to a material element of an offense when:
(i) if the element involves the nature of his conduct or a result thereof, **it is his conscious object** to engage in conduct of that nature or to cause such a result; and
(ii) if the element involves the attendant circumstances, he is aware of the existence of such circumstances or he believes or hopes that they exist.

(b) *Knowingly*
A person acts knowingly with respect to a material element of an offense when:
(i) if the element involves the nature of his conduct or the attendant circumstances, **he is aware** that his conduct is of that nature or that such circumstances exist; and
(ii) if the element involves a result of his conduct, **he is aware that it is practically certain** that his conduct will cause such a result.

(c) *Recklessly*
A person acts recklessly with respect to a material element of an offense when **he consciously disregards a substantial and unjustifiable risk** that the material element exists or will result from his conduct. The risk must be of such a nature and degree that, considering the nature and purpose of the actor's conduct and the circumstances known to him, its disregard involves a gross deviation from the standard of conduct that a law-abiding person would observe in the actor's situation.

(d) *Negligently*
A person acts negligently with respect to a material element of an offense when **he should be aware of a substantial and unjustifiable risk** that the material element exists or will result from his conduct. The risk must be of such a nature and degree that the actor's failure to perceive it, considering the nature and purpose of his conduct and the circumstances known to him, involves a gross deviation from the standard of care that a reasonable person would observe in the actor's situation.

Williams, provided valuable commentary on an earlier draft of this chapter. I am likewise grateful to my fellow conference participants for their insightful comments and questions.

(With these provisions cf. MPC §§1.13.(9)–(16); 2.03; 2.04. Generally speaking, homicide committed purposely or knowingly is murder; homicide committed recklessly is manslaughter; homicide committed negligently is negligent homicide (MPC §§210.1–210.4)).

Appendix 2

Plato and Aristotle on Volition

1. Plato's homicide law (*Leg.* 865a–874d) categorises killings as follows: (1) 865a–866d: (violent and) unintentional killing (τὰ βίαια καὶ ἀκούσια, 865a2–3); (2) 866d–869e: killing in anger (θυμῷ, 866d5), itself divided (867a–b) into (a) killing by those who act *on the spur of the moment and without a preconceived intent to kill* (ὅσοι ἂν **ἐξαίφνης** μὲν **καὶ ἀπροβούλευτως τοῦ ἀποκτεῖναι** πληγαῖς ἤ τινι τοιούτῳ διαφθείρωσί τινα **παραχρῆμα** τῆς ὀργῆς γενομένης) (and who immediately regret the act), which is an εἰκών of unintentional killing, and (b) killing by those who delay vengeance for a slight in word or deed and *after some time kill with preconceived intent* (ὕστερον ἀποκτείνωσί τινα **βουληθέντες κτεῖναι**) (and who do not regret the act), which is an εἰκών of intentional killing; (3) 869e–873d: intentional (and fully unjust) killing (τὰ ἑκούσια καὶ κατ' ἀδικίαν πᾶσαν γιγνόμενα), which (unlike in Athenian law) is ἐκ προνοίας in the full sense of the phrase (cf. 871a1 ff.: νόμος ὅδε εἰρῆσθω τῇ γραφῇ· Ὃς ἂν ἐκ προνοίας τε καὶ ἀδίκως ὀντιναοῦν τῶν ἐμφυλίων αὐτόχειρ κτείνῃ κτλ); (4) 873d–874a: killing by non-humans; (5) 874a–b: killing by an unidentified killer; (6) 874b–d: lawful (justifiable) killing (ὧν δὲ **ἐφ' οἷς τε** ὀρθῶς ἂν καθαρὸς εἴη [*sc.* ὁ ἀποκτείνας]). The cases in category (6) (the killing of a nocturnal thief within the house; of a clothes-snatcher in self-defence (λωποδύτην ἀμυνόμενος); of the rapist of a free woman or child by the victim or the victim's father, brother, son, or husband; or in defence of one's father, mother, child, sibling, or spouse against lethal force, provided that the defended person be innocent of wrongdoing) and the special cases that open category (1) (public athletic competition, warfare or training for war, doctors) are circumstantial; category (6) contains justifiable homicides and the beginning of category (1) contains excusable homicides. Category (6) with its justifying circumstances is so important to Plato ('s Athenian Stranger) that he sets it off as Section 2 of the homicide law (with all preceding—categories (1) through (5)—as Section 1: οὗτος δὴ νόμος εἷς ἡμῖν ἔστω κύριος περὶ φόνου κείμενος, 874b4–5).

2. Arist. *Eth. Nic.* 1135a23–33, 1135b8–27: λέγω δ' ἑκούσιον μέν ... ὃ ἄν τις τῶν ἐφ' αὑτῷ ὄντων εἰδὼς καὶ μὴ ἀγνοῶν πράττῃ μήτε ὃν μήτε ᾧ μήτε οὗ ἕνεκα, οἷον τίνα τύπτει καὶ τίνι καὶ τίνος ἕνεκα, κἀκείνων ἕκαστον μὴ κατὰ συμβεβηκὸς μηδὲ βίᾳ

(ὥσπερ εἴ τις λαβὼν τὴν χεῖρα αὐτοῦ τύπτοι ἕτερον, οὐχ ἑκών· οὐ γὰρ ἐπ' αὐτῷ)· ἐνδέχεται δὲ τὸν τυπτόμενον πατέρα εἶναι, τὸν δ' ὅτι μὲν ἄνθρωπος ἢ τῶν παρόντων τις γινώσκειν, ὅτι δὲ πατὴρ ἀγνοεῖν· ὁμοίως δὲ τὸ τοιοῦτον διωρίσθω καὶ ἐπὶ τοῦ οὗ ἕνεκα, καὶ περὶ τὴν πρᾶξιν ὅλην. τὸ δὴ ἀγνοούμενον, ἢ μὴ ἀγνοούμενον μὲν μὴ ἐπ' αὐτῷ δ' ὄν, ἢ βίᾳ, ἀκούσιον. (…) τῶν δὲ ἑκουσίων τὰ μὲν προελόμενοι πράττομεν τὰ δ' οὐ προελόμενοι, προελόμενοι μὲν ὅσα προβουλευσάμενοι, ἀπροαίρετα δὲ ὅσ' ἀπροβούλευτα. τριῶν δὴ οὐσῶν βλαβῶν τῶν ἐν ταῖς κοινωνίαις, τὰ μὲν μετ' ἀγνοίας ἁμαρτήματά ἐστιν, ὅταν μήτε ὃν μήτε ὃ μήτε ᾧ μήτε οὗ ἕνεκα ὑπέλαβε πράξῃ· ἢ γὰρ οὐ βάλλειν ἢ οὐ τούτῳ ἢ οὐ τοῦτον ἢ οὐ τούτου ἕνεκα ᾠήθη, ἀλλὰ συνέβη οὐχ οὗ ἕνεκα ᾠήθη, οἷον οὐχ ἵνα τρώσῃ ἀλλ' ἵνα κεντήσῃ, ἢ οὐχ ὅν, ἢ οὐχ ᾧ. ὅταν μὲν οὖν παραλόγως ἡ βλάβη γένηται, ἀτύχημα· ὅταν δὲ μὴ παραλόγως, ἄνευ δὲ κακίας, ἁμάρτημα (ἁμαρτάνει μὲν γὰρ ὅταν ἡ ἀρχὴ ἐν αὐτῷ ᾖ τῆς αἰτίας, ἀτυχεῖ δ' ὅταν ἔξωθεν)· ὅταν δὲ εἰδὼς μὲν μὴ προβουλεύσας δέ, ἀδίκημα, οἷον ὅσα τε διὰ θυμὸν καὶ ἄλλα πάθη, ὅσα ἀναγκαῖα ἢ φυσικὰ συμβαίνει τοῖς ἀνθρώποις … ὅταν δ' ἐκ προαιρέσεως, ἄδικος καὶ μοχθηρός. διὸ καλῶς τὰ ἐκ θυμοῦ οὐκ ἐκ προνοίας κρίνεται· οὐ γὰρ ἄρχει ὁ θυμῷ ποιῶν, ἀλλ' ὁ ὀργίσας.

I call intentional … that which a person, among things in his power, does with knowledge and without ignorance of the person to whom he does it, the instrument with which he does it, and the end to which he does it—for example, whom he is hitting, with what, and to what end—each of the aforementioned occurring neither by chance nor by compulsion (as, for example, if someone else took his hand and struck a third person, he is not intentional, since it is not within his power). The person struck may be his father, and he may know that it is a person or one of those present but not know that it is his father; a similar distinction must be made in the case of the end and concerning the act in its entirety. That which is unknown, or not unknown but not in one's power, or done by compulsion, is unintentional. (…) Among intentional acts, we do some by deliberate choice and others not by deliberate choice. We do by deliberate choice what we have deliberated upon; all acts not deliberated upon are not by deliberate choice. Of the three types of harm in interactions, those that occur in ignorance are errors when the person acted upon, the act, the instrument, or the end is not what the actor supposed: he thought that he was not throwing to strike, or not with this instrument, or not this person, or not to this end, but the result was not the end he had in mind—for example, he threw not to wound but to prick—or that the person he struck or the instrument with which he struck was not what he had in mind. Now, when harm occurs contrary to reasonable expectation, it is an accident; but when it occurs not contrary to reasonable expectation but without vice, it is an error (for a person commits an error when the origin of the offence is in him, but suffers an accident when the origin is outside him). When he acts knowingly but not deliberately, it is an unjust act, such as all acts done on account of anger and other emotions that are necessary or natural for people. (…) But when he acts by deliberate choice, he is an unjust and bad person. Therefore, acts resulting from anger are rightly judged not to be the result of forethought, since the initiator is not the one acting in anger but the one who caused the anger.

Cf. *Eth. Nic.* 1109a32–35, 1109b30–1114b25; *Rh.* 1368b9–12, 1373b33–1374a17, 1374b4–10, 1375a7.

Bibliography

American Law Institute (1985) *Model Penal Code: Official Draft and Explanatory Notes: Complete Text of Model Penal Code as Adopted at the 1962 Annual Meeting of the American Law Institute at Washington, D.C., May 24, 1962*, Philadelphia.

Cantarella, E. (1976) *Studi sull'omicidio in diritto greco e romano*, Milan.

Carawan, E. (1993) 'The Tetralogies and Athenian Homicide Trials', *AJP* 114, 235–270.

Carawan, E. (1998) *Rhetoric and the Law of Draco*, Oxford.

Daube, D. (1969) *Roman Law: Linguistic, Social and Philosophical Aspects*, Edinburgh.

Dawe, R.D. (1982) *Sophocles: Oedipus Rex*, Cambridge.

Decleva Caizzi, F. (1969) *Antiphontis Tetralogiae*, Milan.

Dittenberger, W. (1897) 'Antiphons Tetralogien und das attische Criminalrecht: II', *Hermes* 32, 1–41.

Dittenberger, W. (1905) 'Zu Antiphons Tetralogien', *Hermes* 40, 450–470.

Dover, K.J. (1994) *Greek Popular Morality in the Time of Plato and Aristotle*, Indianapolis.

Gagarin, M. (1978) 'Self-Defense in Athenian Homicide Law', *GRBS* 19, 111–120.

Gagarin, M. (1981) *Drakon and Early Athenian Homicide Law*, New Haven.

Gagarin, M. (1997) *Antiphon: the Speeches*, Cambridge.

Gagarin, M. (2002) *Antiphon the Athenian: Oratory, Law, and Justice in the Age of the Sophists*, Austin.

Glotz, G. (1904) *La solidarité de la famille dans le droit criminel en Grèce*, Paris.

Griffith-Williams, B. (2013) *A Commentary on Selected Speeches of Isaios*, Leiden.

Harris, E.M. (1990) 'Did the Athenians Regard Seduction as a Worse Crime than Rape?' *CQ* 40, 370–377.

Loomis, W.T. (1972) 'The Nature of Premeditation in Athenian Homicide Law', *JHS* 92, 86–95.

MacDowell, D.M. (1963) *Athenian Homicide Law in the Age of the Orators*, Manchester.

MacDowell, D.M. (1990) *Demosthenes: Against Meidias*, Oxford.

Maschke, R. (1926) *Die Willenslehre im griechischen Recht*, Berlin.

Miller, S.G. (2004) *Ancient Greek Athletics*, New Haven.

Pearson, L. (1978) 'Hiatus and Its Effect in the Attic Speech-Writers', *TAPA* 108, 131–145.

Pepe, L. (2012) *Phonos: l'omicidio da Draconte all'età degli oratori*, Milan.
Phillips, D.D. (2008) *Avengers of Blood: Homicide in Athenian Law and Custom from Draco to Demosthenes*, Stuttgart.
Phillips, D.D. (2013) *The Law of Ancient Athens*, Ann Arbor.
Robinson, P.H. (1997) *Criminal Law*, New York.
Sealey, R. (1984) 'The Tetralogies Ascribed to Antiphon', *TAPA* 114, 71–85.
Stroud, R.S. (1968) *Drakon's Law on Homicide*, Berkeley.
Todd, S.C. (2007) *A Commentary on Lysias, Speeches 1–11*, Oxford.
Wolff, H.J. (1946) 'The Origin of Judicial Litigation among the Greeks', *Traditio* 4, 31–87.
Wyse, W. (1904) *The Speeches of Isaeus*, Cambridge.

CHAPTER 18

Abuse of Inheritance Law in Isaios?

Rosalia Hatzilambrou

Isaios is probably the Attic orator who is most reckoned to have abused the law. The seeds of doubt regarding Isaios' honesty in the treatment of law were implicitly planted by Dionysios of Halikarnassos, who wrote that Isaios τοὺς δὲ δικαστὰς καταστρατηγεῖ, τοῖς δὲ πράγμασιν, ὑπὲρ ὧν ὁ λόγος, ἐκ παντὸς πειρᾶται βοηθεῖν ('Isaios outwits the dikasts with his stratagems and tries by every means to help the case in the course of which the speech is delivered'),[1] and that ἦν δὲ περὶ αὐτοῦ δόξα παρὰ τοῖς τότε γοητείας καὶ ἀπάτης ('he had a reputation among his contemporaries for trickery and deception').[2] According to the ancient critic, Isaios and Demosthenes are suspected of chicanery because of their τέχνη and δεινότης, that is, rhetorical skill and forcefulness. But since Isaios based much of his argumentation on legal provisions, he could have been suspected of using deceitful arguments not only about the facts of a case, but also about the law. Dionysios did not specify, but his ἐκ παντός ('by every means') could certainly have justified the arousal of suspicion regarding Isaios' treatment of law.

It was, of course, William Wyse who in the Preface to his monumental work on Isaios in 1904 declared that its main purpose was 'to show by analysis of the extant speeches that ancient scholars had a juster appreciation of the orator's art than is shown by modern writers on Greek Law, for some of whom Isaeus' unsupported statements appear to carry the authority of decisions of a Supreme Court'. His scepticism regarding Isaios' attitude to the law surfaces throughout the commentary and is sometimes expressed through very sharp remarks.[3] Although scholarship since the sixties has reacted against the Victorian scholar's evaluation of Isaios,[4] I believe that the heavy shadow of Wysean

1 Dion. Hal. *Is.* 3.

2 Dion. Hal. *Is.* 4. Dionysios does not reveal the names of Isaios' contemporaries who held such a derogatory view of Isaios' means of persuasion, apart from Pytheas (Dion. Hal. *Is.* 4) who was actually in conflict with or antagonistic to Demosthenes, traditionally, and probably truly, attested to be a student of Isaios.

3 See for instance, Wyse 1904: 276, 393 and 560.

4 Harrison 1968: 122, Thompson 1976, Avramovic 1997, Cobetto Ghiggia 2002, Ferrucci 2005, Edwards 2007, Griffith-Williams 2013.

 | DOI:10.1163/9789004377899_020

scepticism still falls across the corpus of Isaios' works and has an impact upon its study. Thus a primary aim of this chapter is to offer some arguments against Wyse's biased stand on the treatment of law by Isaios. To achieve this, I will attempt to sketch out Isaios' attitude regarding the use of law in his speeches. I shall discuss some controversial instances of quotation, paraphrase or invocation of legal statutes in the Isaian oratorical corpus from speeches 3, 6, 7, 8, 10 and 11. And I shall conclude by claiming that with one probable exception Isaios did not abuse the law in his extant speeches, in the sense that he did not *intentionally* use an existing law *wrongly*.

The corpus of Isaios' orations consists of eleven speeches composed for inheritance cases and preserved in medieval manuscripts, a large portion of another speech quoted in Dionysios of Halikarnassos' essay *On Isaios* and traditionally included in the editions as his twelfth speech, and about thirty small fragments attested in lexicographers, Dionysios of Halikarnassos and papyri. In these texts there are references to twenty-five different legal statutes pertaining mostly to succession law, as one would expect, and the subject of adoption and the *epiklēros* daughter. The available evidence, which has been studied in detail by Edwards, suggests that Isaios concentrated on a particular area of the law, namely inheritance and the related area of citizenship rights.[5] It could be taken for granted that such specialisation was conditional upon very good knowledge of (or rather expertise in) Attic inheritance law. Isaios based his argumentation, which was occasionally rather extensive as in orations 3, 7, 8, 11, on provisions of Attic law, if he had confidence that the law favoured his cause.[6] In such cases, he was not discouraged from advancing strong legal argumentation by the fear of alienating his client from the audience of dikasts, who would view the latter's legal expertise with dislike.[7] When his claims could not be supported by legal evidence, usually because the dispute involved specific facts, he does not appear to have resorted to abuse of law but to have employed other kinds of argumentation and evidence, for instance the continuity of the *oikos*, the challenge of a will, the observance of religious custom, character evidence and family feuds.[8]

Attic legislation on succession, which was attributed to Solon, was notoriously vague. *Athenaion Politeia* mentions the law τὸν τῶν κλήρων καὶ ἐπι-

5 Edwards 2006.

6 Harris 2013: 192–196, has convincingly argued that the argumentation in Isa. 1 is mainly legal.

7 This is the well-known *topos* of the amateur litigant, on which see for instance Carey 1994: 27–29.

8 On this kind of evidence in Isaios' speeches see Griffith-Williams 2012: 145–162.

κλήρων as the one reputedly considered as 'worded not simply nor clearly'.[9] Plutarch in his *Solon* restated that '[Solon] drafted his laws obscurely and ambiguously strongly aiming at enhancing the power of the popular courts.'[10] Thus when composing speeches for inheritance cases Isaios often needed to interpret laconic and ambiguous statutes and apply their provisions to cases that were almost by definition complicated. His interpretation of some vague statutes, as suggested by the available evidence for verdicts in the law cases in which his clients were involved, was the expected one, at least as regards his primary audience. This is indicated from orations 3, 8, 11. Actually, in these three speeches the argumentation advanced is mostly, if not almost completely, legal.

There is a strong probability that Isaios' client was successful in bringing the action for false witness (δίκη ψευδομαρτυρίων), on which occasion he delivered the third speech, since he had earlier brought a successful action of the same type against another witness in the same controversy. Although Athenian dikasts were not bound by decisions in previous trials, it would have been odd if they had not taken seriously the outcome of a recent trial instituted by the same type of action between the same groups of litigants.[11] And although there is no indication that Isaios composed the speech for the first action for false witness, he admittedly adduced much (if not all) of the argumentation put forward at the successful first trial.[12] As for the outcome of the eighth speech, some indication is provided by inscriptional evidence. The speaker's younger brother and co-claimant of Kiron's estate could be identified with another Kiron (named after his mother's father), who was a creditor for 600 *drachmas* in ca. 330, as attested in a *horos*.[13] His ability to be a creditor for such an amount might be an indication that Isaios' client won the case.[14] Regarding the verdict of the

9 *Ath. Pol.* 9.2: ἔτι δὲ καὶ διὰ τὸ μὴ γεγράφθ[αι το]ὺς νόμους ἁπλῶς μηδὲ σαφῶς, ἀλλ' ὥσπερ ὁ περὶ τῶν κλήρων καὶ ἐπικλήρων, ἀνάγκη [πο]λλὰς ἀμφισβητήσεις γίγνεσθαι καὶ πάντα βραβεύειν καὶ τὰ κοινὰ καὶ τὰ ἴδια τὸ δικαστήριον. ('And also, since the laws are not worded simply nor clearly, but like the law about inheritances and *epiklēroi*, it inevitably results that many disputes arise and that the court decides on all business both public and private'). Of course the view that Solon intentionally made the laws ambiguous is immediately dismissed by pseudo-Aristotle in the *Ath. Pol.*, who stated that obscurities in the legislation are extant, because it is difficult to make general rules about human conduct. On the treatment of Solon in the *Ath. Pol.* in general, see Gehrke 2006: 276–289.

10 Plut. *Sol.* 18.3: λέγεται δὲ καὶ τοὺς νόμους ἀσαφέστερον γράψας καὶ πολλὰς ἀντιλήψεις ἔχοντας αὐξῆσαι τὴν τῶν δικαστηρίων ἰσχύν.

11 Cf. Harris 2013: 246–273.

12 See 3.11–12, 14, 17, 18.

13 Finley 1952: 134 no 53 (= *Hesperia* 7 (1938) 93–94 no 14).

14 See Edwards 2007: 134.

trial in which Isa. 11 was heard, we learn from a speech in the Demosthenic corpus (Dem. 43) from the opposing side, delivered in a subsequent action, that Isaios' client, Theopompos, won the case initiated by an εἰσαγγελία κακώσεως ὀρφανοῦ—a public action for maltreatment of an orphan—and thus managed to defend, enjoy and transfer to his son the estate of Hagnias he had previously claimed and won, because his interpretation of the law on the intestate succession was accepted as correct. Specifically, he effectively argued that the provision μέχρι ἀνεψιῶν παίδων of the law meant both 'children of first cousins' (i.e. first cousins once removed) and 'second cousins' (i.e. children of a parent's first cousin), hence he, as second cousin of the deceased, was within the required degree of kinship (ἀγχιστεία). Furthermore, he persuasively showed that the statute set limits to the principle of representation and that the line of succession stopped at second cousins. Consequently, a second cousin of a deceased did not transmit his rights to his children, therefore the son of Theopompos' deceased brother, the orphan for whose maltreatment he was prosecuted by another of the boy's guardians, was outside the requisite degree of kinship and was not entitled to inherit his father's share.

Of course, we should always bear in mind that Isaios is a professional speechwriter, and that rhetoric was apparently employed in the presentation of legal provisions and their application to a case. Rhetorical skill can be traced, for instance, in the discussion of the particular stipulation of the law on wills (περὶ τῶν διαθηκῶν) in the third speech that deals with the daughters of the testator. Isaios aimed at demonstrating that his client's opponents, assuming that they had acted in accordance with the law, treated Phile over a long period as illegitimate. The law on wills is referred to in 3.42: οὔτε γὰρ διαθέσθαι οὔτε δοῦναι οὐδενὶ οὐδὲν ἔξεστι τῶν ἑαυτοῦ ἄνευ τῶν θυγατέρων, ἐάν τις καταλιπὼν γνησίας τελευτᾷ. ('For anyone who dies leaving behind legitimate daughters is not entitled to make a will or to bequeath anyone any part of his estate without including his daughters in it'). It is subsequently read by the clerk and is quoted again by the speaker in 3.68:

> ὁ γὰρ νόμος διαρρήδην λέγει ἐξεῖναι διαθέσθαι ὅπως ἂν ἐθέλῃ τις τὰ αὑτοῦ, ἐὰν μὴ παῖδας γνησίους καταλίπῃ ἄρρενας· ἐὰν δὲ θηλείας καταλίπῃ, σὺν ταύταις. οὐκοῦν μετὰ τῶν θυγατέρων ἔστι δοῦναι καὶ διαθέσθαι τὰ αὑτοῦ· ἄνευ δὲ τῶν γνησίων θυγατέρων οὐχ οἷόν τε οὔτε ποιήσασθαι οὔτε δοῦναι οὐδενὶ οὐδὲν τῶν ἑαυτοῦ.

For the law clearly states that if someone does not leave any legitimate male children, he can dispose of his property as he pleases. But if he leaves daughters, he can dispose of his property with them included. Con-

> sequently, only together with his daughters can someone give away and dispose of his property. Without including his legitimate daughters, a man can neither adopt nor leave to anyone any of his property.

The repetition is not pleonastic. Isaios mentions it tactically, when he reviews the misconduct towards Phile, first of his opponent in this legal dispute, Nikodemos; and then of the opponent's main witnesses, that is, Pyrrhos' uncles. The particular stipulation of the law appears to be accurately quoted by the speaker in § 68, where immediately after the quotation, Isaios offers his interpretation. In § 42 the interpretation alone is given by the speaker, presumably because the law is then officially read by the clerk. Isaios manages to base the strongest argument of his speech on two words of the law on wills, namely on the σὺν ταύταις. He exploits the laconic and general phrasing of the law, in order to prove the deceit of the opponents. Specifically, Isaios argues that the law obliged fathers with a daughter, when adopting a son, to stipulate that the latter marry the daughter, otherwise the adoption is invalid. The orator leaves no doubt about the correctness of his interpretation. The διαρρήδην which introduces the law in § 68 adds a tone of finality to the whole argument. It stresses on one hand the clarity of the law and on the other the accuracy of its quotation. The content of the semi-period that follows the quotation of the law (οὐκοῦν μετὰ τῶν θυγατέρων ἔστι δοῦναι καὶ διαθέσθαι τὰ αὑτοῦ) sounds totally acceptable, for it appears to be a mere repetition of the stipulation supplemented appropriately, in order to build an independent and comprehensible clause. However, the subsequent negative semi-period is not exactly synonymous, although presented by Isaios as such, for it emphatically (notice the sequence of negatives) conveys a more absolute interpretation of the law (ἄνευ δὲ τῶν γνησίων θυγατέρων οὐχ οἷόν τε οὔτε ποιήσασθαι οὔτε δοῦναι οὐδενὶ οὐδὲν τῶν ἑαυτοῦ). The latter intentionally replaces in the argumentation of Isaios the stipulation of the law, and is actually introduced instead of it in § 42. Notable, finally, is the accumulation of tropes and figures of speech in § 68 (*paronomasia*, *antistrophē*, chiasmus, *anaphora* and antithesis) which help Isaios' interpretation sound plausible.

The quotation of the particular stipulation on the *epiklēroi* daughters in 3.42, 68, also in 10.13,[15] reveals a tactic of Isaios regarding the use of law and its

15 Isa. 10.13: καὶ τῷ μὲν πατρὶ αὐτῆς, εἰ παῖδες ἄρρενες μὴ ἐγένοντο, οὐκ ἂν ἐξῆν ἄνευ ταύτης διαθέσθαι· κελεύει γὰρ ὁ νόμος σὺν ταύταις κύριον εἶναι δοῦναι, ἐάν τῳ βούληται, τὰ ἑαυτοῦ· ('Again, her own father, if he had no male children, could not have disposed of his estate without her: for the law ordains that he is entitled to leave his property with his daughters to whomever he wishes'). Cf. also Dem. 43.51: "Οστις ἂν μὴ διαθέμενος ἀποθάνῃ, ἐὰν μὲν παῖδας καταλίπῃ θηλείας, σὺν ταύτῃσιν, ἐὰν δὲ μή, τούσδε κυρίους εἶναι τῶν χρημάτων. ('Whenever a

interpretation: namely that he suppressed limitations on the provisions of the statute he was citing, enforced by other laws in effect or even urged by social practice, if these limitations were irrelevant to his case. It has been argued, for instance, that in 3.42 and 68 Isaios probably offers an absolute interpretation of the law, since the adoptee was not obliged by law in all cases to marry the daughter of the adopter, on the condition that she is somehow included in the dispositions, e.g. through provision for her dowry, and indeed a generous one.[16] Menander's *Dyskolos* lines 731–739 are adduced as the closest parallel. They read: ... ποιοῦμαι σ' ὑόν, ἅ τ' ἔχων τυγχάνω / πάντα σαυτοῦ νόμισον εἶναι. τήνδε σοι παρεγγυῶ· / ἄνδρα δ' αὐτῆι πόρισον ... 737–739: κηδεμὼν εἶ τῆς ἀδελφῆς εἰκότως. τοῦ κτήματος / ἐπιδίδου ⟨σὺ⟩ προῖκα τοὐμοῦ διαμετρήσας ⟨θ'⟩ ἥμισυ / τὸ δ' ἕτερον λαβὼν διοίκει κἀμὲ καὶ τὴν μητέρα ('I adopt you as my son; all I happen to own consider yours; I entrust this woman to you; you must find a husband for her ... and care for your sister, as you should. Divide into two my possessions; give one half to her as dowry; take the rest and support myself and your mother'). However, this does not constitute a parallel case. In *Dyskolos* most probably we have a case of adoption *inter vivos*, while in Isa. 3 it is a case of testamentary adoption. Maffi firmly believes that in a testamentary adoption there was no such option; the adoptee had to marry the daughter of his adopter.[17] My own belief is that in a case of testamentary adoption when *one* daughter is left, the adoptee could avoid marrying the daughter of his adopter only if the latter had for a good reason stipulated so in his testament. In *Dyskolos* the adoptee is the son of the wife of his adopter by her earlier marriage, who was forbidden to marry his half-sister by the same mother. In Isa. 3 Phile and the adopted son of her father were first cousins; such a marital union was not considered incestuous and so forbidden. In *Dyskolos* the adopter himself made specific provisions for his daughter and her dowry, while in Isa. 3 there is no indication that Pyrrhos did the same for Phile. Additionally, we should not arbitrarily apply general legal effect to the stipulation on the *thēssa epiklēros*[18] attested in Dem. 43.54, which states the requirement for the nearest kinsman (not the adopted son) to marry a poor *epiklēros* or else to dower her.[19] To sum up, it has been argued that

man dies without leaving a will, if he leaves behind female children, [the property shall go] with them, but if not, the following are entitled to have his property.')

16 Rubinstein 1993: 95–96.

17 Maffi 1991: 218.

18 See, for instance, Cudjoe 2010: 35, 49, 51, 201–202.

19 Dem. 43.54: τῶν ἐπικλήρων ὅσαι θητικὸν τελοῦσιν, ἐὰν μὴ βούληται ἔχειν ὁ ἐγγύτατα γένους, ἐκδιδότω ἐπιδοὺς ὁ μὲν πεντακοσιομέδιμνος πεντακοσίας δραχμάς, ὁ δ' ἱππεὺς τριακοσίας, ὁ δὲ ζευγίτης ἑκατὸν πεντήκοντα, πρὸς οἷς αὐτῆς ... ἐὰν δὲ μὴ ἔχῃ ὁ ἐγγυτάτω γένους ἢ μὴ ἐκδῷ, ὁ ἄρχων ἐπαναγκαζέτω ἢ αὐτὸν ἔχειν ἢ ἐκδοῦναι. ἐὰν δὲ μὴ ἐπαναγκάσῃ ὁ ἄρχων, ὀφειλέτω χιλίας

Endios in Isa. 3 had the legal capacity either to marry Phile or to dower her and give her in marriage to somebody else. The topic falls short of firm evidence to allow for definite conclusions, but on balance it is likely that Isaios offers the expected interpretation of the particular stipulation of the law on wills when *one* daughter is left.[20]

A similar attitude towards the quotation of a legal provision could be observed in 3.64–65, where Isaios enhances an *argumentum a fortiori* by citing the law on the ἐπιδικασία (adjudication) of the *epiklēroi*:

> τὰς μὲν ὑπὸ τῶν πατέρων ἐκδοθείσας καὶ συνοικούσας ἀνδράσι γυναῖκας (περὶ ὧν τίς ἂν ἄμεινον ἢ ὁ πατὴρ βουλεύσαιτο;) καὶ τὰς οὕτω δοθείσας, ἐὰν ὁ πατὴρ αὐτῶν τελευτήσῃ μὴ καταλιπὼν αὐταῖς γνησίους ἀδελφούς, τοῖς ἐγγύτατα γένους ἐπιδίκους ὁ νόμος εἶναι κελεύει, καὶ πολλοὶ συνοικοῦντες ἤδη ἀφῄρηνται τὰς ἑαυτῶν γυναῖκας. εἶτα τὰς μὲν ὑπὸ τῶν πατέρων ἐκδοθείσας διὰ τὸν νόμον ἐξ ἀνάγκης ἐπιδίκους εἶναι προσήκει·
>
> Women who have been given in marriage by their fathers (and who better than a father to judge what is in their best interests?) and live with their husbands, even in the case of those who have been married in this way, if their father dies without leaving them legitimate brothers, the law decrees they should be adjudicable to their next of kin. In fact, many married men before now have been separated from their wives for this reason. Thus, women who have been given in marriage by their fathers must necessarily by law become adjudicable.

On this legal ground, Isaios adds that many husbands are said to have been deprived of their own wives. Nobody would doubt that the legal principle on the ἐπιδικασία of the *epiklēros*, a legal procedure initiated by her father's next of

δραχμὰς ἱερὰς τῇ Ἥρᾳ. ('In regard to all *epiklēroi* who are ranked as *thētes*, if the nearest of kin does not wish to marry her, he is to give her away in marriage with a dowry of 500 *drachmas* if he is a *pentakosiomedimnos*, 300 if a *hippeus*, and 150 if a *zeugitēs*; in addition to what she owes ... And if the nearest of kin fails to marry or give her away in marriage, the *archōn* is to compel him to marry or give her away. And if the *archōn* fails to compel him, he is to owe 1,000 *drachmas*, consecrated to Hera.').

20 If the father of more than one legitimate daughter, and indeed the aforementioned legal stipulations speak of female issue in the plural (θηλείας, σὺν ταύταις), decided to dispose of his property by means of adopting a son, he had in all probability to regulate by means of written provisions the share in his estate of all of his daughters, since it is self-evident that the adopted son would marry (or had already married) only one daughter. But this situation does not of course apply to Isa 3.

kin, is correct, hence again Isaios felt confident of presenting it with a tone of finality (διὰ τὸν νόμον, ἐξ ἀνάγκης, κελεύει). Suspicion has been expressed that Isaios does not tell the whole truth regarding the ἀφαίρεσις of the *epiklēros*, in the sense that he does not mention any restrictions to the right of a next of kin to claim a married *epiklēros*. It is likely that a woman who had already been married by ἐγγύη before her father died could be treated as *epiklēros*, at least if she did not yet have a son, and that her father's next of kin could still claim her in marriage, forcing a divorce from her existing husband.[21] In all probability, if there had been male, or even female issue according to Karabélias,[22] of the original union, such a claim was barred.[23] There is no extant legal provision that states the aforementioned restriction, while the best indication is still Terrence *Adelphoe* 650–659. Ter. *Ad.* 650–652: *haec virgo orbast patre. / hic meus amicus illi genere est proximus. / huic leges cogunt nubere hanc*, and 657–659: *commenta mater est esse ex alio viro / nescioquo puerum natum, neque eum nominat; / priorem esse illum, non oportere huic dari.* ('The girl has lost her father. The friend of mine is her next of kin, and the law requires her to marry him ... The mother has made up a story that the girl has a child by some other man whom she doesn't name; she says that this other man has a prior claim, and the girl shouldn't be given to my friend.')[24] This particular restriction could well have

---

21 The logic behind this law reported by Isaios here could be that if the marriage of a woman, who had been married by *engyē* exogamously before the death of her father, had not produced issue, there was a high risk that the *oikos* of her father would be left *erēmos*. Thus, the Athenian law, which had an explicit interest in protecting the *oikoi* (cf. Dem. 43.75, *Ath. Pol.* 56.7), allowed the next of kin to dissolve the marriage of the woman and claim her himself, since he was regarded in law as the person whom the deceased would have wished to perpetuate his *oikos* by letting one of his sons be posthumously adopted by his dead father-in-law. To the best of my knowledge Maffi is the only scholar who has doubted the existence of the *aphairesis epiklērou* as a legal institution; for his arguments see Maffi 1990: 21–36.

22 Karabélias 2002: 150–157.

23 The rationale behind such a restriction on the right of *aphairesis epiklērou* could be that the existence of issue indicates that the union is fertile and could provide the deceased with a posthumously adopted son. The continuation of the *oikos* of the *epiklēros*' father must have depended on the willingness of her husband to make proper arrangements and ensure that an adoption took place. I think that the latter must have been under strong moral obligation and social pressure to carry out the posthumous adoption of a son of the *epiklēros*, especially if their marriage had produced more than one male heir. If this is taken into account, one can better understand the rules reported by Plut. *Sol.* 20, namely that the husband of an *epiklēros* was required to sleep with her three times a month, while another one permitted the court to dissolve her marriage and choose a more suitable mate, if the man to whom she had been adjudicated is unable to perform his marital duties.

24 On the evidence of this text see Paoli 1976: 363–366, Karabélias 2002: 151–153.

been observed in Athenian society and courts, because then the main purpose of the institution of the *epiklēros*, that is, the continuation of the *oikos* and the tomb cult of the deceased father, would be achieved, provided of course that a son of the *epiklēros* was transferred into the *oikos* of her father by posthumous adoption.[25]

Additionally, Isaios' reliability as a source of law has been questioned, because he does not mention that a married *epiklēros* with no children could renounce her rights and remain with her husband; this is a case attested in 10.19. However, I seriously doubt that such an option, if it was actually practised, was a legal provision and not the outcome of a private agreement. Anyway, Isaios did not abuse the law by not listing all possible restrictions to the *aphairesis epiklērou*, enforced either by legislation or custom. But by writing πολλοὶ in 3.64 he probably hinted at them. Some husbands at least were not deprived of their *epiklēroi* wives, either because they were their next of kin anyway, or because in their case some restrictions were observed. Finally, the argumentation in 3.64–65 appears to focus on the period of the betrothal of the alleged *epiklēros* to Xenokles (see the potential aorist indicatives ἂν ἐπέτρεψ-εν/αν, Ξενοκλέα λαβόντα ἔχειν). If this is correct, the restriction to the dissolution of the marriage of the *epiklēros* because of the existence of children is not relevant, thus its non-appearence in 3.64–65 should not be regarded as an intentional omission.

Another 'legal' statement by Isaios has been disputed, namely the one stated in 10.9: οἶμαι τοίνυν πάντας ὑμᾶς εἰδέναι, ὦ ἄνδρες, ὅτι κατὰ διαθήκας αἱ εἰσαγωγαὶ τῶν εἰσποιήτων γίγνονται, διδόντων τε αὐτῶν καὶ υἱεῖς ποιουμένων, ἄλλως δὲ οὐκ ἔξεστιν. ('I think you are all aware, gentlemen, that introductions of adopted children are carried out in accordance with a will, in which men dispose of their property and adopt sons, and no other procedure is legal'). The assertion is based on the Solonian law of wills, attested *in extenso* in [Dem.] 46.14, which reads:

> ὅσοι μὴ ἐπεποίηντο, ὥστε μήτε ἀπειπεῖν μήτ' ἐπιδικάσασθαι, ὅτε Σόλων εἰσῄει τὴν ἀρχήν, τὰ ἑαυτοῦ διαθέσθαι εἶναι ὅπως ἂν ἐθέλῃ ἂν μὴ παῖδες ὦσι γνήσιοι

25 See also Schaps 1979: 28–33. As Rubinstein 1993: 89, explained, the fact that we know of only one posthumous adoption of this kind, namely that of Euboulides the third into his maternal grandfather's *oikos* attested in Dem. 43, 'need not mean that such adoptions were only exceptionally carried out; it may rather reflect the fact that these adoptions would rarely or hardly ever be disputed. … And undisputed posthumous adoptions are less likely to have been recorded in the sort of sources we have for the institution in the fourth century.'

ἄρρενες, ἂν μὴ μανιῶν ἢ γήρως ἢ φαρμάκων ἢ νόσου ἕνεκα, ἢ γυναικὶ πειθόμενος, ὑπὸ τούτων του παρανοῶν, ἢ ὑπ' ἀνάγκης ἢ ὑπὸ δεσμοῦ καταληφθείς

anyone who had not been adopted with the result that he could neither renounce nor claim by adjudication [an inheritance], when Solon entered upon his office, may dispose of his property as he wishes, if he does not have legitimate male children, and if he is not mentally incompetent because of lunacy, old age, drugs, illness, or under the influence of a woman, or under constraint or has been deprived of his liberty.

This law clearly speaks of the right of testamentary disposition only, which can be taken to include testamentary adoption. This is the line taken by Isaios here, but he goes further in insisting that the wording of the law is such as to permit only this mode of adoption.[26] The fact that the very same law is appealed to in the forensic speeches as the law permitting adoption *inter vivos* (as for instance in Isa. 2) indicates that there was no written legislation establishing the right to employ this or any other procedure of adoption. Regarding the legislation on adoption *inter vivos* Rubinstein notes 'the institution of an heir by means of adoption *inter vivos* could be conceived of as one way of "disposing of one's property"'.[27] In the tenth speech Isaios aimed at attacking a posthumous adoption (that of Aristarchos II), which violated according to the speaker the rights of an *epiklēros* and her son. Since in all likelihood there was no provision in law expressly regulating that type of adoption, which must have developed as a matter of custom, the law is not misrepresented in 10.9 where Isaios maintains that there is no legal provision for posthumous adoption.[28]

Likewise, Isaios appears to ignore social practice and stick to the letter of the law, when it favours his argumentation. This is the case in 6.28: τοῖς γὰρ φύσει υἱέσιν αὑτοῦ οὐδεὶς οὐδενὶ ἐν διαθήκῃ γράφει δόσιν οὐδεμίαν, διότι ὁ νόμος αὐτὸς ἀποδίδωσι τῷ υἱεῖ τὰ τοῦ πατρὸς καὶ οὐδὲ διαθέσθαι ἐᾷ ὅτῳ ἂν ὦσι παῖδες γνήσιοι ('for nobody writes down in a will any bequest of anything to his own natural sons, because the law itself gives a father's estate to his son and does not even allow anyone who has legitimate children to make a will'), and 10.9: γνησίου γὰρ ὄντος αὐτῷ Δημοχάρους ὑέος οὔτ' ἂν ἐβούλετο ταῦτα [δια]πρᾶξαι, οὔτε ἐξῆν δοῦναι τὰ ἑαυτοῦ ἑτέρῳ. ('for as long as he had a legitimate son, Demochares, he would not have wished to do so, and he was not allowed to give his property to anyone else'), where Isaios asserts that the law does not allow someone with legitimate

26 I particularly thank Prof. C. Carey for his comment on this point.
27 Rubinstein 1993: 17. See also Ruschenbusch 1957: 270.
28 On posthumous adoption see Rubinstein 1993: 25–29, Griffith-Williams 2013: 203–205.

children to make a will, while in fact fathers with legitimate sons did make dispositions.[29] Well known examples are the wills of Konon (attested in Lys. 19), Diodotos (see Lys. 22), Pasion (see [Dem.] 36, [Dem.] 45 and 46) and Demosthenes the elder, which were drawn up by Athenians with legitimate sons.[30] With the exception of the one left by Pasion these wills were considered legal and were not disputed by the sons of the testator. Biscardi,[31] followed by Rubinstein,[32] has argued that the law on wills restricts to childless men the right to dispose freely, and thus it would allow the interpretation that a man, even if he left legitimate sons, was permitted to make certain dispositions which would be valid, provided that he had satisfied their claims. Even if this interpretation was accepted as correct in the fourth century, the law would be understood to allow *certain* testamentary dispositions (and not the whole estate, as would have been the case in 10.9) to somebody different from the testator's legitimate children, while in 6.28 the testator in the opponent's story appears to have disposed of his property to a legitimate son. In these contexts, Isaios cannot be accused of having abused the law on the wills by offering the most absolute interpretation of it.

Isaios often had to address claims of which there was no endorsement in the written legislation. In this case, the logographer had to resort mostly to comparative legal arguments, as for instance in 10.10, where in order to support his statement, correct in my opinion, that a minor was not allowed to draw up a will, Isaios cites the law that forbade a child to make a contract: ὁ γὰρ νόμος διαρρήδην κωλύει παιδὶ μὴ ἐξεῖναι συμβάλλειν μηδὲ γυναικὶ πέρα μεδίμνου κριθῶν ('For the law expressly forbids a child or woman to make a contract for more than a *medimnos* of barley'). Similarly, in 8.30–34 he had to support his contention that descendants (ἔκγονοι, in that case children of a predeceased daughter) take precedence over collaterals (συγγενεῖς, in that case children of a brother) in the order of succession and inheritance. Isaios puts forward two arguments by analogy that make use of extant law. The first (8.31) is that if the speaker's mother had outlived his grandfather, Kiron, whose estate was being adjudicated, she would have become *epiklēros* and her father's property would have gone to her children, when they had completed two years after puberty. However, the speaker's mother predeceased her father, thus she never became

29 The law quoted in [Dem.] 46.24 stated that fathers with legitimate sons could make wills, but these would become valid only if their sons die during their minority.

30 See Wyse 1904: 515, Todd 1993: 225–226.

31 Biscardi 1983: 32–33.

32 Rubinstein 1993: 84. In Schaps's 1979: 22 words: 'A man with sons could bequeath sums of money to others; what he could not do was appoint a principal heir other than his sons.'

epiklēros. Her sons certainly inherited her dowry, but did they also inherit rights to her father's estate? An explicit provision on the particular issue was not in all probability included in Attic legislation, therefore Isaios advances another legal argument. Since direct descendants are responsible for the maintenance of parents and grandparents, and according to the law which is actually read out, are liable to prosecution for neglect (κάκωσιν) if the latter are lacking the necessities of life, the descendants should inherit their parents' or grandparents' estate, if there is one.[33]

Likewise, absence of a specific legal prohibition enabled Isaios to argue effectively in 11.27 (and 34) against the plaintiff's assertion that orphans are not allowed to sue their guardian,[34] and that therefore his ward never brought a private suit against Theopompos (supposedly a δίκην βλάβης) on the grounds of a broken agreement. Wyse rightly stated (1904: 698) that 'a minor could only sue and be sued through his guardian, and a guardian could not be at the same time prosecutor and defendant'. However, this ward had another guardian, the one who actually brought the public action for maltreatment of an orphan against Theopompos and who according to Isaios was not prevented by any law from getting satisfaction from Theopompos through a private suit on behalf of the ward. It appears that there was no legal provision regulating the authority and responsibility of each guardian in a joint guardianship.[35]

Finally, Isaios cannot be considered guilty of abusing the law when he did not recognise a mother's right of inheritance from her son in 11.17:

> οἱ δ' ὑπὲρ τῆς Ἁγνίου μητρὸς γένει μὲν ἐμοὶ ταὐτὸ προσηκούσης (ἀδελφὴ γὰρ ἦν τοῦ Στραττίου) νόμῳ δὲ ἀποκλειομένης, ὃς κελεύει κρατεῖν τοὺς ἄρρενας, τοῦτο μὲν εἴασαν, οἰόμενοι δ' ἐμοῦ πλεονεκτήσειν μητέρα εἶναι τοῦ τελευτήσαντος ἔγραψαν· ὃ συγγενέστατον μὲν ἦν τῇ φύσει πάντων, ἐν δὲ ταῖς ἀγχιστείαις ὁμολογουμένως οὐκ ἔστιν
>
> but those who supported Hagnias' mother, who is related in the same degree as I am (for she was Strattios' sister) but is excluded by the law that gives priority to males, left out this point, and thinking they would gain an advantage over me wrote that she was the mother of the deceased—

33 On the legal argumentation in 8.30–34 see Wyse 1904: 607–609, Ferrucci 2005: 189, and Griffith-Williams 2013: 98–102, 134–137.

34 Isa. 11.27: … τῆς δὲ πρὸς ἐμὲ λήξεως ἐμποδὼν εἶναι τοὺς νόμους (οὐ γὰρ εἶναι τοῖς ὀρφανοῖς κατὰ τῶν ἐπιτρόπων) … ('and also that the laws prevented a legal action against me, because orphans are not allowed to bring actions against their guardians.').

35 See also Thompson 1976: 39.

this is the nearest of all blood relationships, but as everyone would agree is not within the prescribed degrees of kinship.

In fact, the law on intestate succession attested in Dem. 43.51 does not mention mothers among those who inherit *ab intestato*. Wyse supposed that in the age of Isaios the law could be interpreted as containing 'an implicit recognition of the rights of a mother',[36] but the dikasts, who awarded the estate to Theopompos, would have disagreed with such an interpretation. And Isaios does not contradict himself and violate the law on succession, when in 11.29–30 he argues that Hagnias' mother was entitled to inherit. In the majority scholarly opinion, what the logographer meant here is that Hagnias' mother could claim the estate by virtue of her second cousinship to her son on the father's side.[37]

I asserted earlier that Isaios, with one probable exception, did not abuse the law in his extant speeches. The exception consists of a misinterpretation of a provision in the law on intestate succession, attested in 7.20: πατρῴων μὲν οὖν καὶ ἀδελφοῦ χρημάτων τὸ ἴσον αὐτοῖς ὁ νόμος μετασχεῖν δίδωσιν· ἀνεψιοῦ δέ, καὶ εἴ τις ἔξω ταύτης τῆς συγγενείας ἐστίν, οὐκ ἴσον, ἀλλὰ προτέροις τοῖς ἄρρεσιν τῶν θηλειῶν τὴν ἀγχιστείαν πεποίηκε. There Isaios argued that 'the law gives the sister and the sister's son an equal share of their father's and their brother's estate, but for the estate of a cousin or any other more distant relative, the share is not equal, but the law gives the right of succession to the male relatives in preference to the female.' The specific provision of the law on succession attested in Dem. 43.51[38] that gets misinterpreted here is the one that states that κρατεῖν

36 Wyse 1904: 693.

37 See Harrison 1968: 141–142, Thompson 1976: 41–42.

38 The text of the law as preserved in Dem. 43.51 reads: ὅστις ἂν μὴ διαθέμενος ἀποθάνῃ, ἐὰν μὲν παῖδας καταλίπῃ θηλείας, σὺν ταύτῃσιν, ἐὰν δὲ μή, τούσδε κυρίους εἶναι τῶν χρημάτων. ἐὰν μὲν ἀδελφοὶ ὦσιν ὁμοπάτορες· καὶ ἐὰν παῖδες ἐξ ἀδελφῶν γνήσιοι, τὴν τοῦ πατρὸς μοῖραν λαγχάνειν· ἐὰν δὲ μὴ ἀδελφοὶ ὦσιν ἢ ἀδελφῶν παῖδες, ⟨***⟩ ἐξ αὐτῶν κατὰ ταὐτὰ λαγχάνειν· κρατεῖν δὲ τοὺς ἄρρενας καὶ τοὺς ἐκ τῶν ἀρρένων, ἐὰν ἐκ τῶν αὐτῶν ὦσι, καὶ ἐὰν γένει ἀπωτέρω. ἐὰν δὲ μὴ ὦσι πρὸς πατρὸς μέχρι ἀνεψιῶν παίδων, τοὺς πρὸς μητρὸς τοῦ ἀνδρὸς κατὰ ταὐτὰ κυρίους εἶναι. ἐὰν δὲ μηδετέρωθεν ᾖ ἐντὸς τούτων, τὸν πρὸς πατρὸς ἐγγυτάτω κύριον εἶναι. νόθῳ δὲ μηδὲ νόθῃ μὴ εἶναι ἀγχιστείαν μήθ' ἱερῶν μήθ' ὁσίων ἀπ' Εὐκλείδου ἄρχοντος. ('Whenever a man dies without leaving a will, if he leaves behind female children, [the property shall go] with them, but if not, the following are entitled to have his property. If there are brothers [of the deceased] by the same father; and if there are legitimate children of the brothers, they are to obtain their father's share. And if there are no brothers or children of brothers ⟨those born⟩ from them are to obtain a share in the same way. And males and the descendants of males have precedence, if they have the same common ancestor, even if they are more distantly related [to the deceased]. And if there are no [relatives] on the father's side

δὲ τοὺς ἄρρενας καὶ τοὺς ἐκ τῶν ἀρρένων, ἐὰν ἐκ τῶν αὐτῶν ὦσι, καὶ ἐὰν γένει ἀπωτέρω ('males and the descendants of males have precedence, if they have the same common ancestor [as the females], even if they are more distantly related [to the deceased]'); for instance, the son of the brother of the deceased, though remoter in degree, had priority over the sister of the deceased. There is nothing in the law to suggest that the same principle of succession did not apply to the direct line and to collateral relatives, and I doubt that the incomplete and corrupt law as preserved in Dem. 43.51 is responsible for our ignorance of a possible change of principle.[39] What is more, Isaios himself in his paraphrase of the same law on intestate succession in 11.1–3 does not confirm that the principle of the precedence of males and the descendants of males was applicable only to first cousins and to relations more distant than first cousins.[40] And although I agree with Griffith-Williams when she concludes that it is difficult to believe

[of the deceased] as far as the children of cousins, those on the mother's side are entitled to inherit in the same way. And if there is [no one] on either side within this degree of kinship, the one who is nearest on the father's side is entitled to inherit. And there is no right of succession for any illegitimate child of either sex, either in regard to religious rites or civic privileges, from the time of the archonship of Eukleides.').

39 The law is omitted in SF, two of the primary witnesses of the texts in the Demosthenic corpus. For the restoration of the text after ἀδελφῶν παῖδες the following supplements have been suggested: ἀδελφὰς ὁμοπατρίας καὶ παῖδας by Meier and Buermann, ἀδελφὰς ὁμοπατρίας καὶ παῖδας ἐξ αὐτῶν λαγχάνειν ἐὰν δὲ μὴ ἀδελφαὶ ὦσιν ἢ παῖδες ἐξ αὐτῶν, ἀδελφοὺς τοῦ πατρὸς καὶ ἀδελφὰς καὶ παῖδας by Lipsius and Paoli, ἀδελφὰς ὁμοπατρίας καὶ παῖδας ἐξ αὐτῶν λαγχάνειν ἐὰν δὲ μὴ ἀδελφαὶ ὦσιν ἢ παῖδες ἐξ αὐτῶν, ἀνεψιοὺς καὶ παῖδας by Bunsen, ἀνεψιοὺς πρὸς πατρὸς καὶ παῖδας by Ruschenbusch who takes (rather arbitrarily) ἀδελφοὶ in the text of the law to denote both brothers and sisters. Taking into account the text in Isa. 11.1–3 (see below), I would tentatively favour Bunsen's supplement. On the question of the authenticity of this law and on the supplements suggested see Harrison 1968: 145 n. 3 and 146 n. 1, Ruschenbusch 2010: 103–109, Scafuro 2011: 27–30, 160 n. 84.

40 Isa. 11.1–3: ὁ δὲ νόμος περὶ ἀδελφοῦ χρημάτων πρῶτον ἀδελφοῖς τε καὶ ἀδελφιδοῖς πεποίηκε τὴν κληρονομίαν, ἐὰν ὦσιν ὁμοπάτορες … ἐὰν δ' οὗτοι μὴ ὦσι, δεύτερον ἀδελφὰς ὁμοπατρίας καλεῖ καὶ παῖδας τοὺς ἐκ τούτων. ἐὰν δὲ μὴ ὦσι, τρίτῳ γένει δίδωσι τὴν ἀγχιστείαν, ἀνεψιοῖς πρὸς πατρὸς μέχρι ἀνεψιῶν παίδων. ἐὰν δὲ καὶ τοῦτ' ἐκλείπῃ, εἰς τὸ γένος πάλιν ἐπανέρχεται καὶ ποιεῖ τοὺς πρὸς μητρὸς τοῦ τελευτήσαντος κυρίους αὐτῶν, κατὰ ταὐτὰ καθάπερ τοῖς πρὸς πατρὸς ἐξ ἀρχῆς ἐδίδου τὴν κληρονομίαν. ταύτας ποιεῖ τὰς ἀγχιστείας ὁ νομοθέτης μόνας, συντομωτέρως τοῖς ῥήμασιν ἢ ἐγὼ φράζω. ('But the law concerning a brother's property has given the right of inheritance first to brothers and nephews, if they are descendants of the same father. … In the absence of these, it second names the sisters by the same father and their offspring. In their absence, it gives the right of succession to the third degree, cousins on the father's side up to the children of cousins. If this degree is also lacking, it goes back again and gives the right to succession to the estate to those on the mother's side of the deceased, on the same principles as it originally gave the right of inheritance to those on the father's side. These are the only rights of kinship the lawgiver recognises, in more concise wording than my paraphrase.')

that Isaios had thought it worth misrepresenting the law in order to enhance an argument which was not central to his client's case and related only to a hypothetical situation, 'given the risk of discredit to his client if even some of the *dikastai* noticed the error',[41] I still cannot find arguments to corroborate Isaios' interpretation of part of the law on succession in 7.20.

To sum up, in this chapter I have attempted to sketch out Isaios' attitude regarding the use of law in his extant speeches, which could be summarised as follows: (a) Isaios merely interpreted vague statutes and his interpretations, as some verdicts, known or for good reason supposed, indicate, were the expected ones, at least as regards his primary audience, (b) he employed legal arguments, mostly comparative, when there was no legal provision relevant to his case, (c) he stuck to the letter of the law when it favoured his argumentation, (d) he suppressed limitations on the provisions of the statute he was citing, if they were irrelevant to his case, and (e) as one would expect, he made effective use of rhetoric when presenting and interpreting statutes.

But he did not resort, at least systematically, to abuse of law, only to manipulation of factual details, perhaps, because he realised the truth of what he wrote in 10.22, that χαλεπὸν γὰρ πρὸς νόμους καὶ δίκαιον πρᾶγμα ἀντιλέγειν ἐστί ('for it is difficult to speak against law and justice').[42]

Bibliography

Avramović, S. (1997) *Iseo e il diritto attico*, Naples. (Originally published as *Isejevo sudsko besedništvo i atinsko pravo*, Belgrade, 1988.)

Biscardi, A. (1983) 'Osservazioni critiche sulla terminologia διαθήκη-διατίθεσθαι', in Dimakis, P., ed., *Symposion 1979: Vorträge zur griechischen und hellenistischen Rechtsgeschichte* (Aegina, 3–7 September 1979), Cologne, 23–35.

Carey, C. (1994) 'Rhetorical Means of Persuasion', in Worthington, I., ed. (1994) *Persuasion: Greek Rhetoric in Action*, London, 26–45.

Cobetto Ghiggia, P. (2002) *Iseo: Contro Leocare (sulla successione di Diceogene)*, Pisa.

Cudjoe, R.V. (2010) *The Social and Legal Position of Widows and Orphans in Classical Athens*, Athens.

41 Griffith-Williams 2013: 61–62. On this point see also Harrison 1968: 147–148.

42 All English translations are from the Loeb Library apart from Isaios' and Demosthenes' cited works which are from Edwards 2007 and Scafuro 2011 respectively. I would like to thank Prof. E.M. Harris for his useful comments. My thanks are also due to the S.A.R.G. of the National and Kapodistrian University of Athens for its financial support.

Edwards, M.J. (2006) 'Isaeus the Rhetorician: A Forgotten Classic', in Calboli Montefusco, L., ed., *Papers on rhetoric VII*, Rome, 67–80.

Edwards, M.J. (2007) *Isaeus*. Austin, TX.

Ferrucci, S. (2005) *Iseo. La successione di Kiron*, Pisa.

Finley, M.I. (1952) *Studies in Land and Credit in Ancient Athens 500–200 B.C.: The horos Inscriptions*, (repr. 1973, with a new intro. by Paul Millett), New Brunswick.

Gehrke, H-J. (2006) 'The Figure of Solon in the *Athenaion Politeia*', in Blok, J. and Lardinois, A.P.M.H., eds (2006), *Solon of Athens: New Historical and Philological Approaches*, Leiden, 276–289.

Griffith-Williams, B. (2012) '*Oikos*, Family Feuds and Funerals: Argumentation and Evidence in Athenian Inheritance Disputes', *CQ* 62, 145–162.

Griffith-Williams, B. (2013) *A Commentary on Selected Speeches of Isaios*, Leiden.

Harris, E.M. (2013) *The Rule of Law in Action in Democratic Athens*, Oxford.

Harrison, A.R.W. (1968–1971) *The Law of Athens*, 2 vols, Oxford.

Karabélias, E. (2002) *L'épiclérat attique*, Athens.

Maffi, A. (1990) 'È esistita l'aferesi dell'*epikleros*?', in Nenci, G. and Thür, G., eds (1990) *Symposion 1988: Vorträge zur griechischen und hellenistischen Rechtsgeschichte* (Pisa, 6–8 June 1988), Cologne, 21–36.

Maffi, A. (1991) 'Adozione e strateghie successorie a Gortina e ad Atene', in Gagarin, M., ed. (1991) *Symposion 1990: Vorträge zur griechischen und hellenistischen Rechtsgeschichte* (Pacific Grove, Cal., 24–26 September 1990), Cologne, 205–238.

Paoli, U.E. (1976) 'La legittima aferesi dell'epikleros nel diritto attico', in *Altri studi di diritto greco e romano*, Milan, 363–376. (Originally published 1946.)

Rubinstein, L. (1993) *Adoption in IV. Century Athens*, Copenhagen.

Ruschenbusch, E. (1957) 'Δικαστήριον πάντων κύριον', *Historia* 6, 257–274. (Reprinted in Ruschenbusch, E. (2005) *Kleine Schriften*, Wiesbaden, 17–31.)

Ruschenbusch, E. (2010) *Solon: Das Gesetzeswerk. Fragmente, Übersetzung und Kommentar*, Stuttgart.

Scafuro, A.C. (2011) *Demosthenes, speeches 39–49*, Austin.

Schaps, D.M. (1979) *Economic Rights of Women in Ancient Greece*, Edinburgh.

Thompson, W.E. (1976) *De Hagniae Hereditate: an Athenian Inheritance Case*, Leiden.

Todd, S.C. (1993) *The Shape of Athenian Law*, Oxford.

Wyse, W. (1904) *The Speeches of Isaeus*. Cambridge.

Glossary of Legal Terms

The glossary does not aim to be comprehensive but rather to cover legal terminology employed in the volume, for the benefit of students and readers less familiar with Athenian legal terminology and procedure (and for Greekless readers). For a more thorough glossary of legal and semi-legal terms our reader can be directed to Todd's (1993) glossary.

***agōn* (*timētos and atimētos*)** lit. 'contest' but as a legal term, lawsuit; *agōn timētos* and *atimētos* designate (respectively) an 'unassessed action' (with a fixed penalty) and an 'assessed action' (in which the judges choose between penalty proposals from the two parties); cf. *timēsis* below.

anakrisis preliminary hearing, literally 'questioning', 'interrogation', conducted by the relevant magistrate after the issue of a formal summons by a litigant.

androphonos murderer, homicide, lit. 'manslayer' cf. *phonos* below.

antidosis exchange of property, a procedure in which any Athenian selected for a liturgy (see under *leitourgeia* below) could put forward another on the ground that he was richer and had been erroneously overlooked. It took the form of a challenge to exchange properties; the individual challenged could either perform the liturgy, accept the exchange of property and leave the challenger to perform the liturgy (since he was now in possession of a property which he had claimed was sufficient to sustain the cost) or refuse both and allow the issue to be settled by *diadikasia* (q.v.).

antigraphē in Athenian law, a 'counterplea' submitted by the defendant to the relevant authority responsible for the preliminary proceedings leading to the trial, also 'counter-prosecution' brought by the defendant against the prosecutor.

antomōsia lit. 'oath [of two people] against each other', the litigants alone swore the *antomōsia* in Athenian trials. It seems that they swore about the truth of the pleas in the evidence handed in. In homicide cases the oath taken was termed *diomosia*.

apagōgē summary arrest (lit. 'leading away'), a public action available in relation to a number of offences but especially associated with the *kakourgos* (q.v. below), involving a self-help procedure in which the individual arrests the perpetrator and conducts the subsequent prosecution, if the offender denies the offence. A necessary condition for the employment of the action is for the offender to be caught *ep' autophorōi* (q.v. below), that is, in highly incriminating circumstances. Cf. *lōpodytai* below.

apographē 'schedule'; a public action available against people allegedly in possession of state property, commencing with a written list of the property in question. The successful prosecutor received a portion of the value of the goods in question.

aphairesis action of the man who takes his daughter away from her husband, that is, initiating a divorce, or of the next of kin of claiming an *epiklēros* (q.v.) who is already married and terminating the existing marriage.

aphairesis eis eleutherian lit. 'removal to freedom'; a self-help procedure involving direct intervention by a third party to oppose the (allegedly wrongful) seizure of an individual as a slave.

apophasis (verb *apophainein*). The literal sense is 'declaration' but as a legal term it is used for a procedure dated to the fourth century., under which the *Areiopagos* (q.v. below) was empowered to investigate any matter related to public security and produce a report to the Assembly recommending a particular action to be implemented.

archōn lit. 'ruler', the term can refer to any official but usually (especially in the plural) designates a specific group of prestigious public officials selected by lot, comprising the *archōn*, the *basileus*, the *polemarchos* and the six *thesmothetai.*

Areiopagos in full 'the Council of the Areiopagos/ Hill of Arēs' (*he Boulē hē ek tou Areiou Pagou*), named from its meeting place west of the Acropolis. The contemporary term Areiopagos, though convenient, is late; classical sources invariably use the full designation 'the Council of the Hill of Arēs'. Its main function in the classical period was as the most important of the Athenian homicide courts. It heard cases of intentional killing where the victim was a citizen, those involving poisoning or arson resulting in death, and wounding with intent. *Cf phonos* below.

asebeia an offence concerning impious or sacrilegious actions, which could be prosecuted by various procedures including *graphē asebeias* (public action against impiety).

ateleia honorific exemption from liturgies, q.v. below.

atimia lit. 'loss of honour', i.e. loss of citizen rights, which could be partial (for instance as a penalty for failure to obtain 20% of the votes in a public action) or total, either as a specific penalty or as the automatic (and reversible) consequence of owing a debt to the state.

ballantiotomoi 'pickpockets'; they were classed as *kakourgoi* (q.v. below) and liable to *apagōgē* ('leading away'), q.v.

basileus one of the nine *archōns* (see on *archōn* above) with predominantly religious duties.

blabē damage incurred by the prosecutor as a result of activity of the defendant. The *dikē blabēs* a private action (see *dikē* below) for damages, could be employed against this offence.

Boulē 'Council', the board of 500 which acted as a steering body for the *Ekklēsia* (q.v. below). It also performed a wide range of executive functions and had a (circumscribed) judicial role. The term is also used for the Areiopagos but only where the context precludes ambiguity.

Delphinion both a shrine (the temple of Apollo and Artemis) and the location of one of the homicide courts; the Delphinion tried cases where the defendant admitted killing but claimed that the homicide was lawful. Such cases were heard by the *ephetai*, q.v. Cf. also *phonos* below.

dēmos according to context, either the Athenian people as a whole or the masses. Inscriptions use the word to designate the popular Assembly (see *Ekklesia*). *Dēmos* ('deme') is also used for the local units (urban districts or villages) which were the smallest political units of the democracy.

desmōtērion prison. The supervisory authority in Athens was the Eleven (q.v. below). The *desmoterion* has been tentatively located to an area south west of the Agora.

diadikasia 'adjudication' (lit. 'judgment between'), a private suit between rival claimants to a right or disputants about liability for a financial burden; unlike *dikē* and *graphē* this action had neither prosecutor nor defendant and (in inheritance cases) could have multiple parties.

diaita arbitration. Arbitration took two forms, public and private. Public arbitration (that is, a hearing before a publicly appointed arbitrator), was a preliminary proceeding required in certain cases. Private arbitration was optional and involved the selection by actual or potential litigants of one or more individuals to resolve the dispute.

diamartyria 'affirmation' (often but misleadingly translated 'affidavit'), a move to bar an action, involving a witness statement that the action could not be brought because of facts known to the witness; it could be countered by bringing a *dike pseudomartyriōn* (q.v. below) alleging that the statement was false, and failure to counter with this suit terminated the original action.

dikai emmēnoi 'monthly cases' (including mercantile and mining suits), variously explained as cases where plaints were admitted monthly or (less likely) cases where the verdict was delivered within a month.

dikastēs (pl. *dikastai*) A citizen serving in a *dikastērion* whose functions combined those of a modern judge and juror. According to the type of case they were hearing, the *dikastai* sat in panels of 201 or 401 (for private cases) or 501 or more for public cases. *Dikastai* were enrolled for a year at a time. The minimum age for a *dikastēs* was 30.

dikē (pl. *dikai*) both a generic term for a legal action (*dikai dēmosiai/idiai* = public/private actions respectively) and the specific term for a private case, in which only the victim (or the relatives in the case of homicide) could sue.

dikē aikeias a private action for battery, lit. 'abuse', 'mistreatment'.

dikē biaiōn a private prosecution for 'acts of violence', including (perhaps specifically) sexual assault.

dikē blabēs a private action for damages.

dikē epitropēs a private action for 'guardianship' (*epitropē*), that is, for misconduct as a guardian, brought by a ward on reaching majority.

dikē exoulēs action for 'ejectment', available to claimants to property, goods or money awarded to them by a court (or to the legitimate offspring of a dead man) if barred from taking possession; if the action succeeded, the person barring was liable to pay an assessed sum to the claimant and an equal sum to the state.

dikē kakēgōrias private action for slander (lit. 'bad speaking', *kakēgoria*), confined in Athens to a number of specific expressions or allegations which were forbidden by law (*aporrhēta*, 'not to be uttered').

dikē klopēs a private action for the offence of stealing private property; the offence could be prosecuted only by the victim of the theft. For other procedures involving theft of public property see also *klopē* below.

dikē metallikē (pl. *dikai metallikai*) 'mining suit', that is, actions relating to the state-owned mines; like the *dikai emporikai*, these actions had favoured status, in that they were *dikai emmenoi* (*q.v.* above).

dikē parakatathēkēs a private case against a person who has allegedly refused to restore something entrusted to him.

dikē phonou action for homicide; a private action, not available to *ho boulomenos* (q.v. below) but brought by the victim's relatives and marked by a unique and complex set of procedures.

dikē pseudomartyriōn an action for 'false testimony' (not 'perjury', since witnesses did not in most cases depose on oath); it was a private suit, brought by a litigant against a witness for his opponent. The penalty consisted of damages to the prosecutor but three convictions resulted in *atimia* (q.v. above).

dikē sitou private action for maintenance (lit. 'grain', 'food'), brought by the *kyrios* (q.v. below) of a divorced woman, if her husband failed to return her dowry; the defaulting husband was compelled to return the dowry or pay a high rate of interest (18% p.a.), thus converting it in effect to a loan; the alternative was to bring a *dike proikos*, a private action for the return of a dowry (*proix*) on divorce.

dikastērion one of the popular courts, which dealt with the majority of legal actions in Athens apart from special cases such as those of homicide.

dokimasia scrutiny to determine eligibility for citizenship/deme membership (on reaching majority) or for office (after election or selection by lot).

dokimasia rhētorōn 'scrutiny of public speakers', a public action brought against those who address the Assembly, alleging that the defendant is ineligible on the ground of disqualifying conduct, punishment on conviction being the confirmation of *atimia* (q.v. above).

echinos a clay container in which the evidence was held sealed ahead of the trial, one container for each litigant's evidence.

eisphora levy on assets of the wealthy usually in time of war.

eisangelia 'impeachment', a name given to two distinct actions. Impeachment for political offences involves a prosecution made before the Assembly or the Council (though in the latter part of the fourth century these were transferred to the courts) and requiring a special enabling decree; but the title is also given to a public action available against those who harmed people in certain vulnerable categories (heiresses, orphans, parents) which was brought through the courts like a *graphē* (in fact our sources call it indifferently *graphē* or *eisangelia*). The two forms of *eisangelia* were alike in that there were no penalties for failure to proceed or to obtain 20% to the votes.

Ekklēsia the formal meeting of the adult male citizens, usually rendered 'Assembly' in English; our sources use the word *dēmos* rather than *Ekklēsia* to refer to decisions made by the Assembly.

(The) Eleven an office of eleven men, in charge of the prison in Athens and of the execution of prisoners who had been sentenced to death. They also presided over trials of *apagōgē* (summary arrest, q.v. above) and *endeixis* (denunciation, q.v. below).

embateusis The right to enter into possession of a dead man's estate without legal formality, enjoyed only by a direct descendant of the deceased or a son adopted *inter vivos*.

endeixis 'denunciation', a public action used principally against people exercising rights to which they were not entitled; it seems often to have been a preliminary to *apagōgē* (summary arrest), q.v. above.

enklēma oral and later written statement of claim, which included the names of the parties, the type of action and, if applicable, (in an *agōn timētos*, q.v. above), a suggested penalty.

engyē a pledge or surety, especially in the context of formal betrothal, the normal preliminary to marriage (except for an *epiklēros*, q.v. below), contracted between the bride's *kyrios* and the prospective groom.

ep' autophorōi a formal condition for the use of certain procedures, such as *apagōgē* (q.v. above). The meaning of the term is 'red-handed', that is, 'in highly incriminating circumstances'.

ephetai the 51 judges who presided over homicide cases in courts other than the Areiopagos.

epidikasia Formal procedure by which an uncontested claim to an inheritance was approved by the Athenian courts. Cf. *diadikasia*.

epicheirotonia general term for voting (lit.: 'raising one's hand'); in fourth century. Athens the term used for a vote of confidence in officials that was cast in every prytany (q.v.).

epiklēros 'heiress' (more literally 'with an estate attached' or 'attached to an estate'), that is, a woman whose father died leaving no male issue; the modern term is misleading in that it implies executive property rights, while in Athens it was the duty of the nearest male relative to marry her in order to continue the family of the dead man. Claiming an *epiklēros* followed the same procedure as claiming an estate, and in the case of rival claimants the issue was decided in a *diadikasia*, q.v. above.

epōbelia a penalty consisting of one-sixth of the sum at issue (one obol on the *drachma*, hence the name) paid by the unsuccessful prosecutor to the defendant in some private cases.

euthynai examination of an official on the expiry of his term of office to check for financial or other irregularity.

exōmosia oath indicating inability to undertake an official act, in court the oath of disclaimer sworn by a witness declining to testify, asserting that he had not been present at the events in question or was ignorant of the relevant facts.

graphē 'indictment', lit. '(charge in) writing', the most common kind of public action, often used in our sources as a generic term for public actions.

graphē hetaireseōs a public action against someone exercising citizen rights after having prostituted himself.

graphē hybreōs a public action for outrage, *hybris*, theoretically available against any insulting behaviour but in practice confined to physical violence; the offence is invariably deliberate and appears to differ from battery (*aikeia*) in involving either a desire to humiliate or a reckless indifference to the status of others.

graphē kakōseōs orphanou public action against a person who maltreated an orphan.

graphē nomon mē epitēdeion theinai 'indictment for bringing an inexpedient law', a public action available in the fourth century against proposers of laws deemed not in the public interest.

graphē paranomōn 'indictment for illegality', a public action available against anyone moving a proposal in the Council or the Assembly which contradicted existing legislation in substance or procedure, used against both laws and decrees in the fifth century but confined to decrees in the fourth century, after the creation of *graphē nomon mē epitēdeion theinai*, q.v. above.

graphē pseudoklēteias a public case against the summons witness (*klētēr*, see also *klēteusis* below) for lying on the grounds that the summons has not been served.

hellēnotamiai treasurers of the Delian League, ten in number, who collected the contributions from the allied cities.

hetairēsis 'prostitution' in association with Athenian (male) citizens; it was an offence, if a citizen attempted to exercise his citizen rights having prostituted himself. The procedure used in such cases was the *graphē hetairēseōs*, q.v. above.

horoi boundary stones marking the boundaries of public territories and private land in Athens and the Greek cities, in general. They were inscribed limestone slabs which could also mark public mortgages on houses and properties.

ho boulomenos lit. 'the one who wants/wishes', 'anyone who wants/ wishes', the global term for the volunteer prosecutor in public actions.

hypōmosia a sworn statement: in court proceedings one party could apply in person or through a representative for an adjournment under certain circumstances; in the Assembly/ Council a man could provide a sworn statement to declare that a decree was illegal (and attack it through a *graphē paranomōn*, q.v. above) and also block the introduction of a law which was claimed to be inexpedient (*graphē nomon mē epitedeion theinai*, q.v. above).

kakēgoria See *dikē kakēgōrias*, above.

kakourgoi 'felons', lit. 'evildoers', a class of property criminal liable to summary arrest and execution in the event of confession before the relevant magistrates (the 'Eleven') or conviction by a court after denial.

klēteuein/ klēteusis procedure (probably involving proclamation by a herald) open to the litigant in the event that a witness refused either to depose or to take the *exōmosia* (q.v. above).

klopē (verb *kleptein*) 'theft'. The offence could be prosecuted by private action (*dikē*) and certain types of theft seem to have been prosecuted by a public action (*graphē*), possibly confined to cases involving the stealing of public money. It should be noted that the existence of a *graphē* for theft in general has been doubted by some scholars.

kyrios 'guardian', the adult male who acted in official and legal contexts for those (women and children) who lacked legal capacity.

leitourgia (pl. *leitourgiai*) translated as 'liturgy' in English. A public service, such as acting as a trierarch, gymnasiarch, or *chorēgos* (chorus producer) performed as a duty by the wealthiest Athenian citizens.

logographos professional writer of speeches for litigants to deliver in court.

lōpodytes (pl. *lōpodytai*) 'clothes strippers/stealers', that is, muggers/footpads who set upon and strip people. They were classed as *kakourgoi* (see above) and so subject to *apagōgē* (q.v. above).

martyria (verb *martyreō*) 'witness statement', 'testimony'.

moicheia an offence of illicit sexual intercourse with a free woman against the will of her *kyrios*. The offence could be prosecuted by a public action, the *graphē moicheias*.

nomothetai 'legislators'. Panels used to scrutinise new legislation proposed and new legislation subject to repeal in the fourth century.

Palladion homicide court which heard allegations of unintentional killing, as well as killings of a metic, a slave or a foreigner (with or without intent).

paragraphē a private action which seeks to block a suit; the defendant in a legal action countersues the prosecutor in a separate hearing, alleging that the suit is barred on technical grounds; success in the suit bars the initial prosecution, which goes ahead in the event of failure of the *paragraphē*.

phasis 'disclosure', 'presentation' (lit. 'revealing', 'showing'), a public action available against certain (mainly financial) offences.

phonos 'homicide'. Cases of homicide were heard in different courts in Athens, based on the presence or absence of intent to kill (as alleged by the prosecutor), the status of the person killed or the nature of the defence. See *Areiopagos*, *Delphinion*, *Palladion*, *Prytaneion* and (*en*) *Phreattō*.

(*en*) *Phreattōi* a place near Pireus (east side) where trials for cases of intended homicide (*hekousios phonos*) took place in Athens for those homicides who had already been exiled for unintentional homicide (*hekousios phonos*). The defendant made his defence speech from a boat, as he was not allowed to enter Attica.

polemarchos ('polemarch') one of the nine Archons with duties especially in relation to resident aliens.

pōlētai 'sellers', financial officials particularly of property confiscated after judicial verdicts and makers of public contracts in Classical Athens.

proagōgeia 'pimping', a serious offence in Athenian law, according to which anyone involved in the procuring of free boys and women was liable to the most severe penalties (that is, death).

probolē a legal procedure available in a limited number of cases, including acting as a *sykophantēs* (q.v.) and committing an offence relating to a festival, which consisted of a hearing before the Assembly. There was no penalty involved at this stage, but conviction could be followed by a trial before a *dikastērion*.

probouleuma preliminary motion before the Assembly by the Council.

prodikasiai preliminary hearings in homicide cases, held by the *Basileus* in three successive months.

proeispherontes extremely wealthy Athenians who undertook the obligation to pay the amount of *eisphora* (property tax) levied at a certain time in advance and they then recovered the respective sums from those liable to *eisphora*. *Proeisphora* was a liturgy, q.v. above.

proklēsis challenge; challenges played a major role in Athenian litigation and served either as a means of terminating litigation or acquiring additional evidence; two which figure prominently are the challenge to swear (or accept) an oath and the challenge to submit slaves for torture or accept the opponent's offer of his slaves for torture.

Prytaneia 'prytany', period of one-tenth of the Athenian administrative year, designated from the term of office of the *prytaneis*, the contingent from one of the ten tribes, each tribe serving in rotation as standing committee of the *Boulē* (Council).

Prytaneion a civic building in Athens whose functions included housing a homicide court where cases of homicide caused by animals or inanimate objects were tried; the court was manned by the *ephetai* (q.v. above).

psēphisma a decree of the Assembly.

rhētōr 'public speaker', term used from the late fifth century for an active political figure.

sykophantēs sycophant. A term used pejoratively of a vexatious or officious litigant; not to be confused with modern English 'sycophant'. The etymology and precise meaning are unclear.

synēgoros (pl. *synēgoroi*) 'supporting speaker', one who spoke on behalf of a litigant, delivering either the main speech at a trial or a shorter epilogue after the litigant had spoken for himself.

thesmothetai (sing. *thesmothetēs*), literally 'law-giver'/ 'legislator', a title given to six of the nine *archōns*.

timēsis the procedure in which the court decided on the precise penalty a convicted defendant had to pay or suffer, in cases where the law did not prescribe one. At this stage of a trial, the prosecutor and defendant each delivered a speech proposing a penalty, and the court voted in favour of one of the two alternatives.

trauma 'wounding', normally found as *trauma ek pronoias* (intentional wounding). Cases of *trauma* (*graphē traumatos ek pronoias*, public case) were tried in the Areiopagos.

triērarchia trierarchy, one of the liturgies; a trierarch had to pay for the manning and upkeep of a trireme (warship) for a year, and was in principle expected to command it himself.

Coinage Terms and Relative Values

6 obols = 1 *drachma*
1,000 *drachmai* = 1 *mna* (usually translated as 'mina')
6,000 *drachmai* = 100 *mnai* = 1 talent

General Index

Index of Names and Places

Index Locorum